A WITCH HUNT

IN OKLAHOMA

The Raye Dawn
Smith Story

by Jody Ortiz

A WITCH-HUNT IN OKLAHOMA: THE RAYE DAWN SMITH STORY

DISCLAIMER

WHILE THIS BOOK IS A NON-FICTION, THE AUTHOR'S OPINION IS EXPRESSED THROUGHOUT THE BOOK. THEREFORE, THIS BOOK IS PRESENTED AS THE OPINION OF THE AUTHOR. IT IS NOT INTENDED TO REPLACE NOR CONFIRM LEGAL OR INVESTIGATIONAL FINDINGS.

GRATEFUL ACKNOWLEDGEMENT IS MADE TO THE FOLLOWING FOR PERMISSION TO REPRINT PREVIOUSLY PUBLISHED MATERIAL:

Craig Key, *A Deadly Game of Tug of War: The Kelsey Smith Briggs Story* published by Morgan James Publishing, LLC. ISBN 978-1-60037-312-1

ISBN: 978-1-962490-04-7

Cover/Interior Design by:
Morbid Panther Designs

Edited by:
Julie Jones and Sherri Heath

Table of Contents

Dedication

There are numerous victims as a result of this particular group of bullies. But this book is dedicated to the only victim who matters – Kelsey Smith-Briggs.

Kelsey, you were abused by the man charged with sexual assault and murder. You continue to be abused by people who refuse to call you by your legal name and who use your image and a false story to promote themselves for personal and financial gain. May God forgive them all.

My prayer is that this book helps to free your mommy from prison and brings peace to your grandma Gayla who still cannot tell a story about you without tears.

I would also like to thank Kelsey's cousin, Sherri Heath, who has been a true example of strength and forgiveness for me since my involvement in this case. This book would not have been possible without her wisdom and input.

Special Note

Throughout the pages of this book, you will read posts from the bullies that were found on blogs, Web sites, and in e-mails. These posts are presented as close to their original format as possible and include the post author's spelling, grammar, and typos.

Also, if you see brackets such as these [ ], most likely it is because a name has been changed or information has been removed for privacy reasons from the book author. The same can be said for some … segues within the book. Most are from post authors, but some are from the book author to protect privacy.

While reading through this book, you will notice there are few descriptions of the characters other than a handful of pictures. For years, these bullies have remained faceless in their hate. Few names or faces are actually known.

To read the e-mails in their entirety, go to FreeKelseysMom.com.

Trigger warning: This is a true story of a two-year-old child who died while home alone with her stepfather. Topics of rape, murder, stalking, harassment, and death threats, etc are discussed.

Introduction

December, 2011

I have struggled for several months over whether the information in this book should be released. As I continue to question why people believe the false stories that have been circulated about this case (even though evidence proves the contrary) I have finally concluded that in order to understand how lies have prevailed, one must first explore the lies as well as the methods of conditioning and torture that were used to perpetuate them.

When thinking of the magnitude of conditioning that paved the way for the wrongful conviction of Raye Dawn Smith, Kelsey's mom, I analyzed how Hitler was able to condition the Germans into believing that Jewish people were soiled and spread disease. The hate that seethed from his soul spread into normal society. And, over a period of years, and through constant reinforcement of his opinions, he manipulated human beings into behaving like animals. After such conditioning, one starts to wonder if there is some truth to the lies. Those with no personal experience or facts on which to base their opinion will tend to believe the stories without seeking the truth for themselves.

Conditioning draws from the energy that is all around us. There is good energy that comes from being around someone who radiates peace and goodness or from reading something that is positive and motivating. Negative energy diminishes your value as a person and every negative statement or action creates the same type of thoughts within your mind. If the words are about you, they can make you feel worthless or like a lesser person, no matter how strong your self-

I

esteem. It takes time, prayer, and a lot of inner reflection to remember that the person that is described is not you. This is something that took years for me to learn and overcome.

If the words are about someone else, your initial reaction may be to doubt them. But, after they are repeated by what *appears* to be several individuals day after day, you get sucked into that energy and your mind creates a truth from the stories. It is easy to get swept into the chaos and lose the part of yourself that first wanted to advocate for something good. *If so many people agree, it must be true* is what your mind tells you. But is it? Many times when people read so much negativity, they lose touch with reality and start to believe the bullies or abusers. Bullies become even more powerful, and they feel better about themselves by tearing someone else down. And people follow suit.

When no other facts are available, what is told is thought of as the true story. Sadly, many are misled to support a vendetta instead of a cause for something good.

This form of conditioning was used via a Web site entitled "Kelsey's Purpose" that was created immediately after two-year-old Kelsey Smith-Briggs's alleged sexual assault and murder on October 11, 2005. Through this online venue, Kelsey's paternal family garnered public support through fabricated stories of a "war hero" coming home from Iraq to bury his child and a "doting grandmother" who was the only one who fought to save her. With nothing to contradict these misrepresentations, the public devoured the stories and took Kelsey's paternal family into their hearts. They fought for this family from small town Meeker, Oklahoma and did their bidding without question. The result? What they termed "bashboards" were formed by bullies with the sole purpose of destroying reputations and lives...all in the name of justice. But justice for whom? When motives and facts are exposed, this question can be answered within the contents of these bashboards.

Motives Exposed

After Kelsey's death, her paternal family, the Briggs, teamed up with Kelsey's stepfather, the same man who had been charged with her sexual assault and murder.[1] Together, they worked to condition hundreds of people who never met anyone involved in the case to hate the child's mom as well as her entire maternal family just as much as they did. They told stories, which were believed by members of the media and then passed on to the unsuspecting public without any proof or evidence of truth. Even today they continue to state that Kelsey's stepfather was alone with Kelsey for fifteen minutes on the day of her alleged sexual assault and murder. They also state that fifteen minutes is not enough time to rape a child. Even if their story were true, common sense tells us that rape can occur within seconds. Why continue to contradict the known facts or common sense?

We know that Kelsey's mom left Kelsey home alone with her stepfather, Mike Porter, between 2:30 pm and 2:45 pm. Mike Porter did not make his first call for "help" until 3:09 pm. Mike Porter's story that you will see him repeat throughout "anonymous" postings on the bashboards were aimed to condition the public to believe that he was alone with Kelsey for only fifteen minutes. He repeatedly posted this story to set a precedent that he did not have enough time to sexually assault Kelsey. His plan worked because his version of the events were repeated by certain members of the media, and are still repeated to this day.

I became involved in this story after working with Judge Craig Key on his book entitled *A Deadly Game of Tug of War: The Kelsey*

---

[1] See Appendix B Exhibit 1

Smith-Briggs Story. He had been the Judge that ruled over the custody battle for Kelsey between the paternal family (the Briggs) who used abuse allegations as their weapon of choice, and the maternal family (the Smiths) who only saw signs of abuse coming from the Briggs family. The Smiths were so caught up in saving Kelsey from the Briggs and her father, Lance, who had pleaded "no contest" to abusing Kelsey's mom that they missed the real abuser, Mike Porter. He was welcomed into Kelsey's home and would soon become her stepdad.

At the time of Kelsey's death, I lived outside of Oklahoma City and spent most of my time working as an editor and ghostwriter as well as running a transcription company that provided work for fourteen part-time transcriptionists. The news was something I never watched. So when Judge Craig Key called me and asked about my knowledge of the case, I had to Google his name. I was a perfect candidate for the job because I had not been tainted by the negative and false media reports or the stories that had been circulated around the Web. That was March of 2007. By June of that year, I decided I wanted to meet Raye Dawn Smith. Shortly before her trial in July of 2007, I was able to secure a private meeting with Raye and her mom, Gayla. I felt their grief and pain. I saw the truth in their tears and throughout the pages of Kelsey's baby book that Raye had lovingly prepared.

Mike Porter agreed to thirty years in prison, which is ten times the state's average plea, so that he would not have to face a jury trial.

IV

On 3-5-2006 Kathie Briggs said, "Our DA has already stated on camera his case against Mike Porter is strong."

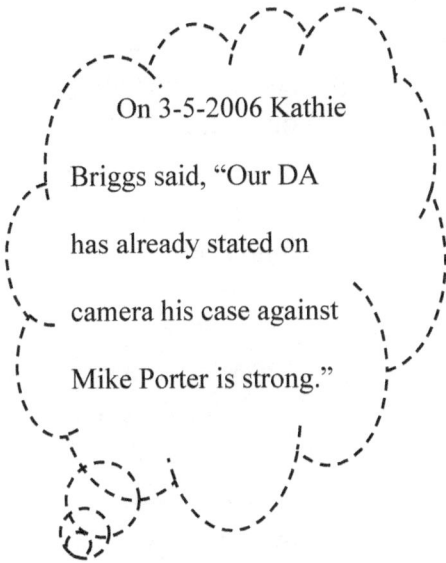

Earlier in the year Mike Porter had been given a plea deal that included imprisonment for thirty years for enabling child abuse. This deal was signed just days after the contents of his computers as well as his external hard drives were reported to the officials.

The combination of child pornography that was reportedly found on his computer and his fascination with anal sex, which matched Kelsey's alleged injuries from the sexual assault, assured a win for the prosecution if he went to trial. A newspaper article reported that District Attorney Richard Smothermon wanted to take Mike Porter to trial, but Kelsey's paternal family, the Briggs, "desired a plea."[2] This same article referenced Kelsey's paternal grandmother, Kathie Briggs as she wept over Porter's fate. She stated that he had "shown remorse" so it was "hard to see" him like that.

When Kelsey's mom, Raye Dawn Smith, went to trial in July of 2007 in front of a media-tainted jury, she was given a twenty-seven year sentence, also for enabling child abuse. The reaction from the Briggs family, and Kathie Briggs in particular was very different than the tearful reaction to Mike Porter's fate. They rejoiced and were overheard yelling that they would not have to share any of the fifteen million dollars with Raye. Kelsey's father, Lance Briggs, had filed to

---

[2] "Plea Made in Kelsey's Death" Web posted from *Shawnee News Star* by Kim Morava found at
http://www.thetruthaboutkelsey.com/MP%20Plea/Plea%20Reaction%20Page.htm

become the executor of the two-year-old's estate just seventeen days after her death. What is in a two-year-old's estate? Toys? Clothing? What did he plan to gain? He then filed multiple lawsuits, including one against the State of Oklahoma for fifteen million dollars. If Raye were to be convicted in connection with Kelsey's death, she would not be entitled to half of the winnings. This gave the Briggs a reason to want Kelsey's mom in jail. They would stop at nothing to see their goal achieved.

After watching the reports of Raye's twenty-seven year sentence, and the Briggs' reactions in the media, I wanted to help. I created FreeKelseysmom.com and became the new target for the bashboard bullies. The life that I loved soon came to an end. Those who had been conditioned to destroy turned their attention to me since they had successfully imprisoned Raye, and the growing mob still craved justice. Since I had never been involved with anything social on the Web, their attacks blindsided me. The energy that was focused on me was suffocating and I had no defense against it.

Once I stood up to spread word of the wrongful conviction of Raye Dawn Smith, I became involved without realizing the snake pit I was entering. Even more disturbing to me is the fact that I was sucked into their pit for a short period of time. I made comments that I regret and I was unkind on more than one occasion. The hate was so strong that it seeped into lives of individuals who are normally peaceful and loving.

For this reason, I have written this book to expose the hate that most of us never see in our daily lives. Let it serve as a reminder that our words—once posted—will forever haunt us. Raye and her family members as well as an unknown number of individuals have been harmed by the actions born of hate. May those who participated in these "bashboards" one day find peace and forgiveness.

An Overview

July 2002 through April 2006

Kelsey Shelton Smith was born into a broken home on December 28, 2002. Kelsey's mom, Raye Dawn Smith, divorced Kelsey's dad Raymond Lance (Robinson) Briggs, before Kelsey was born. Raymond, who goes by "Lance," was born and raised with the surname of Robinson, but he changed his name to his stepfather's surname—Briggs—just before marrying Raye and without a legal adoption.

Raye had allegedly suffered physical and emotional abuse at the hands of Lance during their two year marriage.

Raye stated about the relationship: "I married Raymond Lance Briggs July of 2000. I lost my first child that month at three months due to a blow to the stomach by the fist of Lance. Other than that time he had hit on me several times leaving black eyes, a bruised rib, my hair pulled out, and a lot of my stuff throughout the house that all meant something to me he would break. He even threw my Pomeranian dog against the wall at one time. He busted my nose at the river in front of all of our friends one summer.[3] I finally got enough of all of that and left. I went to live back with my parents. Lance a few weeks later broke into the house we lived in while we were married and broke a bathroom mirror, threw groceries all over the kitchen, threw stuff in the pond, in the creek, and plus stole some school albums…"

---

[3] See Appendix B – Exhibit 2

In early 2002, Raye and Lance separated and she began dating another man before the divorce was final. When Raye discovered she was pregnant, she prayed that the baby did not belong to Lance, but a paternity test proved he was the father. The parties went to court and a hyphen was added to Kelsey's last name. She would be known as Kelsey Shelton Smith-Briggs, taking the name of Lance's stepfather along with her maternal family's name. (Kelsey was a suggestion from Raye's grandmother, Mildred, and Shelton was Raye's father's middle name.) Kelsey's new legal name and double birth announcements (one for baby girl Smith and one for baby girl Briggs) would be telling of the battle for Kelsey that would create an explosive atmosphere that would allow an unforeseen tragedy to end her life just months before her third birthday.

Kelsey lived a fairly normal life for the first two years with no allegations of abuse from either family. Things changed when Raye started dating a man named Mike Porter in the fall of 2004 at the same time that Kathie Briggs, Kelsey's paternal grandmother, was awarded grandparent visitation. Bruises were noticed on Kelsey by her daycare worker after she returned from her visits with Kathie. Raye describes seeing bruises on Kelsey's legs that looked like "finger marks" and a bruise on her ear. Raye states that she assumed they were from Kathie or Lance or that Kelsey had a medical problem and bruised easily—a test determined the latter was not the issue. Kathie states that she assumed Raye was to blame. Because of the tension that was a powder keg ready to explode if one side dared to withhold Kelsey during a scheduled time for her to be with the other family, the families did not get along well, nor did they communicate on Kelsey's behalf. The situation grew far worse when a former friend of Kelsey's maternal grandmother told her to "get ready" because Lance and Kathie were going to "seek custody of Kelsey." This warning was later echoed in court when Kathie stated on the stand that Lance's new wife told her that she didn't want to have children of her own, "she'd just keep Kelsey." Statements such as these that were based on hearsay only added to the tension.

In January of 2005 Kelsey broke her clavicle (the most commonly broken bone in children) reportedly after a fall from her crib. At the end of January, bruises and scratches on her bottom that were discovered approximately four hours after Kathie and Lance had Kelsey at their respective homes were termed "abuse" by her paternal family when she was taken to the emergency room. Kelsey was then taken from Raye.

Four months passed with Kelsey in Kathie's care and Raye seeing Kelsey during supervised and then unsupervised visits after Raye fully cooperated with the state's Department of Human Services (DHS). Reports show that she completed every course and every evaluation she needed to accomplish in order to regain custody of Kelsey.

Hearings were held in Judge Key's courtroom, with one person missing from each and every hearing, Kelsey's father.

Abuse allegations continued to be made against Raye that were unfounded, "screened out," and termed "normal childhood injuries" by child welfare workers. Kathie stated in court that she undressed Kelsey and took pictures of her and that she had three to four witnesses view Kelsey's entire body each time she would arrive at her home and each time she left. Witnesses state that Kelsey began counting her bruises and self-mutilating by biting and scratching herself and picking at her fingernails and toenails—one toenail she had completely picked off on the day that she died.

Judge Craig Key described Kelsey's strange behavior in his book about the case. He stated as follows:

Although she was in protective custody, it was apparent that Kelsey wasn't adjusting to being in the Briggs home. A red flag was raised for me, as a judge, when DHS told me Kelsey's hair began falling out in clumps while in the care of Kathie Briggs. Kelsey's hair was falling out to the point that she had a bald spot on the back of her head the size of a baseball. She began self-mutilating by biting her arms, and as clearly

3

stated in Kelsey's obituary submitted by the Briggs, she was apparently biting the Briggs family as well. Kelsey's behavior and hair loss during this time were all documented by DHS...Why Kelsey acted differently while in the custody of Kathie Briggs is unclear. Why Kelsey was timid, lethargic, and asleep during almost every DHS visit is also unclear. But what's clear is the tug-of-war was starting to get to the child both mentally and physically. [4]

In April of 2005, Raye married Mike Porter. Her father had lost his battle with cancer the previous year and with everything Raye was facing in fighting for her daughter, she needed someone to be a knight in shining armor for her. Mike Porter fit the description. He had custody of his eight-year-old daughter and regular visitation with his son who was slightly younger than Kelsey. Mike Porter claimed that he was a college graduate (untrue) and he inherited the family business after both of his parents died. He seemed to be just what Raye and Kelsey needed in their lives.

Just days before the marriage ceremony, Kelsey sprained her ankle while at the zoo with her maternal aunt and she was returned to Kathie's home with a doctor's note. Four days later when Raye picked Kelsey up from Kathie's home, Kelsey refused to walk. Kathie claimed she took a couple of steps and then crawled for the rest of the week. Kathie didn't think anything about it. She had taken Kelsey to the emergency room for a bump on her nose, but she didn't see a need for a second opinion when Kelsey couldn't walk.

Raye took Kelsey to a doctor when her legs became progressively worse and the doctor stated that the first fracture was consistent with Kelsey's fall at the zoo and that her other leg had been injured more recently and was from overcompensation. Kelsey then went through two sets of casts. Raye and Gayla Smith, Raye's mom, had the casts put on, and Kathie had the first set removed after only six days. After

---

[4] Key, Craig. *A Deadly Game of Tug of War: The Kelsey Smith-Briggs Story.* Garden City, NY: Morgan James Publishing, 2007. p. 51-52.

Kelsey's legs were determined to be broken from abuse by a doctor Kathie had found and reportedly told that Raye was abusing Kelsey, Kelsey was removed from Kathie's home and placed with her maternal grandmother, Gayla.[5]

According to records and witnesses, Kelsey lost weight and hair while with Kathie. A bald spot the size of a baseball was discovered. Once removed from Kathie's home, Kelsey reportedly improved.

After DHS viewed Kelsey's interactions with both Kathie and Raye during separate supervised visits at the DHS office and reported their findings at a hearing in June in Judge Key's courtroom, Kelsey was returned to Raye's custody with three child welfare services assigned by the Judge to watch over Kelsey and visit her home on an almost daily basis.

A total of five agencies were involved in Kelsey's life at this point, and they were: Court Appointed Special Advocates (CASA), Comprehensive Home Based Services (CHBS), Department of Human Services (DHS - Oklahoma's child protective service), the District Attorney's office, and a Guardian ad litem. None of the services in Kelsey's home ever brought to Raye's attention that there was anything unusual going on in her home. The "experts" didn't suspect abuse, and neither did Raye.

Once Kelsey went home with Raye, Kathie quit visiting Kelsey. It was reported that she did not want to be supervised because she did not like what was said about her in court.

In August of 2005, Kelsey, Raye Dawn, and Mike Porter were in a hit-and-run accident.[6] The man who hit the truck was pulled over a

_____

5 See Appendix B - Exhibit 3
6 See Appendix B – Exhibit 4

few blocks from the accident and was charged with drunk driving and leaving the scene of an accident. He caused over $14,000 in damage, bending the frame of Mike Porter's truck and shattering the back glass where Kelsey was sitting.[7] Against the rules, Kathie attended a visit with Kelsey and her stepmother shortly after the accident. Kathie took video and pictures of Kelsey's injuries from the accident to later use to gain custody of Kelsey, but they have since been used to show "abuse."

Kelsey lost her appetite and started to deteriorate after the accident, so Raye took Kelsey to specialists and signed her up for play therapy in an effort to determine what was happening to her daughter.

On October 11, 2005, Raye and Kelsey were napping together in the master bedroom. Raye only had two pull-ups left and Kelsey was in the process of potty training. She had an accident just before their nap, so Kelsey went to sleep wearing only a long, black t-shirt and no underwear or diaper.

Mike Porter arrived home from work between 2:30 and 2:45 PM. Raye awoke to Mike Porter standing above her and she left Kelsey in her bed sleeping while she drove the forty- to fifty-minute round trip to pick up Mike Porter's eight-year-old daughter from school in a nearby town.

When Raye returned home, Kelsey was in the arms of a first responder, and was being passed to an EMT. Raye screamed and ran to the ambulance. She noticed that Kelsey was wearing a pull-up. Mike Porter later stated that he had put it on her because he didn't want anyone "thinking anything" about her not wearing pants. He told Raye that he found a pull-up on the bar, but Raye states the pull-ups were in a bathroom closet.

---

[7] See Appendix B – Exhibit 4

On that day, Mike Porter described Kelsey's episode as a seizure, and nobody in the family questioned it since Kelsey had been reportedly having seizures for a while.

Kathie Briggs stated on 3-5-2006: "We heard another rumor today that a deal could be made for the mother. This is not justice for Kelsey if that happens…"

Kathie Briggs reportedly called the sheriff's office on the night of Kelsey's death and stated that it was murder and that her ex-daughter-in-law, Raye, had done it. She had already begun a quest to put Raye in prison for murder. Later, it became clear she was willing to take down anyone who got in the way of her stated mission.

Autopsy results showed that Kelsey had suffered from a possible sexual assault and that her death was from "blunt force trauma to the abdomen," which meant she had been murdered. (A second autopsy confirmed the sexual assault.)

Two obituaries would announce Kelsey's death; one for Kelsey's maternal family (the Smiths), and one for her paternal family (the Briggs). There were even two funerals at the insistence of Kathie Briggs. The difference in how the child was treasured is mirrored in the descriptions of her short life. The Smiths listed what they loved about Kelsey. The Briggs stated that she "loved to bite."

Published Oct. 15, 2005 - Kelsey Briggs

A funeral service for the Briggs family and friends of Kelsey Briggs, 2 1/2, will be 10 a.m. today at Parks Brothers Funeral Home, Prague.

Kelsey was born Dec. 28, 2002, to Lance Briggs and Raye Dawn Porter.

She died Oct. 11, 2005, at Prague Hospital. She loved swinging and gymnastics and riding her John Deere tractor. She also loved to bite.

Kelsey is survived by her father, SPC Lance Briggs of Fort Benning, Ga.; paternal grandparents, Royce and Kathie Briggs of Meeker; stepgrandpareents, [Susan and Jack] of Shawnee; aunts and uncles, Shirica Howard of Meeker, Jeanna and Randy Fowler of Meeker, Robynn and Gary Stell of Meeker and Shawn and Kristy Middleton of Shawnee; great-grandparents, Carl and Edna Briggs of Shawnee, Joy Batt and Joy Rose, both of Shawnee, ... and the late Raymond L. Batt; and numerous other family members and friends.

Kelsey Shelton Smith

Kelsey Shelton Smith departed this life on Oct. 11, 2005, at the tender age of two years, nine months and two weeks, at her home in Meeker.

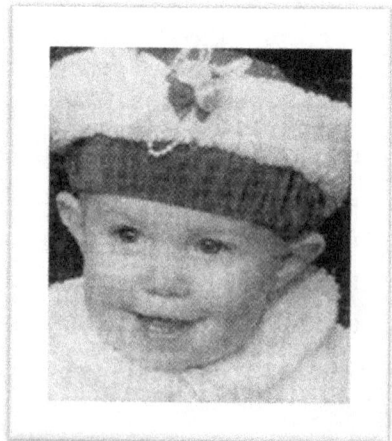

8

Kelsey was born Dec. 28, 2002, in Oklahoma City to Raye Dawn (Smith) Porter and Lance Robinson (Briggs).

Kelsey loved to dance and do the cha-cha with her mommy. She loved playing with her brother and sister and loved riding roller coasters with mommy. She would do anything as long as her mommy did it with her. She was always waiting on Grandma Gayla because they would do everything together that people could possibly think of. Kelsey always looked forward to her cousins, Merissa and Sierra, coming to stay the weekend with her. Kelsey's favorite movies were "Shrek," "Stuart Little 2" and "Monsters Inc." Most of all, she loved to lie down and sleep with her mommy, whether it be just a little nap or all night long.

She was preceded in death by her papa, Ray Shelton Smith; grandfather, Erdis Elvis Fowler; great-grandmother, Alta Smith; great-grandfather, Arthur Dee Smith and great-great-grandmother, Belvis Lucretia Winter.

Survivors include her mommy, Raye Dawn (Smith) Porter; stepfather, Mike Porter; sister, [Mike Porter's daughter]; brother, [Mike Porter's son], all of the home; father, Raymond Lance Robinson (Briggs); grandmother, Gayla Smith of Meeker; great-grandmother, Mildred Fowler of Meeker; grandmother, Kathie Briggs of Meeker; great-grandmother, Bernice Rose of Shawnee and many, many aunts, uncles and cousins.

Service will be 2 p.m. Saturday at the Assembly of God Church in Meeker with the Rev. Charles Pearcy officiating. Burial will follow at New Hope Cemetery in Meeker under the direction of Parks Brothers Funeral Service in Meeker.

Viewing and visitation will be 9 a.m. to 12 p.m. Saturday at Parks Brothers Funeral Chapel in Prague.

A guest book is available to share your memories on-line. Please visit [Web site link removed for privacy].

Shortly after Kelsey's death Mike Porter was charged with first degree murder. The charge of sexual assault was added in April of 2006 after the second autopsy confirmed "signs of forcible sexual assault."

Five years later, the focus is still on Raye. Many question why Kathie hates Raye so much that the hate spills over to Raye's family and supporters. Is it because she's jealous of Raye's close family? Was it due to her inability to get Kelsey to love her, when she clearly preferred to be with her own mother, instead, even though Kathie tried so hard to take her away from Raye? Is it because Raye jilted her son and exposed him as a man who beats women? I am one among many who have researched this case and I don't understand why the focus has always been on Raye, the devoted mom who wasn't home at the time of her daughter's alleged rape and murder and not on the man charged with sexual assault and murder.

After Mike Porter's plea in February, 2007, *Shawnee News Star* reported, "If it wasn't for the Briggs family's desire to accept the agreement, Smothermon said he would have taken this case to trial."

These are the questions that have come to my mind as well as the minds of others who have attempted to piece together the puzzle that surrounds Kelsey's short life and her tragic death. In asking these questions, I have become the next target in the campaign of hate.

The rational mind simply doesn't comprehend such a situation except to suggest, in this author's opinion, that Kathie Briggs isn't really focused on finding justice for her granddaughter so much as she has an unhealthy but passionate rage toward her ex-daughter-in-law. And the reason for that? Alas, hate is never a rational thing.

Kathie Briggs's Web site and its Members

October 2005

Kathie Briggs started her Web site within weeks of Kelsey's death. She quickly gained supporters with her version of the events, which is that she fought to save Kelsey, but nobody would listen, while her son—the "war hero"—arrived home from Iraq to find his daughter dead. I'd have to admit, it is a good story. Too bad it's just that...a story.

Though the Web site named for Kelsey displayed thousands of threatening and harassing comments made by Kelsey's paternal family members and their supporters, unbelievably, there is an even more sinister side to Kathie Briggs and her followers. There is always a secret place where they show their true characters, under aliases and out of the public's eye. They label these places their "bashboards" and through their emails with Mike Porter we learned that Kathie Briggs is "addicted to" the morbid and unruly side of her "cause."

After reading the negative comments, the pure, unfiltered hate, and about what I believe to be crimes that Kathie Briggs and her group have instigated and participated in for years, you'll shake your head, as I do, and wonder how these people could possibly claim to be victims of a fight they started, and are still carrying on amongst themselves in a public venue for all to see, six years after Kelsey's death.

Lies Beget Hate

Our nation's founders created laws to protect our right to speak freely. As part of that freedom, we are allowed to express our opinions and feelings about a topic without fear of reprisal. But when that freedom is misused and turned into a campaign of hate, people who abuse their rights to publicly crucify someone should not be allowed to hide behind "anonymous" or "concerned citizen." They should be forced to put their name to the hate so that the victim can seek a resolution.

In 2005 a hate group was formed in Oklahoma. The members were bold and fierce in their comments; some posted under their real names, but most used "anonymous" or an alias. They didn't see themselves as a hate group, but to someone looking in, the hate is all that is seen. It wasn't the typical type of group one visualizes when thinking of hate. They didn't target a specific race, religion, nationality, or sexual orientation. Their targets were in a special class: people Kathie Briggs hated. It was that simple. At the time, those who followed along with the plan didn't realize what they had gotten themselves into because it was masked behind the beautiful, innocent face of Kelsey. They used her pictures as their avatars so that when people read the awful words about Raye Dawn, they would associate them with Raye Dawn's own daughter. Disturbed doesn't even begin to describe my feelings on this subject. When I look at certain pictures of Kelsey, I don't see the child. Instead, I see hateful comments and actions. What's even more disturbing is that I'm not the only one who feels this way. I never met Kelsey, so I look at some pictures that Kathie Briggs and others hide behind and I feel disgust. It bothers me deeply that Kathie Briggs would do that to her own grandchild, but it was never about Kelsey, only revenge.

Their first target was, of course, Raye Dawn. She's the woman they portrayed as the "evil mother" who didn't care about anyone but herself. Next on the list were Raye Dawn's mother and grandmother, two upstanding and respected women in their community—two widows who were portrayed as self-absorbed women who were too busy with their boyfriends to see what was happening with Kelsey. Then there was the Judge who was said to have "sent Kelsey to her death." According to these people, he's a monster who doesn't care about children. That is far from the truth. As if that isn't bad enough, they added the charge that he was bewitched by Raye Dawn's beauty and charms. In reality, he's a happily married man with a beautiful wife he adores. Since Kathie Briggs's supporters did not know anyone involved, they readily believed her lies. Let's not forget the doctors, state workers, Kelsey's daycare owner, and so on. The list grew to include everyone that had contact with Kelsey throughout her life but had not conformed and bowed down to Kathie Briggs, apologized, and begged for forgiveness. She wanted to hear, "Kathie Briggs, you were right."

I've read post after post where Kathie Briggs and her followers stated "if the Judge would just apologize, he would still be on the bench" or if Kelsey's maternal great-grandmother, Mildred, would apologize for not doing more to save Kelsey, then she would not be harassed. On one occasion, Kathie Briggs stated, "I know one day I should forgive Raye Dawn for what she has done. I hope I can, but how do you when that person won't take responsibility for her actions and then ask to be forgiven?" My question is: How does Kathie Briggs know what Raye Dawn has confessed or if she's asked God's forgiveness? His forgiveness is all that matters. Kathie Briggs claims to be a Christian. Shouldn't she know about forgiveness?

Kathie Briggs seems to have forgiven Mike Porter. She stated that Mike Porter showed remorse so instead of going to trial, he was given a plea. Instead of a lynch mob going after him with picket signs in-hand, prayer requests for him and his family were extended. According to witnesses, Kathie Briggs even had tears in her eyes at Mike Porter's plea hearing stating, "It's hard to see him like that." The man was charged with murdering and sexually assaulting her granddaughter. But because he showed signs of remorse, he was to be forgiven. It still to this day makes me shake my head in disbelief.

In the hundreds of posts seeping with hate from their bashboards, Kathie Briggs neglected to mention that she quit visiting Kelsey because she was asked not to use her phone during the visits. Also, she reportedly didn't like what was being said about her. She made up stories such as her "rights to Kelsey were taken away" and she was told she "couldn't appeal the decision to return Kelsey to the home of Mike Porter and Raye Dawn," but emails written by Kathie Briggs herself tell a different story.[8] Kathie Briggs wanted to blame everyone but herself or any member of her family and rally for hate against everyone who didn't bend to do her bidding.

Within the long list of targets, the name and office that was only briefly mentioned was that of the district attorney. Kathie Briggs has gone after everyone else involved in the case, including Kelsey's guardian ad litem and the attorney whom Raye Dawn had retained during the custody battle for Kelsey. However, after she made a public threat against the district attorney and he succumbed to her wishes, he was deemed "a good man" from that point forward. Why? Kathie Briggs's son, Lance, filed multiple lawsuits and even tried to get people disbarred, but the district attorney snuck under the radar with no lawsuit and no complaints to the state bar. It was the district attorney's office who wanted to remove all services from Kelsey's home just one month before her death because they did not see any issues that were concerning to them. Yet they filed charges against Raye for enabling? But for some reason, the district attorney became Kathie Briggs's strongest ally in her fight as well as someone whom she has referenced as her personal attorney after she made the threatening statement, "I wonder if our District Attorney does not get a conviction if this will be an issue in his next election?" After an abundance of threats, he went after Raye on charges his office did not support while Kelsey was alive. I suppose he knew how to play the game and keep his job, even if it meant going against his sense of right and wrong. He was manipulated, as were many others. He became another marionette in Kathie and Lance Briggs' puppet show.

---

[8] See Appendix B – Exhibit 5 and "The Naked Truth Bound in Scorn" to read the emails

Unfortunately, those who joined the Briggs' "cause" thought they were getting justice for the death of a child. They thought they were building an organization to bring awareness to child abuse and to help other children who found themselves in situations like Kelsey's. That's what they thought they were supporting. An argument I've made since July of 2007 has been the fact that people can only learn from mistakes made if they are going to use Kelsey's true story to ensure others don't make the same mistakes. Until Kathie's and Lance's lies were exposed, only those who were closest to the paternal family knew that their cause would never create real change because the story was untrue. Today, those who blindly supported Kathie Briggs in her mission call it being "Kathie'd." They were deceived into participating in a statewide hissy fit and they didn't know it. Some of the people involved in the hate group now know what they were a part of and they feel terrible about helping it grow into what it became. They were manipulated. They saw a beautiful child who had been allegedly sexually assaulted and murdered and their hearts went out to the child's paternal family. They believed the stories they were told about Kelsey's maternal family being nothing but uncaring monsters. They knew nobody who was involved, so they were easily deceived. It happens. Therefore, I want to clarify that some of the names have been changed, in part, because I would never want to harm those who thought they were doing the right thing. Those I have gotten to know honestly thought they were helping children. But the mission became clear. Soon after Raye Dawn went to prison the billboards came down, as well as some of the "Justice for Kelsey" signs. The group that was supposed to be helping children started to deactivate after Raye Dawn's trial and people woke up and realized what was happening around them. Their duty was done. Raye Dawn was convicted. It was never about the children.

Recently, a witness told me that someone who is well-respected in the state for working against child abuse posed the question, "Could Kathie Briggs have been the one to break Kelsey's legs?" According to the evidence, Kelsey was in the custody of her maternal aunt when she sprained her ankle. But she was in the custody of Kathie Briggs when her other leg became injured and the double casts became a necessity. Will we ever learn the truth about her injury?

People are realizing they were deceived. So as I present evidence of the hate that was churning on Kathie Briggs's Web site and in other places, the hate is the focus, not the Web site members. Many of those members have different views today and wish they could go back and change what was said and done. Despite the turn of events, a few continue this same pattern of hate to this day, with no sign of ever stopping. They feed on the hate. They love it! It was the hate that destroyed me and many others and there has been and still is an abundance of it.

The Bashboards

2005

When putting Raye's story together, I was given a stack of papers approximately two feet tall that was nothing but evidence of this hate campaign against Raye Dawn and her family. For the first few weeks, I was overwhelmed. Of course, I wanted to include every awful word, but it's just too much. After months of editing, I believe I've included just enough to clearly illustrate the intense hate targeted at Raye Dawn and others, and then at myself. All of the posts and statements included in this book are in their original format. They may include typos, etc., but I did not want to change how these haters expressed themselves verbally, so I left them as is.

I recently learned the term "conditioned." Some of the posts may seem random or harmless to someone who isn't personally affected by the words. But for those of us who have been bullied, words that seem harmless have a deeper, darker meaning. We have been "conditioned" to read the hate and threats that are between the lines.

While reading the following posts, one may see a family that desperately wanted justice for a dead child. However, known facts in the case, such as Kathie Briggs's accusations against Raye Dawn starting on the night of Kelsey's death, give us insight into the actions to come. Even with the arrest and charges of murder and sexual assault for the man who was home alone with Kelsey at the time of her alleged rape and murder, Kathie Briggs's initial thoughts of what happened never changed. Her mind was made up and she would work day and night to convince Oklahoma, and then the world, that she was right, despite the facts or the evidence. Is that "Justice for Kelsey"?

Some of the first mean-spirited words were left on Kelsey's online condolences guestbook. The funeral home was eventually forced to close the memorial for Kelsey because the negative comments against Kelsey's maternal family were deemed inappropriate.

The following message of love was left by Raye Dawn's second cousin, Sherri Heath on October 16, 2005. Notice the family had no idea that Kelsey's death had been caused by Mike Porter. On the day of the funeral, and for some time afterward, they thought Kelsey had died of a seizure. She stated,

What a joy it has been these past 2 ½ years watching Kelsey grow and be a part of our large family! In many ways, she showed us how to be strong, loving, kind, and happy as a child of God should be. We will forever hold in our hearts the hugs and smiles she has given us. Mike and Raye, we want you to know that we are praying for comfort and strength during this difficult time. There will be trying times ahead, and we pray that God will wrap his arms around you both and keep you safe. We love you

Gayla, Kelsey's maternal grandmother, left the following message on the same day:

Kelsey, Grandma misses you so much and will with each passing day. We had so much fun together. It's like you knew you didn't have long so let's get it all done. We would brush hog the pasture, mow the lawn, go fishing together, haul off the trash, or take in a movie and when we sang Jesus Loves Me or the BIBLE you'd just snap those little fingers and we'd have a big time. Grandma is going to miss your 4 or 5 calls a day at work. You were such a blessing. You were the one that completed our 5 generations of girls – I'm so thankful we took the time to have that picture made. Kelsey, the day God called you home, Mommy told me you were sitting in front of the door waiting on me to come get you and take you to the movie. I guess God had something more important for you than us going to the movie. I know you lub Grandma so much.

After Kelsey's mommy, Raye Dawn, left the following heartfelt message, even more strangers and "anonymous" people flooded Kelsey's memory board with negativity.

Kelsey, Mommy loves you very much. You know who really loves you and took care of you. The people who matter know you were very happy to be home with mommy, because no matter where we were if we were together we were home and not many two year olds tell their mommy everyday that they lub them so much. Kelsey, life will never be the same because you were my life. You were a very special baby who touched a lot of people's lives in such a short period of time. Mommy is going to miss seeing those bluz eyes every morning when you wake up and all through the rest of the day. We had a special bond that only you and I will understand, besides grandma. Kelsey, you are my baby and I know you will visit me daily. I know you're busy having fun teaching PaPa the ChaCha and I know life in heaven is far greater than here, so save mommy a spot and when God calls for mommy I know you'll be there to take me by the hand to say, 'mommy we're home again.' Mommy

Raye Dawn's loving message to her daughter was followed by a message from someone who didn't know the families, and didn't care who would be hurt by the mean-spirited words.

Lance I do not know you at all, or Kelsey's mother I don't even want to know her or know who she is. I am a Prague resident and you had a beautiful little girl, when I heard about it, It brought tears to my eyes how could this happen to a child, they will find out who did this and when they do they will get theres. I hear you were a wonderful father. Kelsey is in heaven looking down at you and your family she is yalls guardian angel im sorry for your loss you and your family are in my thoughts and prayers. Unknown October 16, 2005

On November 11, 2005, just one month after Kelsey's passing, Kelsey's Purpose's home page relayed the following message:

21

*My granddaughter Kelsey was born after her parents were divorced.
I wondered why this child would be put on this earth after the
two people who were not meant to be together had already
gone their separate ways. I knew she had a purpose, but what
could it be? When my son was called to active duty and sent
to Iraq I was sure that I knew. God was giving Kelsey to us
because her father was not coming home. I was wrong.
Kelsey was the one who did not make it. She died just days
before her dad was to return. After nine months of abuse, she
joined the other little angels in Heaven. It was then that I
knew her purpose…She was put here to make a difference –
to make sure other children are protected. This website is
still being developed. We plan to have more pictures and
information about Kelsey, links to agencies and
organizations who can help prevent child abuse, and a
message board dedicated to sharing information between
people who are dedicated to the welfare of children
everywhere. Please check back soon!*

By November 18, 2005, the campaign was in full swing. The
following e-mail was sent to sixty-one of Oklahoma's teachers:

*From: Justice for Kelsey Subject: Justice for Kelsey Briggs -
Oklahomans are outraged by the senseless and preventable
death of Kelsey Briggs. Please help get Justice for Kelsey
and prevent other children from suffering from child abuse. A
demonstration will be held on Monday, November 21, 2005
at the…County Court house at 11:30 am and then move to
the…County DHS office at 12:30 pm. If you are wondering
why Raye Dawn has not been charged in the death of Kelsey,
contact the District Attorney's office at 275-xxxx or fax them
at 275-xxxx. A website www.Kelseyspurpose.com has been
set up with links to various websites to assist Oklahomans in
holding the agencies and people that failed Kelsey
accountable. Included in this e-mail are a poem written for
Kelsey and a speech that was given by Kathie Briggs at the
State Capital on November 8, 2005. The hope is that they will
inspire Oklahomans to make their voices heard for Kelsey
and other children suffering from child abuse. Please*

forward this e-mail to your family, friends, and coworkers to make a difference in a child's life. Thank you!

Included in the e-mail was a poem about Kelsey that targeted Raye as the monster and a speech given by Kathie Briggs at the State Capitol. The speech gave details of Kelsey's life, according to Kathie Briggs. It ended with the statement, "Not only should the perpetrator be held accountable, but everyone who had knowledge

NOTE from Sherri Heath:

Britten Follet helped mail those letters out per her announcing it on her tv station with a cart full of letters…helping this poor grandmother…..Kathie had already contacted the media to help her hate campaign!

of the abuse and those who failed to help." If Kelsey's story were told including every detail of her final months, Kathie Briggs, Lance, and their family members would also fit her description of those who should "be held accountable."

At some point in November of 2005, a poll was added to the Kelsey's Purpose Web site that posed the question: "Do you think Raye Dawn had any doing in hurting Kelsey? The possible answers were: "Yes- by not protecting her from Mike Porter," which garnered 16 votes or 57.14% as of December 12, 2005, and "Yes – by

enduring[9] it herself" had 9 votes or 32.14% with "No" obtaining zero votes and lastly "Not sure" with 3 votes or 10.71%. Following are some of the captured posts that explain the voters' answers: One of the captured posts was from "LazyHusker" which stated, "…This is only an opinion…" The signature at the bottom of the post stated, "May Kelsey's Memory Live On! Keep Fighting For Kelsey! An Eye For An Eye!" As the button that I received from the Oklahoma Coalition to Abolish the Death Penalty states: "An eye for an eye leaves the whole world blind."

From the posts it was evident that people were joining forces with the Briggs family, even though they knew nothing about either family or any details of the case other than what they had seen in the media and what was being shared on Kelsey's Purpose. A gag order was in place, but that did nothing to deter the witch hunt that was brewing. Weeks passed and torches were lit and nothing stood in their way. Everybody else followed the rules and remained silent but the group was determined that Raye was going to be charged with something. Witnesses state that Kathie Briggs repeatedly said, "Raye Dawn has to go to prison, if only for one day! She just has to go to prison!"

Raye's family soon learned that Raye would have no claims to any monies awarded from Lance's multiple lawsuits if she was convicted of a crime in connection with Kelsey's murder. That meant Kelsey's paternal family would stop at nothing to get her convicted, even if that meant teaming up with the man charged with Kelsey's alleged sexual assault and murder.

The Man Charged with Murder and the Grieving Grandma

Mike Porter was arrested within days of Kelsey's murder. After the discovery was made that Kelsey's death was not the result of a seizure, as the maternal family had been led to believe by Mike Porter himself, the Oklahoma State Bureau of Investigation conducted

---

[9] Emphasis by book author

24

interviews of both Mike Porter and Raye Dawn simultaneously and in separate rooms.

Mike Porter had been acting guilty with multiple phone calls to the medical examiner's office the day after Kelsey's death, demanding the results of the autopsy. He was reportedly upset that the autopsy would be thorough. At one point, the person he spoke with at the ME's office quit answering any questions, noting that only the person guilty of or charged with the crime would behave in the way that Mike Porter had on that day. Also, according to witnesses, Mike Porter pretended to attempt suicide on two occasions: first with a gun that he "overlooked" in a drawer he opened and then slammed shut when he threatened to shoot himself, and then with a full bottle of Tylenol he supposedly swallowed that was later found under a nightstand. He acted equally suspicious during his interrogation.

Raye Dawn was interrogated with the same amount of suspicion as Mike Porter because, as the investigator phrased it, Kathie Briggs was "calling everyone in the world and saying Raye Dawn was guilty." Investigators were supposedly presented with hearsay evidence of Raye Dawn's "violent tendencies" that made her the main suspect for the crime, in Kathie Briggs's opinion. Days after Raye Dawn lost her child she was treated like a criminal and told gory details of her only child's death with Kathie Briggs's finger pointing at her as the perpetrator.

At the end of Raye Dawn's interview, she was informed that Mike Porter had refused to take a lie detector test. Raye Dawn was willing to take one, but since she was pregnant, they wouldn't give her one. Since Raye Dawn had fully cooperated and repeatedly yelled, "Tell me what I need to do!" investigators brought Mike Porter into the room with Raye Dawn and discussed the fact that he refused the lie detector. Mike Porter stated, "It's not that I'm not cooperating. We're just at an impasse." After hearing his uncooperative stance, Raye Dawn stormed out of the room and the video of Raye Dawn's interview ended shortly afterward with the investigator trying to get more information from Mike Porter. He would not budge. Days later, when Raye Dawn returned to the OSBI office for her second interview, the first words from the investigator included an apology for how she was treated in the previous interview. The investigator stated, "I didn't know what happened. I only had the autopsy results."

Recent reports have been released claiming that during the simultaneous interviews, Mike Porter was writhing in pain due to his grief over the loss of Kelsey, while Raye Dawn was talking about her big house and great life, and basically being a cold-hearted, uncaring mother. This is untrue. From what I viewed, those things were never said during her interview. They also claimed that Raye Dawn never cried, yet, from the beginning of the interview, she continuously wiped tears from her cheeks. These reports have clearly been created just to promote hate against Raye Dawn—a hate that Mike Porter helped to build with misrepresented and untrue accounts of events.

Mike Porter is a smart man. He quickly learned how to play the game. After his release on bond less than two months after being arrested for the first-degree murder of Kelsey, he became an active member of Kelsey's Purpose. What had started as a cry for justice against both Mike Porter and Raye Dawn soon turned to a united roar, with Mike Porter a member of "team Kathie Briggs," doing her bidding. He even earned her trust to the point where she gave him a ride to her daughter's apartment for a private meeting with just herself and Mike Porter to discuss not Kelsey's death, but according to Kathie Briggs, possible civil lawsuits.

On August 15, 2007 I posted the following comment regarding their meeting:

I was watching Oprah a while back and I saw a segment where Oprah had guests who had family members or loved ones murdered. The guests confronted the perpetrator on the show and asked them questions. The questions they asked were things like: 1. What were his/her last words? 2. Was he/she in pain? 3. Was he/she scared? 4. Why did you do it? etc. etc. I have a real problem with someone who meets with the murderer and sexual abuser of their grandchild 90 days after that child has been murdered and abused and only asks for information about the Judge and DHS. She also exchanged numerous emails with Mike Porter, not one of them included any of the above questions. The 15 million dollar lawsuit, the multiple suits against doctors, DHS, CASA, etc. and the fact that apparently I guess Lance doesn't have a job but lives off of donations tells me that it's all about the money for these people. Why didn't they use the two life insurance policies they had on Kelsey to help with the rest of the funeral expenses they created? Raye Dawn had a site up a while back. I think it's pretty much shut down now, but on her site she called the charity 'Kathie's Purpose.' At first, I thought that was an exaggeration, but the more I dig into this case, the more clear it becomes to me that Kathie and Lance do have a purpose, otherwise she would have asked the last person to see her grandbaby alive what happened instead of what can I use against the authorities and the system so that I can create a lawsuit.

After Kelsey's death, it didn't take long for members of Kathie Briggs's forum to start questioning the paternal family's actions, as well as their intentions. On November 24, 2005, and almost two years before my post, the question "Where Was The Family During All Of This?" was posed with an explanation for the question. The member stated,

Kelsey's story hit me like a ton of bricks...I was an abused child for nine years...and where was the news coverage then? I had no family. Just a drunken father...Kelsey had a ton of family or that was what the news media portrayed...It took this sweet, beautiful little girl dying to have the news media show up???? And why instead of them (The Media) showing up for Thanksgiving Dinner at this wonderful families home to talk about this tragedy after the fact...where were all these loving family members at when she needed them??? ...where were YOU people? You claim you loved her but apparently you did not help her in a way that may have saved her life! If your hands were tied, by the court system or bureaucracy or

27

whatever, then so be it. That is something that is
understandable and accepted – to a degree.

The story that was being told was that the paternal family didn't
have access to Kelsey in her final months because their rights were
taken away. As proven throughout the evidence found in my first book
on this case entitled, *The Naked Truth Bound in Scorn*, this was untrue.
They gave up their rights. However, this outsider smelled something
fishy with the constant media attention. Why did Kelsey's case garner
so much attention when she wasn't the only child in Oklahoma who
had died after abuse allegations? Was it the portrayal of Lance as a
war hero who was in Iraq instead of in a hospital in Georgia being
reportedly treated for substance abuse and suicide threats at the time
of Kelsey's murder? A witness recently told me that when Cherokee
Ballard interviewed Lance while joining his family for Thanksgiving
dinner, she requested to use the medals and awards earned by Lance's
now former friend as a backdrop for the interview because Lance "had
not yet received any awards." I'm told this friend declined her request.

Jeanna, Kelsey's paternal aunt and Lance's older sister, responded
to the question with this bold statement:

Perhaps this will shed some light on where were all these loving
    family members at when she need them??? The real question
    is, where were Kelsey's maternal family members? In
    addition to Royce and Kathie Briggs' pleas, many, many,
    family members and members of our community also begged
    and pleaded for the protection of Kelsey. Kathie Briggs (in
    addition to other people) spent hours and hours every day
    calling and writing to everyone that she could think of to
    help. Royce and Kathie Briggs, along with Lance's wife,
    [April], and [April's] parents, hired an attorney and did all
    that they could to try to help Kelsey. They did everything that
    they could possibly do under the laws of the state of
    Oklahoma.

Once Kathie Briggs voluntarily gave up on her visits with Kelsey
in June of 2005, she addressed an email to hundreds of people that

included the following statement regarding appealing the judge's decision to return Kelsey to Raye's home, *"Our attorney says we can appeal this decision and is shocked at how the ruling went...We want to appeal, but at this time our financial situation will not allow for that. My son knew while he was gone he could save money for his family and get his truck fixed."* Does that sound like someone who did "everything that they could possibly do under the laws of the state of Oklahoma"?

Two days after the question was asked on Kelsey's Purpose, Kathie Briggs joined the discussion. She stated,

I can certainly understand why so many have questions about what did happen or what should have happened in this case. This story is so long and complicated it was very difficult to summarize it in my speech in front of the Capital...Our Governor is from the same home town as most of my family, and because this situation was not important to him he has lost many votes...Yes, the media is covering a story and it is a business, but what would you suggest we do to get the story out there? It was not a dream of ours to put our family in the spot light of the media...Our family could grieve in private and mourn her death and go back to our own lives, but ... If we need to sit in front of the cameras or write letters and answer questions we do so proudly...We might not be understood by all and we might get criticized from some...We appreciate all of the messages pro and con to our cause...

Since this statement, two people have reportedly been asked, "Don't you know who I am?" by both Kathie and Lance Briggs. I believe the protest of not seeking fame is challenged by this revealing question.

Threats

2005

Threats of lawsuits have been made toward anyone who spoke up against the Briggs. Members of their family have played the role of victim, each time their version of Kelsey's story has been questioned, while the hate for Raye and her family has been a never-ending tide.

For the past three years Kathie Briggs has made claims that she has been stalked, harassed, defamed, and so on. Any backlash that she's received from the public attacks she's launched against dozens of people can, in no way, compare to the pain she's created. For instance, shortly after Kelsey's death, one of Kathie Briggs's supporters left messages on the answering machines of Kelsey's maternal grandmother, as well as her great-grandmother.

The following was a message left for Mildred, Kelsey's maternal great-grandmother:

Now listen here you old pig! You are spending all that money defending old Raye Dawg, why didn't you spend half a little of that money takin' care of Kelsey? You think the citizens of Meeker are hot? You ought to come up here to Oklahoma City, you old pig, and see how we feel. We are mad as hell! And we are going to do something about it! We are going to keep this out in the public and continue to fight for Kelsey till we don't have another breath in us! If you had took half the money you are spending on Raye Dawg and spent it on Kelsey! People like you make me sick!

A few days after Mildred received this message, her phone rang and she answered. No one said a word. The only sound was that of a baby crying.

Gayla, Kelsey's maternal grandmother, received a message that was addressed to her male friend. The person stated,

I just want you to know I'm a grandmother from Oklahoma and the story on Kelsey Briggs has just upset me so badly. I talked to all of my friends and neighbors and we will never buy from [business name withheld for privacy]. You're harboring a murderer and you're harboring somebody who sat by and watched it and I hope that it cuts into your pocketbook, because maybe if it cuts into your pocketbook, you might get rid of both of them. I don't know what kind of guy you are, but someone who harbors a baby murderer tells me a lot about that person.

A second message soon followed:

Well, I can't believe you're still living with a (inaudible)...whore and a baby beater and raper. Good lord! Somebody was looking the other day and saw a real estate sign out there and somebody was taking down the name. One of the neighbors ran out and said, 'Don't buy that house! They harbor a baby raper!' Boy, you must be low. None of them ain't good looking. Hell, I think (inaudible) are better than old Gayla and Raye Dawn! Why don't you give one of them a shot? They haven't killed anybody yet. You sorry thing! Good bye!

On December 9, 2005 a letter addressed to Gayla's friend arrived with a picture at the top of the letter of Kelsey that was displayed on Kelsey's Purpose. It read,

Look at that adorable innocent little face, so full of wonder, hope, magic and love. Children are so innocent, they believe in the tooth fairy, and Easter Bunny and Santa Clause. They have not learned to hate or show prejudice and everyone is their friend. They turn to the adults in their life for love and protection, without asking for anything in return. Children are our future. What kind of monster, punches a baby in the stomach, ending her life?? What kind of monster breaks both legs of a toddler??? I cannot imagine such an individual. I keep asking myself why, why, why???? And again, I ask

32

myself, 'How could you protect and shelter an individual responsible for beating a toddler?' I hope you can sleep at night, knowing you have two women in your home, one abused Kelsey and the other ignored Kelsey's bruises and broken bones. I heard your girlfriend was too wrapped up in you and your money to pay any attention to what was happening to Kelsey. I am putting the word out to boycott your realty company to all my friends. Hope you guys enjoy the holidays together. A Grandmother.

Kelsey's great-grandmother, Mildred, received a message from another one of Kathie Briggs's supporters, Debbie. She had once been Mildred's daughter-in-law, and she had warned the Smiths of the custody battle that the Briggs started planning months before the first allegation of abuse. She is also the mother of Mildred's grandson and the mother-in-law of Kathie Briggs's oldest daughter. The statement that she left on Mildred's answering machine was clearly pre-written, and it included accusations against Kelsey's maternal family. The message ended with this warning: "You'd better be doing something else and praying A LOT!"

As time went on and Kathie Briggs became a regular face on the nightly news, it seemed some of her supporters felt as if they were rubbing elbows with a local celebrity and only wanted to please her by generating more hate for Raye and her family. There was a unified roar for justice. Mike Porter's voice soon became the loudest of all. His $1 million bond was reduced to $250,000, allowing him to bond out of jail. Some say it was done at the request of the paternal family so they could communicate with him.

Pretending to be his sister, he became a part of the forum and later the paternal family's "bash board." In the beginning, he was blamed, along with Raye. Kathie Briggs and her family members wanted him to "pay." Once Kathie Briggs's forum was flooded with posts from Mike Porter supporters, which coincidentally, started at around the same time Mike Porter was released on bond, the tone toward Mike Porter changed while the hatred for Raye grew even more intense. It's clear from communications that Mike Porter manipulated Kelsey's paternal family by sharing "stories" with them of things Raye and her family members had said and done. He knew exactly what they wanted to hear. Some posts by his "supporters" mimic statements he makes later as himself. Therefore, my suspicion is that it was actually him.

Kelsey's Purpose

November and December 2005

Discussion of the impromptu poll continued well into December of 2005 with nobody questioning the choice of words used in creating the poll. If 32% of the Kelsey's Purpose members honestly believed that Raye had "endured" the abuse herself, as the poll suggested, then she too should have been seen as a victim and not made out to be the monster. But this group's hatred for Raye seemed stronger than their intellectual ability to reason.

November 20, 2005

Shirica Posts: 21 Re: Poll - The truth is none of us know what happened in that house on the hill on October 11ᵗʰ. We all have our theories and our gut wrenching beliefs, but only the one who inflicted this horrible pain upon this beautiful child and God know the truth. On the night Kelsey died our family stood in a circle in the living room holding hands. We were led in prayer by a family friend. During the prayer it was said, "Let what was done in darkness be brought into light." I have held onto that prayer and repeated it every day. God has bestowed so many blessings upon our family following Kelsey's passing, I have to believe that he will continue to do so. I have to believe that God will continue to work through our family, the investigators, the District Attorney and so many countless others so that we can know who inflicted the cries that went unheard upon this most precious gift from God.

Shirica's message—while moving—is confusing to me. At the time of her post, Mike Porter had been charged with murder. The mystery was solved. Why continue to question the facts that investigators had uncovered? Perhaps the next post and its insinuation give us a clue.

35

Misty LT is said to have met Mike Porter through Kelsey's Purpose and their "bash board." A few private messages have been shared with the public, but from other private messages on Kelsey's Purpose, Kelsey's paternal aunt claims to have learned of a relationship between this married woman and Mike Porter. Kelsey's paternal aunt stated that this person was ready to leave her husband and move her three children in with Mike Porter. This illustrates how hard the paternal family worked publicly to portray Raye as the one guilty of abusing and murdering Kelsey.

November 22, 2005

Misty_lt Posts: 1 Re: Poll - Hi everyone. I do not know the family, but I live in Chandler and for some reason Kelsey popped into my head tonight and thoughts were reeling about this horrible thing that has happened to your family. Maybe because I've had my own dealings with DHS in this county and the courts, I don't know, but Kelsey was in my head so I decided to look at web sites and see what I could find about her story and this is where I ended up. "Raye Dawn claims she knew nothing of the abuse".....or....."Michael Porter still maintains his innocence and claims that the abuse was coming from Raye Dawn all along", etc....Now I realize that one blames the other, but usually when there is a divorce case filed or something that has high media attention such as this, one is usually standing up pointing fingers loudly. And we haven't heard anything out of Raye Dawn at all. Is this going on behind scenes?? I read the deposition of the FBI agent and everyone's story that they told the FBI agent and I have to question if Michael is the one that did it. But really I just wonder if either one of them are speaking out about it? By the way, I have 3 children of my own and 2 of them are twins. My twins were born 3 months early and almost didn't stay in this world with me. And I remember how painful that was, but I will never pretend to act like I know what you're family is going through or even come close to knowing, but my prayers are with you and my thoughts are obviously with you and Kelsey and she obviously did a little dance in my head tonight and tuned me into your story and website for some reason. I don't know any of the Briggs or Smith families, but with the things that I've read and the strength that I've seen, I wish I did.

December 1, 2005

The following is a post from the angry grandmother who harassed Mildred and Gayla with threatening messages. Lance was able to get Kelsey's records unsealed, but only from himself and his mother. As you'll read in Kathie Briggs's emails to Mike Porter, she read and re-read Raye's letter to the Department of Human Services (DHS). The records were not released to Lance for Kathie Briggs's "amusement," but it seems that is what they have become.

As of the date of this book, the public does not have access to the records...six years after Kelsey's death. If they were available, I believe a lot of opinions would be changed.

Cheryl Posts: 13 KUDOS TO LANCE BRIGGS - I was watching the news last night and I saw where Lance Briggs was bringing a $15 million dollar lawsuit if Kelsey's files were not unsealed within 30 days. I shouted out, "Good for you Lance!" I admire Lance and the entire Briggs family for not letting the untimely, unnecessary and preventable death of Kelsey be brushed under the rug and forgotten. O you can be sure, Judge Craig Keys, Patti J. Bonner, DHS, CASA, Michael Porter and Rae Dawn would love to see all the Briggs family fade away and silenced forever. Kudos to lance and all the Briggs family for continuing to fight and speak for Kelsey!! There are many people, like myself, that are following this story and we are sickened and grief stricken over what happened to Kelsey. Sometimes at night I have trouble sleeping when I think of Kelsey and her final days. I just wonder how Judge Craig Keyes, Patti J. Bonner, CASA, the spokesperson for DHS, Michael Porter and Rae Dawn sleep at night??? My opinion is that a couple of the people I just mentioned need to be charged with Kelsey's murder along with Michael Porter.

Debbie Posts: 3 Re: Where was the family during all of this? - In knowing and being related by my children to both sides of Kelsey's family, I can say first hand that the Briggs did everything humanly possible to help Kelsey. There was not a stone left unturned to try to help this little girl. I can not say that on the maternal side of the family. The mothers side was and still are so worried about what their family is going to look like or what people are going to think that they could not comprehend that little Kelsey was being hurt by one of their "own". No one has a right to say anything about how Kelsey's paternal family handled this horrible situation. They have handled it with more grace than anything that I've ever seen. I could not possibly have done what this family ahs done to try to protect Kelsey. I just wish that DHS, Judge Key and all other top officials would have listened to them before it was too late for Kelsey. Maybe with everyone's help, we can prevent this from ever happening to another child.

From page 4 on Kelsey's Purpose subject titled "Poll":

Debbie Posts: 3 Re: Poll - You asked where is Raye Dawn's mother and Kelsey's paternal grandmother during this time? The paternal grandmother is Kathie Briggs. I'm sure that you meant the maternal grandmother, Gayla Smith. You'd have to know Gayla. She was too involved with herself to have any significant involvement with her children, much less grandchildren. To put it as she put it "they are grown now (children) and I'm through raising them". She's had too much dating to do to see what was happening towards the last of Kelsey's life. This was a "win" situation getting Kelsey back with Raye Dawn. Didn't matter to the Smith family how they did, just so that they won. Guess Gayla and her real estate boyfriend, ... will see just how it is dealing with Raye Dawn on a daily basis since Gayla and Raye Dawn are both living with him in OKC. That is really funny since she told me about this time last year that he didn't want any kids or grandkids living with them. Gayla thinks he has money and he thinks she does. Boy are they going to have a

38

rude awakening. I really don't know how Raye Dawn is even affording any attorney myself.

December 2, 2005

Cheryl Posts: 14 Re: Poll - I figured that the maternal grandmother was too involved with her "new" boyfriend and could not be bothered with the fact that her grandbaby was being beaten and tortured on a daily basis. I had her figured out when I saw her in court with her daughter. I bet they went home that night and watched themselves on the television and then asked each other, 'How did my hair look? Didn't my make-up look good?" You could tell they were both self-involved with how they looked on television. Poor Kelsey, she never had a chance with that family. **What really scares me, is that Rae Dawn in pregnant with her second victim.**[10]

The next character to be introduced into this never-ending drama is Ashley, the daughter-in-law of Raye's former co-worker who became the state's main witness against Raye. She was also "Enough is Enough" on the Free Kelsey's Mom forum. She started the bash board that Mike Porter and the Briggs discuss in their intimate e-mails in which they also bad mouth her. She added her own spin to the rumor mill with the following story.

Posts: 14 Re: Poll - I'm not sure how true this is, but I have heard that Gayla asked a friend of her's whom is a foster parent to take Kelsey so that no one would see the bruises on her. I have also heard that Rae Dawn would make comments at work about how Kelsey was in her way and how they (Rae Dawn and Michael) couldn't do anything with her around and how she would say it with such anger. I would hope that if someone thought their child was in their way, they would give them to someone else who did want them, but then again doing this would have cut off her child support. I'm so outraged at the fact that Kelsey's maternal side is not

---

[10] *Emphasis added by book author*

39

wanting "Justice" also. And if they are, sorry but I don't see it! Think about it, if your daughter has been murdered & your & your innocent ~ then why the hell are you avoiding the press?????? Why are "statements and appearances" only being made when they know there is a raly or protest?? Just what are they hiding?? Why not join in on seeking Just for Kelsey?? If she is innocent then why not join with everyone else and do what ever it takes to get justice for Kelsey?? Why aren't they yelling at the world to help change the laws??? Why not back up Lance and help him ~ He is Inocent in all this we all know for a fact! Bottom line here is obvious......................Why tell the world your pregnant and what you expect to get out of your divorce ~ This is about Kelsey!!!! (Remember her??) I'm so disappointed in our system! Lance fought for us! He risked his life for us ~ for you and for our country! He was brave and unselfish and for what???? For us to let him down in a way that is far to unforgiveable!!! He was willing to die for our country!!! and our country, our system allowed his child to be murdered! Then noone had the decesy to contact him to get him home! It is like saying "Hey go fight for us, but don't expect us to fight for you!" I feel WE ALL OWE it to LANCE to contact as many people as we can about Kelsey's case, not just once or twice, but over and over again and to stand behind him and his family 100% as they seek Justice for Kelsey and try to protect many others. God Bless Lance & his Family!

December 4, 2005

Seebeebrat74 Posts: 2 Re: Poll - Amen Ashley, God Bless him and Kelsey. May the system he swore to defend give him the justice Kelsey didn't get.

After Kelsey's death all that the media seemed to want to focus on was Lance Briggs, this war hero who came home to bury his daughter. As his older sister, Jeanna, pointed out on Kelsey's Purpose, this persona of Kelsey's father was a way to draw attention to their version of the story. In June, 2007 a brave reporter stepped up and wrote about the untold events surrounding Kelsey's life as well as the truth about the Briggs in a newspaper that is dedicated to fighting injustice. The *U.S. Observer* has given me permission to reprint the section of the article that addresses Lance Briggs, specifically, in its article entitled, *"Kelsey Smith-Briggs - Murder and Exploitation – Prosecutor Smothermon Presses False Charges?"* [11]

Lance: Biological Father

A father should never have to bury his child. It chills the bones to even conceive of such a painful ordeal. In the process of unraveling Kelsey's story we cannot forget the hurt surely felt by people in her life. Yet, in the unraveling we cannot fully understand Kelsey's ordeal without uncovering the world into which she was born. That world, whether he wanted it to or not, very much included her father, Lance.

"You want to play games? You decide!" – Lance Briggs

Research has shown that an intact and happy home is by far the best scenario for children. Why then did Kelsey's mother, Raye Dawn, divorce Lance in the first place? Wouldn't Kelsey seeing her mother and father together have been best? It was a long record of physical and mental abuse that preceded Raye's escape. Make no mistake; Lance is a vicious physical abuser with a long laundry list of offenses.

---

[11] *US Observer* "Kelsey Smith-Briggs - Murder & Exploitation - Prosecutor Smothermon Pushes False Charges?" by Barry Jon, Investigative Reporter

*Lance threw Kelsey's mother against the wall and choked her with
      his arm for not "super-sizing his McDonald's Value Meal."*

---

*Lance reportedly, violently punched the pregnant abdomen of
      Kelsey's mother causing a miscarriage in the summer of
      2000. Police were called repeatedly during the marriage for
      assaults on Kelsey's mother and advised her more than once
      to get a protective order. Lance pled to assault charges and
      was court ordered twice to attend anger management classes
      for his assaults on Kelsey's mother and later on with [a
      former] girlfriend... The final blow, according to police
      records, came in May, 2002 when Lance threw Kelsey's
      mother against the wall and choked her with his arm for not
      "super-sizing his McDonald's Value Meal." What a hero!
      The injuries to her collar bone and neck were observed and
      photographed by police. When Kelsey's mother, Raye Dawn,
      filed for divorce, her pregnancy with Kelsey was so early on
      she was unaware of it. According to witnesses, Lance
      repeatedly, and against a temporary relief order, broke into
      her house and destroyed and stole personal items of hers only
      to leave them to be found in a nearby field and creek. On one
      occasion, his mother even returned items that had gone
      missing when Lance claimed to have had no involvement. Yet
      he kept leaving notes asking her to take him back or
      threatening, "You want to play games? You decide!"*
*Lance's second marriage...was so terrible that the divorce was
      finalized only one month after the death of Kelsey. However,
      Lance doesn't confine this physical and mental abuse to his
      wife. Lance was arrested just last year [summer of 2006] for
      assaulting two women when he broke into a former
      girlfriend's house and dragged her by her hair into the front
      yard and now yet another protective order is in place. Police
      records reportedly show he even had a loaded gun with him.
      How many charges and how many protective orders have to
      be filed before a pattern of violence is established and
      properly dealt with?*
*When Kelsey's mother, Raye Dawn, discovered her pregnancy, she
      attempted to shield this child from the chaos of the Briggs
      family. In the end, it was Kathie, not the father, who pushed
      for paternity testing. Originally, Lance didn't want anything*

more than standard visitation. He didn't push for custody; he didn't show up for hearings and he even reportedly told people that he hoped the baby wasn't his so he could move on with his life. These are not the actions of a loving father and certainly not the wonderful man he's been portrayed as. Lance even admittedly lied to authorities regarding his military movements to avoid suspicion.

Upon Kelsey's death, authorities attempted to contact Lance with the terrible news of his daughter's death, but were unable to locate him. We hear over and again of how Lance discovered the news of Kelsey's death right after getting off the plane from Iraq. Horrific news, but Lance and his mother Kathie appear to have been lying regarding his location and status as an American soldier. Lance wasn't fresh from Iraq, but rather sources inform us he had been testing positive for drugs and was spending time in a military drug rehab center at Fort Benning, Georgia. Sources go on to tell that he was being threatened with a dishonorable discharge if he did not voluntarily leave due to possible military drug charges and physically assaulting a superior officer in Germany. Lance claims to have received an honorable discharge, but according to an Observer source he was discharged for being "no longer fit for military service." Lance was initially scheduled to be back well before Kelsey's fatal day with Mike Porter, but was fighting his own demons and not for our freedom. We encourage Lance to release his un-edited DD214 and his full military records to disprove our military sources – a small task for the hero his mother claims.

Not only should we be angry that the disgraced military service of Lance is being hoisted to war hero status, but we should be livid that it is being done on the memory of a slain little girl. This illustrates the level to which the Briggs have dropped in their attempt to use anything to pull at the public's heartstrings to fulfill their agenda – an agenda of vengeance towards Kelsey's mother, Raye Dawn, for divorcing and filing charges against an abusive man. This is a man who couldn't even protect his own marriages from himself.

43

As further proof of this deception, the following is from Craig Key's Book titled, *A Deadly Game of Tug-of-War: The Kelsey Smith-Briggs Story:*[12]

Lance Briggs's Military Career in Iraq Unverified

The sacrifices that our military service men and women make for our country are tremendous and should never be minimized. Yet, at the same time, to falsely portray someone as a war hero shows blatant disrespect to those serving in our military. Lance Briggs has been portrayed as walking off the airplane in Georgia to learn of the death of his daughter. I mean no disrespect, but if we're going to look at the full picture of this case in this book, I must outline what's been learned regarding Mr. Briggs' military career.

As you will recall, in the fall of 2004, Kathie Briggs petitioned the court to be allowed to exercise Lance's visitation with Kelsey if and when Lance was away on active military duty. Kathie was granted her request. Julie, the owner of the daycare center where Kelsey stayed, began seeing and documenting bruises on Kelsey from the time Kathie's visitation began.

It was at the February, 2005, hearing that I began to question Lance's military obligation. I was told Lance was in Meeker until the morning of the guardianship hearing, and then left to return to Fort Leonard Wood, Missouri. However, he returned to Oklahoma that same night. In all of my judicial dealings with the military, any time a service member's child is being abused, the Red Cross can typically arrange for emergency leave to allow a soldier to attend to his family situation. I was never presented with a viable explanation for Lance's absence during this hearing.

What continued to raise red flags was how Lance was in Oklahoma randomly throughout March and April, including returning for his birthday. It was as if he could control his military obligation to be at home whenever he pleased, but why did he always miss Kelsey's court hearings? During Kathie's DHS supervised visits in May, 2005, it was odd to me that Lance

---

[12] Key, Craig. *A Deadly Game of Tug of War: The Kelsey Smith-Briggs Story.* Garden City, NY: Morgan James Publishing, 2007.

called during many of her two hour visits, yet when Kathie was continually asked by DHS for Lance's contact information, she always had an excuse as to why she could not provide the information requested. How is it that Lance always knew when to call, yet Kathie did not know how to reach him?

Because of the lack of cooperation from Lance's family, at that point, DHS became doubtful that Lance was actually stationed in Iraq. Not only did DHS hit a stone wall where the Briggs family was concerned, but they also received no response from repeated attempts to contact Lance through the military.

It was the CASA worker who learned of Lance's location. The CASA worker had gone to pay her insurance bill in Prague, Oklahoma, where Lance's sister worked. It was discovered that Lance had been in Fort Benning, Georgia, at a military hospital for observation. Lance's family expressed how upset they were at the amount of medication Lance was taking, because it was having a negative impact on him.

Finally, on September 23, 2005, Lance contacted DHS. He informed DHS that he was injured while driving a truck in Iraq. He stated his orders were sitting on someone's desk, and he should be home in the next two weeks. Why was the public told Lance was injured in Iraq, but his sister let down her guard and informed the CASA worker of his actual whereabouts?

Lance called DHS again on October 6, 2005, and apologized for having lied about what happened to him and his location. He admitted that he had been in Fort Benning, Georgia since at least September, 2005, and not in Iraq.

The next call DHS would receive from Lance was shortly after Kelsey's death. Lance asked the DHS worker how that worker would feel if he broke into the worker's house and killed a member of his family or his children. Lance went on to say it was not a threat, but a promise, and that worker needed to advise me that my children and family would pay as well. Because of this and other threats by Lance, the office of Inspector General guarded the Lincoln County DHS office for months, and I was required to hide my children and have 24-hour protection by the sheriff's office.

Sadly, Kelsey's Purpose members had no information about the false stories or Lance Briggs's violent past. They only knew what the Briggs wanted them to know. So the hate against Raye grew to a raging boil while the sympathy for the Briggs grew beyond anyone's expectations, and spilled over to include the man charged with Kelsey's murder.

Malena Posts: 10 Re: Poll - I hope I can voice my opinion here without hurting any of the Briggs' feelings. I also believe that Raye Dawn was the one the hurt Kelsey, she knew what was going to happen the day she left Kelsey with Mike. Mike and I have been friends since we were in elementary school, he was my neighbor for 12 years. My mother was also best friends with his mother, and worked at their company. I do not know Raye Dawn, but we have many mutual friends. These friends also know Mike, and they ALL agree that she would do something like this, not him! Don't get me wrong, I believe that Mike had to know what Raye was doing to Kelsey and did nothing to help her, so he is also guilty. They both must be punished. I think that the police in Meeker just needed to make an arrest in the case, so they arrested Mike just because he was arrested and was the last one with Kelsey. I have talked to Mike, very briefly, the day he was arrested and in my heart I don't believe he was the one that hurt that baby. I pray about Kelsey every night, that justice will be served and that the truth will surface. I know I wrote this before, but I can't believe that Raye Dawn hasn't been charged with anything, anything at all! She is walking around free right now, demanding this and that from Mike, while he sits in jail. Makes me sick! I would do anything to take that baby away from her! It does surprise me too that the Smith family isn't seeking justice for Kelsey. They are too busy trying to protect Raye and their reputation. When I saw her family on tv you could tell they are just trying to protect her, they act like they didn't see the bruises or that anything was wrong with Kelsey. If Raye Dawn has nothing to hide then why is she hiding so much? I know there are a lot of rumors going around and I don't know who has come forward and who hasn't. I have heard, though, that Raye Dawn got in touch *with an old friend of hers the day after Kelsey died and told her two different stories about what happened. I know about this because the old friend and I have a mutual friend, who told me about it. I have tried to relay this info. To others, but I don't know if it has gotten to anyone yet. Lance, I read in the paper that you are bring a $15 mil tort claim against the state, GOOD FOR YOU! God bless!*

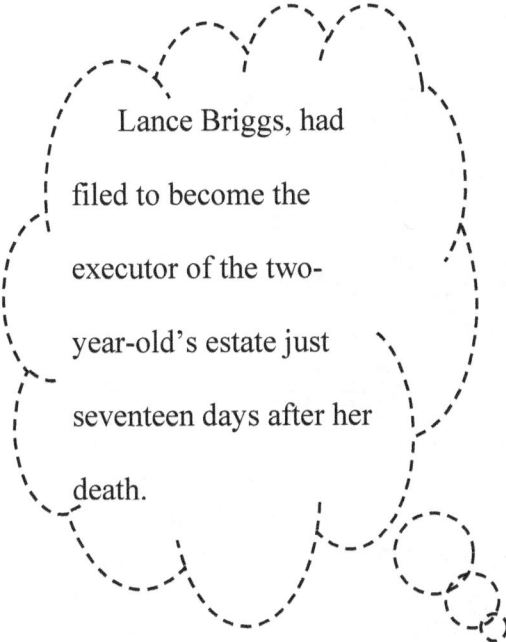

Lance Briggs, had filed to become the executor of the two-year-old's estate just seventeen days after her death.

Malena Posts: 10 Re: Poll - You are so right, Ashley. This is about Kelsey, and Raye is only thinking of herself and what she can get out of it. Disgusting! She doesn't deserve to be a mother!

The same article that released shocking information about Lance Briggs that had been hidden from the public also shared information regarding the real Mike Porter and his soon to be strongest supporter, Kathie Briggs, as follows:[13]

---

[13] *US Observer* "Kelsey Smith-Briggs - Murder & Exploitation - Prosecutor Smothermon Pushes False Charges?" by Barry Jon, Investigative Reporter

Michael Lee Porter: Death by Deception

Michael Porter swept in as a confidence artist in shining armor. He was college educated (so he said), brilliant in his business dealings (miserably false) and had his own home (in foreclosure). Kathie has admonished Kelsey's mother for not verifying all of this, yet she herself publicly denounced one of her own "would be" supporters for attempting to do the same thing regarding her.

Sadly, it wasn't until after Kelsey's death that Mike Porter's house of cards came crashing down. Even before Kelsey's mother knew of the suspicions surrounding Kelsey's death she called for an autopsy because she "wanted to know what her daughter died from." Yet, Mike Porter immediately questioned the need. Mike Porter faked heart attack symptoms not once, but twice as the events following Kelsey's death unfolded. He raved to DHS and investigators in a letter on what a wonderful mother Raye Dawn was, but plea-bargained to "allowing abuse" as if someone was left unpunished. Even after his arrest Mike Porter was quite comfortable having Raye Dawn and her mother watch over his own children. Yet, sources tell us that Richard Smothermon, the District Attorney may be calling him to the stand as a "credible" state witness stemming from his plea agreement. (He was used as a witness against Raye and the jurors believed him even after Richard told him while he was

on the stand, "You know that I believe you sexually assaulted and murdered Kelsey." Mike Porter answered, "Yes.")
It's been reported to us that Mike Porter's own daughter shared with
   a school guidance counselor that her father told her "not to
   talk about what goes on at home" and that he would act
   loving towards Kelsey when her mother was around but
   would hit Kelsey when Raye Dawn was gone. She watched as
   her father hit Kelsey's head against a brick wall when her
   mother was gone. One of Kelsey's young cousins once
   witnessed him take Kelsey into a room and close the door
   and when they came out Kelsey was crying. This monster
   closely guarded his abusing secret like he did so many other
   lies.

Kathie Briggs: For the Love of Money

Kathie spent so much effort getting DHS, CASA, and the judge to
   chase Kelsey's mother that sadly the
   gathering darkness of a real killer
   slipped in almost unnoticed.
When police in our nation's capitol focused on
   tips that a shooter was using a white
   mini-van to randomly execute innocent
   people, the real killers went unnoticed
   until police changed their focus. Scott
   Peterson had family and friends so sure
   of the great man he was, all the while
   hiding a financial downfall that ended
   with him killing his own wife and
   unborn child. Even Ted Bundy, one of
America's most notorious serial killers, was able to keep his
   family in the dark, yet Richard Smothermon wants us to
   believe that trained DHS and CASA workers could overlook
   Mike Porter but Kelsey's mother, Raye Dawn, "should have
   known." Raye Dawn was forced to focus on protecting her
   life and daughter from the manipulations of Kathie and
   Lance.

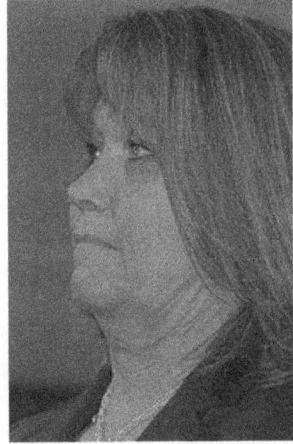

"Take these kids or I will kill every one of them!" – Kathie Briggs

All too often when marriages fall apart the love and the feelings of extended family are shut out of the debate. The blessings of grandchildren are ripped from the nurturing wisdom of grandparents and these relationships are left empty and broken. But in contrast there can also be the meddlesome mother-in-law that has reached mythic proportions in every culture on the globe. Kathie wants you to focus on the dejected grandparent concept and prays her exploits as the meddlesome in-law (that appears to have been taken to criminal proportions) will go unnoticed. Three things tell us about the nature of a person: past record, actions and motives. We are directly questioning her record, her actions and her motives regarding her persecution of the mother of Kelsey, Raye Dawn.

Even though Kathie publicly questioned why anyone would "take the time to verify" details of the case, we decided to do just that and began to compare what was being said with what our investigation uncovered.

Kathie claims she was the one who sought out DHS for help with her own children when they were young. She argues, "This decision was my own and not court ordered." This is correct. In fact, according to witnesses, she drove down to the Pottawatomie County courthouse with her four young children and exclaimed, "Take these kids or I will kill every one of them!" DHS records and a sworn and signed affidavit attest to this. She is exactly right; it was her decision to abandon her own children, but once she threatened their lives in front of DHS workers it was no longer her choice.

Kathie spent two years (uncommonly long) working her DHS plan to get her children back. She was frequently given gas money and even driven by [a] health department worker, just so she would visit her own children. Kathie also claims that the judge in charge of her case praised her as a shining example when, in reality, Judge Carter never did so. This is her past record with DHS; this is her record with her own children, and this is how she revises truth.

Kathie has become the queen of revisionist history. She likewise affirms, "I am very proud of the children I raised and the adults they have become." So you're proud of a son who

50

*pleads no contest to assault charges on more than one
occasion with more than one woman, who attends "court
ordered" anger management twice, who reportedly gets
beaten up for groping a woman in a bar, who admits to lying
to authorities regarding his whereabouts, who doesn't show
up for custody hearings, who gets relieved of military service
for drugs and assault?*

---

*"The information known by Kathie Briggs demonstrates knowledge
gained through harassing/stalking activities." - Meeker
Police*

---

*Kathie sued for the same visitation rights with Kelsey that she was
already freely receiving without court intervention – any
other statement is a verifiable lie. Kathie stalked Raye Dawn,
following her to work, to her school and to her house long
before she ever claimed Kelsey had any signs of abuse. In
fact, in the report to the District Attorney when DHS was first
called to investigate, Kathie stated "she had not seen
bruising on Kelsey on any occasion prior." Yet, she would
now have us believe that a nurturing mother of two years
with no history of abuse or violence suddenly turns on her
daughter. When DHS was called in after Kelsey broke her
collar bone (the most commonly bone broken in children)
Kathie called the Meeker Police and stepped up her stalking
and harassment. Sources at DHS have stated that their
offices received so many calls from Kathie that proved
blatantly untrue they began to disregard them. Some of the
calls reported abuse during times that Kathie didn't even
know a DHS worker was present. And these calls haven't
ended with the death of Kelsey but have continued, only now
stating abuse of Raye's son, whom she has never seen outside
of DHS supervised visits due to the malicious prosecution by
Richard Smothermon, the District Attorney.*
*Kathie would also call in erroneous police reports as well. On one
particular occasion, police stated they received a call from
Kathie claiming that Raye Dawn was driving erratically and
at excessive speeds. Kathie didn't realize an officer was on
that exact road and he saw nothing to substantiate Kathie's
claim. Kathie even alleged that Raye Dawn had the wrong*

license plate on her vehicle having switched it with another, which was likewise proven false. Moreover, in the official police report of the incident, the officer stated, "I believe that Kathie is continually following and stalking Raye Dawn in attempts to gain any information possible to use against [her] in the custody battle for the child. The information known by Kathie demonstrates knowledge gained through harassing/ stalking activities."

Kathie lists three main points in her abuse claims regarding Kelsey's mother, Raye Dawn: broken color bone, two broken legs and bruises from head to toe (the mother is not suspected in the abdominal injury resulting in Kelsey's death). Let us examine those three points from the position of evidence and not innuendo.

The mother took Kelsey to the emergency room when she complained of pain and was unable to use her arm freely. The broken collar bone and bruises were attended to and she was released from the hospital with no suspicion of abuse. The Briggs family, who were locked in a heated custody battle, returned her to the same ER and the same doctor four days later and complained of abuse. The doctor documented all bruises and the collar bone and referred it to the police to investigate. When questioned at the preliminary hearing if he thought abuse had occurred, that same doctor stated it was "not my job to determine what happened. That's for the police." He was required by law to contact authorities simply because the Briggs used the word abuse. Both the police and

DHS investigated the incident and cleared Kelsey's mother of all suspicion, having determined the break to be nothing more than a childhood accident. **Time lines show Kelsey's legs broken while with Kathie Briggs; reason why DHS removed her from Kathie's custody?**

Even more compelling is the evidence surrounding Kelsey's two broken legs. Evidence and DHS time lines substantiated by Kathie show that Kelsey was delivered to Kathie with a doctor x-

rayed and diagnosed sprained ankle, but very much walking. Kathie herself states Kelsey "took three steps and fell down, then didn't walk the rest of the week" but sources tell us that Kathie took her to gymnastics classes several times during her stay. If Kelsey "stopped walking" why did Kathie take her to gymnastics, refuse to take Kelsey to the doctor and just give her back to her mother? Worried, the mother (not Kathie) reported this to DHS and took Kelsey to the ER where her legs were discovered fractured. The doctor diagnosed their cause as "complications from the sprain due to overcompensation" and cast both legs. Back in Kathie's custody Kelsey was taken under false pretenses to another doctor where Kathie had Kelsey's casts removed seeking a different diagnosis - what did Kathie know that the mother didn't? Then Kathie returned Kelsey to her mother without casts. The maternal grandmother then took Kelsey immediately back to the doctor to have the casts put back on so her legs would heal properly, and the doctor who removed the casts is part of the DHS investigation. At this point, DHS began to suspect Kathie, or at the least someone in her house, but realized there was almost no way to prove it. This is why DHS specifically removed Kelsey from Kathie's guardianship to place her in foster care. Very important to note is that three doctors directly disagree with one another on the fractures. Dr. Barrett and Dr. Koons examined Kelsey and determined their cause was over-compensation due to the sprained ankle, but the doctor that Kathie sought out, Dr. Sullivan disagreed. However, because one doctor said there was a possibility of abuse, DHS was required to act. (Kathie's aunt testified at the June, 2005 hearing that Kathie had told the doctor that Kelsey was abused by her mom, Raye Dawn. The doctor confirmed this in his deposition, which led to him noting the break was from "abuse.") Kathie once again was using anything possible against Kelsey's mother, but this time it backfired because timelines show Kelsey was with Kathie when the fractures occurred and not with her mother.

As for the bruises from head to toe, the pictures that Kathie has amassed are a showcase of every scrape and scratch, every bump and fall that a two-year-old can do over an 8-month

53

time span and culminate with the results of an auto accident. The photographs that Kathie has plastered anywhere she can find a flat surface are from what she even called "a very active child." Even the blood vessel burst in her eye was a direct result of the auto accident.

NO ONE from the Briggs family bothered to show up for Kelsey's final "public hearing"

During the next several weeks, all of Kathie's and the mother's visits were monitored at a DHS facility. Here is yet another red flag; during all of these monitored visits with Kathie, Kelsey was documented to have continually hidden from Kathie, thrown things at her, run away from her, yelled at her and tried to bite her, until finally on July 6, 2005 Kathie, without warning, simply did not show up for her scheduled visit with Kelsey. When questioned, [April], Lance's former wife stated Kathie "would not come to the office because DHS told in court what a bad person she was and she did not want anybody to state any more bad things."

Interestingly, DHS workers continually tried to gain contact information for Lance from Kathie, but she kept avoiding the request stating that he was moving around so much in the military this wasn't possible. However, during many of the supervised visits at DHS, Kathie would receive phone calls from Lance. Somehow he was able to coincide calls during visits, but could not keep in contact with DHS. In fact, Kathie spent so much time on the phone talking to various people during several visits with Kelsey that records show observers finally had to reprimand her for it.

So let us cast our eyes on the documented visits with Raye Dawn, the mother. Kelsey played games with her, laughed, snuggled next to her to watch movies and was notably happy with her visits that ended in "hugs and kisses." What did Kelsey know that we didn't? Kelsey's actions were not erratic during these visits; they were consistent with both her mother and with Kathie. We have heard the proverb that children are good judges of character and this child spoke volumes.

Kathie even purposely lies about her access to Kelsey after she was given back to her mother in June of 2005. Kathie claims that

54

*the court blocked the Briggs family from seeing Kelsey, yet
our investigation revealed that this is an outright lie. For
being as vigilant as she claims, how could she overlook her
access for three months before Kelsey's death? In reality, NO
ONE from the paternal family showed up to a public hearing
to discuss restricting overnight stays outside of the mother's
home because doctors were concerned about what might
have been seizures that began to manifest. But Kathie knows
she had access. It is in the court documents and she even
exercised this once after an auto accident where Kelsey was
in the car.*

---

*Kathie's front – Kelsey's Purpose - reportedly slapped with **"cease
and desist"** order by Attorney General for **"misuse of
funds."***

---

*What Kathie doesn't want the public or her supporters to know is
that the DHS record does not show a pattern of abuse by the
mother, because that abuse was never there. It shows a
pattern of her own deceit and manipulation of the system
which she learned with her own children. We already know,
according to Kathie's testimony and others' to DHS, that
Kelsey was not being abused before DHS involvement. Judge
Craig Key and DHS workers poured over the records for
countless hours before Kelsey was finally returned to her
mother in June of 2005. Yet now the DHS worker is being
ridiculed by Kathie out of one side of her mouth while telling
reporters that her testimony at the preliminary hearing was,
"the most compelling." You cannot have it both ways.*

---

*The Briggs family openly mocked DHS worker during preliminary
hearing testimony!*

---

*Now, here is the real kicker; Kathie and Lance have filed a $15
million lawsuit against DHS for allowing the abuse and
death of Kelsey. If they win, they will have to give half of the
settlement to the mother, Raye Dawn. However, if Raye
Dawn is convicted of anything regarding the abuse/death of
Kelsey, then Kathie and Lance get to keep it all. You don't
think $7.5 million dollars isn't a motive? The squeaky wheel*

gets the oil, or in this case, the cash. Kathie's embellishments and outright lies are out of revenge and she now seeks to destroy the life of a grieving mother while lining her own pockets. Even her attempt at a non-profit has been sent a "cease and desist" order from the Attorney General for "misuse of funds." A fact she has tried to hide from supporters, but is finding several in her ranks are discovering this for themselves. Call and ask her how her son, Lance, continues to purchase more and more possessions while remaining unemployed. (The suit was later settled out of court and is discussed in the chapter titled, "Putting a Price Tag on Kelsey." Kelsey's Purpose has also since changed its name to the Kelsey Briggs Foundation where Kathie and her daughters are on the board...a paid position.)

Beware a mother scorned. That's what stands out. Even in the father's seeming lack of interest, Kathie sought and seeks anything she can set her hands on to destroy Raye Dawn's life -attempting to gain any information possible and revising history to use against her. The police even saw this. These actions had nothing to do with the well-being of a child. It had to do with the selfish nature of an individual who was so angry for having been seen through that she came out spitting venom. Of course, we're sure she'll simply say the evidence is lying.

Ongoing Deception – Kelsey's Purpose?

December, 2005

On December 7, 2005 a "Concerned Citizen" voiced an opinion similar to "Malena's," which of course placed all of the blame on Raye and none on the man charged with murder.

> *Concerned Citizen Posts: 3 Re: Poll - The chances of justice being carried out in this case are getting smaller by the day. As far as the OSBI is concerned I don't believe they have looked any further than Michael Porter. I grew up with Michael and I know he is no murderer or accomplice to murder. I've heard second and third hand stories that, if people had the guts to come forward with, would mean jail time for Raye Dawn. If everyone just sits back and keeps quiet they will convict Michael and Raye Dawn will be free to ruin another child's life. An innocent child is dead and many lives are horribly altered. The time for family, friend, employer loyalty is long past. Our only loyalty should be to the truth.*

Lance's youngest sister was apparently disturbed by the good reports regarding Mike Porter's character. She stated as follows:

> *Robynn Posts: 4 Re: Poll - I am sorry but I just cannot sit here and listen to all of these people who say they knew Mike Porter and never thought he could be involved in the murder of my niece. I knew Raye Dawn through school as well and was even on our high school Pom squad together. I never thought I knew anyone that could ever be involved in hurting a child. It makes me sick to know that any human is even capable of any kind of crime against a child. For the people who don't know who I am. I am Lance's little sister. I am in no way trying to be rude or discourteous to anyone who has said*

anything of this nature. I do appreciate all of the support our family has received from everyone. Just continue to pray the justice willb e done for our precious angel.

By this time, the Oklahoma State Bureau of Investigation (OSBI) was being flooded with letters accusing Raye of murdering Kelsey, even though she was not home at the time. Lance's sisters sent letters pleading for OSBI agents to charge Raye with murder because they "just knew" it was Raye who was guilty. Ashley, the daughter-in-law of a star witness against Raye—and one that the district attorney seemed to believe even though she presented false testimony against Raye—added to the plea for Raye's arrest.

Ashley Posts: 14 Re: Poll - I believe that if there are people out there who know for a fact, either by hearing something from the person directly or by having seen anything that is incrimidating or odd behavior that the NEED TO COME FORWARD and contact the OSBI ~ in my books failure to do so makes you just a guilty for killing Kelsey! Make up your mistake by talking with the OSBI now. Tell them what you have seen or heard. Like I said, I believe failure to do so makes you just as guilty as the one who commited this crime. Mike or Raye Dawn ~ both are guilty! And so are you if you know anything and your not talking to the OSBI. Whether you think Mike did or didn't do it, or you think Raye Dawn did or didn't do it. The signs were obvious ~ and neither of them helped. If you look at some of the rapist or murders, some of them were well respected, everyday people who fooled even the people closest to them. You really can't say you know anyone ~ and if you do are you sure enough to bet your life on it???? How about your kids life, or even your grandkids??? Think about it…… We all have our hunches and our own thoughts about the case. But we don't know for sure because we were not there! We need to remember KELSEY and the purpose here. We Need Our Laws To Change! This needs National attention!!! We All Owe It To Lance and to Kelsey!

58

A witch-hunt in Oklahoma   Jody Ortiz

The signs were obvious, for those who believed the Briggs'
story…story being the key word in this scenario.

*Malena Posts: 10 Re: Poll - I am sorry, Robynn, if I have hurt any
feelings with what I have said about Mike. True, none of us
know what really happened that day. I know if I was in your
shoes I would feel the same way. I also just want truth and
justice for Kelsey.*

While the Smiths were grieving the loss of Kelsey and working
with investigators to bring her justice, Kelsey's Purpose became
convoluted with support for the man charged with Kelsey's murder,
providing the Briggs family with a powerful army that would stop at
nothing to bring hate against Raye.

December 8, 2005

*KJ3 Posts: 8 Re: Poll - Robynn I think people just want the truth and
want to make sure the right person pays for the murder. I
agree that know one thinks that their friend, neighbor, or
family member could do such a crime, but the fact is we don't
know. We just all want justice for your precious little Kelsey.
Being a mother of 3 myself, I just know I would want the right
person to spend the rest of their life behind bars, I think that
is what everyone else who has wrote about Mike wants too!!
They just want everyone to know the Mike they know not the
one that the media has portrayed. Maybe he did do this
noone is saying that they didn't they just want to believe that
he didn't until there is more proof that he did. We are not
trying to hurt your family by writing things about Mike we
just want justice like you do. I personally have worked very
hard at trying to get this story nationalized. I want your
family to make a difference and change our system. We will
all keep fighting for you guys!! I pray every night the the
whole truth will come out and that people who are not telling
everything will come forward and that your family will make
a difference and find peace in that.*

59

Brenda Posts: 8 Re: Poll - The system that failed Kelsey and your
family in the first place is the same system that is supposed to
bring the correct person to justice so I think it is
understandable that any of us might not be so trusting that
justice will be served. The OSBI only does what the DA's
office tells them to and that is information we were given by
the OSBI this morning. Given that there are some specific
people who some of us think should be talked to and those
people haven't been then it seems the investigation is only
going where someone wants it to. Enough said. Robynn,
please know that Kelsey, Lance and your family are foremost
in our thoughts and prayers. The fight to correct the system
in Oklahoma so that Kelsey's purpose is fulfilled will be long
and difficult and we can all join together in that fight.

"JusticeforMike Porter" seemed to be a less educated character in
Mike Porter's sudden support system.

justiceformike Posts: 7 Re: Poll - every time we asked Raye Dawn
what was wrong with Kelsey she would always tell us Kelsey
was sick or she had just went to the doctors and so on she
always had excuses for us can anyone tell me what eveidence
they have against Mike besides he was the last one with her.
that dont make you guilty maybe he found her that way he
says she was having a seizer and Gayla flat out lied when she
said she had never witnessed her having one because she had
told us that Kelsey had a couple while she was with Gayla. I
just dont understand why they have arrested Mike and not
investegated anyone else. Raye Dawn should be sitting right
there in jail netx to him intell the investagation is over.

Shirica exploded in a moment of candidness that we would rarely
see from the Briggs family.

Shirica Posts: 21 Re: Poll - As much as I hate to say this, there is
evidence against Michael that is not public knowledge at this
time. OSBI has assured our family that they have the person
who murdered Kelsey in custody. I know it is difficult for
people to wrap their minds around the idea of Michael being
guilty. I know how easy it is to automatically think Raye
Dawn is the guilty one, but none of you have seen the

evidence. Yes, Raye Dawn is less than appealing to so many of us and yes, Michael appears to be a good father to his own children, but so was the BTK serial murderer. He was a strong member of his church and was wonderful to his own children. They did not know he was raping and murdering women his own daughter's age for thirty years. It is VERY difficult to put our faith in this system, but what other choice do we have? OSBI was not involved before and the state medical examiner was not involved before. We have to believe they are better equipped to handle this than the Meeker Police and Lincoln County Department of Human Services were. Again, if you feel you have information to prove otherwise, please come forward and contact the OSBI or the DA.

Aunt bean [Jeanna] Posts: 8 People are not always who you think they are - There have been many posts about the character of Michael Porter. Our family understand how those who know Mike feel the need to support and defend him. Our family has felt the need to defend ourselves and our character against the lies that Raye Dawn, her mother, her grandmother, her uncle, her sister, and yes, her husband have said about our family for the last eleven months. They have spread many, many lies in order to make Raye Dawn look like the poor innocent victim of the "evil, psychotic" Briggs family. In defense of some of Raye Dawn and Mike's family members, they were only going by what they were being told (although they did not attempt to verify what Raye Dawn, Raye Dawn's mother, Raye Dawn's grandmother, Raye Dawn's uncle, and Mike were telling them). I am sure that many people would be shocked at some of the things that Mike has done and lies that he has told in order to get Kelsey back with her mother. Mike has behaved in ways that showed poor character with no appreciation for what is right and what is wrong. I do not doubt Mike was a good son, a giving boss, a kind friend, or a loving father to his biological children. Yes, many think that Mike's character is wonderful, but they have not been in court against him, Raye Dawn, and her family. Even if he did not hurt or kill Kelsey, did you ever think that Mike was capable of allowing a two year old child to be mentally and physically abused? Yes, it would be very scary to have your

*fate decided upon in the Lincoln County Court system. Trust
me, our family is very wary of the court system too. I am sure
that Mike is scared to death to have his fate sitting in the
hands of the courts. For he knows all too well how easily the
courts can be manipulated. He knows firsthand because he
knowingly, willfully, and whole-heartedly participated in the
corruption right along with Raye Dawn and her family. Mike
was willing to do anything that it took to get Kelsey back to
Raye Dawn. Yes, maybe the things that they did are weighing
very heavily on his heart right now, but that isn't going to
bring Kelsey back. I am not going to go into the details of
what they did, but it will come out in court. My family
suffered a great deal because of the actions of the Meeker
Police, DHS, the judge, Raye Dawn, her family, AND
MICHAEL PORTER. Let's face it, if Mike had not
participated in the dirty underhanded tactics used to get
Kelsey away from the Briggs family he would not be sitting in
jail today! Kelsey would not be dead today. By now she
would be living with her daddy, sleeping in her beautiful
room, wearing her abundance of cute clothes and shoes,
playing with all of her toys and swinging on her swing set.
She would be living in a home where all she knew was love,
happiness and security. Most importantly, she would be
ALIVE. I do not know if Mike killed Kelsey. I do not know if
Mike ever hurt Kelsey. That is not for me to decide. I have
not seen all of the evidence, but I do know that they have
evidence against him. I do know that Mike should be in jail.
For how long, I do not know. I am sure that it will be very
difficult for Mike's loved ones to hear the evidence against
him. It would be hard for anyone to learn that someone they
love did terrible things to an innocent, helpless child. It will
also be very difficult for some of Raye Dawn's family to hear
the truth about her too. Whether Mike ever laid a finger on
Kelsey or not, by allowing the things that happened to that
child to happen, he did terrible things to Kelsey. I myself still
cannot wrap my head around the fact the Kelsey was
murdered. I still can't wrap my head around the fact that
Kelsey was abused, or any child for that matter. My head just
won't go there. But I know that it happened and that people
must pay the price for it. I did not intend to make anyone*

*angry, but frankly I am at the point where I don't really care
anymore. When I just held my five year old daughter in her
bed as she cried herself to sleep again because her precious
cousin Kelsey is in Heaven, I don't really care a whole lot
about what other people think anymore. My daughter's heart
is broken. Everyone who truly loved Kelsey and many who
didn't even know her have broken hearts right now. So I am
sorry if I do not have a whole lot of compassion for Michael
Porter. Like the rest of my family, I too do not want the
wrong person convicted of first degree murder. I want
Kelsey's true killer convicted of first degree murder, whether
that is Mike or Raye Dawn. I want others who let it happen
and contributed to the corruption to be put in jail for a very,
very, very long time. Whether Mike killed Kelsey or not, he
contributed to her death. Period! This post was last modified
12-10-2005 11:34 PM by aunt bean*

This passion filled plea is a far cry from the pleas for Raye's arrest
that were subsequently sent to the investigators by the Briggs family
members. Why feign concern about true justice for Kelsey while
hindering the investigation with fabricated stories and gossip? Her
passion touched someone.

Kelsey's Purpose December 9, 2005

*Cm74820 Posts: 1 Re: People are not always who you think they are
- Jeanna, Your niece is dead and your family has been
through a terrible ordeal. I agree you should have to worry
about stepping on toes or hurt feelings. Mike in some way
contributed to Kelsey's abuse and death whether people want
to believe it or not. They should put themselves in your shoes.
I don't think you should be expected to show a whole lot of
compassion right now for Mike.*

A pattern that is still ongoing today is to blame Raye for
everything. Even for controlling a man three times her size.

Kelsey was picked up from Kathie's four days after this picture with two broken legs.

Justiceformike Posts: 7 Re: People are not always who you think they are - Mike only new what Raye and her family told him and what he seen with his own eyes. When the court battle was going on I remember there being wrong doing on both sides of her family that was going on

Cheryl Posts: 13 Re: People are not always who you think they are - Your family has a right to be angry and upset. A precious baby was murdered. Everyone who is familiar with this story should be outraged. There are two people responsible for Kelsey's murder. I don't know who did what or when, I just know both are as guilty as the other. I have a problem with anyone who tries to defend or make excuses for the two people responsible for Kelsey's death.

Shirica Posts: 21 Re: People are not always who you think they are - That is where you are wrong. There was not wrong doing on both sides of the family. Like you said, he only knew what he was told and saw and you only knew what you were told by him. All wrong doing toward Kelsey was going on in the Smith/Porter home and not eh Briggs home. There are no ifs, ands or buts about it. That child was SAFE in our presence.

Remember, they were trying to cover their own actions so any accusations from them should not weigh too heavily. Criminals rarely tell the truth about their crimes. They are more likely to point the finger in the other direction. This post was last modified: 12-09-2005 09:56 AM by shirica

"A red flag was raised for me, as a judge, when DHS told me Kelsey's hair began falling out in clumps while in the care of Kathie Briggs." Judge Craig Key

Though Raye had not been charged with a crime, Shirica referred to her as a criminal.

Justiceformike Posts: 7 Re: People are not always who you think they are - WELL SEE RAYE DAWN TOLD US YOU ALL WERE STALKING AND CAUSING TROUBLE FOR THEM THAT'S ALL WE KNEW WHAT ABOUT THE TROUBLE THAT WAS HAPPENING BEFORE MIKE CAME ALONG?

The angry grandmother who had harassed Gayla and Mildred did not approve of the name "Justiceformike."

Cheryl Posts: 13 Re: People are not always who you think they are - I have a real problem with someone who posts under the name of "Justice for Mike" on a website devoted to a precious, adorable toddler that was murdered. Michael Porter was the only person arrested and jailed for the murder of Kelsey. I believe that Rae Dawn Porter needs to be occupying the jail cell next to her husband. However, with that said, you need to have some sympathy for the family of Kelsey. Posting crass comments under the title of "Justice for Mike" shows no signs of class, sensitivity or sympathy for a family that is already suffering and in pain over the loss of a baby. As for "Justice for Mike", he is getting his justice!! What about "Justice for Kelsey"?? If you think Mike is so innocent, then put your money where your mouth is, and post his million dollar bail or start your own website dedicated to Mike, but stay off this website that was started in memory of Kelsey Smith-Briggs.

Justiceformike Posts: 7 Re: People are not always who you think they are - I DO HAVE SYMPATHY FOR THE FAMILY AND IM SORRY FOR THERE LOSS BUT I BELEIVE JUSTICE SHOULD BE SERVED FOR BOTH SIDES. WE ALL HERE NEW KELSEY AND LOVED HER VERY MCUH SHE WAS HERE OFTEN WITH US AND I DON'T THINK IM DISRESPECTFUL BEING HERE IM SORRY FOR YOUR STATEMENT IM NOT HERE TO UPSET ANYONE AND I DONT FILL I HAVE.

"Concernedcitizen" kept the conversation going against Raye Dawn by claiming,

Posts: 3 Re: People are not always who you think they are - A big problem that those of us that know Michael are having is with things that are said to have happened before he ever came into the picture. Once again, if people would only come forward I think a lot of light could be shed on what kind of mother Raye was. I've heard from those that know Raye Dawn and her mom well that they are world class manipulators. Why is it so hard to believe that they manipulated Michael? So he reacted to what Raye Dawn and Gayla told him without checking into it first. Yes, he should've formed his own opinions and not just taken what they said as the truth, but he was doing what he thought he needed to to protect his family. I'd be interested to know what lies Raye Dawn and Gayla told Michael about the Briggs family. Something I'm curious about is the character of Raye Dawn. Is there anyone out there who can stand up and say that Raye is a wonderful person and mother who could never harm her child? I've actually heard people say "I can believe she would do something like this." I've even heard it said

66

that a few days after Kelsey died she was already bragging about how much money she was going to get out of Michael. For those of you that talk to the OSBI – are they even looking at Raye?

The rumor about "what Raye could get out of Michael" started at the place of her former employment. It was the same place where her grandmother, Mildred, still works, as well as where Kelsey's Purpose member Ashley's mother-in-law worked and created a story she would later tell on the stand against Raye.

December 9, 2005

A letter was sent to Gayla's friend from Cheryl, the angry grandmother who believed the lies of the Briggs. A picture at the top of the letter was one of Kelsey from the Kelsey's Purpose Web site.

Look at that adorable innocent little face, so full of wonder, hope, magic and love. Children are so innocent, they believe in the tooth fairy, and Easter Bunny and Santa Clause. They have not learned to hate or show prejudice and everyone is their friend. They turn to the adults in their life for love and protection, without asking for anything in return. Children are our future. What kind of monster, punches a baby in the stomach, ending her life?? What kind of monster breaks both legs of a toddler??? I cannot imagine such an individual. I keep asking myself why, why, why???? And again, I ask myself, "How could you protect and shelter an individual responsible for beating a toddler?" I hope you can sleep at night, knowing you have two women in your home, one abused Kelsey and the other ignored Kelsey's bruises and broken bones. I heard your girlfriend was too wrapped up in your and your money to pay any attention to what was happening to Kelsey. I am putting the word out to boycott your realty company to all my friends. Hope you guys enjoy the holidays together. A Grandmother.

The Only Grandmother Allowed to

Grieve

December, 2005

One word that both the Briggs and Smith families use to describe Kelsey is "active." Raye told me that Kathie Briggs gave Kelsey some type of medication at all times—reportedly so that Kathie could keep up with her—and that Kathie even suggested that Raye put Kelsey on Ritalin. While the Briggs talk about Kelsey's "mischievious [sic]" side and how she "loved to bite," the Smiths describe her as a child who "wanted to do everything" and she "could light up a room." While the Briggs still work to portray Kelsey as an unloved, abused child, the Smiths focus on who Kelsey was as a person.

Kjbriggs Posts: 13 A Grandma's broken heart - I have not been on this site for a couple of days. Sometimes it all gets a little over whelming. The not knowing is what gets to you. Kelsey was two, she was loving, smart, and a little mischievious at times. She kept me smiling even when she did exactly what she wanted to do. Everytime I pull this site up and see that little face I smile at her very memory. I look at her pictures all day long, I rub the paper it is printed on in hopes of a little comfort. It pains me to see her picture on a sticker on my van and to think it is out there in the cold. I watch her videos because that is all I have of my little angel. I cannot tell you how heart broken we feel, we put on our brave faces and we face each day with the hopes we might get an answer to what happened to Kelsey. We fight for the truth to come out, that is something we have been doing for months. Who could ever hurt this child over and over again? Once could be considered an accident, but more than once is a definite crime. Raye Dawn was given two chances to love and care for her child, God gave her the first one and the Judge gave her the second one. Our attorney stated they would be stupid to hurt her again with everyone watching. Yet, again and again it went on. People in this town took the day off work so they could go sit in the Courthouse and support this mother. They did not know if she was a good parent, they did not look at the pictures or the facts. More people wrote letters on her behalf asking that Kelsey be placed back with her mother. They did not know the facts either, they only knew what Raye Dawn and her family wanted them to know. **This case has never been about Kelsey, it has always been about the mother.** Do you have any idea how many people feel guilty right now for their hand in her eventual murder? I knew Raye Dawn as a child and loved her as a daughter-in-law. She was wrapped up in herself for most of her life, she was not perfect, but I never thought she would abuse her child. **I have heard nothing but good things from those who know Mike Porter. We were excited that Raye Dawn was dating someone that appeared stable. We wanted Kelsey to have two homes where she felt loved and secure. I did not know him, but I knew he had two children that he loved, so I never thought Kelsey would be in danger.** All of that changed on January 14th, what we saw was shocking. Some of you saw the pictures on the news, well I saw the child. I saw her little bottom beaten with sores on it, I saw bruises on both sides of her face, legs, back and bottom, twenty nine total. I put a brace on her back to help heal her broken collar bone and I saw her spirit change that weekend. We could not believe this was happening and that was only the beginning of this nightmare. I saw my son's protective nature kick in when he saw his little girl in this condition. Our fight began that night to keep Kelsey safe. Our fight began that night with a system that began in our own town and went on to help in failing Kelsey. We all know the story got worse while people continued to look the other way. This tragedy has changed the lives of many people. It pains me to know there are two other children and one on the way and they will suffer for this crime. There are a lot of answers dating back to that night that I still do not have. All I know is someone is guilty of murder and some one is guilty of failure to protect child abuse murder. I cannot defend either one until I know all of the facts. I do not want either one to be punished for the other *ones crime. What I really want is to sit in my rocker and to read a book to Kelsey, or to just hold her and tell her that I love her one more time. More importantly I would love to see her Daddy hold her one more time. He loved that little girl with all of his heart and he lives everyday with guilt knowing he was not here to protect her. It was out of his hands and this investigation is out of our hands. All we can do now is let Mike and Raye Dawn fight for their lives as they took away the opportunity for Kelsey to fight for hers. I am grateful for all of the postings pro or con to either side. It is a difficult situation for the family and friends of everyone involved. That is why **I asked to have this message board**, I wanted everyone to have the opportunity to share their views. We do not have to agree, but we do need to be respectful to the family members of all involved who are suffering and feel helpless in this situation. Kathie Briggs This post was last modified: 12-09-2005 1:49 AM by kjbriggs[14]*

In this post, Kathie Briggs refers to Lance Briggs's "protective nature." Yet, he failed to attend any of the hearings for Kelsey, even though he was in town for at least one, and, reportedly, in January of 2005 when his wife begged and pleaded with him to stay home and fight for Kelsey, his answer was that it "didn't concern" him. These very words were used by Kathie Briggs in the spring of 2005 home visit with the state's Department of Human Services (DHS). Two DHS workers visited the Briggs' home to check on Kelsey's progress and to meet—for the first time—with Lance Briggs. Kathie Briggs told them, "It didn't concern him, so he went about his day." The similarity of the words quoted from Lance by two different sources lends validity to how it appears Lance viewed his daughter's welfare…it didn't concern him.

This would not be the only deception in this post. After spending over four hours in the care and custody of Kathie Briggs and without a diaper change, Kelsey was given a bath at approximately 10:30 pm

---

[14] *Emphasis added by book author*

71

on that January night that Kathie mentioned. What appears to be a diaper rash in the original photos was called "abuse" and blamed on Raye. Raye states that it was she who demanded that Kathie Briggs find Kelsey's shoulder brace when Kathie removed it before the doctor recommended time. What a spin-master she was becoming while creating this alternate universe in which she and her son were the protectors and not a part of the problem.

Ashley Posts: 13 States Evidence - I have heard that Raye Dawn is turning states evidence and thus this is why she is not in jail and that this will help her get away free. Please help me understand this. I'm not sure what this all means and if it is even true.....

Hope Posts: 7 Re: States evidence - If that is true it means she will testify against Michael. She will testify that he committed all of the abuse. Was there ever any abuse from Michael to Raye Dawn? That may become part of her testimony.

Ashley Posts: 13 Re: States evidence - I have "heard" that Raye Dawn was the abusive one in all her relationships that she has had. But that is just hear say....Why can't (or maybe he can) Mike testify against Raye Dawn?? Sorry if this thread is out-of-line

Stephanie Posts:5 Re: States evidence - If Raye Dawn and Mike both accuse the other of doing the final deed than it will be harder to convict one of them of first degree murder therefore they cannot be put to death...Right?? What happens then? They both end up going to jail..if we are lucky..but they will not be in there for life!! Our legal system stinks..if you have enough money and friends you can get away with anything...even..MURDER..And It's like they are both just worried about their own tails. I would be sobbing every freaking day...not worrying about what I was going to get out of my divorce etc. Kelsey was/is such a sweet and beautiful little girl..if they have a heart at all everytime they close their eyes to go to sleep they will see her sweet little face and feel the pain that they put her through..I know that I would..sorry if I have said anything that I shouldn't have but I'm tired of people acting like they had no clue and it was such a shock that she was being abused..what the heck a normal child doesn't get broken bones etc. like that all of the time..the lies..they need to remember that, "the truth will set you free" maybe not free from jail but your spirit will be free. Thanks for letting me vent. God bless

~DGW~ Posts: 1 What if..... - Kelsey wasn't being abused, and her death was an accident?!?! Could it be possible that the bruises, broken collar bone, and fractured legs could have been an accident? Being a mother of two and have worked in child care for the past 15 years I know how easy it is for a little one to get hurt playing. We have all seen the video tapes of Kelsey in action at the day care, playing and so full of life. Nothing was going to slow her down, as she had the world to conquer. Her little friends bouncing around her, in what looked to be like some sort of controlled chaos, bumps and bruises were bound to happen. My girl friends daughter broke her collar bone a the age of 5. It happen more often then we would like to think. Could it be that her Grandmother, terrified that she was going to lose her son while he served in Iraq wanted to do anything to get custody of Kelsey for her own peace of mind? She reported the bruises and gained custody for a short while. I wonder while Kelsey was in her custody did she attend any type of child care facility and did the bruising stop completely? Families get so twisted in their own battles between one another they put the childern in the middle. It sounds like Kelsey was a victim in more ways then we think. We also seen video of Kelsey and Mr. Porter, he looked like a caring parent and she seemed to be content to be with him, even secure enough to fall asleep on his chest while they both rested on the couch. I would think if he was beating her she wouldn't want be any where around him. I read the affidavit Mr. Porter gave, and sad as her death is, could it of been an accident of him trying to save her? In a panic, he presses to hard on her frail little body while trying to perform CPR. Nobody knows how they would react in a situation like that, we'd like to think we've be able to keep our composure and do what was right, but we don't know for certain until we're in such a nightmare. I pray the truth come out and some how her families find the peace within their hearts to carry on. God bless you Kelsey and your family.

The previous post came from someone who seemed to be attempting to analyze the known facts and then create logical explanations. The Briggs had knowledge at this time of the alleged sexual assault and the bruise on Kelsey's bottom where it was said to be "held open." Why continue to allow doubt of what really happened?

Stephanie Posts: 5 Re: What if... - Well, the Medical Examiner pronounced Kelsey's death a homicide...I'm sure that the ME knows the difference between an accident and a homicide..that is their job. They deal with this stuff every day. There is different type of bruising, temperature of the body, blood in the intestines, etc. maybe you should find out what all an ME has to do and look at. It might change your mind. I have 4 children and I also know that kids get bruises and broken bones but when it is repetitive that is when there is a problem..regardless of whether the family was fighting over her blah blah etc. she was KILLED and guess who DIDN'T do it!! Obviously the people who WERE reporting the abuse. Also, you don't give CPR in the abdomen..ask any person with medical experience not Joe Bob from down the street but a real MD..it takes quite a bit of force to do that kind of job. Just my own opinion...thanks

The "nine months" of injuries that the Briggs tout as abuse were mostly reported to DHS by Raye as she worked through her treatment plan. She was required to report every scratch, bump, or bruise her two-year-old daughter obtained. Kathie Briggs's latest claim is that she only made "one or two" calls to DHS to report injuries to Kelsey. If that's true, how were they the ones who "WERE reporting the abuse"?

Additionally, the forum members had been led to believe that Kelsey's body was covered in bruises at the time of her death. This has been proven untrue through court testimony and evidence as well as in pictures of Kelsey after her death in which she only wore a pull-up. Pictures that even I have seen and confirmed that she was not "covered in bruises." There were normal childhood looking bruises on

74

her body at the time of death. This issue became confused because the coroner was presented a body that was badly bruised. As investigators told Mike Porter, "There was bruising, a significant amount of bruising that they found underneath the skin, so it was…the bruising hadn't made it to the outer layer of skin yet." According to the investigators, whatever injuries had caused the bruising occurred immediately before Kelsey's death. This was yet another misrepresentation to the public by the Briggs and their media friends to garner hate for Raye, even though she was not home at the time the injuries were said to have been inflicted.

Hopefully Posts: 7 Re: What if..... - One broken bone maybe… but not continued broken bones and bruises over a 9 month period. I believe Kelsey told who hurt her legs. It was not an accident. What does a child abuser look like? Can you see their horns? I have worked with abused children for over 23 years and I don't care what a parent does to them they still want to be around them 99.9% of the time. Just because she appeared to be content means nothing. Is it true the EMSA professional said that no one had tried to perform CPR on her before they got there? I want Justice for Kelsey and answers for her family. That is the very least they should get at this point. None of us were there and we don't really know what happened. We can only speculate but it doesn't take a rocket [remainder of post lost in printing]

Stephanie Posts: 5 Re: What if.... - ~DGW~ (no name) you know what…I'm kinda glad that you wrote..it just makes everyone want to fight harder for justice..maybe more people need to get upset and take action..so good job being what/who you are!

*Admin Posts:7 Re: What if..... - I continue to be amazed at people like ~DGW~ who post comments attacking our family on a board that we[15] own and operate. I am tempted to delete her post, but I want everyone to see Kathie's response. Unlike some people, we have nothing to hide. **We don't care who did what to Kelsey.**[16] We just want to know the truth and to*

[15] Emphasis by post author
[16] Emphasis by book author

make sure that whoever abused Kelsey never gets the change to hurt another child. Michael Briggs <u>*admin@kelseyspurpose.org*</u>

Stephanie Posts: 5 Re: What if.... - ~DGW~ and everyone else...it's all opinions here be brave post your name with your personal opinion..it will make you feel good ☺ I just wish the people who aided in Kelsey's death would be brave. I pray that they will.. "justice" Kelsey didn't deserve to die..and the people who are brave will fight for her memory and others.

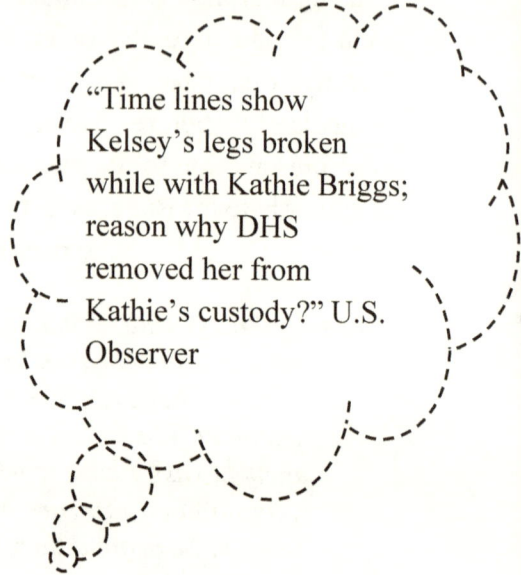

Kjbriggs Posts: 13 Re: What if.... - I normally do not reply to each post, but this one certainly warrants a response. First of all let me make this very clear. I

"Time lines show Kelsey's legs broken while with Kathie Briggs; reason why DHS removed her from Kathie's custody?" U.S. Observer

raised four children and it was never a goal of mine to raise another one unless it was necessary. I wanted all of my seven Grandchildren to have good caring parents so I could be the Grandmother. I know children get bumps and bruises, but rarely do they get twenty-nine bruises unless in an accident and rarely do children get many bruises that the mother cannot explain. Kelsey was an active child and she did fall, run and play just like most two year olds. The diference is when she did those things at our home there was rarely a mark. I did worry my son would not return home, who wouldn't, but that did not mean I wanted to take Kelsey from her mother. Kelsey would have gone home on June 6th and Raye Dawn would have started with a clean slate had the legs not been broken. That is a goal we were all working towards. I had already spoken with Raye Dawn about giving up my two weeks summer visitation so Kelsey could go home and get adjusted with her new family. I already had been awarded Lance's standard visitation while he was gone and was grateful for that. Had the bruises and broken bones stopped after January and after the mother completed her service program with DHS, Kelsey could have had a normal life with her mother. **You stated she would not have been sleeping on Mike's chest if she was scared of him, how do you know that? Children just want to be loved and if you show them affection after scolding them they usually respond.** *You sound as if you are a friend of the Porter's or the Smith's to have made some of these remarks against me, and if those are your views I am happy you had a place to share them. However: before you assume you know what my intentions were please check your facts. My goal was always to put Kelsey's best interest first. If that meant she should live with another family member to keep her safe, that was okay. She was safe and happy in our care that did not happen while livin gin the same house as Mike and Raye Dawn. The bruises on Kelsey did not come from CPR, there are many facts that have not been released to determine this was not an accident and it was not a seizure as some would like to believe. I hope you will follow along as new facts are revealed and then maybe you will understand why we had no choice when fighting for Kelsey. I only wish all of her family members would have fought as hard as we did for Kelsey and maybe she would be alive today. We are devastated by this tragedy, but we do know that this family did all we knew to do within the law and not everyone can say that.*[17]

Kathie Briggs hinted about the release of information on the sexual assault. But Mike Porter would become involved before that big piece of the puzzle was revealed. So many were misled, even Kelsey's step-grandmother would surely not share this same opinion today.

[Susan] Posts: 11 Re: What if.... - I know for a FACT that it was NEVER Kathie's & Royces or Lances & [April's] purpose to "take" Kelsey away from Raye Dawn. All they ever tried to do was to protect Kelsey and love her and keep her safe. I too

---

[17] Emphasis added by book author

77

have had Kelsey at my house and your right she was a VERY full of life and always bouncing around. I have seen her fall, run into things and never have the severity of bruising and number of injuries that she had starting in January. The Briggs NEVER put Kelsey in the middle. DHS, CASA & the maternal side are the ones that put Kelsey in the middle. The paternal side had nothing but Kelsey's safety and well being as their number one priority. As Kathie stated, if all of Kelsey's family members had fought as hard as the Briggs instead of trying to cast blame onto the Brigg's or instead of turning their heads and ignoring what was right in front of them Kelsey would still be here today! IF Kelsey's death was an accident...then WHY isn't the maternal side speaking out to about that? Who's STILL fighting for Kelsey? I think actions speak louder than words!!! [Susan] (Kelsey's Ninni)
KJ3 *Posts: 8 Re: What if.... - I'm sorry but the post by DGW really upset me. It is obvious that the Briggs family wanted nothing but protection for their granddaughter. This was not about making a grandmother have peace of mind because she thought her son was not coming home, it was about her having peace of mind because her sons daughter was being harmed. I know there was abuse in that home. Who it came from I don't know, but even being a friend of Mike's, I will not...[rest of post lost in printing]*

Susan's husband, Jack, was the first cousin to the governor's wife. This political tie gave the Briggs family influence in our state for several years while they misled everyone about the facts in the case. Sadly, many judges and lawmakers have yet to get the memo that the veil of lies has been lifted.

[Susan] December 5, 2005 - I contacted the State Capital and ask about hanging a Christmas ornament on the Capital's Christmas tree in memory of Ms. Kelsey. I was told that the tree is located on the 4th floor and that anyone could hang an ornament. What I'm doing is this: I got a fairly good size clear glass ornament and I'm going to put a picture of Ms. Kelsey inside of it, and tie it with some really pretty ribbon, then I'm going to write In Memory of Kelsey 2002 – 2005. I didn't know if anyone else would be interested in doing this

or not. It's just an idea I thought I'd share. Also, April is child abuse awareness/prevention month. We would like to have another rally at the capital sometime in April. We would like to get some VIP's (doctors, lawyers, etc.) to speak out about child abuse. So if anyone has any ideas or contacts, let me know!! We have enough time to make the next rally EVEN bigger than the one we had in November!!! Thanks, [Susan] (Kelsey's Ninni)

Stephanie Posts: 5 Raising Money? - Hi, I was just wondering if anyone was going to make anything to help raise money..like posters with awareness info. etc. bumper stickers with Kelsey's site on it etc. If so let me know..I would like to purchase something..and help in anyway I can..just let me know..I am a stay at home mom with 4 wonderful kids..I love children..Kelsey was such a cutie..I only saw her a couple of times but she was/is anjelic. God bless..my prayers are with you all

Just short of two months after Kelsey's death Kathie Briggs's interest was piqued. She was not an active participant on the forum and most of her posts seemed to be sympathy-seeking. As of November 20, 2005, Shirica had posted a total of twenty-one times. Weeks later, Kathie Briggs was only at thirteen posts. What could have prompted a rare response? Perhaps the topic heading gives us a clue.

Kjbriggs Posts: 13 Re: Raising Money? - I have had several people inquire about donating money. At first a, "Justice for Kelsey" fund was discussed by some family members. We did not want any negative responses towards our effort and felt others might turn the intent into personal gain on our part. At that time we chose not to open an account. We have had buttons, yard signs, and stickers made mostly at our own expense. There have been some who have given money and that money went directly towards these items. Since then the demand for stickers and buttons has increased and the offers of help have continued. We do not want to sell these items, but we have decided we will graciously accept the offers of help. Yard signs and stickers have been printed by a very generous man in Shawnee. He totally donated the rally signs

79

to support our effort. He has only charged us his cost on the stickers and I do not want to take advantage of his generosity so I only order 200 at a time. Anyone wishing to order a yard sign should contact him directly at [business name and phone number withheld for privacy]. We are working on buttons at this time. We will probably have the pictures printed with Kelsey's name on them and will mail them out as needed. The buttons themselves can be purchased at Wal-Mart and the picture can be inserted. At this time that appears to be the most cost effective way. For those who have asked to send donations please do so to: Briggs [home address removed for privacy] Please send your name and a return address so we can properly thank each one. It still amazes me at the kindness of so many people we have never met. Each day we feel we have been blessed by something or someone new. The word, "thank you", do not seem to be enough. It is because of these blessings we are able to get up each day. For this I am forever grateful. Kathie Briggs This post last modified 12-10-2005 10:52 PM by kjbriggs

Until the time that Raye went to prison, the Briggs had multiple signs in their yard. One giant sign was attached to their chain link fence that brought it to the attention of every passerby that it was the home of Kelsey's paternal grandparents...supposedly their claim to fame.

Donna Posts: 1 Re: Raising Money? - I read the article in the Sunday Oklahoman on Kelsey. I was appalled how Rae Dawn and her mother seemed more upset that Michael Porter had lied to them in regards to the foreclosure on his home than they were with Kelsey's murder. I hope the next time I see Rae Dawn and her mother slither into court Rae Dawn will be handcuffed. They are both guilty and both knew what was going on.

Lance's older sister, Jeanna, revealed the reason behind the false "war hero" image that her family and the media had painted of Lance in her following post.

*Post date uncertain...print date December 12, 2005 - aunt bean
[Jeanna] Posts: 8 Thank you - I sit here tonight, as I do most
nights, trying to figure all of this out. I try to figure out why
God chose Kelsey for this. Why did God choose our family
for this? I know that he chose Kelsey because she was so
special and so extraordinary, yet it is still so heartbreaking.
Did he choose our family because he knew that my mom and
dad would do everything that they possibly could to protect
their grandchild, and that they would never give up? Did he
choose the Briggs family because Grandpa and Grandma
Briggs have proved the Briggs family with the ultimate
example of how to handle adversity with faith dignity, and
respect?* **Did he call Lance to active duty for the protection
of his country in order to give Kelsey's story the edge that it
needed for the media?**[18] *Did he bring [April] and Lance
together so that Kelsey could have the greatest Ninni and
PaPa that would fight for her and her cause with with such
unconditional love and valor? Did he break the hearts of
Kelsey's precious, precious cousins in order to make them
stronger and more compassionate? I wonder so much why he
chose Lance. He has been through so much personal pain
and turmoil in his life. He has made mistakes, yet he turned
out to be such a loving and giving father. How is it possible
for him to get through this? I spoke to a chaplain a few days
after Kelsey's funeral. I was so worried about Lance and how
he was going to get through this. His pain was so raw and so
unimaginably overwhelming. The chaplain told me that God
has been preparing Lance for this all of his life. He said that
every event that has ever happened to Lance has been in
preparation to help him get through the unbelievable,
unfathomable, heartwrenching pain of losing his only child in
such a manor while he was gone honoring his duty to his
country. God has given Lance's heart a sense of calm and
peace. The unimaginable pain is there, but God is getting
Lance through this minute by minute and hour by hour. I
have seen the prayers of so, so many working in Lance's life,
Kelsey's Grandma and Papa's life, Kelsey's Ninni and
PaPa's life, Kelsey's cousins and all of her family. Our*

---

[18] Emphasis by book author

family is truly, truly blessed. We are…[remainder of post lost in printing]

Kathie Briggs could not allow her daughter to get the attention she craved. She followed Jeanna's post with her own, asking for sympathy and prayers for Mike Porter's children. This was just days before the first emails between Shirica and Mike Porter, but as you'll soon learn, Kathie Briggs and Mike Porter had already been communicating via their "bashboard."

Post date unknown. Print date December 12, 2005 - Message: The other children - I have been blessed with seven Grandchildren. Six live in Meeker and one now lives in Heaven. I know Kelsey is safe and protected and I have comfort in knowing my other six are cared for by loving parents. What does break my heart is the pain they are suffering with the loss of their cousin. We are a very close family and the children all love each other very much. They do not understand what has happened or why, they have questions daily and cry often. Kelsey's stocking hangs by the fireplace with an ornament hanging on it that reads: I love you all dearly Now don't shed a tear I'm spending my Christmas With Jesus this year. They look at it and wonder how Kelsey is going to get her presents. One of them is worried no one will hold her hand as she crosses the streets in heaven. They cry themselves to sleep night after night. They are angry that they cannot play with her again. They are angry that Uncle Lance doesn't have a little girl to be with him anymore. Kelsey knew she was loved by these children and couldn't wait to play with them. She enjoyed going to Gymnastics with [her cousin], she thought she was so big. We could not wait to see her in dance class. So many dreams shattered for no reason. I cannot tell you hard it is to answer these questions in hopes they understand. Our family will never forget the enjoyment we got from this child. She was only here for a short time, but she made a lasting impression on so many. We feel blessed that God picked our family to know and love our precious Kelsey. He gave us a gift that we will treasure forever. I ask that you all pray for my Grandchildren as they face the holiday season without

*Kelsey and with more and more questions. **I also ask that you pray for the Porter children.**[19] We have all come through some difficult times, but there are still days ahead that will take courage and faith to get us through. Thank you, Kathie Briggs*

The Briggs and Mike Porter – Unlikely Allies

On December 29th, Mike Porter stepped up his defense efforts by privately contacting Shirica, Lance Briggs's sister, pretending to be his own sister. He seemed practiced in talking about himself in the third person. So practiced, in fact that he continued his charade even after revealing to the Briggs that it had been him all along.

He stated:

Let me say our family's thoughts and prayers are with you everyday...The only thing that gives us any comfort is we know the truth – Michael DID not do this. I know that is a comfort that your family does not have right now. We also understand that Kelsey was taken from your family by someone and the same person is now trying to take Michael from us. However, there seems to be a great lack of interest in prosecuting the guilty party...What we should ALL be concerned about is the reluctance to prosecute other parties. We know what kind of person Michael is – proud, gullable, trusting, blind at times – yes. Capable of hurting a child – never. The truth is there – search your heart for it...We will continue to support your Kelsey and your family in our prayers and actions. We would like to keep the lines of communication open; and for that to happen our communications should be kept in confidence. I hope you will respect and honor this request. God Bless You and your family.

---

[19] Emphasis by book author

Shirica immediately answered his plea:

You and I had a nice heart felt discussion and you made a request to me. I will not go into details because I do not know who all has access to this address because I know Ashley has access to it, but I will say this. I cannot help without getting the confirmation I need and only Mike can do that for me. I am not saying I have groundbreaking information, I do not, but I cannot grant your request without mine being granted.

The public and private conversations continued with Shirica questioning Mike Porter's trustworthiness. She wrote the following words to the man charged with the murder of her niece:

...It is tragic what we all have had to endure at the hand of Raye Dawn. Mike, I truly understand your fear to speak with me. I would not blame you for not contacting me. I was just in hopes you might trust me to do so...I know trust is something you are probably not big on these days. I feel the same way. Just know my heart and prayers go out to your family, especially your precious children...

The email ended with Shirica's home and cell phone numbers. Mike Porter, pretending to be his sister sent this prompt reply. My question is, when had Shirica spoken with Mike Porter before the emails? Some say that Mike Porter's bail was reduced from $1 million to $250,000 at the Briggs's request. Did she visit him in jail? Perhaps there is truth to the rumors. Mike told her:

We all appreciate your discretion after you spoke with __ME__ last time. We don't worry about anyone bringing us harm...The threats are constant and expected, and we know they do not come from anyone who loved Kelsey. The last thing Kelsey would want is more violence or heartbreak. What is the one thing you need to know, Shirica? If it is in my power to tell you I will. Please understand that our phones are most likely tapped. Michael does not eat or sleep because he misses Kelsey, [Mike Porter's daughter and son] so much – not telling you that for sympathy, but because it is the truth. Many don't realize that this has destroyed so many families...How to explain to a 2 year old why someone would ever take any child's life? Especially their own? One they 'loved'?

Mike Porter was conditioning the Briggs to believe that despite the evidence and the fact that Raye was not home, that she had anally raped her own daughter and murdered her as a result. His plan worked. Shirica responded, "I need to hear it in his voice. I have seen it in his eyes but I need to put the two together."

"In person would be best – but how?" Mike Porter asked, and then he answered his own question with the start of a plan...a plan to escape facing the death penalty.

We need to think about where and when. We all know why this will be a huge obstacle to overcome – trust is not something Michael feels he will ever be able to afford again – look at where trust in Raye Dawn has gotten all those who loved Kelsey. Trust is the main factor here – breaking confidence will not change anything that Michael is going to do – that will be done for Kelsey. All it will do is close down the lines of communication between our families – and that is never a good thing...Michael was pulled into this battle by Raye Dawn, and Raye Dawn always made it about a fight between families – and of course you would never believe the things he was told...Michael would give his life in a second for Kelsey to get to see her father again. But he refuses to give his life so the person who is responsible can walk free to do this again.

Shirica seemed impatient for the meeting as she played along with Mike Porter's game, pretending he was his sister.

Do you feel up to meeting somewhere this evening? ... I posted a reply on the bashboard stating I had changed my mind in wanting to be contacted. Please disregard what I wrote. I just did that because I have already had a nosy person email me to see if I had heard from him. I do not in any way want people to know what I am doing here. This is strictly between

US!!! I have not and will not even mention it to ANY
members of my family. This is from one big sister to another.

Shirica eventually met with Mike Porter. She claims Mike Porter was worried about dying for what Raye Dawn had done. The district attorney was seeking the death penalty against him. Mike Porter also told her things Raye Dawn had allegedly said about Shirica's family. Mike Porter is a manipulator who knows how to play Kathie Briggs, and he played her so well that he never went to trial and never faced the death penalty. The emails and the game continued as Mike Porter won over Kelsey's paternal family. He made sure that all of the negativity was directed toward Raye and her family instead of himself. The plot thickened as they soon became an important part of his defense team. Months before Kelsey's body was exhumed for a second autopsy that resulted in the added charge of sexual assault, Mike Porter saved his own life by using the family that had sworn they were only fighting for "Justice for Kelsey." The media told Oklahomans that the Briggs had been the *only* family to fight for Kelsey. If only the public had known the truth!

Seeds of Conspiracy

January, 2006

By January of 2006, it seemed the plot against Raye Dawn was in full swing. Rallies and protests were held to bring public awareness to Raye Dawn and the Judge, and their charge of "failure to protect Kelsey," a charge of which the paternal family thought they alone were innocent. Mike Porter seemed to stay under the radar with prayer requests extended for his family by Kathie Briggs and her daughters. Those closest to Raye Dawn had their suspicions that something odd was happening between Mike Porter and the Briggs family, but they did not know the unlikely allies were communicating privately or that Kelsey's paternal family was aiding in Porter's defense. Further, a witness recently told me that Kathie Briggs confided in her by stating that the only way to ensure Raye would go to prison was to give Mike Porter a plea deal. While reviewing the evidence of the obvious plot against Raye Dawn that was formulated and implemented by Mike Porter and his new friends the Briggs (Kelsey's paternal family), the actions of this group now make sense. They substantiate the fact that their mission had nothing to do with Kelsey, but instead Kathie Briggs's desire to see Raye behind bars.

Evidence regarding the sharing of information about the murder case against Mike Porter started with an email Kathie Briggs' daughter, Shirica, sent to him on Sunday, January 1, 2006. From the language used, there had clearly been communication before this email. What was said is unknown.

Not sure if you know this but OSBI interviewed CG on Thurs. I will be willing to discuss this further later.

Porter snapped at the bait.

*I assume you mean Raye Dawn's ex? I hope he wasn't stupid enough
        to lie about things...Can you give me any more info?*

Shirica obliged.

*...He said OSBI was very mean and rude to him...He said Mike lost
        his temper and walked across the room and hit him across
        the face so hard it knocked him down. [Raye Dawn's ex] said
        he knew at that point he had two choices, get the @%*! Beat
        out of him or leave so he left. He said that Mike had gotten
        jealous over something to do with Lance...*

Mike Porter grew defensive as he continued the charade of being
his sister.

*[T]hat is a bald faced lie about why they had a disagreement...all
        these people that are lying are going to be in deep trouble
        when they get hit with obstruction of justice charges...you
        know the way I feel about the Smiths trying to trash other
        people? BRING IT...Let them talk their same old bullshit
        about them being the victims...Shirica, Mike knows the lies
        that the Smiths spread about your family – these will come
        out!!!! Let them act desperately...I HOPE they try to trash
        our family...*

Shirica took Mike Porter's words as truth.

*We kinda figured Raye Dawn's ex was not telling the complete
        truth...It shows so much of what kind of people we are
        dealing with...[Raye Dawn's ex's] intention with telling that
        story was to add to the fact that Mike was 'very jealous of
        Lance and he has a temper'...I will not lie and say Lance was
        a complete victim and was not at fault, he was...She made
        him out of his mind crazy at times and she is going to exploit
        that for all it is worth. She is going to do the same thing to
        Mike...When the story in the paper comes out about Lance
        and Raye Dawn it is not going to be pretty. She stated that
        Lance beat her and tried to choke her because she forgot to
        supersize his french fries...Lance went to jail...Raye Dawn
        did not have any injuries except for the red mark where he
        put his forearm on her to keep her from hitting him...Mike*

88

needs to be prepared for what is coming his way. They are EVIL people. Have you given any thought to us meeting?"

A story that was later told was that Raye put lipstick on her neck to simulate an injury. However, the Polaroid picture clearly shows bruising to Raye's neck and collarbone. Why continuously blame Raye for everyone else's faults or admit that she was injured in private conversations, but tell the public she was not?

It seemed through their communications that Mike Porter and Shirica were developing a bond from their mutual hatred for Raye. Porter planted seeds that would later develop into the Briggs' version of Kelsey's death.

...Raye Dawn would always try to make Michael hate Lance...As far as Im concerned she can say what she wants about Michael – because there are enough people who know it is bullshit. She is the alcoholic, she is the one who is a sex addict – she is the one with anger problems, she is the jealous one, and she is the controlling, possessive one, and she is the one who killed Kelsey...She is fooling herself if she thinks badmouthing Lance, your family, or Michael is going to convince anyone that she didn't kill her daughter and that she gives a care that she is gone...If she says anything about Michael that is not a fact, she will be sued for slander and libel – I would recommend you all do the same. We will not let her try to destroy him – he is already accused of murder because of her...

The topic skipped as Shirica discussed the upcoming article and the allegations of sexual assault on the niece she loved against the man she was helping.

...I am supposed to prepare a statement from our family and give it to them in the next day or two and Lance is doing the same...Lance is having a very hard time with it because it is going to make him look like a monster for hitting her over french fries...He just wants people to realize that after they split up he went through weeks of anger management and also checked himself into rehab...The comments about the

89

*supposed sexual abuse are quite hard to bear and I feel for
Mike everytime someone makes a comment about his unborn
child. I know people are just venting and do not mean any
harm but man is it hard to read some of it. I do find some of it
entertaining as well. I am not sure if you realize but
'hangemhigh' on the blog is Jeanna's mother-in-law
[Debbie]. I believe Mike's attorney has already spoken to
her. I did not want you to think it was a new avenue to
explore. I will warn you that she thinks truejustice is Mike
and is trying to lure him out a little. Please continue to post
on there, I think you are doing a great job with fueling the
Raye Dawn talk. I have had more than one person e-mail me
about it being him and wanting to know if I have been
contacted by him...The person who started the blog is also
trying to find out the identity. I told her I knew for sure it was
not Mike and for her to leave it alone...No one has thought
anything of 'nterstedinthetruth' I just knew for some reason it
was you and thought I would take a chance... My mom said
that she wished she could just let you guys know one
thing...Sometimes there are things written on the website or
blog by us that may seen anti-Mike and she does not want
you to assume that automatically means any of us think Mike
is guilty of Murder, it is sometimes necessary to say such
things to try to get a reaction out of people to get them to
talk, more specifically, to draw out Raye Dawn and her
family....I have also talked to OSBI and have heard some
things from them that are hard to take. I do want to warn you
about a thing are two where that is concerned but not on
here. I would also love to be able to give you some insight
from the DA, but again, not on here...*

It was still January 1st and the conversation continued with Mike
Porter defending Lance.

*but he knows it is a lie – he knows he didn't hit her over french
fries...If she truly didn't hurt Kelsey then she would be
working with you – But her driving force is her hate for your
family...I would love to know what your insight from the
OSBI is. I do know that they very much WANT it to be
Michael that did this, that was obvious from day one – of*

90

course they do not want to admit that they could be
wrong…Insight from the DA would be great too – but I would
be wary of anything the OSBI tells you, they've been very
dishonest so far. The fact is, if there was CONCLUSIVE
evidence that Michael did this, then they NEVER would have
set a bond for him, much less reduced it. They are attempting
to build a circumstantial case against Michael, and the DA
has admitted as much. But my question is why? Why pick
him? Because he was there? Why was he there? Why was he
left there with Kelsey? Could he really have done everything
they say in 15 minutes or less?

This attempt at Porter's 15-minute precedent was still being repeated, though it did not correlate with the known facts. To this day, it is repeated as fact even though it is not. Nineteen minutes would have been the minimum amount of time he was alone with Kelsey with 39 minutes as the maximum. No one can confirm the exact amount of time because when Porter arrived at his home and woke Raye, she did not look at the clock. Porter told her that he would arrive at 2:45 pm, but he claims he left work at 2:30 pm, which he admitted to investigators that his place of business was less than five minutes from his home. Questions have arisen of whether he was actually at work that day because a witness for him stated he was not.

The exact amount of time he was alone with Kelsey does not matter. It is still more than enough time to rape a child. As well, Porter knew he could build doubt in Shirica's mind about his presumed guilt. The following day she answered him.

I am not hesitant to tell you about the DA and OSBI necessarily
because I am worried about the security of this website…I am
needing to have my feelings confirmed before I can be too
forthcoming with evidence to help him…I would not be able
to live with myself if I thought I was helping Kelsey's
murderer get out of being punished. I think you know how I
feel where Mike is concerned but I still need to be a little
more sure…I think it was great that you have started posting
as anonymous on the bash board…Do not be too trusting. I
would hate for someone to contact you who was up to no

good...Again, I do hope you understand about my not giving you all of my insight just yet.

Porter was trying to hold it together, but his desperation was coming to the surface in this message to Shirica:

I certainly understand your position..I did not mean to imply that I wanted you to help Michael...I know he is no saint...but the things that they will say and are already saying about him are not true...the truth is the DA or the OSBI does not have conclusive evidence...not to say they won't do their best to build a strong circumstantial case against him...but if there was clear and convincing evidence at this point we both know he would not be out on bond... I wish more than anything that I could grant you some comfort by knowing or convincing you that Michael is innocent...but the fact remains if EVERYONE who has facts and truth comes forward then our brother will not be convicted of this crime...I try to imagine Michael if [the mothers of his children] killed one of his children...The only picture he can look at of Kelsey's is on your family's website...I don't know what he would do if that wasn't there...

Though posts from the bashboard at this time had been printed and collected, there were far too many to include.

Knowing what Porter was charged with – sexual assault and murder of a two-year-old child – this statement is unsettling. Also, according to the report on the content of his computers, he had visited Kelsey's Purpose almost as many times as he had visited several pornography Web sites...including some with child porn. Porter continued:

> *I honestly feel the public backlash is going to be huge against the Smiths...especially from what I have seen on the blogs...the DA will not be arresting her...so sad...It makes me angry so I know it has to anger your family..the thought that Raye Dawn could weasel out of this like she has everything else in her life....I know Michael is innocent and the thought that NO one will be held accountable for this makes me shudder...just because the DA and OSBI were swayed by God knows what? Do you want to meet?*

The e-mails that were turned over to the district attorney did not include any correspondence from January 2nd to January 10th. The conversation throughout all of the e-mails seems to be spotty. Either some of the e-mails were withheld by Kathie Briggs's family or the district attorney, or the communications were solely by telephone and in person during the obvious lapses in time. The logical answer is that some were withheld. A few of the e-mails are in answer of a subject to which there is no original message with the same subject heading, just an answer.

One of the stories that Mike Porter told Shirica was of a listening device. He claimed that Gayla (Raye's mom) put something from the black market somewhere in Kathie Briggs's home so she could eavesdrop. Gayla and her family assume that this story developed from something Mike Porter had told them. Kathie Briggs seems to be paranoid and he played on that fact. On January 10th, Shirica questioned him about the location of the alleged "device":

> *...Would you happen to know if it was possible for them to still use that listening device if it was still in the room? Or record phone conversations?*

Mike Porter answered.

*I do not know if they could use it...but I know if it was still there you
      could find it. It wasn't a fancy one..I'm pretty certain the
      range was limited...*

Mike Porter and Shirica discussed an upcoming rally for "justice
for Kelsey" that he wanted to attend. He claimed his sister and
daughter were on their way to the rally when his daughter got scared
because of what people thought of her father. Shirica responded.

*...I have a question or two. Has your attorney requested the phone
      records for your home and Gayla's phone to see if she was
      making calls instead of sleeping? Do you know if it is true
      that Gayla was planning to take Kelsey to the movies that
      evening? And, you mentioned a 911 tape. We were told that
      one did not exist. They said Lincoln County does not record
      911 calls. Do you know if that is true? My sister and I have
      come up with a plan to try and get something going with the
      DA. Not sure how successful we will be but I will let you
      know if anythig comes of it. The problem is Lance. He is the
      one who has to request certain things and he is still VERY
      angry. ..We are doing what we can. Keep your fingers
      crossed. I have let Jeanna in on our conversations. She is just
      as trustworthy as I am I assure you. She is a very take charge
      and get some action done kind of person that I knew would be
      beneficial...*

Mike Porter focused on the possibility of a 911 tape. Was he
concerned or relieved?

*I was so caught up in one part of your e-mail I missed another part.
      You were told that Lincoln County does not record the 911
      calls??? Is this possible? How do they make sure they are
      doing the job correctly? I can't believe that if it is true..I will
      try to find out tomorrow if it is true...I know the 911 tape
      would open some eyes.....*

Or perhaps a recording could send him to prison.

Jeanna joined the private conversation with a message to Mike Porter.

I posted this last night for everyone who is wanting Raye Dawn
arrested right now-I posted it especially for Mike. 'We do not
want to have Raye Dawn arrested before the time is right. I
know that everyone wants her arrested RIGHT NOW!! Trust
me, I do too. However, I do not want her arrested before the
case against her is rock solid for the appropriate crime. I do
not want the OSBI with sufficient evidence to support it. We
just have to be patient and have faith that everything will
work out in the end. We have to pray that God's will and his
justice is served in this case. I have said on here before and I
truly mean it—God may have arrested Mike first in order to
open his eyes and get his heart and head in the right place
for him to be used by God. I believe that God is using Mike to
be Kelsey's voice and tell her truth. It is a huge burden to
place on him, but Mike put himself in the position for it. Now
God is giving Mike the chance to do the right thing and be
used by God to be Kelsey's voice. As hard as it is, we must all
be patient and let Him bring justice for Kelsey.'

Mike Porter replied (still pretending to be his sister).

Michael did read and 'hear' it – there was a post that followed that
said 'Spoken like a true believer. The love for Kelsey and the
strength of the person is evident from this post..We will
continue to have faith and be strong – thanks to posts like
these.' I think that this post would echo Michael's exact
feelings. Thank you for your advice. Michael cried like a
baby after reading that....it could not have been said better.

On January 11th, Porter questioned Shirica about the "bashboard's" disappearance. Shirica responded in defense of the man charged with the murder of her niece.

I had it shut down...I think it started out as a good thing, but I feel it
has gotten out of hand. And honestly, I am worried about
you. I am so afraid you are going to hurt yourself and your

95

case. I do not want to see that happen. I hope you
understand...

The following day Shirica vented to Mike Porter about her
family's supporters… some of the same people still support the family
to this day.

…It is funny how people can hide behind a fake name and say all of
the things they say but if they were to see you or Raye Dawn
on the street, they would not dare. They would never have the
nerve to say what they say on those blogs in person. I am
sorry. I am just having a very poor attitude toward the whole
situation right now…Especially the ones who are power
hungry and the ones who suddenly want to be able to say they
know any of us. The people are sick and they need to get a
life.

Mike Porter turned the conversation back to his defense.

I understand what you mean….I hope the DA has what he needs to
charge Raye Dawn now..he has all the reports he was
waiting for.

Shirica responded.

If Jeanna was to talk with Richard [the district attorney] is there
anything that you would want him to know or anything you
would want her to say that you feel he needs to know, but you
cannot tell him yourself? He gave her his personal email
address…I hope you did not think I was telling you what to
do or anything with that bashboard. I was just afraid Ashley
was getting a little too powerful with it and the knowledge
she was gaining. I feel that if you and mom will stay off of
there it will die out and she will lose out on that power trip of
hers. Unfortunately, I cannot tell her what I think of her these
days because she does have too much information and I do
not want to make her too mad, but I would just love it if
someone would call her out and post her name on there. I bet
she would not find that too funny…How are you? I thought
the medical report [Kelsey's autopsy] may be hard to handle
for you. It was for me. have you read it?

The medical report to which she referred included the evidence of sexual assault. The medical examiner was not comfortable calling it that, though later a second autopsy confirmed it. Even so, the investigators told Raye that the tear in Kelsey's anus that went all the way to her vaginal wall was connected to the bruise near her anus where it had been "held open." How could Shirica read that evidence and still have a civil conversation with the man the investigators said was responsible?

Mike Porter feigned sympathy while painting a mental image for Shirica to envision Raye as the perpetrator and not him.

> *...If anyone wants to really know what happened in those nine months – Michael knows...The site will die out, I agree. The medical report was unbearable. I could not sleep at all last night – I prayed all night that God would allow the DA to hold Raye Dawn accountable with the findings of the report. I can not imagine what she had to endure. I do not understand how any one could do that to Kelsey – and the thought of Kelsey looking at Raye DAwn and wondering why kills me. He needs to know that there is alot more to this story than whatever he has been told by Raye Dawn...*

Shirica continued to protect Porter.

> *Just so you know, you can change your identity all you want on the site but the host of the site knows who you are every time you get on there by your IP address. She lives in Meeker and she as a VERY big mouth. She knows it is you and she is telling people. Her name is Ashley...You should really think before you get on there again.*

As previously mentioned, Ashley's mother-in-law was one of the main witnesses against Raye. She came up with a story that Raye admitted to abusing Kelsey after Kathie Briggs spoke with her. Her sister was in the same prison as Raye when she was first incarcerated. She sought Raye out and apologized for the fact that her sister had lied in order to help convict Raye.

A Common Goal

It was still January 12th when Shirica contacted Mike Porter with what she termed "discouraging news."

... I must now add a bit of news that you may find somewhat discouraging...I have news from the DA. There will not be an arrest until the week of your hearing so quit hoping it may be next week. He apparently has another trial on Tuesday he needs to focus on. He does not seem to understand the importance o this case, so I guess it is time to remind him. I am having everyone I know send him a postcard letting him know that this case WILL make or break his career. I will be urging him to get with the program and start making this case a priority. You might suggest doing the same to your supporters. Mom will be on the news at ten on channel 4 and 9 tonight. Please do not lose your faith. I have this hope for seeing Raye Dawn in her stripes being paraded into court they way you were except I hope there are cameras in her face when they do it. I know that hope will come to light. I know it will.

Mike Porter quickly replied.

...THAT SELFISH BITCH!!! the news about the DA is discouraging. I guess the most discouraging thing is it is hard to believe anything that the DA says anymore. For the last month it has been next week, next week, next week. Now he has everything he said he was waiting on, the OSBI report, the ME report, and he still stalls. If anything the ME report only makes it more obvious to me that Raye DAwn is guilty. How could I have done all that in 12-15 minutes??

Mike Porter had told investigators that he had done laundry, washed dishes, and that he went to the garage to possibly remove tires he was hoping to sell. He also claimed that he turned off the upstairs lights. Porter's known characteristics and the fact that the laundry had not been touched lent to the fact that his claims were untrue. He was merely building an alibi for himself. When he mentioned "all that," he was referring to the numerous chores and activities he said he had done after Raye left the house so that people would question how he could have done "all that" as well as the sexual assault and murder of Kelsey. Without an alibi, he fabricated one, but he was not thorough enough in his thought process to ensure that his story matched what could be found in his home.

Mike Porter then contacted Ashley, the person who controlled the "bashboard" with the following message:

I hope that any information that you recieve from the website will be confidential and not be used in ANY way to jeopardize justice for Kelsey. This CAN NOT happen. I know the IP addresses of those who post are probably available to you. But my point is, I feel your heart is in the right place regarding Kelsey. I think I know who you are, but the fact is it doesn't matter. I know that you may know people that are for Raye Dawn, but we all should want justice for Kelsey no matter who it involves. I hope you don't take this e-mail the wrong way, I just wanted to make sure your intentions were completely honest and you would never exploit any of the things that were said or any of the information obtained from the board to help someone who does not deserve helping. To many people this is our life and not something that is happening to someone else. I am in no way questions your motives, I just want to make my feelings clear. God Bless.

On January 13th Shirica was eager to share evidence with Mike Porter.

what do you know about a hand print bruise?

Porter quickly responded with a question.

when would this bruise have been on Kelsey?

Shirica replied, clearly worried that her correspondence with the man accused of Kelsey's murder could be discovered.

I am not sure. I really kind of need to talk to you because I am not
*   sure I can tell you what I know in this email. It is just a little*
*   too bazarre. I just wondered if a hand print bruise meant*
*   anything to you at all.*

Porter responded with a new accusation against Raye.

the only thing that I know about a hand print bruise is very very old.
*   Before me. If it is something recent then I have no clue what*
*   you mean. If you want you can call me at 602-xxxx.*

On the same day, Shirica contacted Mike Porter but this time the
news was good.

I do not mean to tease you with this next piece of information, but we
*   have been told by OSBI that the possible reason for the stall*
*   from the DA is that he is not just looking at making ONE*
*   arrest. He is looking at making multiple arrests. Now, you*
*   know how things are said and they may or may not come to*
*   light, but that would be a nice explanation as to why they are*
*   not moving quickly. I personally would love to see more than*
*   one person arrested. Be patient. I know that is hard to do...*

Porter responded with his usual flattery.

We can only hope that people will be held accountable for their
*   failures. We already know I will be and I will face that...You*
*   and your family continue to amaze me.*

The Witch Hunt

January, 2006

By January 10, 2006 the "angry grandmother" who had been so vocal about her opinion on the case that the Briggs had created against Raye and her family had then turned her attention to the next person on Kathie Briggs's list, Judge Craig Key.

Cheryl Posts: 26 Council on judicial complaints I wrote a letter to Eric Mitts, Director of the Council on Judicial Complaints regarding Judge Craig Key's decision in placing Kelsey back into Rae Dawn and Michael Lee Porter's home. I received a letter saying they had received my complaint against Judge Craig Key and that it had been forwarded to members of the Councial of Judicial Complaints. It also stated I would be advised when proceedings on my complaint were completed. My 84 year old mother telephoned to lodge a complaint against Judge Key and they sent her an instruction sheet on filing a judicial complaint along with the complaint form was very simple to fill out, but it does require a notary for your signature. I encourage everyone to either mail or fax a letter or telephone and request a Judicial Complaint Form to complete. Here is the address: [address removed by book author] I have heard it is almost impossible to remove a judge from office, but I enjoy a challenge. There is power in numbers and if we all call, write or fax a complaint, I think we will see a change made.

Tommi Posts: 225 Re: Council on Judicial Complaints I think it would be possible to get a judge suspended if there is something that they have done that is unethical.

Kathie Briggs had been telling the media and public that Judge Key had sent Kelsey back to Raye's home against DHS recommendation after Kathie had been successful in removing her from Raye's home. An issue arose when it was revealed that the judge acted in what he thought was Kelsey's best interest after DHS and others started to question if indeed Kathie Briggs was the abuser after Kelsey's leg was injured in Kathie Briggs's care and custody. Shortly afterward, Kelsey was removed from the Briggs home and placed with Raye's mom, Gayla. This was an important detail in the story that the Briggs did not share.

On January 16, 2006 a letter was distributed to residents in the neighborhood where Gayla and Raye had taken refuge with Gayla's friend. The misinformed author repeated information that had been distributed throughout the media that has since been proven inaccurate and misrepresented. At the top of the letter were two pictures of Kelsey. In one picture, she had a bump on her nose. The other was of her with a big, white bow on her head with her face lying in her arms. On the second page was a picture of Kelsey in her swing after the hit-and-run accident caused by a drunk driver in August of 2005. All three pictures had been taken by her paternal family.

Dear resident: I am a concerned citizen that would like to make you aware of a couple of people that you currently have residing in your neighborhood. They are residing with [Gayla's friend's name was listed as well as his home address]. Some of you may have heard recently in the news the story of little Kelsey Briggs that was murdered in her own home.

A list of "injuries" from the first autopsy was given. She continued:

Her step-father Mike Porter was arrested in October and charged with her murder, but was later bailed out in December. Her mother has yet to be arrested on any charges. The mother, Raye Dawn Smith, is widely SUSPECTED to be the actual person that abused and killed Kelsey and not Mike Porter. It is expected that Raye Dawn's arrest will come in the near future, most probably in the next 3 weeks, for the murder of little Kelsey. You will have to read the entire story of the day of her death to make a judgment for yourself, however, it is

102

*also widely believed that it would have taken Kelsey more
time to die than in the short amount of time that Mike Porter
had her in his care that day, before he called 911. This would
only leave one other person responsible for her death, Raye
Dawn. It was also speculated that Kelsey had been sexually
abused before her death; however, the Medical Examiner
was unable to determine if this was actually the case, due to
the extreme damage done to that area of her body. Raye
Dawn and her mother, Gayla are still out living as free
citizens, living their lives day to day as they want, and they
are living IN YOUR NEIGHBORHOOD. Raye Dawn is
pregnant again, due to give birth sometime in the next couple
of months. The reason I am writing this to you, is to make
sure you are informed that you have a SUSPECTED
murderer and possible SUSPECTED child molester living in
your neighborhood, especially if you have children. Both
Raye Dawn and Gayla formerly lived and worked in Meeker,
however, after the death of Kelsey they fled Meeker and are
now living with [Gayla's friend]. It is SUSPECTED that
Gayla helped her daughter cover-up the abuse, and
manipulated and lied to people in order to get them to go to
court for Raye Dawn and lied that she was a good mother
and should get Kelsey back. It is also SUSPECTED that
Gayla is now helping Raye Dawn cover up the murder of her
daughter. Kelsey's Purpose www.Kelseyspurpose.org is a
website set-up by the paternal family…and is dedicated to
finding justice in the death of little Kelsey, and also working
to make reform of current child welfare laws so this does not
happen to anyone else. They have been asking everyone to
display the Justice for Kelsey signs in their yards and
businesses, and they have stickers available to put on your
car, or where ever else you wish. I am asking you to have it
in your heart to display a sign in your yard for little Kelsey,
and a sticker on your car. The stickers are small hearts with
her picture on them saying 'Justice for Kelsey'. You can
request both at the above website, and someone will send or
deliver them right out to you. None of us can just turn our
backs because we don't want to get involved or because we
simply don't want to hear about this horrific case. Little
Kelsey did not ask to be put through this, and I am sure she*

would have like to have turned her back as well. We all have to fight to find justice for this little girl, and all the other abused children in Oklahoma and around the nation. If you have any questions about the case, you can also go to the above website and the family will be glad to answer them for you. I AM NOT RELATED TO THE BRIGGS, SMITHS, OR ANY OF THE OTHER FAMILY OR FRIENDS INVOLVED IN THIS CASE. THEY DID NOT PUT ME UP TO THIS, NOR DO ANY OF THEM HAVE ANY KNOWLEDGE OF THIS LETTER. I HAVE TAKEN IT UPON MYSELF AS A CONCERNED CITIZEN TO INFORM YOU. As I have said, everyone spoken of in this letter is purely 'suspected', and everyone is innocent until proven guilty, however if you look at the case I think you will see everything I have stated is the truth. You can go to the above website to read up on the case, or any of the local news channels have plenty of articles on Kelsey's death. Sincerely, An anonymous concerned citizen of Oklahoma

Within the contents of the letter, and among other misleading statements, this anonymous person claimed that the injuries inflicted upon Kelsey would have allowed her to live for several minutes. Not true. Investigators as well as the medical examiners stated that with a four inch tear in her pancreas Kelsey would have been curled up in a ball and screaming immediately after the injury from the pain. She would have remained in a fetal position, screaming and crying until the point that she passed out, which would have been moments before her death. Both Mike Porter and Raye told investigators that when Raye left the home, Kelsey was on her back asleep. Mike Porter told the investigators one story and the Briggs another. Yet the Briggs family continues to defend him. Why?

At approximately the same time this letter was distributed, Cherokee Ballard—a former reporter with the local NBC affiliate—did a newscast from the entrance of Gayla's neighborhood with a "Justice for Kelsey" sign as her focus. Ms. Ballard stated that the signs had been "spotted all over Oklahoma City" and surrounding areas. According to witnesses who collected the signs, the only area the signs were found was in Gayla's neighborhood. According to OKC.gov, Oklahoma City covers an area of 622 square miles (an area larger than New York City, Houston, or Atlanta). [20] How did Ms. Ballard just happen upon signs that were only present in one neighborhood and do a report on it if Kathie Briggs and her group knew nothing about the letter, as the author claimed? Also, how did Raye and her family stand a chance against a growing mob that had members of the media willing to cover "stories" that promoted their campaign against Raye?

On January 25, 2006, Gayla's friend wrote a letter to Raye's attorney. The tone of the letter clearly illustrates the frustration felt by Raye's family due to the negative, untrue media reports and the backlash of hate from Kathie Briggs's supporters as well as the fear of charges or arrest of Raye if the family dare speak up and put an end to the lies. Kathie Briggs was quickly gaining power in the state and everyone was afraid of her...and still are to this day.

Dear [Raye's attorney]: As you know, Raye Dawn and Gayla live with me. You are aware of the letters and phone calls that have been directed at me over the past several weeks and now the letter sent to all home owners in my subdivision has taken me to my 'fight back' point.

I have watched both Raye Dawn and Gayla struggle with the loss of Kelsey and have felt bad for them every time Kathie Briggs has been on TV ranting and raving about how they need to 'arrest just one more person'. I have offered comfort to them and even though I have been approached by the news media, I have kept quiet. Now under attack by the cult from Meeker, it is time I defend myself.

I composed a letter that I have attached for you to review. Gayla says it will get Raye Dawn arrested. I don't think so. I think it will, if anything, get Kathie Briggs to put up or shut up. I have agreed with Gayla that if you think it will get Raye Dawn arrested, I will not print it. I am going to offer it to the Shawnee news paper and the Oklahoman. If they will not

---

[20] http://www.okc.gov/info_tech/gis/index.html

*print it on their own, I will purchase space to have it printed.
I will do this only if you think it will not get Raye Dawn
arrested. I am not speaking for anyone in this letter other
than me so I see no harm. I also am going to hand deliver the
letter to Richard Smothermon [the district attorney] and to
the OSBI and will mail copies to [the Judge] and last but
certainly not least to Kathie Briggs.*

*They are attacking me and I WILL NOT allow it. I have done nothing
wrong.*

*Your opinion is appreciated and I will be glad to talk to you about
the letter. Feel free to call me anytime at my office or on my
cell or at my home.*

[Attached open letter]

*This is an open letter to Kathie Briggs and all of the misled people
she has persuaded into thinking that Raye Dawn killed her
child.*

*Because of a court order, Raye Dawn has kept quiet about the
horrible tragedy of losing her child. Fact is Raye Dawn and
the entire family is devastated. The family was cautioned
about saying anything as not to jeopardize the justice system
in its efforts to properly work the case. As a favor to them, I
too have not said anything that may cause prejudice. That is
until now.*

*Over the past several months I have been the target of harassment.
Letters have been sent to my office. Phone calls on my
answering machine accusing me of harboring 'sluts', 'baby
killers' and 'child beaters'. Now someone has started
sending anonymous letters to every home owner in my
neighborhood with the same accusations. Kathie, I have done
nothing to you. I hardly look at you when in public court. I
have never commented publicly about you. That is until now.*

*I have a challenge for you. You pick the place and time for a public
debate about Kelsey and Raye Dawn. I'll bring the cookies
and Kool Aid. First though, I will arrange for a licensed
person to give both of us a lie detector test asking us 15
questions of the other parties choosing. This test will be made
public at the debate.*

*Ready yourself for questions such as 'who was Kelsey in the custody
of when her legs were broken?' You say it was Raye Dawn
but why was it that she wanted to crawl when Raye Dawn
picked her up for Raye Dawn's scheduled visit? Who took her
to the hospital to have the casts put on? We both know it was
Raye Dawn. And who took Kelsey to the doctor to have them
removed just one week after they were put on? The day you
picked her up you took her to 'your' doctor to have them
removed. Why? When Raye Dawn got Kelsey back, Raye
Dawn took her back to the doctor to have them put back on.
And 'why did Judge Key take Kelsey away from you in late
April and give her to Gayla?' The public is going to love that
answer.*

[Actually it was child protective services that removed Kelsey, but
the answer would be the same.]

*You scream you want the DHS reports released to the public? No
you don't. You say that only because you know they would
not because the courts would not let them be released. You
know, the reports that states what the DHS worker wrote
while viewing the visitations. The ones that said that Kelsey
could not wait to see her mother and they sat and played the
entire hour while during your visits, Kelsey hid under a table.
One time she had a blanket over her head. One time she slept
during your entire visit. And one time she even bit you. I
loved the blurb you put in Kelsey's obit saying she loved to
bite. Here is a clue for you; she NEVER bit anyone from her
mother's side of the family. You have painted a picture that
depicts everyone on Kelsey's mother's side of the family as a
group of people that sat around and beat on Kelsey. You
ready for another shocker? Raye Dawn smacked Kelsey only
once on her diapered bottom. Raye Dawn NEVER raised a
hurtful hand to Kelsey. All of her bruises were accidents that
are explainable and I plan on explaining them to you and to
your followers. Unless you want to open the files to your
followers first and explain them that way. Remember, you
were care taker from January thru April and all of Raye
Dawn's visitations were supervised visitations. That means
that at least one other person, not counting Mike Porter, had*

to be present at all times. Mostly there were two and three people around. Something that you forgot to tell the media when you had a microphone in front of you. And prepare to talk about your web site. The accusations that your group has made. I can set some of those rumors straight now. The truck did not get repossessed. It was sold. Raye Dawn has not been to any bar or casino in Meeker or the surrounding area and the baby she is carrying is Mike Porter's and not Judge Key's. I did not pay off Judge Key so Raye Dawn could get Kelsey. She is not having a 'fling' with someone with the OSBI, and that is not why she has not been arrested. Gayla did not get fired from her job. She quit to marry me. And to pick on Gayla's mother, Mildred, is really a long shot. That lady has more class and dignity, as does Gayla, in their little toes than you have in your entire being. Neither one of them had two children from two different men so close together that they went through school at the same grade at the same time. And neither of them is on or ever has been on welfare. Nor have they made one cent from Kelsey's death to spend on themselves. Can you make that statement? Hint: that will be a question on your test. Be sure to review your copy of the custody trial from last September. If you have lost your copy, I will get one for you. Everyone will absolutely LOVE this one as well. It really shows you for your true colors since you did not even show up at the hearing knowing what was going to be said. You can also answer the question as to why you want Raye Dawn charged. Since you were not there and have not a clue as to what happened that fateful day. Could it be because that if she is charged, you will be able to keep all of the money you have sued the DHS for, assuming you win, and if she is not charged, you will have to split it with her? Just for the record, I believe that DHS did its job properly and Kelsey's death was a random act of violence. But then, this is something that we can discuss later.

Now you can invite anyone you want to this meeting. Naturally we will want [the district attorney] there. At least he will be able to meet all who have been sending him all of the anonymous letters. I will also invite the OSBI. They have not interviewed Gayla, Mildred, Raye Dawn's brother and most of the family so they can hear what is said. You ever wonder why they *have not charged Raye Dawn? Could it be that after interviewing Raye Dawn, and other key witnesses and viewing documents that they don't feel that she had anything to do with Kelsey's death? I will also invite Judge Key. He may not come and I would not be surprised if he did not but at least I will let him know that he is welcome. He may want to send someone else in his place to ask you questions and that will be fine with me. Naturally we will want [Representative S.] there to witness who he is representing in the 'Kelsey Bill' he will be sending to the House and Senate. Funny how there is not a drop of Briggs [your husband's] blood in Kelsey but the bill will be named after the Briggs. Let's also invite the Meeker police. I would love to hear what they say about your following Raye Dawn and filing numerous false reports on her. You said under oath in court that you did not do that. Another question for the lie detector. And bring your son. Let's ask him about his beating Raye Dawn and destroying her apartment after their divorce and before he joined the military. You can invite the news channel that seems to burn up the highway just to hear you throw fuel on a fire. [Channel four, our NBC affiliate] You know, the TV station that was sued and lost a slander case some time back and paid over $800,000 to a restaurateur who promptly left Oklahoma. I'm not too fond of you inviting the reporter that works for that station either, but you can. You know the one that was arrested in California some time back but they managed to keep it under wraps here [Cherokee Ballard]. I would really like to hear her definition of 'investigative reporting' since she has not talked to anyone from the mother's side of the fence. She did manage to drive out to interview a couple of your 'workers' at the entrance of my subdivision just to let people know where Raye Dawn lives. She did not have to do that. She could have called me and I would have given her permission to tell where I live. Be sure to invite the news paper people. They need to be there to get their story straight as well.*

Anyway, you have the challenge. Any place. Any time. Lie detector first. Your 15 minutes is up. Time to put up or shut up. And I will do something that 99% of the letters to the OSBI and [district attorney] and 100% of the letters sent to me don't

109

*have. That being a signature. JUSTICE FOR KELSEY! With
this meeting, Kelsey's family will have it, and if the court
system does its job, she will have hers as well.*

While the forum members continued to take action in the "justice
for Kelsey" campaign, the Briggs found a new financial backer in the
man charged with Kelsey's murder.

Pictures of the Victim Sent to the Man Charged with Her Murder

Mike Porter soon learned another way to get in with Kathie Briggs
and her family…money. He offered to purchase a billboard for their
cause. Shirica sent at least 43 pictures of Kelsey to the man charged
with her murder. Within months of receiving the pictures, Kelsey's
body was exhumed for a second autopsy and a sexual assault charge
was officially added to Mike Porter's Murder in the First Degree
charge.

On January 17th Mike Porter told Shirica:

*I would like your family to pick the picture of Kelsey that will be on
the billboard on I-40…She is so beautiful in all of her
pictures but I want to use one that is special to your family…*

Jeanna, Lance's older sister, e-mailed Mike Porter on the same day
in an attempt to control him.

*I am going to tell you the same thing that I just told my mother.
Neither one of you have anyone to blame but yourselves when
Raye Dawn's attorney can anticipate EVERYTHING that
either of you (especially you) have to say on the witness
stand. Both of you are handing their defense to them on a
silver platter. I can get on the bashboard any day of the week
and know who is who. Do you think that Raye Dawn, Gayla,
or [Raye Dawn's attorney] cannot determine that either? I
will be damned if I am going to sit by quietly and watch Raye
Dawn walk away scott-free because two people have to
communicate about this case via the Internet. Trust me-I*

*would like all of the answers too, but I do not want them in a
format where everyone, including my relentless, obsessed,
mother-in-law [Debbie] and all of the rest of the free world
can figure out who is who. Communication can be
accomplished privately. It may be too late to salvage the
damage that has been done. I understand the need to get
one's story told, but telling it to Raye Dawn's defense
attorney and obsessed freaks is not eh place to go about it.
We all know how strong their powers of lying and
manipulation already are. Let's not give them any more
power than they already have.*

Mike Porter responded in agony. His emotions were obviously
running high.

*ARGG!!! I can't take it anymore. The DA is not going to charge
Raye Dawn!!! God it is too much. I can't take not being able
to speak these things. The fact is he should have all the
evidence he needs to charge her. Nothing I can say will
convict her. The truth will be told no matter what. But it
seems like the burden is too much to bear sometimes. These
things weigh on me everyday like a ten ton truck. I pray and
pray, I guess I should have saved your post about about
being Kelsey's voice. Damn!! you are right. I need you and
Shirica as big sisters also. I am sorry. I have faltered. It is so
hard to bite my tongue, it makes me so mad at the justice
system that the truth has to be rationed out or justice will not
be served.*

Jeanna emailed a warning to Shirica:

You, or, we, have got to get some people under control.

Shirica responded by sending Mike Porter some false hope.

*the psychic says it will happen tomorrow at 10. If it does that is
going to freak me out but make me very excited at the same
time. She will supposedly turn herself in. I guess we will see if
she is right.*

Mike Porter replied with information about Kathie Briggs. She had reportedly yelled, "Take these kids before I kill every one of them" just before she gave them up for two years. As a witness has sworn, she had to be begged to see her children as well as to work to get them back before she lost them forever. With Kathie Briggs's public criticisms of Raye's parenting abilities, while Kathie repeatedly cried, "I raised four children," her own DHS records were in fact called into question.

> *that would be too good to be true. By the way, I was with my attorney today. Something I wanted you to know – I was told that Raye Dawn called [the CASA worker] and requested that she give her the info from your mothers old custody thing. I know that whatever Raye Dawn does or tries to do to your family one makes her look worse, I just wanted you to know...Why she would still think anything that your mother did however long ago even MATTERS I have no clue. It seems to me and everyone else that she is preparing her defense, almost trying to justify why she did what she did. I will say an extra prayer tonight that the psychic is right, but it will be scarier to me if she is right, I think, but scary in a good way. the things you told me the other night stuck with me, she knew things that NO one could know. She knew that I did not kill Kelsey and the only two people living that know that for a fact are Raye Dawn and myself. She knew about the handprint and today when I got to my lawyer's the FIRST thing they asked me for out of the blue was a HANDPRINT. There is pretty convincing evidence in my opinion that Raye Dawn's hands made the bruising on Kelsey.*

Mike Porter was clearly falling apart emotionally. As the evidence against him continued to build, his time became limited. He had Kelsey's paternal family on his side, but how long would it last?

From the first mention of Kathie Briggs's desire to communicate with Mike Porter, her interests were clear. She wanted to know who she could sue and if she could take down Raye's entire family. On her forum she hinted at her intentions when answering a question about a possible lawsuit against Mike Porter. She stated:

RE: suing - That is a good question. Kelsey was injured and murdered in their home. I have been told the home was only in Raye Dawn's name so I would doubt Lance could sue Mike. They only lived there for a little more than a week. The house could have still been insured by Gayla.

If it isn't an attack on Raye, Gayla is always the next best target.

On Friday, January 20, 2006 Shirica wrote to Mike Porter about Kathie Briggs's interest in seeing Gayla face charges as well. She was determined that Kelsey's entire maternal family would pay…in some way. Also, Jeanna's admonishment of Porter's and Kathie's behavior on their beloved bashboard clearly pressed the unlikely friends to communicate out of the eyes of the public.

My mom has a specific question she would like answered…She wants to know if you and/or Raye Dawn ever had Kelsey during the time that Gayla had her in her care…Mom is also interested in starting some private correspondence other than what you two are doing on the awful bashboard. If you are interested in doing the same to keep it out of public viewing you can email her at…Do not sit by the tv today expecting an arrest. Mom's talk with Smothermon [the district attorney] did not go well yesterday.

An hour later, Mike Porter responded to Shirica:

I emailed your mother. She has not responded…Can you tell me about the talk with the DA?

Shirica answered.

Mom said she will not be on her computer until atleast 4:00 today. She said the DA is having a press conference at 2:00 so she is supposed to go to that. I guess he is going to pretty much say if you have info step forward, enough with the anonymous tips. Either put up or shut up pretty much. I don't think he is going to release any groundbreaking news or anything.

At ten minutes past four Mike Porter answered. He was still pretending to be his sister in some of the e-mails and kept referring to himself in third person. Perhaps this would be his defense if he slipped up and said something incriminating. He could claim, "I didn't say it."

Well the DA is sadly mistaken...he has only heard one side of the story, which is Raye Dawn's side...we both know that if the DA is fooled and does not file the correct charges against her, the truth will not make sure Raye Dawn is held accountable. Nothing that Raye Dawn can say will convict Michael. The DA was not convinced fromt he evidence that Michael did it...We can't do the DA"s job for him. If he ever wants the truth, then he will talk to Michael. He is trying to build a case to back up what he has already done, and that is wrong. He has already charged Michael, and rather than start form scratch, talk to Michael and Raye Dawn, and do a thorough investigation with both of them as primary suspects, he is gong to use Raye Dawn to build his case against Michael, which will seriously hurt the credibility of the whole case. He can't know the truth unless he talks ot Michael – Raye Dawn will never say anything that incriminates herself. It would be truly sad if no one was held accountable because the DA did not do his job and pursued a one sided case, which it looks like he is on course to do.

Thirty-three minutes later, Mike Porter e-mailed Kathie Briggs.

We had been wanting to contact you for some time now. There are so many things that need to be said, but I will just tell you that I will answer any questions that I can for you. We know that you all want and deserve the truth. I know the correspondence must be hard and many people would not understand but here goes...

Kathie Briggs answered his e-mail later that same evening, showing compassion for his situation...the man charged with the murder of her grandchild.

...First of all this is a little strange. Why we either one have a desire to communicate may seem strange, but when you grasp at

*straws for answers your willing to put yourself out there...I
would like to sit and ask point blank questions and get very
honest point blank answers, but I also don't want to take
advantage of your situation. Basically there is nothing I can
do to change the criminal investigation. Facts are facts and
that is what it is based on. I am sure you know I am not
convinced the proper person has been charged with the right
charge...I am actually looking for answers for the civil case
at this point...If there was enough information to put some
others in jail for failing Kelsey then I would be willing to talk
to the DA about deals. I am sure you know who all I am
interested in, but mostly Gayla or any family member,
Meeker Police, DHS, CASA, CHBS, Judge Key, [another
judge], [Raye Dawn's attorney for the custody battle] and
[Kelsey's doctor]...Don't answer anything you are not
comfortable with, I am not trying to put you in a bad position.
Even with the situation the way it is, I don't think it right to
take advantage of you. You are young, you got caught up
with a family that snowed you big time. I understand how that
can happen. I honestly don't have much information on how
the investigation is going. One minute I feel they are going
after Raye Dawn for the right charge and sometimes I
wonder what they are thinking...Once again let me say, you
are young, you don't have the guidance of your parents, and
I am trying not to take advantage of that. Part of me has
compassion for you...I am not here to make you feel worse...
I don't want my feelings for Raye Dawn and her family to
over shadow my willingness to accept the fact that maybe
they did nothing wrong. I had no idea they hated me and our
family the way they do...At any point you are uncomfortable
communicating with me, please let me know and I will
understand your decision.*

Within minutes of receiving the e-mail from Kathie Briggs, Mike
Porter eagerly replied.

*Well here goes. This is the hard part. The criminal investigation is
being bungled severely. Every lawyer in the county knows
this. The DA is destroying his case day by day...Raye Dawn
was NEVER pursued as a primary suspect in this*

investigation – even these last two months have been them basically going through the motions…The fact is Richard Smothermon [the district attorney] could just as easily charge Raye Dawn with the murder as me…Basically, his press conference sounded to me like he is already preparing people for the possibility that he may choose not to even file against her. He was passing the buck saying 'if you all don't give me info then I can't arrest her'. He has just as much evidence against her as me, and then he would have her actions since Kelsey's death, which speak volumes. I know you have been fooled in the past, we all were. I know you want people hels accountable, but it HAS to start with Raye Dawn. Anything esle is not justice. As far as the answers, I have them all. I would rather talk to you or someone in person…I never hurt Kelsey. Never did, never could, never would – in a million years…Basically by me being in jail for two months that made people who knew better think twice about my innocence…I am going to nail everyone to the wall that I can in the criminal case to see what they have to say…the thing you need to know is that I will give you the answers and I want people held accountable…

A meeting must have been planned in an e-mail that was not turned over to Raye's attorney. The following day, Mike Porter told Kathie Briggs:

Would you still be interested in meeting tomorrow? I am not opposed to Shirica coming. I feel the strongest need to talk to you. Let me know and I will plan accordingly. So many questions need to be answered.

The e-mails continued for several days as the tone between the grandmother of a murdered child and the man charged with her murder grew to be friendly, playful, and even more compassionate. It's not clear which one of them was the manipulator and who was being manipulated, but it appears they both thought they had the upper hand. Kathie's words reflected the tone of the many letters received by OSBI and the DA within days of Kelsey's death. They pressed to have Raye charged with murder, and it seemed that Kathie would not give up on her mission.

The Meeting

January, 2006

Kathie Briggs responded to Mike Porter's request to meet in person. Obviously they felt the need to discuss the case where nobody could discover what was said. Kathie responded to Porter without concern for the child that was in his care, even though he had been charged with the murder of her own grandchild.

Tomorrow is fine… You should spend as much time with [your daughter] as possible since she has been through so much. I am supposed to take Richard [the district attorney] a time line on Monday sometime, but I can work around that… I don't know what your transportation is like so let me know. I am pretty flexible. I will be up for another 30 minutes or so. I took a tylenol pm and it should be kicking in soon.

Mike Porter stated:

I do not have [my daughter] tomorrow. I will have my son however. It is whenever it is convenient for you. Monday I will be at my office. I will wait to hear from you… As you know my life is pretty devoid of activity. I know you have much more to do so you tell me the day and I will work a time out… I can hand you your civil case on a silver platter. I do not say this to persuade you to help me. I just want you to know that I am having my lawyer subpeona EVERYONE that was involved in the case. And another intersting side note – one of my attorney's personal missions in life is to get [Raye's attorney during the custody battle] disbarred. The information is there to do it. I want what you want. I will do everything in my power to make sure everyone who is responsible is held accountable – financially or criminally – no matter who that may be.

Kathie responded.

118

*I don't know if you sent anything because of my aol problems. Try
again if you did or send Shirica a message on her phone 788-
xxxx or what ever you want. Just let me know if today is
possible.*

Porter answered, giving Kathie a taste of what was to come if she
would only meet with him.

*Tomorrow is better for me. [my daughter] is with me today. I just got
the mail, sorry for the delay in responding. I will try to work
something out tomorrow, the difficult thing is I can't drive
right now. I will call you or S if I can make it to work. I can;t
respond to the things you said in your first e-mail right now
but there are answers.*

Kathie Briggs asked:

Are you bringing your son to Shawnee tonight or in the morning?

Porter responded with another story in which Raye was the murder
suspect and not him. Both Raye and Gayla state that they were never
at Quail Springs Mall at the time this alleged encounter took place.

*I am bringing him to Shawnee tonight. I agree, I do not want to be
on a clock either. We will work it out this week. My schedule
is pretty much open – I generally go into work at about 7:00
and stay till 6:00. I agree about not being in the north side of
OKC. The first time I went out fo the house after all this was
the day after Christmas – my sisters drug me to a movie and
withn 3 secomds of walking in Quail Springs Mal I saw Raye
Dawn and Gayla. She had the nerve to look at me and just
chuckle like "I got away with it." I just new the stalking
rumors would start. Truth be told I would never be within ten
miles of her if given the choice. Unfortunately with what I
have to do that will not be possible. Kathie, I can assure you,
you would be wasting effore if you try to consider the
possibility that the Smiths may have done nothing wrong.
Wrong was done. More is doen everyday. The web of
deception is woven deeper and deeper everyday. I will
contact you or Shirica about meeting this week.*

Jeanna, Lance Briggs's older sister and Kathie's eldest daughter, sent Mike Porter, the only suspect in the murder case, an e-mail from a governmental e-mail address where she is employed.

I truly believe that Richard wants the truth and true justice for Kelsey. I believe that he is open to ANYONE who has evidence in this case. He has stated to me that he would rather see a guilty person walk free than a wrong person convicted. At this point, I have to believe that he really means that...Kelsey's voice needs to be heard and her true story needs to be told.

Mike Porter replied, calling Raye a "murder suspect." This allegation was ruled out within days of Kelsey's death.

conversation with attorney was not hopeful. Bottom line is this – Richard [the district attorney] knows who the single biggest source of information is. Richard has made NO attempt to talk to this person. Richard is placing weight on Raye Dawn's testimony when she is the other murder suspect. Better lawyers than him feel he is looking for a way out of arresting her. No good attorney would attempt to prosecute a murder case withour hearing all sides. Feelings were echoed of if [the district attorney] had any information he needed verified there is one source to have that done, whether it is info on Michael or Raye Dawn. Raye Dawn has had her chance to tell the truth, and she obviously has not done that or she would have been arrested. The feeling is that by placing the burden of proof back on "anonymous" tipsters, the buck is being prepared to be passed. The DA has put himself in this position. The truth will be told but I am afraid that our desire to believe that the DA is genuinely concerned with prosecuting the correct party may be in vain. If he was interested he would contact the proper parties and arrange it. It is HIS job to do this. Michael WILL tell the truth, but he will not be allowed to take the first step. If Richard wants to know the truth about Kelsey he will either file charges or contact the proper people.

120

On the following day, Kathie sent an e-mail to Mike Porter questioning him about his work schedule and providing him with information that makes her appear to have been stalking Raye and her family, an allegation she had faced in the past.

Do you actually stay at work each day? So the evening is better? You better not let you wife know you are working, she might want all of your earnings. I saw you mother-in-laws car at Mildreds again last Friday. They have come to town several times lately. You should get a giant sticker made for your window at work. That might send them over the edge. Have you seen the stickers they have made? I expect a sign up at Mildreds any day. The bash board was interesting last night, but Debbie ... should not let them get under her skin, that is what they want. They never stick around after they post something. I am going to Smothermons later this afternoon, that is if I get this time line done. I hope he worked on the case over the weekend and is ready to sign the warrant. Do you know what is going on Firday? Is it or isn't it a pre-lim?

Raye Dawn had her attorney write up a stalking complaint on [Lance's second wife] as soon as she and Lance got married. So we have been a part of her game for a long time. I read the e-mail Raye Dawn wrote to the DHS and it is almost amusing. There is no train of through there. The things she brings up are crazy. She complained about Lance offering to buy Kelsey a coat. He did that because she handed Kelsey to him with a T-shirt on, no jacket and it was 18 degrees outside. He was offering to help and she turned it around. She always turned everything around. I don't understand why she let things get so out of hand.

She filed that epo on Lance when they split up and then had him come back for several days and hide his truck out. Jeanna finally went and got him and told him the first time she got mad she would call the cops on him and he would be in jail. He came back here and that was the end of that until Kelsey came along. We really thought we were rid of her until we found out she was pregnant. Then we didn't expect Kelsey to really be Lance's. I never understood why a child would be born under those conditions, but I am so glad we had the opportunity to know her. She was such a joy for the short

121

time we had her. She certainly was "Miss Personality". Let me know what day, time, and place is good.

Mike Porter's reply included his usual phrase of "murder suspect" in relation to Raye. The fact is that the only murder suspect was charged with Kelsey's murder. Possibly he was trying to convince himself as well as Kathie Briggs.

yes I do stay at work each day. Life has been forever altered for all of us, but sometimes the only thing we can do is try to live the best way we know how. The fact is I am lost without those children. Being a father is the only thing that has ever really mattered to me. I know that this means nothing to you because you feel I failed Kelsey. I did trust Raye Dawn with her life, which was a mistake. I don't make much money now, I never did. Every penny I had I spent on the children and Raye Dawn. We would argue all the time about her priorities. She would come to work to pick me up and all the kids would be in the backseat hungry and she would be eating a hamburger. Trying to explain to Raye Dawn why children should come first is like talking to a brick wall. The money I would budget each week for food and gas she would spend on beer and cigarettes. It was a constant battle. Her statements now are so ridiculous about my "jealousy o Kelsey". Quite the opposite actually. When i talked to her about the kids, it was all of them I felt she was neglecting, not just mine. There was never something that I did for or gave to my children that Kelsey did not get first. the only thing that gives me any comfort, and believe me it is a tiny comfort, is knowing that the minute amount of time that I was allowed to spend with Kelsey I feel she had fun and felt safe with me. My time with the children was spent focusing on the children, going to the park, playing in the yard, whatever they wanted to do. Raye Dawn would sit inside and drink, or sit on the porch and drink. She made fun of me ad called me a kid because i would rather be spending time with the kids than anything. In hindsight everything is so clear. Debbie has only played into Gayla's hands with the stupid grudge thing. But it makes me as mad at the DA and the OSBI as anyone. They should not be deterred from speaking to people because the mother of a murder suspect convinces them that the people who will speak about them have a grudge. The biggest mistake Richard is making besides not talking to me is assuming Raye Dawn's testimony will have credibility with a jury when she is a murder suspect. As far as I know Friday is a "telephonic status conference". I am not sure if appearances will be made or not. The sad thing is, many of the things I will tell you would be amusing if they were not so tragic with what we know now. I know how she turned things around. Every time I begged Gayla to help me with Raye Dawn will be turned around on me. Every fight we had about the kids and her obsession with your family will be turned into jealousy of Kelsey and jealousy of Lance. My acceptance of her friendship with [her ex] will be turned into jealousy of him. I doubt everything she ever told me now in hindsight. She told me that [J] broke up with her because he couldn't handle her having a child. But in hindsight, I see he broke up with her because she lied to his family about who's Kelsey was!!! That is the thing about Raye Dawn, the things she says will always have about 20% of actual facts in them. I have a question about you all finding out Kelsey was Lance's. Did Lance know about [J]? And does the DA know about the [his family] and how they were lied to and believed that Kelsey was their grandchild? If that doesn't show how much she hates your family. I had contemplated having them subpeonad, I am reluctant to because they are innocent people, but then again this is too important to consider people's feelings. I can assure you that your schedule is busier than mine. Here is my schedule – work every day from 7:30 – 6:00. My sister picks me up at work at 6:00. after that would be fine, during the work day would be fine if I had transportation but the Spawn of Satan has taken care of that for me. I do not want to be in a rushed atmosphere, and I know you don't either. Honestly you tell me the day and I will make it happen.

Porter's claims were interesting considering that after his arrest he asked Gayla to take his children knowing that Raye was living with

123

Gayla at the time and reportedly hoping that Raye would continue to act as their guardian. He was building a case against Raye and he could not allow the real story to come to light when the Briggs hated Raye and her family so much. Kathie Briggs's response was filled with compassion.

Sounds as if you are having a particularly bad day. They seem to come more often and I understand, please feel free to vent here anytime. I do believe we were both mislead into thinking a lot of things. I am trying to remain open minded and I am willing to rethink some of my previous beliefs. I gave Raye Dawn the benefit of the doubt many times and now I realize she did not deserve any of it. I don't know what happened in Kelsey's life while she was in Raye Dawn's care. There was an excuse for everything. Raye Dawn stated in court the first time in February that if you tell a child something often enough they will repeat it, she made the same statement in June. That told me that Kelsey was brainwashed to say what she had been told over and over. Think about that. I could be a total idiot for listening to anything you say, but something tells me we were both wronged by the same family. I have been looking at the DHS reports today and each time I catch something new. I saw red flags from the beginning of this, but no one would listen.

You are right our lives will never be the same. All we can do now is figure out what went wrong and make her pay. At this point I do believe Raye Dawn and Gayla are very evil and they have manipulated people to long. It has to stop before more innocent people pay the price. I do worry about your new baby and the life they will inflict on him/her. I also worry about the two children you already have. Raye has ruined so many lives all because she hated our family.

The whole thing is she had no reason to hate as she did. Most of the things she has said are lies. She and Lance did have a crappy marriage, but it wasn't one sided. Truth be known Lance tried to help her stop drugs many times. H wanted to just have a normal marriage, that is why he went to rehab. When he did not continue to want Raye, that is when the hate came in. She did not want him, but she could not stand the fact that

124

he did not want her. She couldn't stand the fact that he found someone else and did normal things. That they treated Kelsey like a child should be treated and there was nothing negative she could really prove. She had no problems with me until I asked her to sign a piece of paper so I could see Kelsey after Lance was deployed. She wanted me to trust her, but I knew better. She would have let me see Kelsey, but it would have been at her convenience and [his new wife] would have never been allowed around her.

*She would never have let us see her on a holiday and I could not take the chance of Kelsey not being a part of the family. It wasn't fair to her to know her cousins were close and she was always on the outside. This was never intended to be against Raye, it was for Kelsey. A concept Raye could never have thought of. Smothermon was busy when I took the papers in so I did not speak with him. Raye and Gayla were at Mikdreds along with about four others cars today. Shirica saw Raye and Gayla in her car leaving Mildreds going into Meeker around 5:30 and [Raye's cousin] was behind them. You need to realize [Raye's cousin] is not going to come through for you. They are up to something. They keep trying to pull stuff and it doesn't work. First they tried to put something in the paper and she would not do it. They got mad. Then they wanted the OSBI to banish the bash board and that did not work. Something is in the air and if they don't put the little **hussy**[21] in jail soon we are probably going to be the target of their next scheme.*

I don't mean to be nosey, but are you not allowed to drive? I am trying to figure out a meeting time. The next evening I have is Friday. The days are fairly flexible. Let me know what is actually the best for you.

Mike Porter played on Kathie Briggs's sympathy:

Today was bad. I get more and more frustrated everyday, as we all do. I am so disillusioned with our justice system. I know I am preaching to the choir here, but the fact that people are able to suppress the truth is almost maddening. Some days I feel

---

[21] Emphasis by book author because this is the same word used on their "bashboard" by an anonymous person

125

like there are too many people who know the truth for it to be completely hidden, but hen there are days like today when I think it doesn't matter what I or anyone else who loves Kelsey does, because evil always wins. I know you may have felt I was the one who hurt Kelsey. There were always excuses, and the harder I pressed Raye Dawn on what happened, the angrier she got. So finally I just insisted on going to the doctor to hear for myself. My aim is not to get you to believe one way or the other. All I can do now is tell the truth if I am given the chance and hope the people who are able to hold everyone accountable will do so. [My attorney's] researchers tell me everyday that Raye Dawn exhibited many classic signs of a child abuser, and they can tell this just be reading the DHS reports. I saw Raye Dawn drive by my office today twice. I do not expect [her cousin] to come through for me. I am hoping she will tell just enough of the truth to blow some of Raye Dawn's bullshit away. The fact is, [her cousin] can't deny that she would come over to the house once a week at least. Every time she would come over, her and Raye Dawn would go "drive around". She would leave her daughter with me and I would have all the kids with me. I have neighbors who witnessed this. That never bothered me that they would leave the kids with me. The truth be told I would rather have spent all my time with the kids than Raye Dawn. But if I would have been this horrible person [her cousin] would have seen it and never would have trusted me with her daughter. Her daughter would cry when she would leave our house because she loved me so much. I don't expect her to say that she thinks Raye Dawn killed Kelsey. But I do expect her to tell enough of the truth that people will know Raye Dawn is full of shit. I know they are up to something, and I don't really care. Let them do what they want. The only people in that town who support them are Mildred and [Raye's cousin]. Raye Dawn is ashamed to go into [her former employer where the key witness against her—Donna—who lied about her worked] becase she knows how they feel about her. Everyone who spoke up for her regrets it. The OSBI was given some good info from Donna ... that proved Raye Dawn lied about the timeline on the leg injuries and the zoo trip. ...from Meeker News is on my

126

witness list. She saw Raye Dawn blow her top when [she] refused to print an article Raye Dawn wrote trashing Lance and your family a couple of days after Kelsey died. I can meet with you tomorrow, I do not mind. I can get a ride to meet you, depending on where it is. I do not have a problem with Shirica's apartment, but I want your word I will not be recorded. I have already told you that I will give you any and all testimony I have that will aid in making sure everyone is held accountable for Kelsey's death. I am not driving at this time as I have no vehicle and my license has been suspended – long story. I feel the need to speak to you and I would like to do it as soon as possible. Just tell me where Shirica's apartment is and I will see if I can make it there, if it is local.

Kathie Briggs responded with directions (for the man charged with her granddaughter's murder) to her (unmarried) daughter's apartment.

There will be no recording devices, I know you are use to dealing with the Smiths, but the Briggs do not operate that way. I would like to take a few notes just because I am old and my memory left with Kelsey. If that will bother you I won't do that. Shirica's apartment is where Raye's was…Shirica's is on the back row, the second one from highway 18 and has a Kelsey sign in the window. We really don't have to meet there if that makes you uncomfortable. I know you may need to work and if you would rather wait I don't mind.

Just so happens the day that Mildred, Raye, Janet, and [Mildred's sister] were at the Meeker News to put the trash article in the paper, my daughter Robynn was there too. We knew we needed to put Kelsey's thank you in the paper by noon and we had to leave town so I pulled in from of your office and Robynn went in. I waiting and waiting and wondered what was taking so long. About that time I saw Raye and Janet come out and thought "oh my gosh", then a few minutes later Mildred and [her sister] came out. They had parked over by Mildreds truck and were in Gayla's car so we had no idea they were there or we would have waited. Robynn came walking out laughing, then they went to [Raye's former place of employment] and said Robynn was stalking her. We would have expected no less.

127

*I hope [your attorney] is having someone go through the reports and
    the stuff Raye has written to prove the girl is unstable. We
    can't be the only ones who see it.*

*I just read the three page e-mail from Raye Dawn in the DHS files
    again. **Everytime** I read it I am amazed. She skips around,
    she is crazed.*

*I had the OSBI go to [Raye's former place of employment] and talk
    to the women there. Rita is one of them and she was a Smith
    supporter before. Donna…[a state's witness against Raye
    and the mother-in-law of Ashley, the person who ran the
    bashboard that Shirica and Porter discussed in their emails
    as the one they were afraid of] called me and talked for a
    long time about things Raye stated while working there.*

*Debbie … played right into their hands last night and then changed
    her name to Joan. She was so obvious. **I wish I wasn't
    addicted to that stupid bash board**,²² I know there has to be
    better things to do with my time. I do enjoy getting on
    Kelseyspurpose, each time I see her smiling face it makes me
    smile. I have met many nice people from this site. We had a
    meeting tonight to discuss more rally's in April. Let me know
    what is best for you.*

Mike Porter prepared Kathie Briggs for the emotional display he
was saving just for her.

*How does 1:00 sound? I see no need in waiting. The more I put it off
    the more chance I have of talking myself out of doing it.
    Richard told [my attorney] today that he still ahs every
    intention of arresting her, he just does not want it to be for
    too little. The thing is he can amend charges, but I believe
    that they can only be amended down, not up. If he does not
    charge her with murder then he never will. So Robynn
    overheard all this in the newspaper office? That is almost
    comical. That was the same day that Raye Dawn was at [her
    previous place of employment] telling everyone that she was
    going to own [my company] and that all my friends would be
    working for her. I wish I could have seen the look on her face
    when the truth hit her that she would never be able to have a
    part of that place. I still honestly believe when she retained*

---

²² Emphasis by book author

*[her new attorney] she hired him in the hopes of filing a
wrongful death suit. [Her attorney] is well known as a
personal injury lawyer, but not so much as a criminal lawyer.
I can guarantee you that when the they found out I had
nothing to take they had to have panicked. I can't even
imagine what that lawyer cost them, probably at least a
$50,000 retainer, and that is without her going to trial. The
sad thing is Gayla would spend every dime to protect Raye
Dawn rather than admit that she needs help and get it for
her. To me, anyone who can't see that Raye Dawn is a
sociopath is blind. I was at the funeral. I SAW her with my
own two eyes. She can turn it on and off like a light switch.
People in that family actually badmouthed me because I was
so distraught at her Kelsey's funeral. It was surreal. You
know the sad thing, there was so much evidence at thae house
that could have been used against Raye Dawn that is gone
now, stacks of letter s that she would write after she had
sobered up from one of her drinking rages, so may things that
becasue Kevin wanted to arrest me so quickly will never
come to light. I could have handed her on a silver platter, but
since they let her clean out all the evidence like they always
do, all I have left is my word, which is damaged because I
stood behind raye Dawn even when I had doubts. I will do my
best to control my emotions tomorrow but I can't promise
anything. I can't turn my feelings on and off like Raye Dawn.
Although I did not kill Kelsey and I do not feel I should spend
the rest of my life in prison, a part of me feels a great deal of
responsibility and regret. I was already faced with the facts
that I believed Kelsey died in my arms, but I would have
coped with that because I knew I did everything I could
THAT day to save her. But then for people to not only say
that I didn't try to help her but that I actually took her life is
almost impossible to take. The fact is Raye Dawn will always
be the same person, she will never change. I am not the
person I was when I was with her. I tried to make her change
and be the paretn she should have been, but eventually, well I
will stop there, I am just venting, nothing of use and certainly
nothing you want to hear. Let me know if 1:00 will work and
I will be dropped off there at that time.*

People who attended Kelsey's funeral have relayed the strange antics of Mike Porter from that day. Raye had left him immediately after investigators told her that Kelsey had been murdered. That didn't stop Porter. He showed up at the funeral carrying a doll that had been Raye's as a child. She had passed it down to Kelsey. Porter never tried to comfort Raye. As Raye reviewed her notes on what she wanted to say about her daughter, Porter snatched the paper from her and questioned why there was nothing about him. At the cemetery, Porter stood away from everyone else, holding Kelsey's doll. Even though Raye and her family members were sorting out the events and trying to come to terms with what actually happened to Kelsey, Porter's behavior that day lent to thoughts of his guilt.

Kathie Briggs seemed eager to meet. She has admitted to picking Mike Porter up from his place of business and driving him to her daughter's apartment. Her hate for Raye and Gayla was evidently stronger than her love for Kelsey.

*Do you live close to something? I can meet you in the City. This should not be this hard. **I don't have a problem with picking you up.** It is not like I feel unsafe. I am up for a while. If you write back with a plan that is okay, if not I will hear from you tomorrow or later today since it is already tomorrow. If you write back with a plan that is okay, if not I will hear from you tomorrow or later today since it is already tomorrow. If you can meet earlier on Wednesday that is okay. Don't chicken out, **I don't bite, that was Kelsey's trademark.** I don't know if this is proper for us to visit. I have no idea what Lance or [my husband] would say and I don't want to know right now. **I don't know why I have compassion for your situation, but I do.** I know what it is like to be at the end of the Smiths tactics. You know how they work so you should have an advantage, then again, knowing how sneaky there are can be scary. **Gayla is the one that should be ashamed of herself for taking advantage of someone so young.**[23] It really makes me sick the way they think they are beyond accountability.*

---

[23] Emphasis by book author

They have been in Meeker so many times lately and that is odd. I think Smothermon does want to arrest her for murder, and at one time I thought it was a done deal. I think you can arrest up, but not positive. There is no statue of limitations on it. Did you know that Raye got an audio of the funer from [the funeral home]? I think I will see if Smothermon will get a court order for it. It will show psycho woman in action. I saw [your attorney] leaving either the court house or the DA's office today. Has he had a meeting with him ever? I still have faith in this and you should not give up. I am not closed minded, but so far I am not convinced she doesn't need to be charged. I guess you can confirm my gut feelings when we meet. Let me know something. This should not be so hard, dang!

Mike Porter's emotions took control in his reply.

We can meet earlier Wednesday if that is ok. Raye got an audio recording of the funeral? She is a sick puppy. The audio will not prove how cold she was. A video recording would porve that beyond a doubt. I will never give up. Kathie, you should have serious concerns about her being charged. I have said it time and time again, I will accept any responsibility that is mine in this. We all owe that to Kelsey. But I will not accept responsibility so the person who killed Kelsey can walk free. I really hope you have serious doubts about it, because if the DA chooses to prosecute me he will be prosecuting the wrong person for Kelsey's murder. I hope that shakes you to your core like it does me. I know everyone wants to believe that stuff like this only happens on TV, but it happens right here in Meeker America. The fact that Raye Dawn has already fooled so many is very scary. When I was first arrested, my feeling was utter shock but I had faith that the truth would be revealed. As time passed, fear began to sink in. The fact is Raye Dawn fooled the one person she had to fool from the beginning, [the O.S.B.I. investigator]. The are using a statement Raye Dawn made about Kelsey was fine and breathing when she left. DId you see in the DHS reports about the interview with [my daughter]? Why would Raye Dawn tell [my daughter] on the way back from picking her

131

*up from school that Kelsey was eating the raisins and she
was fine when she left? I can't figure that one out. At that
point she should not have known anything was wrong, if she
did not do anything, right? I still don't get why Richard has
not considered her statement in the News Star about "she
knew something was wrong when she left". You can call it
ESP, you can call it a premonition, you can call it mothers
intuition, but I call it bullshit. Where was her mother's
intuition for all this time when I was supposedly hurting
Kelsey? AHHH!!! This is so ridiculous. You should not be
convinced by a long shot. If Raye Dawn was able to convince
you that she was innocent by convincing the DA then that
could be her single biggest coup. I don't know what the DA
has or tells you he has, but [my attorney] has people and
proof and he knows what the DA has and says he is using it
to prosecute the wrong person. Raye Dawn and her followers
assume that because [my daughter] is on the list she will be
testifying against me. I am afraid they will be sadly mistaken
in court. Any testimony [my daughter] would give would
make Raye Dawn look so much worse, but the OSBI never
asked any of these people anything about RAye Dawn. [My
daughter's] grandma tried to tell the OSBi about all the times
she came over to pick [my daughter] up and Raye DAwn
would be sleeping and the kids would just be running loose
and how EVERY time she came over Raye DAwn had a beer
in her hand. You know what [the investigator] said "Well just
becuase she drinks that doesn't make her a bad mother" SO
apparently alcoholism is a desirable trait in parents now
according to [the investigator]. [My daughter] saw Raye
Dawn slap me so many times, and she knows what kind of
parent Raye Dawn is. She knows we fought about her
drinking and her not putting the kids first. Anyway, sorry to
unload on you again. I do not have a problem meeting you. I
do not know if I will be able to confirm any feelings you have,
but I can tell you the truth. I can tell you if Richard gets this
wrong then THE PERSON WHO KILLED KELSEY WILL
GO FREE. HOW DOES THAT MAKE YOU FEEL? THAT
SOULD SCARE THE HELL OUT OF YOU. IT SCARES THE
HELL OUT OF ME. SOMEONE KILLED KELSEY AND SO*

FAR BY AND LARGE THEY HAVE MANAGED TO ESCAPE SUSPICION FOR THE ACTUAL CRIME.

Among his stories, Mike Porter admitted that Raye had "escaped suspicion." Why continue to refer to her as a "murder suspect" when only the Briggs believed her to be that? He knew it was not true.

Kathie Briggs liked what she was hearing. Mike Porter was speaking her language.

First of all, I want Raye Dawn in jail and I want her charged with murder... [24]*I want the DA and everyone involved to prove to me beyond a reasonable doubt that she was not responsible. I am not falling for the Smith lies, not this time. I am going to try and have an open mind in case I am wrong. I do feel you are being sincere, but it would not be the first time I fell for the wrong story. I don't want you to think I am doubting you, I don't actually know you and I have to be prepared to accept the fact that you could also be manipulating me. I don't think you are, but look how gullible I have been over the past year. I tried to save Kelsey from an abusive life and everytime the very people that could help her listened to the Smiths. I know they are evil and manipulative people. It makes me sick that we did not sue other means to protect her, but we felt being ethical law abiding citizens and telling the truth would help. We were out played and Kelsey paid for it and all I can do is fight for the truth now. I think we are both on the same page for that. I don't know what the DA has in mind. He hasn't given me that information in black and white. I hope when I go in there tomorrow he will have read through more reports and he will have her phone records like I requested. I really wanted her in jail by now and the wait is making me nuts. Honestly I want her and Gayla in jail, they both failed Kelsey in my books. I will not stop until every last person that had knowledge of wrong doing is help responsible. **If you are willing to help me do that I am willing to help you.***
The funeral home gives people a copy of the audio just as part of the package. It is kind of eerie, but I guess some people actually

---

[24] Emphasis by book author

*want them. We got one too and I can't see myself wanting to
     hear it anytime soon.*

*Lance is working to get witnesses that saw Raye mistreat Kelsey to
     come forward. I know they are out there and if the father of
     this child can make them feel guilty for staying quiet then that
     is the tactic we will use. What exactly is the DA telling [your
     attorney]? Have they discussed Raye's part in this? I don't
     have any records with [your daughter's] interviews in them.
     That must be the OSBI records. I know Smothermon has the
     video tapes of all of the interviews with the OSBI. The DA
     knows I don't trust anyone in this and I will question every
     move he makes. I feel he wants the truth, he just wants
     enough of it to get a conviction. What would make Raye get
     an attorney for wrongful death if she thought Kelsey died of a
     seizure? She probably thought she needed to file before
     Lance did.*

*I heard [Raye's attorney] does do murder charges and he was good.
     Raye certainly did not fight to hard when Lance fought
     executive rights to Kelsey. They never asked for Raye to have
     the rights, they asked for a neutral party to be in charge.
     Lance's attorney was finally able to bring up the fact that
     Raye lied in court about being pregnant when she got
     divorced and it was not denied. They called her to the witness
     stand and her attorney would not let her go. That was a great
     day for us after we watched the news. I love Nick Winkler [a
     Fox reporter who has reportedly dated Britten Follett].*

*Anytime on Wednesday would be fine. Not before 10:00, I might be
     cranky if I have to get around early. Do you need me to park
     around the corner and drive you over there? Let me know. I
     am home today with a sick child so I will be checking this all
     day.*

It was January 24, 2006, and just three months after Kelsey's
death. The man charged with her murder responded to his new friend
that same day.

*They will never be able to prove beyond a reasonable doubt that she
     did not do it – there is nothing that will exclude her. We have
     already talked to doctors who have told us that the state I
     saw Kelsey in when I found her was most likey a form of*

shock from the massive trauma she suffered, and convulsions are common with this. I am sorry if that is too graphic, but the first time I saw the ME report I threw up. The fact is the things that happened to Kelsey would have been very hard to do in that short of a time period. One hting that you probably do not know is that in my interview with [another investigator] at OSBI – he told me that they knew Kelsey was gone when I got there and that Raye Dawn killed her. I know these are police tactics, but the fact remains he said this. Now answer me this – who could instantly grasp the possibility that their spouse killed their child? Someone who had to and knew exactly what they had to say, that is who. But he knew that at that time I was not in a state of mind to grasp that Raye Dawn killed Kelsey. I was in denial and shock. The other thing that he did to me which was very unfair was he left open the minute possibility that her death could have been accidental. He kept saying, what happened, did she fall off the trampoline, etc. So no matter how small the possibility was that it could have been an accident, that was the hope that I clung to. The alternative was to believe that my wife who I loved beat her own child to death and left me there to take the blame. If [the investigator] would have told me the whole truth, the state she was in and that it was obvious it was no accident, then I could have at least tried to get my mind around it. he kept saying, you're thiking emotionally, you need to be rational. I do not know anyone could have been rational at that point, but apparently Raye Dawn was. Kathie, I rode home in the same car with raye DAwn after that interview and I cried and screamed at her to tell me what happened. She said "I don't want to talk about it". She was calm as can be. It is terrifying to me in hindsight looking back at some of her actions. There are plenty of people who have seen Raye Dawn mistreat Kelsey. [My attorney] knows the DA will arrest her, he tells me to be patient. He says they jumped the gun with me and the mistakes they have made are very damaging to their case in general. He feels he will file on her before Friday, but for what we do not know. Since the DA will not talk to me, I would guess it would just be failure to protect. The DA will never know the whole truth until he sits down with me. Raye

DAwn got the attorney as soon as she found out it was ruled a homicide, but my point was simply that [her attorney's] law firm is more well known for civil and personal injury suits than for criminal defense. He is not that good of a lawyer because he let Raye DAwn make several damaging statements in the press, but he seems to have gotten that curtailed by not lettign her open her mouth anymore publicly. I can assure you Gayla needs to be in jail too, if for nothing more than the actions she has taken to cover up for Raye Dawn. How about 11:00? i can have someone bring me over there, it should not be too hard to find. No on will know what I am doing for the same reasons no one will know what you are doing.

Less than an hour elapsed before Kathie Briggs answered Porter.

Don't worry about getting to graphic, I need to know everything my grandchild suffered from. I have already seen one of the autopsy photos. The DA covered her face for me, was a little hard to take, but it is her and if she can endure the pain, I can surely hear about it and look at the damage. I owe it to her to know everything she suffered. I really hope Lance does not have to see any of that in court. Hopefully they will just have the pictures for he jurors and not display them. Lance did not want to see her after she died. He couldn't handle the fact that his child had been cut on. We had a closed casket service, but later [his ex-wife] needed to see her for closure. I don't know if it is a good thing not to have seen her or not. Sometimes it seems like it really did no happen. We had to go so long without seeing her and sometimes it seems like she is still here and we just can't diagram without seeing her and sometimes it seems like she is still here and we just can't see her. The ME report was much worse than I expected. I cannot look at the diagram without seeing her face. I see Kelsey there not an outline.
[Your attorney] is probably right, I hope to know more tomorrow about the DA thinks. He certainly isn't getting any vibes from that family that we think she is innocent. I really feel he wants her in jail for life one way or the other.

I hope [your attorney] is right, maybe tomorrow we will be together when we get the call she is in jail. 11:00 will be fine. You can call me at home if something comes up. I don't think my phone is tapped, don't know why it would be. You can also call my cell phone if you would be more comfortable 788-xxxx.

That is strange behavior on the way home from the OSBI. Where was Gayla? Didn't Raye know what the autopsy was for and did it concern her? When they took Kelsey that night did she act funny about it? Did she sleep that night like nothing was wrong? We were all in such shock, we couldn't sleep, or eat for days. We could not force food in Lance. He just kept looking at her pictures and screaming that she isn't smiling now. Watching him get off that plane was so painful. It was a long trip on the way up there just dreading it. [His ex-wife] and her family met us there and he would not even look at her. Was very weird. I noticed several cars at the house on the news. Did Gayla and the other family members come up there or did they just ignore you?

Kathie Briggs e-mailed Mike Porter again on the 24th to discuss his offer to sponsor a billboard.

[Lance's ex-wife] called this morning because her company is putting a billboard up for six months and with that contract they are able to have a Kelsey one for free. Then this morning they found out you are putting one up too. Shirica called Lance and told him you wanted to do this and he approved it. Then we [Lance's ex-wife] said her company would not probably do it if there all is one up. I told her to have the company go ahead. I know they are expensive and you really need to put your money towards your children or other expenses. We are not saying we don't appreciate the idea, but this really is to much money for one person to do. ***I don't want this to hurt your feelings.*** *Maybe we could come up with another idea that could get the same results you are looking for. There is a lady outside of meeker going to Shawnee where the old taxidermy place was and she said we could put up a big sign there. It would not be a billboard size, but could get a statement across.* ***You could have a large one***

137

and attach it to the outside of your business.[25] *Your employees can have yard signs made. I am really wanting to get them all over Meeker. I just wish people in this town were not so scared of speaking out. Let me know what you think. I have to tell you if Lance has approved letting you do something that is a big accomplishment. I mean BIG! I did not know how he would react.*

Kathie Briggs later posted a statement on her forum defending her actions in regards to Mike Porter. She stated, *"It made me sick when he plastered his place of business with Kelsey's stickers. I knew he was doing it for a big show and we used his desire to please us to gain information about many things."* Presumably, she had forgotten that it was her suggestion for him to do so, or perhaps this was another deception.

Porter responded, offering even more financial support to "please" the Briggs.

Well, then if they go ahead and do it then I will hold off. But money is not an object, not meaning i that I have it but meaning that me and my family will do everything in our power to make sure that people do not forget about Kelsey. It does not hurt my feelings at all, I just wanted it done. I tried to have it done from jail, but that was very difficult. Everything I do for Kelsey has to kept hidden at thispoint and it is extremely frustrating. I could tell these people how the system can be manipulated. I have seen the enemy up close and I know how they do what they do and how they are able to hide it. I know the signs now and the excuses everythign else. I know the things DHS could have done to prove Raye DAwn was hurting Kelsey and to keep her safe. i can't tell you how it makes me feel that Lance approved my involvement as limited as it can be at this point. I will never be able to give him anything but maybe the small comfort of knowing the truth and and a promise that I will do everything I can to make sure the people who failed Kesley are held responsible. I know these things are nothing next to his wish to hold his

---

[25] Emphasis by book author

precious daughter once more, but it is all I have to give. I will give my life it means the person(s) responsible will be held accountable. Kelsey life was worth a thousand of my lives. But I WILL not give it so these same people who are responsible can be free. I think that many people's biggest hesitation is they do not feel that someone who was completely manipulated should go to prison for the rest of their life. I am not saying that I have a great deal of support in that town but I will tell you that people that have known Raye DAwn her whole life do not believe in her. Wanna know what I tell people? I tell them Justice for Kelsey means something different to everyone. To me, Justice for Kelsey means holding the people responsible who were BEHIND the deception and the lies and the abuse, and the people's who's JOB it was to protect her. I know that I was not the one who abused Kelsey, and I know I was not eh one(s) who were behind the deception. I was a pawn, but that does not relieve me of responsibility. I will never claim complete innocence like Raye DAwn has. I AM INNOCENT OF MURDER. So when I put up Justice for Kelsey signs, that is what it means to me. I think some people think that by putting up signs they are agreeign with a certain notion of who should be punished. I know that all the signs mean is "Let's get justice for Kelsey, whatever that may be and whoever may be responsible" The signs are not partial, and that is why it is so absurd that the Smith's feel the need to get their own. The signs do not say "Raye Dawn killed Kelsey". They say "JUSTICE FOR KELSEY". Only a guilty person would not support that cause. I honestly can't believe they have been so vengeful even now. In hindsight if I really was the one abusing Kelsey you would think that you would be the first person Raye DAwn would calland apologize to for being fooled and allowing it to happen. But don't hold you rbreath on that one. Her actions speak volumes to me, and I think to any sane person they do also. I guess I am either starting to question the DA's true intentions or his competency, I am not sure which one yet. I did hear something form someone, and I usually do not listen to what is said, but the source on this has been a very reliable source in the past. This person I heard this new bit of info from was the one who called me the

*day before I was arrested ad told me it was gonna happen. I
was told that the DA was made aware of a statement that
Raye DAwn made to a man at a bar in which she admitted to
killing Kelsey. It apparently was made with sarcasm, but the
fact that she would joke about it seems kind of sick to me. I
know she was seen at [a bar] in Shawnee a month or so ago
with [her ex-boyfriend] so the statement seems feasible. She
is not above confessing, becasue I can tell you she is very
smug about this whole deal. When I saw her at Quail Springs
Mall she laughed. Not a reaction you would expect form a
mother who sees her daughters supposed killer. I was
shaking and almost went into cardiac arrest. I still want to do
something to support what you all are doing. I guess I could
make an anonymous donation to [the sign shop], say so the
next 100 yard signs or so would be paid for and stickers
also?*

The e-mails seemed to skip in sequence when two days later
Kathie Briggs responded to an e-mail with the subject "Thank you."
This is just one example of the questions that arise of which party
withheld evidence.

*You are welcome, I enjoyed our visit. I know it wasn't easy for you. I
am on my way to meet Cherokee Ballard in a few minutes for
a story on Lance.*
*I looked at some reports last night too, and I have a question about
the checks. I found an entry that stated you told them that
your check book had been stolen. Is that something you told
the DHS to cover for Raye?*
*I did not get the feeling I wanted when I left the DA's office. He is
going out of town all next week and it will be after that before
he gets back to work on this case. My trust issues are flaring
up again.*
Gotta go, I will check with you later.

Porter responded on the 28th.

*About the checks – I was missing a book of checks and I had been
told by my neighbors that they had seen a woman who still
liked me lurking around our house. I thought they may have*

been stolen, but it is probably more likely Raye DAwn took a book of checks. I was not great with checks or I could have proved it. I will be able to tell with the carbons from BancFirst. I knew that I had either lost a book or had a book taken. I could not fathom at the time that it might have been Raye Dawn. But yes in hindsight I was covering for Raye Dawn I guess in a way, because I knew the likelihood that the person who stole the checks would have written a check at the same liquor store Raye always went to was slim. I have one for you – the DA is subpeonaing phone records FINALLY. Do you remember Raye Dawn's phone number at the apartment? This would help prove many things such as she would call ...(an RN) about Kelsey's injuries. I could not remember it, and I thought you might have it written down in some old notes. If you don't want to give it to me I understand, but it will help in the case against Raye Dawn.

On the following day Porter contacted Kathie Briggs and referred to the video of the interrogation of Raye Dawn. Kathie soon had the video in her hands of both Raye's and Mike Porter's interrogations. Jeanna made copies and distributed them to their followers...one copy was then given to me. When asked where she got the video (which was against the law for her to have it), Kathie stated that Porter's attorney had given it to her. Porter told her:

I will help however I can you know that. But if you had access to the OSBI report you would be puking right now, just like I have been since I saw it. And I have not seen Raye Dawn's obviously, but if the DA is talking about not filing against her then I would think all you would have to do is mention to him that you will be requesting access to the OSBI report at the conclusion of the investigation and I would think that would change his tune. [My attorney] has told me that he can not choose not to file against her since the OSBI has issued an arrest affidavit for her. I am not sure what exactly is going on, but I believe Jeanna was on the bash board and I was trying to get her to keep an open mind because I feel there IS GOOD evidence to prove that Raye Dawn killed Kelsey. I had mentioned when I spoke to you that the DA may not be telling you everything, including his dealings with raye

*Dawn, and all the evidence that is NOT favorable to his
position. I know you do not trust anyone, nor do I. I am not
asking you to trust me, I am simply asking you to remain
skeptical of everything. There is so much more. Kelsey's
voice is there, in the information, he just has to look and hear
it. Being close minded will NOT work.*

Kathie responded that same evening. The communications with
Kathie Briggs and Mike Porter seemed to take place mostly late at
night. This was also true for the busiest time on their bashboard.

*I wish I could see the OSBI reports. I was wondering how he could
keep from arresting her if they had issued an affidavit. I was
wondering what the charge was that they recommended. So
you only have a copy of yours? How are you to prepare a
defense without both? I do believe Jeanna misunderstood
what she thought Smothermon was saying and she has
written an apology. We are always skeptical of everything we
hear. Things are not adding up and that is what is turning in
my head. I really need to know some of the things that I asked
you. If you are not comfortable telling me that is okay. I am
trying to piece together some of the things she told me. My
thought is Raye Dawn is not alone in this and I want to see
what others knew as well. I am just like you, grasping at
straws. One more question though, you told me Judge Key
told [Raye Dawn's attorney during the custody dispute] that
Raye would be getting Kelsey back, but how much ahead of
time did she know that? You do realize if they were trying to
help Raye Dawn then that it could still be going on. Craig
Key will be trying to cover his butt.*
*Remember when I told you someone said they saw someone take
something out of that house during the funeral? Well, today
there was a fire back behind that house. I don't know if it is
related in anyway, but if that was a piece of evidence it could
have burned. Does that house have insurance?*

Kathie Briggs and Mike Porter exchanged several lengthy e-mails
discussing the same issue—their mutual desire to have Raye Dawn
arrested. Porter responded.

I will meet with you agian and tell you anything you want to know, no beating around the bush. You let me know if you want to do this and we will sit down and get down to business. You can make notes if you wish. The truth I will tell you will be the same truth I will tell the DA, if I ever have the chance. Jeanna did not need to write an apology, I just know how much faith you all are having to put in him and I am afraid that his true intentions may let you all down. I understand how you feel about me and nothing I can do can change that. The things I am going to do are not going to be for you or anyone else, they will be for Kelsey. Her mother does not love her enough to tell the truth about her life, but I do. I do not expect you to believe everything I tell you, but I have faith that you will know the truth when you hear it. I believe Shirica knew the truth when she heard it, but that is of course just my belief. I WANT JUSTICE FOR KELSEY. WHAT IS HAPPNEING RIGHT NOW IS NOT JUSTICE. WE NEED AN INDEPENDENT REVIEW OF THE DECISIONS THAT ARE BEING MADE. RAYE DAWN HAS BEEN PROFILED AS A SOCIOPATH. TO HER, SOMETHING SHE COULD USE TO MAKE HERSELF FEEL GOOD AND EXACT REVENGE ON LANCE AND YOUR FAMILY. I AM SORRY TO PUT IT IN THOSE WORDS, BUT THAT IS THE DEFINITION. I KNOW WE ALL KNEW KELSEY WAS SO MUCH MORE, BUT RAYE DAWN NEVER HAD THE CAPABILITY OF KNOWING HER LIFE HAD VALUE. KATHIE, I WISH YOU UNDERSTOOD HOW I FEEL. THE ONLY PERSON WHO KNOWS THESE THINGS AND IS NOT AFRAID TO TELL THEM IS BEING IGNORED, BECAUSE HE HAS BEEN CHARGED WITH A CRIME. DOES IT MAKE ME LESS CREDIBLE BECAUSE ONE MAN THINKS HE WILL HAVE A BETTER CHANCE OF GETTING A CONVICTION BY PROSECUTING ME THAN BY PRESECUTING A MOHTER WHO HAS MANAGED TO PUT DHS, A JUDGE, A CASA WORKER, A CHBS WORKER, AND AN OSBI AGENT IN HER POCKET? I am sorry that you were misled into believing he actually wants to prosecute Raye Dawn. As far as the OSBI reports, I am only allowed to see mine because that is all that he can used in my prosecution. I feel like there is ENOUGH in mine to prosecute her. I know you are trying to prove she has lied to cover things up, but she has proven that herself. She has changed her story about the collarbone NO fewer than three times. I am going to try to reach out to [Raye's sister-in-law], and see if she will AT LEAST admit that Kelsey did not hurt her foot/ankle at the zoo. Ihad heard that Gayla and [her friend] were no longer together, but I do not know for sure. That would be something, if the life Gayla lived was finally catching up to her. She would not be able to support herself and Raye Dawn without [her friend], and she probably would not even be able to afford the lawyer. Sad that all the DA would have to do would be to file charges and if he filed against both of them, then Gayla would have to make the choice between herself or her daughter, then the truth might come out. Even if it didn't bring the truth out, it would make Gayla show what kind of mother she really was. Kathie, Gayla knew – she knew something was going on. She had seen Kelsey from he time she was born, how could she not? What movie was she going to? Was there even a cartoon movie out at that time? She has lied since to cover for Raye Dawn, and to me that is enough for at least an obstruction of justic charge, if not failure to protect. I never knew Kelsey before she was abused. My sisters thought something was strange the first time they met Raye Dawn. We wnet out to dinner and Kelsey was talking or something, and Raye Dawn WENT off on her. My sisters were like "Whoa". Raye Dawn looked at them after she went off, and said "She's really shy and quiet". She obviously was not. But they knew then that she wanted to control Kelsey and make her be a certain way that she was not. She did not want Kelsey interfering in her single life, which was odd because I wanted us to do things all together, but on nights I would not have my children she would insist on "getting rid" of Kelsey. On nights she couldn't and I wouldn't stay with her or let her stay with me I know she had to be angry at Kelsey. DO you think your source on Gayla and Raye staying at Mildred's is reliable? I could see Gayla making Raye move there but I could not imagine Gala living living there. And the thing about evidence being removed...they cleaned that house out THE DAY I was arrested. They can say they were "in shock" and

"grieving", but they were not. The day I was arrested, they
loaded up some of my kids things and dropped them off at
Alesha's parents house, and SWEPT that house clean. That is
COLD, LOGICAL thinking. I know evidecne was destroyed,
but what can we do? The DA made sure of that. If they would
have came ot me before they arrested me and wanted to go
through the house I would have let them, no questions asked.
I did not remove or tamper with anything in that house. It
was all I could manage to do to eat and try to sleep. Raye
Dawn's letters which she wrote after she would snap, the
laundry that was being done, the alcohol, all the pictures I
took of Kelsey's bruises, those things are ALL gone. Thank
the DA for that.

When Raye and her family arrived at the home after Kelsey's
death, they were met by police and investigators who were collecting
evidence. Here, Porter tried to convince Kathie Briggs that there was
no evidence that his story about doing the laundry was true because
Raye had destroyed it. How could she when the police were in the
home while she was at the hospital rocking her dead child? Several of
Mike Porter's stories that he told the Briggs in an effort to save himself
from the death penalty have been repeated as fact. Could the Briggs
hate Raye so much that they can no longer distinguish fact from lies?
Do they hate Raye so much that they took his stories as fact without
question? Or did they see this as an opportunity to garner more hate
for Raye, despite the truth?

Kathie Briggs answered with more information about her stalking
tendancies.

I just had a report that possibly Raye Dawn and Gayla are staying
with Mildred. You know how rumors are, but Gayla's car has
been there for the past three days. I just want you to know if
we don't get some sort of proof that Raye Dawn lied about
the different accounts of abuse or someone who saw her
drink and drive or something, she might walk. You are the
only one who can help me figure this stuff out. I was thinking
last night about the time Kelsey busted her nose and Raye
Dawn said she fell in her aprartment. Do you know about

145

that? Several lies will make a big difference. My hopes of justice seem to be fading where the Smiths are concerned. If you know of something Gayla knew about and did not report it needs to be known. Basically she will be having another child and will go on with her life if the answers are not there.

Porter responded with desperation in his plea of innocence. He had no concrete proof to back up his claims about Raye and her alleged abusive tendencies. This suited the Briggs, but it was not enough for the district attorney to press charges.

I do not know what to say except the answers ARE there. They are righ in front of the DA. The only thinkg I can think of is they may not be being viewed objectively. Raye Dawn lies about each separate instance 3 times AT least fromt he reports I have seen. The DA obviously feels he has the right person for the murder. He is seriously mistaken on that. But with him believing that, the OSBI in my opinion has already proven Raye Dawn lied about several of the istances in question. Only she knows what happened on a few of these instances, and whether she says she was lying to cover for me or whether she lied to cover for herself like I know she did, she STILL LIED, and it is right there in black and white. There is an OSBI report on Raye Dawn 3 inches thick full of lies and misinformation uncovered. So now you see that you may have been mislead by the DA also? He may be hesitating to file charges because he knows that [her attorney's] defense for failure to protect will be "If you charge Raye awn then you have to charge everyone." This is not a denial of guilt, but it is still a powerful defense because it would force the DA to prove the level of involvement of each person thoroughly. He may be scared to file charges, but in NO ay does that mean that he does not have what he needs. If he says I was abusing Kelsey, then she is automatically guilty of failure to protect, bacuase it would mean every story she said was a lie. I hope you umderstand my level of frustration with this case now. The total reluctance and noe DENIAL to actually pursue the possibility that Raye Dawn killed Kelsey. It is terribly sad for me to see how badly this case has been handled. You know that I care about justice more than myself. [Raye's sister-in-

*law] would have come forward if I would not have been
charged. The DA took that. She was one of the only links to
the actual lies that Gayla and Raye Dawn have told, she
knew so many of them and would have exposed them. The
things I know about Raye Dawn do not make her guilty of
failure to protect. I know the DA has told you and your family
he would rather see a guilty person walk free then prosecute
an innocent person, but that is absolutely what he is doing. I
am sorry that you may have been mislead and the DA does
not care about holding the right people accountable. I was
telling you in a way that I already knew that. This case is
about a conviction, and his record. If he goes after everyone
he should, he is scared he will not win those cases. The
evidence is there to prosecute Raye Dawn for murder and or
failure to protect, I guarantee you that. She has changed her
story 3 times on every account. Her timecards that she was so
desperate for from [her former employer] and Donna's
calendar prove she lied about the zoo. Gayla saw Kelsey be
abused since last July and did nothing. How do you prove
that except it happened? She said herslef she would do
anything to get Kelsey back fromyou, she didn't care what it
took. I guess we may need to talk again to discuss some
things, if you are up to it. Let me know what you think.*

By the January 30th, their conversations suddenly seemed cold.
Mike Porter wasn't providing Kathie Briggs with concrete evidence
that he was telling the truth, and she had already expressed her
impatience in having Raye charged and arrested for murder. It is
unclear why Kathie Briggs suddenly changed her nurturing,
protective, and often playful tone with Mike Porter. Could it be that
she realized people would one day read their communications? Was
she starting to see through his web of lies? Whatever the answer, to
this day she repeats his lies as fact. She told him:

*I have been thinking since we met. I don't think it is a good idea and
I am not comfortable with this. You could be baiting me for
information, you could be lying to me to get me to lend
reasonable doubt with your information. Basically I am
doing the same thing. I am using you to find out what*

happened to my granddaughter. It is wrong of me. You might be innocent of murder, you might be guilty. I was not in that home that day and it is wrong for me to assume a position either way without all the evidence. If you are innocent it is wrong for me to put you in a position to lose your attorney. If you guilty it is wrong for me to give you my time. You avoid every question and that tells me you are just baiting me more and more. Basically my trust if very little. I cannot change what happened in the criminal aspects of this case. I want to know who failed Kelsey from January until October 11th. I will have to trust the court system and our DA to do that. I want Justice for Kelsey and I cannot get it by doing anything unethical.

Within minutes, Porter responded.

I understand. But just know that I want the same things as you. I will answer any question that you have and I have told you that, but I would prefer not to do it by e-mail at this time. I will leave my offer on the table. It will remain there. If you choose to never take me up on it then I understand. I am sorry if you felt I was avoiding your questions, I certainly have not tried to. So much has been lost because people would not communicate. It would be a shame if we still could not after everything. I am in no way baiting you. I told you in the beginning I do not want nor do I expect any help from you in any way. My offer for help in holding people accountable stands and will stand. No matter what happens to me I will not stop until I have exhausted every means I have to make sure people are held accountable. Please know that. Again, thank you for the things, and I have not and will not ever try to bait you. To what end? 12 people will decide my fate, and you will not be one of them. I know that. I will die knowing I DID NOT hurt Kelsey, and there are people who can not say that for themselves. I am sorry I have not made my true intentions clear to you. I certainly understand your lack of trust, but I made my offer for help to you with a pure heart.

Porter could not bare the loss of his biggest supporter. He messaged her the following day.

And I am not sure which questions you felt I was avoiding. I can't go back through and check e-mails because I delete them after I respond. But here are a couple questions I know you had. Number one, yes Raye Dawn had a cell phone. Yes Raye Dawn had a toddler bed/crib. The bed had side rails that you could raise or lower. She had the side rail removed and used it like a normal bed for Kelsey. She claimed to me that that night she had turned the open side towards the wall, so Kelsey would had to have climbed over the high side that was facing out. I had NEVER sen her do this before. Her story on the collarbone has already changed so many times who knows what happened. We were at [my friend's] house when Kelsey leaned on the unlatched screen door. That was one of the very few times I ever saw Kelsey fall or hurt herself. [Raye's sister-in-law] lied about the zoo because Raye Dawn asked her to. Kelsey did NOT hurt her foot at the zoo. Craig Key told [her attorney] AT least three weeks before the court hearing that "He was going to fix things". Basically [her attorney]made it clear to Raye Dawn that it was well in hand and all she had to do was show up. You were there, you knew the Judge had his mind made up. The Judge came up to Raye Dawn in the hallway and said "I created this monster, now let me take care of it." I heard this with MY OWN EARS. I do not ever want it saud that I was not willing to do whatever it took to make sure the people who failed Kelsey are held accountable. If you have any more questions, then feel free to ask them, AND I WILL RESPOND IN WRITING. I WILL ASK NOTHING OF YOU. I care more about justice for kelsey than myself, I would have thought I made that very obvious. If I do not hear from you then I will know that you do not feel I can help you in this cause. Thank you for your time.

Mike Porter and Kathie Briggs continued their mission on their beloved "bash board."[26]

---

[26] Read the e-mails at www.RayeDawnSmith.com and www.FreeKelseysMom.com.

Raye Dawn "Bashboard"

February, 2006

Originally, Kathie Briggs and her group started two separate "bashboards." There was one that focused on Mike Porter and one with Raye as the main topic of discussion. Since Mike Porter and his supporters were a part of the group, the Mike Porter board did not last long, but the Raye board buzzed day and night with hate for Raye and her entire family. While Kelsey's maternal family members were still in mourning, her paternal family members were apparently having fun with Mike Porter and his supporters at Kelsey's maternal family's expense.

There are several posts in which they pretend to be Raye's family members, specifically her mother, in order to make fun of them. Following is just a sampling of the posts that were captured.

Posted by "stinky pete" Friday, February 3, 2006 @ 12:04 AM - I wonder who all will be in the interview tomorrow night. Did they all meet at Mildred's again?

As you will recall from the e-mails between Kathie Briggs and Mike Porter, Kathie always seemed concerned with the location of the Smith family members and how often they were seen at each other's homes. This insight makes the previous post seem eerily familiar.

Posted by "Webster" Friday, February 3, 2006 @ 12:05 AM - Could someone take a dictionary to their interview so they can look up "seizure"

The next posts came from people who found comedy in Gayla's grief over the loss of her granddaughter, Kelsey. They pretended to be her to add to the harassment. The fact that Kathie Briggs admitted that she not only posted on the bashboard but that she was addicted to it, makes this behavior even more questionable. Considering she was Kelsey's other grandma, shouldn't she be grieving as well?

Posted by "Gala" Friday, February 3, 2006 @ 12:08 AM - Hey, that is my house too now that [Gayla's friend] has kicked us out and traded me in for a new model. What is so wonderful about 60 year old women anyway?!?!

Posted by "The Real Gayla" Friday, February 3, 2006 @ 12:14 AM - excuse me but I am only 54!! And I think I have preserved well, considering I cake on 3 inches of make up daily. My nightly dips in formaldehyde help to slow the aging process. If it wasn't for those I would look 95.

The focus was continually on Raye, but someone tried to bring the group back to reality. This post was ignored.

Posted by "Anonymous" Friday, February 3, 2006 @ 12:57 PM - If mike was a great dad, he would have turned raye's ass in for beating her child. He was NOT innocent of knowing these things were going on...come on people!

Posted by "Anonymous" Friday, February 3, 2006 @ 12:59 PM - I have a confession to make: I love Lance. Never realized that before and it may be just because my heart breaks for him. I dream of him and dream of us having a child together. When people ask how many kids we have, we say 2 because Kelsey will never be forgotten. Before you all say I'm after what ever money he may get, well your wrong. I would take him the way he is today, even if he did not have a cent to his name. I'm not sure if it is true love I feel or just love for him because of his pain and I feel the need to comfort him and love him. Please do not bash me I just wanted to get this off my chest. Never knew it before or even thought of it before, but now it just seems we could be happy together.

*Posted by "?" Friday, February 3, 2006 @ 1:01 PM - Wow anon
    who are you*

The haters then focused on Raye's grandmother, Mildred, a sweet,
soft-spoken lady who has never had anything bad to say about anyone.

*Posted by [unknown person] Saturday, February 4, 2006 @ 12:31
    AM - Mildred didn't "knowingly" harm Kelsey. That's the
    key word. She didn't know what she was doing. That's
    right...that's the ticket, she didn't even know that she didn't
    have a seizure at the funeral.*

*Posted by "Anonymous" Saturday, February 4, 2006 @ 12:32 AM
Mildred is common knowledge around Meeker and especially
    around [Raye's former place of employment and where
    Mildred still works to this day]. She used to be a fine
    upstanding woman.*

The place where Raye had worked became a hot topic of
conversation because the person who ran the bashboard, Ashley, was
the daughter-in-law of Donna, the state's main witness against Raye.
At the time of the bashboard, she worked there with Mildred. This is
the same witness that seems to have spoken with Mike Porter. Kathie
Briggs told Porter she had spoken with her "for hours" before Donna
went to investigators with her story that changed from its original
version at the time of Kelsey's death. It's interesting how the Briggs
managed to come up with witnesses that would tell stories about Raye
that they did not tell when the investigation began.

*Posted by [unknown person] Saturday, February 4, 2006 @ 12:33
    PM - Med – Mildred would be left out of it if she would just
    come out and tell the damn truth. If she would come out and
    say "I am just supporting my daughter and granddaughter. I
    do not know what went on in that house. I know Kelsey was
    abused and I do not know what went on in that house. I know
    Kelsey was abused and I do not know who did it. I know it
    was not Lance or Kathie. I will support my family and that is
    all. I will not lie for them, or withhold information for them. I
    will tell everything that I know, even if it makes my daughter*

153

*or granddaughter look bad. Yes, Raye Dawn is an alcoholic
and yes I tried my best to cover it up. Yes she has slept
around and treated people like shit generally. No she was not
a good mother most of the time. But I do not believe she
killed Kelsey so I will support her." IF MILDRED SIAD
THAT THEN I WOULD SAY "EVERYBODY LEAVE HER
ALONE AND BASH RAYE DAWN AND GAYLA." BUT SHE
WIL NOT DO THAT SO SHE DESERVES WHAT SHE
GETS. SHE HAS DONE JUST AS MUCH TO COVER SHIT
UP AS ANYONE.*

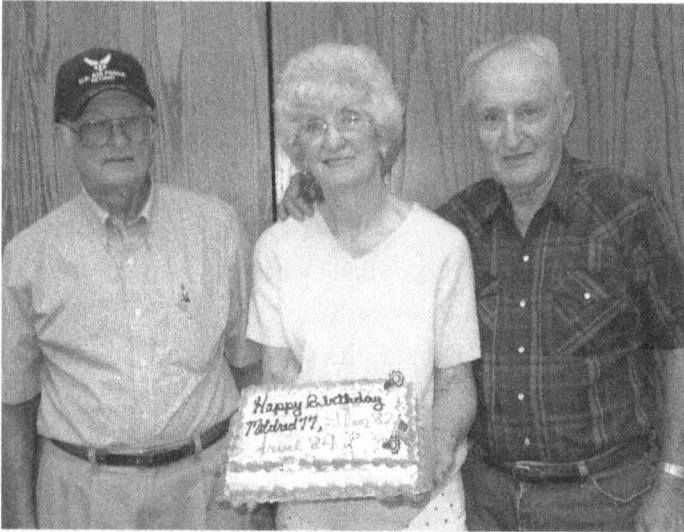

Mildred with her brothers on her 77th birthday

Within the printed pages I was given of their bashboard, Gayla
noted on the paper alongside the following post, "I have never been
on here. They are posting my name." One of the stories told to garner
hate for Gayla was that she stole from her employer and tried to burn
down the building. They were becoming even more creative with their
stories. An imposter wrote:

Posted by "Gayla Smith" Saturday, February 4, 2006 @ 12:58 AM -
NO, I do not live with Mildred. I am simply staying there for
a few days. There is a good reason. I just can't tell you what
it is. [My friend] and I are still together. He could never get
rid of me even if he tried, which he has. I did not embezzle
any money form my cousin's company. I simply permanently
borrowed it. But I quit because I had a nervous breakdown. I
am so worried and so scared because Raye Dawn did nothing
wrong and we have NOTHING to hide. Me and Raye DAwn
are so upset over this. It took us a whole 3 hours to get over
Kelsey's death. I know we don't cry anymore, but we are just
STRONG women. I have to go now, I have to take my mask
off. It is staring to droop.

In Mike Porter's emails with the Briggs, he frequently typed
Raye's name as Raye DAwn. If I had to guess who this was, I'd say it
was him and he obviously loved all of the negative attention toward
Raye and her family because that meant less hate toward him. The
attention turned back to Mildred with the next hate-filled post. At
Raye Dawn's trial, Kathie Briggs stated under oath "not that I know
of" when asked if she and her supporters had bashed Mildred on their
"bashboard."

Posted by "Anonymous" Saturday, February 4, 2006 @ 12:59 AM -
Granny Grunt should just marry [her friend] or what ever the
heck his name is and move out of Meeker if she cannot
handle the crap her daughter and granddaughter have
created for her.

These bullies left no stone unturned as they discussed Gayla's
husband, Ray, and allegations against the way he was treated as he
battled terminal cancer for years before he died before Kelsey's
second birthday.

Posted by "Anonymous" Saturday, February 4, 2006 @ 1:03 PM - I
do have to admit. Mildred did wait for a while before she
started "seeing" [her friend]. Can't say the same for Gayla.
Ray was sick in bed and she was doing her thing. Taking
"vacations" to Arkansas. Hmm...isn't that where her and

[her friend] went together? What would you expect though. Raye Dawn would be boning that married guy while her daddy was downstairs knocking on that headboard wanting his medicine.

Posted by "Gaila Swine" @ [unknown date and time] - I am sorry everyone. I was stupid and did not realize that Raye Dawn did not really have enough money to buy that house. I was stupid when...[remainder of post lost in printing]

An email from a family friend had some of the following posts attached. In the text this person wrote:

Well, Kathie just could not stand not having a place to put Raye Dawn down. She has endorsed and even posted on a new blog authored by that Faith... It is called "How was Kelsey, let down?" It claims to not be a bashboard but the 1st post is a slam on Raye Dawn. Imagine that. It's address is http://pub6.bravenet.com. Kathie is really a piece of work, she is so obvious in her manipulation.

Posted by KJBriggs Saturday, February 4, 2006 @ 12:30 PM - I would like to state that The Briggs and [Kelsey's step-grandparent] families do not want anyone threatening The Smith family. This will not get us to our goal of Justice for Kelsey. We have learned the best method for getting answers is to work together. Gayla was right. Mildred is 74 years old and no one should be calling her and leaving hateful messages. Just because Gayla herself screamed and yelled at my father-in-law who is 82 and my mother-in-law who is 77 and had the Prague police ask them to leave the hospital the night Kelsey died does not make it right. I was taught to respect the elderly and if she wasn't taught the same thing that does not mean we would condone the same actions. We do not know what Raye Dawn's role was in Kelsey's death on October 11th. We are waiting for answers just like everyone else. We do not want harm or undue stress to effect the health of her unborn child. Janet stated that they cannot grieve. Join the club, this family cannot either. I think the only difference is we are not consumed with the guilt of not fighting for

Kelsey's safety. So I am asking that all hate mail and calls to stop. Take that energy and fight for Justice. This is an election year and we have lots of campaigning to do. We also have rallies coming up on Kelsey's behalf. We hope all will attend to listen to Kelsey's story and to learn how they can help other children in abusive homes. The bottom line is once again we know this is not about the Briggs/[Kelsey's step-grandparent] families. It is about Kelsey. We only wish the others felt the same. Kelsey was the victim. She is the one the family members should be talking about. If more had been worried about her when she was alive this would not be an issue now.

Justice for Kelsey

February 14, 2006

While the bashboard continued with hate fueled by Mike Porter and the Briggs, members of Kelsey's Purpose moved forward with their justice for Kelsey cause. Many of these members were kept in the dark about the existence of the bashboard as well as the man who kept it going.

Susan Re: Judge Key's re-election 8:03 AM - Has anyone heard if anyone is running against Judge Key? We have GOT to convince someone to run against him! I was told that Key's campaign "platform" when he ran for office was....I KNOW you are ALL going to find THIS hard to believe, Child Protection, he also said that child abuse prevention was his NUMBER 1 priority! So what happened? Or was this just his empty promise to get elected? I personally will help WHOMEVER runs against him and give them 110% to help them campaign against Key.

Aunt bean [Jeanna] Posts: 30 Re: Judge Key's re-election 8:33 AM - I will join you in that [Susan].

Someone Who Loves Kelsey Posts:2 Re: Judge Key's re-election 9:43 AM - Here is the article that talks about Judge Keys' election victory and the "campaign platforms" he used to get elected. Funny how politicians rely on us as voters having such a short term memory. Maybe he just needs to know that we remember the promises he made to get elected – the same promises he broke when he sent sent Kelsey back to her mother against the advice of 4 doctor's and DHS.

Meanwhile, back at the bashboard…

Posted by [unknown person] Tuesday, February 14, 1006 @ 2:31 PM - You are right 2:25. Gayla is really messed up. She still

159

keeps secretes from her mother so she can misuse her. They like to keep Mildred in the dark.

Posted by "Anonymous" Tuesday, February 14, 2006 @ 2:40 PM - Poor poor Mildred. They better hold a press conference for her. She needs peoples sympathy for her getting left out in the dark.

Posted by "Anonymous" Tuesday, February 14, 2006 @ 2:42 PM - How could Gayla see poor Kelsey abused and not do or say something. Poor little Kelsey. Did you ever think maybe Gayla was rough with Kelsey too? It is possible. I think of that baby every day and cry alot. I know all of you do too! Thanks for trying to get justice for Kelsey. I wish I could do more.

Posted by "Tired of waiting for Justice" Tuesday, February 14, 2006 @ 2:44 PM - So ture. Mildred has ALWAYS been in the dark pertaining to what the Smiths are doing. She IS a good woman, but she has been misguided by all this and stands by someone, or some people that she should not stand by and she SHOULD know better. But you've got to remember, she IS 74 years old and I'm sure that her mind is staring to fail her. I just hope she doesn't think that her darling Gayla will take care of her when she needs it.

Posted by "Anonymous" Tuesday, February 14, 2006 @ 2:44 PM - Anon – 2:42. If you are in Oklahoma you can do more. Do you check Kelsey's purpose for upcoming rallies and events?

Posted by "Anonymous" [unknown date and time] - I am sure that Gayla will take care of her – the same way she took care of her "beloved".

One of the popular stories that the bullies loved to share was the accusation that Gayla murdered her husband, Ray. Raye told me that her dad had fought cancer for years, starting when she was in high school. The cancer had spread to various organs before he finally gave up the fight. I have watched hours of home videos in which Ray could barely talk after the cancer was found in his throat. Moments of this

160

close, but struggling family were captured as Gayla sat at his side helping him eat. (The following pictures are fuzzy because I took them from home videos)

Kelsey didn't want to leave her Papa's side.

Gayla helps Ray eat while their youngest daughter, Rachelle (on the left) smiles as Kelsey walks to her mommy, Raye Dawn

161

For these bullies to even insinuate such a monstrous act about Ray's widow is beyond belief. The evidence is clear that she doted on him and did what she could to take care of him. But nothing seemed off limits for this blood-thirsty gang.

Posted by "Tired of Waiting for Justice" Tuesday, February 14, 2006 @ 10:55 PM - There would have been absolutely no way in Hell that Gayla or Raye Dawn would have EVER given Kelsey up to Lance or Kathie, well it'll be the same way with this baby. Exactly the same way. IF this baby makes it that long.

A handwritten note on the printed pages of this bashboard stated, "Mike Porter" next to the "Tired of Waiting for Justice" posts. Porter referred to his son that Raye was carrying at the time of Kelsey's death. Kathie and her crusaders worked hard to ensure that the child would be taken from Raye and Gayla the moment he was born.

Posted by "Anonymous" Tuesday, February 14, 2006 @ 10:57 PM - I really do not think that Gayla will try to get that baby if RD goes to prison

Posted by "Tired of Waiting for Justice" Tuesday, February 14, 2006 @ [unknown time] - Want to make a bet on that one?

The bullies were attempting to create ties and more stories to push bias and cover-up. Sadly, this is still being done today.

Posted by [unknown person] Tuesday, February 14, 2006 @ 11:39 PM - [first part of post lost in printing]...was also reported that some dresser was taken out to the woods in the back of the house during Kelsey's funeral.

Posted by "Anonymous" Tuesday, February 14, 2006 @ 11:41 PM - Did anyone know that Raye's sister use to date Judge [G]?

Posted by "Anonymous" Tuesday, February 14, 2006 @ 11:44 PM - Really? Did anyone know that [Mike Porter's attorney] and Judge [G] used to be law partners? And what furniture would they have been burning? And what dresser would have

162

been taken out during the funeral? And who would have done it?

Posted by "Anonymous" Tuesday, February 14, 2006 @ 11:47 PM -
    Don't know, just know that a dresser was seen being removed
    and it was reported to the DA. It could have had journals or
    any other evidence in it.

Posted by "Anonymous" Tuesday, February 14, 2006 @ 11:50 PM -
    Yes, I did know that and the information about Janet is not a
    rumor, it is fact.

Posted by "Anonymous" Tuesday, February 14, 2006 @ 11:56 PM -
    Well that is strange. I would have thought that people who
    were in the house after the funeral would have noticed a
    dresser missing.

The Smiths

February, 2006

Sherri Heath—Gayla's cousin and someone who has been a strong advocate for the Smith family—wrote an e-mail to Gayla on February 15, 2006 warning her of Kelsey's Purpose members' next steps in getting what they saw as justice.

Sherri Heath and her husband Bill, a 20-year veteran of the military, celebrate their 25th wedding anniversary

Gayla, I just want you to know that I got this info from Kathy's website. You might want to inform your lawyer and possibly the DA. There certainly are a lot of strange people out there!!! Hang in there, we are still with you both~~~ xoxo Sherri

Sherri's message was followed by a post from Kelsey's Purpose. This seemingly new member with only two posts on the forum had inside information. Where was the protest against Mike Porter's release from jail?

Mygift9602 Posts: 2 Peaceful Protest Friday, February 16, 2006 - I have learned today, that there is going to be a grand jury hearing next week, in the later part of the week for Raye Dawn's charges. What they are, is unknown. This amounts to either, Mr. Smothermon cannot solve the case himself, and feels like he must do this, or he is taking the easy way out of this mess. We must question his motive in doing this. He needs to be reminded of his professional and humanitarian duties to Kelsey, and that if Raye Dawn gets off on whatever charges she is facing, his career as a D.A. is over. In my opinion, this case has been handled very unprofessionally, and sloppy from day one, and I don't think he is taking this for its seriousness. I am staging a PEACEFUL rally tomorrow at 3 p.m. at D.A. Smothermon's office in Shawnee. It is located at [address removed for privacy] in Shawnee. I need at least 20 – 30 people there, with signs to join the protest. The more, the better. I also realize that this is VERY short notice, and it is hard for people with jobs, and kids, as I have both, but we HAVE to do this, and do it during business hours. If you are interested or have any questions, please private message me. I apologize for the last minute notice, but I JUST found this out. It will be on the news tonight. I think on all channels, but I do not know the time. PLEASE, anyone that can join us, please do so! We need to show Mr. Smothermon that we will not stand for Kelsey to have died in vain, and for her mother to walk free! He needs to be reminded of his duties, and reminded that he IS an elected official. All of you that say you want to help, THIS is your chance. Stand up for little Kelsey, and let your voice be heard! Let him know we will NOT stand for this injustice!

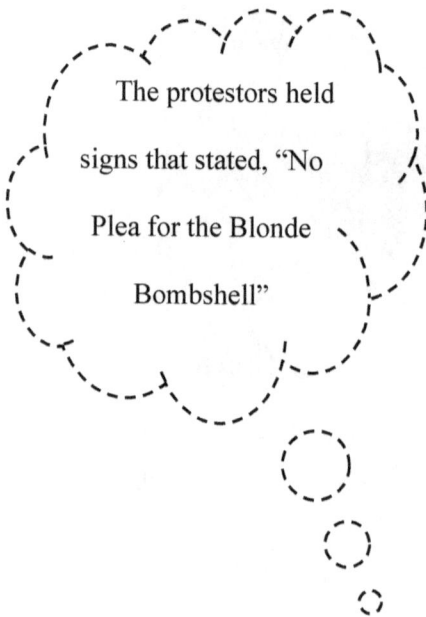

The protestors held signs that stated, "No Plea for the Blonde Bombshell"

The following pictures are from Kelsey's Purpose's first rally at the state capitol. This was just weeks after Kelsey's death.

Kathie Briggs just weeks after Kelsey's death

Misinformation

February, 2006

On the bashboard, Debbie began rallying the troops to contact the investigators about Raye and how guilty this group had deemed her to be.

Posted by "junior" aka Debbie Wednesday, February 15, 2006, @ 10:13 AM - I think that you're right about OSBI investigator. Who can we contact to get someone that actually cares about this case enough to actually solve it and not cover it up.

Posted by "A voice for Kelsey" Wednesday, February 15, 2006 @ 10:16 AM - We need to know who the supervisor is for the OSBI in Lincoln County. They need to be called and made aware that we KNOW about the mess that is going on, and we demand that someone who actually cares about the case, is put on the case.

"A voice for Kelsey" was how Jeanna had referred to Mike Porter in their e-mails. Was this him or one of the Briggs?

Posted by "Anonymous" Wednesday, February 15, 2006 @ 10:16 AM - He may care but he is not investigating impartially. There is one investigator that believes that Raye Dawn could never do this and that affects his judgment, and it shows up in his interviews. There have been several people that have said he even defends Raye Dawn in the interviews. Not professional at all.

A new story being told was that Gayla was in the room with Raye when she was questioned by investigators. This was as false as the story of Porter's daughter being "interrogated for several days." Mike Porter tried to gain sympathy, or perhaps he would use that as an excuse if his daughter made allegations against him.

169

Posted by "A voice for Kelsey" Wednesday, February 15, 2006 @
       10:17 AM - I cannot believe that she was allowed to stay in
       that room! That never happens. Look at what [Porter's
       daughter] went through. She was taken away from her family
       and interrogated like an adult for several days.

Posted by "junior" aka Debbie Wednesday, February 15, 2006 @
       10:18 AM - I would think that they're (the OSBI) probably in
       districts like other state agencies with the main office on
       OKC There should be something on the state website for
       them.

Posted by "Anonymous" Wednesday, February 15, 2006 @ 10:20
       AM - Yep, [Porter's daughter] wasn't allowed a coach. I
       know who the agent is but nothing will happen about it.
       Someone else was supposed to be doing the bulk of the
       interviews, but they put this same clown back on the lead
       spot. What a joke. Ask the people at [Raye's former
       employer] if he cared about anything they had to say.

Posted by "A voice for Kelsey" Wednesday, February 15, 2006 @
       10:23 AM - And that pisses me off because it was hard
       enough to get people at [Raye's former employer] to talk
       anyway.

In the e-mails with Kathie Briggs and Mike Porter, Kathie
admitted to talking to Donna—a woman who had worked with Raye—
for hours. According to the O.S.B.I reports, her story to investigators
at the time of Kelsey's death was that Raye told her that Kathie had
accused Raye of spanking Kelsey with a hair brush after what
appeared to be a diaper rash was found on Kelsey in January, 2005.
After Kathie Briggs spoke with this State's witness "for hours," the
story changed and suddenly Raye had told her that she had spanked
Kelsey with a hair brush. This woman's daughter-in-law ran the
bashboard and her story changed, yet she was treated as a credible
witness against Raye. The plea deals that the district attorney offered
Raye before her trial and on the last days of her trial involved Raye
admitting to spanking Kelsey with a hair brush. Raye said, "I didn't
do it. I won't take it." She would not admit to a crime she did not

commit. Had she taken the plea deal, she would be a free woman today. But she did not abuse her child and would not take a false plea. Why did the district attorney not recognize that this witness's story had changed?

Posted by "Anonymous" Wednesday, February 15, 2006 @ 10:24 AM - If they would have done Raye Dawn like they did [Porter's daughter], who is an 8 YEAR OLD, then she would have sang like a bird. If they would have separated Raye Dawn from her Mommy dearest and put her in a strange place and hammered on her with complete strangers who knows what would have happened. But wait, Raye Dawn had rights. [Porter's daughter] didn't. She was just a child.

Posted by "junior" aka Debbie Wednesday, February 15, 2006 @ 10:28 AM - I think that Lance should file some sort of formal complaints/lawsuit whatever against the OSBI and against that agent.

Posted by "A voice for Kelsey" [unknown date and time] - Well, if the DA is smart, and we already know the answer to that, then he will ask her to take…[remainder of post lost in printing]

The person who provided the next post was misinformed. Gayla was never questioned. She was immediately ruled out as a suspect. But as usual, if it was stated by the bullies, it was fact.

Posted by "v" Wednesday, February 15, 2006 @ 10:39 AM - There seems to be a persistant rumor on this blog that I would like to lay to rest. Gayla, Mike and RD were all questioned separately by the OSBI and I might add at length. If you speak to the agent in charge he is not fond of any of the parties involved in this case. In fact he is rather insistant that if you have not actually seen something and not just heard something that your information is useless. You may have truthful information but if it is not 1ST hand it cannot be used in court. That may be why some of the Lewis employees feel that the agent is not interested in what they have to say. If it is not 1ST hand I saw this type of evidence he cannot use it. He

171

*is not a very friendly individual so his demeaner is rather
cold.*

*Posted by "junior" aka Debbie Wednesday, February 15, 2006 @
10:43AM - The problem with that is, that everyone that
knows Raye Dawn knows that she was not going to hit and
beat on her child in front of someone. She might drink in
front of her, but she was smart enough to beat up on her in
front of her own relatives. And it's certain that no one saw
her kill her.*

*Posted by "iq" Wednesday, February 15, 2006 @ 10:43 AM - I
don't care what his demeanor is like. Don't try to make
people think they have useless info. And they will be treated
poorly by this guy if they call. If you have something,
anything, call the osbi or da and let them sort out what is
useful and what is not.*

*Posted by "A voice for Kelsey" aka Porter [unknown date and time]
- That is very funny, because I talked with a very credible
person yesterday, in relation to the case, and they said the
SAME investigator that was supposed to be removed from the
case, is still being sent out to question people, and that he is
not interested in what anyone...[remainder of post lost in
printing]*

*Posted by "junior" aka Debbie Wednesday, February 15, 2006 @
10:46 AM - I did talk to an asst. D.A. which was totally
worthless in the matter, he wasn't even familiar with the
case. The OSBI never even called me back to tell me that they
weren't coming to interview me. I think it's because I wasn't
"convenient" right there in Meeker. But, I would have went
there.*

*Posted by "Beyondmybelief" Wednesday, February 15, 2006 @
10:48 AM - Junior, Do you have 1st hand knowledge that can
be used?*

*Posted by "A voice for Kelsey" Wednesday, February 15, 2006 @
10:50 AM - Junior, if you call and try to talk to the DA and*

*try OSBI and can't get either to listen, then try calling
Cherokee Ballard. That is what [Porter's friend] did, and her
story did get heard, after that.*

*Posted by "v" Wednesday, February 15, 2006 @ 10:50 AM -
Anybody can go up to the OSBI anytime they want to and talk
to the agent. If you have credible and useful information then
quit bitching about the OBSI and get your ass up there. I am
so sick of people blaming others for not listening. Sounds like
a Oh Poor me on this blog.*

Mike Porter and the Briggs had discussed the fact that Debbie was
ruled out as credible with the investigators because she had a "grudge"
against Gayla. Notice how the "v" character immediately recognized
"junior" as Debbie. This lends a hint as to the identity of "v," because
"Beyondmybelief" does not pick up on the identity of the person
posting.

*Posted by "junior" aka Debbie Wednesday, February 15, 2006 @
10:52 AM - Most of my knowledge, is already noted thru a
letter written. Gayla told them that I had a "grudge."*

*Posted by "v" Wednesday, February 15, 2006 @ 10:53 AM - OK
Debbie*

*Posted by "Beyondmybelief" Wednesday, February 15, 2006 @
10:53 AM - Junior, do you have 1st hand knowledge that
could be helpful in this case?*

*Posted by "junior" aka Debbie Wednesday, February 15, 2006 @
10:57 AM - V, now that you've decided who I am, who are
you? Gayla had sent me lots of emails, which I forwarded on
that told a lot about what Raye Dawn was doing during the
months before and the first few months of abuse. I had first
hand knowledge from her. She wasn't lying then to me. I
didn't have a grudge against them when I went to court in
June to testify against Raye Dawn, but as we all know how
Kelsey's story ended up, yes, I do have a grudge against
someone taking the life of a child and some selfless bitch*

173

standing up for her own child and feeling telling other
relatives lies about the
Briggs family just to
make themselves look
better. Gayla is
nothing in my book
anymore, but an
accomplice in a
murder.

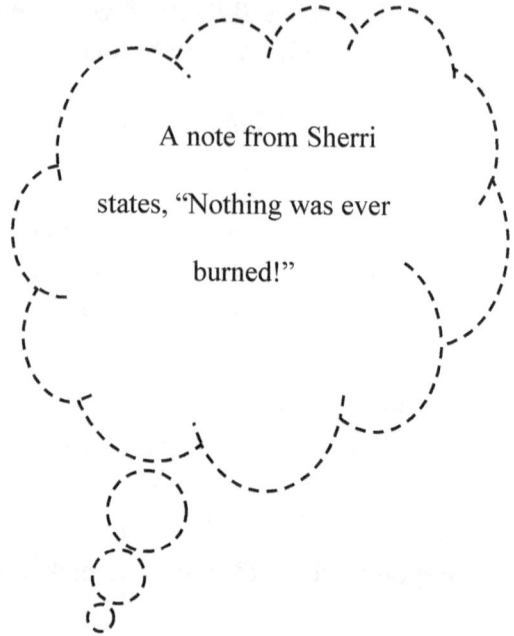

A note from Sherri states, "Nothing was ever burned!"

Posted by "beyondmybelief"
Wednesday, February
15, 2006 @ 10:59 PM
- Junior, What did the
e-mails say?

Posted by "junior" aka
Debbie Wednesday,
February 15, 2006 @
11:01 AM - And
another thing that I can't understand is why people would
stand up for these murderers! Now, I'm hearing that they
burned a lot of the evidence. They knew exactly what they
were doing when they did that. They're not real smart, but
they're not exactly stupid, just devious and conniving. Gayla
has Mildred so snowballed that she doesn't know which end
is up.

Posted by "Anonymous" Wednesday, February 15, 2006 @ 11:01
AM - You know V, we all want everyone to talk, but you don't
have to attack someone like that, and if WE WANTED
PEOPLE TO KNOW WHO WE ARE, we would post under
our names. Why attack her like that? She has come out and
said these things and I think it is TRUE that there is a bunch
of cover up going on in this case, and people ARE being
shruged off!

Posted by "A voice for Kelsey" aka Mike Porter Wednesday,
February 15, 2006 @ 11:02 AM - Gayla and Raye Dawn are
not book smart, but very "street" smart and criminally smart.

174

Posted by "junior" aka Debbie Wednesday, February 15, 2006 @ 11:03 AM - V, are you not going to talk anymore? If V is Gayla, she's probably in deep thought right now trying to remember all the many many emails that she sent me at work. I'm not going into what the contents were on this website.

Debbie testified against Raye Dawn at a 2005 hearing. As Judge Craig Key pointed out while I worked on his book entitled *A Deadly Game of Tug-of-War: The Kelsey Smith-Briggs Story*, Debbie's testimony was filled with gossip and stories, nothing credible. Debbie was the person who had warned the Smiths at the end of 2004 that the Briggs family was gearing up for a custody battle, and they had better get ready. Debbie had also been a part of the Smith family for several years due to her marriage to Gayla's brother. This created a common tie between the families because Debbie's children are Mildred's grandchildren and Raye's cousins. Due to the hate that Debbie caused within the family and the hateful message she had left on Mildred's answering machine where she read from a pre-written statement, her grandchildren, which are also grandchildren of Kathie Briggs, have missed out on Smith family events. Debbie has tried to make amends by showing up at Mildred's brother's doctor's office and stating how she missed the family and sending cards to various family members. These tokens of affection and repentance are soon over-shadowed by hate-filled statements about the Smiths that she still posts on the Internet today.

At the end of her testimony in 2005, she stated that she was Gayla's best friend. Gayla quit speaking to Debbie because of her testimony. Therefore, her next statement is simply an exaggeration and an attempt to add to the hate of her "best friend." People on the outside looking in do not realize the complex relationships between these two families or the ties that bind them together, such as Debbie and her obvious contempt for Raye and her family members.

Posted by "junior" aka Debbie Wednesday, February 15, 2006 @ 11:07 AM - Yeh, I should have rethought that statement.

*That's impossible. I do know what Gayla is truly like and I
will tell whoever will listen to me. Those two, Gayla and
Raye Dawn are NOT going to get away with this murder. I
cannot believe that I was on their so called side when Kelsey
started getting all those bruises and broken bones and Gayla
told me that the two broken legs were "no big deal." She
didn't care about Kelsey, all she cared about was "winning"
Kelsey back and getting her back to Raye Dawn. She's such a
fake, liar and an absolute pitiful lowest scum of person alive.
I could care less what she thinks of me. I was her sister in
law for over 17 years and I know her very very well.*

*Posted by "c" Wednesday, February 15, 2006 @ 11:10 AM - Where
did V go???*

*Posted by "Anonymous" Wednesday, February 15, 2006 @ 11:12
AM - V or he probably went to call Mildred at work.*

*Posted by "A voice for Kelsey" aka PorterWednesday, February 15,
2006 @ 11:17 AM - At least you're a big enough person to
stand up now and tell what you know. I just cannot believe
that they treated little Kelsey the way they did.*

*Posted by "V" Wednesday, February 15, 2006 @ 12:06 PM - Never
talked to Gayla about this. I figure the truth would lie
somewhere in between. It usually does with a family dispute.*

*Posted by "Anonymous" Wednesday, February 15, 2006 @ 12:11
PM - None of those witches have ANY care about any of this
because they truly think they are going to get away with this
murder. NOT if I or any of the others of us can help it! And if
those emails have in them what she says they do, that is
VERY valuable information and I pray to God that someone
takes heed to them!*

*Posted by "abc" Wednesday, February 15, 2006 @ 12:12 PM - I'm
part of the family and the family "dispute" was over the
treatment of Kelsey and Gayla did not like anyone
questioning anything that they did.*

Next, "iq" had obviously struck a nerve with the bullies. Whatever was said was either deleted before the posts were captured or lost in printing.

Posted by "flubug" Thursday, February 16, 2006 @ 7:42 PM - Anonymous (7:13), I was always taught there is no such thing as a dumb question. To iq (7:04), Who are you? The blog police? Please don't let your halo choke you. Passing fancy? Well la-de-damned da. You have such an over inflated opinion of yourself it's laughable. What have you done to help get justice for Kelsey? Have you gone to the OSBI, DA? Talk about me throwing out hypothetical situations? What inside info do you have and what have you done to show more than a "passing fancy" and make a difference? At this point the only thing that those of us on the "outside" have is theory-based on what we've seen and heard in the media, on this site and from personal conversations with other folks interested and shocked about what's happened to that precious little girl. Those of us with this so called "passing fancy" as you describe it have as much right to be here as you and express our thoughts, concerns and throw things out for the bloggers to ponder and discuss (key word: DISCUSS). Again-what makes you think you're so special that your interest in Kelsey's case is more than a passing fancy? You "sound" like one of those people that if someone doesn't agree with you then they are wrong, they are an idiot, they are the one that "doesn't get it", and this is all a joke to them. From what I've heard from you so far it sounds like to me the only way you can give yourself any sort of self-esteem is to belittle others and try to make yourself look smarter by attempting to discredit them and make them appear stupid. As for me...it's still a free country & if I choose to throw out "things" for people to discuss I will. I don't care what you think or don't think. Again-you aren't the blog police and until you are I suggest you find someone else to aggrevate-I will address your nonsense no more.

On February 20, 2006, Mike Porter sent the following e-mail to Kathie Briggs regarding an upcoming Grand Jury against Raye Dawn. He reminded her where her loyalty lies.

*I just wanted to tell you I will be praying for you this week. I hope
the Lord will allow the truth to come out in that courtroom so
people can be held accountable. You will be one of the only
chances for Kelsey's voice to be heard in that room. Raye
Dawn will be working against you and the truth, but you
already know that. Good luck and God Bless you*

Media Attention for Kelsey's Purpose

February, 2006

The focus of Kelsey's Purpose turned into efforts to attract the interest of bigger media. The Briggs had befriended two Oklahoma journalists—Britten Follet and Cherokee Ballard—which kept their version of Kelsey's story in the statewide news. But that wasn't enough for this attention-seeking family.

Tina-mother3 Posts: 1 I didn't know what to do so... - I e-mail some talk shows, newspapers, and news channels. I don't know if I'll get a response or not. I hope this will help in some way. I hope there will be Justice for Kelsey. I'm sure there will be with her grandma Kathie and all her family on her side fighting for her. I wish you guys all the luck in the world. Don't ever give up fighting for her.

Mother3 Posts: 2 Re: I didn't know what to do so... - I think what you did is awesome what better way to get the word out. Hopefully there will be justice for Kelsey, my prayers are with her family.

Kathiew Posts: 2 Dr. Phil...contact info - Here is the contact info for one of the producers at the Dr. Phil show. Please call and email her with info regarding Kelsey's case. Maybe we can get some national attention from Dr. Phil. [Contact information removed for privacy]

windy Posts: 190 Re: Dr. Phil...contact info - I will add this to one of our days of the weeks contact. How about on Monday? We'll use this for Monday. Thank you for the info!

I_dare-U2_move Posts: 30 February 21, 2006 1:02 PM Talk shows I have emailed - I have emailed the following talk shows about this story and I'm just waiting for responses but when I get them I will post them on here - Oprah, Montel Williams,

179

20/20, Ellen, The View (all 4 ladies individully), KOTV Channel 6 news in Tulsa, KJRH Channel 2 news in Tulsa, FOX 23 Channel 5 or 23 news in Tulsa, Good Morning America, World news tonight, Dr. Phil, Nancy Grace, Nightline, Primetime, Muary Povach, 60 Minutes, CBS Evening News, Today Show, Dateline NBC, NBC Nightly News

On the bashboard, the bullies seemed to be discussing the jurors that would attend the upcoming grand jury against Raye Dawn. It seems they were worried that the jurors had not been tainted by the false stories.

Posted by "sew&sew" Wednesday, February 22, 2006 @ 11:10 AM - To All: I would presume the Judge or whoever is presiding over the GJ would provide instructions to the jury although I'm wondering if a GJ isn't a "standing" jury. In other words you're a GJ member and therefore "on call" when one needs to be convened just don't know..guess I should go to the web-site (LOL). That being said we will just have trust that even if for some unbeknownest reason a juror hasn't heard about Kelsey that it wil be okay. If you stop & think that might not be such a bad idea..they come in with no pre-conceived "notions" & should therefore be able to look at all evidence with a clear head-maybeeven "pick up" on something that has been missed or can/would even ask some pretty hard-nosed, comment sense... "you've got to be kidding me" questions. We'll just have to be patient and see what happens.

Posted by MistyLT Wednesday, February 22, 2006 @ 11:10 AM - When I leave for lunch and have to go by the post office, I will check out the courthouse and see if there's a lot of people there. I don't know these people so I don't know what anyone drives to be able to tell who's there though.

Posted by MistyLT Wednesday, February 22, 2006 @ 11:11 AM - Think they'll go out for lunch here? ;)

Posted by "I want justice for Kelsey" Wednesday, February 22, 2006 @ 11:12 AM - It's in OKC, I've been told.

Back on Kelsey's Purpose

On February 23, 2006 at 2:29 PM Jeanna issued a paternal family statement about their victory in getting charges brought against Raye Dawn and the family's dealings with Mike Porter. Less than one year after this post, Mike Porter was given a plea deal for thirty years on the charge of enabling child abuse, reportedly at the request of Lance Briggs. Jeanna stated as follows:

Raye Dawn will be charged tomorrow morning with one count of enabling child abuse and one count of child neglect. Both are felony charges and could be punishable by up to life in prison. My sister received a disrespectful e-mail from one of our members questioning the intentions and integrity of our family in regard to the criminal proceedings in this case...It is my understanding that rumors are being posted on other sites regarding our family's dealings with the District Attorney and some of the responsible parties in this case. Unless you read a statement on this site that is posted by a Briggs family member, consider it a false rumor. Our family has not and will not entertain ideas of negotiating deals or plea bargains in this case. Kelsey was not given a deal and neither will anyone else. Those responsible for her death and abuse should be punished to the fullest extent that the law will allow...Our family is working hand in hand with our District Attorney... We stand behind him and support him. Today's announcement was just one more step in the long journey ahead...

The post was followed by a statement from Kathie.

Raye Dawn, the biological mother, was charged with two felonies, One was Child Neglect and one was Enabling Child Abuse. After new evidence that came out charges were amended. She is now being charged with felony Child Abuse which is more serious than Child Neglect. In the alternative she is charged with Enabling Child Abuse. This means the jury will have a

*choice. She either abused her child or allowed her to be
abused. Either charge can put her in prison for life. In
Oklahoma life is 45 years. This is an 85% crime which means
she could be eligible for parole in 37 years if convicted and
sentenced to life. She would be 64 years old at that time. It is
possible a jury would give her less time, but that will depend
on the evidence presented...*

The "new evidence" was the claim from the bashboard owner's
mother-in-law, Donna, who suddenly changed her story about the hair
brush. The district attorney told witnesses that he "had to charge Raye
with something." Perhaps his memory went fogging when reviewing
the sudden change in this witness's claims. The "bash board" picked
up on the news right away.

*Posted by "sew&sew" Friday, February 24, 2006 @ 6:42 AM - Quit
bitching so much aoub thwat hasn't happened yet. If RD gets
off with a "slap on the wrist" even after a jury trial I should
think the folks you can "thank" would be the jury-won't they
set her punishment? Sure, I'm guessing the DA may make a
recommendation for punishment but I don't know if the jury
is obligated to follow that request if they don't believe it is
severe enough. If you don't like the sentencing guidelines
then I suggest you figure out who "wrote" them (the State
Legislature?) and do what you can to change them. But then
wait-that would require "us" to get off our butts and actually
DO something instead of bitching wouldn't it? Please not I
included MYSELF in that question. Why keep beating up the
DA? Granted he may be worthless but at least TRY to be a bit
more supportive-what would that hurt? A lot of you who
bitching about what "punishment" will or won't be dealt out
to RD were on here raising hell that RD would never be
charged in the first place (guess you were wrong). I know it's
hard to see all this happen (especially when we think it could
have been done differently)—but couldn't just one day be
spent bashing RD & Mike & less bashing the "system" that
finally got off it's ass and is doing SOMETHING (which to
me is still better than nothing). *&^%)%$#*

On the day before the charges were filed against Raye, the district attorney held a press conference during which he stressed that the charges he had filed against Mike Porter and Raye were appropriate for their culpability. He stated that Mike Porter murdered Kelsey, and Raye "should have known and could have prevented her abuse or death." Britten Follett, a friend of the Briggs family and a reporter for our local FOX station, attended the press conference. She stated that she was told the district attorney was considering Murder 1 charges against Raye. The district attorney denied ever stating that as a possibility.

Posted by "sew&sew" Friday, February 24, 2006 @ 6:42 PM - TO ALL: MY 6:42 COMMNETS WERE TO NO ONE IN PARTICULAR BUT TO THE BLOGGERS IN GERNAL. I'M EXERCISING MY FIRST AMENDMENT RIGHTS (AS YOU TOO ARE ALLOWED TO DO)

Posted by [unknown person] Friday, February 24, 2006 @ 8:41 AM - [first part of post lost in printing] ...Shorty, we'll have to agree to disagree because I disagree with you. A child is not breathing and you waste time calling the mother-in-law. Somethings not right with that picture. Please don't defend Pudge-Boy. He is a child abuser.

Posted by "sew&sew" Friday, February 24, 2006 @ 8:44 AM - Shorty (8:39) I agree w/what you have to say regarding the bond & date. Not being privy to the DA or his thought process (or even the legalities of such a "move"—if there are any), we can only presume things were done in accordance with law, statutes or something. Perhaps someone w/some legal experience in such matters can come on here and offer some sort of reasonable explanation to explain it.

Posted by "A voice for Kelsey" aka Mike Porter Friday, February 24, 2006 @ 8:48 AM - I for one, would NOT call ANY of my relatives before 911. BUT, in his defense, he may have panicked, and just called Gayla, although MY OPINION is that, that is not the truth. We have to have faith in the DA because there is no other choice. WHAT else can we do? We have had protests, written letters, called him...he know people expect justice in this case! We will just have to wait and see what evidence he has against Mike...we just don't know! And he CAN go back and charge Raye Dawn with more severe charges at some point, should it warrant it.

Posted by "sew&sew" Friday, February 24, 2006 @ 8:53 AM - TO ALL: Can/would any of you agree that if we could get more folks with "bonafide" legal experience on here talking it would help to diffuse some of the anger as to how things have been done (i.e. charges againist RD, possible sentencing for RD, Mike's situation w/bond, dates being changed, etc.)? Everyone needs and should be be angry about what happened to little Kelsey—I'm just thinking our anger needs to be channeled into figuring out constructive ways to ensure that Kelsey's memory is honored and to prevent what happened to her from happening to some other little child.

Posted by [unknown person] Friday, February 24, 2006 @ 9:29 AM - Tasha....if you go back and read this here is the answer to your question....Richard Smothermon is the "District Attorney" so it is several counties hes in control of...the people appointed him to do this we go to vote who the district attorney is

Posted by "A voice for Kelsey" aka Mike Porter Friday, February 24, 2006 @ 9:31 AM - Yes, Christina, and next time, if he doesn't get justice for Kelsey, he needs to be voted OUT! In my opinion, he already failed her by not charging the mother with abuse last year! Christina, I am still trying to call the person you told me to the other day...do you know what I'm talking about?

Posted by "sew&sew" Friday, February 24, 2006 @ 9:43 AM - Shorty (8:59) I realize I cannot (and shouldn't) make everyone focus on what I think they should focus on. I just want folks to think about if the Briggs family is (at least for now) supporting the charges against RD & Mike Porter then we need to show them respect by what we say & how we say

*it regarding charges/sentencing on RD. Does that make
sense?*

*Posted by "A voice for Kelsey" aka Mike Porter Friday, February
24, 2006 @ 9:45 AM - Yes, its nice to meet everyone and put
a name with the face. I WISH we were at that courthouse this
morning with big signs "Justice for Kelsey" to greet her! I
wanted to SO bad, bust couldn't take off work.*

*Posted by "A voice for Kelsey" Friday, February 24, 2006 @ 9:47
AM - Yes, Sew – I think the Briggs just feel at this point they
don't have a choice but to trust the DA, and go along with
what he does...really, WHAT can they do right now? Now,
later on is a different story, if they feel justice has NOT been
served.*

In 2007, someone told me that Mike Porter had been a part of the
bashboards and that everyone knew he was there. She stated they all
"had fun" with him. When I read posts like these where he leads the
conversation where he wants it...on charging Raye, I wonder how
anyone could have considered conversing with the man charged with
Kelsey's murder "fun"!

*Posted by "sew&sew" Friday, February 24, 2006 @ 9:53 AM -
AVFK (9:47) Gosh – you said exactly what I wanted to say!
FOR ME...I feel the best way I can support the Briggs family,
show them & Kelsey respect is to support their trusting the
DA and how things have proceeded the last few days. In my
mind that means keeping my personal views on what I think
the charges should/should not have been and any possible
sentencing.*

*Posted by "Anonymous" Friday, February 24, 2006 @ 10:15 AM -
Can someone post a link to the Oklahoman article? And will
the news channels be showing RD on the news at 11:00 or
12:00?*

*Posted by "Anonymous" Friday, February 24, 2006 @ 10:20 AM -
http://newsok.com/article/1769916/?template=home/main*

Posted by "treemonkey" Friday, February 24, 2006 @ 10:21 AM - The news channels should have some coverage at noon to my understanding.

Posted by "proud mom" Friday, February 24, 2006 @ 10:23 AM - Paper said this morning that Raye Dawn is due to have her baby in the next six weeks!

Posted by "sew&sew" Friday, February 24, 2006 @ 11:08 AM - About 10 minutes ago Channel 4 [Cherokee Ballard's channel] had a "blurb" that RD has been formally charged. Said they would have complete details on their noon broadcast.

Posted by "Anonymous" Friday, February 24, 2006 @ 11:13 AM - Thanks sew&sew for keeping those of us who are out of state the informed of the immediate news broadcasts. I can't see it until much later. Thank You, I appreciate it.

Posted by "A voice for Kelsey" aka Mike Porter Friday, February 24, 2006 @ 11:15 AM - I wish they would tell us WHAT she pleaded

Posted by "treemonkey" Friday, February 24, 2006 @ 11:18 AM - Didn't it just start?

Posted by "Anonymous" Friday, February 24, 2006 @ 11:18 AM - I think it's more or less a given she'll plead not guilty.

Posted by Kathie W [unknown date and time] - I just read the article at the following link - http://newsok.com/article/1769916/?template=home/main - I have been involved in the legal profession in California and am familiar with the way the system works. I just want to caution people from getting too worked up about comments made by Raye Dawn's defense attorney. He's a lawyer and it's his job to say anything to defend his client it's all "smoke and mirrors" so to speak. He knows the law just as well as the DA knows the law. Even IF Raye Dawn "didn't know" that Kelsey was being abused, the...[remainder of post lost in printing]

Though few people shared their real names, "L Anthony" signed the next post, causing me to question his or her true identity.

Posted by "sew&sew" Friday, February 24, 2006 @ 11:37 AM - Treemonkey (11:34) In my opinion you are 100% correct. Blood is thicker than water as the old saying goes. It's my opinion the reason they continue to give her their undying support (at lease publicly) is to save THEIR faces-in other words they are guilty as well simply by association (blood ties)...L. Anthony

Posted by "sew&sew" Friday, February 24, 2006 @ 11:38 AM - TM: did what I say make sense???

Posted by "treemonkey" Friday, February 24, 2006 @ 11:52 AM - Yep

Posted by Anonymous Friday, February 24, 2006 @ 11:53 AM - Raye dawn is out on $25,000 bond

Posted by "treemonkey" Friday, February 24, 2006 @ 11:54 AM - How do you know this?

Posted by "A voice for Kelsey" aka Mike Porter Friday, February 24, 2006 @ 11:55 AM - You have GOT to be kidding me? This is a JOKE and a TRAVESTY! That is NOTHING. Kelsey's life is worth NOTHING to these people. Is this true?

Posted by "Anonymous" Friday, February 24, 2006 @ 11:56 AM - She never shed a tear.

Posted by "Anonymous" Friday, February 24, 2006 @ 12:18 PM - She SHOULD have been brought in in handcuffs!

Posted by "shorty" Friday, February 24, 2006 @ 12:19 PM - Did they say anything about conditions or did she just pay and go on her way?

*Posted by "Anonymous" Friday, February 24, 2006 @ 12:19 PM - I think we need to start calling TODAY Judge Engle's office and tell them this is a bunch of BULL****! Seriously, this is CRAP!*

Posted by "Christina" Friday, February 24, 2006 @ 12:20 PM - Yeah! Where does he think he is in nascar? And as far as Judge Engle goes he was the one who was the judge for her when she filed the protective order on lance and Kathie and he was the judge when mike filed for divorce from her.

Posted by "Christina" Friday, February 24, 2006 @ 12:21 PM - I can't wait to see her charges on odcr they still aren't on there yet

ODCR is the State of Oklahoma's Web site that lists all criminal charges. Why was this group so excited about charges against Raye while they "had fun" with the man charged with murder as well as an added charge of sexual assault? Wasn't it supposed to be about "justice for Kelsey"?

Posted by "proud mom" Friday, February 24, 2006 @ 12:25 PM - Maybe the judge should have been key, he could of make up for giving Kelsey back to her, by locking her ass up today.

Posted by [unknown person] Friday, February 24, 2006 @ 12:35 PM - Cherokee [Ballard] even sounded disgusted when she read how much bond was set at.

Posted by "pissed of bitch" Friday, February 24, 2006 @ 12:38 PM - Well its nice to know that the state of OK is great when it comes to law, welfare of children. But who cares what happens to these children more will be born right who cares is mothers beat or allow their kids to be beaten. Lets just keep giving them chances slap there little hands and tell baeting your kid is a no no. TO THE JUDGES IN LINCOLN COUNTY YOU SUCK ASS

Posted by "Christina" Friday, February 24, 2006 @ 12:45 PM -
HEY EVERYONE THAT WANTS TO BEAT THEIR
CHILDREN AND THAT ALLOW ABUSE TO HAPPEN GO
TO RAYE DAWNS ATTORNEY BECAUSE IT SEEMS HE
CAN GET YOU OUT OF EVERYTHING!!!!

The hate against Raye became even more sickening. Yet, still no mention of Mike Porter, except to possibly get his opinion on the day's events.

Posted by "Christina" Friday, February 24, 2006 @ 12:46 PM -
Does mikes sister or any of his family get on here anymore?
What do they think of all this?

Posted by "A voice for Kelsey" aka Mike Porter Friday, February
24, 2006 @ 12:54 PM - I am REALLY mad right now. I want
to know WHAT was that judge's reasoning for letting her off
so easy?

Posted by "proud mom" Friday, February 24, 2006 @ 12:55 PM - I
am so mad that I have ate a hole box of girl scout cookies for
lunch.

Posted by "shorty" [unknown date and time] - It is sickening. But at
least she was charged. I was beginning to think it would
never...[remainder of post lost in printing]

Posted by [unknown person] Friday, February 24, 2006 @ 1:11 PM
- Don't worry! Justice will prevail. The hearing today is all
procudural...Be patient.

Posted by "sew&sew" Friday, February 24, 2006 @ 1:20 PM - TO
ALL. I have no idea why the bond was set at $25K-but again
there is another example if a LAW, MANDATE,
GUIDELINE, ETC. needs to "toughened" up then kick those
folks who can do something about it in the ASS! In my mind
that would be those bozos sitting up there at the State Capitol
writing all these "laws"....does that make sense????

Posted by "Anonymous" Friday, February 24, 2006 @ 1:29 PM -
Every time I have seen Raye Dawn on T.V. I mean
EVERYTIME-She always has such a MEAN EXPRESSION
on her face. Even in the videos with Kelsey. Has this girl ever
been happy? A mean expression every time!! Did she take
everything out on Kelsey? What made this girl so mean and
miserable? Just very curious.

Posted by "TINA G" Friday, February 24, 2006 @ 1:33 PM - Can
someone tell me how they se the bond amount for the charge?

Posted by "Anonymous" Friday, February 24, 2006 @ 1:34 PM - I
can see her being charged with murder and trying to blame it
on her hormones from being pregnant! Like all other mothers
who kill their kids, they try to get out of it by some lame
excuss!

Posted by "Anonymous" [unknown date and time] - Kathie W. I
know it is a bit early. But in your opinion. How long of a
prison sentence do you think Raye Dawn will recieve. Can
you just make a wild guess. What would be the average
sentence…[remainder of post lost in printing]

Posted by [unknown person] Friday, February 24, 2006 @ 2:36 PM
- Sew, at this point, just seeing her makes me want to PUKE.
I think I would have held it for the NOT GUILTY and let it go
all over them!

This "sew&sew" character has me baffled. At first, I presumed it
was Kathie Briggs because I have seen several of her posts where she
discussed how she sewed clothes for her grandchildren. However, the
"DAwn" version of Raye's name, and the added "L. Anthony"
signature to cover tracks, plus the uncontrolled rage behind the posts
make Mike Porter a likely candidate. This character seems to have
cornered the market on sucking up to the Briggs…something Porter
had mastered. He did have multiple computers that were confiscated
by investigators so he could have posted simultaneously, ensuring his
choice of discussion. Could this have been another one of his aliases?

Posted by "sew&sew" Friday, February 24, 2006 @ 2:38 PM - If Mildred & [her friend] was to be pissy I suppose that's their right. Would seem their Pissiness would be better spent though bitch slapping that worthless daughter of Mildred's and kicking Raye DAwn in the ass. Their vileness is sorely misplaced if you ask me. Their own family is what has brought them to their sorry state...if they want to pint fingers & start assigning blame they have no further to look than within their own gene pool!!!!

Posted by "sew&sew" Friday, February 24, 2006 2:42 PM - I hope that the Briggs family now has drawn the line in the sand with these idiotic, self-rightous, self-serving, lying, cheating, scheming, back-stabbing asses. The Briggs family has set the standard for real class and Christian behavior if you ask me. They have turned their check time & time again with the Smith clan has struck out at them...In my mind they no longer have to do that I think if I were them I'd start filing VPOs againist each & every member of that Smith family that even dares to give them a sideways glance. That's what I'd do but you know what? The Briggs family is a class act—I can't say I have that much going for me. Let's continue to pray for the Briggs family—they are going to need it now and for many months to come. It's bad enough they did everything within their power to save their beloved Kelsey and the system failed them...now they have to put up with even more insulting behavior by RD & her jackass clan.

Posted by "A voice for Kelsey" aka Mike Porter Friday, February 24, 2006 @ 2:45 PM - I have said many times, they are WAY better than me...I would not have had any class when it came to dealing with them! The BRIGGS are the UPSTANDING CHRISTIANS!

Posted by "sew&sew" Friday, February 24, 2006 @ 3:24 PM - Anon (3:20) It's unfortunate the poor baby has to suffer because of it's worthless mother isn't it? If her baby has health problems (God forbid) then the stupid, lying, idiotic bitch has no one but herself to blame (what am I thinking-she never does anything to hurt anyone else). L. Anthony

The sequence of some of these posts is confusing because posts had been deleted before they were printed. The Smith family members have several boxes with posts just from Kelsey's Purpose and the bashboard. Unfortunately, it would take months to put it all in order. But you get the idea from these representative posts of the hate that was building against Raye and her entire family, and most importantly who was behind the hate.

Posted by "sew&sew" Anon (3:30) I'm sorry-you don't deserve me getting pissy. That aside in reality I think that all of us have have genuine pity and feel sorrow for that little unborn baby. We can only hope that he will be placed with a loving, deserving family that will raise him with plenty of hugs, kisses, and love...I honestly believe if that baby is left with RD and/or the Smith clan he will suffer the same horrific fate as precious little Kelsey.

Posted by "treemonkey" Friday, February 24, 2006 @ 3:28 PM - I really doubt raye dawn is stressed. She is as cold as ice and emotionless. She is probably out partying it up right now.

Posted by "MistyLT" Friday, February 24, 2006 @ 3:28 PM - Sewnsew, I'm sorry, that was me up there using your name lol. I guess instead of typing my own name in, since I was talking to you, I accidentally typed your name in. sorry ;)

Posted by "Lana" Friday, February 24, 2006 @ 3:44 PM - I hope that Raye Dawn isn't partying it up for the baby's sake, but also for her own. I heard that one of her conditions of bond is that she is not able to drink ANY alcohol until she goes to trial, which could be a year away. If she is caught drinking she will have to go to jail.

In the courtroom, Mildred asked Kathie Briggs, "Do you ever sleep?" The Smiths knew of the bashboards and the fact that most of Kathie's post on Kelsey's Purpose and the bashboard were in the middle of the night. Kathie jumped up and yelled, "I'm being harassed!" Jeanna then called her husband, Randy, who is Debbie's son and Mildred's grandson and she whined to him about being accosted in the courtroom by his grandmother. This would not be the only story blown out of proportion, nor the only wedge the Briggs would use to separate Mildred's grandchildren from her. In December of 2010, Mildred sent Christmas cards that contained money to her great-grandchildren. Jeanna returned the cards to Mildred, unopened. I often wonder if Randy knows what his wife and mother-in-law have done to his family.

Posted by "Anonymous" Friday, February 24, 2006 @ 6:23 PM -
The friend of mine that works at the courthouse said that she saw what Mildred did to Kathie Briggs and one of her daughters and what [Mildred's friend] did to Lance and [Susan's husband, Jack]. She said it was unbelievable and disgusting. She said that they were full of hate and venom. She said that the Briggs family had to ask for deputies to keep them away from them and out of their faces.

Posted by "Anonymous" Friday, February 24, 2006 @ 6:25 PM -
Anon 6:23. Please tell me what happened. Please!

Posted by "Polly" Friday, February 24, 2006 @ 6:30 PM - It is true
that Mildred and [her friend] approached the Briggs family in the hallway in court.

Posted by "Anonymous" Friday, February 24, 2006 @ 6:32 PM -
[Mildred's friend] acts like he's some 7 foot tall, 400 pound guy! He acts like when he walks up people should shutter and be scared.

Posted by "Anonymous" Friday, February 24, 2006 @ 6:35 PM -
OH this is the UPSTANDING CHRISTIAN WOMAN? HA, they are a joke!

Posted by "sew&sew" Friday, February 24, 2006 @ 6:38 PM -
Anon (6:32) Anyone who's been on this blog for a while knows there is no love loss on the Smith side of the house towards the Briggs. Do the Smith clan realize they are hurting "their cause" more than helping it by lashing out at the Briggs family. I can't think of anyone other than the

Smith's that do not support the Briggs family in anyway shape or form…[portion of post lost in printing]…IGNORED ALL OF KELSEY'S abuse and then the Smith family wouldn't be put in the embarrassing situation of having to defend that rotten, lying, scheming, black-hearted bitch of a woman known as Raye Dawn. L. Anthony

Posted by "Anonymous" Friday, February 24, 2006 @ 6:40 PM - She said that Mildred walked straight up to Kathie and said something in her face and just kept standing there glaring in her face. The other Briggs family members were telling her to go away and stop it. So then Mildred walked up to Lance's sisters and got in her face and just stood there in her face glaring at her but wouldn't say a word and the lady whose face she was in didn't acknowledge her. [Mildred's friend] walked straight up to Lance and got right in his face and pushed his body up against Lance's and was saying some stuff to him but she couldn't hear what it was. She said that [Jack] tried to get between them and pull [Mildred's friend] away From Lance. The Briggs family was telling them to just keep walking and leave them alone. Then after the deputies came to stay with the Briggs family, [Mildred's friend] came back and got in [Jack's] face again and the deputies threatened to remove him if he didn't get away from the Briggs'. She said that she couldn't believe [Mildred's friend] and Mildred behaved that way.

Posted by "Anonymous" Friday, February 24, 2006 @ 7:08 PM - EVERYONE, AFTER HEARING THAT STORY, NOW WE KNOW WHY GAYLA AND RAYE DAWN ARE THE WAY THAT THEY ARE. JUST LOOK AT MILDRED'S CLASSLESS, AGGRESSIVE BEHAVIOR. THAT EXPLAINS IT ALL!!!

Posted by "Anonymous" Friday, February 24, 2006 @ 7:10 PM - A CHRISTIAN??? NOT HARDLY.

Posted by "Anonymous" Friday, February 24, 2006 @ 7:12 PM - I used to think that Mildred had a little bit of class. Now I know that she doesn't. What a disgrace.

194

Though only the Briggs and their closest supporters were in the courtroom, the bullies believed the over-dramatized story without question.

Posted by "sew&sew" Friday, February 24, 2006 @ 7:15 PM -
Anon (7:08/7:10) (AND ALL) I want to say something here so
please bear with me. I used to know Mildred Fowler...I say
"used to know" because the Mildred Fowler of "today" is
certainly not the Mildred Fowler I thought I knew some 30
odd years ago...her mother (Grandma Winters) and sister
(Jeri Murray Hardison) would be turning over in their graves
about all this. I do not know what happened over the years to
make Mildred this way...maybe she was this way all along
and just kept it to herself or only those closest to her knew the
real her. It's sad for me as the Mildred Fowler I thought I
knew was a kind, generous, loving good hearted woman. It
would appear that is not the case.

The tiny courthouse was flooded with reporters. Hallways were blocked and microphones were shoved into the faces of Raye, who was pregnant at the time, and her family members. Their only interest was to get everyone out of the way so that Raye could walk down the hallway without being harmed. Yet this turned into another tragic story of the "evil Smiths."

Posted by "Anonymous" Friday, February 24, 2006 @ 7:15 PM -
Channel 5 showed the Smiths pushing the reporters, shoving
notebooks in front of the cameras to keep them from filming,
shoving camera men and acting like a bunch of classless,
white trash bullies. Julie... was taking her whole body and
shoving Britten Follet all the way down the hall. I honestly
couldn't believe what I saw.

Posted by "Anonymous" Friday, February 24, 2006 @ 7:18 PM -
Total embarrassment. Just think of your grandma behaving
that way. How humiliating I wish sew&sew could have been
there to bitch-slap Mildred and [her friend]!! Ha Ha Ha

Posted by "sew&sew" Friday, February 24, 2006 7:18 PM - Anon (7:15) You know what..their behavior does nothing to "help" their cause. By treating the Briggs family like crap, by treating the news media like crap, by treating EVERYONE in general like crap all they will do is seal Raye Dawn's "fate" even more than it already is if they had nothing to fear or hide then they would conduct themselves with more dignity and class wouldn't you think?

Posted by "sew&sew" [unknown date and time] - Anon (7:18)-Don't think I wouldn't have if I thought I could have gotten away with it...I guess the "trick" would be to have them throw the first punch...then couldn't I get away with bitch slappin' them? L. Anthony ☺ You know-self defense and all that!

Once again, posts were lost in printing. But you get the general idea of the topic of conversation from "sew&sew's" answer...which I believe to be yet another alias of Mike Porter. His "get away with it" comment is very telling.

Posted by "sew&sew" Friday, February 24, 2006 @ 7:28 PM - Anon (7:24) Rats-well I guess that would screw up my self defense plea wouldn't it? Maybe we'd better come up with another idea so I can bitch slap them and get away with it! L. Anthony

Posted by "Anonymous" Friday, February 24, 2006 @ 7:29 PM - What in the world happened to Mildred? Was like that all along probably. She was just playing the nice grandma role in the past maybe. Wow, Kathie probably didn't know what to do with all of that inappropriate behavior.

Posted by "Anonymous" Friday, February 24, 2006 @ 7:30 PM - You guys really need to quit saying that you want to "bitch slap" them. They will take that as a threat and have this site shut down and investigated. You are breaking the law.

Posted by "Anonymous" Friday, February 24, 2006 @ 7:34 PM - Oh for crying out loud. It is obvious that we are joking.

Lighten up a bit. I've been crying for days over Kelsey's death. I was enjoying the laugh.

Posted by "Jim" Friday, February 24, 2006 @ 7:42 PM - Sew&Sew, You and I think a lot alike. BUT your comments at 555???? What would happen if Mike said anything about what RD was doing to Miss Kelsey? RD and her family would say that Mike was doing it. Gayla would say she saw it and maybe one of good friends (ha-ha) would agree, then where would Mike be. I have been in a spot like that. Sometimes you just have to hope things will change for the better.

Posted by [unknown person] Friday, February 24, 2006 @ 7:55 PM - [first part of post lost in printing] ...mean anything to me, mainly because my daughter is 2 and says things like that all the time and she is NOT abuse! For instance. Her daddy will ask is mommy mean and she will say yeah mommy mean. Same if I ask her if daddy is mean. Her legs were broken for god sake, anyone could hurt her. Raye is acting like a murderer and Mike is playing all inocent when in fact I hope they BOTH rot in prison for the rest of their lives!!!!

The next post alerts us to the fact that the bashboard now had a new owner. I am somewhat confused about the sequence of ownership, because it seems that bashboards would go up and then disappear. I witnessed this first-hand once I became involved. It is my belief that at this point Misty LT, the woman rumored to have had a relationship with Mike Porter, took over the bashboard. Soon tension would arise between those who posted on the bashboard and the Briggs family members.

Posted by "sew&sew" Friday, February 24, 2006 @ 7:55 PM
Anonymous (7:53) Tell you what...I'm not going to lose any sleep over it if you promise not to. I understand your concerns and out of respect for your feelings, out of respect for LJBD (as this is her site) I will "knock it off". I apologize AGAIN if I have offended anyone. If the Smith's care to sue me then they can...I am not afraid of them or anything they think they can

and cannot do to me. I would hope they have bigger concerns than me!!!

Posted by "Anonymous" Friday, February 24, 2006 @ 7:57 PM - Maybe Kathie and Lance should sue Mildred and [her friend] after that incident today!

Posted by "sew&sew" Friday, February 24, 2006 @ 7:59 PM - Anon (7:57) Be careful that you don't annoy the Smith family by making that recommendation (oops)!

Posted by "Anonymous" Friday, February 24, 2006 @ 8:00 PM - They should get VPOs against them.

Posted by "Anonymous" Friday, February 24, 2006 @ 9:55 PM - Can you guys believe that the Smiths' are blaming the Briggs? HOW STUPID IS THAT? The Briggs haven't even seen Kelsey in HOW MANY MONTHS? These people are idiots!

Posted by "sew&sew" Friday, February 24, 2006 @ 9:56 PM - Anon (9:47) I wouldn't even presume to try and figure out what the man was thinking. I suppose reading & interpreting (spelling?) the law can be subject...sort of like 2 people reading a passage in the Bible...each individual takes what they need/want and "fits" it to suit their needs...he may have followed the "intent" of the law but didn't, wouldn't or couldn't follow the spirit of the law. Does that make more sense?

Posted by MistyLT Friday, February 24, 2006 @ 9:58 PM - Can anyone tell me who these people are? The man in the red shirt that escorted RD into the court house by the arm after she was booked, the girl that was pushing Britten, and the big girl in the neon green shirt?

Posted by "Anonymous" Friday, February 24, 2006 @ 9:58 PM - Excellent way of putting it sew&sew.

Posted b misty_lt Friday, February 24, 2006 @ 9:58 PM - Anon 9:55 – Well they have to blame the Briggs bc it can't be the Smith's fault.

Posted by "sew&sew" Friday, February 24, 2006 @ 10:01 PM - Anon (9:55) I for one believe the Smiths are blaming the Briggs...the question is WHAT are they blaming them for? Loving their granddaughter and trying to protect Kelsey from their evilness? They will do or say anything to try & divert the issue to someone else. They want to try & point fingers at everyone else in the hopes of making themselves look like the victims(s). The victim here is little Kelsey...the Briggs family has done nothing but try to help that child...in doing so, the truth about RD and the Smith clan is coming to the surface for all the world to see!

Posted by "anon947" Friday, February 24, 2006 @ 10:01 PM - Sew and sew, I understand your point but the law is clear the overriding consideration in all cases of abuse is the best interest of the child. It doesn't take a rocket scientist to know that if abuse is going on in a household it's not in a child's best interest to be returned to that home, but apparently key couldn't see that. He needs to go. PERIOD!!!!

Posted by "sew&sew" Friday, February 24, 2006 @ 10:02 PM - Anon (9:58) Thank you!

Posted by "sew&sew" Friday, February 24, 2006 @ 10:04 PM - Anon947 (10:01) I agree with you...I was just trying to throw out a possible explanation for his actions...he's the only one that can "justify" why he made the ruling he did. Actually I think he did...but I can't recall what he said. Maybe someone else "on here" and be specific as to Key's justification for making the ruling he did.

Posted by "MistyLT" [unknown date and time] - I think I will be sending a reminder via Lincoln County News next week to DHS to remind them that this woman is getting ready to have a baby.

199

Posted by "sew&sew" Friday, February 24, 2006 @ 10:22 PM -
Anon (10:19) Wow! I forgot about that but you're right!
Wasn't that nice of them to FINALLY remember little Kelsey!
Hope they didn't strain themselves pinning on their buttons!

Posted by MistyLT Friday, February 24, 2006 @ 10:24 PM - Well
channel 5 did the best coverage of that where they showed
everything that was REALLY going on, and on that footage I
ever heard some guy say "Go ask Kathy Briggs".

Posted by "Anonymous" Friday, February 24, 2006 @ 10:26 PM -
The fat girl in the green shirt is Sarah..., RD's cousin. The
guy in the red shirt is Curtis..., RD's older brother. The man
in the navy or black shirt that was trying to block her was
[Gayla's friend]. The woman with long blonde hair is Janet,
RD's older half sister. The girl with the long brown curly
hair is Rachelle, RD's younger sister. The old hardlooking,
bitter woman in the red and black is Mildred Fowler. The old
man in the black leather coat is ..., Mildred's boyfriend.
Everyone knows Gayla's helmet head.

Posted by MistyLT Friday, February 24, 2006 @ 10:29 PM - Wow,
thanks anon.

Posted by "sew&sew" Friday, February 24, 2006 @ [unknown date
and time] - They can "hide" all they want but in this case it
won't do them any good. If RD and the Smith clan have done
nothing to be ashamed of then in my opinion they should
have...[remainder of post lost in printing]

Before Kelsey's death, Raye's younger sister, Rachelle, had a miscarriage. Of course, in the mean-spirited eyes of this pack of wolves, her miscarriage became an abortion. Mike would also tell the Briggs that Raye had aborted his child before she was pregnant with his son. Though this has been denied by the Smiths, and there is no proof to back up his claim, it is repeated as fact.

Posted by "Lilly" Friday, February 24, 2006 @ 10:42 PM - Does
anyone know if Rachelle is still pregnant or did she abort
another baby? I think that DHS should take RD's baby as

soon as it's born. It sucks that if you know the "right" people, appear to have money, or the right lawyer you can get away with everything!!

Posted by "Jim" Friday, February 24, 2006 @ 10:42 PM - I think that Lance Briggs is pretty tough, and has a lot of self control. If something like this happened to my oldest son while I was on my way home from Vietnam, I don't know how I would have handed it. Knowing my temperament at that time. I would taken maters in my own hands. And my exwife would have been the first one to go, then her family. Fro the Briggs family, we all pray for justice. But the way this smoke screen has been set I don't think we will...I hope I'm wrong.

Posted by "Anonymous" Friday, February 24, 2006 @ 10:45 PM - The lady that tried to get [Mildred's friend] to stop was Jeanna Fowler. She is Lance's older sister. She is also married to Mildred Fowler's grandson.

Posted by "Anonymous" Friday, February 24, 2006 @ 10:48 PM - Well, I for one will be there on April 14th to support the Briggs! This wont happen again. If enough justice for Kelsey supporters show up, we can outweight the venom! NOT that we all have to go in the courtroom, but we all can be there and support the family, and outweight the stupidity!

Posted by "sew&sew" Friday, February 24, 2006 @ 10:48 PM - Kelsey (10:42) I don't have inside access to how much money the Smith clan does or does not have—if anyone in that family had some money it would be Mildred. I say that as it is a well known fact that Gayla embezzeled money from a former employer. True...she inherited her late husband's business so I guess there could be some money there—don't know how much as there would be overhead in keeping the business up & running. It's all illusion with the Smith clan if you ask me. They are the sow's ears trying desperately to make themselves into silk purses. I honestly don't think they will get away with as much as they think they will (but stranger things have happened). I say that because the general public and townsfolk of Meeker are "on to them".

Shifting the Blame

February, 2006

At midnight on February 26, 2006 Kathie Briggs e-mailed Mike Porter regarding his unanswered email to her from just days before. She stated that she had spent the week "planning for the grand jury"…a grand jury that was a closed proceeding. What was there to plan? Things obviously weren't going as she had schemed. What more did she want? Raye had been charged with a crime and she would most likely have a trial. Was that not good enough? Porter was out on bond. Where were the protests against him walking the streets?

> *I just read your message as I spent the week planning for the grand jury. I would also like to know if you would be willing to give a sworn statement to Lance's attorney about Judge Key. I think it is time to start bringing these people down. I can assure you if you don't help they will not be there for you. It would be your way to get some of these people to held accountable. Smothermon keeps saying if Raye Dawn cooperates she could receive a deal. You should think about the same thing. I spoke to my attorney about this and he would be willing to do a deposition with or without your attorney. You wished us luck for the week. I can tell you we did not have it, but whats new.*

Porter responded immediately.

> *You know I will do this – the last thing I told you was my offer still stands. You know I will do anything that will help you in your fight. I will make NO deal that involves me admitting to something I did not do. I will admit to all the culpability that I have in this – I told you that from day one. All I ask of you is that you tell everything that you know also. Please Do not hold things back that will prove RD's guilt when the time comes. I will let you know this week.*

Porter then answered a post that was not captured on the bashboard...presumably by Kathie Briggs.

Posted by "sew&sew" Sunday, February 26, 2006 1:01 AM - Anon (12:16) If I could take your grief and pain away I would but you know I can't. I've lost people I've loved more than anything (but not a little child). For me it was not only grieving about losing them but I was grieving for myself. Why? Because I was left behind to face the fact that I knew that in this lifetime I couldn't see the person I loved. What got me through?

Simultaneously, Kathie Briggs posted a family statement. The billboard she mentioned is the same billboard that she had suggested for Porter to sponsor. Did he? Also, if you will recall from the e-mails, Porter agreed to take an "anonymous donation" to the sign shop. Between her public and private conversations with Mike Porter in the wee hours of the morning, I'm with Mildred. Did she ever sleep?

Posted by "Briggs family" Sunday, February 26, 2006 @ 1:01 AM - I have had several people contact us about a protest. My opinion is this...it concerns me that Raye Dawn will never spend jail time. I do believe she needs jail time. She deserves no deals as Kelsey was not given a deal. She did have better offer, but Judge Key messed that up. We are having a town hall meeting on March 11th in Shawnee and hope for a great turnout. The location has been found, but I cannot remember where it is. We have a billboard going up for Kelsey on 177 in the next two weeks. We are also needing to get more and more people to commit to yard signs. We have distributed 14,000 stickers, yet there are so many cars that do not have them on them. We have received some donations and that has been amazing and we appreciate it. We have ordered close to 1000 stickers a week and still have a big demand. We were lucky to have an anonymous donor take $200 to the sign shop. We will be making big signs for the Meeker area. People on this site have been very supportive. Even though we don't post often, we do read as often as we can. Thank you.

Posted by "Anonymous" Sunday, February 26, 2006 @ 1:04 AM -
Gayla mentioned in court that Raye had support from her two
sisters and her brother and then as she paused she said and
her other brothers. It is as if she forgets the other two boys. It
also seems Raye has forgotten about Ray Smith. She was
holding hands with her new Daddy. How quaint.

Posted by "sew&sew" Sunday, February 26, 2006 @ 1:04 AM -
Briggs Family (1:01) Have the pins arrived yet???

Posted by [unknown person] Sunday, February 26, 2006 @ 1:06 AM
- I was thinking about the signs today as I was driving
through Meeker on 18. I didn't notice any on the way in or
out and then I thought ya know, I don't have one either and
then was trying to remember where people said to them. The
girl that lives across the street from me is pregnant and has 3
children that were abused. Apparently the guy hasn't
disappeard bc B.A.C.A. converged upon our houses the other
day and came to me and explained what was going on and
brought our children some gifts and let mine take pictures on
the bikes so I was also thinking about getting her one too.
Don't know when I'll get back out of Chandler but are there
any signs near here?

Posted by "Briggs family" aka Kathie Briggs Sunday, February 26,
2006 @ 1:10 AM - Mildred Fowler was nice enough to get in
my face at court and ask me if I ever sleep at night. I finally
replied as she would not move. I told her "yes I do". Fact is I
sleep very little since Kelsey was removed from our home. I
spent everynight on the net writing any and everyone asking
for help for Kelsey. No one listened and Kelsey has moved to
heaven. I still have a hard time sleeping as the wheels in my
head are constantly turning. Tonight I did break down and
take a sleeping pill and it is starting to kick in. So if my post
makes no sense just remember I am not use to these drugs.

Posted by "sew&sew" Sunday, February 26, 2006 @ 1:10 AM -
Anon (1:04) Well it is hard no doubt for her to keep track of
that...she is busy thinking about her nappy hair and nappy
makeup.

206

Posted by "Anonymous" [unknown date and time] - There will be a few big signs on Hwy 18 just north of Meeker very soon.

Posted by "Ashley" [Donna's daughter-in-law and the person who originally started the bashboards] Sunday, February 26, 2006 @ 1:19 AM - I need 100+ people to commit to doing a protest on March 17th or 18th. PEACEFUL of course. You must remember who we represent! We need to let the D.A. know that "DEALS" are out of the question. Kelsey was not given a deal and neither should anyone else! Please let me know if you can attend, children welcome!

Posted by "MistyLT" Sunday, February 26, 2006 @ 1:20 AM - At what time Ashley and what days of the week does that fall on?

Posted by "Anonymous" Sunday, February 26, 2006 @ 1:20 AM - Ashley – please pick a day when the DA will be in his office. I will have people there. Count me in for AT LEAST 5 people. ☺

Posted by "Anonymous" Sunday, February 26, 2006 @ 1:25 AM - The DA is not usually there on Saturdays. Fridays are not good TV coverage days either. Is there any way to do it after three on Mon, Tues, Wed, or Thurs?

Posted by "Anonymous" Sunday, February 26, 2006 @ 1:26 AM - The DA does not work on Saturday

Posted by "sew&sew" Sunday, February 26, 2006 1:27 AM - AG (1:24) I don't know but most "public" offices are closed on the weekends. There are of course exceptions to that rule...I would guess you could call his office to find out...

Posted by "sew&sew" Sunday, February 26, 2006 @1:30 AM - TO ALL: I promise to attend and promise to be good I swear I will not cuss, spit, get in people's face or otherwise make an ass out of myself or do anything to disrespect Kelsey & bring shame to her family.

Posted by "Anonymous" [unknown date and time] - He may have already cut the deal by then. I still do not get what he means by cooperating IF he does not need her in Porter's case then why even bother with her? Why not just prosecute Mike and then depending on the oputcome of his trial prosecute her for her charges or for another charges or for another charge also? He is talking out of both sides of his mouth. HE says...[remainder of post lost in printing]

Posted by "Ashley" Sunday, February 26, 2006 @ 1:31 AM - Ok, well lets make it March 16th @ 4:00pm then maybe a week before Raye's trial we can do it again in Chandler at the court house for the judge to see. We need 100+ people to commit to this.

Posted by "Anonymous" Sunday, February 26, 2006 @ 1:34 AM - I think Richard puts his foot in his mouth every time he speaks. He is tough on child abuse – parents have a moral responsibility – but then does not object to a $25,000 bond for a charge that carries up to life in prison. WTF??? HE does not need her to convict Mike but then he would offer her a deal? A deal for what exactly? Her Cooperation at this point is blame it all on Mike. That does not seem very helpful or credible.

Posted by "sew&sew" Sunday, February 26, 2006 @ 1:34 AM - Anon (1:31 & 1:31) Hey-who knows what he's up to? He may just be playing old RD & her attorney...I cannot believe with his career on the line as it is now that he would do anything even more stupid to put it in further jeopardy. Guess we'll just have to wait and see.

Posted by "Anonymous" Sunday, February 26, 2006 @ 1:36 AM - Misty – you go up to the atrium and then take a right. I have not been there Since October 15th – I tried to go 2 weeks ago but could not do it.

Posted by "Ashley" Sunday, February 26, 2006 @ 1:36 AM - Ok CHANGE THE PROTEST TO MARCH 9th @ 4:00pm...that *way it is just before Porter's court appearance. We can go to the court to support the Briggs family and Kelsey's Purpose, however, we MUST be respectful and stay outside and stay peaceful. We represent Kelsey and the Briggs and no matter what is said to us from the other side we must remain strong and respectful. Remember that is Kelsey's family also and that we must be respectful to Kelsey's memory.*

Posted by "sew&sew" Sunday, February 26, 2006 @ 1:37 AM - Ashley (1:31) Count me in...see my 1:30 post please.

Posted by "Anonymous" Sunday, February 26, 2006 @ 1:37 AM - Hey that is Richard Smothermon. HE is a very important man. President Elect of the Oklahoma District Attorneys Association. I think the power has gone to his head. Maybe it is time for us voters to let him know that we are watching in a big way.

Posted by "sew&sew" Sunday, February 26, 2006 @ 1:40 AM - Anon (1:37) I've been saying that for several days now. What these folks need to remember is that we, as taxpayers, are in effect...their employer! If they cannot or will not do their job then we need to "fire" them and find someone who will.

Posted by "Anonymous" Sunday, February 26, 2006 @ 1:40 AM - Porter will not be at court on March 9th. But you can be there anyway. ☺ I think the person who needs ot hear our voice is the DA. And Apparently [Judge E]. I can tell you this – that bond was not standard for these charges. AND [Judge E] being as new as he is would not have set bond that low without direction from Richard or one of the other Judges.

Out of the prying eyes of the bashboard members, Kathie Briggs answered Mike Porter.

It is my against my better judgement to do this, but I still have questions and i want answers. I will only tell the truth, but I can tell you after yesterday I am ready to accept the fact that something has got to change. The royalty treatment was uncalled for. I feel the DA is going to make her a deal and I

209

cannot accept that. The bottom line is I do not know what happened in that house. I too will need to wait for the trials and will go from there. I cannot change it and I cannot help you in the criminal defense, however I will tell the truth as I have always done. If you are willing to talk to him, can I set up an appointment? My main focus is getting a sworn statement against the Judge first. [Raye's first attorney in the custody battle] and [Kelsey's doctor]. Then of course I want to know everything you know about connections between all of these people such as [the CASA worker] and DHS. Did [Raye's attorney] get to the Judge? How did that come about? I have been told cooperation will go along way when deciding sentences and I cannot believe it could hurt you to play their same game. You may feel I am out of line to ask you for this information, but I still believe you want to help. I hesitated to contact you again, but what went on in that court room was unreal. There was no problems with the Porters and the Briggs in court and would not anticipate any in the future. Your family can feel comfortable around us and we would be willing to sit next to them without hesitation. This crime is not the fault of other family members. Stupid [Gayla's friend] kept hollaring ask Kathie Briggs. Julie pushed Britten Follet in the hall and that was uncalled for. The other thing I want to know is how much fraud was involved in buying that house and why don't you bring that out? Those people need to be reported if they committed fraud. I realize it involves you as well, but what have you got to loose at this point? Richard seems to think he works for them too, and if we cannot prove some of the things they have done wrong they will still smell like a rose. I know you know things and I am still here ready to expose others. I need your help in where to look. The civil case can start soon. YOU ARE not the only witness against the Judge, but it would really help. He did Kelsey wrong and you can make that right.

Porter answered Kathie Briggs is the final e-mail that would be released to Raye's attorney.

It has always been against my better judgement. But some things are more important than others. I only ask you to tell the truth. I know you will. I can tell you that we have put some things together that will mean NO deal for RD and much more. But that is neither here nor there. And I am sorry if you ever felt I was trying to use you for info – I simply wanted you to see that Richard is very reluctant to even prosecute RD and I beleive that you know that now. I know you can offer no help to me and would not and I have never asked you to and never will. Yes I will tell you everything that I know. I would like to put it in writing for mysefl first. And I can not risk losing [my attorney]. He has promised to help me prove the truth about what we know happened that day. You are not out of line at all. You know my feelings about this – I do not want to put it in e-mail. There was a time when I would have but my trust is non-existent now. Kathie – I do want to help. I never had anything to gain by speaking to you and everything to lose. But my main concern is proving what I know to be true. I could not beleive what I saw on the news. They should have been thanking Richard for gettign the star treatment. Instead they were pissed and blaming you STILL. Not one word about me – the one who supposedly killed Kelsey. Crazy. Kathie – the proof of fraud on the house is there. But at this point I will look vindictive if I say, well Look at this Richard. I will tell everything I have done wrong when the time comes – I promise you that. The phone records will help tremendously and I will share those with you – I just need to figure out how. I think the phone records may show some collusion with the Judge or [Raye's attorney], I am not sure. Let me write out everything I know and send it to you. Here is what I need from you – Your solemn word that you will not share that information until I say so. Give me an address to send the info to you and I will do it and then if you think that it is worth me being deposed we will do it. BUt PROMISE you will keep the info between you and your attorney – then it will fall under the confidentiality clause.

The unlikely friends seemed to be questioning each other's trust and motives. This did not stop them from their public relationship via the bashboard.

*Posted by "Anonymous" Sunday, February 26, 2006 @ 1:51 AM - I
    heard the pre-lim has been set for April.*

*Posted by "Anonymous" Sunday, February 26, 2006 @ 1:52 AM - IS
    the prelim on ODCR?*

*Posted by "Anonymous" Sunday, February 26, 2006 @ 1:53 AM
Maybe they are trying to kee it under wraps. Lord knows enough
    people already assume Porter is guilty.*

The following post echoed Kathie Briggs's words to Mike Porter
in her e-mail just moments before when she told him, "There was no
problems with the Porters and the Briggs in court and would not
anticipate any in the future."

*Posted by "Anonymous" Sunday, February 26, 2006 @ 1:53 AM -
    There has never been any problems with the Briggs and the
    Porters in court. I think we can figure the common
    denominator as who causes the problems. The Smiths a true
    example of white trash.*

*Posted by "Ashley" [unknown date and time] - Anyone can come
    and protest or show their support. I don't care what side your
    from. Personally it is not about sides it is about Justice for a
    little girl was murdered. I don't care who thinks who did it –
    I care about Justice. Everyone should want Justice for
    Kelsey.*

Ashley then posted the plans from the bashboard to protest Raye's
possible plea deal to the Kelsey's Purpose forum.

*Ashley Posts:84 February 26, 2006 2:12 AM - March 3rd – Changed!
    - WHAT: Peaceful Rally/Protest - WHEN: March 3rd @
    4:00pm - WHERE: Shawnee court house - WHY: To let the
    DA and Judge know that a deal in this case is unacceptable.
    Kelsey was not given a deal and noone else should be either.
    The way they handle this case will determine their reelection!
    NEED: 100+ people to commit and show up! The more that
    show up will prove to them just what they have to lose.
    Please let me know if you can come join in with us. The*

Briggs family is ok with this taking place. You want to help and this is your chance! Kelsey needs us all!!!! Thanks! Ashley This post was last modified: 2-27-2006 10:44 PM by aunt bean [Jeanna].

Christina Posts: 41 Re: March 3rd – Changed! - I will be there!

Meanwhile, back on the bashboard, it was business as usual, and by business I mean trashing Raye and her family.

Posted by "Deb" Sunday February 26, 2006 @ 11:52 AM - Sew&Sew, Thanks for the compliment/funny early this morning or late last night, whenever I read it. I was crying reading all this on here, catching up from last night so I needed a laugh. Yes, I believe that the term rally should be used. But I'm from those olden days too where protest reminded people of the hippies and the vietnam war. Even thought the Smith family is making a "war" out of this and don't know why "precious" has to be charged with anything because she is grieving and the mother of Kelsey. Mother is a term of endearance and not to be taken lightly. Just because R.D. gave birth to Kelsey, doesn't make her a "Mother". She didn't protect Kelsey so she failed and I think that Kathie Briggs said it right on tv when she said that Raye Dawn had 2 chances being a mother to Kelsey. First chance was given by God and the 2nd chance was given by Judge Keys and she failed at both. She WILL fail at proving that she was a 'good' mother also. Good mother don't allow their children to be hurt or killed. Good mothers fight for their children. It's obvious that Raye Dawn was NOT a good mother.

Posted by "Anonymous" Sunday, February 26, 2006 @ 12:00 PM - No she wasn't. She was a bad mother. Poor little Kelsey landed a bad one. At least she experienced love from the Briggs. Thats more than alot of other abused children have.

Though she was an admittedly active participant and "addicted to" the bashboard, Kathie Briggs put up a public front of the grieving grandma that was only concerned with "justice for Kelsey." Yet, she could not pass up the chance to express her true thoughts of the

213

Smiths. The most fascinating part of this post is where she refers to herself in the third person. I suppose she had a lot of practice with anonymous posts and she slipped, or she had just learned a few tricks from the man she had stayed up late at night e-mailing, Mike Porter.

Posted by "Briggs family" Sunday, February 26, 2006 @ 12:24 PM - It is nice that people think we are doing such great things, be we are only doing what seems like the only thing to do. We do not expect praise for our actions, we just have to do whatever we can to show that Kelsey did have a family with dignity. She deserved at least that. We will not let her memory die, she only lived here on earth for two years, but she will be in our hearts forever. What ever can be done to honor her, we will do. The Kelsey Briggs law is only a start. Kelsey is now very powerful, no one listened to her before, but they are listening to her now. Thank you for all of your support. What would we do without it. We have been fighting the tactics of the Smith families for so long and it is hard to plan for their next move, as we cannot think in the same manner as they do. What happened in the court on Friday was uncalled for. It is not anything we would ever had imagined. They have accused us of threatening people, stalking, and harassing and yet when we are sitting there minding our own business, they try to start trouble. We will let them provoke us that way. That old man and woman obviously need therapy. I honestly feel bad for Mildred, she is 74 years old and her mind is slipping. Must be a difficult time to know her granddaughter has been charged with such a serious charge. But to still blame Kathie Briggs shows her mind is slipping. We should probably pray for her to get back to reality. What a sad thing it must be to put on the image of an ultimate Christian woman and then blow it in one encounter.

Posted by "Anonymous" Sunday, February 26, 2006 @ 12:28 PM - Deb – and your post is even making the assumption that ALL RD is guilty of was not protecting Kelsey. That is yet to be determined.

Posted by [unknown person] Sunday, February 26, 206 @ 12:40 PM - My first post of the day---I just heard an old song on tv. Miss Dolly wrote that I think fits RD. The title was "I will Oil Wells Love You. THAT FITS>>>

Finally, a voice of reason...

Posted by "KJ" Sunday, February 26, 2006 @ 1:38 PM - I would like to add my thoughts about Mike calling his mother in law before calling paramedics. I live several miles outside of Meeker. I realize that living this far from town results in precious miniutes being wasted waiting on medical help. When my child was hurt with potential life threatening injuries last year, I didn't call the paramedics. When I saw that my child was in trouble I immediately swooped her up and put her in my car and called *55 on my way to the hospital in Shawnee. The OHP met me on Highway 18 on the north side of Meeker and escorted me through all the traffic and lights on the way to the hospital ER physicians were waiting on me at the entrance. I want to be clear that I do not condone moving an injured child and rushing them to the hospital in any circumstance. Driving while in a state of fear and high adrenaline is very dangerous. My point is, living rurally, you think about things differently and you realize how long it could take to for help to arrive. I am very close to my mother and she is such a powerful prayer warrior in every time of stress in my life. But it never crossed my mind to call her when my child's life was in danger. My only thought was getting my child medical help immediately. It was only after arriving at the hospital and knowing my daughter was in the hands of medical professionals that I called my mom so that she could pray. I find it very, very odd that Mike called his mother in law before calling paramedics. Why would he do that? He absolutely should have called paramedics first. To do anything other than seek medical help first shows a different area of concern than Kelsey's welfare.

Posted by "Jim" Sunday, February 26, 2006 @ 1:45 PM - K.J., Gayla beat the first responders there. I think I would call the

215

closest help. I live a little farther out then their house, and I know there is someone closer then the fire station that I would call at certain times of the day. I don't know just what I would in a spot like that, thank God I have not.

Posted by "KJ" Sunday, February 26, 2006 @ 2:13 PM - So is Gayla in the medical profession? I guess when she arrived she knew what medical treatment to administer. That must be why he called her first.

Posted by "KJ" Sunday, February 26, 2006 @ 2:14 PM - I suppose if my mom were a medical professional and knew she could arrive before paramedics then I would have called her first too.

Posted by "KJ" Sunday, February 26, 2006 @ 2:32 PM - Was the mother in law a physician? Was she a paramedic? Mike was already doing CPR. Did she have medically advanced training more than CPR (which was already being done) that would have benefited Kelsey? If the answers to those questions are no then I must question why Mike Porter did not call paramedics first.

Mike Porter had told the investigators that he performed CPR on Kelsey. Yet there was no evidence to back up his claim. When his friend arrived, he was standing outside the home with Kelsey on his shoulder. When Gayla arrived, he still stood there, waiting, with several vehicles in the driveway. Gayla said one of the vehicles was her truck and the keys were in it. Why did he not take Kelsey to the hospital?

The topic suddenly changed to the fact that the house that Porter and Raye had purchased from Gayla was up for sale.

Posted by "sew&sew" Monday, February 27, 2006 @ 8:06 AM - TO ALL: Here's my thought for anyone even considering buying "Hell House". Hire and independent inspector. Have them go over that house, septic, well system with a fine tooth comb. Ensure the sf is correct and take it from there. Don't trust any home inspector that [Gayla's friend and realtor] (bitch) recommends!!!! Oh-don't know if it's true but I understood that Mike's name was never put on the house...if that's correct then he wouldn't necessarily have to sign papers to sell as I understand it.

Posted by "sew&sew" Monday, February 27, 2006 @ 8:07 AM - COME ALONG WITH ME TO FANTASY ISLAND: I think it would be lovely if we could raise enough money to buy Hell House. We could then invite everyone we know & love as well as the Smith clan to the housewarming. Of course the housewarming would entails about 100 gallons of gas and a match. L. Anthony

Posted by "sew&sew" aka Mike Porter Monday, February 27, 2006 @ 8:10 AM - FANTASY ISLAND TRIP NUMBER 2: Raise enough money to hire the best forensic team in the country to go over Hell House with a fine tooth comb. Granted I'm sure it's been cleaned from top to bottom but still I bet the CSI team from Las Vegas could find SOMETHING to kick RD & Mike's butts. Dang-I gotta quit watching so much TV!!!!! ☺

Mike Porter worked to get the bashboard members riled up and back on the hate Raye train yelling "no deals," because Kelsey did not get a deal. Later, Porter would benefit from a deal. However, the bullies could not have a rational discussion.

Posted by "A voice for Kelsey" aka Mike Porter [unknown date and time] - I am asking EVERYONE TODAY to write and call both the DA and Judge [E] in regards to Kelsey's case. Tell them that this $25,000 bail that was set was in insult to little Kelsey, and that the public WILL NOT accept any preferential treatment of Raye Dawn. She SHOULD NOT have been given a two day notice that she was going to be required to turn herself in and she should have been arrested, just like the criminal she is suspected of being. PLEASE tell them that NO DEALS should be made with this woman. Kelsey got no...[remainder of post lost in printing]

*Posted by [unknown person] Monday, February 27, 2006 @ 11:11
AM - [first part of post lost in printing]...the welfare of this
new baby. We all have to do this in numbers! There should be
no deal-no reason for it. The DA's case is solid against Mike
w/ou Raye Dawn's testimony, or so he has said-NO DEALS,
period! Let the jurors decide what she gets!*

Back to the conspiracy theory...

*Posted by "Anonymous" Monday, February 27, 2006 @ 12:22 PM -
The D.A. is in on it. Judge [E] is in on it. Raye Dawn will
walk. The Smith's know this. This case has got to go national.
They are corrupt. Richard Smothermon and Judge [E]. WE
need the help from someone big.*

*Posted by "on the positive side" Monday, February 27, 2006 @
12:35 PM - I for one am going to pray that Richard
Smothermon, and all the others involved in investigating, and
solving this case, have far more information than we do, and
are doing the best for Kelsey and the Briggs family. I believe
that the Smiths have shown the kind of people that they are by
disgracing Kelsey's name with their actions, just as the
Briggs have honored her. I will pray that justice is done for
Kelsey.*

*Posted by "Anonymous" Monday, February 27, 2006 @ 12:52 PM -
There is no positive side to this...there is undercover stuff
going on, and we as citizens HAVE to stop this now!*

*Posted by "Anonymous" Monday, February 27, 2006 @ 2:07 PM -
Undercover, pay-offs, Ha, you guys watch too much TV.*

*Posted by "Anonymous" Monday, February 27, 2006 @ 2:24 PM -
I'm not talking about pay-offs. I'm talking about a group of
men trying their best to cover each others asses and to
appease everyone involved. This is no joke. There is a lot of
underhanded stuff going on here. Don't be so naïve. Both of
those people should be behind bars right now and neither one
of them are! Bottom line. That speaks volumes to me. What
the hell is going on in Oklahoma. People, Pull yourselves*

together and get out there with signs and raise some hell. Get the media out there to cover it.

Posted by "A voice for Kelsey" aka Mike Porter Monday, February 27, 2006 @ 2:28 PM - Anon, you are exactly right! This is EXACTLY what is going on, and anyone that thinks we're being ridiculous or funny about this is NAÏVE. This is exactly what's going on. They are afraid that someone is going to get hung out to dry over all the wrong-doing in the case, and so there are trying to cover each other's asses, PERIOD. I don't know who posted that comment about watching too much TV, but I guess YOU DON'T WATCH ENOUGH about Kelsey's story to know we're speaking the truth, OR you are a cheerleader for those responsible. Don't post on here unless you are here to help us!

Posted by "Anonymous" Monday, February 27, 2006 @ 2:41 PM - Smothermon, [Judge E], Key have communicated with each other and are working it so the situation plays out a certain way. The path of least resistance and to the benefit of themselves. It is obvious, so obvious. In their minds, none of what they are doing has anything to do with Kelsey it has to do with Judge Key. The 25,000K bond shows that [Judge E] is corrupt. Someone made sure he set that bail amt. So R.D. wouldn't have to stay in prison. National coverage is the ticket to justice. GET OUT THERE EVERDAY FOREVER AND PROTEST!!! Work it out in shifts. Some people do Mondays, some do Tues and so forth and so on. Protest over the bail amt! protest that Mike Porter is out of jail. These are specifics to draw attention to. I mean for Gods sake a person charged with first degree murder out on bail!!! It's unheard of. PROTEST THESE THINGS EVERYDAY! Take a shift.

With all of the hate directed toward Raye, Mike Porter's role and his charges were somehow forgotten. Someone finally expressed a rational opinion about Mike Porter being free on bail. Why wasn't this the topic of discussion all along?

Posted by "Anonymous" Monday, February 27, 2006 @ 3:05 PM - Those guys are all professional friends of one another. They like to keep everything cordial. They have coffee together and dinner or they may frequent the same country club. They speak and know each other. They are on friendly terms. This is not about Kelsey. This is about them! And whats best for THEM! How would they feel if Kelsey was their granddaughter or daughter? A BIT DIFFERENT, I can tell you that without a doubt.

Posted by "Anonymous" Monday, February 27, 2006 @ 3:07 PM - PROTEST THE DECISIONS THAT ARE MADE IN THIS CASE, IF THEY ARE NOT RIGHT. SIMPLE AS THAT.

Posted by "sew&sew" Monday, February 27, 2006 @ 5:08 PM - What harm would it do to also start complaining to the State Attorney General (Drew Edmonson), the State Legislators, and the Oklahoma Bar association on the DA and judges? It sure can't hurt can it?

Posted by "Anonymous" Monday, February 27, 2006 @ 5:24 PM - That's a good suggestion. But everyone has to do it. One of two letters aren't enough. It has to be 50-100. Is everyone willing to sit down. Write letters that are written well, typed well, folded the correct way etc. It takes time and effort. And not just one but 100. A list of the specific things that are wrong need to be organized, communicated and letters sent. Just like the protesting, one day or just a few people isn't enough. Also the complaints need to be organized and founded in whats normal or average in the law. And if the decisions that have been made are not the normal or average, then why? Why are these two people being treated differently?

Posted by "sew&sew" Monday, February 27, 2006 @ 5:38 PM - Anon (5:24). YOU HIT THE NAIL ON THE HEAD! I'm going to do some research and get some info on here on how to contact the folks suggested in my 5:08 post.

Posted by "Kathie W" Monday, February 27, 2006 @ 6:10 PM - Here is the letter I am sending: Richard L. Smothermon, District Attorney Pottawatomie County Courthouse [address removed for privacy] Dear Mr. Smothermon: I recently came across a case in your district involving a small child, Kelsey Smith-Briggs, who was apparently killed by her parents, Michael Porter and Raye Dawn (Smith) Porter. I live in California and have no direct connection to the case whatsoever. However, the facts of the case are intriguing and upon further investigation on it seems that the case is quickly gaining a vast following from all over the United States. I did some research on the case, and am struck by the seeming lack of diligence practiced by the Meeker, Oklahoma police, DHS, the judicial system, and even your own office's investigation. I believe that this case will soon become spotlighted by national attention, which will unveil all of the facts since child abuse was first suspected in Kelsey's case, nearly a year before her death. I urge you to do everything in your power to thoroughly investigate and prosecute Raye Dawn Porter, as well as Michael Porter. As I said, I am in no way connected to the Meeker community, but upon my own investigation, it seems apparent that there is a cover-up going on regarding Raye Dawn Porter. As this case continues to gain national attention, I hope you understand that you and your community will be scrutinized by many across the country. You have the power now to acknowledge the mistakes that have been made in this case, continue to investigate thoroughly noting any and all inconsistencies in the parties' statements which are obviously self-serving after the fact, bring any and all appropriate charges against those involved in Kelsey's death, and prosecute Raye Dawn and Mike Porter to the full extent of the law. Finally, please take action to the full extent of the law in protecting the unborn child of Raye Dawn Porter. With 20/20 hindsight in mind, the law should err on the side of caution in light of the circumstances and the child should be removed from Raye Dawn's care immediately upon his birth.

Posted by "Anonymous" Monday, February 27, 2006 @ 6:19 PM - O.k. Lets make a list. Everyone add to it. Everyone writes all of these...justice. I made the comments before about the DA taking his time with charges because I truly believe that he was gathering evidence against Raye Dawn. "In the

221

meantime" which could only strengthen his case. But I do understand the frustration of all involved.

Posted by "sew&sew" Monday, February 27, 2006 @ 6:27 PM - Anon (5:24) I'm going to brainstorm here and throw this out as well. If you call to express your concerns, please—be courteous & calm. Keep it simple; state your concerns (i.e. "I've been following the Kelsey Briggs' case & am concerned as to how the DA , Judge...& Judge...handled it". I am now even more concerned that the DA is working "deals" with those charged. As a citizen & taxpayer I do not support this idea and want to express that I do not want it to happen". This is me brainstorming, not trying to tell you guys what to say or not say or even how to say it. You know your concerns and what you want done (or not done)...so be explicit, get to the point & tell them what you EXPECT them to do (investigate, etc.) and tell them what you DO NOT WANT (i.e., no deals, a competency hearing for the DA & judges, etc). Also, some folks are more articulate in their written product. Be polite, some folks are more articulate in their written product. Be polite, concerned and just get to the point about what you are complaing about and what you want done if your choose to write a letter. Something is better than nothing (in my opinion). Again....I'm just brainstorming...I know what I want to suggest to you good folks...just perhaps have fallen short of how to do it. Thank you as always for letting me throw things out here!

Posted by "sew&sew" Monday, February 27, 2006 @ 6:29 PM - Katie W's letter is awesome! I'm thinking now you all can take my brainstorming ideas and ignore them! LOL

As "Kathie W" stated herself, she was outside of Oklahoma and did not know anyone involved in the case, or what Raye did when the news cameras were shoved in her face. A previous poster claimed that she always looked "mean," but now she "smiled and waved to the cameras"? This must have been another story taken as truth on this bashboard. This gang mentality was hindering the investigation with Mike Porter begging them to send letters and complaining about

Raye's treatment while the Smith family members worked for true justice for Kelsey and the imprisonment of Mike Porter. "Kathie W" posted another sample letter, ensuring that the bashboard bullies would convey the correct message to the recipient.

> Posted by "Kathie W" Monday, February 27, 2006 @ 7:56 PM -
> Another "sample letter"...haven't proof read it and may not
> have all the facts correct (I'm tired). Just trying to throw out
> some ideas. Dear_____I have been
> following the Kelsey Smith-Briggs case closely. As the case
> has unfolded, it is apparent the many mistakes were made in
> the case, including...(DHS failing to listen to numerous
> complaints of abuse, obvious injuries from abuse being
> justified as "accidents", etc.) Additionally, obvious conflicts
> of interest took place during the investigation that hint at
> serious corruption in the community's legal system. One
> example is allowing Dr. Kelly Koons to testify regarding
> Kelsey's injuries in the case involving returning Kelsey to her
> mother, Raye Dawn Porter. Dr. Koons is the sister of
> Kelsey's Raye Dawn's attorney, which is an obvious conflict
> of interest. Based on her testimony and against the
> recommendation of DHS, Kelsey was returned to her
> mother's home, where she was murdered four months later.
> Recently, Raye Dawn Porter was provided the luxury of two
> days' notice prior to being charged with two felonies, and
> was allowed to turn herself in just prior to appearing in court
> on the charges. Her arrest took an appalling 4 months after
> Kelsey's death. To add insult to injury, her bail was set at an
> abysmal $25,000 for her part in the murder of her innocent 2
> year old daughter. I witnessed her demeanor on the new
> following that hearing where she smugly smiled and waved to
> the news cameras as she left the court parking lot. It is
> apparent that even she knows that the system has allowed her
> to continue to be treated preferentially with no real
> accountability. It is an outrage and sends a strong negative
> message about our political system in Lincoln County to the
> thousands and thousands of people following this case across
> the nation. Most importantly, it is a disgrace to the memory
> of Kelsey Smith-Briggs. It seems that the system continues to
> fail her...

Kathie Briggs made a large production about Kelsey's doctor being Raye's attorney's sister (Raye's attorney during the custody battle, not her defense attorney). According to reports, Kathie Briggs did what she had reportedly done with every one of Kelsey's doctors…she told each doctor that Kelsey was abused and that Raye Dawn was the perpetrator. When Kathie discovered the relationship between Kelsey's doctor and Raye's attorney, she had a fit. She did not realize to who she was speaking or telling stories. She later had Lance Briggs file lawsuits against Kelsey's doctor, which were thrown out of court.

Posted by "A voice for Kelsey" aka Mike Porter Monday, February 27, 2007 @ 9:08 PM - There is a complaint form you can get from the Oklahoma Bar Association that is especially for judical complaints and also one for lawyer complaints. Their fairly easy to fill out. If each and every one of us fills one out, they will get the message that we wont take these corrupt judges anymore. What about the DA…is the State Attorney Genral who we complain to?

Posted by "A voice for Kelsey" aka Mike Porter Monday, February 27, 2006 @ 9:18 PM - Kathie W – We cannot tell you. HOW MUCH we appreciate people like you taking time to write letters, and even share them with folks so they too can write and call. Some people know what they want to say, but cant put it into words. We need people like you on our team. PLEASE, I am asking EVERYONE on here to write these letters and call, and send the sample letter to anyone that you think would do the same. If they have a response in numbers, it will have a great effect! PLEASE, we have to do this for little Kelsey. She deserved so much more in her little life, and she deserves so much more now! She as cheated before her death, and she's been cheated now. ☺

Posted by "sew&sew" Monday, February 27, 2006 @ 11:18 PM - You know what I think? This is the best group of folks around. Oh yeah, once in awhile we get some b.s. from "you know who" and her clan…but as long as we all stick together we can get a lot done. I'm thinking…isn't there something on

224

Oprah's web page about Kelsey? If so, it might not hurt to post a request there for folks to write our legal reps...the more nationwide this goes the better. Heck why not send it to the Washington Post or New York Times? Nothing ventured nothing gained I say!!!! I think it's time we really start putting the screws to these folks.

Posted by "sew&sew" Monday, February 27, 2006 @ 11:19 PM - Another thought...get this info to Rose O'Donnell...she is a big advocate for children...she might take an interest.

Posted by "sew&sew" Monday, February 27, 2006 @ 11:24 PM - AVFK (9:08) Why not send one to the State Attorney General & one to the Oklahoma Bar Association? Nothing to lose in my opinion!!!

Posted by "Anonymous" Monday, February 27, 2006 @ 11:31 PM - The state attorney general has no oversight power. He is basically the lawyer for the State of Oklahoma. The only oversight to DA's is the OBA. As for Judge's good luck. They have to screw up SO royally to come under review it is not even funny. Like Judge Key did.

Posted by "Anonymous" Monday, February 27, 2006 @ 11:39 PM - A grand Jury would be the best idea and would expose the truth – the Attorney General would never call for it. Richard would insist it was not necessary.

Posted by "sew&sew" Monday, February 27, 2006 @ 11:41 PM - Anon (11:39) Okay-but then someone above the DA should be empowered to call one shouldn't they? Any idea who that might be? Thank you!

Posted by ""Anonymous" Monday, February 27, 2006 @ 11:43 PM - It would be the attorney general I beleive that we as citizens can prompt one but I think it is a signature thing. A Grand Jury would expose how incompetent these officials have truly been. I am telling you Richard cancelled the grand jury because of what he was afraid it would lead to. The GJ was the most powerful fact finding weapon in his arsenal and he chose not to use it.

Posted by "sew&sew" Monday, February 27, 2008 @ 11:46 PM - Anon (11:43) I agree with you on the Smothermon/GJ fiasco. I'm just wondering about the procedures or what it takes to get a Grand Jury called to investigate him & perhaps the judges as well. Maybe you've answered my question & I'm just too thick brained to "get it".

Posted by "sew&sew" Monday, February 27, 2006 @ 11:56 PM - I went & found this on who can call a grand jury. Section II-18 Grand Jury. [sew&sew posted the entire section of the law on grand juries]

Posted by [unknown person] Tuesday, February 28, 2006 @ 12:14 PM - She will go down – trust me on that. She is not afraid because she is too stupid to be afraid. She has gotten away wioth everything she has ever doen in her life and she thinks she will get away with this too. Didn't you see her smiling and waving when she left the courthouse? She thinks this is all a joke. Sad excuse for a mother.

Posted by "billygoat" Tuesday, February 28, 2006 @ 12:15 PM - Where does your smugness and cockiness come from? You people are so damn arrogant its pathetic. You know, you would think raye dawn and her family would want justice for Kelsey too instead of constantly having people talk her up. What a bunch of self-centered losers, they don't enen KNOW the true raye dawn.

This next statement came from someone who obviously did not side with the gang of bullies. Did Raye smile and wave? I'm not sure. I have only seen clips of her with a serious face or crying. Raye knew about the bashboard and what this gang was trying to do to her. But she did not realize that Mike Porter's voice had been one of the loudest of all.

*Posted by "Anonymous" Tuesday, February 28, 2006 @ 12:16 PM -
She was smiling because the judge believed her and knows
she didn't do it. She is glad that he can filter truth from lies.*

*Posted by "Anonymous" Tuesday, February 28, 2006 @ 12:16 PM -
She is a great mom? WOW. If your definition of a great mom
is either abusing her child or allowing her to be abused for 9
months then the world needs a whole lot fewer GREAT
MOMS. Smith family definition of a GREAT MOM =
alcoholic slutty woman who either abuses her child or lets
her child be abused and does nothing and then claims she is
the victim. Let's just hope that her greatness as a mom does
not lead to another child death. She has already got rid of 2.*

Raye had actually been pregnant twice. She was just a few weeks
pregnant when she says that Lance got mad at her in front of one of
his friends and he punched her so hard in the stomach that she fell
backward onto the bed. She miscarried later that night and when she
went to the hospital for the constant cramping, she was pulled aside
and reportedly told that the embryo detached from the uterus. How
was that her fault?

*Posted by "A voice for Kelsey" aka Mike Porter Tuesday, February
28, 2006 12:17 PM - Anonymous 12:08, you are as
IGNORANT as you sound. IF Mike is the one that abused and
killed baby, the mother knew...there is NO WAY she didn't,
and you are a stupid fool to think she didn't, and is totally
innocent. She didn't deserve Kelsey and she doesn't deserve
this baby. And she only getting special treatment (low bail,
ability to turn herself in, 2 days notice, etc) because of who
she is and because there is a bunch of underhandedness
bullshit going on. BUT we as supporters of justice for Kelsey,
will continue seek justice for her, and NOT let this injustice
occur. We WILL raise hell and make sure that ALL these
people responsible in her death and held accountable.
$25,000 for bail is an insult to Kelsey – all her suffereing and
her horrible death. Once again, she only got that because of
her buddies in the Lincoln County legal system. And her
family – well they ALL showed their asses that day, and
showed what they are about. Now go on and find Julie, Sara,*

and the rest of you idiots that believe this woman is innocent – you are ALL going to pay when judgement day comes for failing Kelsey so miserably. Its good you show up here from time to time to liven up this board! It gives us the incentive to keep doing what we are. Obviously you and the rest of the supporters aren't doing SHIT to help find justice for Kelsey.

Posted by "billygoat" Tuesday, February 28, 2006 @ 12:17 PM - Great mom, thanks for the laugh.

Posted by "Anonymous" [unknown date and time] - The Judge believed her? DO you think the Judge has anything to do with this? She plead not guilty whih means her fate will be up to a jury. If you wanna know how common people feel about her and her innocence go look at any poll taken and look at the 97% of people who feel she should rot in prison.

Once again, posts are missing. But you get the point.

Posted by [unknown person] Tuesday, February 28, 2006 @ 1:06 PM - That was a powerful post by anon 12:44. If people cant close their eyes and picture their own children being beaten and take action then there is not much hope.

Posted by "A voice for Kelsey" aka Mike Porter Tuesday, February 28, 2006 @ 1:18 PM - I just heard from a close personal friend that one of the justice for Kelsey supporters from VIRGINIA called Judge [E] yesterday to talk to him about Kelsey's case. Following their conversations, she is VERY worried about ANY justice being served from that little girl. He is very smug and takes child abuse very lightly. Its as if he has not a care in the world for what Kelsey went through, nor any of the other abused kids. ALL of us need to call and write TODAY, ask them when his term in up, and that he WILL be voted out if he gives this mother ANY preferential treatment – in my opinion, he already has, but these judges continue to play God, and this has to be stopped. Like anonymous said above, Kelsey needs us, and we ALL have to stand up and do something about this. CALL, WRITE, and commit your time for on hour TODAY to a protest! PLEASE, we have to be this little girls voice!

The hate for Raye and her family from this gang had spread from coast-to-coast. Judges, the district attorney, and investigators were flooded with phone calls and letters from people who appeared to hate Raye just as much as the Briggs even though they knew no real facts in the case and were being told false stories. How quickly they were deceived by Mike Porter and the Briggs. He was trying to escape the death penalty. The Briggs hated Raye and had other motives.

Posted by "Anonymous" Tuesday, February 28, 2006 @ 1:24 PM - Can we legally take out a one page add in the chandler or Shawnee paper telling people not to vote for these people again and what they are all about.

Posted by "Anonymous" Tuesday, February 28, 2006 @ 1:32 PM - NO, they will sue you for liable.

Posted by "billygoat" Tuesday, February 28, 2006 @ 1:38 PM - She may be completely right but I wouldn't put alot of anything into his reaction to her. no offense to her, but he is probably a busy man and was not real concerned with someones thoughts from Virginia, maybe he is like this to everyone, I don't know, but in all honesty, I wouldn't expect him to act overly concerned during a phone call such as that.

Posted by "Anonymous" Tuesday, February 28, 2006 @ 1:40 PM - Judge [E] would not even be presiding over her trial.

Posted by "Anonymous" Tuesday, February 28, 2006 @ 1:51 PM - You can take out an ad in the paper and say we will not be voting for these people because of the ay they handled the Kelsey Briggs case and then stat the facts – Stepfather out on $250,000 bond. Grand Jury called and then cancelled. Mother allowed to turn herself in and then given a ridiculous bond amount and allowed to walk free too. The DA's statement that he has not decided whether or not to take the baby or not. As long as the statements are factual it is ok. I would make the last line of the AD – "WE THE VOTERS OF

229

*THIS DISTRICT ARE WATCHING THE EVENTS OF THIS
CASE VERY CLOSELY. WE WILL NOT STAND FOR
DEALS, FAVOROTISM, OR SPECIAL TREATMENT OF
ANYONE DIRECTLY OR INDIRECTLY INVOLVED IN THE
DEATH OF KELSEY BRIGGS."*

*Posted by "billygoat" Tuesday, February 28, 2006 @ 1:56 PM -
How do you know its not [Judge E]? If not him, who?*

*Posted by "MistyLT" Tuesday, February 28, 2006 @ 1:58 PM -
Sounds like a good idea*

*Posted by "billygoat" Tuesday, February 28, 2006 @ 2:03 PM - I
read in the Shawnee paper today that it cost the city $2,100
for 3 full pages to list the warrents last weekend. We are
talking about $700 a page. Looks like we to start taking up
donations now!*

*Posted by [unknown person] Tuesday, February 28, 2006 @ 4:40
PM - How is this Kathie's fault? I don't get it.*

Mike Porter kept the topic of his son on the front burner. The group
started gearing up in February for the huge campaign they would push
once the baby was born.

*Posted by "Anonymous" Tuesday, February 28, 2006 @ 4:44 PM -
The baby can be taken more easily after she's convicted. If he
is still alive.*

*Posted by "Anonymous" Tuesday, February 28, 2006 @ 4:47 PM -
The Smith's think it is Kathie's fault. Gayla's boyfriend said
that on TV. So did Raye Dawn's brother Curtis on Channel
25. They honestly blame Kathie instead of blaming Raye
Dawn and Mike. Hell even Mike's family thinks he was
wrong for not protecting Kelsey even though they know he is
innocent of killing her. The Smith's are the only ones stupid
enough to make this about RD and Kathie and not Kelsey.
And anon @ 4:38 – I would not put too much stake in what*

Smothermon says. He does not keep his word much. He is working a deal with her right now.

Posted by "Anonymous" Tuesday, February 28, 2006 @ 4:47 PM - I don't even know how Raye Dawn can walk around and function since Kelsey is gone. I would want to die.

Posted by "Anonymous" Tuesday, February 28, 2006 @ 4:49 PM - I am sure she is not stupid enough to hurt the baby while she is still Public Enemy #1. But that would be a hell of a way for our DA to find out he was wrong.

Posted by "Anonymous" Tuesday, February 28, 2006 @ 4:51 PM - She was functioning fine the day after. That is a fact. She is not a normal person. But you listen to the Smith's and she is the picture perfect mom. If she is a great mom then I had a crappy Mom and I am SO glad I didn't have a great mom. A mother is someone who puts their children above all else. Raye Dawn has NEVER done that she was not taught how to. I still don't' get how they think it's Kathie's fault Kelsey was abused and killed under Miek and Raye Dawn's care. The Smith's are just bad people who want to be bad. It's ridiculous.

Posted by "MistyLT" Tuesday, February 28, 2006 @ 4:52 PM - I only see one charge on ODCR. I'm going to assume that they just don't have the other one there yet.

Posted by "Anonymous" Tuesday, February 28, 2006 @ 4:54 PM - Ask [Gayla's friend] He was adamant that is was Kathie's fault. He fits in very well with that family's victim mentality. HE must feel like a hero – he gets to save two white trash damsels in distress.

The "white trash" portrayal of the Smiths came from the Briggs and their friends in the media. It's always interesting when people who spend time with the Smith family members before they learn who they are. They do not fit the picture that the media painted. On the other hand...Judge Key's replacement on the bench had refused to get involved in the case when Kelsey was alive. She called Kathie Briggs "white trash" and said she did not want to work with her. Her tune changed when Kathie Briggs became her ticket to winning the election.

Posted by "Anonymous" Tuesday, February 28, 2006 @ 5:01 PM -
Anon-4:12, you said "us people" are all talk and no action.
Believe me when I say, if the general public had a say in raye
dawns case…justice would be swift and harsh you can take
that to the bank.

This would be just one of many threats to Raye's life by this gang.

Posted by "billygoat" Tuesday, February 28, 2006 @ 5:03 PM -
Tryin to be a hero and winds up still being a zero but I'm
[Gayla's friend]
BITCH!

Posted by "Anonymous"
Tuesday, February   "Richard seems to
28, 2006 @ 5:11
PM - But Raye   think he works for them
Dawn thinks she is
a star and everyone   too…" Kathie Briggs to
loves her!! Didn't
you see them wave   Mike Porter
to their admirers as
they drove off from
the courthouse?
Everybody loves
her! (Well, the DA
and Judges do
anyway)

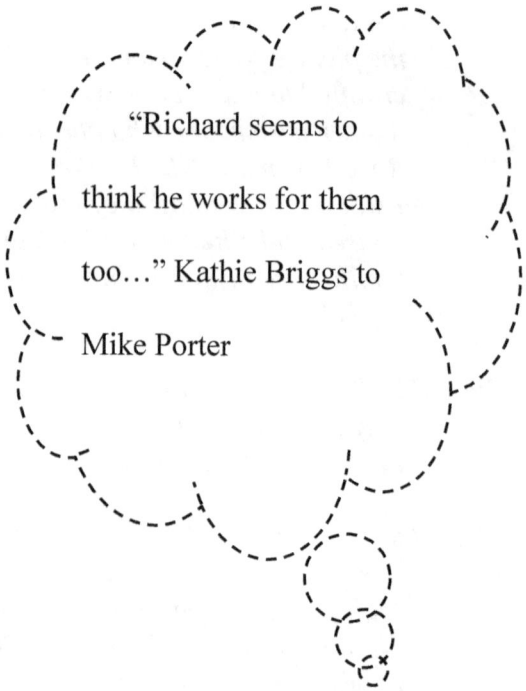

Posted by "Anonymous"
Tuesday, February
28, 2006 @ 7:26 PM - Funny but sad and true. RD has two
lawyers now. [Her attorney] and Richard.

Posted by "sew&sew" Tuesday, February 28, 2006 @ 7:42 PM -
Looks like it was one "heck of a day"! It is so obvious when

RD & her clan get on here isn't it? If RD is such a great mom I would hate to see a bad one wouldn't you? And isn't it curious they find it so necessary to sing RDs praises yet have little to say about Kelsey? Well, no really it isn't strange...because RD is a "victim", she has always been a "victim" and will always continue to be a "victim". They can try & blame Kathie for crap all they want. The ONLY THING AKTHIE BRIGGS IS "GUILTY" OF IS LOVING HER GRANDDAUGHTER AND TRYING TO GET HER AWAY FROM THE ABUSE those dumbasses were allowing! They are just pissed off because Kathie stepped in to try & get Kelsey away from the abuse when they KNEW about it and did nothing! What a bunch of ignorant, stupid, trashy morons. In my mind Raye Dawn believes she did nothing wrong ("they hate me because I'm beautiful" attitude). Well little girl-you may be decent looking on the outside but you are one ugly bitch on the inside!

Someone had obviously seen enough of the hate and lies.

*Posted by "Anonymous" Wednesday, March 1, 2006 @ 2:57 AM -
FUCK YOU ALL BITCHES YOU ARE A BUNCH OF NIT-PICKING, CANNABALISTIC, GOSSIP FREAKS. YOU CAN'T MIND YOUR OWN BUSINESS, AND IT IS STARTING TO REALLY PISS ME OFF. YOU'RE RIGHT, LET JUST BE DONE. LET THE COUNTY SEAT DO IT. YOU GUYS NEED TO BACK THE HELL OUT. NOW FUCK YOU.*

*Posted by "Anonymous" Wednesday, March 1, 2006 @ 3:06 AM -
ONE MORE THING, I THINK PEOPLE SHOULD KNOW WHO YOU ARE. SO BE EXPECTING THAT INFORMATION SOON. YOU'VE HURT A LOT OF INNOCENT PEOPLE AND THEY DESERVE JUSTICE AS WELL. PICK THAT ONE OVER.*

*Posted by "MistyLT" Wednesday, March 1, 2006 @ 5:48 AM -
Hmmm, such anger at 3:00 in the morning. Anon 3:06 – Not to be a smartass but I'm just curious as to if you do not like*

this site then why are you here, and why are you here at 3:00
in the morning?

Posted by "Anonymous" Wednesday, March 1, 2006 @ 7:48 AM
That was Raye dawn or her family. It's obvious.

But it wasn't Raye or her family members. They read the various
bashboards and printed posts, but they never participated. They
worked with the OSBI and the district attorney to try to get the
bashboards (including the Kelsey's Purpose forum) shut down, but to
no avail. When I first became involved in fighting the hate, I was
continually called a Smith. Since Raye was in jail, they called me
Rachelle. Anyone who could see past the hate had to be a Smith in the
eyes of these bullies.

Posted by "treemonkey" Wednesday, March 1, 2006 @ 7:53 AM -
Funny how raye dawn or her "support group" get on here
talking smack at a time they knew there would be no one
here. Seems they must have a hard time sleeping at night
hmmm, wonder why?

Posted by "Anonymous" Wednesday, March 1, 2006 @ 8:06 AM -
What does she mean by, "I think people should know who
you are." I don't think "people" would mind since 98% of
the population feel the same way we do. And the other 5%
have Smith as a last name. I'm really scared!!! Ha! Ha! Ha!
What a freak show!

Posted by "treemonkey" Wednesday, March 1, 2006 @ 8:17 AM -
They should know who we are, but they posted under anon.
yep, that sounds like them special treatment for themselves
and screw everybody elses rights.

In the next post, the "Rainbow" is mentioned. It is the small town
of Meeker's gas station, coffee shop, and presumably gossip mill.

Posted by "MistyLT" Wednesday, March 1, 2006 @ 8:19 AM - They
don't like this board bc people talk. Okay, but do they go into
the Rainbow or anywhere else when people are talking about
this and scream at them to stop? I'm pretty sure we all still

have freedom of speech even though they government is slowly taking that away too.

Battle for the Bashboard

March, 2006

As of March of 2006, the bashboard was owned and operated by Mistylt. She was a mother of three children, married, and a woman the Briggs claimed was in love with Mike Porter. Although the Briggs family members had participated in and were "addicted to" the bashboard, it was soiling their reputation. The damage being done was even worse than what they were doing as themselves on their Kelsey's Purpose forum. They were the state's bullies, whether they did it under their own names or hid behind anonymous identities. But I guess they did not realize it at the time. The Briggs were trying to pass a law and promote themselves as upstanding citizens. They had to at least put on a public display of shutting down their beloved bashboard.

| *kjbriggs*
Kelsey's Grandma
⭐⭐⭐⭐⭐

Posts: 1,208
Group: Administrators
Joined: Nov 2005
Status:
Reputation: | **RE: Governor Proclaims "Kelsey Briggs Day"**   Post: #20

This is some of the wording on the Proclamation we received last night.

Whereas, despite efforts to protect young people from harm, lives are lost each year to child abuse and neglect, with 51 Oklahoma children dying in 2004 alone, and

Whereas, the horror and tragedy of child abuse was felt once again on October 11, 2005, when two-year old Kelsey Briggs was senselessly taken from this world; and

Whereas, while no one can ever bring back Kelsey or erase the pain of her loss, the tragedy of her premature death has focused new attention on the horrible crime of child abuse; and

Whereas, with the help of that attention, the hard work of dedicated citizens and the grace of God, it is hoped that child abuse can not only be reduced but ultimately eliminated from our society.

Now, therefore, I Brad Henry, Governor of the State of Oklahoma, do hereby proclaim April 29, 2006, as "Kelsey Briggs Day" in the State of Oklahoma. |
| 04-28-2006 09:03 AM | 🔒 PM   🔍 FIND |

Was it a sudden change of heart and they realized that Mike Porter was guilty? Or were they once again protecting him as Shirica and Kathie stated in their e-mails? Shirica posted the following message on the Kelsey's Purpose forum:

Shirica Posts: 63 Statement Regarding the Bashboard - I would like to stress to everyone who visits our site, that the Briggs Family (me especially) in no way supports the bashboard

237

*that has been set up. When **it was originally created with the permission of the Briggs Family** but has since then requested it be removed. It has not been removed even though we were told it could be taken down anytime we felt it was not appropriate. Well, it is most definitely not appropriate and the Briggs Family is strongly against its existence. I have told everyone who will listen to me that **it is nothing but a place for Mike Porter to twist his truth and get people to have reasonable doubt to keep him from being convicted of murdering our precious Kelsey**. I will not be a part of that and I strongly urge the rest of you to do the same. Turn your energy into something positive. Our family has asked yet again for it to be shut down only to find out that it is still there but it is being run by a different member of this site. I find that to be quite disappointing. That bashbaord has caused our family pain and yet it is still there. The new person who is running it has recently apologized to our family for jumping to conclusions that were incorrect (conclusions that were discussed on that bashboard) and yet it is now being run by that same person. How sincere was the apology? Please forgive me if this post seems harsh, but I cannot stress enough how strongly I feel about this issue. Anyone posting on it, I am afraid, could be asking for trouble. It is being monitored by many who are interested. I would hate for people to be on there posting stuff that should not be posted that could end up in court defending what they have said. Please, please take our wishes into consideration and join with me to ban this awful site. I do apologize if I have offended people by posting this, but so many other people are being offended by posting on the bashboard. I feel the emotions that came out in court last week may only be the beginning and I feel a lot of the anger that is being expressed between the different families involved is partly **because of the hate that is being generated on that basbhboard**.[27] Please consider what I have said. Thank you for your time and God bless each and every one of you. Shirica*

---

[27] Emphasis by book author

Instead of the bashboard shutting down, it sprung to life in protest. Mike Porter and Misty would not follow orders. People were buying the story he was selling and he needed the support to save his life.

Posted by "Soccermom" Wednesday, March 1, 2006 @ 8:33 AM - I don't know if anyone has touched on this yet but if you search on odcr.com it shows that Raye Dawn filed for a protective order against Kathie & Lance on Oct. 12. Does that sound like a grieving mother or a guilty murderer who is afraid the people who actually loved Kelsey might come after her?

Posted by "Anonymous" Wednesday, March 1, 2006 @ 8:39 AM - This was just one of many of her questionable actions.

On the day of Kelsey's death, Lance Briggs reportedly called a supervisor at DHS and stated that he would break into his home and kill him and his family and then break into Judge Key's home and kill him and his family. Because Lance made the call from the mental facility he had been placed in at Fort Benning, Georgia after allegedly threatening to commit suicide when his wife told him she wanted a divorce, the authorities took the threat as credible. Since there was a history of violence between Raye and Lance with Lance pleading "no contest" to assaulting Raye, it was suggested that she file a protective order against him. Judge Key's home was guarded by the sheriff department and he had to send his kids to stay with relatives and have no contact with them for their safety. The authorities also guarded the DHS workers and their offices. How could Raye being afraid for her safety with Lance making such threats be seen as suspicious?

To make matters worse, the hate group went after Raye's son. Kelsey's Purpose member, Windy, did not know the Smiths or Raye Dawn. Like all of the others, she only knew the stories that Mike Porter and the Briggs had told. I commend her and the others who thought they were acting in the best interest of Raye's unborn baby. However, hopefully these people have learned their lesson about

239

getting involved where a child is concerned when they don't know the full story. After the Kelsey's Purpose members flooded everyone with protests about Raye and her close relationship with Gayla, Raye's son was taken away and put into foster care. When Gayla went to court to try to get guardianship, DHS had three to five attorneys present. Gayla's attorney had never seen such representation. Were they influenced by public opinion and by people like Windy who were fooled by the lies? Clearly, she also believed the "war hero" story about Lance. She posted the following on the Kelsey's Purpose forum:

Windy Posts: 190 Please call & write DHS & DA - I have put some thought into the statements that D.A. Richard Smothermon quoted to the Daily Oklahoman last Friday, following the release of Kelsey's mother on bond. I am VERY concerned about his statement that he hasn't decided what steps he will take to make sure this mother's newest baby, once born, will be safe. He said he hasn't given any thought to asking DHS to remove the child from this mother once he is born. "Right now, all that's up in the air" he quoted to the paper. This mother was charged, by him, with child neglect, and enabling child abuse. Yes, it is true that she has not been found guilty of these charges, however, this baby is due to be born in the next six weeks. Her next preliminary trial is set for April 14, 2006, however, there is not indication as to when this trial will begin. I can tell you that the death of Kelsey, and the manner in which she was forced to live, then die, has touched me deeply. I am extremely scared for this newest child's life and well-being. I cannot bare to think of another child being brought up in this atmosphere and live through the life that Kelsey was forced to live. I am asking you to please call OK County DHS and demand that they take notice that these charges have been filed against the mother, and step in and remove this child. You should call the OK County DHS office, and write those in the highest up positions to catch their attention. The contact information is as follows: DHS: [phone number removed for privacy] Howard Hendrick (he is THE head of DHS in Oklahoma) [email removed for privacy] [Two DHS employees' email addresses removed for privacy.] We also need to contact the D.A. Richard

Smothermon, and let him know we EXPECT him to do his job with this newest baby and make sure it is safe. Tell him a deprived petition needs to be filed. If you are unsure of what this is, here is a link that will tell you: http://www.policy.okdhs.org/ch75/Chapter...rocess.htm The D.A. filed a deprived petition against Lance Briggs, last year, when he was fighting for our country in Iraq – this man was off fighting a war and was not even ehre to do anything wrong. Here is the contact info for the D.A. Richard Smothermon, DA [Address and phone number removed for privacy] Remind them that as DHS, they do not need ANOTHER Kelsey Briggs case against them! I am begging you to PLEASE do this for this little baby. He is soon to be born into a very controversial life, even before has time to understand all of this. We owe this to him, and to Kelsey, as this is her little brother, to save yet another innocent child's life from evil and harm. We owe this to them, and to all the children of Oklahoma! They deserve to be loved, be safe, and to live their childhoods, as children should! Thank you from the bottom of my heart! Windy

Cnlsmom Posts: 7 March 1, 2006 @ 3:58 PM Re: Please call & write DHS & DA - Unfortunately DHS has no common sense. They spend all their time harassing people who don't need their interference and in the mean time, the children who do need their help get ignored. Too many people use the child welfare system out of spite and to get even with people...they need to come to there senses and recognize those children who need their help and focus on them...sorry I just had to make the comment.

MistyLT Posts: 6 March 1, 2006 @ 9:39 PM Re: Please call & write DHS & DA - Windy, I am sending the emails now. I have a suggestion though. Since she now lives in Oklahoma County, shouldn't be sending an email to the OK County DA, since he is the one that needs to file the deprived petition?

Windy Posts: 190 March 2, 2006 @ 7:33 AM RE: Please call & write DHS & DA - You know, that is a GREAT question. I don't see why we shouldn't. Here is his information: Wes

241

*Lane, DA for Oklahoma County [address and phone number
removed for privacy] Lets all do this too. We have to help
this little baby, that cannot help himself! I am sure this DA is
VERY aware of this case, but may not be aware of the entire
situation with this newest child.*

*Goldtoothgovernmentman Posts: 22 Re: Please call & write DHS &
DA - DHS cannot pick up the child without an order signed
by a judge. And no judge will be able to sign the order until
the child is born. As long as a child is in the mother's womb,
Child Welfare cannot intervene on the child's behalf. This is
one of the most frustrating things about the laws under which
we work. A pregnant woman can do anything to herself
(drugs, alcohol, smoking, failure to seek medical attention)
and until the child is born, CW law has no effect or
jurisdiction. Just one of the many things I know I have
suggested by changed. So remember, you can write the DA of
OK Co. now, but be sure to keep writing as the time for the
child's birth gets near. You can also write to the Juvenile
Judge, as it will require that Judge's signature on the pick up
order. The only other option is for the police department to
go to the hospital after the birth and place the child in
protective custody. That probably won't happen since the
child is protected while in the hospital. Everyone keep up the
good work.*

The gang of bullies was so loud and fierce in their protests about
Raye's new baby that they were able to convince those in charge to
test the baby for fetal alcohol syndrome, which came back negative. It
is still rumored to this day to be an ailment of this innocent child. Why
were they working so hard to interfere with the well-being of Raye's
unborn child while Mike Porter's children were spending nights with
him? Where was their protection from the man charged with Kelsey's
murder?

While Kelsey's Purpose members focused on taking away Raye's
baby before he was even born, a power struggle over the "bash board"
that Kathie read, posted on, and was "addicted to" soon erupted with
Misty, a Mike Porter supporter. Kelsey's Purpose members did not

realize that the forum administrators could read private e-mails and reportedly, Mike Porter and Misty had developed a more than just a friendship before she took over the "bash board."

Posted by "Anonymous" Thursday, March 2, 2006 @ 12:31 AM - We are not back. We never went away.

Posted by "Anonymous" Thursday, March 2, 2006 @ 1:06 AM - Okay boys and girls. I will have to make a few changes to the site tomorrow to get LJBD's name off of it and stuff like that, but the site is still up and will stay up.

Posted by "Let Justice Be Done" Thursday, March 2, 2006 @ 1:16 AM - You may have to leave it under my name for a few days and let them know that the site will stay but it will be a new address since you have to change the name.

Posted by "sew&sew" Thursday, March 2, 2006 @ 7:01 AM - THOUGHT FOR THE DAY: IF YOU DON'T LIKE WHAT SOMEONE HAS TO SAY QUIT LISTENING.

Posted by "sew&sew" Thursday, March 2, 2006 @ 7:26 AM - I think today is the day that "Kelsey's Law" will be presented to the legislation for approval.

Posted by "sew&sew" Thursday, March 2, 2006 @ 7:32 AM - To All: Wes Lane should be contacted but since the crime was not committed within his jurisdiction he may not be able to do anything (which is sad 'cause it looks like to me he's a little bulldog-he'll tear ya up).

Posted by "MistyLT" [unknown date and time] - Doesn't matter, he's still the DA in the county that she is living in and he needs to do...[remainder of post lost in printing]

Posted by mimisluv Posts: 2 Response from Jim Inhofe - Dear Mrs. Moore: Thank you for your recent correspondence regarding the tragic death of Kelsey Briggs. As your voice in Washington, I appreciate you taking the time to share your views with me. Like you, I was deeply troubled by the heartbreaking news of Kelsey's untimely death. As a father of four children and grandfather of twelve grandchildren, I understand the motivation of your fears and concerns. In Federalist Paper No. 39 regarding the Constitution, James Madison reminds us that, "in relation to the extent of its powers, the proposed government cannot be deemed a national one; since its jurisdiction extends to certain enumerated objects only, and leaves to the several States a residuary and inviolable sovereignty over all other objects." There is nothing more conservative than this principle of preserving local powers against centralized national government. Therefore, I have always believed that the state and local governments know better the needs of their people than we in Washington do. Such criminal legislation as pertains to the case of Kelsey Briggs falls within the purview of the State of Oklahoma. As Congress continues to address criminal issues on a national level, I will look for opportunities to strengthen our laws. Together, I pray, we can make both Oklahoma and our country a safer place to live.

Kelsey's Purpose was gaining attention and getting financial support from several organizations including the following event where Lance Briggs accepted a $6,000 check from the sponsors. It was never turned over to Prevent Child Abuse Oklahoma, the organization, which was their umbrella at the time, and when later asked where the funds had gone, Lance denied knowing what had become of them. Members of the Kelsey's Purpose organization also questioned missing funds when a total of $10,000 disappeared with no explanation from the Briggs.

Events for Oklahoma:

03/01/2006 through 04/04/2006

Casino Fun Poker Run

Shawnee, OK

244

Sponsored by: Kelsey's Purpose

Poker run to benefit Kelsey's Purpose (Kelsey Briggs) Sponsored by: The Maria Ward Foundation. High hand paying out $600, low hand paying out $100. ENTRY FEES, $20 for singles, $30 for couples. Door Prizes, 50/50 pot Auction. Start at the Shawnee VFW [address removed for privacy] ending back at VFW. 1st bike out at 11:00, last bike out at 12:00, last bike in at 5:00. Map and locations handed out at Buy-In. For more information contact: [names and phone numbers removed for privacy] Website: Kelseyspurpose.org

Meanwhile, back on the bashboard...

Posted by "deannabmean" Thursday, March 2, 2006 @ 1:07 PM - If Raedawg lived in okc when Kelsey died she would be in jail with mike. Neither would be out. Like Irvin Box said, in his 30 years of practice he has never seen someone make bail that killed a baby like this. Little prick [Gayla's friend] has no legal pull here in okc. Raydawy and Graylegs would just be two low class whores like they are.

Posted by "MistyLT" Thursday, March 2, 2006 @ 1:16 PM - It just occurred to me that [Gayla's friend] is in the same position as Mike. He is Gayla's new love, eh came into the middle of something he knows nothing about, he is siding with Gayla and RD bc he loves Gayla, he standing up for them all the while looking stupid because he doesn't really know what he's talking about and how RD really is, is doing everything he can to keep that baby with RD and saying she deserves to raise that baby...hmmm, sound familiar? [Gayla's friend], I think you've been caught up in the "fight" and are getting sucked in and manipulated by your blinded love. Better watch out. If she kills that new baby she may pin it on you.

With the pressure from the Briggs to shut down the bashboard...a public stance, anyway...Mike Porter stopped being "Kelsey's Voice" and joined the sea of anonymous participants.

Posted by "Anonymous" Thursday, March 2, 2006 @ 1:21 PM - Apparently Misty Raye Dawn is innocent. Children are completely safe with her. I guess people who weren't there believe that Raye Dawn could not have hurt Kelsey.

Posted by "yo mama" Thursday, March 2, 2006 @ 1:42 PM - I know for a fact that the Briggs family has asked that this site be shut down!!!

Posted by "HEY EVERYBODY!!!" Thursday, March 2, 2006 @ 1:47 PM - THE KELSEY BRIGGS ACT WAS PASSED INTO LAW TODAY!!!! HOORAY!!!!

Posted by "Anonymous" Thursday, March 2, 2006 @ 2:08 PM - What happened to the site?

Posted by "JNDMOM" Thursday, March 2, 2006 @ 2:47 PM - I BELIEVE THAT KELSEY'S FAMILY ASKED THAT THIS BASHBOARD DIASAPPEAR. WHY IS IT STILL ON? ALL OF THIS HURTS THEM AND YOU SHOULD RESPECT THEIR WISHES. IF THIS WAS YOUR FAMILY WOULD IT STILL BE ON? TAKE IT OFF! THIS IS ABOUT KELSEY, NOT YOU GUYS. THERE ARE OTHER WAYS TO TALK TRASH AND VENT.

This is the first example I have seen of the bullies turning on each other. But it would not be the last.

Posted by "Anonymous" March 2, 2006 @ 3:20 PM - Letjusticebedone is no longer the owner of this site.

Posted by "Anonymous" March 2, 2006 @ 3:35 PM - So?

Posted by "Anonymous" March 2, 2006 @ 3:40 PM - So, I don't think I need to spell it out.

Posted by "Anonymous" March 2, 2006 @ 3:54 PM - I asked and the new owner has not been contacted by anyone about shutting the site down.

Posted by "JNDMOM" March 2, 2006 @ 4:02 PM - WHY DOES IT MATTER WHO IS RUNNING IT? THE BRIGGS FAMILY ASKED FOR IT TO BE SHUT DOWN!

Kathie Briggs posted on the "bash board" as "Anonymous" and then changed to her actual name and posted the exact same post. She must have realized she blew her cover immediately after posting.

Posted by "Anonymous" March 2, 2006 @ 4:19 PM - For the record...our family has in the past asked for this site to be shut down. Many innocent people connected all three families involved been hurt. Comments expressed have either been misguided rumors, opinions, meant as humorous, or just a need to vent. Once again we are asking for this site to be shut down. There are sites for more constructive methods of venting about this case and child abuse.

Posted by "kjbriggs" March 2, 2006 @ 4:21 PM - For the record...our family has in the past asked for this site to be shut down. Many innocent people connected all three families involved been hurt. Comments expressed have either been misguided rumors, opinions, meant as humorous, or just a need to vent. Once again we are asking for this site to be shut down. There are sites for more constructive methods of venting about this case and child abuse.

Posted by "JNDMOM" March 2, 2006 @ 4:31 PM - THANK YOU. NOW THERE IS NO REASON FOR ANY CONFUSION FOR SHUTTING THIS DOWN.

Posted by "Anonymous" March 2, 2006 @ 4:55 PM - JNDMOM- Did you ever think that your bossiness and you coming onto someone ELSE'S site and telling them what they should do with it may have something to do with the fact that is still up? Or do you think the fact that this is someone's personal blog and people are entitled to post personal blogs without other people's permission might have something to do with it still being here? Do you police the internet looking for blogs where someone might have said something bad about Michael Porter or Raye Dawn and tell them to shut their site down? You could at least be a little bit more tasteful about it since it's not yourblog. I for one do not think this site should be shut down. We do have freedom of speech and I plan to exercise mine and I plan to do it on this site if the owner does not shut it down. Everyone has always had the right and been asked to email the owner of the site if something here is said that shouldn't be and those people were banned. Most blogs wouldn't even give you that option.

Posted by "MistyLT" Thursday, March 2, 2006 @ 5:11 PM - I am taking care of it.

Posted by "Anonymous" Thursday, March 2, 2006 @ 5:54 PM - Taking care of what? Shutting it down or or you the new owner?

Posted by "Anonymous" Thursday, March 2, 2006 @ 5:56 PM - MistyLT: What happened to your site?

Posted by "MistyLT" Thursday, March 2, 2006 @ 5:56 PM - The website has been changed.

Posted by "MistyLT" Thursday, March 2, 2006 @ 6:08 PM - I took it down because I was trying to make one that was easier to navigate and post on. NO such luck.

Posted by "sew&sew" Thursday, March 2, 2006 @ 6:15 PM - TO ALL: I just saw the 6:00 report that Kelsey's Law has been passed in the House & will now go to the Senate for approval. Kathie Briggs is an amazing woman, who despite all that has happened maintains her dignity. Kudos to Kathie and all the Briggs family.

Posted by "MistyLT" Thursday, March 2, 2006 @ 6:20 PM - Is there a place we can read the full law?

Misty must have posted a comment about Raye using meth. Raye has admitted to using drugs while she was with Lance, but she quit using drugs once she escaped his abuse. Gayla stated that when Raye and Lance were married, Gayla discovered that Lance was even

248

growing his own drugs. Raye's father made him destroy all of it. Lance has been in rehab multiple times, but not Raye. From the moment she left him, she quit using drugs on her own and she did not require rehab. These bullies, however, call her a drug addict. Isn't a drug addict someone who requires help in order to quit, like Lance? If Raye were a drug addict, wouldn't she continue to do drugs after she left Lance?

Posted by "Anonymous" Thursday, March 2, 2006 @ 6:25 PM - MistyLT – I think your comment about meth being a serious problem with what's goin on with things today was true. I seen on the news today where a man has been arrested for killing his girlfriend's 15 month old daughter because the gf refused to buy the boyfriend meth and he took it out on the baby.

Posted by [unknown person] Thursday, March 2, 2006 @ 7:07 PM - [first portion of post lost in printing]...intentionally hurt Kathie, Lance, the whole family or even disrespect Kelsey in keeping it up?

Posted by "JNDMOM" Thursday, March 2, 2006 @ 7:16 PM - This was a good idea to begin with. But there are so many people on here that have ruined it. I understand that some have been banned. But I'm trying to get you to understand that this is constantly causing problems. Its hurting people. People that have already been hurt more than they should have been. This was meant to help, not create more pain. I'm not trying to tell you what to do. I'm trying to help the Briggs and [Kelsey's step-grandparents]. They have told you that they don't want it. Why can't you respect them enough to do this?

At last! Someone admits that the bashboard had harmed several people. But that did not stop the bullies. Their intent was to harm Raye and her family. The other people harmed were possibly considered mere casualties of their war.

*Posted by "MistyLT" Thursday, March 2, 2006 @ 7:18 PM - This board was never meant to hurt any of the Briggs and **it is not just about Kelsey anymore.** There is no disrespect to Kelsey here either just because people want to discuss the case and discuss child abuse. The site has been changed. No disrespect meant to you JNDmom, but this site was not put here because of kelseyspurpose. I remember LJBD's post on kelsyespupose when she made this site. **It was a site to be able to say the things that kelseyspurpose was not meant for.**[28] This blog is no different than the people who stand around everyday talking about this case and their opinions of it. I hear worse things from people that are actually related to RD's family everyday than I read on this board. Rumors and trash talking are going to happen with or without this board so the blame shouldn't really lie here.*

Posted by "MistyLT" Thursday, March 2, 2006 @ 7:30 PM - And I really resent the fact that you say it is disrespectful to Kelsey to keep a board up about child abuse. I have not seen you go to any of the other boards where members are actually copying posts from this board into those boards and tell them to shut it down.

Posted by [unknown person] Thursday, March 2, 2006 @ 7:31 PM - Why haven't you asked the other sites to shut down? Because this one gets the most attention?

Kelsey's law had been passed and the Briggs family members wanted to portray themselves as advocates and not bullies. They wanted to bury their past, but Mike Porter and his friend did not want to lose his new supporters. This site had provided a platform for the Briggs and Mike Porter to share stories to garner hate. It caused people doubt his guilt and to believe that Raye was in fact the guilty party, even though the investigators did not believe so due to facts and evidence. The Briggs had something to hide. They did not want their

---

[28] Emphasis by book author

true nature to be revealed to the public. As they had stated, they wanted to save Mike Porter from himself.

Posted by "JNDMOM" Thursday, March 2, 2006 @ 7:40 PM - Most of the time its not about child abuse. If it were, there wouldn't be a problem would there? People talking trash is unavoidable. It's the point that this is Kelsey's family and they have asked for it to be taken off. By fighting to keep it up is not genuinely caring about them. And if you are not the 4:55 Anon, then Im not talking to you.

I can't help but chuckle while reading this next post. It comes from an alternate reality than what has been presented throughout the pages of this book.

*Posted by "Anonymous" Thursday, March 2, 2006 @ 7:45 PM - The Smith's hate the Briggs and it it not because of this blog. They always have and always will. **The Briggs have always made it clear that they do not condone this site or bashing anyone.**[29] Just because they may disagree with people's opinions that post on here does not make it disrespectful for people to voice their opinions. The Briggs have opinions about thing and they are free to voice theirs and they are respected when they do. I for one have the utmost respect for the Briggs family but I will not quit saying what I think just because they have an opinion that differs.*

Posted by "JNDMOM" Thursday, March 2, 2006 @ 7:57 PM - Misty, Okay look, This is going nowhere Between both of our big moths, we could go on and on and on. I understand that you want to keep the sight. As long as Kelsey and her good family is not being wronged, I could care less. Why cant the owner ask the family if it would be okay to keep it up as long as you guys agree to keeping all of the -----straight. Don't allow people to talk trash. Delete their message and bump them off.

---

[29] Emphasis by book author

251

*Posted by "JNDMOM [Mary B.]" [unknown date and time] - Anon-
But it is disrespectful to them when a member of their family
is being wronged. Obviously they don't like each other if the
site is being used in a way that helps then talk...[remainder
of post lost in printing]*

*Posted by "MistyLT" Thursday, March 2, 2006 @ 8:52 PM - That is
fine. Hell I just got the board today. No one has even given
me a chance yet. - But I will say this because I just read
Shirica's post that she made about me on Kelseyspurpose
and I know she's reading this bc she sent me an email. How
DARE you say that my apology to Kathy Briggs was
insincere! YOU have NO right trying to convince people that
my apology to Kathy Briggs was anything BUT sincere. If it
was not, I would NOT have taken the time to personally email
her and apologize to her 3 days after I had already
apologized to her on this board. Because I do not agree with
your views and opinions does NOT make me the person you
are trying to make me into. You know, I find it ironic that I
have been chewed out today by two people who think what
we're doing is hurtful and disrespectful, but both have done
the same to me by 1) telling me I'm disrespecting Kelsey and
2) by saying that my personal apology and admitting I was
wrong to Kathy was unfelt and insincere. I don't find it right
that you come here and ask us not to do something and then
turn around and do it to me. That's like the pot calling the
kettle black isn't it? - That's the last thing I'm going to say
about it. You don't like this site, fine, but you don't know me
from the stranger standing next to you tomorrow, so do NOT
tell me or anyone else how I feel. I can do that myself and I
do a damn good job at it.*

*Posted by "Anonymous" [unknown date and time] - No one can stop
me from getting on here and voicing my opinion and telling
what I know to be true – no matter what they THINK THEY
KNOW. Shirica got on Kelsey's Purpose and bashed Mike
and that is not supposed to be a place to discuss the guilt or
innocence of anyone. I guess opinions are ok depending on
whose they are.*

Posted by "Anonymous" Thursday, March 2, 2006 @ 9:24 PM - Shirica's neice was MURDERED. She has a right to be upset.

Posted by "Anonymous" Thursday, March 2, 2006 @ 9:30 PM - I DO not disagree with you AT ALL. But her opinions DO not mean that NO one else is upset or NO one else has a right to a different opinion than hers. I respect Shirica and the Briggs' family and THEIR OPINIONS. But they are just that – opinions. And everyone is entitled to theirs. Not just Shirica or the Briggs'.

Posted by "Anonymous" Thursday, March 2, 2006 @ 9:33 PM - I will continue to speak my opinion and what I know to be true based on ALL the facts. I do not mean any disrespect to the Briggs' even though I know some of their opinions are wrong and I will do all possible to make sure justice is served for Kelsey and their family and all those who loved Kelsey.

It appears that someone else recognized Mike Porter in the anonymous post taking up for Misty and a right to his opinion. The next "anonymous" person also caught him. Was it because those were the same words he repeatedly used in private conversations with the Briggs? This substantiates my beliefs about the true identity of this anonymous person.

Posted by "Anonymous" Thursday, March 2, 2006 @ 9:38 PM - You know Mike, you can honor Kelsey and the Briggs' by asking your friend Misty to shut this site down. The two of you can still communicate via email. What is the difference?

Posted by "let justice be done" Thursday, March 2, 2006 @ 9:45 PM - MistyLT please email me.

Presumably, "Let justice be done" must have been Ashley's screen name, or there was a blog owner between Ashley and Misty...two women very close to the case. Perhaps Ashley was persuaded to give up the blog when her mother-in-law became the state's star witness against Raye.

253

Posted by "Anonymous" [unknown date and time] - Not Mike, but I will agree anon @ 9:30. I have watched everyone who disagrees with certain people on here be accused of being Mike. Shirica and the Briggs family are free to tell...[remainder of post lost in printing]

Posted by "Anonymous" Thursday, March 2, 2006 @ 9:56 PM - Can't disagree with you there. But it is also disrespectful to allow yourself to be used as a pawn to cover up the truth even if you do not realize you are being used and you have the best intentions at heart.

Posted by "Anonymous" Thursday, March 2, 2006 @ 10:32 PM - BRAVENET RULES!!!!!!!! No spamming allowed, no harassing, threatening or illegal activities. I have reported this site!

Misty must have set up a new bashboard on Bravenet. Apparently, the old bashboard could not be reported, but this new one could. It still did not stop the bullies. When the bullies don't get their way, they turn on each other and use the same tactics they use on their prey. This, too, I have also witnessed.

Posted by "Anonymous" Thursday, March 2, 2006 @ 10:33 PM - BRAVENET RULES ALSO...All Members must ensure that their member account information is accurate and complete at all times!!!!!!!!

Posted by "Christina" Thursday, March 2, 2006 @ 10:38 PM - The rally is tomorrow at 4 right? Misty can you get on yahoo?

Posted by "Anonymous" Thursday, March 2, 2006 @ 10:40 PM - Good job anonymous at 10:32!!!! Way to go!! Way to suppress that fee specah!!!!! Good for you!!!!

Posted by "Anonymous" Thursday, March 2, 2006 @ 10:44 PM - Way to try to stop people from talking that don't agree with you. RD would be proud.

Posted by "MistyLT" Thursday, March 2, 2006 @ 10:58 PM - I just now signed back on. Are you people blind or what? THE BOARD HAS BEEN CHANGED. **THIS BOARD IS NOT ABOUT KELSEY ANYMORE AND IT IS NOT NAMED TO BE A BASHBOARD.**[30] *IT IS ABOUT OKLAHOMA'S ABUSED CHILDREN DO YOU HAVE A PROBLEM WITH PEOPLE TALKING ABOUT ABUSED CHILDREN?? YOU ARE THE ONLY ONES THAT ARE KEEPING THE BASHING AND BICKERING GOING WHICH IS ALOS AGAINST BRAVENET'S RULES. THIS BOARD HAS NOTHING TO DO WITH THIS CASE ANYMORE EXCEPT THAT KELSEY WAS ONE OF MANY ABUSED OKLAHOMA CHILDREN. Why are you still here bitching about it? You got what you set out to do. You used kelseyspurpose to steer people away from talking on this board and made it a closed post at that so no one could reply to it. The only thing that you accomplished is people are not posting, they're just sending me emails and setting up new sites. Good job. I tried to take the focus off of your case by changing everything n the board and making it an Oklahoma child abuse board and you managed to piss people off by trying to shut them up so they've decided to make their own bash boards.*

Posted by "Anonymous" Thursday, March 2, 2006 @ 11:02 PM - Misty, it is very unfortunate that you are obviously a very angry and unkind person. I was the one who posted those comments and I am not related to Kelsey's family, nor do I associate with Kelsey's Purpose.

Posted by "sew&sew" Thursday, March 2, 2006 @ 11:06 PM - MistyLT (10:58) I'm of the mind that based on what I've seen and heard that Oklahoma might be a good place for any and all child abusers to live. Yep-it's true, our laws are appalling, the judicial and state system(s) set up to protect these children have and will continue to fail miserably. The "legal" eagles may follow the law as written but not necessarily the spirit of the law. Again, anyone wishing to

---

[30] Emphasis by book author

abuse their kids & get away with it might consider certain counties as a decent place to live (i.e. Pottawatomie & Lincoln)

Posted by "Anonymous" Thursday, March 2, 2006 @ 11:08 PM - Who cares if 50 sites are set up. Nothing that is posted on them is even true anyway. If anyone reads all of this and thinks that it is true they are stupid and who cares what they think.

Posted by "MistyLT" Thursday, March 2, 2006 @ 11:08 PM - Oh get over that bs non 11:02. You know damn well why I'm angry right now. Not only have I been told that I'm disrespecting Kelsye by putting up a board about abused Oklahoma children, but after I'm being jumped on for doing it, then I'm being bashed on a board run by the same people. PLEASE. Anyway this board is not here for you to come fill up with this bs. It is about abused Oklahoma children. Do you have something to say about that topic?

Posted by "Jim" Thursday, March 2, 2006 @ 11:10 PM - LJBD, you have mail. I hope I didn't spam, harass, or threaten anyone with that notice....

Members of the bash board made an attempt to appear to be concerned about child abuse in the state with the following posts:

Posted by "MistyLT" Thursday, March 2, 2006 @ 11:10 PM - Sewnsew-I have to agree with you. Since this story woke me up, I've been paying more attention to the stories on the news and I think just about every night I've heard some kind of news where a child has been hurt in one way or another. Did anyone see anything else on the man that killed his girlfriend's 15 month old daughter bc she wouldn't buy him crank?

Posted by "sew&sew" [unknown date and time] - Anon (11:08) I can't be sure of the number but I believe even within the last 2 233ks there have been no less than 2 cases of child abuse the media have been reporting on. Unless an individual is

privy to inside info anything they discuss regarding kids
being aubed is based on what they read, what they hear, or
what they have been told. Remember…where there's smoke
there's fire. I don't agree with you when you say the "nothing
that is posted on them is true anyway." While not every thing
can be "true" I believe statistically some of…[remainder of
post lost in printing]

The bashboard members continued their "prevent child abuse"
charade with Mike Porter leading the pack. This is reminiscent of the
Mike Porter's plan to improve the state's child welfare program that
he e-mailed to Shirica on January 13th. He stated as follows:

We can only hope that people will be held accountable for their
failures. We already know I will be and I will face that. I
attached a few ideas for change. Keep in mind these are
changes that I know would help, and I was on the other side
and saw how Raye Dawn manipulated the system. These are
just a few. I have so many more. I will keep praying for you
all, and if I don't hear from you I will be thinking of you all
tomorrow. My sister will be there, please look out for her if
you are able. She is on Kelsey's side and she is one of the
only people I have left. God bless you Shirica. You and your
family continue to amaze me.

SUGGESTIONS FOR IMPROVEMENT
Unscheduled visits – Once DHS becomes involved in a case, a
worker should make a minimum of 2 unnanounced visits per
week to the home in question. This could be done by a
primary or secondary worker who is knowledgeable about
the case. The theory of only visiting at scheduled times does
not appear to put the child's best interests first. Re-
unification should be a secondary goal – the child's safety
should be first and foremost. Having a child is a priviledge,
not a right. Do not try to make it easy for the parent. Forget
about their privacy, their dignity. Make them prove that they
are a capable parent. Any parent can appear to be a model
parent at 11:15 if they know DHS has an appointment at that
time that day. Scheduled visits do not allow the worker to see
the child in their actual day to day life. Kelsey's situation is a

257

*perfect example. After the CHBS worker began making her
<u>scheduled</u> home visits, on one occasion she saw Kelsey out in
the lawn unsupervised 20 feet from an often traveled street.
And this was when the parent <u>knew</u> the worker would be
there. Imagine what she would have learned about the child's
situation if the parent did not know when the worker would
arrive. This is a huge change that needs to be made – and it
would be so easy to do. Send a worker out to the home – stop
in – see if there is anything wrong.*

*Family mediation – After DHS becomes involved in a case, DHS
should have someone skilled in family mediation. Let adults
sit down in a room together, with a mediator and talk about
what is going on. People may think this is a little risque', but
here is what it would accomplish. First off, it would make it
very clear to everyone involved who honestly has the child's
best interests in mind. Secondly, it would help pave the way
to communication, which is sorely lacking in most cases,
Kelsey's especially. So much could be changed by people
who have the child's best interests in mind sitting down and
talking. Too often the only time that "opposing" sides see
each other is in court, and this does not breed
communication, it breeds contempt. In Kelsey's case, I think
a family mediation session would have been helpful, and
telling. It would show who honestly wanted to know what was
happening to Kelsey and who just wanted to shirk
responsibility and point fingers.*

*Daily Logs – This is something that DHS recommends, but it should
be mandatory. Make a parent who has had services
recommended keep a detailed daily log of their activities
involving the child that day. This would do two things. The
first thing it would do is hold the parent accountable for any
injuries to the child. If parents were made to keep a daily log,
then it would be nearly impossible, or at least very obvious if
the parent tried to alter their story about an injury to the
child. Secondly, it would help the parent be responsible.
Wouldn't a parent think twice about something if they knew
that they had to record everything that they did? This ties in
to the workers stopping by unannounced. The workers who
stop by could pick up the logs. This should be mandatory.
Again, having a child is a priviledge, not a right. DHS makes*

it to easy to keep your child. After abuse has been confirmed, make the parent <u>work</u> to show that they are a fit parent. A child's life is too valuable to let parent's go through the motions. Eventually, a web journal could be added to the DHS website to help with the logistics and amount of paperwork. A parent who is receiving services from DHS could receive a username and password. They could log on each day and complete their daily log of what happened that day. There could be a section for "critical incidents" and this should raise a red flag in the whole system and dispatch a worker immediately. Having it in writing is prudent. Doing the same thing verbally is not as effective. Things are always lost in translation, and anyone who has ever worked with DHS knows that there are many times you will have to tell the same story over and over. Putting it in writing increases accountability. The logs would have to be backed up by the unscheduled visits.

Mike Porter's plan also read like an O.J. Simpson "How I got away with it" outline. Were any of these suggestions used in Kelsey's law? Since even attorneys have had a difficult time determining how the law has benefited the state, or how the proposed changes have anything to do with what actually went wrong in Kelsey's case once the facts are known, it is as of yet to be deemed undetermined.

No Plea for the Blonde Bombshell

March, 2006

The following e-mail was sent from a friend of the Smith family to another Smith supporter:

From: [A friend of the family] To: [Another family friend]
Friday, March 3, 2006 12:24 PM
Subject: new blog address
MistyLT from Chandler has shut her site down and has taken over the blog. The new address is http://iuxbehave.bravejournal.com. She does allow bashing. I have asked her why she is not afraid of a suit since both families know who she is and the other owner was. We will see what her response is. She is as far as I know Misty…from…if she is using her maiden name. Her dad is the chief of the…Fire Dept. He was on TV against last night and I noted the spelling of his last name. … Keep this information in case [Gayla's friend] wants to pursue this. Further research should be done on her if he wants to continue to get it shut down. Both the Briggs and us want it to be shut down. They claim to be for Kelsey but they are not, if they were they would shut down the site since they claim to respect Kathie Briggs. Such hypocrites.

Posted by "Anonymous" Friday, March 3, 2006 @ 8:28 AM - Well I'll be damned. Who would have ever guess that it would be the Briggs instead of the Smith's would try to silence people and harass them until they shut up.

Posted by "MistyLT" Friday, March 3, 2006 @ 11:04 AM - Only some people.

Posted by "Anonymous" Friday, March 3, 2006 @ 12:19 PM -
Misty are you not concerned that both families know who you
are? Are you not afraid of a law suit? LJBD was.

Posted by "MistyLT" Friday, March 3, 2006 @ 12:26 PM - There
are no grounds here for a lawsuit, so what does it matter?
And no, I'm not concerned that people know who I am. If I
were, then I would have tried to hide it. Are you concerned?

Mike Porter and Misty started planning this protest via their
bashboard. Now, Kathie Briggs was joining in. when asked in a later
deposition, she denied planning the event. (You can read her
deposition at www.RayeDawnSmith.com)

Kathie Briggs posted the following on her Kelsey's Purpose
forum:

Kjbriggs Posts: 183 March 3, 2006 3:37 PM "Walk for Justice"
March 11ᵗʰ ⁻ Many have asked that we have a protest of some
sort on a Saturday. What we have chosen to do is have a
"Walk for Justice" next Saturday, March 11ᵗʰ before the
Child Abuse Fair. We will meet at Brooke Insurance at 2102
N. Kickapoo in Shawnee (across from Sonic) at 11:00 a.m.
We will then simply walk up and down the street with our
signs asking for justice for Kelsey. You can bring your
strollers for your children and those who choose can walk
around in a small area in the parking lot. The plan is to also
have a firetruck to display Kelsey banners. Please do not
make threatening or inappropriate signs. This could last
about one hour and that will give everyone time to eat lunch
and get to the fair. Our message should be clear that child
abuse is a crime and failure to report child abuse is a crime.
Those who turn their backs on child abuse and let children be
hurt should be punished along with the perpetrator. Thank
you, Kathie

*Kjbriggs Posts: 183 Re: "Walk for Justice" March 11th - Okay,
        brilliant is not a word ever used to describe anything I have
        ever done before. That might get a chuckle out of my family. I
        want everyone to know that it will not be necessary to cross
        streets during this walk if you have children with you. There
        is enough parking area for us without putting the children in
        danger of cars. I really hope as many as possible will be
        there. We heard another rumor today that a deal could be
        made for the mother. This is not justice for Kelsey if that
        happens. It sends a very bad message for all who witness
        abuse and do nothing. Once they know they will be held
        accountable maybe they will put their children above
        perpetrator. I urge all of you to call the Attorney General and
        any other elected official with your outrage at this possibility.
        <u>Our DA has already stated on camera his case against Mike
        Porter is strong and he does not need Raye Dawn.</u>[31]*

---

[31] Emphasis by book author

*Therefore; he does not need to make a deal with someone
who did not protect her child for nine months of documented
abuse. We would like to believe Mr. Smothermon is working
for Kelsey, but we have believed in our system in the past and
Kelsey died. The Judges in Lincoln and Pott. Counties need
to know they cannot be soft on child abuse. It has to become
a serious issue. Please once again write, call, fax and e-mail
those who will be making these decisions on Kelsey's behalf.*

Then why request a deal for Mike Porter and not let the district
attorney take him to trial? In Kathie Briggs's deposition at
RayeDawnSmith.com, she stated that her family could not handle the
appeals process. Former Kelsey's Purpose members state that it was
the only way to see that Raye Dawn was charged. Why such public
deception?

*Windy Posts: 190 March 7, 2006 10:13 AM Reminder to write DA
and Judges - Just a reminder, if you haven't done so, please
write the DA and judges in Kelsey's case and remind them
that NO DEALS are accepatable. Kelsey go NO deals, and
those responsible should get NO deals! The information for
all of them is below:*

*Richard Smothermon
[address and phone number removed for privacy]*

*Judge E...
[address and phone number removed for privacy]*

*Judge V...
[address and phone number removed for privacy]*

*Judge E... and Judge V... are not allowing faxes to be sent to them,
so PLEASE mail these today! Your efforts are greatley
appreciated! Judge V... is the one who should be hearing the
criminal trials and could be the one to hear any plea
agreement. Please write him. We need them ALL to know that
they cannot be soft on child abuse, and we as voting citizens
will not accept this type of behavior from them. God bless
you and justice for Kelsey!*

Beverly Posts: 153 March 7, 2006 Re: Reminder to write DA and
*   Judges - Today, I sent off three letters to, Richard*
*   Smothermon, Judge E...and Judge V... I was wondering if I*
*   should wait a week and send three more? A few letters don't*
*   get much attention, but a lot of letters gets a lot of attention.*
*   So please everybody send this letters.*

Windy Posts: 236 March 8, 2006 Re: Reminder to Write DA and
*   Judges - Beverly, Thank you SO much for all this hard work.*
*   Yes, send more. That's what I do, send them every week!*
*   Thanks a lot!*

Zoe's Meemaw Posts: 239 March 8, 2006 Re: Reminder to write DA
*   and Judges - I sent my letters off yesterday*

kjbriggs	**Kelsey's Billboard posts merged here**	**Post:** #1
Kelsey's Grandma	Kelsey's billboard became a reality today. Teri, her parents, and I along with channel 4 were there for the unveiling of this message for others.	
Posts: 1,221 Group: Administrators Joined: Nov 2005 Status: Offline Reputation:	The billboard has Kelsey's name on one side, her picture in the middle and states "child abuse kills" on the other side. It is also hot pink like her stickers and has the website at the bottom.	
	The billboard is located on I-40 westbound between the Kickapoo and Hwy 177 exits just west of Shawnee.	
	We wanted the message to be simple and clear. Something to get people's attention as they drive by 70 miles an hour. Child abuse does not always kill a child physically, but it does kill their spirit. It can scar a child for life and the fight to help others has only begun.	
	This post was last modified: 10-01-2007 09:24 PM by kjbriggs.	

03-09-2006 05:54 PM	PM FIND	QUOTE REPORT

Channel 4 is our local NBC affiliate and where Cherokee Ballard was a reporter. Cherokee was so close to the Briggs family that she had Thanksgiving dinner with them.

As always, the Smith family watched the Briggs family and their followers closely so that they could report to Raye's attorney. Sherri sent the following e-mail to Gayla.

From: Sherri To: Gayla March 14, 2006 8:45 AM
Subject: ANOTHER BILLBOARD??!!
Here is some info. Surely we can stop the exploiting of Kelsey's
*   picture up on the sides of the roads! Doesn't [Raye's defense*

*attorney] have any ideas legally??? It just sickens me to see
Kathy doing this!*

[The following post was included in the email]

*KJBRIGGS Posts: 191 Re: Kelsey's Billboard - I have another
billboard just outside of Meeker I am working on. It is
smaller, but will have a similar design with a different
picture. I spoke with the company today and I am waiting on
the exact cost. At this time the full cost is $400 per month
with a production and installation fee also added. I hope to
get at least 12 to 18 different businesses to sponsor a month.
The money can be sent to the Oklahoma Prevent Child Abuse
organization and put in Kelsey's account so they can receive
a tax credit. As soon as I get more details I will let you know.*

kjbriggs	**Another Billboard**	**Post: #6**
Kelsey's Grandma ★★★★★☆	The Meeker billboard went up today. It has the same message about child abuse as the other one, but is smaller. We used a different picture this time. Our small town of 900 has lost two children to murder in less than five years. We think one was too many and two is a reason to make a statement.	
Posts: 1,221 Group: Administrators Joined: Nov 2005 Status: Offline Reputation: ▮▮▮▮▮▮▮▮▮▮		
	This post was last modified: 04-14-2006 08:06 PM by aunt bean.	

tp://kelseyspurpose.org/forums/showthread.php?tid=449 (2 of 16) [7/17/2009 2:09:02 PM]

:lsey's Billboard posts merged here

04-12-2006 11:24 PM   PM   FIND   QUOTE   REPORT

kjbriggs	**RE: Kelsey's Billboard**	**Post: #21**
Kelsey's Grandma ★★★★★☆	I would like to clarify the previous post. I was not told by the billboard company that the maternal family was making all the calls. This information came from one land owner to a member of Kelsey's paternal family. I do know the maternal family wanted the billboard removed. It is hard to look at, I personally hate that my own granddaughter could be on a child abuse billboard. The fact is she was abused and she is dead. If people see that sweet little face and think just a little about the consequences of their actions it will make it a little easier for me to see. This billboard was not put up to bash the maternal family. Is was put up to let people know what a tragedy these actions bring.	
Posts: 1,221 Group: Administrators Joined: Nov 2005 Status: Offline Reputation: ▮▮▮▮▮▮▮▮▮▮		
	I would also like to point out the highway the billboard was on will be under construction soon. This was a blessing in disguise. We have the option to put it on another Meeker site or move it to OKC. We are currently waiting for the locations we have to choose from.	

10-12-2006 01:17 PM   PM   FIND   QUOTE   REPORT

Sherri contacted Prevent Child Abuse Oklahoma and spoke with the director who stated that the organization had no knowledge of any billboards and that they would never approve one.

kjbriggs Kelsey's Grandma ☆☆☆☆☆☆ ☐ Posts: 1,221 Group: Administrators Joined: Nov 2005 Status: Offline :putation: ❚❚❚❚❚❚❚❚❚❚	**RE: NEW Kelsey-Billboard** **FYI** Before the other family runs to the Attorney General let me say.....this billboard will contract under Prevent Child Abuse Oklahoma.	Post: #47
09-01-2007 10:13 AM	🔲 PM 🔍 FIND	💬 QUOTE 📄 REPORT

I was contacted by this same organization when I first became involved due to the fact that I questioned the legality of the organization because the Briggs requested earmarked donations, which are illegal. Kathie Briggs repeatedly instructed donors to put Kelsey's name in the memo so that it would go into "Kelsey's account." This is called "earmarking," and it is against the law. The director assured me that there was not a specific account for the Briggs. Donations were made, and even if Kelsey's Purpose or Kelsey's name was in the memo, it was deposited into the general fund and then distributed fairly. This is what I was told, anyway. Perhaps this director told the truth and Kathie did not receive a specific dollar amount from the fund. This could explain why over $6,000 from the poker run went missing and was never turned into the organization. Since Kelsey's Purpose did not operate under a 501 c 3, they could not accept cash donations and claim them as tax deductible. This is the reason that Prevent Child Abuse Oklahoma agreed to umbrella their cause.

A few years later the group reportedly had a falling out with the Briggs because they wanted it to be all about Kelsey with her pictures and name everywhere. Prevent Child Abuse Oklahoma wanted it to be about all abused children, not just Kelsey.

Though the Briggs later claimed they were "letting Kelsey rest" by removing her name from their organization, Briggs family members are now on the board of the Kelsey Briggs foundation, which is now a 501 c 3 and is still accepting donations.

Shirica	RE: "Walk for Justice" March 11th Post: #15
Administrator	Today was incredible. Thank you, thank you,
★★★★★☆	thank you to everyone who helped make today such a
	success and thank you to everyone who came out and
Posts: 207	participated. We gave out 1600 stickers today and
Group: Administrators	even received a few donations. The fair was a huge
Joined: Nov 2005	success. I cannot believe how many people were
Status: Away	there. And the Walk for Justice was phenomenal. You
Reputation: ▊▊	all are AMAZING!!! And thank you to Rep. Steele and
	Rep. Morgan for coming and speaking. You guys are
	doing an incredible job. Keep up the good work. There
	is still so much left to do. Our voices are being heard
	and our presence is being felt. We will not go quietly in
	the night.
	THANK YOU!!!

03-11-2006 07:26 PM   PM   FIND   REPORT

The Naked Truth Bound in Scorn

March, 2006

While the Briggs family members used their forum and bashboard to garner intense hate as their weapon against Raye and her family, the Smiths reacted by attempting to have their voices heard amongst the loud roar of the witch hunt.

On March 16, 2006, Sherri sent the following letter to Raye's attorney in a desperate plea to control the building hate:

[Raye's attorney], We, as family members of Kelsey Smith-Briggs, find it appalling and sickening that Kathy Briggs is blatantly exploiting Kelsey's picture on interstate billboards, T-shirts, banners and buttons. Kelsey should not be the 'poster child' for abused children. We, as Kelsey's maternal family, feel victimized and harassed. Raye Dawn should have a say about where and how pictures of her daughter are being publicly displayed. She is the mother and had joint custody with the state of this child. Why have those rights been taken away from her? We understand she has been charged with enabling and neglect, which we disagree with. The truth will come out in court. In the meantime, what can our family do to stop this exploitation of Kelsey?? Kathy Briggs thinks Kelsey's purpose was to be an advocate for abused children. We witnessed the fact that Kelsey lived a happy life for 2 ½ years, full of love for and from her family. She should not be exploited as an abused child. Justice for Kelsey is being served with the stepfather who has been charged with her murder. Justice for Kelsey is NOT being served by corrupting the public's opinion of Kelsey's mother and maternal family. Raye Dawn has NEVER been charged with child abuse. She did everything in her power to work with the State to find out who and why abuse allegations were being made. The State could not even figure it out! Please help us protect Kelsey

269

now as an abused child in the public eye. Her memory does
not need to suffer anymore. This unconsented exploitation
should be discontinued immediately. I have copied part of the
Oklahoma Constitution concerning harassment and stalking:
F. For purposes of this section:
1. "Harasses" means a pattern or course of conduct directed toward
    another individual that includes, but is not limited to,
    repeated or continuing unconsented contact, that would
    cause a reasonable person to suffer emotional distress, and
    that actually causes emotional distress to the victim.
    Harassment shall include harassing or obscene phone calls
    as prohibited by distress to the victim. Harassment shall
    include harassing or obscene phone calls as prohibited by
    Section 1172 of this title and conduct prohibited by Section
    850 of this title. Harassment does not include constitutionally
    protected activity or conduct that serves a legitimate
    purpose;
2. "Course of conduct" means a pattern of conduct composed of a
    series of two (2) or more separate acts over a period of time,
    however short, evidencing a continuity of purpose.
    Constitutionally protected activity is not included within the
    meaning of "course of conduct";
3. "Emotional distress" means significant mental suffering or
    distress that may, but does not necessarily require, medical
    or other professional treatment or counseling;
4. "Unconsented contact" means any contact with another
    individual that is initiated or continued without the consent of
    the individual, or in disregard of that individual's expressed
    desire that the contact be avoided or discontinued.
    Constitutionally protected activity is not included within the
    meaning of unconsented contact.

Also, copied is a portion of Oklahoma's victim's rights: Statutory
    Rights of Crime Victims – Rights of Crime Victims 19 Okl. St.
    Ann. & 215.33
Oklahoma Statutes Annotated Title 19. Counties and County Officers
    Chapter 7A. District Attorney 2. To receive protection from
    harm and threats of harm arising out of their cooperation
    with law enforcement and prosecution efforts, and to be

provided with information as to the level of protection available and how to access protection;

Please advise us how we may protect Kelsey's memory and her victimized, emotionally distressed family members. Best Regards, Sherri

On March 17, 2006 the Governor included Kelsey's case in his executive address. It seemed to be never-ending and all one-sided. A letter to the editor of the local newspaper as follows:

To the Editor: I am the ex-wife of Raye Dawn Smith's deceased father. I have known Raye Dawn her whole life and knew Kelsey too. Kelsey's violent death has affected this whole family in a profound and long-lasting way. We as citizens have a few questions. I'm concerned about the fact that the man charged with Kelsey's murder is free on bail. It seems all the TV media has been more about Raye Dawn, who has not been charged with murder, while little concern or TV media attention has gone toward the person who actually has been charged with her death. Little has been heard from the maternal side of Kelsey's family, yet we are forced to see ongoing footage and copy driven by her paternal side. Why? Why is the paternal family not voicing their concerns about Mike Porter, the individual who has been charged with first-degree murder? Fact: he had his bond lowered 75 percent. Fact: he is allowed to see his daughter with DHS supervision. Has that stipulation been followed to the letter of the law? Fact: Mike Porter was not to be in contact with any state witnesses. Is this stipulation being followed? Kelsey's paternal grandmother has stated on TV that she is concerned

271

*for his safety! I have never heard her or any of the TV media
voice the same concern about Raye Dawn, Kelsey's mother.
How can this be about justice for Kelsey? If this was all
about justice for Kelsey, it seems we, as Americans, should
all be asking these questions. Kelsey's maternal side would
like to remind the media and the public that Raye Dawn
Smith has not been charged with murder. Is this justice for
Kelsey? As a mother, grandmother and an American, I am
concerned about our rights as citizens and the fact that
anyone who has been charged with murder of a child is
walking around free, in contact with children. Where is the
justice here? I implore the people of Oklahoma to look at all
the facts and not be caught up in the TV media hype that has
surrounded this emotionally charged tragedy. Justice is an
American freedom meant for all. Lillie*

This letter was followed by an e-mail from Raye to the editor.

*From: Kelseysmom1228 To: Shawnee News-Star March 16, 2006
      1:40 PM*
Subject: Wanting you to hear from me
*I am writing to you in regards to my awareness that you have
      received a short letter from my daddy's ex-wife about some
      issues that have upset our family tremendously. I understand
      that you have wanted to talk to my mother and I and we are
      very sorry that we have not been able to talk and tell our side
      of things. You must also understand though the situation I
      have been in. I have lost my beautiful baby who was turning
      into a beautiful little girl and have yet to be treated like the
      victim I am. I loved Kelsey with all of my heart, she was my
      best friend, and if I had any idea that he was hurting her I
      would have taken her and ran like the wind leaving everyone
      and everything else behind. It seems to me that people have
      heard the story that Kathie Briggs has told and refuse to hear
      anything else. I feel as if I have talked until I am blue in the
      face about what all I was trying to do in helping my daughter
      and it has gotten me no where, except for charged with
      "SHOULD HAVE KNOWN". Everyone over looks that she
      was enrolled in play therapy and I got her acceptance papers
      in the mail the day she died and she was set up for an EEG in*

272

November to see if in fact she was having seizures. I WAS TRYING!!!!!!!! Okay people and the DA say how could I have not known, but then turn around and let the man who is charged with 1st degree murder of my two and a half year old daughter see his children as he pleases. Well, if I SHOULD HAVE KNOWN then heaven forbid if something was to happen to one of his kids while in his care who would then be charged with SHOULD HAVE KNOWN? Another thing that has gotten me upset is that this person that has been charged with Kelsey's murder is out doing as he pleases just living a normal life and going to work everyday and working with a state witness to whom is his best friend. I thought this guy had to have restrictions to be out on bond or would go back to jail. Once again I am following my rules I am given, but he is not and no one seems to care. Also his bond is set at $1,000,0000.00 and then is lowered to $250,000.00 so of course he gets out of jail, but do you see or hear Kelsey's paternal grandmother; the great Kathie Briggs; out protesting about that? Of course not. But I thought she was out looking for "Justice for Kelsey". I know you have no control over all of this, but I just wanted to let you know about some stuff that has us all VERY UPSET. Thank you for your time and I am looking forward to hearing back from you VERY soon. Thank you, Raye Smith

From: Sherri To: Gayla March 17, 2006 12:21 PM
Subject: Get Together
Hello! I was wondering if we could get together sometime this week
end. I don't want to be the official PR person, but I do have
some ideas. Course, I would be cheaper!! Ha ☺ We should
get a "time-line" of the last year of Kelsey. I know Raye
Dawn has a calendar, and surely we can use some of the
DHS records to back up some dates. What if we start
chronological order of who was with Kelsey and when and
start feeding it to the media (newspapers first) and have
documents to back it up. Also all the classes Raye Dawn took
during this time verses other "caretakers" of Kelsey. Things
like that. It's time for Raye Dawn and you to start defending
your rights as a good mommy and grandma!! Surely your
lawyer can get Lance's military records. I've heard some
interesting things about him and the military....also, do you
know when Kathy left her kids on the courthouse steps? I
would like to get ahold of those documents too. It's time to
turn this thing around. Luv you all, Sherri

From: Sherri To: Gayla March 17, 2006 1:12 PM
Subj: Interesting...
Thought you might need to know this.

[The following post from Kelsey's Purpose was included in the
email]

KJBriggs Posts: 201 Kelsey Briggs Week in Wynnewood
Kelsey will be honored April 20th-27th with Kelsey Briggs week at the
...Exotic Animal Park in Wynnewood, OK. One of our
member, Cheryl..., donates money to this animal park and
told them of Kelsey. They were so touched by her story, the
decided to dedicate a week to her memory each year. This is
such a thoughtful offer and another honor for her. I hope to
take all of the grandchildren there that week. We have never
heard of this park and plan to have a new adventure. Thank

*you Cheryl, you are a kind and generous lady. Thank you,
Kathie*

*From: Sherri To: Gayla March 20, 2006 1:31 PM
Subj: Governor's letter*

*I just had to write something! Here is a copy of his article and then
my letter.*

*Protecting Children
March 17, 2006
Few people are comfortable discussing issues of child abuse and
neglect. The very thought of doing grave harm to a child is
repugnant to most human beings, and for good reason.
Children are our most vulnerable and innocent citizens.
Their very existence depends on our protection and care.
That is why it is all the more important for Oklahomans to
face this disturbing phenomenon. Of paramount concern, we
must ensure that our hard-working child abuse investigators
have the resources and manpower necessary to do their jobs.
In my executive budget this year, I am proposing funding for
the Oklahoma Department of Human Services to hire 112
additional child abuse investigators over the next two years.
Moreover, I am calling for a pay raise for these men and
women who have such a monumental responsibility resting
on their shoulders. Oklahoma cannot waver in its resolve to
protect children. Over the past few months, Oklahomans have
read with a mixture of grief and sadness the case of Kelsey
Briggs, a 2-year-old girl who died last October as the result
of child abuse. Perhaps the most tragic aspect of Kelsey's
story, however, is that it is all too common. In 2004, 51
children in Oklahoma died from abuse and neglect. While
such cases are certainly shocking, we must not lose sight of
the fact that no instance of child abuse and neglect is
tolerable. Last year, DHS investigators confirmed 13,328
cases of child abuse and neglect, an increase from 12,347 in
2003. Child abuse destroys lives – both literally and
figuratively – and perpetuates a cycle of violence that can
continue for generations. If you suspect an incident of child
abuse or neglect involving someone you know, please contact*

the Oklahoma Child Abuse/Neglect Statewide Hotline at 1-
800-522-3511. It is critical that all of us recognize the duty
we have to help protect our most precious resource: our
children.

[Sherri's letter to the Governor]

Governor Henry,

I support the changes of the DHS and State Children's protection
laws. I do NOT agree with you referring to Kelsey in your
statements. I am a member of Kelsey's maternal family. We
are the side of the family that has been quiet about this case
due to ongoing investigations. Thanks to Kathy Briggs and
her paternal side of the family, Kelsey has been exploited as
the "poster child" for child abuse. Unfortunately, her
stepfather was the abuser and charged with her murder.
Kelsey was loved very much by her mother and family. Her
mother has NEVER been charged with child abuse. If Kathy
Briggs is suing the state for 15 million dollars, why isn't she
helping abused children NOW verses trying to get the Judges,
DA, CASA workers, and DHS workers all fired??? Governor,
there is so much more to this case than just reading about it
in the media. Please refrain from pointing Kelsey out as the
ultimate child abuse case. Yes, we lost a little family member,
and yes, justice will be served. Justice for Kelsey will NOT be
served by corrupting the public's opinion of Kelsey's mother
and maternal family. We are fighting now to get her pictures
off billboards and posters. It breaks our hearts every time we
see them. Since when does a mother lose rights of her child
even after death? Sincerely, Sherri

Kathie's Purpose

March, 2006

The next step in the gang's plan to destroy Raye was to deliver a petition to the district attorney. I captured posts from the petition that included threats against Raye and Gayla and name-calling. Why was that type of behavior allowed if it was supposed to be from a group that fought abuse? Why were these people not concerned about Mike Porter? Where was the petition against him? Following is a sample of the comments from the over 2,600 signatures captured.

We endorse the <u>SEEKING JUSTICE IN THE DEATH OF KELSEY BRIGGS</u> Petition to District attorney, Lincoln and Pottawatime County.
Read the <u>SEEKING JUSTICE IN THE DEATH OF KELSEY BRIGGS Petition</u>

To: District attorney, Lincoln and Pottawatime County

Any person or persons who fail to report child abuse and has the opportunity to prevent or remove the child from harm and does not do so, shall be subjected to equal punishment as the person or persons who physically caused the death of the child. All individuals who knew of and participated in the abuse and death of Kelsey Briggs, and did not take preventative measures to prevent it, should be punished to the full extent of the law - no deals.

Addresses in this petition are optional, but if possible, please at least post your zip code. Thank you.

Sincerely, <u>The Undersigned</u>

i think they should fri ,she was a baby and never had the chance to know love or life. so why should they have any more mercey than they gave that baby – from zip code 73036

277

she needs to pay – from zip code 73118

*I am a deputy court clerk in Alfalfa County, Ok; I do not believe
     child abusers are ever properly held accountable. Children
     are gifts given to us to care for and protect. The legal system
     has let them down terribly. – from zip code 73728*

*I fail to understand how taking the life of a child allows you to be
     bonded out. Is murder really okay in our great state? – from
     zip code 73026*

*With documented history of abuse what were they thinking puting
     that child back in that home (hell)? – from zip code 73065*

*they should all be punished especially the mother for what she did to
     that poor little girl – zip code unknown*

*An eye for an eye. You take a life, (or allow one to be taken) you
     should give yours in return. – from zip code 74855*

*Her mother deserves to be sentenced for allowing this to happen. –
     from zip code 74859*

*Kelsey's death is a horrible disgrace! The judge, all DHS workers,
     the hospital and medical workers, the Meeker Police
     Department. have all FAILED ! I am ashamed of all of you!
     Most of you were paid public servants who are a disgrace to
     mankind ! May God show mercy on your sorry souls..... –
     from zip code 89117*

*The government seems to have different standards concerning the
     step-father and mother. The mother is pregant, but that does
     not make her a mother or innocent. She is a violent sort who
     many feel actually caused the death. It does not appear that
     is even being considered. Why? – from zip code 73026*

*I work in ER in Odessa,TX Isee abuse all yhe time hang the suckers
     for Kelsey and all others that no longer have a voice!!!!!! –
     from zip code 79761*

278

I have seen people do lesser crimes that have done life and yet I
afraid that all that have been involved in this incident will get
a slap on the hand. I personally feel that the mother and the
mothers mother have a lot more to do with this childs injuries
than is being admitted or let know. The stepfather is guilty
too, but I think he is getting the shaft. All involved need to be
dealt with. – from zip code 74855 (Meeker)

The mother should be hung as should the stepfather!!!!! – zip code
unknown

NO DEALS. Do what is right for Kelsey, not what is easiest for you.
– from zip code 73118

Kelsey's mother has NO excuse ! – from zip code 74864

hang them both!! – from zip code 74033

i feel so sorry so the father, it made me cry to read about the little
girl. I hope that her mom and her step-dad rotten in prison!!
– from zip code 73541

This little girl shouldn't have died..senseless.Kelseys mom should be
ashamed of herself...hope you rot in hell – zip code unknown

I think this woman should be held responsible and be in jail as well I
also think that she should get life in prison with out any
chance of parole. Also sterilization so she cant produce and
hurt anymore children again. – zip code unknown

Fry him, this was uncalled for what a rotten man this person is, and
the Mom where the hell was she when all this crap was going
on. How sick, you both deserve to die!!!!!! – zip code
unknown

Though 99% of the petition signatures with comments focused on
hate toward Raye, some, such as the one above, also mentioned Mike
Porter. Because he had been charged with murder, why would the

focus be on Raye and not him? Could it have something to do with the hundreds of false stories circulating the Internet by Kelsey's Purpose members?

They started their campaign on the Kelsey's Purpose forum and asked for volunteers to get signatures for their petition. One witness who joined the group at a grocery store stated that a woman walked in front of Kathie Briggs while entering the store. Reportedly, Kathie turned to her and asked, "Don't you know who I am?" This same question would allegedly be asked later by her son, Lance Briggs, while shopping at a local department store. Was the local fame their new purpose?

Windy Posts:190 Poll – Volunteers for petition - I'm taking a poll to see how many people would be willing to go to the Shawnee Wal-Mart or other large businesses there and get a petition signed to take to the DA in the very near future. We feel like other avenues that have been used to reach the DA are not being noticed, and a petition is a strong way to get attention. How many of you would be willing to spend a couple of hours on a couple of days, gathering signatures?

Zoe's meemaw Posts: 7 Re: Poll – Volunteers for petition - Saturdays would be good for me.

Tommi Posts: 125 Re: Poll – Volunteers for petition - Bring it on, sister, I'm right there with ya. State capitol here I come!!!!!!

Faith Posts: 59 Re: Poll – Volunteers for petition - I can take Tuesdays or Wednesdays

Rwoody Posts: 1 Re: Poll – Volunteers for petition - I could do it on a Monday from 9-2

Little Rae Re: Poll – Volunteers for petition - I can spend some nonwork hours in Shawnee and I'll also get the petition around McLoud. I think this is a great idea!

Shirica Posts: 84 Re: On-line petition - Windy made a request for someone to volunteer to take the petitions to Smothermon's office on Tuesday around 2:00 pm. Is there anyone that can do this? The office is in Shawnee. You may not even actually speak with Smothermon. It could just be that you will be handing them to his secretary and leaving but Channel 4 [Cherokee Ballard's channel] will be there so you could possibly be speaking on camera. Windy said she would take off and do this if no one else could, but she has already taken off so much for other things and she lives in Piedmont. That is a long drive. Please let me or Windy know if you are willing to do this.

Sherri alerted Gayla to the bullies' new plot.

From: Sherri To: Gayla March 20, 2006 3:33 PM
Subj: petition
You do know that they got hard copy signatures at Firelake and Wal-mart, and then this online petition also. Crazy people...

Another tactic for Kelsey's Purpose members involves what they call "Kelsey Saturday." On this day, members of the group set tables outside of stores and pass out pamphlets of the Briggs' version of Kelsey's story.

Yhiannah Posts: 35 March 26, 2006
Kelsey Saturday
A Statewide Stand Against a Statewide Problem

Who: Any member of Kelsey's Purpose who desires to participate
What: A statewide stand against child abuse on a Saturday to be called "Kelsey Saturday"
When: April is Child Abuse Awareness Month. Right now, the tentative scheduled date is Saturday, April 29th.
Where: Various sites throughout Oklahoma
How: Each member of Kelsey's Purpose who desires to participate will be responsible for gathering a group to hand out Kelsey stickers in their areas of the state. (Possibly ask local civic groups to help) This means a statewide stand against child abuse will be seen. When a date is officially set, media will be

281

*notified so the public is aware of when and where we'll be
   located.*
*Other possibilities: ask local groups who work with children if they
   would like to be present.*
*More information to follow! If you are interested in being part of
   Kelsey Saturday, please send me an Instant Message or email
   me at kelseysaturday@yahoo.com*

Yhiannah Re: Kelsey Saturday
*I talked to Kathie abut my idea yesterday and she ahs given her okay
   to proceed with it. Thank you Kathie! The idea originated
   about a month ago when I realized how many of us there are,
   and lots of us in different areas of the state. Then recently, I
   started seeing posts saying, "can we do a sticker handout
   here?" It seemed logical to coordinate an effort to make it a
   statewide presence, and now the time has come. Thus, the
   idea of Kelsey Saturday was born. I've tentatively set the date
   for Saturday, April 29th. This gives us plenty of time to form
   our groups, get organized and notify the media. When people
   see a gathering of individuals for a cause in one location, I
   feel they tend to think "oh, isn't that nice," and go about
   their day. But if we are seen in various locations throughout
   the state, people will really take notice and think "Wow!
   These people are serious about standing up for their cause!"
   We will be assembling our own groups, but it is a
   coordinated effort on the same day. This way, the stickers are
   not just concentrated to one area of the state. People
   everywhere are wanting these stickers, so let's make it a little
   easier for them to get one! So...if you're interested, please
   respond. I'll be checking the website and instant messages on
   a daily basis. I've also got an email address set up for Kelsey
   Saturday: kelseysaturday@yahoo.com. Please be patient
   with me on responses, there is just one of me and many of
   you. ☺*

Every year Raye and her family members write to lawmakers and
beg them to put an end to the Kelsey day and Kelsey Saturday. The
message that is shared is a false story of Kelsey's life and donations
are taken for the Briggs family. It is deplorable that they continue to
use Kelsey in this way. Volunteers have told us that they must

purchase their own stickers and pamphlets, yet the money that is raised is going where? That is a question that many are starting to ask. In 2008, I personally contacted Yhiannah and pointed out the misinformation in her brochures, but they have not been changed.

From: Sherri To: Gayla April 3, 2006 @ 5:42 AM - Subj: Info~

Found this today on the website~~
Kjbriggs Posts: 216 Re: Kelsey's Billboard - The new billboard near Meeker will be located on Highway 18. It will be between the stoplight and the cemetery going south to Shawnee. Thank you, Kathie

A little more~~
Kjbriggs Posts: 216 Re: Kelsey's Billboard - I was able to get the billboard in Meeker for a discount. The fee will be $200 a month plus a $540 production fee. I will be sending out letters to locally owned businesses and asking them to sponsor a month or what ever they can. This billboard should go up in April sometime. Thank you, Kathie

From: Sherri To: Gayla April 4, 2006 6:28 AM
Subj: KATHY INFO~~ Gayla, Here is some info for April 11th from Kathy's website. Julie S. and I are working on a way to STOP the billboard from coming to Meeker. It looks like it will be on the back side of the "Vision Bank" billboard just south of town. I think they have started on it. So, when anyone is driving to Shawnee will see the Kelsey billboard. We called City Hall and there has not been anyone applying for a permit for one. We were thinking of getting a petition signed to NOT put one in Meeker community since there is so much animosity between the families. I would like ...(the lawyer) to let us know exactly what we need to do legally so we can have that to back us up. Could you contact him about this soon as you have a chance? The Meeker town planning meeting is April 13th, and then the town board meets on the 17th. We would like to go in both times (as many as we can to come) and either have the petition or legal papers to fight Kathy with. Let me know. Thanks!! Sherri

The Smith family was not alone in trying to make efforts to bring attention to the unfair measures that had been taken in the "justice for Kelsey" campaign. The judges released a court order to ban buttons in the courtroom, weapons, or cell phones. To control the media, they specifically stated there would be no cameras or interviews in the courtroom and that witnesses could not be photographed without their permission. An order that was soon tossed aside was that the jurors were not to be contacted, even after the trials were over. Judge E. told the press, "I realize it's a fine line, because we have several competing rights. Among them are a defendant's right to a fair trial, freedom of the press, assuring the protection of jurors and witnesses and the public's right to access the courthouse without being hindered by hallways jammed with cameras." This did not stop Kelsey's Purpose members.

Windy Posts: 212 Volunteers needed for April 11 project - As many of you know, April 11 is the day we all gather at the Capitol for the childabuse awareness day, and visit with the legislators and senators. One of the members on this site is putting together some "token" packages, along with Kelsey's story to give to legislators and senators. She needs some help putting these together. She has planned on doing this on Saturday evening. She lives near Harrah. Please let me know if you can donate some of your time to go over and help her put these together. There are 200 to do! Thank you so much! Windy

From: Sherri To: Gayla April 4, 2006 9:11 AM - Subj: MORE KATHY

Yhiannah Posts: 53 Re: Kelsey Saturday – Your Help is Needed! GREAT NEWS!!! The flyers have been forwarded to all registered student organization presidents on the OU campus AND the OU Volunteer Office. We shall see what the response is. I know our groups in the metro areas have colleges, let's see about asking them to participate as well! I contacted Student Life. All campuses should have one. I'm so excited!!!!!! ~Jamie

284

Battle for Raye's Baby

April 11, 2006

Raye Dawn gave birth to Porter's son. He was born at about 4:20 p.m. and weighed 7 pounds and 4 ounces. Raye's attorney told the press, "We are cooperating with the Department of Human Services." He also stated he hoped they would make their decision of custody or visitation on the facts of the case and not "outside influences" or "wild speculation." The baby boy was born within 15 minutes of Raye's sister, Rachel's baby. Gayla told the press, "It's been kind of wild. I have two beautiful, healthy grandbabies. They're just gorgeous. I'm just so excited." Richard Smothermon told the press that Raye's baby would be taken into protective custody because of Raye Dawn's criminal charges. He stated, "She is innocent until proven guilty, but our main concern right now is for the safety of the child." Family members were being considered as possible placement of the boy.

Kelsey's Purpose members had attacked Raye and her entire family. It was now time to go after the most innocent and helpless of them all, Raye's newborn son.

Slyon Posts: 20 Re: Concerns about new baby - The paper also said that her sister Rachelle delivered 15 minutes after her, lets all pray for this new baby girl also.

Mygift9602 Posts: 5 Concerns about new baby - I am putting this post on here to ask everyone to email the head of the Lincoln County DHS, Debra..., and ask her what she plans do to ensure the safety of Kelsey's mothers newest child. I am not certain that the baby has been born, but considering that we are almost in the middle of April and the baby was due last month, I am pretty sure she has had this child already. Ms. W..'s district will be responsible for the safety of this child, since the charges that are against Kelsey's mother were done in Lincoln County. Her email address is: [address removed for privacy]. We need to ask her exactly what she is doing to make sure this child is safe, and we need to urge her, if she already hasn't, to remove this child and give it a safe home. Remind her that we DO NOT want another Kelsey. Also, please copy Howard Hendrick, the head of Oklahoma DHS, on your emails. His email address is [address removed for privacy]. Please take a moment and write to them. This little boy AND Kelsey are depending on us to make sure he is safe. This is Kelsey's little brother and none of us want to see him end up the same way poor little Kelsey did! Thanks!

Susan Posts: 87 Re: Concerns about new baby - Maybe I shouldn't say this and if the administrater needs to delete it thats fine. The suggestion to write to Debra ... and Howard Hendricks is a great idea. But don't count on anything happening. These are the two people that probably received the MOST emails and phone calls about Kelsey's safety and we all see how well they protected her.

Kjbriggs Posts: 262 Re: Concerns about new baby - [Susan] is right, they did ignore our pleas for help.[32] Let's hope they learned from that mistake and don't fail this baby. I would recommend that you find out the name of the supervisor for Oklahoma County and also cc a message to them. The more people held accountable the better. It does seem strange to think they will do their jobs now after letting Kelsey down, but it is worth the try.

Windy Posts: 252 Re: Concerns about new baby - This makes me cry this morning. I would never wish that any mother have their baby taken from them, because it is the moment that we wait for, for so long after 9 months of feeling the baby inside you, and being excited and wondering what the baby will look like, and be like. Unfortunately, this mother has proven that she does not have the same motherly instincts that normal

---

[32] See "The Naked Truth Bound in Scorn" for Kathie Briggs's e-mails to DHS and lawmakers where she states that they would not fight for Kelsey because of how she had been treated and because Lance Briggs needed to fix his truck instead of hire an attorney

mothers have, and cant love a child in the same manner we can. I hope that this morning as she wakes up, without her newest child, that she thinks about the hell she put little Kelsey through, and feels sorry for the things she did. I hope she feels the pain of something being torn and stolen from you, the same way Kelsey's happiness and life was torn and stolen from her. I pray that she gets right with God, admits to the things that she did, and asks for forgiveness. And I pray the most for this little boy who was given life into such a turbulent situation, and most likely will face the fight of his life, torn between families, for the rest of his life. I pray that God keeps him safe, and will provide him with a loving, safe home. I know Kelsey is looking down on him, watching out for him!

Mktate Posts: 2 Re: Concerns about new baby - The system finally got something right and its about time lol and the good thing is that raye dawn won't be able to abuse this baby.

The members of Kelsey's Purpose did achieve their goal. The baby was removed from Raye and put into a foster home where he was starved and neglected. At less than one month old, he almost died. Once he was placed with Raye's family member, DHS received at least three "anonymous" calls about abuse and neglect. No one was safe from these bullies.

Misty_lt Posts: 1 Re: Concerns about new baby - I also felt this way and cried for this baby because he will not get that loving bond with his parents that most babies get after they are born. Although I am glad he is safe. The news article states that they are interviewing family members for placement. That makes no sense to me at all and I hope everyone prays for this baby that they will not do to him as they did Kelsey and place him with the same family members. If they were to give him to Gayla, it would be the same thing as placing him back into RD's hands.

Sixesmum Posts: 74 Re: Concerns about new baby - Welcome baby [name removed for privacy]! My fear is that they will let the maternal family look after the baby. The same family that apparently didn't see the bruises or broken bones on Kelsey. That doesn't sound to me like a family that will take good care of this baby. I pray for a SAFE and loving home for this baby.

Jenny310 Posts: 75 Re: Concerns about new baby - I feel the same way. He has a big fight ahead of him. Hopefully, they know better than to place it with ANYONE who had contact with Kelsey, yet contends they didn't know.

Windy Posts: 96 Re: Concerns about new baby - Stop Elena. You are one of the very few people that can make me cry. Stop it! I think [Raye's baby] will be okay. If by some chance Raye Dawn does get [her baby] back, she wouldnt hurt in fear that someone is always watching. Same with Gayla. If she doesn't get him back, then I pray that he will get a chance to live in a house full of loving parents and family. He has a better chance of finding a happy family to bring him up as their own than being involved with the family he is in now. Besides, his big sister is watching over him and she is a very powerful little girl.

Remembering4U Posts: 4 Re: Concerns about new baby - I'm with the majority of you, this is such a horrible and joyous occasion. Part of me is so saddened by the fact that this little baby is going to be thrown into a system that is proven not to work effectively, but so thankful that he is being properly protected. In a perfect world a mother should always be with her children. They grew inside you and the bond and protectiveness you feel in unexplainable. But unfortunately in this case the mother is lacking these iniate instincts! I just pray for [name of Raye's child removed for privacy] and that the system does not fail him.

Edge5511 Posts: 252 Re: Concerns about new baby - Quoted text: If by some chance Raye Dawn does get [her son] back, she wouldnt hurt in fear that someone is always watching. Same with Gayla. End quoted text. I agree Kelsey's mom. But let them be the vindictive people they are. We need to watch and if they give that baby to a family member that has been proven to know about the abuse, we need to BURN the phone lines up at DHS. I would THINK that they wouldnt be this careless again, but you never know.

Yhiannah Posts:92 Re: Concerns about new baby - We pray they do anyway. I'd like to be optimistic about what will happen, but with the current DHS leadership as it is, I'm skeptical..... But by our efforts, this will CHANGE!!!!

Jenny310 Posts: 75 Re: Concerns about new baby - Zoe's Meemaw always makes me cry!!! Let's just send our letters and emails now demanding he not be placed with those "blind" people! I can't bear the thought of another baby being hurt!!!!!

Edge5511 Re: Concerns about new baby - Mary, I think you're wrong. People like Raye Dawn don't think about consequences when they are hurting a child. A blind rage takes over. As long as she is drinking, doing drugs and sleeping around, she'll be a danger to that baby.

April 14, 2006
Governor Henry, I am a cousin of Raye Dawn Smith's. I am aware that letters, faxes and emails have been pouring in to you and many other State departments from the "Kelsey's Purpose" organization regarding the safety of Raye Dawn's baby [name removed for privacy]. The Maternal side of the family is VERY upset and the State has taken [Raye's son] away from not only his mother, but also his grandmother Gayla and the rest of the family. I hope you know that MANY of Raye Dawn's family members have adopted children and are or have been foster parents. How can you place [Raye's son] with strangers???? What political motive do you have??? Does this family have to protest on the courthouse steps with banners and posters to be heard also??? If you are listening to the letters and complaints from the paternal side of the family and their so-called non-profit organization that are not registered as such in this State, just remember that they have a pending law suit against the DHS and State agencies for 15 million dollars. Here are some names of the maternal family members who have adopted children or have qualified

as foster parents: [name removed for privacy] (adopted 3 girls), [name removed for privacy] (adopted 1 boy), [name removed for privacy] (adopted 2 girls), [name removed for privacy] (foster parent qualified), [name removed for privacy] (adopted 1 girl), [name removed for privacy] (adopted 1 girl), [name removed for privacy] (adopted 1 girl), Gayla (foster parent qualified)

You cannot tell my family or me that we do not care about child abuse of children in this State of Oklahoma. ALL these family members adopted through this State and or became foster parents. Most of the children involved were neglected or abused children. This family needs answers for your actions. If we do not, we WILL be heard through the media, newspapers or such. This is just not right! I will be faxing you copies of statements from the "Kelsey's Purpose" organization's website about how they feel about his new baby. You cannot tell me they are not after Raye Dawn and her entire family. It's pretty clear they are. It's not about protecting children who have been abused, it's all about Raye Dawn. There is definitely a vendetta against her. Raye Dawn has been charged with enabling and child neglect. She has not been convicted. She is being treated as if she has been sentenced and convicted already. How can you say you have a Family Reunification Program in this State but yet place [Raye's son] with strangers when there is so many of us willing to take care of him that qualify with the State and are willing and wanting to protect him??? Why are you making this new mother, Raye Dawn feel like a failure already with this child??? What benefit comes from this? It is our opinion that this is NOT the best interest of [name removed for privacy], Raye Dawn or this family to place him in custody with strangers. Please advise us of what we need to do to resolve this issue. I do know that Gayla Smith has done EVERYTHING by your guidelines to be able to have [Raye's son] placed in her home. Raye Dawn also has abided by your rules. This family needs a response to this letter and a plan of action of what will be happening to ensure [Raye's son's] placement. Regards, Sherri, Maternal Family Member

Missing Funds

April, 2006

Meanwhile on Kelsey's Purpose…

*Kjbriggs Posts: 306 Re: Kathie - Thank you for spreading Kelsey's
story. This will help bring awareness to this sad issue. We
cannot let the end of April be the end of child abuse
awareness. This is a subject we must talk about and take
action on all year long. Please encourage people to join
Kelsey's website and share their comments or suggestions.
Thank you, Kathie*

Along with their other efforts, Kelsey's Purpose members were
making plans to put their flyers all over the State of Oklahoma. They
required money to go to Kathie Briggs, personally, in order to get the
flyers printed. Donations poured into the Briggs' mailbox and were
said to have disappeared. As mentioned previously, one witness
claims that as much as $10,000 went missing and Kathie Briggs
claimed it all went to purchase stickers. Yet I was told that the stickers
were not provided by Kelsey's Purpose. Kelsey Saturday hosts are
required to purchase their own stickers. It seemed that Kelsey's
Purpose was turning into a business rather than an organization
fighting abuse.

*Kjbriggs Posts: 576 April 17, 2006 Re: Lifesaver Flyers - The
address to get the flyers ordered is: - [Kathie's mailing
address removed for privacy] - Thanks, Kathie*

*Yhiannah Posts: 138 Re: Kelsey Saturday~~Your Help is needed -
Charlie still has some of our stickers at the shop. If anyone
has businesses or individuals who were interested in
donating, several options are available. FOR TAX
DEDUCTIBLE RECEIPTS, DONATIONS MAY BE SENT*

*TO: Prevent Child Abuse Oklahoma [address removed for privacy] *Please write kelseyspurpose in the memo space so it will go in her account. TO DONATE WITHOUT NEEDING A TAX DEDUCTIBLE RECEIPT, DONATIONS MAY BE SENT TO: Kathie Briggs [address removed for privacy] TO DIRECTLY HELP WITH THE COST OF STICKERS, PLEASE CONTACT: Charlie's Sign Shop [address and phone number removed for privacy] Payments can be mailed or made by debit/credit card over the phone. *If you are calling to donate specifically for Kelsey Saturday, please specify this when you call. Charlie has a separate list set up for this event. TO PAY BY PAYPAL: Ashley... has graciously offered us the option of sending money through paypal to her account and she will see that it gets to Kathie. Log in to PayPal (accounts are free). Ashley's email for PayPal is ...family@valornet.com. Donations are appreciated and the money will go to the stickers, signs, rallies, or any other things we can do to keep Kelsey's story out there. If you have donations, please let me know which group and how many stickers you have donations for. Any questions, please let me know.*

Ashley was the same person who ran the bashboard. She was also the daughter-in-law of Donna, the state's main witness against Raye. Her support of the Briggs was taken a step further when she provided her Paypal account for donations for Kathie Briggs. Not one of these aspects came into question at Raye's trial. This would have been important for her defense.

The following post from Kelsey's Purpose provides proof that volunteers purchased their own "Kelsey" supplies. So where did the donations go?

Julie B. Posts: 19 Re: Kelsey Saturday~~Your Help is Needed! - Hey everyone- I just handed out over 100 fliers to fellow classmates at OU. They were already talking about the stickers when I came to class today. A couple of the girls are in sororities and they really want the stickers. They also are disgusted by what happened to Kelsey and this one girl took a stack of extra fliers to give to her friends. The word is getting out there and it gives me goose bumps to think of the impact Kelsey is making on everyone. She is definitely with us in spirit. Office Max made me pink copies of Jamie's flier for 5 cents a copy and I've almost gone through 300 of them. I am going to go by there after I meet with Jamie about somethings. Our newspaper here on campus wants a press release from Jamie to see if they can print the story. Everyone pray that they put it in, because it's up to them what they decide to print. Tomorrow I am going to hit all of our public schools to put a flier in the teacher's breakrooms. I got permission to do that yesterday. I will also do to churches, doctor's offices, and all of the social services agencies. My little girls daycare has them on dispaly in their lobby and wants stickers so I said I would order 200 for 25.00. We are on a roll here in Norman...

Kelsey's Purpose members sought to spread their "cause" everywhere, even in small towns that are barely a blip on the state map such as Little Axe. Their true agenda? Reaching possible jurors across the state. But, as you will see, not at the expense of Kathie Briggs or the thousands in donations she was said to have collected.

Izabelmammy Posts: 15 Re: Kelsey Saturday~~Your Help is Needed! - Hello Everyone, I live in the Little Axe area. On April the 29th we are having the Spring Thing at Little Axe on Highway 9 North of the highway near the casino. I found a paper about it. They are having a Chili Cook off, Horse rides, horse shoe tournament, blood drive, food fair, games, garage sale etc. The paper I have says a non-profit booth is available for $15.00...I have a lung disease and if it is really hot I won't be able to stay out in the heat long but maybe if we have enough people interested in coming out there to the booth we can rotate the help. You can e-mail me and let me know if this is something of interest to Kelsey Saturday. I think we could probably post the location on here and maybe another article in the newspaper (good job, Julie) and maybe alot of people would show up and maybe make donations also. Let me know and I will find out if we can get a booth and more details. [name and email address removed for privacy]

*Kjbriggs Posts: 306 Re: Kelsey Saturday~~Your Help is Needed! - I
    will be available to help part of that day in Little Axe. When
    you get the booth secured[33] let us know the time and we will
    get some things ready. This is a wonderful idea. Perhaps
    others can help after they finish at their post. I will get
    buttons ready. Julie, You make me tired just reading about
    your energy. You must be young!! Thank you, Kathie*

*Izabelsmammy Posts: 15 Re: Kelsey Saturday~~Your Help is
    Needed! - The lady at the Little Axe Chamber says the
    festival starts at 10am. She says most people start getting
    there and setting up things about nine. So I will say that I can
    be there at that time. I will glad to pay for the booth as well
    as some stickers or whatever. My grandaughter...has a
    soccer game that day so my daughter won't be able to help
    until after the game but she is willing to help. My other
    daughter probably can help also if she does not work. Just
    give me suggestions on what we will need and want in the
    booth and I'll see it is done. Any and all help will be
    great...The more people we have the louder message we can
    send. I have not been able to be at any of the rallys or
    anything so tell me what is best to do.*

Without an offer to pay for the booth or this volunteer's expenses,
Kathie Briggs then turned her attention to Kelsey's daycare owner,
Julie. She had been a vocal supporter of Raye Dawn and attended court
with the Smith family. In the fall of 2004, when Kathie Briggs got
visitation of Kelsey, Julie noticed finger mark bruises on Kelsey's
legs. She took pictures and reported the Briggs to DHS. These pictures
somehow disappeared. But Julie's suspicion of Kathie Briggs and her
support for Raye would make her next on the target list. Julie's
daycare would soon close its doors forever.

---

[33] i.e., when you pay the $15 to rent it

DHS Changes

April, 2006

*Kjbriggs Posts: 306 RE: DHS messed up again! - We all know or
should know that not reporting child abuse is a crime. What I
would like to know is how often does a person get charged
for failing to report it? What happens when a licensed DHS
day care states they took pictures of what they suspected as
abuse and did not report it? It happened in our case. What
happens when a licensed DHS day care tries to bill the father
for payments she has already received from the state? It
happened in our case. Charges have not been filed as of yet,
and it is not out of the question that they could be, but why
doesn't DHS take action? They were informed of both of
these problems along with others. These are not allegations
that do not have documentation to back them up. All of this
was presented in court. Thank you, Kathie*

The following excerpt regarding Julie's role comes from Judge
Craig Key's book, *A Deadly Game of Tug of War: The Kelsey Smith-
Briggs Story*. Kathie Briggs wanted to blame DHS, but even the
experts were confused due to the cloud of suspicion that followed
Kathie.

*The most independent supporter of Raye Dawn's to testify at the
February 4ᵗʰ hearing was Julie, the owner of Kelsey's in-
home daycare. She had taken care of Kelsey since before her
first birthday until the battle for the little girl turned ugly.
Prior to this time period, she did not know anyone involved in
this case, yet at one point, she had to order Kathie Briggs
never to return to her home.*
*According to Julie, when Kelsey first started with her daycare, she
was a funny and busy kid. Kelsey was very active and
climbed on everything. Julie couldn't even place Kelsey in a
portable crib for naptime, because she would climb out.*

Instead, she had to be placed on the couch or on a mat on the floor.

From Julie's observations, Raye Dawn was a good mother and had always been appropriate with her daughter. When Julie started noticing bruises on Kelsey in August of 2004, she wasn't overly concerned. Kelsey was very active, fair skinned, seemed to fall down a lot, and bruised easily. However, when the bruising became more consistent, she became alarmed.

According to Julie's observations, in late August to early September, 2004, around the same time Kathie Briggs was granted grandparent visitation, Kelsey had a couple of bruises on her upper leg. In October, 2004, she had one on her arm and one on her upper thigh by her buttocks. As was Julie's custom, she called the DHS daycare licensing supervisor and reported the increased occurrences of bruising. DHS told her to keep track of who Kelsey had been with at the time she noticed any bruising.

At the direction of DHS, Julie made notes that the bruises would show up on Mondays after Kelsey had visited Lance and Ashley, or Kathie Briggs for the weekend. This concerned her because she hadn't noticed bruises on Kelsey before Kathie's weekend visitation had been awarded.

Julie contacted Raye Dawn about her concerns and asked if she noticed the bruises. Raye Dawn confirmed that she had seen them. According to Julie, Raye Dawn was also concerned, because when Kelsey returned home after one visit with the Briggs, she thought some of the bruises were slashes like finger marks over Kelsey's knees, and some looked like finger marks on her buttocks.

In January, 2005, after Kathie got the emergency guardianship custody order, she went to pick Kelsey up from Julie's home daycare. According to Julie, Kathie jumped out of her car, instantly became angry, and started yelling at her. Julie held on to Kelsey as Kathie grabbed her little arm and tried to rip her loose. Julie was afraid that Kathie would hurt Kelsey by pulling on her in that manner, so she let Kathie take little Kelsey.

Once Kathie snatched Kelsey from Julie's arms, Julie told Kathie that she was not to come back to her property. Julie felt that because she ran an in-home daycare and other children she cared for were present, they did not need to witness Kathie yelling and screaming at their caretaker.

As Kathie angrily stormed off, she informed Julie that Kelsey would not be returning to her daycare and Julie could feel free to fill Kelsey's spot.

I always found it interesting that according to Julie, Kelsey did not hold her arms out to Kathie or act like she wanted to go with her. Julie came to the hearing to support Raye Dawn because she had seen, first hand, Kelsey's reaction to Kathie.[34]

Meanwhile on Kelsey's Purpose...

Tommi Posts: 226 May 7, 2006 RE: DHS - I agree with what Kathie said. Maybe a parent can make a mistake that hurts a child. Maybe with the right resources, that parent can become the kind of parent who has the INSTINCT to not hurt their child. Unfortunately, I think those cases are few and far between. A repeat offender should have their parental rights severed. I also agree with Jean when she says that removing a child from their home is traumatizing. I disagree that it is less traumatizing for a three year old boy to be held in a bath tub full of scalding water and remain with his parents, than to endure being separated from that "parent." We need to think of the children's rights. A three year old cannot make the decision as to what is best for him. He may think the child welfare worker who came and took him from his home is the boogieman. That's okay as long as he is still alive to think that. The three year old I am referring to isn't. I will stand by the fact that you cannot teach instinct to someone. If a parent doesn't have the instinct to keep them from biting their child, they never will. I use the term "biting" because of a child that was removed from her mother because she was biting her. after several months, she was given back to the mom. Less than 2 weeks later, the girl is returned to her grandmother with adult teeth marks on her face.

---

[34] Key, Craig. *A Deadly Game of Tug of War: The Kelsey Smith-Briggs Story.* Garden City, NY: Morgan James Publishing, 2007.

Kelsey was returned to Raye with bite marks and scratch marks on her body. When Raye reportedly asked what happened, Kathie Briggs made statements such as "she shouldn't have sat on the cat." Yet, Kathie Briggs claims to have taken every injury to Kelsey seriously. Did she?

Malena Posts: 29 May 7, 2006 Re: DHS - When a child is taken out of the home due to some form of abuse, why wouldn't the grandparents automatically get the right to take the child? Can anyone answer this for me? Seems to me like that would be the best answer if the grandparents are stable, loving and can care form the, right?

Kelsey's Purpose members did not have access to Kelsey's DHS records. They only knew the story that was being told. Kathie Briggs claimed that she could not fight the fact that Kelsey was placed back with Raye and Mike Porter just months before her death. But the truth was that she did not want to be supervised with Kelsey and Lance wanted to spend money fixing his truck—not fighting for his daughter.

Evidence of Sexual Assault Ignored

May, 2006

As efforts turned to Raye's baby and removing her from Raye, Richard Smothermon told the press that he hired the best expert in the United States to perform a second autopsy on Kelsey, but he had kept it a secret to spare the family further grief of seeing Kelsey's body exhumed and reburied on the news. He stated of the expert, "He reviewed all the evidence and had an opinion. The autopsy was necessary to support his opinion."

Gayla reportedly told the press that she could not imagine the horror that Kelsey was put through by Mike Porter. Apparently, Smothermon told Judge E that the autopsy was necessary because of certain injuries that were found in the first one still posed questions. Allegedly, he wanted to establish the exact nature of Kelsey's injuries and a better timeline since Porter insisted the injuries occurred before he arrived home that day.

According to the autopsy, Dr. Hawly wrote, "…The association of this injury with non-accidental trauma in children is well-known. The mechanics of the injury require a constrictive blunt impact force, squeezing around the circumference of the mid-abdomen, like a seat belt worn too high on the abdomen during a motor vehicle collision. The stage of organization of the pancreatic pseudocyst would be consistent with that original injury having occurred in August (traffic collision about 8/25/05) and death on October 11, 2005…*Patterned injury of forcible sexual assault is present*, as well as a significant medical history of numerous remote healed fractures and other blunt impact injuries." According to Dr. Hawley's notes, the information he received from Smothermon led him to write, "What I learned from a

300

review of the available records was that this 2-year and 10-month old child died while in the custody of Michael Porter."

Even with the release of this disturbing information, the bashboard once again focused on Raye and her new son and not on Mike Porter, the man free on bond who was now facing sexual assault charges as well as murder charges against Kelsey.

Posted by "Anonymous" Monday, May 22, 2006 @ 6:16 PM - Gayla is getting the baby, yes. Isn't it disgusting?

Posted by "Anonymous" Monday, May 22, 2006 @ 8:18 PM - I wonder who told you Gayla is getting the baby? I think someone lied to you. Or you are a Smith and it is just wishful thinking. ;) Either way I am sorry.

Posted by "Anonymous" Monday, May 22, 2006 @ 6:22 PM - No girl- Seriously!!! She's getting the baby. I swear! No, I am not a Smith.

Posted by "Anonymous" Monday, May 22, 2006 @ 6:24 PM - If she was getting the baby she would already have him. So you just reduced your word to rubble. I don't doubt that she thinks she will, and probably told everyone so. But I think there are still a few people left in this world with some common sense. Thank God.

Posted by "Anonymous" Monday, May 22, 2006 @ 6:24 PM - I heard that Gayla is no longer allowed to live with [Gayla's friend] if she has the baby.

Posted by "Anonymous" Monday, May 22, 2006 @ 6:26 PM - Mark my words. Gayla will have that baby by the end of the week.

Posted by "Anonymous" Monday, May 22, 2006 @ 6:27 PM - I guess we will all see who is right after the court hearing.

Posted by "Anonymous" Monday, May 22, 2006 @ 6:28 PM - Ok. Well then we will start a countdown. When Friday comes and

301

she still don't have her then will you be here to say you were wrong? Didn't think so. Lol

Posted by "Anonymous" Monday, May 22, 2006 @ 6:29 PM - Do you even know when the court hearing is? You guys crack me up. Keep up the good work with the misinformation. You are doing a swell job.

Posted by "Anonymous" Monday, May 22, 2006 @ 6:29 PM - SHE IS GETTING THE BABY FOR A FACT...I am not making this up. That is all I am going to say about that.

Posted by "Anonymous" Monday, May 22, 2006 @ 6:30 PM - Just show up Friday to admit that you are wrong ok. You do not know so much as you think you do.

Posted by "Anonymous" Monday, May 22, 2006 @ 6:31 PM - If you actually knew anything you would know when the court date is. But you don't. Or you would know you sound like a fool.

Posted by "Anonymous" Monday, May 22, 2006 @ 6:34 PM - Anon at 6:31 – see the other anon at 6:31. When is the court date? If you know then say it.

Posted by "Anonymous" Monday, May 22, 2006 @ 6:35 PM - I just mean that it does not affect me if the baby goes to Gayla, Mike's family, or a foster home. I do not know enough about what goes on in any of their homes to make a decision of preference. I am just telling you what I know because of VERY reliable leaks of information.

Posted by "Anonymous" Monday, May 22, 2006 @ 6:37 PM - You need to re-examine your definition of reliability. And when is that court date? Con on "insider". Fill us in. Please.

Posted by "Anonymous" Monday, May 22, 2006 @ 6:38 PM - So my offer remains. When Friday comes and Gayla does not have the baby will you be here to admit that you were wrong? I doubt it. That would make a first.

Posted by "Anonymous" Monday, May 22, 2006 @ 6:38 PM -
Honestly, I was not given the exact date. I didn't ask either. I
just know that it is this week. If you don't believe me – I
really don't care one way or the other.

Posted by "Bunch of BS" Monday, May 22, 2006 @ 6:38 PM - Anon
6:26 – Are you bothered by it or do you just like to start shit?
Does it make you angry? If it does, it sure doesn't show in
your posts. IF you think Gayla is getting that baby, have you
spoke up to anyone? Or do you just fin it funny?

Posted by "Anonymous" Monday, May 22, 2006 @ 6:45 PM - If the
date has come and gone, I would believe you. I never said
that I could be wrong. I work in a law office where I get to
hear a lot of things about this case. I know what I hear. I am
smart enough to know not to ask questions about key pieces
of information that I do not hear.

Posted by "Anonymous" Monday, May 22, 2006 @ 6:48 PM - You
work in a law office and you are disseminating important
information on a blog? Whoa. You are either stupid or a liar.
And I told you were wrong. But you refused to believe it. It
wouldn't be so bad if you were just like, "hey I heard this, I
don't know if it is true or not".

Posted by "Anonymous" Monday, May 22, 2006 @ 6:5? PM - First
of all, there are thousands of law offices in Oklahoma and
you have NO way of telling which one. I could work for
[Porter's attorney], I could work for [Raye's attorney], or I
could work for Joe Blow. You would be VERY surprised
where leaks are being made in this case.

Could this person possibly work for the district attorney?

Posted by "Anonymous" Monday, May 22, 2006 @ 6:55 PM - My
money is on Joe Blow. Because your information sure does
blow.

Posted by "Anonymous" Monday, May 22, 2006 @ 6:55 PM - You
will all see that they are giving the baby to Gayla as a foster

303

parent situation. That is the truth. Don't get mad at the messenger for it. Blame it on D.H.S., I guess. They are messing up again.

Posted by "Anonymous" Monday, May 22, 2006 @ 7:02 PM - If what you say is true Anon 7:00 – then I would really hope that I am wrong and they do not give the baby to Gayla. I am just telling you what is going around my office from a VERY reliable source.

Posted by "Anonymous" Monday, May 22, 2006 @ 7:04 PM - Gayla is getting the baby. This is the truth. That is why Gayla and [her friend] aren't together in the same living space. So they would give her the baby.

This would not be the first leak of legal information. Kathie Briggs transcribed her version of Raye Dawn's OSBI interview from just days after Kelsey's death and posted them on the Internet. This is a crime. When asked where she got the copies of the video, as previously mentioned, she stated "Mike Porter's attorney." Could these leaks be related?

Sherri contacted Raye's attorney to inform him of the group's latest plans.

Thought you might want to know…this is posted on the Fox 23 News in Tulsa. I emailed it to Gayla, and she wanted me to fax it to you. Sherri

Kelsey Briggs Day at Bell's Amusement Park Posted June 6, 2006 11:16 AM - Members of a group called "Kelsey's Purpose" in memory of 2 year old Kelsey Briggs from Meeker Oklahoma who died from child abuse on October 11, 2005, will be at Bell's Amusement Par July 22 2006 from 1pm- 11pm for a day they are calling "Kelsey Briggs day at Bell's Amusement Park" passing out Kelsey's bumper stickers, buttons, and flyers and a portion of the money that Bell's makes that day will go towards Kelsey's Purpose to help get a traveling billboard here in Tulsa. If you have any questions please contact Jamie at [phone number removed for privacy]

.... For more information about Kelsey's Purpose please visit our website www.kelseyspurpose.org.

Crdb169 Posts: 69 Kelsey Day at Bell's Amusement Park - I just spoke with..., owner of Bell's..as many of you know, they sustained much damage from the June 6th storm. He said they are hoping to be open by the end of next week, so we can be assured that July 22 will be good. He asked how many tickets we would like for our members for general admission on Kelsey Day...so...let me know how many you want and I will tally them up and let him know.

The public persona of Kelsey's Purpose members was one of a group that cared for children and fought against abuse. The side hidden in the shadows was that of a group that had turned into abusers themselves. They continued on their bashboard.

Posted by anon500: -Sunday June 4th 2006 @ 10:53 pm- I saw Mildred and ... the Crank on the news. They've got major problems for someone so old. They don't have to worry about Mildred giving them too much money.

Posted by anon500: -Sunday June 4th 2006 @ 10:56 pm- They've got to campaign for the next child of theirs. Let's see...set a court date and how many months does the child have left. Those beautiful pictures of Kelsey everywhere. Too bad she wasn't as cute as her mother. When you're ugly inside, it shows on the outside. Look at grandmommy dearest Smith, some ugly thing musta whupped on her.

Posted by Anonymous: -Sunday June 4th 2006 @11:00 pm- What did Mildred and [her friend] have to say on the news??

Posted by anon500: -Sunday June 4th 2006 @ 11:20 pm - ......With Kelsey a poster child for child abuse, Raye Dawn could be the poster parent for alcoholism, Drug addiction and BAD parenting skills and Child abuse. I think we need to start a new fund and have Raye's picture on there with all those charges. Big Billboard, and then a put an X thru the middle of it. They could say, daughters, don't turn out like some mothers.

*Posted by Meeker ite: -Monday June 5ᵗʰ 2006 @ 8:15 am - ....Carl
     sold Leedar about 1 month ago. Has anyone noticed his dads
     car lot has gotten bigger since then. He's got money now.
     They still don't know who burnt there building down just a
     little while after Gayla got fired for embezzeling. Some of the
     people that were named on the witness list deeply regret
     being duped by R.D. & Mildred. One of my parents grew up
     with Mildred and said that she never took care of her own
     children that she was always pawning them off onto one of
     her sisters. They were a great inconvenice for her. Another of
     my family grew up with Gayla went to school with her. They
     said she was always very mean and hateful and always
     thought she was above everyone else. She to had a bad
     reputation just like R.D. so see the apples didn't fall from the
     tree. That loving family would go over and prop Grandma
     Winters up in the morning leave her alone then stick her in
     bed at night. Were they too tight to put her where she could
     have nursing care just as they Elvis and Ray. Do they think
     dying alone is the way to go. Is it money with them or what.
     Do you leave someone that's over 100 alone to fin for
     themselves. I had a lot built up.*

*Posted by "Anonymous" Friday, June 9, 2006 @ 4:38 PM - Why do
     you think Gayla should be charged? I think that she may also
     be guilty, but I was just wondering what your view is.*

*Posted by "Anonymous" Friday, June 9, 2006 @ 4:39 PM -
     Everyone in Meeker thinks that Gayla and Mildred both
     should be charged.*

*Posted by "Jane Doe" Friday, June 9, 2006 @ 4:43 PM - From
     what Gayla has told people and on the tv, she seems like the
     type that would lie for her own daughter just to protect her
     children from anyone else and in the meantime, she didn't
     protect Kelsey. If she truly was there and saw Kelsey often,
     she should have seen all the signs of abuse and by now
     changing her story and saying that she saw how Mike was
     jealous, etc., she is just as guilty as Raye Dawn.*

306

Posted by "Anonymous" Friday, June 9, 2006 @ 5:09 PM - I agree that Gayla seems like quite the B*tch in this situation.

Posted by "Anonymous" Friday, June 9, 2006 @ 5:11 PM - I think it's a run for the money on who's the most responsible of that family, they are all non caring human feces.

These people referred to Raye's family as "non caring human feces." Yet in this next post, they aligned themselves with the man charged with Kelsey's murder and newly added charge of sexual assault.

Posted by "Anonymous" Friday, June 9, 2006 @ 5:13 PM - Does anyone know who's got the baby now? Does Gayla have it yet? Poor child, if she does. Surely Mike wouldn't allow that.

Posted by "Anonymous" Saturday, June 10, 2006 @ 12:06 AM - Oh wouldn't this be funn?!?! Mike Porter is found innocent but Raye Dawn is found guilty and goes to prison for a very, very, very long time. She becomes ugly, haggard, and a girlfriend. Mike goes to the Briggs' to express his sympathy and regrets. He gets close to one of the Briggs daughters. They get married and raise [name of child removed for privacy]. The rage and bitterness becomes more than Gayla and Mildred can stand. They get arrested for plotting to murder Kathie. They are convicted and sentenced to the same penitentiary as Raye Dawn!!!!!

Parts of this theory had actually occurred. Whose fantasy was this? Mike Porter's or one of the Briggs family members? Less than one month after evidence of the sexual assault that Kelsey had suffered was made public and the charge of sexual assault was added against Mike Porter, he was referred to as "hot."

Posted by "Anonymous" Saturday, June 10, 2006 @ 12:07 AM - I guess that's how you get everyone to be quiet, say Porter is hot haha Porter's hot, Porter's hot

Posted by "Anonymous" Saturday, June 10, 2006 @ 12:08 AM - Wow 12:06 – you put a lot of thought into that lol

307

Kathie Briggs posted the following announcement on the Kelsey's Purpose forum:

Posted by kjbriggs June 14, 2006 10:52 PM Baby [name removed for privacy] I have been given information concerning Kelsey's baby brother, ... It seems he has been admitted to an Oklahoma City hospital. I do not have anymore information at this time. Please pray for this baby. I know his guardian angel is watching over him, but he needs our help too. We will keep you updated if we receive any new information on [name removed for privacy]. Thank you, Kathie

At the time of this post, Raye's son had been in foster care where he was starved and neglected. The Smith's question is how did Kathie Briggs get sealed information on a child who was in foster care? The bullies on the bashboard picked up the news.

Posted by "Anonymous" Thursday, June 15, 2006 @ 9:30 AM - So is [Raye's son] really in the hospital?

Posted by "Anonymous" Thursday, June 15, 2006 @ 10:05 AM - In the hospital for what??

Posted by "Anonymous" Thursday, June 15, 2006 @ 10:22 AM - I am just going by the post on Kelsey's Purpose

Posted by "Anonymous" Thursday, June 15, 2006 @ 12:00 PM - Somebody needs to call Cherokee Ballard, Britten Follett, and Nick Winkler to investigate what is going on with the baby.

Posted by "Anonymous" Monday, June 26, 2006 @ 11:02 PM - The Smith family still thinks that Kathie killed Kelsey. They are some real dumb rears (to put it nicely.) It's amazing how many people have came forth and talked about how they can't stand Gayla and just put up with her because of Ray. Now that he's gone, they don't have to put up with her crap.

Posted by "Anonymous" Monday, June 26, 2006 @ 11:03 PM - The Smiths are not really highly educated people. They just know how to swindle people out of money.

Posted by "Anonymous" Monday, June 26, 2006 @ 11:04 PM - I think that [Mildred's friend] gets on this site. I'm sure that he tells Mildred what everyone says. Probably same way with [Gayla's friend] and Gayla. She's not really very educated in computers. She only had the job at Leedar because she was the owner's cousin. Until she took his money anyway.

Posted by "Anonymous" Tuesday, June 27, 2006 @ 11:21 AM - Raye Dawn was seen with a mystery man yesterday. I feel sorry for that guy.

Posted by "Zoe's Meemaw" Tuesday, June 27, 2006 @ 11:26 AM - I also heard she had a new boyfriend. I heard he was a black man and that Mildred Fowler will have a fit over Raye Dawn dating a black man! He has no idea what he has gotten himself into.

This was just another rumor, but it gave the bullies something else to use in their ongoing hate campaign.

Posted by "Anonymous" Tuesday, June 27, 2006 @ 11:33 AM - Mildred is the "ultimate Christian woman" She would never judge someone based on their skin color. She loves everyone. So they say.

Posted by "Zoe's Meemaw" Tuesday, June 27, 2006 @ 11:49 AM - Occupying a church pew ever Sunday, does not a Christian make. Actions speak louder then words and the actions of Mildred Fowler, [Mildred's friend], Gayla, Raye Dawn, Michael Porter and [Gayla's friend] are anything but "Christian". These people scare me and I don't think Christians are supposed to be scary.

Posted by "Anonymous" Tuesday, June 27, 2006 @ 11:51 AM - Poor [Raye's son]. This family only act like they want him for appearance sake. He really needs someone who will love him especially if he really has Fetal Alcohol Syndrome.

Posted by "Anonymous" Tuesday, June 27, 2006 @ 11:53 AM - Raye did not want Kelsey and took her for appearances and look how she treated her. If this child has a disability and Raye remarries it scares me to think how she will allow him to be treated.

Posted by "Anonymous" Tuesday, June 27, 2006 @ 12:19 PM - We will have a booth at the Blackberry Festival this weekend with Kelsey stickers. Anyone in that area please come by and say "hello". The Blackberry Festival is in McLoud. One of our members will also have a BUG in the car show with Kelsey magnets on it.

Posted by "Anonymous" Tuesday, June 27, 2006 @ 12:37 PM - Is it true that Raye Dawn is living in Tecumseh with her sister?

DHS visited Rachelle in her home and went through the process of an investigation due to "anonymous" calls. They had been told that Raye lived with her. This was not the case.

Posted by "Anonymous" Tuesday, June 27, 2006 @ 12:40 PM - I saw the cutest lime green BUG on Saturday at Lake Stanley Draper for the Kelsey's Purpose rally. I had Kelsey stickers on it. Is this the BUG? It was absolutely adorable.

Posted by "Anonymous" Tuesday, June 27, 2006 @ 12:41 PM - Scary to think that DHS would let her be around Rachelle's baby with criminal charges pending. I heard that Rachelle had to get assistance for her baby too. Whatever happened to working?

Posted by "Anonymous" Tuesday, June 27, 2006 @ 12:50 PM - Just curious? Do any of the Smith women (Gayla, Raye Dawn, Rachelle) currently work? How are they sopporting themselves? And did I read correctly, Gayla Smith, actually embezzled from her own brother's company? Is this true??

310

Posted by "Anonymous" [unknown date and time] - Raye Dawn and
Rachelle supposedly work. Gayla might show houses for her
man if anything. They are supported by the men in their life
as usual.

Raye's family members hosted several yard sales to pay for her
defense. Kelsey's Purpose members stalked these sales and listed the
items that were sold on their bashboard. One reformed Kelsey's
Purpose member stated that she stalked Raye under Kathie Briggs's
orders.

Posted by "Anonymous" Tuesday, June 27, 2006 @ 1:33 PM -
Where have I been? EBay?? What kind of things would
anyone want to purchase from that family? Plus, I believe
court costs, legal fees and attorney fees can be quite costly.

Posted by "Anonymous" Tuesday, June 27, 2006 @ 1:44 PM - What
are they selling Raedawgs scratch and sniff panties? Or
Mildew Fowlers scratch and sniff dentures? I know Gayla is
making some money showing Prick ...'s homes. On her
knee's.

Another rumor started by the Briggs involved who paid for
Kelsey's funeral. Kelsey had two funerals because the Briggs family
insisted on their own.

Kathie Briggs posted the following on Kelsey's Purpose in 2007
after Mike Porter was given a plea deal. Her statement was misleading
because at this time, the public still thought that Lance was in Iraq at
the time of Kelsey's death and not in a mental institution in Georgia.
It made a better story.

Post: #1 - Kelsey's Story Part 2 - I want to update some information
on Kelsey's story. Most have read the thread Kelsey's story in
summary. I want to walk some of you through our lives since
Kelsey's death. Some I have already told, but I will start with
October 11, 2005 for anyone new to our site. October 11,
2005 started out as a normal day. We knew Kelsey was with

311

*her mother and we could not see her at this time. We also
knew her father would return from Iraq anytime and his
visitation had been promised to resume. We also knew
Kelsey's mother was very upset about this. On this day I am
working on Halloween costumes for my grandchildren. I get
a call from my good friend at the beauty shop telling me
Kelsey had been taken by ambulance to the ER. Her son-in-
law had gone to the Porter home to look at some tires. When
he arrived Mike Porter was on the front porch in a panic
because Kelsey was not breathing. He was on the phone with
911 and asked his friend to help him. Kelsey's maternal
grandmother had been called prior to the 911 call and
arrived on the scene. She had Kelsey in her arms when the
first responders arrived. Kelsey's mother had gone to pick up
their other child at school. When she arrived back home she
saw them putting Kelsey in the ambulance and she rode with
them to take Kelsey to the hospital. With our current situation
with DHS I called the CASA volunteer to check on Kelsey. I
am deeply concerned because she looked so unhealthy in
August on our last visit. I called the CASA worker again and
she told me Kelsey had a seizure when in fact she had
already died. We got that news when my daughter contacted
a friend that worked in the hospital for an update. All I could
do was fall to my knees and scream. I was trying to make
some phone calls, but could barely remember any numbers.
My daughter showed up and about that time Lance called
from Fort Benning, Georgia. He was that close to being
home from the war. I had to tell him his only child had died
from a seizure. He was screaming and begging that it wasn't
true. He hung up the phone and we called the base and asked
them to locate him. We also contacted Red Cross to get him
home. Word got around fast and many people started to show
up. Food was being delivered before we realized it was
dinnertime. None of us were hungry, but some tried to eat
anyway. The Army managed to get Lance a flight home at
11:00PM that night. My 80-year-old in-laws and my sister-
in-law drove to the hospital to see if we could get any
information. When they arrived Gayla Smith started
screaming to have them removed. No one in the maternal
family had the courtesy to call and let us know Kelsey was*

312

*gone. Neither did DHS or the CASA volunteer. They were
surprised that the OSBI and the Prague police were all there
for this seizure. We picked Lance up from the airport that
night. He was a broken man when he walked off that plane.
He could barely stand and once again begged us to tell him it
wasn't true. On the way home he called the CASA volunteer
to ask question. He wanted to know if Raye Dawn and Mike
had been properly trained to handle seizures. He just did not
understand how this could have happened. He did not
understand why she was in this home in the first place. He
told the CASA volunteer he would like to meet with the Judge
and ask him. We drove Lance to his house. He went in alone
at his request, to a house that had a wife and a child in it
when he left. He was now facing a divorce and an empty
bedroom where his daughter once played. The following day
our phone was ringing non stop. The media was showing up
on our doorstep most of the day. We would not speak on
camera at this time. We had still been told the seizure took
her life. My personal suspicion was something else had
happened. After the way she looked the last time we saw her
it was obvious something was seriously wrong and we tried
to tell DHS. I really thought Raye and Mike would do
something to Kelsey and DHS would finally realize it and
give her back to our family. I never dreamed she would
actually die. We did not know that cause of death and the
autopsy had not been released so I did not tell Lance until we
had confirmation. We got our confirmation when the media
called and asked if we wanted to make a statement about the
"Homicide". It took our family awhile for this to soak in.
Some of our family members met with the OSBI to do
standard interviews. We continued to get calls from the
media wanting interviews, but we did not want to go on
camera until after Kelsey had been buried. The news was
covered with her story. We had three televisions recording
the news several times per day. We found out Raye Dawn had
taken out an EPO against Lance and myself. We did not
understand this, but felt she was trying to keep us from the
funeral. At this time we knew we needed to have our own
memorial service for Kelsey. Our attorney was out of state
and sent us to another one in OKC. He called the District*

Attorney and the Sheriff to arrange our own service. We had four hours to make the arrangements. Family members had several phones going at once contacting people. On October 15, 2005 on what should have been a celebration of my 50th birthday we got dressed for the funeral of an innocent two-year-old angel. The church was packed with more than 250 people. If you go to the thread "A Grieving Parent" you will know how difficult this was on Kelsey's Daddy. Two weeks later the stepfather, Mike Porter, was arrested for first-degree murder. I stood across the street and watched while they put him in handcuffs and took him to the county jail. We finally did some interviews and were treated very well by the media. People from all over the state were sending cards and calling. We started this Website soon afterwards to make it easier for the contacts. We had a second phone line installed to help handle the calls. For days we had to have someone here to help answer all of them. In December Mike Porter's bond was reduced from one million dollars to $250,000. He was out before Christmas. He had filed for divorce from Raye Dawn from jail. In February Raye Dawn Smith was charged with felony child neglect and felony enabling child abuse. Both hold a possible life in prison sentence. Her bond was $25,000 and she never spent one minute in jail. Her family blamed us for her mistakes. The courthouse was full of tension. In April Kelsey's body was exhumed for a second autopsy. The results showed she had been sexually abused. New charges were then filed on Mike Porter. Also in April, Raye Dawn Smith gave birth to a baby boy. He was taken into foster care where he remains at this time. Mike Porter's pre-trial was set. It took most of one day to present enough evidence to hold him over for trial. Raye Dawn testified against him. Listening to the doctor describe the autopsy was very hard on all of us. Raye Dawn waived her pre-trial. Trial for Mike Porter was set for February 12, 2007. Two weeks before it was to begin plea negotiations started. Mike Porter was willing to plead guilty to a lesser charge. Our family sat down with the District Attorney and talked about all the reasons we should or should not accept it. We expressed our desire to accept a plea for 30 years for enabling child abuse. This would eliminate the chance for appeals and keep us

from enduring a trial. On February 2, the plea was entered.
Mike Porter will serve at least 25.5 years in prison before he
is eligible for parole. Raye Dawn will face her felony charges
on June 12, 2007. She is charged with the same charge as
Porter plead guilty to and accepted 30 years plus an
additional charge of felony child neglect. This post was last
modified: 02-20-2007 01:28 PM by kjbriggs.

Kathie Briggs admitted to requesting her own funeral for Kelsey. Witnesses who attended stated that Lance Briggs smelled of alcohol, plus the Briggs stated that a family friend gave him something to "calm him down." He could barely walk and had to be partially carried to the back of the church. A later statement claimed that he wanted to sit in the back because "a soldier always sits with his back to the wall." Witnesses state that he was too inebriated to go any farther. Could this be the real reason the Briggs avoided the media that day?

As for who paid for the two funerals, the Smiths purchased Kelsey's plot at the cemetery and the victim's relief fund paid for one of the funerals. The Smiths covered the balance. Although Gayla officially owned Kelsey's plot, the Briggs added a donated headstone. Raye had plans for a stone that would match her daddy's large, heart-shaped stone since the plots are next to each other. The bullies on the bashboard believed the Briggs' stories regarding the funeral.

Posted by "Anonymous" Tuesday, June 27, 2006 @ 1:44 PM -
WHAT!!!! The Smith's never paid for Kelsey's funeral???
You have got to be kidding me!!! My blood is just boiling!
Now let me get this straight. They have money for cigarettes
and alcohol. They have money to pay thugs to beat people up.
They have money to run all over town harassing people about
displaying Kelsey stickers. They had money for bond for Raye
Dawn. Yet, they could or would not pay for Kelsey's funeral
services???

Stories also started circulating that portrayed the Briggs as victims of stalking and hacking. The guilty party...without any evidence of guilt...was always their current target. I experienced this first-hand because I, too, would be accused of crimes that were actually done to me.

Posted by "Anonymous" Tuesday, June 27, 2006 @ 1:48 PM - How evil and demonic do you have to be to hack a murdered child web site? Just ask Judge Key! The red faced brat.

Posted by "Anonymous" Tuesday, June 27, 2006 @ 1:59 PM - I heard they used the victims compensation fund to pay for her funeral. I guess they could do that since that was before the mother was criminally charged.

Domestic Violence

July, 2006

The bullies took a break from the limelight just as new charges of domestic violence against Lance Briggs made a brief appearance in the headlines. The following excerpt is from *A Deadly Game of Tug of War: The Kelsey Smith-Briggs Story*:

One of the ironies in this case is that Marie Larson later dated Lance Briggs. After Marie ended the relationship, Lance was arrested for breaking into her house on July 6, 2006, and dragging her out by her hair. He would later plead to two counts of assault and battery. One was on Miss Larson. The other was on a female friend who was staying at her apartment for Marie's protection due to prior threats by Lance. Once again, Lance is court ordered to attend anger management. [35]

Lance Briggs's mug shot

[35] Key, Craig. *A Deadly Game of Tug of War: The Kelsey Smith-Briggs Story*. Garden City, NY: Morgan James Publishing, 2007.

According to police reports, Lance smelled of alcohol and tested at a .08 alcohol concentration. When the police arrived, he was sitting in his truck with the keys in the ignition. Therefore, he was also arrested for Actual Physical Control. His friend was arrested as well when authorities found a green leafy substance that was said to be marijuana on his shorts. This would be the second time that Lance would face domestic violence charges with the first brought by Raye in 2001 when he pleaded "no contest." Since my involvement, I have learned of five women who claim to have been assaulted by Lance Briggs. Since he is on disability with the military, I have to question whether he would still get a check for being "disabled" if the military were made aware of his ability to allegedly assault four women since he became disabled.

The Briggs released another "family statement" claiming that they had to take a break from their mission. But the break would only last as long as the headlines. On August 15, 2006, Kathie Briggs posted on Kelsey's Purpose about the complaints her followers were filing against Judge Craig Key.

Kjbriggs Posts: 576 Re: Council on Judicial Complaints - Cheryl, Have you heard anything back on your complaint? Seems now would be a good time for anyone with concerns with this Judge running for this seat again to contact this board. Thank you, Kathie

Zoe's Meemaw Posts: 239 Re: Council on Judicial Complaints - Yes, they sent me a letter that they had dismissed my complaint. I later found out, that if you are not directly involved in the court case, you cannot file a complaint. I find it kind of amazing, that they even acknowledged my complaint in the first place, but they did and dismissed it.

Ignoring the Truth

August, 2006

Kathie and her supporters continued with their mission full speed ahead. Their "justice" stickers were on so many cars that one could hardly drive down the street without seeing a sticker. According to a close friend, the group visited a small town in the southern part of the state and stood on street corners, slapping stickers on back windows as cars came to a stop at stop signs. A family member of my friend rolled down the window and instructed the person that he did not want a sticker on his car. He had to repeat the order several times and then the person approached his window and shoved the sticker through the crack. Many people in the small town were reportedly upset about the fact that a sticker had been placed on their car without permission given. For those who had been watching the tactics of Kathie and her group, they knew that their mission seemed to have nothing to do with helping children. This became even more evident after Mike Porter's preliminary hearing when the bashboard opened back up with the sole purpose of ripping apart Raye's testimony against Mike Porter. The fact that the district attorney presented new evidence of Kelsey's sexual assault and asked that Mike Porter's bond be revoked (which was denied) seemed to escape this group because their only concern was a mention of a possible plea deal for Raye. Any attempts to bring up Mike Porter's new charges were squashed and the person who dared bring up the topic was threatened with expulsion from the bashboard.

Posted by the blog owner, MistyLT, on August 23, 2006 @ 1:18 PM
 - I received several emails asking for the comments to be
 opened back so that Kelseyspurpose is not clouded with posts
 about today's events and emotional opinions. I will open it up

for this, but those are the only comments that I will alow. No comments about the new charges or bashing will be allowed.

Posted by What a day August 23, 2006 @ 1:27 PM - been a long time since I've been here haha they let her testify against him? what the…that DA has a screw loose somewhere

Posted by MistyLT August 23, 2006 @ 1:30 PM - Surprises me too that they would use anything she has to say. Of course she's going to say Mike did it, she needs to save her own butt. The report of a plea bargain makes sense for her though.

Posted by "Anonymous" on August 23, 2006 @ 1:34 PM - Seems Richard likes to give plea bargains to mothers who beat their children or know they are beating them. Happened just recently.

Posted by "Anonymous" August 23, 2006 @ 1:39 PM - ok-now where is everyone-I think you all were right-needed to find a different place to chit chat about it-so where is everyone?

Posted by "Anonymous" August 23, 2006 @ 1:39 PM - Yeah it sure did…..…and it will probably happen again…after all…..these people do not really care about these children…….

Posted by "Anonymous" August 23, 2006 @ 1:41 PM - the comment about Porter rolling his eyes and shaking his head-if anyone knew Porter they would know that's part of his personality-raye dawn makes me angry

Posted by "justice81204" August 23, 2006 @ 1:42 PM - She will probably get off and never have to serve anytime in jail.

Posted by "Anonymous" August 23, 2006 @ 1:43 PM - Yes, it is his personality. He rolled his eyes at the thought that Raye Dawn would even have to tell him to take care of Kelsey.

Posted by "Anonymous" August 23, 2006 @ 1:44 PM - Justice – I hate to say it, but you are right. I would be willing to bet $500 Richard has offered her a plea bargain for her *testimony. Kind of makes you wonder why since he publicity stated that he doesn't need Raye Dawn's testimony to convict Porter. HA Must have lost all of the evidence he had at lunch or something.*

Posted by "anon" August 23, 2006 @ 1:45 PM - why they would even listen to anything she says is crazy...she is a liar

Posted by "Anonymous" August 23, 2006 @ 1:46 PM - he had to have offered her a plea bargain – there is no way her attorney would allow her to testify against him and incriminate herself without a plea bargain

Posted by "Anonymous" August 23, 2006 @ 1:50 PM - Does MP just not have the stories or proof that RD participated in the abuse, too? Why is he (and his attorney) so tight lipped? Everyone one else involved has plenty to say (Even with the gag order,) so why don't we hear from them?

Posted by "Anonymous" August 23, 2006 @ 1:51 PM - What good would it do him to go public? No one would believe him. It's not the public's business anyway. He only needs to convince 12 people.

Posted by "anon" August 23, 2006 @ 1:52 PM - so who were the other witnesses today? What did they have to say...does anyone know?

Posted by "Anonymous" August 23, 2006 @ 1:53 PM - First witness was one of the EMT's, second witness was Taber, Porter's friend that came to the house before the ambulance go there. Third witness was Raye Dawn.

Notice that this person said "came to the house" instead "arrived at" or "went to." Also, Porter's friend who was first on the scene was related to Kathie Briggs's good friend at the beauty shop, according to Kathie's post about the day Kelsey died. This was a state witness and a man who still worked for Porter at the time of his preliminary hearing.

Posted by "Anonymous" August 23, 2006 @ 1:58 PM - Either way, their both guilty. I don't know who actually killed her, but they both deserve to be convicted. Neither of them deserve to get off easy.

Posted by "Anonymous" August 23, 2006 @ 2:06 PM - I agree, they both knew what was happening to Kelsey, and one of them was doing it if not both. She's basically saying she thought the abuse was coming from the Briggs, and then realized it was him after the autopsy, if you thought ANYONE was abusing your child wouldn't you do something about regardless of who it is. Her testimony was so over the top, that I don't believe a word.

Posted by "Anonymous" August 23, 2006 @ 2:06 PM - not that comment again – i was so nice not to read that comment over and over again

Posted by "Anonymous" August 23, 2006 @ 2:09 PM - well there's only 18 comments. i'm sure you haven't heard it too many times yet.

Posted by "outsider" August 23, 2006 @ 2:11 PM - Let's just hope that RD is so busy wanting to defend herself that she is spewing without a plea bargain. Just wishful thinking I suppose. Her remark about "I do now" makes me sick. Someone explain to me why the Smiths hate the Briggs family more than the man who allegedly killed Kelsey?

Posted by "MistyLT" August 23, 2006 @ 2:12 PM - Everyone please try to limit your comments to comments about the coverage today. That is the only reason I opened it back up.

Posted by "esha" August 23, 2006 @ 2:31 PM - ahhhhhhhhhhhhhhhhhhhhhhhhhhhhhhhhhhhhh, I just wanted to scream.

Posted by "MistyLT" August 23, 2006 @ 2:32 PM - haha, I just said the same thing to someone else esha.

Posted by "Anonymous" August 23, 2006 @ 2:34 PM - I read on newsok.com that RD admitted that her attorney and the DA have been talking about a plea deal. Totally sucks. Hopefully Richard will give her more then 2 years like he did the other mother recently. The other mother even admitted that she knew about it and she still got 2 years. It's ridiculous!

Posted by "jan" August 23, 2006 @ 2:35 PM - remember this is just a prelim. They will save pretty much all they can for the trial. Today is just to decide if they have enough evidence to have a trial. I read on channel 9 that the judge says yes it will go to trial. That is when most of the real testimony and evidence will come out. I don't think a plea bargain has been made or the family would know about it by this time.

Posted by Starla August 23, 2006 @ 2:36 PM - Makes me sick to think RD was offered a "plea bargain"....no matter for what reason. They still don't "get it"[36] do they?:-? Usually people don't take a plea bargain unless they are worried they can prove the original charge right? This just makes me ill. God be with the Briggs family and especially Lance.

Posted by "Anonymous" August 23, 2006 @ 2:37 PM - The family knows a lot of things that they don't tell people on Kelseyspurpose. Don't fool yourselves.

Posted by "Anonymous" August 23, 2006 @ 2:38 PM - And most of it the Kelseyspurpose members would find very interesting.

Posted by "Anonymous" August 23, 2006 @ 2:42 PM - I think Raye Dawn needs to be sitting where Porter was sitting and Porter should be testifying against her.

Posted by "Anonymous" August 23, 2006 @ 2:45 PM - Agreed

Posted by "Zoe's Meemaw" August 23, 2006 @ 2:54 PM - This is just breaking my heart. Hearing all the details the day of Kelsey's death. I just don't know how the family endures and

---

[36] Underline by book author. Quotations by post author.

continues to be so strong and brave. My heart is literally breaking for this family and that poor baby. This should not have happened and I am just so mad I could scream!!!! Her comment, "I do now" just makes me want to hurl!!! When did she decide "I do now"??? After the plea bargain???

Posted by "Anonymous" August 23, 2006 @ 3:00 PM - People who play the victim role got good at it after awhile. I just pray the truth comes out with about the WHOLE case. I think there are many guilty of the abuse and death of this child and not just Mike Porter.

Posted by "Anonymous" August 23, 2006 @ 3:01 PM - I agree with that anon 3:00

Posted by "justice4kelseybriggs" August 23, 2006 @ 3:08 PM - what i would like to know is in one news article i read, it stated that Raye Dawn said that when she left, Kelsey had no underwear on but when she returned she had on a pullup. Why would you put a 2yr old down for a nap, with no underwear of any kind on? That puzzles me.

Posted by "Zoe's Meemaw" August 23, 2006 @ 3:09 PM - One thing I have learned in life is that we always get what we deserve in the end. Sometimes we get to witness this and sometimes we do not, but you will always reap what you sow in the end. God is watching and he is the ultimate judge and he chooses when and where.

Posted by "DandCsmom" August 23, 2006 @ 3:19 PM - I totally agree with Zoe's Meemaw. Life is one big circle and we always get what we deserve in the end. Eventually it always happens. I try to remember that when I deal with others.

Posted by "Emmasmom" August 23, 2006 @ 3:33 PM - hello, i wonder if i can spell impatient wrong again?

The next "anonymous" person pushes the fifteen-minute precedent once again in an effort to spin the odds in Mike Porter's favor.

Posted by "Anonymous" August 23, 2006 @ 3:34 PM - I used to let my babies run naked sometimes when they had diaper rash. It airs it out and helps it heal. I tend to believe Porter's statement about putting the pull up on Kelsey so the EMT's wouldn't see her naked. This man only had 15 minutes to do all of this to Kelsey. If he had hurt her, I don't see him being sane enough to be able to PLAN putting a pull up on her. Especially knowing she didn't have one on before.

Posted by "Zoe's Meemaw" August 23, 2006 @ 3:38 PM - What is that quote from the bible? "Vengeance is mine, sayeth the Lord."

Posted by "Anonymous" August 23, 2006 @ 3:39 PM - A speedy trial would not be good in this case. Let it run it course and many people testify just may expose the truth about what really happened.

Posted by "DJones" August 23, 2006 @ 3:48 PM - mmmmm, michael still out on bail/same bon. guess smotherman is already getting shot down. this guy must be desperate having to plea bargain w/rae dawn for testimony. appears he is still trying to cover for her.

The following statement is disturbing! But Kathie Briggs would later express the same thoughts about her own grandchild. She convinced her supporters that Raye had sexually assaulted Kelsey and not Mike Porter. How could a grandmother even imagine that scenario?

Posted by "DJones" August 23, 2006 @ 3:53 PM - Justice4....article stated that she testified they had been outside playing with a turtle and that she had just put a big black t-shirt on her for her nap. but, i agree, that laying odwn for a nap would be THE time for a pull up. wouldn't it? unless of course you were doing something to her when someone showed up unexpected and you didn't have time to put one back on......

Posted by "Anonymous" August 23, 2006 @ 3:55 PM - Very good DJones. I'm glad to see there are still some people left with common sense.

Posted by "esha" August 23, 2006 @ 3:57 PM - I pray that she will get hers when the time comes. Does anyone know where the trial will be held?

Posted by "esha" August 23, 2006 @ 3:58 PM - Why would any child be outside or anywhere with out underpants. Just a tshirt. whatever. Good job Djones

Posted by "DJones" August 23, 2006 @ 4:01 PM - thank you, 3:55, that's really the first time I've given an opinion like that and it felt dang good. ;) haven't seen where/when, etc. only that the arraignment will be Sept. 5

Finally, someone with real common sense tried to redirect the misguided conversation where it belonged. Was it not a preliminary hearing with evidence presented against Mike Porter? However, any talk of the real issue at hand was quickly silenced. This group could accuse Raye of anything and get away with it. But as is still the pattern, Mike Porter is protected.

Posted by "Anonymous" August 23, 2006 @ 4:12 PM - Why did the Judge not increase his bail? That monster should not be running around free!

Posted by "MistyLT" August 23, 2006 @ 4:17 PM - 4:12 – NO MORE. I understand that you are able to say this in other places and get away with it, but you WILL NOT here. All parties are innocent until proven guilty. Just because they have charges against them for certain things does not make them true. I did not say anything before about it and had no rules here, but for right now, there ARE rules and this is not going to happen.

Posted by "MistyLT" August 23, 2006 @ 4:19 PM - There are lots of reasons why a judge will not raise bail. You should look into those reasons and then you should investigate this case a little bit closer instead of believing everything that you are told.

Posted by "esha" August 23, 2006 @ 4:20 PM - Well did anyone watch channel 9? I think it make people stop and think and not be so bias

Posted by "MistyLT" August 23, 2006 @ 4:22 PM - I watched it and Irvin Box did a very good job. Maybe it will open some eyes to what is really happening.

Posted by "esha" August 23, 2006 @ 4:25 PM - MistyLT, That guy was freakin awesome. Some people out there are not influenced by what others think. i loved it

Posted by "MistyLT" August 23, 2006 @ 4:27 PM - Yes, Mr. Box is a well respected attorney. I hope people listen to what he had to say, especially about the 3 different opinions about the amended charges. 4:12 If you watched that, maybe it will explain to you why his bail was not raised

Posted by "chris" August 23, 2006 @ 4:29 PM - Do we know what the emt or the friend said?

Posted by "Anonymous" August 23, 2006 @ 4:30 PM - http://www.channeloklahoma.com/news/9724213/detail.html

Posted by "MistyLT" August 23, 2006 @ 4:32 PM - Who was the old man that they interviewed right before Irvin came on?

Posted by "Chris" August 23, 2006 @ 4:35 PM - do u have the link for the irvine box interview?

Posted by "Anonymous" August 23, 2006 @ 4:44 PM - Misty I apologize. I didn't know calling someone a monster was implying that they are guilty. I think Mike & Raye are both Monsters becuase whoever did or didn't do it they other should have reported it. Also, I thought I was following your rules by asking a question about the bail. Don't worry I will

*not make any more posts after this one, I am done with this
site.*

*Posted by "DJones" August 23, 2006 @ 4:46 PM - Mike Taber,
friend, told of how he showed up while mike was outside
waiting for emergency persons after calling 911 and was
crying "Oh my God, what's wrong. Something's wrong......"
and that he was basically hysterical, not knowing what to do.*

*Posted by "Anonymous" August 23, 2006 @ 4:56 PM - I am very
confused as to why Richard would be offering any kind of
plea deal to Raye Dawn after stating he did not need her. The
only reason to offer her a plea deal would be if she had
something he needs for his case. I do not understand why he
would say he does not need her to make his case against
Michael Porter and then offer her a plea deal knowing it
makes him out to look like he is either lying or letting her off
for the sake of letting her off. I do not get that at all.*

*Posted by "MistyLT" August 23, 2006 @ 5:01 PM - And 4:44 you
are assuming that you know. Like I said, I realize that you
are able to say certain things about people on other sites and
no one cares and those sites pick and choose what is allowed.
I have never picked and chose, but I am right now and have
to and will.*

*Posted by "Anonymous" August 23, 2006 @ 5:19 PM - so you will
allow comments about Raye, and not Mike? or both? just
wondering...it seemed a little vague to me.*

*Posted by "Anonymous" August 23, 2006 @ 6:09 PM - no bashing
comments period will be allowed. People's opinions about
the events of today is the scope of discussion. The fact
remains no one knows who did what that day except for the
person who committed the crime, Kelsey and God. The DA
has an opinion and the defense attorney has an opinion. We
are all entitled to our own opinion. No one can know
everything nor should anyone claim to kno everything.
Everything stated on here is opinion. Please keep it restricted*

to your reactions about the news coverage of todays events, i.e. testimony, statements, evidence, etc.

Posted by "Anonymous" August 23, 2006 @ 6:24 PM - misty is that you posting under anonymous?

Misty was caught using more than one name to post.

Posted by "MistyLT" August 23, 2006 @ 6:24 PM - Yeah, what 6:09 said, Umm, thanks lol

Posted by "Anonymous" August 23, 2006 @ 6:26 PM - From everything I have been told it takes next to nothing to get bound over for trial. Is this true?

Posted by "Anonymous" August 23, 2006 @ 6:28 PM - Did the father's family have a reaction to the news that the prosecutor was in the process of working out a plea deal for the mother? After he promised no deals and said he did not need her testimony? Surely he would not do this without the father's consent or at least his knowledge?

Posted by "MistyLT" August 23, 2006 @ 6:32 PM - There was supposed to be an interview at 6 on one of the news channels of one of the grandmothers. Did anyone see it

Posted by "Confused" August 23, 2006 @ 6:39 PM - Is it be assumed a plea bargain was offered or is it a fact?

Posted by "Anonymous" August 23, 2006 @ 6:43 PM -
http://www.newsok.com/article/2835653

Posted by "MistyLT" August 23, 2006 @ 6:44 PM - The media says it's true so it must be true.

At the time or Mike Porter's preliminary hearing, there was not plea offered to Raye. Later, plea offers would include her admitting to the false story told by Donna in which she was said to have spanked Kelsey with a hair brush. Raye said, "I didn't do it. I won't take it." Yet to this group of bullies, "the news said it, so it must be true."

Posted by "Anonymous" August 23, 2006 @ 6:53 PM - From what I have read it sounds like the DA admitted that he was attempting to negotiate a plea deal with Raye Dawn and the defense attorney was pointing out that plea bargains taint testimony and generally make witnesses not as credible. It is basically buying testimony.

Posted by "Anonymous" August 23, 2006 @ 7:00 PM - I was outraged when I heard that the mother would most likely get a deal in Kelsey's case. This seems to be this prosecutor's MO. Let the mom's go free with slaps on the wrist. A mother in Shawnee recently got a plea deal of 2 years from this DA but her child was sill alive and she actually could give timelines for her baby's injuries. I do not understand what the mother in Kelsey's case has that the prosecutor could want. It seems the only way she will admit to any wrongdoing is if she is allowed to walk free. I for one would be disgusted if this is allowed to happen.

Posted by "Anonymous" August 23, 2006 @ 7:12 PM - i also wonder what the briggs think of the plea deal – maybe everyone needs to start writing letters to the da again

Posted by "LadyInMoore" August 23, 20006 @ 7:18 PM - The preliminary hearing went as I expected it to go. The only new evidence was a turtle and pullups. I thought that Kelsey and Raye Dawn went down for a nap after the case worker left. This is the first mention of playing outside. Mildred was very cordial in her speech. She said she is praying for all the families involved. Aren't we all praying for the families?

Posted by "Anonymous" August 23, 2006 @ 7:20 PM - What else did Mildred have to say Lady in Moore??

Posted by "MistyLT" August 23, 2006 @ 7:20 PM - Hi LIM;) what channel was that interview on?

Posted by "LadyInMoore" August 23, 2006 @ 7:22 PM - I was watching Channel 4. I can't remember what all she said. I just got tickled at her for being so stern about praying for the families.

Posted by "LadyInMoore" August 23, 2006 @ 7:31 PM - She was just saying that she wants to see justice done for Kelsey's death. I can't find her interview on Kfor.com

Posted by "Anonymous" August 23, 2006 @ 7:32 PM - Justice does not mean her granddaughter walking free in my opinion.

Posted by "Anonymous" August 23, 2006 @ 7:38 PM - About RD's statement about Kelsey playing with a turtle and then coming in to tell she had an accident....why was a 2 year old playing outside by herself in the first place?

Posted by "Anonymous" August 23, 2006 @ 7:39 PM - Doesn't look like KFOR puts it 5 and 6 news casts on their sites. Guess we'll just have to see if they play parts of it at 10

Posted by "Anonymous" August 23, 2006 @ 7:50 PM - I am surprised Raye Dawn's attorney allowed her to testify without a plea deal in hand. At least one attorney had the scruples to put her through the ringer. Channel 5 reported that her questioning by the defense attorney did not go too well for her.

Posted by "anon500" August 23, 2006 @ 8:02 PM - I do believe that Smothermon is trying to get a plea bargain just so he won't have to "bother" getting her convicted. Maybe in his eyes it's saving the tax payers money. I say "BULL". I don't want my money saved just to let a mother get off with a slap on the wrist. He just doesn't seem interested in doing his job or at least not effectively in my eyes.

Posted by "anon500" August 23, 2006 @ 8:07 PM - Also, I believe that Mildred did that interview just to be in the lime light again. How many times has she been on tv and has changed her "opinion" each time. I believe that it was her first interview that was saying how wonderful Mike was. Now that they think that Raye Dawn might be charged with "something" she has changed her opinion. Mildred's statement changes as the wind blows. Also Raye Dawn stated that today that she didn't remember the hair brush incident. You've got to be kidding.

Posted by "Anonymous" August 23, 2006 @ 8:09 PM - [Porter's attorney] will probably do a number on Raye Dawn on the stand. Her plea bargain won't work so well if they get her to crack.

Posted by "Anonymous" August 23, 2006 @ 8:17 PM - I just saw Irven Box's interview on Channel 9. He is a very good attorney who seems to have a pretty good handle on this case.

Posted by "Anonymous" August 23, 2006 @ 8:21 PM - Im sure both families are deeply hurt and are in sorrow. They all loved little Kelsey. I choose to pray for all of them. The only ones who are responsible is raye dawn and porter. And they need prayer also.

Posted by "Anonymous" August 23, 2006 @ 8:23 PM - My heart goes out to the family of Kelsey Briggs. I sincerely hope that they are able to find peace and comfort someday. The days ahead will be very tough. I pray that people will be able to sort through all the misinformation and falsehoods coming from the prosecution and the defense and get to the truth of what really happened. Kelsey went through so much in her short life.

Posted by "Anonymous" August 23, 2006 @ 8:27 PM - Everyone does need prayer. I will pray for all of them also. God's love is not reserved for those who are without sin, for there are none without sin. There is no person that is better than any other person in God's eyes. He gave his only begotten son to die for all sinners, large and small. God does not sort sinners into categories. We could all better ourselves by praying for not only those who love us but those that hope to do us harm.

Posted by "Anonymous" August 23, 2006 @ 9:09 PM - Someone tell me why Britton Follett is the only reporter that finds it necessary to keep portraying Raye Dawn as the damn victim....I'm sick of listening to her.

Posted by "MistyLT" August 23, 2006 @ 9:12 PM - Very good post 8:27

Posted by "Anonymous" August 23, 2006 @ 9:18 PM - What did Britton have to say about Raye Dawn and the events of today?

Posted by "Anonymous" August 23, 2006 @ 9:23 PM - I don't see how Raye Dawn is the victim. How did Britton say she was, I must have missed that part.

Posted by "Anonymous" August 23, 2006 @ 9:24 PM - You all can jump all over me if you want to but I just don't think Porter did those things. I watched him today and he did not hang his head like a guilty man. He has never ran like Raye Dawn has when confronted with those cameras. That is just my opinion and you can bash me all you want for it. I think sometimes the people who talk the least may have the most to say.

Posted by "Anonymous" August 23, 2006 @ 9:24 PM - News 9 reported that [Porter's attorney] said "that the circumstantial evidence pointed at Raye Dawn and not Mike Porter". I agree with that totally.

Posted by "Anonymous" August 23, 2006 @ 9:27 PM - Oh please. The whole thing reeked of poooooor poor Raye Dawn and the ther man that fooled their family and she didn't testify to save her own butt blah blah blah blah

Posted by "Anonymous" August 23, 2006 @ 9:27 PM - No jumping here 9:24, I agree with you.

Posted by "Anonymous" August 23, 2006 @ 9:28 PM - The sexual abuse angle is the only thing that tilts the scales in Porter's direction. Not by accident I am sure.

Posted by "Anonymous" August 23, 2006 @ 9:32 PM - I think Raye Dawn weakens any case the prosecution tries to present. Her being a chief witness and her absolute lack of credibility. I do not believe a word she says and I do not see how anyone would. I want to see the facts. I would not have cared what she said and that was before the news of her getting a deal. It sounds to me like this whole case is resting on the assumption that her saying Kelsey was ok when she left is true. I want to hear that that was the case medically. I still do not think that anyone can say that. I would not take someone's life based on anything Raye Dawn said.

Posted by "Anonymous" August 23, 2006 @ 9:35 PM - 8:17, did you find that interview online yet? Do you have the link?

Posted by "Anonymous" August 23, 2006 @ 9:38 PM - Someone gave me a blow by blow on the interview. I think it is pretty much common sense if you objectively look at the case. Irven Box is not for the prosecution or for the defense so I think it is interesting to hear what he has to say.

Posted by "Anonymous" August 23, 2006 @ 9:44 PM - I would like to know what Smothermon and [Porter's attorney] asked Hawley in the courtroom.

Dr. Hawley was the medical examiner who performed the second autopsy on Kelsey and confirmed the sexual assault. He gave details of his findings at Mike Porter's preliminary hearing.

Posted by "Anonymous" August 23, 2006 @ 9:46 PM - No one seems to want to discuss what exactly was found in that 2nd autopsy. Hmmm, wonder why that is.

Posted by "anon500" August 23, 2006 @ 9:46 PM - I've been thinking after listening to the news reports online again. They stated that Kelsey had been playing outside and had an accident. Raye Dawn then put her in a shirt, no panties or pullup at that time. How many people would do that? Or, how many parents would be very upset and MAD because they had an accident and then clean the child up and put them to bed. Possibly even punishing them because they wouldn't go to sleep then. After all, mom had to clean her up cause she'd had "and accident". I know this has been brought up earlier here. But, I guess I had to listen again for it to sink in. It all falls into place now.

Posted by "Anonymous" August 23, 2006 @ 9:50 PM - Thanks for bringing that up anon500…you made me think too. if she had an accident, maybe she was punished for that accident and that would explain why there's bruising in some places. 9:28: Since there is no DNA, why would it have to be Porter that did it? All it would take is a sick person as a mother.

Kelsey had three bruises on her body at the time of her death and one on her bottom that was said to have occurred when it was "held open." This evidence was not presented until Raye Dawn's trial, but even then it was ignored by the bullies. Also, there was no DNA because the first medical examiner did not test for it. By the time of the second autopsy, the family was told that there was nothing left to test.

Instead of discussing the real evidence that had been presented and the fact that Kelsey had been sexually assaulted while home alone with Mike Porter, he and Misty worked hard to ensure that all of the focus remained on Raye, even with this new, gut-wrenching evidence against him.

Posted by "Anonymous" August 23, 2006 @ 9:52 PM - That's also assuming that there actually was sexual abuse to Kelsey.

Posted by "Anonymous" August 23, 2006 @ 9:54 PM - I feel that since there was 'an accident' that the mother got very mad, punished her severely and put her to bed. Then, she wouldn't go to sleep so she went overboard punishing her. I think that's what [Porter's attorney] is going to bring out. He'll bring out the fact that Raye Dawn had a terrible temper and went overboard.

336

Posted by "Anonymous" August 23, 2006 @ 9:55 PM - It's a proven fact that there is a larger percentage of times that the mother is the one that does the sexual abuse to a child.

Posted by "Anonymous" August 23, 2006 @ 9:56 PM - Britton's getting a 2nd chance at making Raye Dawn look like the victim at 10

Posted by "Anonymous" August 23, 2006 @ 10:07 PM - Porter was probably rolling his eyes at her stupide LIES

Posted by "Anonymous" August 23, 2006 @ 10:10 PM - I do not believe that there was sexual abuse. The prosecutor in this case found a doctor who would say that there was after the state Medical Examiner refused to unequivocally say that there was sexual abuse. I put no more weight on the prosecution's doctor saying there was than I do on the defense's doctor saying there was than I do on the defense's doctor saying there was not. Alot of people are forgetting that fact. There will be two medical examiners who will disagree with what the new doctor is testifying to.

Posted by "Anonymous" August 23, 2006 @ 10:10 PM - I would have probably been rolling my eyes too if I'd been there. Course, she's been pretty good at lying up until now. She'll be caught in her own lies. The truth a whole lot easier to remember than all the lies that you might have told.

Posted by "Anonymous" August 23, 2006 @ 10:13 PM - I don't know how he sat there and listened to her spew her crap and cry her fake tears. His eyes were probably rolling to keep his head from exploding.

Posted by "Anonymous" August 23, 2006 @ 10:14 PM - I just want to say way to go Raye Dawn for accusing Mike of killing your daughter and then admitting on the stand that "He never disciplined Kelsey. They had a good relationship." Looks like you walked right into that one.

Posted by "anon500" August 23, 2006 10:14 PM - 10:10 I don't feel that it has changed my opinion of "who did it" with the 2nd autopsy. Since there were no proven DNA, it doesn't necessarily point the finger at the step father. It just proves that there was a sick person in that house. If it was Mike, Raye Dawn married him, so she's guilty too. If it was Raye Dawn, Mike should have seen what she was doing long before Kelsey's death. So, he's not innocent either.

Posted by "Anonymous" August 23, 2006 @ 10:17 PM - That's still assuming that she was sexually abused

Posted by "anon500" August 23, 2006 @ 10:17 PM - 10:14 That's looking really bad on Raye Dawn's side. Course today wasn't "about" Raye Dawn. Her day will come. She will create her own "new" charges. If Mike "never disciplined Kelsey", more than likely he didn't kill her either. Think about that.

Posted by "anon500" August 23, 2006 @ 10:19 PM - Regardless 10:17 whether she was sexually abused is kind of beside the point. Kelsey is not here with us because of the attack". I'd prefer to think that she wasn't sexually abused. But, at the same time, it does not point the finger directly at Mike one way or the other.

Posted by "Anonymous" August 23, 2006 @ 10:21 PM - Anon500 – that was me at 10:10. I was just saying I would imagina that there will be plenty of evidence presented that will dispute whether there even was sexual abuse. I do not believe that just because a doctor was found who would say that that is their opinion makes it so. You can go out anywhere and find a doctor that will tell you anything. They all have different opinions. The first ME was apparently not prepared to say that there was sexual abuse. So someone was found that would. I am not saying it did not happen or it did happen. I am saying that there is plenty of doubt due to the fact that sexual abuse is only being alleged by one doctor, basically through a second opinion.

338

Posted by "anon500" August 23, 2006 @ 10:22 PM - There are abused children everyday in the news. The court needs to do something to this parents and NOT PLEA BARGAIN to ANY of them. Let them all get sentenced in the way that the court intended them to be sentenced. Do NOT let them "talk" their way out of a longer sentence.

Posted by "anon500" August 23, 2006 @ 10:26 PM - I think that the State Medical Examiners office have a lot of faults. Their first one in my eyes was the fact that they did NOT want their "findings" questioned in any way on this case and did NOT let them use the state facilities to do another autopsy. That was just inexcusable. If this was on a tv show, you would know that someone got to them first and passed money out to get them not to tell the whole truth. I'm not saying that's what happened here (the money part), BUT, it really looks funny. If they had been SO SURE of their findings they should have stepped aside and said, "sure, go head, use the state facilities (with a charge of course) and do your thing. They DIDN'T do that so it looks bad in the public eye. They are not infallible. Everyone makes mistakes and in this case ONE of the two autopsies was wrong or incomplete.

Posted by "Anonymous" August 23, 2006 @ 10:28 PM - hmmm, so what about the 3rd opinion that says there was no sexual abuse?

Posted by "Anonymous" August 23, 2006 @ 10:29 PM - they didn't say they were refusing to let them use it, they were saying that it wouldn't be possible to do it there

Posted by "Anonymous" August 23, 2006 @ 10:31 PM - So now Porter paid the ME's office off too? Like he did the judge, the doctor and the lawyer in this case? Is that what you were saying? Man, this guy's more loaded than I thought he was. He probably doesn't even know how loaded he is.

Posted by "Anonymous" August 23, 2006 @ 10:34 PM - Why wasn't it possible to do the 2nd autopsy at the State Medical Examiners office in OKC?

339

Posted by "Anonymous" August 23, 2006 @ 10:37 PM - Just because two doctors had different opinions it does not mean that one of the autopsies was incomplete. I just wonder if there actually was anything new found during the second autopsy. I think the new doctor could just have a different opinion based on the first autopsy.

Posted by "Anonymous" August 23, 2006 @ 10:43 PM - so you don't think that even if it was because the ME refused to let them have it there that the ME had a right to be a little ticked off that his expertise was questioned? how long has the ME been an ME? did I hear 30 years?

Posted by "Anonymous" August 23, 2006 @ 10:45 PM - I know a little about law and from what I read it seems the prosecution's case in chief is based on the assumption that the mother's statements about that day are true. It also appears there will be 3 conflicting medical opinions also. This case is far from cut and dry as many would like to beleive. It is going to be a long difficult trial and at the conclusion there still may be unresolved questions. There will be a smoking gun or a clear cut answer as so many would like in this case. It is going to be a nightmare for all involved. I hope you all will pray with me for all those involved regardless of which "side" they may be on.

Posted by "goldtoothgummentman" August 23, 2006 @ 11:23 PM - Just a thought, but could Smotherman be setting RD up for charges of perjury later? I'm sure he knows that she will lie about her involvement, and if he has evidence that she was involved in the abuse, then he could use her to convict MP and then charge her with perjury later. Any attorney out there know how this might work?

Posted by "Anonymous" August 23, 2006 @ 11:28 PM - Any negotiation that her attorney would involve her in would have a provision to protect her from the likelihood that she will perjure herself. Perjury is typically not a crime that is prosecuted anyway. And the thoght that a mother that either

340

knew of the abuse or perpetrated it could get off with perjury charges is disheartening to say the least. The case for enabling would be the easier case to make against the mother or the stepfather. No jury of 12 reasonable people is going to believe that either one of them could not have known Kelsey was being abused. There will be great difficulty determining who was actually perpetrating the abuse, but from a legal standpoint enabling/failure to protect has always been pretty much a lock.

Posted by "Anonymous" August 23, 2006 @ 11:32 PM - I hope that helped Goldtooth. Criminal law is not my specialty but I have worked in law long enough to know a few things. :)

Posted by "Anonymous" August 23, 2006 @ 11:35 PM - Oh, I think you do pretty good. Well versed.

Posted by "Anonymous" August 23, 2006 @ 11:44 PM - In plea deals the witness is usually giving testimony that the prosecutor has instructed them to give or has at least advised them on giving for the purpose of direct examination. It would be unthinkable for Richard to expect Raye Dawn to say what he needs and wants her to say to try to aid in a conviction and not expect to have to offer concessions in return for the aid she is providing to the state's case, such as a guarantee of immunity from any further prosecution attempts related to the case in question. That is why defense attorneys despise plea bargains and informants who are offered reduced time for testimony. It is in effect a legal means for prosecutors to "purchase" testimony, be it through promises of leniency or reduced time. It would be similar to a defense attorney going out and paying an individual to provide an alibi for their client. Anytime a witness receives compensation for any form for testimony one must consider their motive and their credibility.

Posted by "Anonymous" August 23, 2006 @ 11:50 PM - 11:44 sounds pretty smart

Posted by "Anonymous" August 23, 2006 @ 11:51 PM -
    Breathtaking.

Posted by "anon" August 24, 2006 @ 1:21 AM - Plea bargains are
    retarded.......poor little Kelsey didn't get to bargain....why
    should they?

Posted by "Anonymous" August 24, 2006 @ 8:56 AM - I think
    everyone should contact this DA and tell him that we will not
    stand for him to offer another mother a plea bargain for
    allowing someone to beat her child. (405)275xxxx FAX:
    (405) 275-xxxx POTTAWATOMIE COUNTY COURTHOUSE
    [address removed for privacy]

Posted by "Anonymous" August 24, 2006 @ 10:54 AM - The girl
    needs to spend some time in PRISON. I hope the deal he is
    making with her does not clear her totally. I think we do need
    to let the DA know we are tired of people letting someone
    harm their child and getting away with it. It also seems if she
    has already changed her story from previous testimony that
    too is a crime. The lies she told helped killed her child.
    PLEASE WRITE THE DA.

Posted by "Anonymous" August 24, 2006 @ 11:35 AM - I will say
    what I have always said. The DA lied when he said he did not
    need her for his case. It is obvious now. He needs her to play
    the victim role she is so good at playing and get on the stand
    and cry a few fake tears so jurors will feel sorry for her. He
    needs to make them beleive that this is a mother who wants
    juastice for her child instead of what I think she is which is
    someone who will say anything to save her own ass.
    Shameful.

Posted by "Anonymous" August 24, 2006 @ 12:11 PM - We can
    pray the truth comes out in this trial. What concerns me is if
    raye dawn did this crime and is not convicted DHS will
    return her son to her and it could happen to him as well.

Posted by "Anonymous" August 24, 2006 @ 12:17 PM - Based on
    the testimony that was reported from Raye Dawn, I am

convinced now more than ever that she is guilty of this crime!!!I DO NOT support Mike Porter in the least, but I can see the truth. In my opinion, she is so guilty of the charges that Mike Porter is facing. I believe this with all my heart. I can see it in her face. I pray that everone else will see it too.

Posted by "Anonymous" August 24, 2006 @ 12:20 PM - I think if the DA cuts her a deal and allows her to walk people are going ot be outraged especially once the trial gets under way.

Posted by "Anonymous" August 24, 2006 @ 1:02 PM - We must write the DA!!!!!!!!!!!!

Posted by "Anonymous" August 24, 2006 @ 1:14 PM - I think we should support Porter because as we are seeing he did not kill or sexually abuse this child. We do not want an inncocent man going to prison for life or the death penalty for something he did not do.

The public opinion on the bashboards and Web sites had indeed convinced many that Raye was the murderer and not Mike Porter, the man charged with both murder and sexual assault. What proof was the basis for this conclusion? Where are the investigative reports that state that their version of events is even a possibility?

Posted by "Please Don't Plea Bargain" August 24, 2006 @ 1:44 PM - Everyone that I have talked to today (and some of them have previously been Smothermon supporters that have now seen the light) have all been in accordance that Raye Dawn has proven herself even more (if that's possible) guilty than before. She is setting Mike Porter up and by the looks of it, Richard Smothermon is going to come to her aid in doing just that.

Posted by "DandCsmom" August 24, 2006 @ 2:05 PM - I'll repeat something my husband told me which makes perfect sense. "The squeaky wheel gets the grease." In other words, don't CALL the DA. He won't waste his time talking to you. He said, "They need to GO to the DA's office. Preferably 4 or 5 women with their kids in tow and DEMAND to talk to the DA

RIGHT NOW". But before you go, call all of the TV stations in town and tell them that a riot is going on at the DA's office. With news cameras in his face and moms and kids in his office, he isn't going to turn you down. If he does, go throught the door anyway. He said, "If you want to make a difference, make it." Don't just talk. Demand that they stop making plea bargains with moms who either abuse or don't stop people who are abusing their kids. My be a militant approach, but he's friends with the Assistant DA here and said that's the one way to get attention. They don't want bad publicity in front of the news cameras and voters.

Posted by "Please Don't Plea Bargain" August 24, 2006 @ 3:10 PM - Tell us when to be at the D.A.'s office and I'll be there. I don't want him to plea bargain.

Posted by "Anonymous" August 24, 2006 @ 3:12 PM - Someone said much earlier that Mildred was very corial with her speech. That woman needs anger management and some brains.

Posted by "DandCsmom" August 24, 2006 @ 3:19 PM - You Oklahoma girls are gonna have to organize that one. I'm not in your state, but if you can get something organized and get people to commit, I'll be happy to attend if at all possible. It's about a 5 hour drive that I'll be happy to make if we have a group who would be willing to go. What town is the DA's office located in?

Posted by "MistyLT" August 24, 2006 @ 3:22 PM - 2:05, I think you are right. Apparently our letters do nothing. Where could we start? I don't think you're going to get a lot of people to agree to show their faces in this county and do something like that, but I could be wrong. I suppose we could start with the news stations, but then people would have to speak up. Is that going to happen? By the way, I don't have a link to the Irvin Box interview. I could never find one.

Posted by "MistyLT" August 24, 2006 @ 3:22 PM - His office is in Shawnee

Posted by "justice4kelseybriggs" August 24, 2006 @ 3:26 PM - I wonder how many people now believe that the wrong person is charged with the murder of Kelsey Briggs????? I did hear on the news last night that they did NOT give RD a plea bargain and everything she said in court CAN and probably WILL be used against her in court. I have never thought Porter was the one responsible for taking Kelsey's life. He would have had to do too much in fifteen minutes while RD went to pick up his daughter which was NOT a normal thing for her to do.

Posted by "Anonymous" August 24, 2006 @ 3:32 PM - I will show my face and I will committ to be there.

Posted by "Tinam" August 24, 2006 @ 3:33 PM - That last post was from me

Posted by "DandCsmom" August 24, 2006 @ 3:33 PM - I think the first thing you have to do is get a group of women who are willing to meet at a certain time and go to his office together. As I said, I'm in Little Rock so depending on the day/time, I am willing to go. It just needs to be planned enough in advance that I can make sure nothing else is going on. Others need to commit to do the same. There are alot of people who say they want to make a difference and this is a chance for them to do something. Then, we can call the news stations on that day prior to going to his office and tell them something major is going on at the DA's office and they better get down there for a story. News people live for stuff like that. Then we go and tell him we are sick and tired of moms being alowed to plea and basically do no time after allowing people to abuse their kids. They also need to do the time if they are aware of the abuse. As my husband said, "You gotta jump on a few desks now and then." Figuratively speaking, of course.

Posted by "Please Don't Plea Bargain" August 24, 2006 @ 3:44 PM - I'd be there. I haven't changed my mind. I always thought that R.D. did it. The statements that she made yesterday just confirmed it a little more.

345

Posted by "MistyLT" August 24, 2006 @ 3:47 PM - What would be a good dat for you?

Posted by "Please Don't Plea Bargain" August 24, 2006 @ 3:53 PM - I'm pretty much open just very few days in the next month that I couldn't be there.

Posted by "Please Don't Plea Bargain" August 24, 2006 @ 3:54 PM - I'm busy wiring Smothermon a letter now.

Posted by "Anonymous" August 24, 2006 @ 3:55 PM - Is this site now a pro-Porter site? Its disgusting seeing how many people defend this guy? He lived in the very house where Kelsey was slowly beat to death. Whether he is guilty of her murder or not, I don't think he needs to be defended for anything. He failed this child in the worst way you can fail someone.

Posted by "Anonymous" August 24, 2006 @ 4:00 PM - You don't want to give the news channels too much warning. They might call the DA and then he would have a heads up. You also need to check out court times. If he's in court when you show up, he gets off easy. Maybe the best way to know when he is going to be there is to call (anonymously) and just say you need to come in to talk to him about a bad check or something and when is the best time to do that?

Posted by "MistyLT" August 24, 2006 @ 4:05 PM - 3:55, I don't think it's pro-Porter. I think it's about people paying for the right charge. I think it's about people don't believe Porter killed that baby and they don't want Raye Dawn walking for it. I don't think people are trying to get Porter off of his responsibility, they are trying to make sure Raye Dawn takes some responsibility for her actions.

Posted by "DandCsmom" August 24, 2006 @ 4:05 PM - It depends on how soon we need to do that. I could be over there toward the end of next week. Say Friday afternoon. We need to make sure he isn't in court during the time we will be there though.

346

How do you find that out? Is Smothermon the Da there? Seems I read that in one of the articles.

Posted by "MistyLT" August 24, 2006 @ 4:06 PM - *And since Smothermon is an elected official, and works for the people, and he is the one that is supposed to make sure that happen. Since he is not making that happen, he needs to know that he's failing at his job title.*

Posted by "MistyLT" August 24, 2006 @ 4:08 PM - *Hmmm, I'm not sure how we're going to get a group of women and kids in his office and it be a surprise of why we're there. Lol I think if we call to make an appointment, we'll probably get stuck with an Asst DA or a clerk or something.*

Posted by "Anonymous" August 24, 2006 @ 4:11 PM - *Misty- thanks for clearing that up. I'm all about people getting charged with the proper crime. I'm confused as hell as to who I think did what. I really don't have alot of sympathy for either right now.*

Posted by "Anonymous" August 24, 2006 @ 4:13 PM - *neither deserve sympathy, neither are victoms, and neither are innocent*

Posted by "Anonymous" August 24, 2006 @ 4:19 PM - *Okay people, we already know this. So I guess you think the murderer should be able to walk? Who cares as long as Porter pays right?*

Posted by "Anonymous" August 24, 2006 @ 4:22 PM - *i disagree with you 4:13...i do think it's possible after watching raye dawn manipulate so many people that a lot of other people that should have seen it could be manipulated too....if you don't agree with me, oh well...we have 2 different opinions....doesn't make your opinion right and it doesn't make my opinion right*

Posted by "Anonymous" August 24, 2006 @ 4:22 PM - I don't think that storming the DA's office is the solution here. Try praying.

Posted by "Anonymous" August 24, 2006 @ 4:25 PM - Been praying for months. It didn't work. God gave me free will and I plan to use it.

Posted by "Anonymous" August 24, 2006 @ 4:33 PM - Who has ever said "who cares as long as Porter pays"? I think most of us here want justice. Period. I've never heard anyone say they didn't care as long as he was convicted.

Posted by "Anonymous" August 24, 2006 @ 4:36 PM - 4:22, I will agree that RD is a master manipulater, and that she could have fooled many people, but I cannot and will not believe that the person living in that home was manipulated to the point of no responsibility for what happened to that baby...The only way I would believe that is if someone could provide me with medical documentation stating thatperson is blind...again just my opinion, and certainly we are all entitled to our opinions...we will have to agree to disagree

Posted by "Please Don't Plea Bargain" August 24, 2006 @ 4:40 PM - I think that R.D. manipulated people and is still manipulating people. Porter is guilty of not protecting Kelsey too. But, R.D. was initially the one that was supposed to protect her (even from Porter at one point, whom she just conveniently married). I'm sure that Mike wishes that he would have ran like hell from her now and let some other poor stupid bastard be charged with Kelsey's death. sorry, but that's how i feel.

Posted by "Please Don't Plea Bargain" August 24, 2006 @ 4:41 PM - I wasn't calling Porter a poor stupid bastard, although it sounded like I did.

Posted by "Anonymous" August 24, 2006 @ 4:50 PM - I think next Friday is the beginning of a holiday weekend. He might not be there. He does not take care of bogus checks, his people

348

do. He is not going to let you in his office or come out. When the petition was presented to him he had his assistant get it. He will not face the public.

Posted by "DandCsmom" August 24, 2006 @ 4:51 PM - I believe in prayer as well. But I also believe that God expects us to be proactive and look for solutions to our problems. As I've said, I don't live in OK so I don't have access to alot of local news that you all get. I probably haven't heard all that you all have. However, I have seen pictures of that little girl before the abuse started and then after and I have to say that even I can see a change in her. I never never even met that baby but the change is there. It's in her eyes. Her spirit was broken. I also do not know who did the abusing. I do not know whether it was the mother or the stepdad or a combination of both and I'm not about to accuse anyone without knowing all the facts. I do not believe that someone living in the same house who was not a participant, wasn't at least aware of what was happening. That is also just an opinion. I may be right and I may be wrong.

Posted by "Anonymous" August 24, 2006 @ 4:58 PM - I think it is evident that some people don't care who is charged with what and who does how much time, as long as someone pays for her death.

Posted by "Anonymous" August 24, 2006 @ 4:59 PM - And since we knows it's not going to be Raye Dawn that pays for it, then it's going to be Porter, whether he did it or not and people are just fine with that.

Posted by "Anonymous" August 24, 2006 @ 5:07 PM - Agreed 4:40. Raye Dawn testified yesterday that she herself had witnessed one of the seizures that Porter has been accused of making up. There was also a car accident. And she testified yesterday that Kelsey's tummy was not feeling good that day. It leaves me to wonder if everyone around Kelsey thought she was sick and since Raye Dawn had so many excuses for the injuries and doctors to validate thos injuries to Mike....We don't have

all of the facts yet, but the testimony about Kelsey not feeling
well that day stood out to me.

Posted by "Anonymous" August 24, 2006 @ 5:08 PM - That is if we
    are even to beleive when she says Kelsey wasn't feeling well
    that day. I don't know what to beleive from her.

Posted by "Anonymous" August 24, 2006 @ 5:17 PM - 4:59...I don't
    know anyone that would be fine with the fact of Porter
    getting convicted IF he didn't do it. That seems absurd that
    anyone involved with this case would be fine with that
    scenario, unless you are the guilty that he took the fall for. If
    you are referring to Raye and her family not caring who is
    convicted, who really cares what any of their opinions are?
    That whole bunch has already shown their carelessness and
    lack of general intelligence. 99% of anyone involved in this
    case, including all the armchair quarterbacks with their
    "theories", want justice for that sweet innocent little girl. Not
    just a conviction.

Posted by "DandCsmom" August 24, 2006 @ 5:50 PM - Well said
    5:17. I think you're right.

Posted by "Anonymous" August 24, 2006 @ 6:01 PM - All I can say
    is the more and more i hear about Raye Dayn telling how
    stuff went that day Kelsey died leads me to think she is the
    one that killed Kelsey.... :-(

Posted by "Anonymous" August 24, 2006 @ 6:42 PM - I HAVE A
    QUESTION FOR RICHARD SMOTHERMON. WHY
    WOULD YOU COME OUT ON TV AND SAY YOU DON'T
    NEED RAYE DAWN'S TESTIMONY AND THEN ADMIT
    PUBLICLY THAT YOU ARE TRYING TO OFFER HER A
    PLEA DEAL IN EXCHANGE FOR HER TESTIMONY? I
    THINK YOU OWE THE CITIZENS OF THE 23RD JUDICIAL
    DISTRICT AN ANSWER. WHY MAKE THAT STATEMENT
    AND THEN TURN AROUND AND DO THE OPPOSITE OF
    WHAT YOU SAID? WERE YOU LYING THEN OR ARE
    YOU JUST SOFT ON WOMEN YOU THINK DID NOT

*ABUSE THEIR CHILREN BT MERELY STOOD BY AND
LET IT HAPPEN?*

*Posted by "Anonymous" August 24, 2006 @ 8:07 PM - 4:25, the
free will God gave you was salvation. If we come up there in
as a mob group that will not do anyone any good. Only throw
another log on the fire. Trust God and let him be the JUDGE.
Pray without ceasing.*

*Posted by "Anonymous" August 24, 2006 @ 8:12 PM -
DandCsmom, God is our solution to all our problems. =)*

*Posted by "justice4kelseybriggs" August 24, 2006 @ 8:44 PM - To
whoever said that Porter failed Kelsey in the worst way you
can fail someone—you are WRONG—RAYE DAWN failed
Kelsey in the worst way because SHE was Kelsey's
mother....SHE was SUPPOSED to PROTECT her
DAUGHTER AND SHE DID NOT...even if Porter is the one
responsible for the death, Raye Dawn is just as responsible
for not protecting her child. She could not live in the same
house with Kelsey and NOT KNOW that Kelsey was being
abused, and as for the sexual abuse...she changed her and
bathed her and she didn't know that? There is no way. And it
is NOT about "who cares who is guilty as long as someone
pays"...that statement is ludicrous. The one who murdered
this child needs to be convicted and punished justly, and the
one that stood by and did nothing, needs convicted and
punished justly also. There is no excuse for either one of
these adults. There is also no excuse for DHS and Judge Key
failing this child either. They "FAILED TO PROTECT"
plain & simple and they should be charged with felony
failure to protect as should the one that did nothing.*

*Posted by "Anonymous" August 24, 2006 @ 8:53 PM - Maybe if
DHS and courts would of removed this little girl at birth none
of this would of happened and there was reasonable cause to
do so just as there was with her son.*

*Posted by "ok_state_mom" August 24, 2006 @ 9:03 PM - I am
reading this a little late after ya'll were talking about going*

to the DA. My daughter and i will be going thru OKC next
Friday or any other day would be great but i am NOT afraid
to show my face and ask him what the heck!! And I am with
everyone else I don't think Porter killed Kelsey. I feel RD did.
But he needs to be held responsible for not doing anything
about it.

Posted by "anon" August 24, 2006 @ 9:21 PM - Whether it was
Porter or R.D., there is still ONE person who should answer
for his deeds. That's Judge Craig Key. He knew what was
going on with that poor child and sent her to her abusers.
And remember folks, he made up his mind and called R.D.'s
attorney BEFORE listening to the evidence. When does his
day come?

If you will recall from the e-mails between Kathie Briggs and
Mike Porter, the story that Judge Key had his mind made up about
Kelsey's placement before court came directly from Mike Porter
while he placated the Briggs with stories about the people Kathie
wanted to "make pay." The more familiar one becomes with this case
and what has been said by Porter and the bullies, the easier it is to
recognize that the majority of their stories came directly from the man
trying to save himself from the death penalty...as can be seen in many
of these anonymous posts that mention taking Porter's life.

Posted by "Please Don't Plea Bargain" August 24, 2006 @ 9:29 -
6:42 I'm in complete agreement about Smothermon. He lied
to the public about not offering her a plea bargain. If he
does, he can kiss his rear end goodbye in the next election.
There WILL be someone running against him next time.
There are too many people questioning his tactics since
yesterday's hearing. He isn't keeping his words to his
constituents.

Posted by "Please Don't Plea Bargain" August 24, 2006 @ 9:35
PM - I agree justice4KelseyBriggs. What mother would clean
up a child after that child having an "accident" in her pants
and then not put a diaper or some sort of pants on her. That
doesn't fly with me. She's lying....again. Also, about the

towel, R.D. asked Mike if he had gotten it out. So, evidently Kelsey was awake and running around the house while R.D. was either passed out or sleeping or at the very least unaware of what her child was doing. What was Kelsey doing outside playing by herself and had to come inside to tell her mom that she'd had an accident. For God's sake. She was only 2 years old and she was left alone (according to her mothers testimony). I hope that they throw the book at the witch of a so called mother. She shouldn't even ever get unsupervised visitation with her son if that's the way that she's going to "take care" of her children.

Posted by "Please Don't Plea Bargain" August 24, 2006 9:37 PM - 8:53 Raye Dawn didn't' even acknowledge that Lance was the father at that time. She was to busy telling other people that Kelsey was their granddaughter. Another lie and she knew it. But, heck she got free babysitting out of the deal for quite a while. She knows how to work 'em.

To me, among some of the anonymous posts, "Please Don't Plea Bargain" sounds a lot like Mike Porter. Here, s/he mentions Raye's attorney during the custody battle. He told Kathie Briggs that his attorney's mission in life was to see the man disbarred. Who else would be so familiar with this attorney than a man who wanted him disbarred so badly that he had made it his life's mission…or his client. But with so much nastiness and hate, they all sound alike and it's hard to even guess their identities. Possibly it is Kathie Briggs. Who knows! Whoever it is, this person is filled with hate.

Posted by "Please Don't Plea Bargain" August 24, 2006 @ 9:43 PM - Judge Key should be made to pay for his mistakes. Instead he doesn't even acknowledge that he EVEN made a mistake. For God's sake, he's a judge. He couldn't possibly make a mistake. And so what if eh connived with Raye Dawn's attorney,… THE [Raye's attorney during the custody battle] who is still trying to run for mayor of Tecumseh because he obviously doesn't have to work very hard since he doesn't have to win his cases, all he has to do is slip the judge a little, I'll let you guess what and presto, he's victorious. Judge Key is beyond reproach, after all he IS a judge. Who in the right mind would question such a superior person of such high morals? Certainly not us peons that live in his district. After all, we're only the low life people that elected him to office and could put him out of office if we so select to do so. My blood pressure is going up just thinking of these scum of the earth elected officials.

Posted by "Anonymous" August 24, 2006 @ 9:50 PM - justiceforKB...I am the one that stated that he failed her in the worst way. You are right. Raye was her mother and should have protected her no matter what, so therefore, she could be considered the person that failed her in the worst way possible. That being said, he failed her in the closest way possible to Raye's failures. He lived with her for the last 4 or 5 months of her life and did what to help her from this horrific life she had to live?

Posted by "Anonymous" August 24, 2006 @ 9:51 PM - Why was Raye calling her attorney and Kelsey's attorney that morning? She already had Kelsey.

Posted by "nomore" August 24, 2006 @ 9:54 PM - Way to go Please Don't Plea Bargain. I agree all the way. What a great thing we could do if we got rid of this "judge" and did it in the name of Kelsey. Would that not be a great thing? Kathie and others worked so hard to get Kelsey's law past. But there still is a judge that can do this again and again. Are the other children he may send to abusers less precious than Kelsey??? They are all precious in God's eyes. Now is the time. We must make sure Kelsey's death had a PURPOSE....and that needs to be REMOVING THE KEY!!!!!!

Posted by "Anonymous" August 24, 2006 @ 9:56 PM - I know three women that want to go when the trip to Smothermon is scheduled.

Posted by "Please Don't Plea Bargain" August 24, 2006 @ 10:04 PM - Yes, Remove Key From Office. That's a start.

354

Supporters of Kelsey's Purpose won their fight to get a law passed in Kelsey's name against child abuse, with no help from the Smith family or the wonderful Mildred Fowler whom has been on tv numerous times saying that their family is a God fearing family, etc. etc. Yes, they are, but SHE is not acting like it now. SHE is doing just the opposite and is full of hate. She and her boyfriend, ..., need to go to some Anger Management classes and then go to OZ and get a brain. The Smiths and Mildred all owe the Briggs family a giant apology for the way that they have acted ever since Kelsey was first injured. They blamed it all on Lance and Kathie when they didn't even look in their own household for the murderer. Shame on you ladies.

Posted by "Anonymous" August 24, 2006 @ 10:06 PM - Vote for Sheila Kirk! That's another step in truly getting Justice for Kelsey.

Posted by "nomore" August 24, 2006 @ 10:08 PM - Who do you think is supporting Key in the election? Mildred and her clan, of course. How in the world could these people consider supporting the man that sent their "beloved" grandchild and great grandchild to her death? I'll tell how. They are only concerned about winning. Even if that means more Kelsey's will suffer. We must stop this insanity. Remove the Key!!!

Posted by "anon11" August 24, 2006 @ 10:11 PM - we HAVE to do something about this plea bargain deal! if it's a visit to richard then i will try and be there. but something HAS to be done. as it has been said before, kelsey didn't get a deal and neither should raye dawn.

Posted by "hadenuf" August 24, 2006 @ 10:11 PM - Is it ture that this judge called the mother's lawyer before the hearing? What is that about? I hadn't heard anything about that. Does anyone know the story?

Posted by "Please Don't Plea Bargain" August 24, 2006 @ 10:12 PM - We've all heard the comment, a bad egg in the basket or variations. Key is a bad judge in the judicial system. We need to remove him from office. Anyone that cannot publicly admit when he's made an error in judgement on his part should not be allowed to stay in office. He's the bad egg in the basket. He needs to be sent home for his actions. I wouldn't even want to use him as an attorney. But, on the other hand, if Richard Smothermon doesn't prosecute Raye Dawn Smith to the fullest extent of the law, he, also, should be held accountable and removed from office. Elected officials are supposed to be the BEST of the BEST. Key is certainly not in that catagory. We will have to wait in judgement of Richard Smothermon. He's up to bat and hasn't struck out yet.

Posted by "Anonymous" August 24, 2006 @ 10:13 PM - *Yes, the judge talked to the attorney prior to the court date and said that it would be taken care of. It'll all come out in the trial.*

Posted by "anonymous" August 24, 2006 @ 10:15 PM - *The Oklahoma Victim's Bill of Rights states: To be informed of any plea bargain negotiations* http://www.oag.state.ok.us/oagweb.nsf/Villofrights!OpenPage *I thought the father's family stated they would never accept a plea in this case. I wonder how they can reconcile the fact that the DA is now offering one to the mother in exchange for testimony after previously stating he did not need her testimony.*

Posted by "Anonymous" August 24, 2006 @ 10:15 PM - *Mildred doesn't have sense that God gave a goose. She would have Charles Manson signs in her yard if he were trying to run for something. She should wake up and smell the roses. Key returned Kelsey to Raye Dawn and now Kelsey is dead because of that action. Kelsey didn't have to die. I'm asking you Mildred and the Smith family, can you wash Kelsey's blood off of your hands? How can YOU sleep at night?*

Posted by "anonymous23" August 24, 2006 @ 10:16 PM - *You are so right PDPB. Key has shown what he is-a bad apple. Richard is still in the game. He has not struck out yet and he certainly didn't throw the game like Key did. Keep your eyes on Richard, but give him a chance to do his thing. He may have a trick or two up his sleeve.*

Posted by "anon11" August 24, 2006 @ 10:18 PM - regarding the plea deal for RD....it's a long shot but maybe we can all email "The Rant" on KFOR. at least that way we can get the word out to more people about why she shouldn't get to accept a plea.

The Rant is a program that is on our local NBC station. This is also the news channel where Cherokee Ballard was a reporter. Why wasn't this group ranting because Richard Smothermon tried to raise Mike Porter's bond and put him back in jail due to the new evidence of sexual assault but it was denied and he was still a free man and on the bashboard? Why did it always have to be about Raye Dawn?

Posted by "Please Don't Plea Bargain" August 24, 2006 @ 10:19 PM - The way that I read that Bill of Rights, it says that they have to be notified of a plea bargain, doesn't say that they have to consent. "To be informed of any plea bargain negotiations

Posted by "hadenuf" August 24, 2006 @ 10:20 PM - OMG. You mean the actually made a call to the mother's attorney before the hearing? He told her she would win? What has our justice systme come to? What happened to hearing the evidence and THEN making a decision? When does this guy come up for appointment or election or whatever you folks do????

Posted by "Anonymous" August 24, 2006 @ 10:22 PM - Exactly. What I'm saying is that they know about it and they said they would never accept a plea bargain. Are they going to voice something about it?

Posted by "Anonymous" August 24, 2006 @ 10:22 PM - Lance said on tv yesterday that they fully support Smothermon. I just want to know how they can fully support him when they know he's negotiating a plea bargain with Raye Dawn.

Posted by "Please Don't Plea Bargain" August 24, 2006 @ 10:26 PM - I think that the Rant is a very good idea. Don't they have open topic on Thursday nights? Course, it's too late tonight. We could bombard them next Thursday night. Or perhaps suggest that they have that the topic one night. How about it Cherokee Ballard? Are you reading this? You have been a strong voice in getting Kelsey's voice heard. It's really great how the news has kept Kelsey's name in the papers and on the news. We don't want a plea bargain. People all over the state of Oklahoma are talking about this very issue since yesterdays newscast. We are outraged by the insignificance that Richard Smothermon has shown regarding the actions of Kelsey's mother, Raye Dawn. She should be charged, prosecuted and serve time in prison for not protecting her young daughter. Hopefully this will also get national attention.

Posted by "Anonymous" August 24, 2006 @ 10:27 PM - The DA only has to notify the victims family that a plea agreement is on the table. They can fight it all they want to, but he can make it regardless and will. They have told him very firmly they DO NOT WANT ONE. He has told them he has not agreed to one. He could be lying and probably is. He is in this for the career and that is all that matters.

Posted by "Please Don't Plea Bargain" August 24, 2006 @ 10:29 PM - I have no idea how the Briggs family feels about the plea bargain. I can only imagine how I'd feel. They have to believe in Smothermon at this point. He's all they have. There is a saying that goes something like you can take a snake and feed it and nurture it, but it's still a snake in the end. It WILL bit you in the end. I feel like this towards Richard Smothermon right now. Not sure if I believe anything that comes out of his mouth since he has already went against what he said earlier that he "would not plea bargain" with Raye Dawn. The snake.

The following post is another example of the misinformation that these bullies believed as fact. In Judge Craig Key's book, *A Deadly Game of Tug of War: The Kelsey Smith-Briggs Story*, he discussed the

358

fact that he did not go against DHS when he returned Kelsey to the home of Raye Dawn and Mike Porter. DHS wanted her returned to Raye. However, they expressed that they did not want her returned to Kathie Briggs. DHS wanted Kelsey phased into Raye's home. The judge placed Kelsey in the home with five agencies assigned to monitor her progress and report if anything seemed suspicious. Nobody did. In fact, at the September, 2005 hearing that was set to take away all visitation with the paternal family (even though they had only seen Kelsey one time since June, 2005 because Kathie Briggs gave up her visits due to the way DHS reported on her interactions with Kelsey during her supervised visits), the district attorney's office wanted to drop all allegations against Raye and remove the agencies from the home. Kelsey was doing very well with Raye and there had been no red flags reported by the experts who visited Raye's home almost every day. The longest period of time without a visit from June to October was seven days. Kelsey was constantly monitored. Judge Craig Key denied the motion and kept the services in the home. Further, Kathie Briggs and her family could have appealed the decision to place Kelsey in the home with Raye and Mike Porter. As she stated in her e-mail that is in my book, *The Naked Truth Bound in Scorn*, Lance's funds were going toward fixing his truck, so he could not afford to appeal. Kathie stated as follows:

> *Our attorney says we can appeal this decision and is shocked at how the ruling went...We want to appeal, but at this time our financial situation will not allow for that. My son knew while he was gone he could save money for his family and get his truck fixed.*

Why did Kathie Briggs mislead the public and her followers? Why not explain the fact that they could not afford to appeal? Most people would understand her situation and sympathize with it. Why place the blame elsewhere and allow it to escalate to a witch hunt based on lies?

Additionally, DHS did try to notify Lance about Kelsey's situation. They asked Kathie Briggs on numerous occasions for his contact information, which Kathie never seemed to know even though he called her during some of her visits with Kelsey. Lance "was driving around Shawnee," Oklahoma, which is near his home town of Meeker, on the few occasions that DHS did speak with him personally. For someone who was supposed to be overseas "fighting a war," Lance Briggs seemed to be everywhere except Iraq. In late April of 2005, he was in Oklahoma for his birthday. In as early as August— latest would be early September—he was in Fort Benning, Georgia reportedly in a treatment facility. This made DHS and others question if his alleged service overseas was yet another story told by Kathie Briggs. Sadly, the bashboard bullies were not told the entire story. They believed the lies and wanted people to pay with their jobs and through harassment and stalking without knowing the real reason for the witch hunt.

Posted by "Anonymous" August 24, 2006 @ 10:33 PM - Judge Key may have given Kelsey back against DHS recomendation, but it could have been appealed. The DA's office "could have and should have" appealed the decision. They did not notify Lance his child was in state custody and violated his 14th amendment rights. The DA has immunity and they cannot do anything about him or the Judge. WE GAVE THEM THIS POWER AND WE NEED TO TAKE IT AWAY!!

Posted by "Please Don't Plea Bargain" August 24, 2006 @ 10:33 PM - Everyone write a letter to Smothermon and either mail it or take it by his office. We need to make him aware that the majority of his constituents are AGAINST a plea bargain, whether it is with Raye Dawn or Mike. His address is: Richard Smothermon [address removed for privacy] A simple letter showing your support will be most appreciated.

Posted by "Please Don't Plea Bargain" August 24, 2006 @ 10:36 PM - If Smothermon doesn't "do right" in this case, we need to start a petition and take it to the Attorney General getting his ousted from office. I'll be the first on a street corner and I truly believe that I know hundreds of people right now that would sign it from Pott. County. We'll just have to wait and

*see how it goes. He's still up to bat. He's got his day in court
so to speak. He'd better use it wisely.*

Kathie Briggs then posted the following threat on her Kelsey's
Purpose forum:

*I wonder if our District Attorney does not get a conviction if this will
be an issue in his next election?*

Was "Please Don't Plea Bargain" actually Kathie Briggs or Mike
Porter? Any guesses regarding the true identity of this person or the
identity of the "anonymous" person who seemed to echo this
mysterious person's thoughts?

*Posted by "Anonymous" August 24, 2006 @ 10:37 PM - Tell him we
will follow his career and haunt him if he allows her to go
free. He only cares about politics and his career. He thinks
we will forget about this in four years.*

Starla was an outsider who had watched news reports on the case
and searched the Internet to find Kathie Briggs. She would soon
become one of Kathie's closest friends who would later stalk, harass,
and threaten me. She had posted the following threat toward the judge
who was to decide Raye's sentencing a year after these bashboard
posts. (Her name was Ursula in my previous book. The emphasis was
done by her.) Could this threat as well as the previous one from Kathie
Briggs give us more insight into the identity of these bullies?

*I read the report a couple of days ago, and I would think the
recommendation would stand. Uumm...the Judge knows
everyone is watching this case...from ALL over. I believe **he
probably remembers what happened to the judicial career of
the last Judge** that did not pay attention to things related in
this case. I believe he will sentence her to the 27yrs and not
release her. **To do anything but** that, since it is also the
recommendation from the investigators **would be suicidal to
his judicial career.** I doubt he is going down that road.*

*Posted by "Liar Liar Pants on Fire" August 24, 2006 @ 10:38 PM -
How many lies did Raye actually tell in court yesterday?*

Posted by "Anonymous" August 24, 2006 @ 10:40 PM - So you want to wait until AFTER this is over to do something about the lies??? After he's already lied to the people that voted him in??? It will be too late then.

Posted by "Anonymous" August 24, 2006 @ 10:40 PM - Call his office and bombard his receptionist. The number is 275-xxxx. He could just throw the letters in "the file cabinet". If you call the office over and over again the whole place will talk.

How did the previous "anonymous" person have so much inside information about the inner-workings of the district attorney's office?

Posted by "Anonymous" August 24, 2006 @ 10:43 PM - We cannot wait until after it is over. She is going to walk!!!!! Smothermon and [Raye's attorney] were both ADA's in OKC. They are buddies. The "good ole boy system" working once again. Kelsey never gets to win. Raye is the only one that has constantly gotten her way during this entire ordeal.

Posted by "Anonymous" August 24, 2006 @ 10:47 PM - If Richard gives Raye Dawn a plea bargain and allows her to walk and then chooses to use her in the trial, people are going to be outraged at what they will hear about Raye Dawn and what actually happened.

Posted by "Anonymous" August 24, 2006 @ 10:47 PM - What about perjury? When you lie in court to cover up abuse and then later admit you lied so you can now cover up murder? When is that girl going to be held accountable?

Posted by "Anonymous" August 24, 2006 @ 10:49 PM - How can you use a LIAR in court? She is not credible. Is this the best he has?

Posted by "Anonymous" August 24, 2006 @ 10:55 PM - This probably would be the best that he has, that's why he has to cut a deal with a liar just to get his case to the preliminary stage.

*Posted by "Please Don't Plea Bargain" August 24, 2006 @ 11:12
PM - It's sad to say that Raye Dawn is probably the best that
he has. That's not saying much at all. True, we need to
bombard his office with telephone calls. Bombard the media
with our outrage. Kelsey didn't deserve this. Raye Dawn
doesn't deserve a plea bargain. She needs to go to jail for not
protecting and possibly even commiting those horrible acts
against Kelsey. She's not innocent, not by a long shot.*

*Posted by "Please Don't Plea Bargain" August 24, 2006 @ 11:16
PM - We need to have pictures of Raye Dawn with a line
thru it saying no plea bargains!!!! no time for that much
planning though. We need to act now. Get the message out
there. Write letters to the Daily and Sunday Oklahoman.
Write letters to the Shawnee News Star. Let's show people
that we mean business and not are just all talk. Key is going
to be at the Lincoln County Fair. Let's show a non support of
him at his own "tent" there. Bombard him with questions of
why he did this to Kelsey. One after another question from
different people. Find out how he can handle the average Joe
out in the crowd asking questions about why he killed Kelsey
Briggs.*

*Posted by "Please Don't Plea Bargain" August 24, 2006 @ 11:17
PM - For those that get the Meeker News, Key has an ad
there saying what day and time that he will be at the Lincoln
County Fair. I'm sure it's probably in the Lincoln County
News also.*

Cherokee Ballard, the Briggs reporter friend who was with our
local NBC affiliate had turned into the Briggs family's publicist. She
took the initiative that was suggested on this bashboard and showed
up at the fair. For those that live outside of Oklahoma, allow me to
give you a visual of Oklahoma, and insight into why a reporter from
Oklahoma City would even know about a small fair in Chandler.
According to the map below (borrowed from Google Maps), the small
town of Chandler, Oklahoma is forty miles and a forty-one minute
drive from Oklahoma City where the NBC station is located. I realize

it is typical for reporters to travel for a story, but how did this reporter know there was a story in Chandler?

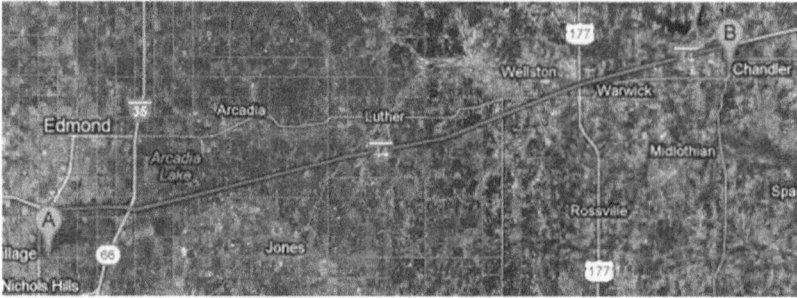

(Map taken from Google Maps)

The following excerpt is taken from my book, *The Naked Truth Bound in Scorn.*

At approximately the same time this letter was distributed, Ms. Ballard did a newscast from the entrance of Gayla's neighborhood with a "Justice for Kelsey" sign as her focus. Ms. Ballard stated that the signs had been "spotted all over Oklahoma City" and surrounding areas. According to witnesses who collected the signs, the only area they were found was in that neighborhood. According to OKC.gov, Oklahoma City covers an area of 622 square miles (an area larger than New York City, Houston, or Atlanta)[37]. How did Ms. Ballard just happen upon signs that were only present in one neighborhood, and do a report on it, if Kathie and her group knew nothing about the letter, as the author claimed? Also, how did Raye and her family stand a chance against a growing mob that had members of the media willing to cover "stories" that promoted their campaign against Raye?[38]

The city of Chandler is nowhere near the size of Oklahoma City. According to the city's Web site, it is a thirty-mile radius.[39] As you

---

[37] http://www.okc.gov/info_tech/gis/index.html

[38] Ortiz, Jody. *The Naked Truth Bound in Scorn.* Oklahoma City, Ok: 2010.

[39] http://chandlerok.com/

364

can imagine, residents in Oklahoma City rarely hear of news or activities in Chandler, and we certainly don't monitor events or fairs in small towns across Oklahoma. On an average day, there are plenty of newsworthy occurrences in our own area. Keeping all of these facts in mind, why would a reporter from Oklahoma City care about activities in Chandler? Could it be for reasons other than reporting a newsworthy story? The following excerpt from Judge Craig Key's book, *A Deadly Game of Tug-of-War: The Kelsey Smith-Briggs Story* gives us more insight.

It was now August, 2006, and at the Lincoln County Free Fair in Chandler I had a booth. Just as in other rural counties, the annual county fair is a big deal. Hundreds of children exhibit animals, produce, or crafts and everyone shows up to participate as a family event.

I ran an ad in the paper telling people they could come ask me about the Kelsey case. The ad read: "Within judicial and ethical limits find out all the facts possible about this case." It was my desire to allow the voters of Lincoln County a chance to ask any question they had involving Kelsey's case.

I was gone from the booth when a reporter for KFOR, Channel Four, the NBC affiliate out of Oklahoma City, showed up and verbally attacked the gentleman and his wife who were working at my booth. The reporter came there to attack me. They were basically just looking to try and force me to talk with a complete disregard for the citizens at the fair.

I wasn't there, so this reporter got into a verbal altercation with the gentleman and his wife who were working my booth. As my associate walked away from them, the cameraman bumped him with his camera. My associate told the cameraman to remove the camera from his face. It was at this point that the cameraman loudly proclaimed my associate to be a "backwards country jackass." He said this in front of women, children, and everyone who was there within our county fair. There was a lady who works at the USDA county extension office, was sitting with her seven-year-old twin daughters right next to this confrontation. In addition, a lady who was working the Farm Bureau booth, plus all sorts of other individuals witnessed the event. The cameraman had no regard for our little county fair, nor did he have any respect for our citizens.

Instead, they wanted to come down and verbally and physically assault me and my people in order to get their story.

During this time, newspaper ads, ran by Sheila Kirk, were distorting the facts of Kelsey's case. The attorney for Kelsey decided to set the record straight, and sent the following letter on September 21, 2006, to the editors of both the Lincoln County News and the Stroud American. Both papers ran the letter he sent as follows:

"To the Editor, As the attorney for Kelsey Smith-Briggs, I am writing this letter to set the record straight regarding several issues pertaining to Kelsey's case. Unfortunately, her death has become a political football and it concerns me that some are pointing fingers without having full knowledge of the facts. Whether you support Judge Craig Key or his opponent, Sheila Kirk, I would encourage everyone to base their decision on the truth rather than emotion. To do otherwise would not serve the voters and citizens of this county. The truth is Judge Key had the legal obligation to return Kelsey to her mother. The Court, as well as myself, were advised that the mother had completed the Individualized Service Plan created for her by the Department of Human Services (DHS), and there were no additional requirements of her. The Oklahoma legislature has declared that it is the official public policy of this state to reunite children with their parents under such circumstances. The truth is that Kelsey's placement with her mother in June of last year was conditioned upon the stipulation and Court order that there would be significant monitoring by various child welfare agencies. That is exactly what happened. The truth is that during the four months that Kelsey was in the care of her mother, none of those responsible for overseeing Kelsey's well-being ever reported to me or the Court that there were any problems with the care she was receiving. The truth is no one ever objected to or appealed Judge Key's ruling to return Kelsey to her mother. Based upon the evidence presented to the Court, and the monitoring and oversight requirement that was put in place on behalf of Kelsey, I do not believe that at that point in time any of the parties involved in the case

366

feared for her safety, much less, her life. No one has a crystal ball or can foretell the future. Judges and lawyers rely on the law and evidence. Everyone knows this. The more Kelsey's tragic situation is exploited and politicized, we will only move farther from the truth of what really happened to Kelsey. The people of Lincoln County should not be pulled apart or deceived by this sad incident. Sincerely, ... Attorney for Kelsey Smith-Briggs"[40]

09-06-2006 10:00 PM		
Kelsey's Grandma	**RE: Campaign issues and promises.**	**Post:**
Posts: 581 Group: Super Moderators Joined: Nov 2005 Status: Reputation:	Many people in Lincoln County may have read the negative report about Channel 4. I would like to set the record straight. Judge Key used Kelsey in his ad to get people to talk to him. When Cherokee Ballard walked in to give him the opportunity to set the record straight on why he sent Kelsey back home he was not in his booth. One of his supporters and his wife were not very hospitable. The tone was not one Sheila would have allowed in her booth. The supporter also grabbed the lens of the camera. It is true the camera man used ONE profane word for which he was suspended for a day. I guess these supporters did not realize the camera was rolling the entire time and the true actions were captured on video. He and Judge Key have made statements in the Lincoln County news trying to discredit her reputation as a reporter. Ms. Ballard has been a great crusader for children over the years and should be applauded for her efforts. I was not present at this time, but was told Judge Key was in the booth until he heard she was in the building and headed out the back door. This was witnessed by more than one person. Another person saw him sitting in his truck until KFOR left. He then returned to the booth shaking hands with this man, patting him on the back and laughing. Thank you, Kathie	
Today 12:15 AM		

As usual, the bullies on the bashboard were not aware of the real motives behind all of the stories, nor did they know the truth.

Posted by "Anonymous" August 25, 2006 @ 12:49 AM - Can we also write and call the Bar association and report Key's action on him Giving Kelsey back to the people that murdered her? He needs to be turned in, I'm sure there is someone we can write or call.

---

[40] Key, Craig. *A Deadly Game of Tug of War: The Kelsey Smith-Briggs Story.* Garden City, NY: Morgan James Publishing, 2007.

Posted by "Anonymous" August 25, 2006 @ 3:12 AM - We need to pray these charges are not dropped against Raye Dawn. Because if they are she could get custody of [her son] and this happen to him.

Posted by "Anonymous" August 25, 2006 @8:47 AM - I would like to know how many people agree to do what? We can sit here and talk about this all day long but we need action. Has anyone done anything yet, if so what? If you haven't, are you planning to? If so, what are you planning to do?

Posted by "DandCsmom" August 25, 2006 @ 8:59 AM - Exactly. We have pretty much determined the problems. What are we going to do for a solution? Whatever we do needs to be a collective effort and an organized effort. We need to agree on something. I am willing to call or write or visit the DA...pretty much whatever the group agrees on. Remember that these people are supposed to work FOR the public. You guys are the ones paying their salaries. They should be looking after the children of your state.

Posted by "Anonymous" August 25, 2006 @ 9:11 AM - I just want to remind everyone that this is NOT the DA's first chance. Akaysha was. And he plea bargained with her mother and her mother only received 2 years. He already had his one chance and he blew it. We cannot allow him another chance with Kelsey.

Posted by "Anonymous" August 25, 2006 @ 10:28 AM - 8:47, this battle is best fought on our knees and this is what we will continue to do.

Posted by "Anonymous" August 25, 2006 @ 10:51 AM - For those of you who want to know why Porter remains free on bail: What is the purpose of the bail? 5The purpose of the bail is to assure the attendance of the defendant, when his or her presence is required in court, whether before or after conviction. Bail is not a means of punishing a defendant, nor should there be a suggestion of revenue to the government.

He is not a flight risk and he is still innocent until proven guilty.

Posted by "DJones" August 25, 2006 @ 11:09 AM - Thank you, 10:51. I think alot of people just want to see someone locked up right now for this atrocity.

Posted by "Anonymous" August 25, 2006 @ 11:17 AM - Understandable. These are only charges and accusations. That does not mean that they are true. Innocent until proven guilty is what seperates us from being communists. For some to say that he should be locked back up is presuming that he is guilty of something that he has not had a fair trial for yet. That is also assuming he will get a fair trial, which doesn't look likely. I think everyone should stop and try to put themselves in the position of an accused. If you were falsely accused of a crime, would it be fair to you to be contained for almost a year when no one has proven those accusations against you? No it would not.

Posted by "Please Don't Plea Bargain" August 25, 2006 @ 11:44 AM - You are right about this not being the D.A.'s first chance. He's already blown it once and he will probably blow it again. I've delivered my letter to Smothermon. I challenge everyone on here to do the same and either mail a letter or take it by his office. Bombarge him with telephone calls. Do whatever it takes. We need to make him aware that this could very well happen again to [Raye's son]. It'll just be a different man next time that does the dirty deed. Raye Dawn will make sure that she is cleared and no one will expect her to do anything like that. After all, she is the "good" mother you know. Like the move The Good Son.

Posted by "Anonymous" August 25, 2006 @ 11:48 AM - Or she will do it herself

Posted by "Anonymous" August 25, 2006 @ 11:51 AM - Could you copy your letter here (without yoru name of course), or parts of it so maybe people that don't feel like they have the time can use it as a base letter for their own?? I am not suggesting

369

to anyone to copy it. I think that would be the wrong thing to do as he would just get tired of reading them.

Posted by "Help Kelsey" August 25, 2006 @ 12:38 PM - The number to the DA's office is 275-xxxx. Please call him, leave a message, let him know this will be the end of his career if she walks. Don't just call once, keep calling. He needs to hear the message loud and clear. Has anyone decided when there will be a group going to his office?

Posted by "Tinam" August 25, 2006 @ 12:39 PM - Why don't we all write letters to him and then a few of u hand deliver them with the media involved, regardless, if he's there or not, it will still get the public's attention and it should be a bag full of letters. We really need to do this!!!! We don't' need him to be there, cause he'll see us on TV later while he's eating dinner.

Posted by "Anonymous" August 25, 2006 @ 12:58 PM - I think we need to pull this off of this board because this blog is read by everyone. And I mean probably the people that you are talking about. I think this needs to be discussed privately and as a group. If you would like to be added to a mail list to get this together, please send an email to Isitreallyjustice@hotmail.com It would be better if you could identify yourself in the email so we will know who you are as to keep others off of the list that don't need to be there.

Obviously, some comments had been removed prior to this post. As per the instructions above, perhaps?

Posted by "Elizabeth" August 25, 2006 @ 1:23 PM - Sorry I asked you to identify yourselves and then I didn't identify myself. I am a member of Kelseyspurpose.

Posted by "Anonymous" August 25, 2006 @ 4:41 PM - Good idea elizabeth-can I ask you how many people have answered you? I hope people are getting involved with this.

Posted by "Anonymous" August 25, 2006 @ 6:25 PM - Why don't they interview [Mike Porter's daughter] she's older and she was with Raye Dawn, Mike, and Kelsey when she would visit ask if she would see anything. Also ask her if Raye Dawn acted strange that day when she picked her up the day Kelsey died

Posted by "Anonymous" August 25, 2006 @ 6:37 PM - [Mike Porter's daughter] has been interviewed.

Posted by "Anonymous" August 25, 2006 @ 6:43 PM - And they still don't know man

Posted by "Anonymous" August 25, 2006 @ 6:57 PM - So ok what it boils down to is say for some weird reason I go out murder a 2 year-old child does that mean I get to roam the streets as a free person. If they don't know who did it lock both of them up they should have known Kelsey was getting abused

Posted by "Anonymous" August 25, 2006 @ 7:13 PM - I will ask again, is there any place we can call or write to tell what Key has done, when he went against DHS and the grandparents wishes not to put Kelsey back with the abusers.

Posted by "DJones" August 25, 2006 @ 7:17 PM - Neither have confessed, neither have been convicted yet and neither are a flight risk, as Mike will hang around to clear himself and RD will hang around to....well......uh.......mmmmmmmm

Posted by "DJones" August 25, 2006 @ 7:22 PM - 7:13 – the family are the only ones that can file charges against anyone. You might contact the governer and see what he is going to do about it, but from what i understand, all we can do is see that he doesn't get re-elected.

Posted by "Anonymous" August 25, 2006 @ 7:27 PM - 6:57 If you wish to live in a communist country, please do so.

Posted by "Anonymous" August 25, 2006 7:29 PM - Agreed 6:57. They would think differently if it were them that were the

371

accused. Especially if they were wrongfully accused of
something.

Posted by "Anonymous" August 25, 2006 7:30 PM - I meant agreed
to 7:27

Posted by "Anonymous" August 25, 2006 @ 8:51 PM - IT'S ALL
BULLSHIT ANYWAY. ALL OF IT.

Posted by "Anonymous" August 25, 2006 @ 8:54 PM - Yep, every
last damn bit of it

Posted by "Anonymous" August 25, 2006 @ 9:04 PM - YEP. Some
people just dont get it. They think they know so much but they
are really clueless. Not stupid at all. They just don't
understand things that they don't feel.

Posted by "Anonymous" August 25, 2006 @ 9:26 PM - You're right.
Not stupid. Or clueless. But they sure know what they feel.
Too bad some are in denial about it.

Posted by "Anon 101" August 25, 2006 @ 10:53 PM - Thank you
[Jack] for speaking out. We all want the truth to come out.

Posted by "Anonymous" August 25, 2006 @ 11:47 PM - What did
[Jack] say?

Posted by "Please Don't Plea Bargain" August 26, 2006 @ 11:16
AM - It was on channel 4 last night. All R.D. supporters are
stupid in my opinion. If they were smart, they could se thru
all that crud.

Posted by "anon15" August 26, 2006 @ 11:19 AM - It seems that
the news stations are having a different outlook on the case
also since Wednesday. I don't' know if it's my imagination or
not, but it seems that they are more negative about RD than
before. Has anyone else noticed that?

Posted by "Anonymous" August 26, 2006 @ 11:20 AM - How can
the news stations not be more negative than before? Raye

Dawn is sinking herself. Evidently her lawyer isn't beating into her what to say too good.

Posted by "Anonymous" August 26, 2006 @ 11:20 AM - That's because they could tell that she was lying.

Posted by "Please Don't Plea Bargain" August 26, 2006 @ 11:22 AM - Maybe the news stations could see thru Raye Dawns lies. It seemed to be quite obvious.

Posted by "Anonymous" August 26, 2006 @ 11:23 AM - Raye Dawn lie? Haha That wouldn't be a first.

Posted by "Anonymous" August 26, 2006 @ 11:26 AM - Were you in court Please Don't Plea Bargain?

Posted by "Anonymous" August 26, 2006 @ 11:26 AM - I heard that Raye Dawn and her family are positive that she'll walk. Elephants fly too, wonder if they've been told.

"Then they wanted the OSBI to banish the bash board and that did not work. Something is in the air and if they don't put the little hussy in jail soon we are probably going to be the target of their next scheme." Kathie Briggs to Mike Porter

Posted by "Anonymous" August 26, 2006 @ 11:35 AM - Anon 10:56 – Just because a motion is made to lift a gag order does not mean that it will be granted. It more than likely will not be lifted in this case.

Posted by "anon15" August 26, 2006 @ 11:38 AM - I don't think it will be lifted either. There's too much media hype. There are people already disobeying the

gag order. Just think what would happen if they lift it? raye
Dawn will want much more media time along with Mildred
and Gayla. Shoot those three hussies will be fighting over the
microphone.

Posted by "Anonymous" August 26, 2006 @ 11:39 AM - I wonder
why it would not be lifted now that the defense wants it
lifted?? Hmmm. That would be interesting.

Posted by "Anonymous" August 26, 2006 @ 11:42 AM - ONCE
AGAIN – RAYE DAWN HAS NEVER BEEN UNDER THE
GAG ORDER – NOR HAS ANY OF HER FAMILY. RAYE
DAWN HAS ALWAYS BEEN ABLE TO SPEAK FREELY
ABOUT THIS CASE. SHE HAS CHOSEN NOT TO. SHE
WAS NEVER UNDER A GAG – AS THERE IS NO GAG IN
PLACE AS IT PERTAINS TO HER CRIMINAL CASE. THE
ONLY PEOPLE THAT ARE UNDER THE GAG ARE THE
ATTORNEY'S IN PORTER'S CASE AND LAW
ENFORCEMENT. THE GAG IS NOT ENFORCEABLE ON
WINTESSES. IT NEVER HAS BEEN.

Posted by "Anonymous" August 26, 2006 @ 11:42 AM - why or who
in the world in the defense wants it lifted?

Posted by "Anonymous" August 26, 2006 @ 11:43 AM - please
don't type in caps, it's hard to read

Posted by "Anonymous" August 26, 2006 @ 11:44 AM - Isn't that
what people want?? To hear from Porter or his attorney?
I've seen it said several times that he looks guilty by not
speaking up, even though he hasn't been able to. Why should
he not be able to defend himself publicly like the rest?

Posted by "anon15" August 26, 2006 @ 11:46 AM - It has been
stated on tv that there is a gag order. If the defense wants it
lifted that would be suicidal to them. No telling what those 3
women will be saying. Mildred goes on tv every time that the
wind blows a different direction. by the way, she needs to get
some makeup that's not white. she looks dead.

374

Posted by "Anonymous" August 26, 2006 @ 11:46 AM - The DA in Porter's case has and continues to disregard the gag order repeatedly directly and through his chosen emissaries. I guess Porter feels that there is a lot of information that the DA is choosing not to make public that should me made public. I really don't know but I think it would be telling if the motion to lift the gag was denied since it is a defense motion.

Posted by "Anonymous" August 26, 2006 @ 11:48 AM - Does anyone honestly thin that it does not help Porter's case every time anyone from the Smith family speaks? Everything they say helps his case. Especially Raye Dawn.

Posted by "anon15" August 26, 2006 @ 11:49 AM - I think that Porter is right by sitting back and not saying anything. Raye Dawn and her family are going to hang raye Dawn. It seems so obvious that she set him up. Especially after hearing that Kelsey was outside playing with a turtle and came inside (what 2 year old is outside by themselves) to tell her mom that she had an accident. That's when Raye Dawn flipped out and started whipping her, and put her to bed and she didn't want to go to sleep, so she kicked her in a whirl wind of anger, Mike came home and she left, leaving him with what she thought was an injured child. She went to far.

Posted by "anon15" August 26, 2006 @ 11:50 AM - I agree 11:48. Everytime that they open their mouths, they are helping Mike's case. Let them talk. They don't realize what they are doing.

Posted by "Anonymous" August 26, 2006 @ 11:53 PM - Does anyone know whether Gayla and Raye Dawn sold that house?

Posted by "Anonymous" August 26, 2006 @ 12:09 PM - 11:46, the lift of the gag order is not going to make a difference in how much those 3 women speak, they are not under a gag order as it is

Posted by "Anonymous" August 26, 2006 @ 12:57 PM - ODCR states the following regarding the gag order in Michael Porter's case: "ATTORNEYS ON BOTH SIDES ORDERED NOT TO SPEAK TO MEDIA ABOUT THIS CASE AND TO ADVISE ANY WITNESSES OR OTHER PARTIES INVOLVED TO DO THE SAME"

Posted by "Anonymous" August 26, 2006 @ 1:00 PM - The witnesses in the case are under the gag order.

Posted by "anon15" August 26, 2006 @ 1:04 PM - I think it would be appropriate to revoke Raye Dawn's bond and either raise it much higher or put her in jail. She has faithfully continued to incriminate herself.

Posted by "Anonymous" August 26, 2006 @ 1:04 PM - The witnesses ARE NOT under the gag order. The gag order is NOT enforceable on witnesses, only attorneys and law enforcement. That is a fact. Advise means to suggest or recommend. That is all. Witnesses can be ASKED not to speak but if they choose to they would not be sanctioned for breaking the gag order as it DOES NOT APPLY TO THEM IN THE FASHION IT APPLIES TO ATTORNEYS AND LAW ENFORCEMENT. I do not care what ODCR says, what I am telling you IS A FACT.

Posted by "Anonymous" August 26, 2006 @ 1:05 PM - I second that. Put Raye Dawn in jail.

Posted by "Anonymous" August 26, 2006 @ 1:06 PM - 1:04. You are dead wrong in this case.

Posted by "Anonymous" August 26, 2006 @ 1:06 PM - Is it enforceable on Michael Porter?

Posted by "Anonymous" August 26, 2006 @ 1:07 PM - I believe that 1:04 is right in this case.

Posted by "Anonymous" August 26, 2006 @ 1:07 PM - I meant the second 1:04 is right.

Posted by "Anonymous" August 26, 2006 @ 1:08 PM - Read what it says carefully and it will be obvious to you. Attorneys are ORDERED not to speak to the media, and to advise any witnesses to do the same. It does not say witnesses are ordered to not speak to the media. The only thing the gag order says in relation to witnesses is that the attorneys is that the attorneys are ordered to advise them to not speak to media – witnesses were not ORDERED to do anything. As a non principal in a criminal case you can do as you please, and that includes speaking to the media of your so choose. Does that clear this up? I hope so.

Posted by "Anonymous" August 26, 2006 @ 1:08 PM - What do you mean its it enforceable? You idiot, the defense wouldn't be asking for it to be lifted if it wasn't. go back to school.

Posted by "Anonymous" August 26, 2006 @ 1:09 PM - He can't file charges on them if they are not ordered to remain silent under the gag order. The witnesses are trying to respect the judge and the DA and not say anything to the media that they should not. [Jack] is not listed on the witness list and has not been asked to remain silent.

Posted by "Anonymous" August 26, 2006 @ 1:11 PM - [Jack] is not listed. What about Mildred Fowler. She is on the witness list and continues to talk. She should be charged accordingly.

Posted by "Anonymous" August 26, 2006 @ 1:11 PM - Witnesses can speak if they so choose. They are protected by the first amendment. No judge can take away your first amendment right if you are a not a principal in a criminal case. Think about what you are saying people.

Posted by "Anonymous" August 26, 2006 @ 1:12 PM - Mildred didn't talk about evidence or specific information about the case. She did not violate any requests.

Posted by "Anonymous" August 26, 2006 @ 1:13 PM - NO witness can be charges with any crime!!! They are not under the gag order. They can choose to follow the advice of the DA and not speak, but they can not be prevented from speaking by the gag order. It is simply a fact.

Posted by "Anonymous" August 26, 2006 @ 1:14 PM - 1:13 is correct. The witnesses are simply trying to respect the court.

Posted by "Anonymous" August 26, 2006 @ 1:14 PM - 1:11 These are the same people that think someone should have to be locked up before being proven guilty.

Posted by "Anonymous" August 26, 2006 @ 1:15 PM - It's a good thing they run our justice system.

Posted by "Anonymous" August 26, 2006 @ 1:15 PM - 1:13that's why the defense has asked for it to be lifted, right, because it doesn't exist. You are really bright.

Posted by "Anonymous" August 26, 2006 @ 1:15 PM - I meant they don't run our justice system

Again, it appears that posts were deleted. They must have been anti-Porter.

Posted by "Anonymous" August 26, 2006 @ 1:34 PM - NO AGAIN second 1:32. Yes, everyone agress that they are BOTH guilty of SOMETHING!!

Posted by "Anonymous" August 26, 2006 @ 1:35 PM - Ok if you don't want to talk about that 1:34, are you still wanting to talk about the gag order. Get over it. People don't want to talk about that anymore.

Posted by "Anonymous" August 26, 2006 @ 1:35 PM - Enough about the gag order already.

Posted by "Anonymous" August 26, 2006 @ 1:36 PM - Amen 1:35

Posted by "Anonymous" August 26, 2006 @ 1:36 PM - Need to invoke a gag order on this site. :)

Posted by "Anonymous" August 26, 2006 @ 1:37 PM - That's funny – and true – 1:36!!!

Posted by "Anonymous" August 26, 2006 @ 1:38 PM - I say we just all meet up and kick the crap out of each other until we agree.

Posted by "Anonymous" August 26, 2006 @ 1:38 PM - I like this site when there is intelligent discussion. When the trash talking starts, I just have to leave. The people who trash talk need to feel better about themselves so they put other people down.

Posted by "Anonymous" August 26, 2006 @ 1:39 PM - And when we still don't agree, we'll just pop open up a 12 pack and call it good.

Posted by "Anonymous" August 26, 2006 @ 1:40 PM - See when people who aren't very bright find that out they make posts like 1:38. It would be better to just say I was wrong, I am not near as smart as I think I am. :)

Posted by "Anonymous" August 26, 2006 @ 1:46 PM - neener neener

Posted by "Please Don't Plea Bargain" August 26, 2006 @ 1:54 PM - My goodnesss...what is happening to this site?

Posted by "Anonymous" August 26, 2006 @ 2:13 PM - It's just getting back to the same old crap that it used to be.

Posted by "Anonymous" August 26, 2006 @ 2:18 PM - I think neener neener was a poke at people who use emotional arguments when they run out of intelligent things to add to a discussion. I know that someone on here has made an appeal for people to join them to take a stance against Raye Dawn receiving a plea bargain. How many of you posting have joined that effort? IF not, why? I will be taking a stand against Raye Dawn receiving a plea bargain. For those of you here who just want to talk, when there is a chance to take action why do you not?

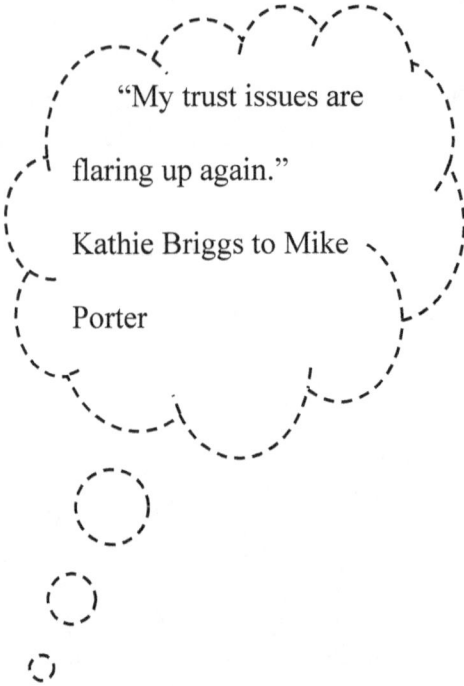

> "My trust issues are
>
> flaring up again."
>
> Kathie Briggs to Mike
>
> Porter

Posted by "Anonymous" August 26, 2006 @ 2:20 PM - I personally am disgusted that more people are not taking a public stand against Raye Dawn getting a deal. Keeping quiet benefits no one. Certainly not Justice for Kelsey.

Posted by "Anonymous" August 26, 2006 @ 2:20 PM - See....a call to action is made....and what is there? Silence.

Posted by "Anonymous" August 26, 2006 @ 2:34 PM - Wow, it seems asking people why they haven't acted or won't act doesn't get much of a response, does it?

Posted by "Please Don't Plea Bargain" August 26, 2006 @ 3:01 PM - what was the call? Or when? I guess I missed that point. I've already took some action towards that.

Posted by "Please Don't Plea Bargain" August 26, 2006 @ 3:04 PM - I am also disgusted about the Plea bargain as you can tell my user name here. I also, want to make sure that I do not "hook up with the wrong people" on here. What I'm trying to say. I don't want to give out my email address to people that are on the Smith side just playing that are snakes to get peoples names that are against them. I might be paranoid, but stranger things have happened.

Posted by "DandCsmom" August 26, 2006 @ 3:13 PM - See the post by Elizabeth. Yesterday at 1:23pm.

380

Posted by "Anonymous" August 26, 2006 @ 3:14 PM - Please Don't Plea Bargain – I know you are one of the people who have chosen to act. I was referring to the people who just come here to voice their opinion in secret and bicker and argue. Elizabeth made a request for people that would be interested in taking stand against a plea bargain to contact her. From what I hear the results have been dismal so far. Many people visit this site, but few are actually willing to take an actual stand on this issue, for reasons unknown.

Posted by "Anonymous" August 26, 2006 @ 3:19 PM - I can assure you that Elizabeth is not the Smith clan and has perfectly honest intentions.

Posted by "Anonymous" August 26, 2006 @ 10:19 PM - What is this about RD leaving Kelsey outside alone? And did I read that she pumished her for having and accident? So she admitted to punishing Kelsey the day she died?

Posted by "Anonymous" August 27, 2006 @ 9:01 AM - RD said she was playing with a turtle outside and came in to tell her she had an accident. RD did not say she punished her. Get your facts straight before you start making stuff up in your questions.

Posted by "Anonymous" August 27, 2006 @ 9:37 PM - I think the point of asking questions is to try to get the facts straight. It was stated as a question, not fact. Wake up on the wrong side of the bed?

Posted by "MistyLT" August 27, 2006 @ 11:13 AM - There is a new day up. Please start posting on it then we won't have to scroll so much.

Battle for the Bashboard – Round Two

August, 2006

From their new bashboard entitled "Oklahoma Child Abuse Cases" A note at the top stated as follows:

Letjusticebedone is no longer the owner of this site and is not responsible for it. All rules and disclaimers still apply. If for any reason you need to email the owner, please send to [email removed for privacy]

Posted by the blog owner at August 27, 2006 @ 11:11 AM - Several people have told me they are having problems being able to post. No one has been banned. If the site tells you your IP address has been banned, I assure you that it has not been. Please go to http://oklahomachildabuse.bravehost.com/, scroll down to the link that say "Who is Failing Our Children" and try to get in from there.

It seems that some of the bashboard bullies were now talking to themselves since they had been ousted by Kelsey's Purpose—for appearance's sake. Now that Kathie Briggs was no longer "having fun" with Mike Porter, she wanted to distance herself from him. Perhaps she knew the district attorney and many others were watching. She would later turn against her friend by turning over private messages from Porter's Kelsey's Purpose account to the district attorney.

Posted by "Anonymous" August 27, 2006 @ 11:22 AM - From what I heard the people in the courtroom knew that Raye Dawn lied every time she opened her moth. People could tell that just by looking at her.

Posted by "LadyInMoore" August 28, 2006 @ 4:46 AM - That is so strange. I didn't have any problems posting. Does anyone have a link to the original autopsy? I would appreciate it if you would post it here.

Posted by "Anonymous" August 28, 2006 @ 8:40 AM -
http://www.channeloklahoma.com/download/2006/011/60 08873.pdf

Posted by "Anonymous" August 28, 2006 @ 8:41 AM - Someone had said something about the way Raye Dawn was dressed in court. What was she wearing?

Posted by "Anonymous" August 28, 2006 @ 10:52 AM - Some of the previous posts have been removed

Posted by "Anonymous" August 28, 2006 @ 3:45 PM - The link to this page has been removed from KP again. I had a hard time getting back here!

Posted by "Anonymous" August 28, 2006 @ 3:47 PM - It seems no one wants to talk. Wonder why?

Posted by "Anonymous" August 28, 2006 @ 3:50 PM - I was wondering the same thing. I guess everybody got tired of the same ole, same ole.

Posted by "Anonymous" August 28, 2006 @ 4:30 PM - That is not surprising that they removed the link again.

Posted by "Anonymous" August 28, 2006 @ 4:31 PM - Yeah, I was just trying to find the thread on JonBenet and apparently it's gone too. I guess that subject was taboo as well. John Karr's DNA didn't match. I guess he was just an obsessed fruitcake.

Posted by "Anonymous" August 28, 2006 @ 4:32 PM - I doubt if everyone is quiet because they're tired of the same ole, same ole. I'm sure there is more influence than that.

383

Posted by "Anonymous" August 28, 2006 @ 4:37PM - I have a feeling KP won't be around much longer. If the members want to keep in touch, one of them better get another site up and running that does not have the name Kelsey Briggs on it anywhere. I think it has expanded more than the family expected. There are too many various opinions on there now.

Posted by "Anonymous" August 28, 2006 @ 4:38 PM - I figured as much as well. God knows we can't have too many various opinions.

Posted by "Anonymous" August 28, 2006 @ 4:39 PM - I've thought about posting using the word 'ALLEGEDLY' as every other word but I figure I would just get banned.

Posted by "Anonymous" August 28, 2006 @ 4:42 PM - Probably so. The only time everyone wants to wait until the whole story comes out and the evidence is when it's a family member. Everyone else is convicted by the public.

Posted by "Anonymous" August 28, 2006 @ 5:54 PM - If you guys are so against Kelsey's Purpose and the family, why do you go there?

Posted by "Anonymous" August 28, 2006 @ 6:00 PM - The new moderator said that the link was removed because links to blogs aren't allowed. They kept Misty's link up for a few days to be nice. Many things are removed because they are trying to focus the site more since it has gotten all over the place. They are trying to make it a little more focused because they have more laws that need to be changed. If legislators are to take them seriously, they need to reign the site in more so than in the past few months.

Posted by "Anonymous" August 28, 2006 @ 6:00 PM - Oh look, someone expressed an opinion that didn't agree and now they don't want to be Kelsey's Purpose members or involved in the fight against child abuse. Who would have ever thought.

Posted by "Anonymous" August 28, 2006 @ 6:01 PM - I never said that. I just asked a question.

Posted by "Anonymous" August 28, 2006 @ 6:04 PM - Honestly, someone could the Briggs' guts but it doesn't mean that they dont' want justice for Kelsey or not want to be involved in the fight against child abuse. There's not a person on here that said they were against Kelsey's Purpose or the family, so why do you ask?

Posted by "Anonymous" August 28, 2006 @ 6:05 PM - That was supposed to say hate the Briggs' guts

Posted by "anonymous" August 28, 2006 @ 6:11 PM - I think the Briggs' have done an exceptional job hosting KP and should be commended for doing so. It is ashame that so many people are getting their feathers ruffled for them wanting to have a better handle on the site.

Posted by "Anonymous" August 28, 2006 @ 6:14 PM - 6:04 – I am sorry if I misinterpreted some of the negative comments. I didn't mean to put words in someone's mouth. My mistake.

Posted by "Anonymous" August 28, 2006 @ 6:20 PM - I am sure that KP is trying to guide that site just as it appears that Misty is trying to do the same by deleting hundreds of posts on here. Sometimes site owners have to do that, even if it isn't liked by everybody.

Posted by "Anonymous" August 28, 2006 @ 6:28 PM - ha i find it funny that misty has now had to remove posts, i think that's the 1ˢᵗ time she's ever done that

Posted by "anonymous" August 28, 2006 @ 6:29 PM - It has to be very time consuming to stay on top of all of it. Because some people will say anything and everything without beginning concerned of hurting the families involved.

Posted by "Anonymous" August 28, 2006 @ 6:32 PM - Anon 6:26 – Why do you find it funny that Misty is removing posts?

Posted by "Anonymous" August 28, 2006 @ 6:32 PM - OK can we talk about something that matters? Like preventing child abuse?

Posted by "Anonymous" August 28, 2006 @ 6:37 PM - just thought i'd never see it happen

Posted by "Anonymous" August 28, 2006 @ 6:39 PM - Some people need some things said to them sometime.

Posted by "Anonymous" August 28, 2006 @ 6:41 PM - Some people criticize others for trying to make a little bit of a difference for a child when they themselves have never taken a major stand for children until now either.

Posted by "Anonymous" August 28, 2006 @ 6:43 PM - It's easy for people to sit back and criticize site owners/operators when they have never tried running one and NO IDEA how hard, stressful, and time consuming it is.

Posted by "Anonymous" August 28, 2006 @ 6:44 PM - This is getting old. It is all opinion on here. Some people would prefer not to read other people's opinions, all the while spouting out their own opinions about other people, living in a constant state of hypocrisy. No persons opinion is worth more just because they may have more education or more intellect. I have met some really ignorant educated people in my life.

Posted by "Anonymous" August 28, 2006 @ 6:45 PM - How would you know 6:41?

Posted by "Anonymous" August 28, 2006 @ 6:46 PM - I definitely agree with you there 6:44.

Posted by "Anonymous" August 28, 2006 @ 6:48 PM - I don't know if you have, but I can guarantee that not everyone who is sitting back criticizing has ever started a major movement against child abuse or some other cause.

Posted by "Anonymous" August 28, 2006 @ 6:48 PM - Running a site is time consuming and stressful. That is no excuse for consistent double standards allowed on a site or thinly veiled references to people's guilt as long as it agrees with the site owner's personal beliefs.

Posted by "Anonymous" August 28, 2006 @ 6:53 PM - Raye Dawn and Mike are both guilty of failing or harming Kelsey and the Briggs family knows that.

Posted by "Anonymous" August 28, 2006 @ 6:58 PM - See that is one example of the double standard. ALL accused persons are innocent until proven guilty, regardless of what anyone's opinions may be on the subject.

Posted by "Anonymous" August 28, 2006 @ 7:05 PM - Where does it end? Why are more people not charged in Kelsey's case? Why is the maternal grandmother not charged? Surely she knew right? Why are the DHS workers not charged? Why is the daycare worker not charged who admitted to suspecting abuse but never reporting it? Why are other family members who saw Kelsey every day not charged? Why is there no public outcry against the office of the District Attorney that never even thought that there were grounds to file any criminal charges for the confirmed abuse until Kelsey was killed? The same office that tired to withdraw from Kelsey's case? Where is the puvlic outcry now that the mother is being offered a plea deal by the same office that chose to never press charges after abuse was confirmed on her in the first place? How many people have things to hide in this case? Why is it ok for people to continue to cover things up and no one says anything?

Posted by "Anonymous" August 28, 2006 @ 7:06 PM - It's not okay. i don't' understand why people aren't speaking up.

Posted by "Anonymous" August 28, 2006 @ 7:07 PM - Especially the people with the most influence

387

Posted by "anon" August 28, 2006 @ 7:20 PM - Who do you think has the most influence?

Posted by "Anonymous" August 28, 2006 @ 7:22 PM - The Briggs of course.

Posted by "anon" August 28, 2006 @ 7:26 PM - Maybe they are taking action but have chosen to be quiet. I am sure they have attorneys advising them when to speak out and when to sit back and say nothing.

Posted by "Anonymous" August 28, 2006 @ 7:52 PM - contrary to popular belief, not every member of KP hangs on every word that comes out of a briggs' family member's mouth. believe it or not, we do have our own opinions and values. and just as you have stated that those charged are innocent until proven guilty; then maybe you shouldn't pass judgement on people you don't know. get to know someone before you start assuming that they have no brains of their own and can't think/speak/live without the guidance of someone else. i believe that the briggs family is a good family, and if it wasn't for the death of kelsey and the families fight for justice, then none of us would even be here discussing this. if this weren't true, then action would have been taken by people long before kelsey's death. if you want to commit to fighting against child abuse…then do it. but remember that the briggs do what they can and the members of KP can stand on their own as well.

Posted by "Anonymous" August 28, 2006 @ 7:56 PM - BLAH BLAH BLAH BLAH

Posted by "Anonymous" August 28, 2006 @ 7:58 PM - 6:58 – You're absolutely right. It's the double standard that bothers me. All or nothing, but don't pick and choose.

Posted by "Anonymous" August 28, 2006 @ 8:51 PM - Fuel the fire 756, fuel the fire.

Posted by "Anonymous" August 28, 2006 @ 9:03 PM - Didn't anyone watch channel 4 news @ 10 friday night? seems there IS someone that isn't afraid to speak up and say they think the DA is doing a sorry job.

Posted by "Anonymous" August 28, 2006 @ 9:04 PM - I missed something...what is this about double standards?

Posted by "Anonymous" August 28, 2006 @ 9:25 PM - Yes I did watch Channel 4 and am thankful that ... [Frank] finally spoke up. What I want to know is why they aren't holding Richard accountable for what happened to Kelsey too

Posted by "Anonymous" August 28, 2006 @ 9:27 PM - A lot of people would like to know that. No one mentions that. Too busy playing politics I guess.

Posted by "Anonymous" August 28, 2006 @ 9:31 PM - I still do not get how the Briggs can say they have complete faith in a DA that is offering the mother of Kelsey a plea bargain? This makes no sense whatsoever to me. Keeping quiet about this does not benefit Kelsey.

Posted by "Anonymous" August 28, 2006 @ 9:33 PM - 7:52 – Did I miss a post where someone said something about KP members hanging on to every word? Or did you need to clear a guilty conscience

Posted by "Anonymous" August 28, 2006 @ 10:04 PM - i'm not even going to bother. it's pointless.

Posted by "Anonymous" August 28, 2006 @ 10:20 PM - figures

Posted by "Anonymous" August 28, 2006 @ 11:50 PM - There are Christian Organizations out there to help children. Just go to where God leds you and move on. It's called "Shaking the Dust!" God bless.

Posted by "Anonymous" August 29, 2006 @ 3:27 PM - Did you all shake the dust?

Posted by "Anonymous" August 29, 2006 @ 8:49 PM - Hmm. Seems there were a lot of questions asked that no one wanted to answer.

Posted by "Anonymous" August 29, 2006 @ 9:47 PM - I just hope someone else besides [Frank and Susan] will have the guts to stand up and say what we all know – offering Raye Dawn a plea deal is NOT ACCEPTABLE UNDER ANY CIRCUMSTANCES!!!!

Posted by "Anonymous" August 30, 2006 @ 1:06 AM - Ok I have to put this on here after everything I have heard I'm really leaning towards Raye Dawn did it and this is why That day Kelsey had an accident in her pull-up Raye Dawn got mad and that may be where the bruises on Kelsey's buttom came from. Then Raye Dawn tries to put Kelsey to sleep for her nap with a big black t-shirt and no pull-up or anything, maybe like most 2 year-olds Kelsey didn't want to take a nap and Raye Dawn got really mad and started hurting Kelsey. But see what's really fishy is Raye Dawn went and picked up Porter's daughter from school wheich she never does and and Porter knew his friend was coming over that day now why would he wake Kelsey up from her nap beath the crap out of her when he knows his fired is coming over doesn't really make sense there. I hope they don't give Raye Dawn a plea deal because they don't know if she did it or not.

Posted by "Anonymous" August 30, 2006 @ 8:05 AM - It's good to see some people think twice about the sexual abuse charges instead of just accepting what the DA says. Shows you have some common sense.

Posted by "Anonymous" August 30, 2006 @ 8:31 AM - i think you'd be surprised how many people are now leaning more towards raye dawn just because of some of the things she said at mike's prelim.

Posted by "Anonymous" August 30, 2006 @ 10:23 AM - The fact is, only a few of the statements that Raye Dawn made on the stand last week were released by the media. She was on the stand for two hours and they printed no more than 8-10 sentences. You cannot make an informed decision based on that.

Posted by "Anonymous" August 30, 2006 @ 11:50 AM - The rest of what Raye Dawn said, that was not in the media shows that she did it for certain.

The truth is that there was nothing different about Raye's testimony than what she told investigators. The bashboard bullies realized that there were few outsiders in the small courtroom. Therefore, few people witnessed the testimony for themselves. These bullies knew that they would get away with deceiving people because they had believed all of their lies so far. During Raye's testimony, she stated that she "knew now" that Mike Porter was abusing Kelsey, not that she knew then. Of course these bullies had to twist her words. Also, it was revealed that Raye and Porter took turns picking up Porter's daughter from school. This is an example of repeating a falsehood to turn it into "truth," such as the statement about her knowing about the abuse. (Her testimony can be found in my first book in the series, *The Naked Truth Bound in Scorn*.)

Posted by "Anonymous" August 30, 2006 @ 12:22 PM - I'm the 106am person I'm not trying to say I take Mike Porters side now I'm just saying the facts are starting to get obvious and Raye Dawns better start watching her mouth cause she starting to get herself into some problems here. The bottom line that still makes it kinda iffy is Porter knew his friend was coming over Raye Dawn left the house to do something she never does it kinda boils down to who did it right there. Plus and I just thought of this at the prelim she said she knew Mike was abuseing Kelsey well WHY THE HELL DID YOU LEAVE HIM WITH HER THAT DAY

Posted by "Anonymous" August 30, 2006 @ 3:11 PM - 12:22 – You were not at the prelim, so you do not know what she said and what she did not say.

Posted by "Anonymous" August 30, 2006 @ 3:11 PM - It was not uncommon for Raye Dawn to pick [Mike Porter's daughter] up from school either.

Posted by "Anonymous" August 30, 2006 @ 3:46 PM - It was uncommon for Raye Dawn to pick [Mike Porter's daughter] up from school alone from everything I have heard. And nothing Raye Dawn says holds any eight anyway. People will see that. The only people who will back anything she says is her mommy or another brainless member of her family.

Posted by "Anonymous" August 30, 2006 @ 3:49 PM - I am sure Porter and his lawyer are jumping for joy that Raye Dawn is actually going to testify. Everyone in that courtroom knew she was lying. You can see right through her lies and fake tears. Porter's lawyer is going to have a field day with Raye Dawn if she ever sees the stand.

Posted by "Anonymous" August 30, 2006 @ 4:18 PM - 3:11 How do you know who was talking to know if they were there or not. Not even the immediate family knew everyone there.

Posted by "Anonymous" August 30, 2006 @ 4:56 PM - Sounds like Raye Dawn's defense will be that her and her family are the only people who tell the truth and it's everyone else that lies.

Posted by "Anonymous" August 30, 2006 @ 6:17 PM - Question if you knew your friend was coming over would you beat your 2 year-old step-daughter up to make her die before your friend came over that just doesn't make any sense there

Posted by "Anonymous" August 30, 2006 @ 7:11 PM - I wonder when the DA is going to announce the plea deal he has agreed to with Raye Dawn?

Posted by "Anonymous" August 30, 2006 @ 8:06 PM - I still can not believe that no one on KP is talking about another mother getting a plea deal from this DA. After months of talking about how everyone that failed Kelsey needs to be held accountable, the person who had the ultimate

392

responsibility to Kelsey gets a free pass, when it is still unclear what her actual role was. Her testimony looks worse and worse. What kind of witness will she make? I just do not get it. It is almost unbelievable.

Posted by "Anonymous" August 30, 2006 @ 9:16 PM - Obviously, you don't really read the KP site, because there is a post from the family asking everyone not to talk about the case because their is a gag order that applies to them. Since it is THEIR site, they can not allow ANYONE to speak about the case on the web site.

There aren't any "Briggs family statements" on the bashboard due to the gag order. But it is clear that they were a part of the discussion. Who else would know the details of what the Briggs thought or were told? Who else would hate Raye and her entire family with such venom other than Mike Porter? Why was the gag order suddenly an issue when multiple gag orders had been issued since the beginning of the case and they were all ignored by the Briggs? What changed?

Posted by "Anonymous" August 30, 2006 @ 9:30 PM - I don't think the Briggs or [Kelsey's paternal step-grandparents, Jack and Susan] will support Smothermon offering RD a plea bargain. And they don't think he's doing a good job.

Posted by "Anonymous" August 30, 2006 @ 9:30 PM - Wonder why they don't want people talking about the plea deal. I agree with you 8:26. Seems something may be happening here and if it's not talked about, then it doesn't exist.

Posted by "Anonymous" August 30, 2006 @ 9:31 PM - 9:30 Is Lance the only one that thinks Smothermon is doing a good job?

Posted by "Anonymous" August 30, 2006 @ 9:32 PM - 9:16 That gag order didn't stop them before. Why now? Why would they not use the KP site to get people to ask why there's going to be a plea bargain for Kelsey's abuser? Yes she was a confirmed abuser. The Briggs are not under a gag order n Raye Dawn's case, there is no gag order in her case.

393

*Posted by "Anonymous" August 30, 2006 @ 9:54 PM - 9:32 you
     sound like Ann...from the Daily Oklahoman! KP did not
     openly talk about the case. There are MANY MANY other
     cases talked about on that web site. If someone asked a
     question then it usually got answered. But, Smothermon
     started being a little bit more strict about the gag order after
     the pre-lim. He ever so kindly (sarcasm here) reminded the
     family that they were under a gag order. I don't think the
     problem is that the family doesn't want a plea discussed
     because it has been discussed on the web site. There were
     two different threads asking people to write Smothermon and
     tell him NO DEAL. What else is there to talk about? No one
     wants a deal for Raye except for her and her dumb family
     members. That is understood.*

*Posted by "Anonymous" August 30, 2006 @ 9:55 PM - Smothermon
     reminded the Briggs they were under a gag order? LOL!!!!
     This coming from someone who can't even remember that
     he's under one himself? I'm sure he did remind them that
     they were under a gag order. He probably doesn't want them
     telling what they know. If I were him, I wouldn't want them
     telling either.*

*Posted by "Anonymous" August 30, 2006 @ 9:56 PM - hahahaha
     wonder why smothermon wanted the gag order to be a little
     more strict after the prelim hehe*

*Posted by "Anonymous" August 30, 2006 @ 9:58 PM - We have
     been over this before, not the gag thing again. The Briggs are
     NOT under a gag. Never have been. Raye Dawn is not under
     a gag. Raye Dawn's plea bargain is immaterial to Porter's
     case. Anyone can speak about the plea bargain. My question
     is why are people not doing it? KP has been a forum to
     discuss who failed Kelsey from day one. Now that the mother
     could walk suddenly the case can not be discussed? I support
     the Briggs. TRUST me I do. But I do not support their silence
     on this matter.*

Posted by "Anonymous" August 30, 2006 @ 10:00 PM - What can Smothermon do to people who speak out? You guessed it...NOTHING. Maybe he has people fooled into beleiving that the gag applies to them.

Posted by "Anonymous" August 30, 2006 @ 10:20 PM - 9:16 – I have read KP from day one. I support the Briggs. The fact is that the case was discussed on there NUMEROUS TIMES. The posts are still there that give details of the case. That is fine. TO use the gag now as a reason for not speaking out about a PLEA DEAL does not hold water. Like I said, I ready KP daily. I think alot of good things have come from KP. I just want to know why the people who should be speaking about the plea deal are not doing it. I have tried to figure out how not speaking benefits Justice for Kelsey and I just do not see how it can. Speaking out is probably the ONLY reason the mother was even charged with a crime. The DA did not want to prosecute her regardless of what he says, that much is obvious.

Posted by "Anonymous" August 30, 2006 @ 10:22 PM - Raye Dawn got herself another attorney on the 23th.

Posted by "Anonymous" August 30, 2006 @ 10:39 PM - I doubt if it was because she didn't want [her attorney]. I bet [her attorney] dropped her ass like a bad habit.

Posted by "Anonymous" August 30, 2006 @ 10:49 PM - No, she still has [her attorney]. But she added Richard Smothermon to her defense team on the 23rd. Since he will be using her to testify he will have to defend her more than [her attorney] ever did. [Her attorney's] job was easy. All he had to do was work out a deal with one of his old buddies. He will never have to defend Raye Dawn in an actual courtroom. Now it's up to Richard to defend Raye Dawn.

Posted by "Anonymous" August 30, 2006 @ 10:56 PM - Ah, sorry, I'm slow ya know. That's very true.

Posted by "Anonymous" August 30, 2006 @ 11:03 PM - He will have to try to cover up every lie she has told to make her look credible. Her performance at trial will be scripted by who?? Yep, you guessed it.

Posted by "Anonymous" August 30, 2006 @ 11:08 PM - She may need more than those two to pull this off..I think her new prosecuting attorney ([Porter's attorney]) will make those two have bad nightmares. I sure hope so..

Posted by "Anonymous" August 30, 2006 @ 11:14 PM - I wonder how [Porter's attorney] stood up in court to Richard? I heard second hand that he was no slouch. I also heard on the news that [Porter's attorney] hammered Raye Dawn. Hopefully that was just the beginning. If anyone is going to expose her for what she is I guess it will have to be [Porter's attorney]. No one else will.

Posted by "Anonymous" August 30, 2006 @ 11:21 PM - I hope no one still questions how badly people need Raye Dawn to get off free and clear in this case. There is SO much riding on her not being found guilty of anything.

What did the bullies think was riding on this? Money? Book deals?

Posted by "Anonymous" August 31, 2006 @ 12:13 AM - God I hope Sutton exposes it all. You are right, no one else is going to.

The next post is reminiscent of a statement from Kathie Briggs regarding a paternal grandmother in Oklahoma that has been making false allegations of child abuse against the maternal family of her grandchild for over ten years. The allegations started when she wanted custody of her grandchild and her son was in prison for the same issues that Lance Briggs faces…drug abuse and domestic violence. Kathie Briggs and her bullies teamed up with her, and when a Grand Jury decided that the child was not being abused, Kathie Briggs posted this on her Kelsey's Purpose forum. "One thing I can say is NEVER count John and Alene out." The following post was on the bashboard. See the similarities? Perhaps the public stance of not discussing the case was just another smoke screen?

Posted by "Anonymous" August 31, 2006 @ 10:01 AM - Don't count the Briggs' out. Trust me, they are working against a plea bargain. This is not a new subject to them. The subject and possibility has existed since before Raye Dawn was even charged. Raye Dawn has been trying to get a deal for months. It was not a surprise to the Briggs family, only to the media and to all of you guys. If it were not for the Briggs family, Raye Dawn would have had a deal months ago. She was asked if her attorney and the DA are trying to negotiate a deal, and they are. They will continue to. Smothermon and the Briggs are trying to get her to serve time in prison and [her attorney] is not. All attorneys try to negotiate deals for their clients. That does not mean that it always gets negotiated into terms that both sides can agree on. The Briggs are taking a break from posting on KP for a while, but that does not mean that they are not working with the DA. They work with him every day. They are not slacking off at a critical time, because for them, every single day has been critical in holding those those responsible accountable for their actions and inactions. As I stated, the idea is not new to them. They have been fighting it since October 11, 2005.

Posted by "Anonymous" August 31, 2006 @ 10:42 AM - Actually, it wasn't a suprise to any of us, I think we all just needed confirmation that it was happening so that our letters would do some good and Richard could not lie about it. But thank you for finally answering some of our questions. Although I do still believe that the only reason Raye Dawn is testifying in this case is bc she has been promised something. There is no way for her to testify without incriminating herself and her attorney would not allow it without some kind of deal.

Posted by "Anonymous" August 31, 2006 @ 11:02 AM - Please continue to write your letters and make your phone calls. Write many times. Call many times. For every call and letter that you generate, the Smith family has a call and a letter to match it. They have been on a campaign for Raye Dawn since before she was charged. Don't let up. It is very important that Richard realize that the general public, not just KP members, will not stand for a plea deal for Kelsey. Kelsey deserves better. All of the children in our state deserve better. Richard has the opportunity to stand up and show that he is not soft on crimes against children in his district. Make him realize that he not only has this opportunity, but this responsibility. The children deserve justice. Kelsey deserves justice. WE WILL NOT SETTLE FOR LESS!

Posted by "Anonymous" August 31, 2006 @ 11:04 AM - I have spoken with someone from the family (not a distant family member, an actual close to the case family member) regarding the plea deal. She stated that Raye Dawn has not been offered a plea deal yet. She also said they they will not support one and they will not support Richard if it happens. They want people to do everything they know to do to get the word out about this plea deal and they want to stop it from happening. I'm not just blowing smoke out my ass here. This was an actual REAL conversation with a REAL family member invoved in the case.

Posted by "Anonymous" August 31, 2006 @ 11:10 AM - Richard is very aware that the Briggs family will not support him if he allows Raye Dawn to plea and walk. Make him aware that will not either.

Posted by "Anonymous" August 31, 2006 @ 11:16AM - So if the Briggs know that Richard has been lying about the plea to the public all along, then why do they trust anything he says? He tells people he does not need her, then why offer her ANYTHING? Let a jury decide what she is guilty of and what her punishment should be. He is taking that decision away from the public. You can not beleive anything he says and this is the bottom line.

The quotes in the bubble below echo the language and spelling of the next two "anonymous" posts. Same people, different bashboard...

Posted by "Anonymous" August 31, 2006 @ 11:17 AM - Richard
needs to know that the public will not allow a man to be
convicted based on lies. He KNOWS that many of things that
she said on the stand at the prelim were lies. Make him not
only hold her accountable for her crimes against Kelsey, but
also for perjury. We cannot allow our justice system to
reward people who lie on the stand. He cannot sweep her lies
on the witness stand under the rug along with her crimes
against Kelsey. HOLD HER ACCOUNTABLE!!

Posted by "Anonymous" August 31, 2006 @ 11:19 AM - I am sorry

"Well the DA is sadly mistaken and all the evidence is there to prove it." "I am afraid they will be sadly mistaken in court." "I beleive that you know that now." "I could not beleive what I saw on the news." "I prayed all night that God would allow the DA to hold RD accountable with the findings of the report." "hold her accountable" "We can only hope that people will be held accountable for their failures." "hold the parent accountable" "the truth will not make sure Raye DAwn is held accountable." Mike Porter to Kathie and Shirica

to disappoint anyone, but Richard does not tell the Briggs
family everything. He tells them what he wants them to know
to keep them quiet. I beleive that they do not support a plea

deal. But if you beleive that he tells the Briggs everything you are sadly mistaken.

Posted by "Anonymous" August 31, 2006 @ 11:23 AM - Richard is scared that if he does not a conviction againt Mike that his career is over. He has to know that if he does not get a conviction against Raye Dawn as well that his career is over. A conviction for one does not cover all of the justice that Kelsey deserves. She deserves justice for what her mother should have done as a mother. Kelsey deserved a good, protective, unselfish mother. It is not her fault that she got stuck with one who allowed money and hatred to get in the way of what was best for Kelsey. Raye Dawn has to be pay for being a sorry excuse for a mother. It is not excusable.

Posted by "Anonymous" August 31, 2006 @ 11:23 AM - Don't' think the Briggs don't know that. They don't trust him as far s they can throw him.

Posted by "Anonymous" August 31, 2006 @ 11:27 AM - If anyone doesn't think that all parties involved aren't skeptical of the other sides and aren't playing strategies, they are sorely mistaken. All sides are working their angles for their best interests. The Briggs' best interest in JUSTICE FOR KELSEY!!

Posted by "Anonymous" August 31, 2006 @ 11:29 AM - The sad thing is that people who should not be convoluting and covering the truth are the MAIN ones doing it. Beleive that.

Posted by "Anonymous" August 31, 2006 @ 11:31 AM - Richard Smothermon has put the Briggs family through so much more than he had to just to get a conviction.

Posted by "Anonymous" August 31, 2006 @ 11:40 AM - Maybe he should charge the right person with murder and we wouldn't be having this conversation.

Posted by "Anonymous" August 31, 2006 @ 11:44 AM - OH no, no. He has done that, remember? He has so much "great" evidence that somehow still needs to put a woman who could not tell the truth if her life depended on it on the stand to try to convict him.

Posted by "Anonymous" August 31, 2006 @ 11:50 AM - If Raye Dawn gavce a shit about her child she would want to testify against the man who supposedly killed her child NO MATTER WHAT. But it is still all about her. That is bullshit and everybody knows it. Richard should tell her ifg she chooses to testify it is completely up to her, but it will not benefit her in any way. She should hope that a jury finds her testimony compelling enough to give her a light sentence, which I HIGHLY doubt. If she wants to testify that is find and dandy, but RICHARD SMOTHERMON SHOULD NOT OFFER HER ANYTHING IN RETURN. A REAL MOTHER WOULD FACE THE MUSIC FOR WHAT SHE DID OR FAILED TO DO. KELSEY DESERVED BETTER THAN HER AS A MOTHER. THE CHIPS ARE DOWN NOW AND WHO IS RAYE DAWN CONCERNED ABOUT? YOU GUESSED IT.

Posted by "Anonymous" August 31, 2006 @ 1:00 PM - Amen 11:50!!!!

Posted by "Anonymous" August 31, 2006 @ 1:25 PM - I just do not see how she keeps fooling people. She has left so many people destroyed. How can someone who is tried to deal with criminals not see her for what she is?

Posted by "Anonymous" August 31, 2006 @ 1:33 PM - Raye Dawn has a way with men. He has probably fallen for her too.

Posted by "Anonymous" August 31, 2006 @ 1:38 PM - Let him know that we will not stand for him allowing her to walk just because she has played him and he has fallen for it.

Posted by "Anonymous" August 31, 2006 @ 1:51 PM - Everyone should let him know. There is no outcry and that is EXACTLY the reason why he will keep offering plea deals to mothers who in his mind dont deserve to be punished because he

THINKS they are "only" guilty of letting their children be beaten. Sad that he thinks that but even sadder that people are not more disgusted by it. He works for us!!!! Whatever he does is ultimately because we as voters of the 23rd Judicial District ALLOW him to do it. DO you think he would have given Akaysha's mom a plea deal if the media was on him and there were hundreds of people protesting it? NO. Do you think he would try to give Kelsey's mom a plea deal if the media called him on his statement that he did not need her testimony? NO. What about if he received hundreds of calls and letters DEMANDING that he not offer pleas in child absue cases? NO. What about if there was a public protest with people carrying signs saying "Parents that dont hear their children's plea's dont deserve plea's!" NO. But instead what is there…….listen carefully……silence. He will do whatever he wants because the majority of people are too damn gutless or apathetic, which is even scarier.

Posted by "Get after it!!!!!" August 31, 2006 @ 2:04 PM - Everyone on there should quit complaining and pick up the phone right now (405-275-xxxx)and let him know Mothers that do not protect should be put in prison. You should not do that just once per day, you should not do it twice per day, but several times. Have your friends at work do the same thing. Send a letter, go buy some post cards. I remember when this first became an issue people all over Shawnee were sending those pre-stamped post cards so his staff could see what people really think and he could not just throw them away. Basically put yourself in gear for an all out public attack with our best sources, mail and telephones.

Posted by "Challenge" August 31, 2006 @ 2:08 PM - If everyone would send a few letters tomorrow they would all be there in a big stack waiting for him when he comes back from a three day weekend. It is all about numbers. Go to the post office and buy 10 postcards, or send 10 letters. Make that postal worker wonder what is going on. You all say you don't want Raye to get a deal then I challenge you to send several cards or make several calls. That is what the Smith/Winters/Fowler families did to the Judge when they wanted Kelsey placed

*back with her. You can bet they are doing it again. We have
to beat them at their own game.*

*Posted by "emmasmom" August 31, 2006 @ 2:13 PM - this has to
be done. everyone needs to get on the ball NOW. call, write,
do whatever you can think of and let him know. because
before you know it, it will be too late. something has to be
done not only for kelsey, but for all of the children in this
state!*

*Posted by "Anonymous" August 31, 2006 @ 2:14 PM - I have been
told that Richard reads letters. Faxes will be trashed. Letters
and post cards would be great. I know that there is media
that is willing to cover this case. Write to the rant, to the
newspapers, to the DA, write to everyone. He has to know
that people are not going to allow him to continue to allow
people to not protect their children.*

*Posted by "Anonymous" August 31, 2006 @ 2:16 PM - You better
beleive that the Smith's have every person that is still willing
to writing letters for them. Pastor's they know, family
members, anyone that they think MAY know someone or has
some influence, they will exploit to get Raye Dawn off. When
they say they are working non stop, you better beleive they
are. To get Raye Dawn off the hook.*

*Posted by "Anonymous" August 31, 2006 @ 2:22 PM - I challenge
each of you to talk to other people about this. I challenge you
see how many friends, relatives and co-workers that you can
get to write a letter or make a phone call about this issue. Go
to Wal-Mart, buy box of envelopes and package of paper. Go
to the post office and buy a book of stamps. Address and
stamp the envelopes and put a piece of paper in it. All that
your friends, relatives, and co-workers will have to do is
write the letter and put it in the mailbox. Do it of our
children. Do it for Kelsey.*

*Posted by "Anonymous" August 31, 2006 @ 2:28 PM - Don't forget
that the Smiths are reading this and are trying their hardest
to counteract it. They are calling the DA and telling him that*

*the Briggs family is on here trying to start and vendatta
against him. Show him that we, the general public, not the
family, are outraged and are not going to stand for this. This
is not about the Briggs', [Kelsey's paternal step-
grandparents], the Smiths, or the Porters, this is about our
children and this is about Kelsey. This is about what is right.
This is about JUSTICE!!!!!!!*

*Posted by "Anonymous" August 31, 2006 @ 2:30 PM - If you wrote
a letter last week, that is great. SEND ANOTHER ONE!!*

*Posted by "Anonymous" August 31, 2006 @ 2:32 PM - SEND ONE
EVERY DAY!!!*

*Posted by "Anonymous" August 31, 2006 @ 2:35 PM - Write a
letter to the editor in your town or city.*

*Posted by "Anonymous" August 31, 2006 @ 6:21 PM - The Lincoln
County Newspaper is willing to run letters to the editor about
the campaign and this case. Their email address is:* [e-mail
address removed for privacy]

*Posted by "removethekey" August 31, 2006 @ 10:03 PM - While
you are writing the LCN be sure and tell the good folks of
Chandler that their "hero" Judge Key sentenced Kelsey to
her fate. Be sure and remind them that he made the decision
before he heard any evidence and that he called RD's
attorney and told him how he was going to rule before he
heard testimony. There's a person who needs to be held
accountable.*

*Posted by "Anonymous" August 31, 2006 @ 10:37 PM - It will take
a tremendous effort to make sure that the mother is even held
accountable. The only way to hold Judge Key accountable is
at the polls.*

*Posted by "Anonymous" August 31, 2006 @ 10:54 PM - Who all
has written letters or called or done anything to prevent the
DA from offering a deal to another child abuser/enabler? I*

GUARANTEE the Smith's made calls and wrote letters today telling Richard how great and how innocent she is.

Posted by "Please Don't Plea Bargain" August 31, 2006 @ 11:49 - I agree with you totally 2:08. The Smith/Fowler/Winter family is calling and writing like the devil (no pun intended) trying to save poor R.D.'s butt. We need to make sure that Smothermon knows that there are more of us out there that wants her convicted than there of people that want her to walk. Send letters and cards and call please! I'd be willing to pay the price every month to the county to get her sorry ass in jail where she belongs!

Posted by "Please Don't Plea Bargain" August 31, 2006 @ 11:50 PM - The Smith family has such distant family members supporting Raye Dawn that they have to have Raye Dawn pointed out to them. They don't even recognize her!

Posted by "Anonymous" September 1, 2006 @ 7:23 AM - It is so obvious that the same person keeps posting here over and over again. Most people in the area have lost faith in any efforts. Porter's defense efforts are futile. As more evidence becomes public he just looks more desperate. I cannot believe his daughter was subjected to being put on TV for all the public to know recognize her. Talk about taking advantage of a child. Smothermon knows there is a very vocal minority when it comes to the plea bargain. Yes I said minority. The majority of citizens want the justice system to be allowed to work without political pressures. That is the only way we can preserve the integrity of the system we all depend on to keep this country from anarchy. Imagine judges making decisions based on a letter writing or calling campaign? If the tables were turned on you the outcry would be just as strong against such a thing. As for judge Key. If KP members had known the reputation the Briggs family had prior to giving Kelsey back to RD they would have understood the difficult decision he had to make. Yes, he made a mistake in his decision but maybe there should have been another alternative. After all people forget that Kelsey was taken from Kathie Briggs and given to Gayla at one point because it could not be

*determined who or how the legs were broken. I am not saying
the Briggs broke her legs by any means but at the time it just
could not be determined where and how it happened. Lance
also had a reputation for skirting the law and violence so
why would you want to put a child back in a home where that
behavior was fostered while he grew up. I just think people
need to look at the larger picture and put themselves in the
place of a judge and current judges that can and should only
make decision based on evidence in court. Yes a terrible
tragedy happened. We are all angry. All sides, but we do not
want our judicial system to sway with a vocal minority ever.*

Since the previous anonymous post was grounded in the known
facts and common sense instead of a call to action that involved a
witch hunt, the bullies automatically assumed the person was Gayla's
cousin, Sherri. It was not.

*Posted by "Anonymous" September 1, 2006 @ 8:16 AM - Sherri,
keep hoping that it's a minority. Cross your finger sand pray
reaaallll hard and it might come true. Better yet, click you
heels.*

Porter obviously took the common sense post personally and he
went on a rant.

*Posted by "Anonymous" September 1, 2006 @ 8:29 AM - The efforts
to have Raye Dawn serve the time that she deserves has
nothing to do with Porter's innocence or defense. You want
fairness in the justice system. Do you think it allows Porter to
have a fair trial if Raye Dawn's testimony is bought by the
DA? Do you think it's fair that since is is a state witness for
Smothermon, that he will coach her as to what to say and
what not to say? Have you not been out in the public and
listened to people when they say that after the prelim, their
opinions were swaying to believing that Raye Dawn
murdered Kelsey? Do you have your head so far up the
Smith's ass that you can't see daylight? It is sad that [Mike
Porter's daughter] had to get on TV. It's sad that she is a 9
year old innocent victim in this story that is paying for
something that she had no control over. Her whole life has*

406

*been turned upside down. I thought the news segment was
great. People need to know the things that Smothermon is
doing to people, including the children, to try to win a case
that he knows he cannot prove without Raye Dawn pointing
the finger at Mike or without [Mike Porter's daughter]
saying that Mike has done something bad to her. So you think
it's okay for Smothermon to harass [Mike Porter's daughter]
for 10 months and try to force her to say something that she
doesn't want to say? Think about if it were your own children
and someone tried their damndest to convince them to say
something so horrible about you that they would have to live
the rest of their lives knowing that they helped convict you
and send you away for life. Especially when that something
they're trying to get your children to say is not true! Think
about if it were your own children that someone tried to
convince for 10 months that you molested them or hurt them
and they know damn well it didn't happen. She is 9 years old!
She should never have to hear those things about her father.
Richard needs to be spanked and stop acting like a junior
high bully to get what he wants. It's not Porter that looks
desperate, it'*

*Posted by "Anonymous" September 1, 2006 @ 8:30 AM - it's
Richard*

*Posted by "Anonymous" September 1, 2006 @ 8:36 AM - If you so
whole-heartedly believe in allowing the judicial system to
work on its own, why have you contacted the DA yourself and
tried to save Raye Dawn's rear? Why has the Smith family
had their own campaign of handing out stamped envelopes at
Leedar and Mildred's place of employment asking people to
write letters on her behalf? Why did they do the same letter
campaign a year ago asking Judge Key to return Kelsey to
Raye Dawn? I agree that the judicial system should be
allowed to work on its own merits. Too bad the
Smiths/Fowlers/Winters do not.*

*Posted by "Anonymous" September 1, 2006 @ 8:39 AM - I totally
agree 829. It's unfortunate that Richard is going after [Mike
Porter's daughter] like he is. If she had something to say, I'm*

407

sure she would have said it a long time ago. This whole thing is ridiculous and it's unfortunate that they wil both probably get away with murder.

Posted by "Anonymous" September 1, 2006 @ 8:43 AM - There is nothing wrong with voicing your opinions to the DA. He should know how his constituents feel. He is supposed to serve the people of the District. Instead it seems sometimes he serves mothers who he thinks allowed their children to be abused. Richard should know that the MAJORITY of people do not agree with giving scum bags plea bargains.

Posted by "Anonymous" September 1, 2006 @ 9:00 AM - I am sure that 7:23 is one of Raye Dawn's family members trying to persuade people to not voice their opinions to Smothermon, while they themselves all the while will be doing the same thing. Don't allow them to dissuade you. Work even harder to show them that the MAJORITY of people feel that Raye Dawn should be held accountable.

Posted by "Anonymous" September 1, 2006 @ 10:38 AM - [Mike Porter's daughter] ahs already given damaging statements against her father in a previous recorded interview. It is the DA's job to interview her once again. Yes, it is ashame it has happened, but this is her father's fault she is going through this. If his ex-whatevers think he is so wonderful why aren't they in court supporting him? He did not have one friend there on his behalf. Why? Because he is guilty and he doesn't want them to hear what all he did to Kelsey. It is Porter himself that has caused his child such heartache.

Posted by "Anonymous" September 1, 2006 @ 10:39 AM - Shame on the Spain family for allowing her to be on the news. Now the few children at school that did not know her father was charged with the murder of a child will now be questioning her. So now who is exploiting who?

Posted by "Anonymous" September 1, 2006 @ 10:48 AM - Judge Key will be at the Lincoln County fair tonight from 5-9. He says he is willing to answer any questions concerning

408

Kelsey's case. Everyone that can should attend and ask him if he knows what remorse means?

Posted by "Anonymous" September 1, 2006 @ 10:50 AM - I have to agree with both 10:38 and 10:39. It is very unfortunate that the she has to be interviewed, but that is the DA's job. It Mike had given Kelsey as much protection as he is trying to offer [his daughter], she would not be in this situation.

Posted by "Anonymous" September 1, 2006 @ 11:08 AM - 7:23 If you had listened to a previous interview it stated the Briggs were fine with Kelsey staying with Gayla. They just did not want her to go back to the Porter home. It has also been reported on KP that the DA has officially cleared them of any involvement in abusing Kelsey.

This was another untrue statement. The Briggs were never officially cleared of anything. In fact, in reports one of the probabilities listed is that Kathie Briggs could have perpetrated some of the abuse herself. Since this was reported by the state, how could she be cleared?

And you shall know the TRUTH and the truth shall make you FREE.
~ John 8:32

Abuse - The Lies

Those under suspicion for the abuse Kelsey suffered were Raye Dawn, Kathie Briggs, and Lance Briggs. Kelsey had been with Raye Dawn, Kathie, and Lance the two times abuse was confirmed and she was with Mike Porter when she was sexually assaulted and murdered.

At Raye's trial, it was made clear that Kelsey was with Kathie when her legs were broken. In an answer to Raye's appeal, the Attorney General agrees that Kelsey was not with Raye Dawn or Mike Porter when her legs were broken. Who does that leave?

Despite claims that Kathie has been cleared of any abuse, nobody has been cleared of abuse in Kelsey's case. Another lie is that Lance was in Iraq during the entire ordeal. However, Lance was in the state and was with Kelsey on the two times abuse was confirmed. He was also in Shawnee on the day of at least one of the hearings and he chose not to attend.

kjbriggs Kelsey's Grandma ★★★★★	**Post: #14**

RE: Documented Facts

That has been my position all along. If you cannot determine the perpetrator leave the child in a neutral location. Judge Key should have left Kelsey with her maternal grandmother.

Posts: 1,107
Group: Super Moderators
Joined: Nov 2005
Status: Away
Reputation: ████████

I will also add, since the murder, I have officially been ruled out as the perpetrator. FINALLY! To bad Judge Key, DHS, the Guardian ad litem, the ADA and CASA could not take the time and use the common sense it took to figure it out. Thank you Richard Smothermon.

06-21-2006 10:06 AM   [PM] [FIND]   Quote this message in a reply

Shirica   **Post: #15**

410

Super Moderator
★★★★★   **RE: Documented Facts**

Posts: 169   One of the amazing things about this case as well is that Lance was listed as a
Group: Super Moderators   possible perpetrator and he was not even in the state, yet I lived in the home at the
Joined: Nov 2005   time with Kelsey and never once was I questioned. My two children were also in the
Status: Away   home. They never questioned them or checked to see if they were being abused by
Reputation: ▯   my parents as well. If they truly thought the abuse was coming from my parents
                    home, then why in the world were they not checking into me or checking on my
                    children? None of this will ever make sense to me, EVER!!!

                    Shirica
                    Kelsey's Aunt Rees

06-21-2006 10:16 AM

This is from the confidential OCCY report. It clearly states that Kathie Briggs was not and has not been cleared of
any abuse toward Kelsey:

After months of reflection and review, the Lincoln County staff demonstrated an attitude of suspicion of the
paternal grandmother, Kathie Briggs. The OJSO has considered the possibility that the paternal grandparents were
somehow involved in one or more of the incidents reported. Within this context, after examining the evidence and
DHS case history the following alternatives must be considered:

a)   Ms. Briggs was the perpetrator of some of the incidents of abuse and child welfare failed to adequately
investigate and document her involvement.

b)   Ms. Briggs was not the perpetrator, but, by her demeanor, persistence, and/or irritation, was able to
negatively influence DHS professional child welfare investigators so that her concerns were not properly
investigated.

c)   DHS staff did not consider the danger to Kelsey significant to warrant a thorough investigation.

d)   DHS staff did not comprehensively review the case to consider the contextual evidence implicating a
different perpetrator.

*Posted by "Anonymous" September 1, 2006 @ 12:05 PM - Hey
Sherry, just how much time did you actually spend with
Kelsey or see RD or Mike interacted with her? When was the
last time that you saw Kelsey prior to her death? Did you see
her? If u did, they why didn't you see that something was
wrong? Could you NOT see that her health had declined
dramatically? If you DID see it, WHY did you choose to turn
your head? WHO did you think was abusing her then? The
Briggs or [Kelsey's paternal step-grandparents] hadn't been
allowed to see her, so it obviously wasn't them! If you
DIDN'T see her decline, then maybe you should go back and
look at pictures PRIOR to her death and PRIOR to August!
You call yourself a Christian? Yet your out there believing
the lies? And what does Kathie's past have to do with ANY of
this? That was 20 + years ago AND her kids were NOT
abused! She made a mistake, well all do, she did what she felt*

was the best thing at the time for her children! At least she hasn't denied it, like the SMITHS continue to do!

How is dumping your children on the state for two years after threatening to kill them "the best thing" for her children? Kathie Briggs didn't deny that she gave her children up. She just changed the story and made herself a loving and caring mother in the process. But was that the truth?

Posted by "Anonymous" September 1, 2006 @ 12:09 PM - to the 7:23 post: judge key did state that he could not determine who broke kelsey's legs. lets say her legs were broken when rd picked her up that THURSDAY from the Briggs.....and yet she didn't take her to the doctor until HOW MANY DAYS LATER? Wasn't it like 4 days LATER? that in itself isn't abuse? come on! OPEN YOUR EYES! what about ALL THE OTHER injuries to kelsey BEFORE her legs were broken? the injuries that the COURT AND DHS found and file chld abuse on rd? what about that? now say that you REALLY DON'T KNOW WHO BROKE HER LEGS? you have to be a smith/fowler or julie or sherry! ☹ ☹ ☹

Posted by "Anonymous" September 1, 2006 @ 12:11 PM - 7:23 Good point. The Briggs did say that. It was also never their intention to keep kelsey away from raye. they just wanted her to not be hurt, they just wanted her to be safe.

Posted by "Anonymous" September 1, 2006 @ 1:27 PM - [Mike Porter's daughter] has not said anything bad about her father and she never will no matter how much people try to brainwash her or force her to say things. Richard wants to use her like a tool but he has already done too much wrong to do that. I am sure [Mike Porter's daughter] would have had plenty of things to say about Raye Dawn too if anyone would haev ever asked her. She will never testify against her father. Being led into saying things is not going to be useful testimony.

Posted by "Anonymous" September 1, 2006 @ 1:27 PM - Support in court does not matter either. The Smith's are the only people that beleive that how many people you have in court matters The facts matter. I am sure none of Mike's family wants to hear the lies and Raye Dawn's fake tears and "poor, poor me" story. Public showings are what the Smith's are about. Not all families work that way. I am sure Porter did not want anyone to have to hear that garbage. Innocence is not based on whether you can fill a courtroom. ;)

Posted by "Anonymous" September 1, 2006 @ 1:37 PM - I hope Raye Dawn's family keeps encouraging her to testify. I hope they keep telling her that people will feel sorry for her and people will beleive her "story". I hope Raye Dawn herself beleives it. Richard better work hard on that script with her. She did not do very good at prelim from what I heard.

Posted by "Anonymous" September 1, 2006 @ 2:05 PM - I was the 7:23 post. I am not a relative of either side nor am I Julie or Sherri. I am a citizen of Meeker that does get out in the public and works here as well. I DO NOT HEAR all the negative things that people claim that EVERYONE is saying here. There are a lot of different opinions here in town on these issues. There is a small, radical, vocal minority that apparently runs in a small circle of friends that wish you to believe differently in their desperate attempt to persuade the legal system to their point of view. If those people are so convinced that RD is lying each and every time she steps foot on the stand that is up to the jury to decide not them.

Posted by "Anonymous" September 1, 2006 @ 2:27 PM - Everyone else hears all the negative things. But I do agree many people in Meeker are two faced. I am sure they would not tell a Raye Dawn supporter how full of crap they think she is. The jury will know she is lying just like every one that heard her speak at the prelim knew. Even Richard. Just from the statements the media printed I can tell it is not going to be pretty. Her testimony will be worthless by the time everyone realizes it changes depending on what she gets out of it.

413

Posted by "Anonymous" September 1, 2006 @ 3:45 PM - Does anyone think that any other child in this world is just as important as Kelsey?

Posted by "Anonymous" September 1, 2006 @ 3:56 PM - 3:45 What are you talking about??

Posted by "Anonymous" September 1, 2006 @ 4:02 PM - Exactly what I said. Sometimes it seems that no other child is anywhere near as important as Kelsey.

This was the last post captured from this particular bashboard. But the bullies would find other places to share their opinions…and still do to this day.

Reigniting Kelsey's Purpose

September, 2006

On September 6, 2006, the Kelsey's Purpose group put the following open letter in the local newspaper. This would be the same newspaper that one of the jurors in Raye Dawn's trial admitted to reading.

This letter stems from news of the recent developments in the pending criminal cases involving the mother and stepfather of Kelsey Briggs. After watching coverage of the stepfather's preliminary hearing held on August 23rd, we were very disturbed by the news that Kelsey's mother is currently in plea negotiations with the District Attorney. This news is even more shocking given Richard Smothermon's past public statements concerning the possibility of a plea negotiation between his office and Kelsey's mother. In that press conference, Richard Smothermon spoke of society's demand that parents be held accountable when they do not uphold their moral responsibility to protect their children. He said that Kelsey's mother knew or should have known her daughter was being abused. His emphatic statements to the media made the recent development all the more surprising. We would like to know why it seems that people who 'ONLY' fail to protect or enable their children to be abused are not considered to be as culpable as the actual abuser? Why would Richard Smothermon even consider any kind of plea negotiation for this woman! What would the reasoning behind it be? Why would he even consider using her testimony? Another recent child abuse case comes to mind, that of another very young child. The mother and mother's boyfriend were both charged in the beating of this child, arrested and each subsequently jailed on a $250,000 bond. The mother in that case was able to give a timeline for each individual bruise, and in exchange for her testimony she

416

received a plea deal of two years from Richard Smothermon. Two years for a mother that stood by and watched as her child was savagely beaten. This leads us to wonder how light the punishment for the mother in Kelsey's case will be? Why is Richard Smothermon sending a message that it is not acceptable to beat children but it but it [sic] is acceptable to stand by and watch or not protect your child? More importantly, why are the citizens of the 23rd Judicial District allowing our District Attorney to send this message? We would encourage all of you to take the time to let your feelings be known. RICHARD SMOTHERMON, WE DEMAND JUSTICE. [The DA's address and phone number were provided.] Paid for by Concerned citizens of the 23rd Judicial District...[41]

The group members made a plan to write the judge and the district attorney that there should be "no plea for Raye," yet not a peep about the man who was accused of raping Kelsey and who was out walking free. This double-standard continued through the time of Raye's trial and spilled over onto me. When I became involved in late July, 2007, I was clueless about the past actions of the hate group. I had no idea what I was getting myself into or how relentless some of the Kelsey's Purpose followers could be.

On September 13, 2006, Shirica posted on the Kelsey's Purpose forum, claiming that Kathie Briggs had "bombarded DHS" with calls. In a later deposition, Kathie claimed she made one or two calls at the most. Which statement is the truth?

Shirica Posts: 171 September 13, 2006 12:58 PM No Subject - You need to understand something – Kathie's focus was never just Raye Dawn. Kathie questioned Michael from the very beginning. She suspected him way more than she suspected Raye. She voiced that many many times. I even personally heard her have a discussion with Raye about Mike not supposed to be being around during the visits. Kathie stated more than once that the abuse seemed to start about the same

---

[41] See Appendix B – Exhibit 9

time that Mike came in the picture. I do not know why so many members of your family assume that it has always been about Raye. It was always about Kelsey and keeping her safe. She told Raye more than once that she never intended to keep Kelsey from her, she only wanted Raye to make sure Kelsey was safe, but that just did not happen, did it? Yes, my mom bombarded DHS but that was because she was trying to protect an innocent child, not make Raye's life more troubled. Kathie is not a vindictive person. She knows what it is like to be a mother and need help. She has been there herself. She knows how easy it is to make mistakes, that is why she always gave Raye the benefit of the doubt. Raye was a part of our family and we loved her. Yes, her and Lance's relationship was a nightmare, but we always loved Raye. She was a part of our family and that is how we viewed her. Even after Kelsey was born she was always welcome into Kathie's home. This situation is just so tragic. I hate it. It breaks my heart that so much turmoil has come from all of this and I hate it that Kelsey's family has to be at odds with each other instead of all fighting together to see that this man pays for what he did.

The topic of discussion on Kelsey's Purpose shifted to money...the root of all evil in this case.

Kjbriggs Posts: 1,393 October 1, 2006 Re: Campaign Issues and Promises - I would also like to share the events of the weekend. We started out on Friday night preparing for the yard sale. Our Tulsa girls made it down to help finish up around 9:00. The garage was full of hidden treasure ready to be sold and donated to Prevent Child Abuse Oklahoma. My aunt, my sister, Lori, Jamie, Liana and Beverly all gave up their weekend to help out. Lori, Jamie, Liana, [Susan] and I then met in Meeker and made our way to Chandler. We walked around the town handing out campaign literature. For those of you not familiar with this town I can tell you it is full of hills. Some people in our little group are experiencing soreness after our walk and it isn't [Susan] or me. Yes, it was the young girls, but they were troopers. They could have been home sitting in front of the TV, but instead they donated their

418

time to Sheila's campaign. After our walk we went back to the festival and listened to good music and visited with Rep. Danny Morgan. We had several people come up to us and ask for stickers including a group of teenagers that put them on their shirts. We left Chandler are 4:00 and headed to Prague. Sheila Kirk hosted a Pig Roast in the park. We had the opportunity to meet and visit with some new supporters. On Sunday afternoon I hosted a Meet and Greet fro Sheila in Stroud. I was touched by a 78 year old woman from Chandler who came to meet me. She called me after Kelsey died to offer her support. I never forgot that call and it was nice to meet her along with the other supporters that stopped by. Lori, Jamie, Liana and her daughter Emma also attended. Everywhere we go to campaign people want to talk about Kelsey. Her short life has made such an impact on the citizens of this county. Some people have been a little confused about the role DHS has played in the case. It is very important that our voters know DHS may have made many mistakes, but the fact remains in ALL reports that DHS DID NOT recommend for Kelsey to be returned to her mother. They also need to know that Judge Key DID NOT have the authority to place Kelsey. The law actually states: If the child is placed in the custody of the Department of Human Services, whether in emergency, temporary or permanent custody, the Department SHALL determine the appropriate placement of the child. Thank you, Kathie This post was last modified: 10-1-2006 10:36 PM by kjbriggs

Kjbriggs Posts: 647 October 11, 2006 Re: Kelsey's Billboard - I know some of you are going to panic when you notice Kelsey's billboard in Meeker is missing. It was brought to my attention that the land owners have been harassed for months over the billboard by the maternal family. To the point they no longer wanted a billboard on their property. This family should not have been put in the middle of this. I have had some contact with the billboard company and even though our contract has seven months remaining I am in the process of choosing a new location. Sometimes when God closes a door he opens a window that is my outlook on this. We now have the opportunity to place the billboard in a location so more people can view it. I had originally wanted to have a traveling billboard and this worked to our advantage. Little Kelsey will be sending her message to many more people in our state. She has been such a blessing to us and we look forward to sharing her with many more. Thank you, Kathie

After Kathie Briggs had gone cold with Mike Porter, he joined Kelsey's Purpose under a new name, "seekingtruth." Since Richard Smothermon had been threatened and publicly scorned over the job he was doing on Kelsey's case, he grew even more serious about making sure that justice was served. Perhaps he thought if he could successfully convict Mike Porter, the Briggs would be satisfied. That would never happen. They had other motives to want Raye behind bars and they would not stop until that happened.

Below is a screen shot of Porter's Kelsey's Purpose account. Notice that Porter registered with this account just after his e-mails with Kathie Briggs ended. His last visit was at the same time he plead guilty to enabling child abuse and went to prison for a thirty-year sentence (ten times the state's average in plea agreements). He had spent a cumulative time of five days, eighteen hours, and forty-one minutes on Kelsey's Purpose. At the time that I found this information, most of his posts had been deleted. I was able to capture a few that focused on blaming moms for child abuse.

Kelsey's Purpose / Profile of seekingtruth

seekingtruth
(New Member)
☆☆

Registration Date: 03-12-2006
Birthday: Not Specified
Local Time: 07-16-2009 at 09:09 PM

seekingtruth's Forum Info		Additional Info About seekingtruth
Joined:	03-12-2006	Sex:
Last Visit	02-01-2007 09:26 AM	Location:
		Bio:
Total Posts:	4 (0 posts per day | 0.02 percent of total posts) (Find All Threads — Find All Posts)	
Time Spent Online:	5 Days, 18 Hours, 42 Minutes	
Rating:	☆	

Since the Briggs were now under the microscope of the district attorney, and Kathie Briggs had turned over the e-mails as well, it was now time to expose Porter's identity on Kelsey's Purpose. Her brother-in-law sent the following message to the DA with private messages from the Kelsey's Purpose forum between Mike Porter, Misty, and other members.

To Richard L. Smothermon from M. Briggs, Administrator,
KelseysPurpose.org November 02, 2006
CC: [Kathie Briggs' e-mail address removed for privacy]; [Jeanna
Fowler's e-mail address at Tinker Air Force Base (the same
e-mail address she used to communicate with Mike Porter)
removed for privacy]
Subject: Recent posts on KelseysPurpose.org by user 'seekingtruth'

Attached is a Word file with the text, timestamps, and IP addresses of
six recent posts by 'seekingtruth.' Internet access for all posts
was through AOL. AOL logs will probably be timestamped
using Coordinated Universal Time (UTC). Our timestamps
are either Central Daylight Time (add 5 hours for UTC) or
Central Stand Time (add 6 hours) as indicated. The third post
was deleted by the author shortly after posting. Fortunately
Kathie was online and was able to save the text of the msg

before it was deleted. The IP address used for posting was not captured, so the one used while deleting the post is listed. I am still collating the information on the earlier posts which were deleted by the user in mid-September. Let me know if you need that too. Also, I am working on capturing the content of the user's private message folder. I will forward this info ASAP. Sincerely, M. Briggs Administrator KelseysPurpose.org

From id Tinam told seekingtruth Subject no subject utc timestamp 10/6/06 2:26am - message I liked your post on the letter that sad little Gayla wrote.

Fromid seekingtruth told Tinam subject re: no subject utc timestamp 10/6/06 2:44am - I tried my hardest to bite my tongue but I just could not. I read this site daily and for family member to come on here and accuse people of hatred was just too much. Ultimately it is a waste of time to try to tell people like that anything. Supporting loved ones is one thing, but to lay blame at the feet of people that tried to help Kelsey is just plain wrong. If they would have cared about Kelsey half as much as they care about Raye Dawn things would be different right now. Some of the things they say like saying that they were trying to figure out where the abuse was coming from just makes you shake your head. Raye Dawn had abuse confirmed on her. In my opinion that is the point when if she did not abuse her child she would have stopped protecting whoever did it. I am sick of them playing the victim role, but that is all they know I guess. It makes me angry and sad at the same time. Kelsey never stood a chance with those people. Didn't mean to vent but those people make me so upset.

Fromid Tinam told seekingtruth re: no subject utc timestamp 10/6/2006 2:56am - Well, your reply is a lot nicer than I would like to be. I will never believe for one second that RD is innocent of anything!!! Personally, after hearing on the news what she said in court in Mike's prelim, I feel that the charges should be reversed!!!! But that's just my opinion!!! I'm very hard on her when it comes to talking about Kelsey, because she was the mother and for that child to be dead is a reflection of her character!!!!!!

Fromid seekingtruth told Tinam subject re: no subject utc timestamp 10/6/2006 12:26pm - I will always believe that she is responsible for Kelsey's death too. Too may things do not add up. I heard about some of the things that were said in court and it sounded like she didn't help herself at all. You would think if anyone should have loved Kelsey enough to tell the truth it should have been her "mother". I have heard too many people say that they saw her mistreat and abuse Kelsey to think it was all the step-dad. I just have to shake my head when I seem them continue to embarrass themselves by bashing the Briggs and supporting the people who failed Kelsey. Talk about going down with the ship, my gosh.

Fromid MistyLT told seekingtruth subject fw: no subject utc timestamp 10/7/06 6:18am - He's standing over the top of me so I can't answer you. R.D. knows just how to get people to like her. She was in no telling how many beauty pageants in her life and up on the state taking dance for over 12 years. She knows just how to smile and win people over. She's very good at it. Very Good. FYI Before Lance had the DNA test for Kelsey's paternity, R.D. was wanting to move to Florida and be a topless dancer. Yeh, I laughed at that one too...she's flat on top...or was. Her mom, along with Carl...'s mom (..., Mildred's sister) had already checked into her staying with Carl's dads brother in Florida. They were going to run away and Gayla was going to help hide R.D. She never did this, but she was very close to it. I'm sure that if it was brought up now, they'd deny anything about it...but it did happen this way. I'd heard that R.D. danced down at the Earlsboro nudie bars for awhile. Don't know for that sure. Her cousin (Justin's dad) told me that.

Misty had gotten the above information from Debbie, Jeanna's mother-in-law and the one that had a grudge against Gayla and her family. Misty then forwarded to Porter the following message from Debbie.

*Fromid MistyLT told seekingtruth subject fw: no subject utc
      timestamp 10/15/06 11:03pm - {quote=Debbie...} Maybe the
      pregnancy made her boobs grow! Haha who knows, but she
      used to be flat. That was what was so funny about the fact
      that she wanted to be a stripper. The whole thing about going
      to Florida was to hide from Lance and his family. Then
      Gayla thought about hiding her out at another part of the
      state. They were really planning on getting her away and
      keeping her "protected" from Lance. Shoot, the whole time
      she was married to Lance, she was very violent towards him.
      Ray went over there many times in the middle of the night
      because she would be drunk and hitting and screaming
      towards Lance. One time she even put her hand thru a glass
      door and shattered it. She's one wild and wicked person, I'm
      telling you. I'm sure that Mike doesn't know all what
      happened with Lance because Raye Dawn isn't going to tell
      him what SHE did. It's always the other way around. Back
      when I still lived in Meeker, I was on my way home from
      work in the middle of the day & Gayla called me (she knew
      that I was going home) and asked me to stop in there to see
      what was happening between R.D. & Lance. They lived in the
      R.D.'s grandpa Smiths old house just south of where Mildred
      lives. Anyways, I pulled in there & R.D. was out in the yard
      just having one of her fits & Lance was just sitting there.
      Course, at the time they had me believing everything that
      they told me about Lance (I found out the truth later) & R.D.
      got in the car & sat there talking to me for a very long time.
      Now, Gayla was at work, Mildred was at work at ... & both
      of them were really upset that Lance was going to "hurt"
      R.D. (because that's what she had told them) yet neither
      bothered to even take off work to go check it out, so I went by
      there. Lance was calm, R.D. wasn't. I told her if the marriage
      wasn't working out, etc., to get out of it. I had figured out by
      this time that she was drinking heavily again, (she did that
      before they got together too) and she was totally out of
      control. She would throw things in the creek behind their
      house (household things) & then say that he broke all her
      collectables (I had bought quite a few of them & they weren't
      cheap, for her for her sr. graduation). She was just totally
      nuts. She needed psychiatric help & I'd even told Gayla that*

424

before she even met Mike. She was out to get Mike & marry him from the first time she met him. She thought he had money & Gayla ALWAYS told R.D. it was just as easy to marry a rich man & fall in love later. Did you see her at Mike's & her arraignment? I haven't went to any of that stuff so I haven't seen her in person since I was at court in 6/05. Are you going to be at the walk this afternoon? I'm going to try to be there...me and my flag chair! Haha{quote}

Fromid Seekingjustice told seekingtruth subject no subject utc timestamp 10/22/06 2:02am - Actually my opinion on the whole situation is that Mike was set up to be the one found alone with Kelsey when she died and that Raye Dawn actually is the one who killed Kelsey. In my opinion and I repeat MY opinion, the charges are flip flopped and Mike should be the one charged with Enabling Child Abuse and Raye should be the one charged with murder. I am, however, a witness in the case so I can not go into detail about the evidence I have seen and heard-on which my opinion is based! I didn't want to post this on the main board simply because I know no one will agree with me and I don't expect them to because we all are entitled to our own opinions. But you are right, everyone on the maternal side who saw Kelsey often should be charged and punished with at least failure to protect!

It seems that Kelsey's Purpose forum members had figured out Porter's identity and they sent him messages, agreeing with his stance. This person, in particular, admitted to having a crush on Mike Porter and she gave him rides to visit his son with Raye after he was put with a Smith family member. This person would also become a new state witness against Raye. Kathie Briggs wanted someone to say that they saw Raye drink and drive with Kelsey in the car. Here she was! Ready and more than willing to come forward with more stories. He forwarded the message to his accomplice, Misty.

Fromid seekingtruth told MistyLT subject Fw: no subject utc timestamp 10/22/06 2:26am {quote=SeekingJustice} Actually my opinion on the whole situation is that Mike was set up to

425

be the one found alone with Kelsey when she died and that
Raye Dawn actually is the one who killed Kelsey. In my
opinion and I repeat MY opinion, the charges are flip flopped
and Mike should be the one charged with Enabling Child
Abuse and Raye should be the one charged with murder. I
am, however, a witness in the case so I can not go into detail
about the evidence I have seen and heard-on which my
opinion is based! I didn't want to post this on the main board
simply because I know no one will agree with me and I don't
expect them to because we all are entitled to our own
opinions. But you are right, everyone on the maternal side
who saw Kelsey often should be charged and punished with
at least failure to protect!{quote}

Fromid seekingtruth told SeekingJustice subject Fw: no subject utc
timestamp 10/22/06 3:17pm - Sorry I just saw this PM. I
completely agree with you. I know several people involved
and I also will never believe that Mike killed Kelsey.
Everything I have seen has pointed at Raye Dawn. I do think
you would be surprised how many people think that. I know
that in the town of Meeker many people think Raye Dawn is
responsible and also in Shawnee where Mike is from most
people believe that Raye Dawn did it. In my opinion he
should be punished but not for something he did not do.

Fromid SeekingJustice told seekingtruth subject Re: no subject utc
timestamp 10/22/06 7:06pm - I'm glad that you can see
where I'm coming from. And yes, both Mike and Raye dawn
should be punished but they should be punished for what they
did-he should not go to jail for murder but for failure to
protect. She should not go for child abuse but for murder! I
also think Gayla should go to jail with her since she
supposedly saw Kelsey so much yet she somehow didn't see
all of the signs of abuse or else she saw them and chose not
to report them because she knew her daughter was the one
who did it and she didn't want to get her into trouble. I used
to babysit Mike's kids and NEVER EVER saw anything on
either of them. They were two of the happiest kids I had ever
met in my life and they had a GREAT dad and they still do.
The only thing Mike did wrong was not help Kelsey. He

should have tried to help her even if it meant upsetting Raye Dawn. I'm sure now he realizes that. Another thing that bothers me is that she didn't go file for divorce. If they arrested my husband and said that he killed my son or daughter I would be a the court house before the police even had him there and I would be filing those papers-but I think she was too worried on covering her own butt to even think about filing for divorce. I'm sorry but none of the things she has done add up to me. But don't get me wrong I do believe Mike should be in trouble also but like you said she should not be in trouble for something he didn't do. Are you from Meeker? Or Shawnee?

Fromid seekingtruth told SeekingJustice subject Fw: no subject utc timestamp 10/22/06 7:33pm - I could not agree with you more. I know Mike very well. I am from Shawnee. I know he was and is a good father. I saw him with Kelsey and his own kids. I think that there are a lot of people that know that this case doesn't add up. I know for a fact that Mike wishes he would have helped Kelsey. I truly believe that if he was charged with failure to protect he probably would have plead guilty because that's how he feels. Like I said, I know him very well and he is not the person that so many people want to make him out to be. I think he should be punished but not for the things he is accused of. I truly believe that it is so obvious that Raye Dawn did it. I just can't see what the DA sees, and I know a lot of other people can not see how anyone could not see straight through her. I think it is sad, sad, sad, most of all for Kelsey and also for the other kids involved. Mike's kids are probably going to lose a father just because he is an easier target for a conviction. Like I said, no one will ever be able to convince me that Mike killed Kelsey. The evidence is just not there. I will always know that Raye Dawn got mad at Kelsey that day and went too far. Plus she knew Lance was coming back and he would take Kelsey from her.

Fromid seekingtruth told MistyLT subject Fw: no subject utc timestamp 10/22/06 7:39pm Now this is getting interesting lol

Those were the final words we would read from Mike Porter other than his statement on his plea agreement.[42]

Kathie and her family members have admitted that Mike Porter is a "liar," "monster," "murderer," and "disgusting." Yet, the focus is always on Raye. *Why?*

Among evidence against Mike Porter was a report on the contents of his computers. It was released just days before Mike Porter accepted a plea agreement that the Briggs family supported. The report showed that on one of the computers numerous pornographic images were found with many of the pictures displaying acts of anal sex (an act that investigators and the district attorney reportedly believe that Mike Porter committed on Kelsey while Raye was picking his daughter up from school). Pornographic videos of anal sex were also found. Among the pornographic pictures were several pictures labeled with Mike Porter's name and they featured an erect penis. One picture, in particular, showed semen in the palm of a hand and had a baby bib on the floor in the background.

On May 16, 2005, less than a month after Mike Porter married Raye, "pdaddy_44" was his alleged chosen screen name in several Yahoo chat sessions with an unidentified person in which graphic language was used and his avatar was a picture of an erect penis with the picture labeled "Mikecock."

The same e-mail address that was used in some e-mail conversations with Kathie was also used to sign into AOL in online sessions during which the Web address www.-porno.com was typed directly into the search bar. This would not be the only pornographic site he reportedly visited. Some Web sites had the name "teen" in them as well as "sex," and he made multiple visits: 979; 740; 447; 424; 102; 60; and 15. In addition to porn, Kathie's Web site featuring Kelsey's picture along with plans to hold rallies and write letters to ensure that Raye was charged was visited on 711 occasions.

---

[42] Details of his arrest warrant can be found at www.thetruthaboutKelsey.com

Aside from the evidence linking Mike Porter to Kelsey's alleged sexual assault and murder, witnesses state that Mike Porter appeared to be guilty at the hospital immediately following Kelsey's death. Among other eyewitness accounts, Mike Porter was reportedly seen by a police officer pounding his fist into a vehicle and yelling, "She'll never forgive me! She'll never forgive me!"

Though eyewitness reports and evidence verify that the correct charges were filed against Mike Porter (sexual assault and murder), he was supported by Kathie and her family members within days of Kelsey's death with e-mails and letters claiming that Raye had murdered Kelsey and that Mike Porter was only guilty of "not protecting" Kelsey. The charges against him reflected the fact that investigators and the district attorney clearly did not agree with their point of view. However, this damaging evidence against Mike Porter was not presented at Raye's trial.

From: The Heaths
To: Smothermon, Richard
Sent: Mon Jan 29 17:06:49 2007
Subject: Mike Porter Plea Bargain

Mr. Smothermon, The news media is having a frenzy about YOU making a plea bargain with Mike Porter. If this is true, then someone has leaked the information to Channel 4 and 25. They are both on their way to Meeker to find anyone who will talk. ... (Raye Dawn's attorney) was NOT notified of this from your office. If this is true, you will have an office full of angry people tomorrow morning. I will talk to the media, not about the case as my gag order indicates, but of the actions of the District Attorney of Lincoln County. I understand you are out of town at this time...I know you have access to your emails. Please respond as soon as you can. The news media WILL talk to someone this evening. Sherri Heath

From: Smothermon, Richard
To: The Heaths

Sent from blackberry wireless device

Sherri, I can not now, nor have I ever been able to control the press in this case. I have been told by Judge V... in no uncertain terms that I cannot speak with you or anyone else about this matter. I have told [Raye's attorney] what I could, even though I am under no legal obligation to do so. For me to respond merely because the press demands it would be irresponsible of me, and if this were your side, you would likewise demand my silence. I hope you understand, but you do what you feel you must. Richard

From: The Heaths
To: Smothermon, Richard

Mr. Smothermon, I am not requesting notification for the media; I am requesting information for the FAMILY of Kelsey. Let me remind you a part of the Oklahoma Victims Bill of Rights: Oklahoma Victims Bill of Rights - As a victim of crime, you have the following rights: To be notified that a court proceeding to which a victim or witness has been subpoenaed will or will not go on as scheduled, in order to save the person an unnecessary trip to court; To have the family members of all homicide victims afforded all of the services under this section, whether or not the person is to be a witness in any criminal proceedings; To be informed in writing of all statutory rights; and To be notified by the Pardon & Parole Board of Pardon & Parole actions if you request notifications; and To be informed in felony cases involving violent crime or sex offenses when pre-trial proceedings may substantially delay prosecution.

Are you saying we the family members do not have rights in this matter? I think we do. The confusion that the media has proposed to us about Mike Porter are unfounded and ridiculous. Surely you can make known to a family member on the maternal side of what is happening to Kelsey's murderer. We DO have a right. Sherri

Kathie Briggs's Mission

February, 2007

Although Porter was now behind bars, Kathie Briggs was still on a mission. She would not rest until Raye was convicted. Her version of Kelsey's story could be found on hundreds of Web sites, including Kelsey's memorial.

A good friend of mine was once an active member of Kelsey's Purpose. She was so active that when Kathie Briggs begged for donations to create a memory Web site for Kelsey, my friend stepped up and purchased the Web site...a decision she later regretted and wished she could take back.

The message at the top read, "This memorial website was created by Kathie Briggs on 2/26/2007." On this Web site was an album of Kelsey's "documented abuse" according to Kathie Briggs. In reality, there were two instances of documented abuse—the diaper rash on Kelsey's bottom in January of 2005 and Kelsey's broken legs. Kelsey had been with Kathie and Lance for four hours before the diaper rash was discovered in January of 2005 and Kelsey was with her maternal aunt at the zoo when one leg was broken. It was proven at Raye's trial that Kelsey was with Kathie Briggs when he other leg was broken. But reality isn't something that sells a story and Kathie's concept of reality does not involve her being a suspect in the abuse of Kelsey, which she was. Therefore, on the Web site were several pictures as described below with Kathie's captions.

Picture of Kelsey with knot on her nose—caption: "Kelsey was elbowed in the night by her eight year old step sister." Here Kathie admits that Kelsey's step-sister elbowed her but she has this listed as "documented abuse."

Picture of Kelsey in a swing with two casts—caption: "Two broken legs in separate accidents." Here Kathie has Kelsey's broken legs listed as "accidents," yet she calls them "documented abuse."

Picture of Kelsey with a bruise on her cheek and reddened eye after the August, 2005 automobile accident—caption: "Two months after she was returned to her mother and two months before her death."

Picture of Kelsey in a swing with the bruise on her cheek after the August, 2005 automobile accident—caption: "August 27, 2005 – swing."

Picture of Kelsey in cheerleading costume—caption: "Days after being diagnosed with a broken clavicle. She is wearing her brace." Kelsey's broken clavicle was never seen as "abuse." The red marks that looked like a diaper rash on Kelsey's bottom were called "abuse." Plus, according to Raye Dawn, Kathie took the brace off of Kelsey several days before it was time. When Raye asked about it, Kathie had thrown it away. Raye insisted that Kathie find the brace and give it to Raye so she could put it back on Kelsey until the doctor said she was healed and no longer needed it.

With Kathie Briggs's story saturating the Internet, she was gaining even more followers on Kelsey's Purpose. This next post is especially interesting to me now considering the fact that Kathie's connection with the Governor was severed when Kelsey's paternal step-grandparents realized they'd been "Kathie'd." The post featured on the top left corner a picture of Kelsey's cheek with the bruising from the August, 2005 car accident in which the family's vehicle was totaled after being struck by a drunk driver. Somehow, Kathie always forgets to mention that part. Instead of making a public service message about drunk driving, she insists on creating evidence with the accident pictures and calling them abuse.

Kjbriggs Posts: 1,239 March 13, 2007 RE: I don't understand! -
*Kelsey's case was marked **HIGH PRIORITY**. If this is what*

*happens when you are high priority what kind of care do the others get? Our **First Lady**...called [the head of DHS] personally and asked him to check on Kelsey. This is how he acknowledged her request. He turned it over to someone else and did not take care of the situation. He snubbed his nose at her request because he can and no one is doing anything about it. If the **Governor's wife** and the cousin to Kelsey cannot save a child the other children in this state don't have a chance under [the head of DHS's] eye. Our **County Director**...knew this was a **HIGH PROFILE** case and she allowed her workers to make the decisions. It was her job as their supervisor to make sure Kelsey was safe. I have emails from her stating she noticed Kelsey's decline, yet she did nothing. She alone could have saved a child's life and she is still in charge of other children. How safe are they? Look at Kelsey's face. Look at the other pictures of her? How could any **HUMAN** not notice a problem? These people have degrees? In what? Thank you, Kathie [Emphasis by post author]*

Kjbriggs Posts: 1,393 Re: Agenda and Events – 2007 - Prevent Child Abuse Oklahoma will start with a breakfast for Legislators at 8:00. I have a call into the Executive Director for more details. I am open to suggestions, but this is what I am thinking. KP members will meet at 9:00 and I will post the location later. This will give more people time to get their children off to school. Some of you are driving a long distance and I want to be considerate of that. At that point we will have a list of contacts that need to be made. We will lobby for 2 hours and then have lunch. We will start again at 1:00 to finish our contacts and to meet with other groups that are in the building. Each individual will depart at their needed times. Last year we had the opportunity to meet the Governor in the afternoon. [a picture of Kelsey on a slide in her casts was in the middle of the post] KP will be distributing newly designed 8.5 x 11 posters to every member of the House and the Senate. These will have a picture of Kelsey in her casts, our website at the bottom along with Kelsey's name and 2002-2005. It will also say, "When is someone going to read them their rights?" I had enough made so that each person in attendance will be able to take one home. Thank you, Kathie

07-21-2006 02:23 PM   [EMAIL] [IM] [FIND]   [QUOTE]

kjbriggs
Kelsey's Grandma
★★★★★

Posts: 1,237
Group: Super Moderators
Joined: Nov 2005
Status: Offline
Reputation: ███

RE: Briggs Family Statement   Post: #5

I heard a rumor earlier today that came from a Smith family member. I want to address it before it goes any further.

I have not nor will I be visiting Michael Porter in prison.

It has also been reported that Michael Porter has been moved for his protection. According to DOC he is still in Lexington and I have not been notified otherwise.

I had a meeting with him in January of 2006 and corresponded by email for a short time following that visit. I soon put a stop to it stating I was only using him for information and I knew he was doing the same and it did not feel right. The correspondence I have from him has become a valuable tool in getting justice for Kelsey. The meeting was at his request and something I chose to do for my granddaughter. I have no further interest in meeting with him in the near future. Until someone proves to me otherwise I still believe he is guilty of the original charges. Our decision to agree to the plea was for personal and strategic reasons I cannot reveal those reasons until the gag order is lifted. At that time I will release more information leading to the plea.

He is expected to testify in Raye Dawn's trial, but I do not know what that testimony consists of. I have not spoken to any of his family members or his attorney concerning his position on the trial.

Thank you,
Kathie

This post was last modified: Today 03:18 PM by kjbriggs

435

Jury Tainting

January 2007 through July 2007

It was July 9, 2007, a characteristically hot summer day in Oklahoma when jury selection commenced. While it would normally take attorneys more than a day for a high-profile trial such as Raye's, the district attorney and Raye's defense attorney had selected the members of this jury before lunch-time. Raye's attorney explained in a sworn statement that the trial judge put restrictions on the process and controlled it in a way in which the jury pool couldn't be questioned to the extent that he would have preferred. Raye's motion for a new trial (found on RayeDawnSmith.com and in *The Naked Truth Bound in Scorn*) explains that the restrictions included the fact that only the trial judge was allowed to question the jury in regards to the media and only three questions were asked: 1) Do you have any prior knowledge of this case? 2) If so, where did you obtain your knowledge? 3) Will your prior knowledge keep you from making a fair and impartial verdict? Raye's defense attorney was not allowed to further the questioning, even after some of the jury members admitted to prior knowledge. The restrictions made the jury selection process swift—too swift! This is unusual in a case of this magnitude because of the constant media coverage, as well as the hundreds of stories on the Internet about the case. And it constitutes a serious issue related to fairness and had a critical role in the outcome, which shows up time and time again as one looks back on how the trial went.

In an effort to try to minimize possible jury pool tainting before the trial, Raye's defense attorney requested a change of venue, which was granted. However, the trial was only moved as far as Creek County, the Bristow division, a straight shot up Interstate 44 and a 34-minute drive from the location of the original courthouse in Chandler, which is in Lincoln County, Oklahoma. So his effort—while appreciated—ended up being somewhat ineffectual.

Kathie Briggs and her gang of supporters left no stone unturned as they blanketed Oklahoma with pamphlets telling their version of Kelsey's story and Creek County was on their list of target areas. The match was ignited in Raye's home county and those who held the torches caused a brushfire throughout the state. Some say the intent was clear—jury tainting.

Someone we'll call "Blue" posted a message on January 30, 2007 regarding the April, 2007 "Kelsey Saturday." They were targeting key cities/towns in counties all over Oklahoma in an effort to ensure they reached the one where Raye's trial would be held. Several cities were listed that were the seats of many Oklahoma courthouses.

32 people have joined the Kelsey Saturday project. Groups are organizing in the following locations:
Norman [location of Cleveland County courthouse]
OKC/metro area [location of Oklahoma County courthouse]
Guthrie [location of Logan County courthouse]
Stillwater [location of Payne County courthouse]
Sapulpa [location of Creek County courthouse. Trial was ultimately held in a Creek County District Court in Bristow, just 20 miles away.]
Pawnee [location of Pawnee County courthouse]
Cleveland [located in Pawnee County]
Weatherford [located in Custer County and about 20 minutes from the Custer County courthouse in Arapaho (Weatherford is a bigger town than Arapaho and is just off I-40, the main highway)]
Elk City [located in Beckham County and about 15 miles from the Beckham County courthouse in Sayre (Elk City is a bigger town than Sayre)]
Woodward [location of Woodward County courthouse]
Lawton [location of Comanche County courthouse]
Tulsa [location of Tulsa County courthouse]...

The following post was also made by "Blue" one week later, on February 5, 2007:

*****Drum Roll Please***** *Kelsey Saturday is growing rapidly.*
        This year I have incorporated delegation. With that
        said......Now Announcing the 2007 Kelsey Saturday Area
        Directors!!

A list of areas across Oklahoma was provided along with the counties that each "director" represented. It seemed only the Southeast portion of Oklahoma wasn't covered. This was verified with the ending statement, **"Southeastern Oklahoma — Available! Contact me!"**

The following map provides a visual of their efforts to blanket Oklahoma with their version of Kelsey's story. The stars indicate Lincoln County, the county where Kelsey was murdered, and Creek County, the location of Raye's trial. The checkmarks indicate counties that were covered with "Kelsey Day" events and their pamphlets and stickers. The dots indicate counties in which volunteers had already agreed to cover at the time of the post. As you can see by this map, this group worked hard to cover all bases once they learned that Raye's trial could be moved out of her home county.[43]

---

[43] *US Census Bureau.* July 18, 2010.
<http://quickfacts.census.gov/qfd/maps/oklahoma_map.html>.

On "Kelsey Saturday," pamphlets are handed out that tell Kelsey's paternal family's version of her story and donations are requested to support "Kelsey's Purpose" now named "Kelsey Briggs Foundation."

As previously mentioned, "Kelsey's Purpose" is Kathie Briggs's Web site. It was established with the stated goal of turning Kelsey into a poster child for abuse with the claim that it was "Kelsey's purpose to die so that other children can live." It has also been used to garner media attention and public support for this purpose. This was played out in so many ways throughout the entire case. It was exemplified in a variety of ways in the entire story of Kelsey's life and during the custody battle and now in Raye's fight for freedom. But it can be seen even as we continue to look at how the Briggs continued to blanket the potential jury pool by tainting it with the philosophy that Kelsey was nothing more than a sacrifice to make her mother a monster that Kathie Briggs was going to see convicted.

Stickers were distributed within the mapped areas of the "Kelsey day" sites that were pink-colored, heart-shaped stickers that display a picture of Kelsey with the Web address to the Kelsey's Purpose Web site and they state "Justice for Kelsey Briggs."

Something I still fail to understand is why demand "Justice for Kelsey" when the man charged with her murder and sexual assault was given a plea deal? This is one of the many questions that have plagued me throughout the time I have followed this case. The argument that they seek "Justice for Kelsey," which is what makes up the content of their pamphlets that still promote things as fact which have since been disproven in a court of law, remains their cry. It is time their specious arguments be challenged.

The Trial Bashboard

July, 2007

I first heard of Kelsey's case in March of 2007 when Judge Craig Key hired me to edit his book. At the time, I was busy with my ghostwriting, editing, and transcription business and I did not have time to watch the news so I knew nothing of the case or the drama that seemed to follow it. This made me a perfect candidate for the job.

Once the realization set in of how unfairly Judge Key was treated in the Oklahoma media, and subsequently, in the public's opinion, I wanted to meet Raye Dawn for myself as well. While working on Judge Key's book, I noted that in the list of Kelsey's injuries, most occurred while she was with her mom. At the time, I didn't know that the list was from Raye's reporting to child protective services about each and every scrape and bump a two-year-old could have while working through her treatment plan to regain custody of her daughter, or that Kelsey sustained injuries while with her paternal grandmother that were never reported so they weren't added to the list. Therefore, the list presents a pattern of injuries that states, "with the mother," "with the mother," "with the mother," and doesn't clarify these injuries were "screened out" or that all but two of them were deemed "normal childhood injuries" and not abuse. That information was shared neither with me nor with the public, and it made Raye seem to be either abusive or careless.

After working on the Judge's book, I had learned the facts and wanted to know more, sensing that possibly the truth wasn't as simplistic as a first glance at the report had made things appear.

I made contact with Raye shortly before her trial. I told my family, "I'm going to meet a murderer," and gave them the address where we were meeting. I had never met a criminal, and I was terrified. But as a mom, I had to know.

At first, both Raye and Gayla seemed to be on their guard as I asked questions about the content of Judge Key's book. It was all I had to go on about the case, and there were issues that were concerning to me. I wanted to know if Raye really cared about Kelsey, or if it was just about herself, as I had originally assumed. Looking back, they had nothing to prove to me. I was nobody in their world. But for some reason, they trusted me, and since then, I've learned that it's not my place to judge.

All of my questions were forgotten as Raye flipped through the pages of the baby book she had lovingly prepared for her daughter. Her face was a mixture of pride and grief. Tears spilled from her troubled, blue eyes. It was almost a form of torture watching the young mother's pain as she showed me the lock of Kelsey's hair. It was half brown, half blonde and thoughtfully placed in this book of a proud mother's memories along with the first flower Kelsey had picked for her mommy and an extended list of Kelsey's firsts that were handwritten to the bottom of the page.

Kelsey's baby book made me feel like a bad mom. Mia was a miracle child, and the only baby I will ever have, and I didn't spend a fraction of the amount of time on her baby book as Raye had spent on Kelsey's.

Kelsey's baby book was kept in a manila envelope filled with cards from Kelsey's birth as well as a list of possible names for Kelsey. At the bottom of the envelope, I discovered a simple, gold wedding band that was too big for Raye's tiny fingers. I assumed it must have belonged to a man. When asked why the man's ring was mixed in with treasured memories of Kelsey's birth, Raye explained that the band belonged to Lance. It had been his wedding ring. She stated, "I kept it so that some day when Kelsey was old enough to understand, I could give her the ring to show her that her parents really did love each other."

I left the meeting with a new realization that Raye did love her child. She was clearly in mourning and confused about what had happened. She thought possibly Kelsey's death was the result of the drunk driving accident they had been the victims of in August, 2005, and a trip to a local amusement park during which Kelsey had ridden many of the rides with a bar across her stomach, and finally whatever Mike Porter had done to Kelsey while Raye was away from home for forty to fifty minutes on that fateful day while picking up Mike Porter's daughter from school.

For the first time, I saw the tragedy from Raye's point-of-view. I felt a new, almost maternal feeling toward Raye. She wasn't young enough to be my daughter. But she was tiny, like a teenager, and she seemed so vulnerable and filled with pain, and I empathized with her on a deep level, from one grieving mother to another.

In the summer of 2007, during the time of Raye's trial, I was busy with my business and had been hired to work on a book for a country music artist. It was an exciting opportunity for me. I had worked with celebrities in the past, but none of the caliber of my new client. He wanted the book finished within a month, so we signed an exclusive agreement. Other than overseeing my contract labor, I did little else but honor my obligation. Trouble started to brew, however, as my mind continually drifted to Raye's trial. I wanted to be there to show my support, and I wanted first-hand knowledge of the evidence as it was presented. The book was an uplifting, motivational book, but my mind and heart just weren't in it.

Always the professional, I trudged forward and did the best I could for my client. Ultimately, I missed the deadline to finish the book, so I lost the job. The loss of that book was the beginning of the downward spiral of my career as my heart took the lead and I searched for ways to "help Raye."

The Blog

Searching Kelsey's name today produces something much different than what one would have found when conducting an online search before July, 2007. I should know because I conducted a search at that time, as some jurors allegedly did. Among hundreds of posts against Raye I counted sixty-three YouTube videos that were touted as "Kelsey's true story." The videos promoted Lance as a "war hero" and loving and attentive father, stating he was in Iraq at the time of Kelsey's death. According to witnesses, this portrayal was nothing but a smokescreen to garner media attention for the paternal family's "cause."

Lance's older sister, Jeanna, confirmed this theory with the following post:

> *Post date uncertain...print date December 12, 2005 Did he [God] call Lance to active duty for the protection of his country in order to give Kelsey's story the edge that it needed for the media?*

This post was made at about the same time a picture was taken of Lance in his fatigues at Kelsey's gravesite. The picture and another similar picture with him standing have been shared repeatedly in the media. It was said to have been taken by his mom. Lance had been out of the military for over two months at the time of this photo.[44] Some have questioned the authenticity of the uniform he wore in the picture, stating that the flag is on the wrong side and that the patch possibly belongs to a unit other than his own.

---

[44] See Appendix B – Exhibit 6

Picture taken by Kathie Briggs in December of 2005

What I believe to be Lance's true character was revealed when he was involved in an accident during the months that Raye was pregnant with his child. The following police report gives us insight into the man the news media portrays as a war hero:

On 8-2-02 at approx. 15:45pm, I, Officer…and Reserve Officer…
responded to a two-vehicle accident in the 200 block of West
Main… Upon arrival I noticed a white male, later identified
as Raymond Lance Briggs, walking away from one of the
vehicles involved, a 1994 Blue Plymouth van. I then noticed
two subjects, one white male and one white female in the
other vehicle, a 2002 Blue Ford pickup. The white male
walking around seemed to be highly agitated, he was walking
with his hands in his pockets, looking at the ground, and
scraping his feet on the asphalt. He was in pacing mode. I
asked if anyone was injured and if an ambulance needed to
be called. The white male threw up his hands and stated,
'Fuck yea, he does,' pointing at the subjects in the Ford
pickup. I then returned to my patrol unit and requested first
responders. I then had [the reserve officer] start traffic
control. I then turned to the injured subjects to reassure the
two parties that help was on the way and to find out what
type of injuries they had obtained during the accident. As I
was standing there trying to get some information, the white
male (Briggs), started to walk up toward the injured subject.
I asked the male subject to step back and I would be with him
in just a minute. At that response, the white male (Briggs)

444

looked at me, threw up his arms and stated 'Fuck you. I don't have to step back. Who the fuck do you think you are? Fuck this shit.' I advised the subject that I was the officer on duty to investigate the accident, and that I would be needing to speak with him in just a few minutes and obtain some information from him. The white male (Briggs) then started to approach my location. I advised the subject to remain by his vehicle and I would be with him in a minute. The white male (Briggs) then stated, 'Fuck you. I don't have to step back. What the fuck do you want? I don't have to tell you anything, Bitch.' The white male continued to pace, and continued to throw his arms up in the air. At this point, [the reserve officer] came over to my location for back up. I then advised the white male subject that if he didn't calm down and do what I asked him to do, I was going to place him under arrest for his safety as well as our safety. The white male responded by stating 'Fuck you. You can't arrest me. I haven't done a fucking thing. I know the fucking law.' He then approached [the reserve officer] and attempted to intimidate [him] by throwing his chest out toward him and flexing his muscles. [The reserve officer] then asked what I wanted to do. I advised, 'Handcuff him.' The white male (Briggs) then replied, 'Yea right. Fucking arrest me. You can't. You have no right. Oh, fuck this shit here.' At this point, he put out both his hands in front of his body in a motion, wrist by wrist, and stated, 'Fucking arrest me then, if you can.' Before another word could be said, another male subject walked up and advised this officer that he was the male subject's brother in-law and that he could take him aside and cool him down, and asked that I not arrest him. I advised the subject that I would give him the opportunity to take the subject off to the side by the curb, sit him down, and try to calm him, but if the subject continued to act in the same manner, I would have no choice but to arrest him. The white male (Briggs) jerked away from his brother-in-law and then stated, 'Who the fuck do they think they are? Fuck you and them. I don't have to do a damn thing. Fuck, leave me alone.' The brother-in-law finally got the subject out of the first responders' way and away from the scene. [The reserve officer] then returned to do traffic control. With first

*responders on scene trying to take care of the injured, I once
again approached the white male subject for information. As
I approached toward his direction, he immediately started in
again, 'Now what the fuck do you want? Huh? Fuck you!' I
advised the subject that I needed to see his driver's license
and insurance verification on the vehicle that he was driving.
The subject began to walk toward the van then reached into
his back pocket and got out his wallet. He stated, 'Fuck, I
don't have it, so fuck you.' I then asked if he had any other
form of identification, so that I may know who his is. He then
replied, 'I got a fucking military I.D. Do you fucking want it?
No, fuck you. You don't fucking need to see it.' He then
slammed his wallet shut. I then asked if I could have his name
and driver's license number. He turned from the van and
started to walk to the curb, continuously throwing his arms
up in the air. He then turned and advised that his name was
Lance and his driver's license number was...He said the
number too fast for me to write it down and I had to ask him
to repeat. He then turned around, threw his arms up in the
air, and stated, 'What, you fucking can't hear either?' He
then repeated the number. I then asked for his middle name,
he advised..., 'shit, did you get that?' I advised, 'Yes, thank
you.' Briggs then turned around and started walking toward
the old gas station on the south side of the road. I then
started to look at the damage done to the vehicle that he was
driving and obtaining tag information. I attempted to see if
the windows had been rolled down or if they had been
shattered, when he started to walk up to the van. I turned and
was attempting to ask him if he had had the windows down or
if they had possibly been shattered when he interrupted by
saying, 'What the fuck are you doing now?' Once I was able
to finish my question, he replied, 'Fucking figure it out
yourself, bitch.' It was determined that he had the windows
down. I then returned to my injured subject to try and obtain
information from them on their identities. I then exited my
patrol unit and attempted to go back to the pickup and I
noticed another disturbance in the location of where Briggs
was located. [The reserve officer] and myself responded to
the disturbance. Upon arrival, I observed Briggs screaming
and yelling at a female subject standing by a car. As I*

approached, he turned away and started cussing another female subject who was sitting on the ground with two small children. It was learned that was Briggs's mother. I continued to stay between the female subject, a sister, and Briggs. I advised Briggs again that he needed to calm down. Again, I was informed by Briggs to fuck off and leave him alone. He had nothing to discuss with me and to fucking leave. Again, Briggs was trying to intimidate my reserve officer and myself by throwing out his chest and flinging his arms around. I then noticed a white pickup pull up and an older male subject get out. I walked up and asked if he was father of Briggs. He replied 'Yes, Royce Briggs [Lance's stepfather].' I then asked if he was the owner of the vehicle. He stated, 'Yes.' I then requested to see the insurance verification. [Royce Briggs] advised that he did not have any insurance on the vehicle, it was uninsured. I then asked the father to try to keep Briggs calmed down while we continued to investigate the accident. Mr. Briggs advised he was not sure he could do that, but he would try. I then returned to Briggs and asked that he come back with me to my patrol unit so that I could finish my investigation by obtaining further information. Briggs replied, 'No, I am not fucking going back to your car. Why the fuck?' I then noticed a slight hint of an alcoholic beverage coming from Briggs. I turned to his sister and asked if he had been drinking that day. She advised no, he had been at his great-grandmother's funeral today. I then returned to Briggs and advised him that we need to go to the patrol unit where it was cooler and try to cool down and that he would be getting a citation. Briggs politely states, 'You can go back to your fucking car and write my damn citation without me being there. Go the fuck back. I'm not going to your patrol car.' I spoke with the family and asked them to take Briggs home and get him calmed down.

This type of display was also evident on an occasion when Lance was arrested. According to the arresting officer, he threatened both the officer and his family members.[45] This is a claim that was also made by Judge Key and the DHS supervisor after Kelsey's death. From

---

[45] See Appendix B – Exhibit 7

Judge Key's *A Deadly Game of Tug of War: The Kelsey Smith-Briggs Story*:

> *I forced myself to go to work the day after Kelsey died. The last thing*
> *I wanted to do was deal with people's problems, but I felt*
> *obligated to do my job. The sheriff called me into his office*
> *that afternoon and informed me they had talked to Lance*
> *Briggs the night before to tell him of the death of Kelsey, and*
> *that he was in Fort Benning, Georgia. The sheriff indicated*
> *that Lance was in some type of a treatment center, and that*
> *Lance had made threats against my family and me. At that*
> *point, the sheriff was concerned because he told me he had*
> *spoken to people who were concerned with Lance's mental*
> *instability. The death threats that were made had come*
> *directly from Lance. It was a threat against my children, as*
> *well as the supervisor for DHS and his family.* [46]

As for the villain in their version of what happened to Kelsey, the focus was always on Raye as an uncaring mother who chose a man over her own child with statements such as "Kelsey was returned to the home of her mother..." However, it was never included that Kelsey's step-father, the man charged with her sexual assault and murder also resided in the home and had been home alone with Kelsey at the time of her alleged rape and demise. The way in which such statements were phrased cast a dark cloud over Raye, and sadly, the darkness is all the general public could see.

The voices trampling and trashing Raye were over-whelming and impossible to ignore. Therefore, Raye had few supporters outside her immediate family and close friends. As I soon learned, anyone who dares to stand up in Raye's defense is quickly shut down with threats of lawsuits or they're inundated with stories that aren't based on fact just to silence the opposing voice of reason.

Consequently, from the fall of 2005 to the summer of 2007, everything that had been attempted to aid Raye's defense or to repair the damage that had been done to her public image was immediately

---

[46] Key, Craig. *A Deadly Game of Tug of War: The Kelsey Smith-Briggs Story*. Garden City, NY: Morgan James Publishing, 2007. p. 91.

flooded and either shut down or taken over by those who opposed Raye. People were afraid of being added to the list of civil lawsuits or afraid of enduring a backlash of terror, and rightfully so. This fear was another catalyst for the lack of support for Raye, and it was echoed throughout the Web on every Web site where "Kelsey's story" was told.

During my search, I also discovered a blog that seemed to be actively discussing Kelsey's case. At the time, I didn't know much about Kelsey's Purpose and its followers, how many people were members, or who was involved with their mission. I just knew the facts. When I stumbled upon the blog, I didn't realize it was a temporary venue where Kathie Briggs's supporters were posting while her Web site was closed to new posts due to the trial. To me, it seemed to be random people sharing their opinions.

The blog began with the following intro: The "Other" Kelsey Posted on *June 12th, 2007.*

Previously posted elsewhere on Tuesday, June 12th, 2007 8:32 pm
Kelsey lived in a pack of wild dogs. And because she lived amongst these people, she did not live for very long: My Question is: Who is the Alpha Dog, the man who terrorizes women or the man who kills a toddler?

After the introduction, the blogger listed an article that discussed Lance's two charges of domestic abuse from 2006 regarding his alleged attack on a former girlfriend who stated he had been stalking her before he reportedly drug her out of the house by her hair and then pushed her friend into a glass window that was said to have been broken by him.[47]

The blog owner seemed to want to present both sides, and he kept the conversation going with over 763 comments in a month and a half—the amount of time that the blog was active.

Certain jury members could have read the blog posts according to witnesses who claim jurors were searching the case online. Also, the scenario that was introduced on the news by a juror who posted on

---

[47] See articles and evidence at the following Web address:
http://www.thetruthaboutkelsey.com/Lance/Lance%20Briggs%20Page.htm

Kelsey's Purpose, was presented on this blog. The juror claimed Raye had murdered her own child and framed Mike Porter. Evidence of this scenario was not included in the evidence against Raye; she was not on trial for murder, but the juror seemed to quote verbatim some posts from the blog and from previous bashboards.

Following are a select few comments from the blog (Any use of actual names is not intentional):

FYI - *July 3rd, 2007- As for the observer. They should be sued. Along with the family pawn that has been passing the papers and the flyers out. I hope the Briggs have a good attorney.*

Karen - *July 5th, 2007 – Kelsey wasn't breathing when Mike Porter went into the room. He said he heard a 'gurgle' sound and when he picked her up she wasn't breathing...*

Jamie - *July 5th, 2007 – Actually her statement doesn't even say he came in and woke her up, it just states that he woke her up. Is it possible that when he came into the house it woke her up?*

[blog owner] - *July 5th, 2007 - Jamie - you are correct - the part of the arrest warrant when MP makes a statement simply says: 'when Mike Porter arrived home Raye Dawn and Kelsey were sleeping in Raye Dawn's bed. Raye Dawn got up and Kelsey was still sleeping.' So Mike Porter did not say she was sleeping peacefully or that he saw her asleep at all. The idea that Raye Dawn started to abuse Kelsey out of jealousy is a possible theory - BUT WHERE DOES IT COME FROM? Since when does being a 'drinking, volatile tramp' make you a child abuser? At what point did the public decide that Mike Porter was innocent and Raye Dawn the abuser? This is an important fact for me in looking at the case. I am not saying Raye Dawn COULDN't be the abuser - she absolutely COULD be but I don't see in these reports conclusive evidence that she is except that Mike Porter is pointing the finger at her [as the abuser] - I read that the Briggs AND Raye Dawn were all cited as either being responsible OR not able to protect Kelsey but that didn't include Raye Dawn alone. All evidence that points to Raye Dawn directly comes from Mike Porter's own version of events. Where DOES Gayla fit in here? Something simply does not add up about these relationships. What does Gayla know that would settle the mysteries of this case? What did she see? WHy did all of* *the family trust her so much (to the point that Mike Porter called HER?) The unknown abuser theory, as frustrating as it seems, makes a little sense - DID ANYONE EVER SEE RAYE DAWN ABUSE KELSEY? and they just aren't talking? DID ANYONE EVER SEE MIKE PORTER for that matter? Did Raye Dawn SEE Mike Porter or vice versa and they simply denied what they saw? Guess we'll never now I am just curious to know how onlookers can be so sure that Raye Dawn is guilty of the actual abuse (vs. enabling or failing to report it or intervene - still a hefty responsibility! AND if this is TRUE She COULD have saved Kelsey.) DId the Briggs make all those calls? and if so why are they being vilified since the abuse DOES seem to have occurred? is it because they are not cleared from inflicting the abuse? Suddenly I am wondering, why is the obvious answer not a possibility anymore: Mike Porter DID IT! Have all the mudslinging, divorce, custody, family-feuding and hatred issues clouded the obvious? I STILL need more evidence, not conjecture, that Raye Dawn committed the crime - I KNOW i could've missed something that makes others so sure - point it out to me!"*

Gracie - *July 5th, 2007 –Just another tidbit of info..Raye Dawn moved out of her mothers house (which at that time also included her younger sister) around the same time she met Mike Porter. Which poses another 'theory' that having to care for a toddler all on her own may have been too much for her to handle.*

The following post is reflective of the juror's statement to the media within hours of her verdict. This juror convinced the jury to make an emotional decision.

Jamie - *July 5th, 2007 – Without a trial and evidence being shown, there is nothing that points at Mike Porter either except for Raye Dawn...From what I gathered, Mike Porter's doctor said Kelsey's injuries were inflicted several hours before he ever got home ...As for the sexual abuse, the ME said he couldn't say whether it happened or not, the DA's hired doctor said it did happen, and Mike Porter's doctor said there was no evidence of sexual abuse. Who do you choose to believe? The defendant's hired doctor or the DA's high paid* *hired doctor? Both of them need to prove something...Since Mike Porter never went to trial, we will never know what made the DA so sure he was the one that did it. From what I understood, there was no medical evidence that pointed at either person and it was all circumstantial. Maybe when the gag order's lifted, the DA will show what he has that made him so sure it was Mike Porter.*

The blog was so accessible and easy to find that the CASA worker who was listed as a state witness in Raye's trial joined the discussion DURING the trial.

[CASA] - July 9th, 2007 –Please go Gracie June 19, 2007. then read the 33 page report that was in The Oklahoman this last week. Just put everything together.
Karen - July 9th, 2007 – [CASA], aren't you supposed to be in Bristow today???
[CASA] - July 10th, 2007 –Who said I was going to Bristow??

Although I suspect by the language of some of those who posted that Kathie was an active participant on the blog, she sent a message to the blog owner via e-mail alerting him of the trial notes that would be online nightly after the trial. Kathie's active forum was closed to new posts at the time, but I was able to read the forum, and apparently so did others. Members of the group seemed to always find a place to express their opinions, and Kathie always seems to know exactly where to find them.

[Blog owner] - July 9th, 2007 – From Kathie Briggs: "I hope you will let your readers know that each night after the trial Fox...will have a page of notes about the trial. Britten Follett, a reporter that has been on this case from day one will be in court daily. She will come home and give a more in depth look about the days testimony." A link to Ms. Follett's notes was posted.
Jamie - July 13th, 2007 – I didn't think twice about the stalking allegations, until Kathie testified herself. How would you

know if Raye Dawn switched tags on her vehicles unless you had known the previous tag numbers? How would you know a previous tag number unless you were stalking someone and writing it down? And then the officer testified the PD was getting phone calls about Mike Porter and Raye Dawn's whereabouts and what they were doing...I do not buy the testimony about the e-mails. There was a lot more to those e-mails and the meeting than what was testified to and if they had actually allowed the e-mail to be presented, I'm sure it would have shed some light. Someone else said on another blog that some of those e-mails contained several pictures of Kelsey that were sent to Mike Porter from the Briggs family. I'm not convinced it was a set up against Raye Dawn, but I do smell manipulative and vindictive. Against who? Who knows...

[Whit] - *July 13th, 2007 – First off, Marcy and [Betsy], the point of this blog is for people to freely express differing viewpoints WITHOUT BEING ATTACKED. Attacking seems to be a Briggs (and supporters)specialty. If you have an opinion, i.e. that the Briggs are unaccountable for the unraveling of this situation, then back it up with an explanation. Acting like an immature child that resorts to name calling when you disagree only discredits your opinion, character and intelligence. I'm not saying you are wrong or stupid, just that the explosive, irrational way you respond is coming off that way. Why do you assume every comment posted is made by a Smith family member? It only reinforces the hateful, assumptive mentality that people suspect of Kathie.*

Ellen - *July 13th, 2007 – [Whit], I agree Craig Key is a IDIOT!! and should be as or more responsible in her death! hes a ASSHOLE and i hopes he rotts in hell! [Betsy], I also agree 'officer Byers is the VILLAGE IDOT' I would like to see them both have the sh!! kicked out of them! I am appalled by both of their actions, they make me sick!*

The following post is definitely from a member of Kelsey's paternal family. The story about the "monitor" in the paternal family's home came from their overactive and paranoid imaginations and the story of Raye stalking the paternal family was supposedly told to

Kathie by Mike Porter. Also, the "all cried out" phrase came from Raye's OSBI interview that the paternal family obtained illegally.

Jill - *July 14th, 2007 – The stalking started with Raye Dawn stalking the Briggs home. She would sit across the road and 'monitor' everything that went on. She had a bug inside the house after a visit with Kelsey...Was she 'cried out' as she claimed...She is shedding more now for herself during the trial. Her out of control sobbing at the trial was so excessive that they had to take a recess. The moment the last juror walked out of the room, her uncontrolled crying ceased immediately. That's amazing that she's able to put her emotions back together so easily...Mommy will 'settle down' and cool off when she's in prison. Justice for Kelsey*

Tony - *July 14th, 2007 - OK, let me understand this, Raye Dawn has planted a wire tap in Kathie's home and sat outside her house with other spyware monitoring everything at Kathie's then she ran this 'game' on her whole family to get them on her side and now people have abandoned ship, right? Actually, it would appear to me that the pack of wild dogs have become rabied because they are not convincing people of their dillusional ramblings. Oh, they probably forgot to tell us about Raye Dawn's formative years in the CIA and the fact she helped Al Gore invent the internet. Was she around when the shopping cart was invented too or did her Dad have a hand in planning the Bay of Pigs invasion in Cuba? This sounds foolish and does not help anyone truly debate this case. I want to thank [the blog owner] for having this site and allowing some people to openly discuss this case. However, I will not be persuaded by 'JFK conspiracy theories'. Does anyone know why Fox 25 took all the prior days notes off their website? It appears to me from the notes that what the TV stations are reporting and what is in the transcript notes on Fox 25 are very diffrent. Look at [the DHS worker] saying really DHS thought Kelsey should have gone home with Raye Dawn, and the fact she didn't think Raye Dawn abused Kelsey, thats not what they said on TV though. Did anyone else catch [Jack] say that 'if they don't get Raye Dawn in Court then God will get her later'. I wonder if maybe it isn't going well for Smothermon?*

Jamie - *July 14th, 2007 – Tony, don't forget that Mike Porter's doctor says something totally different than the other 2, but I don't think the jury will see that either. Smothermon definitely won't introduce it because it blows his theory out of the water.*

ED - *July 14th, 2007 – The facts of this case are that: Kelsey is dead, Mike Porter or Raye Dawn DID it, AND Mike Porter or Raye Dawn is HIDING it. No matter what happened with the family before the fact of death is really irrelevant. Raye Dawn is on trial for allowing someone to hurt her child. She knew and should have done something about it. Regardless of whether or not the families hate each other (which they do of course) that is not what is on trial here. I don't care what else is going on in your life, you TAKE CARE OF YOUR CHILDREN. I don't have any kids but my good friends do and I would put my life on the line for them, and they aren't even related to me. Why can't people realize that we need to take care of our kids? This is a sad case and it will never be a happy subject to talk about, but instead of attacking each other, the Briggs or the Smiths, or anyone else, why can't we try to work together and start preventing child abuse. This situation should have been stopped LONG before Kelsey died. No matter what, she should be here today.*

Jill - *July 15th, 2007 – [Whit] stated that Meeker was no where land and Raye Dawn wouldn't have access to high tech spyware? Are you serious??? You're so uninformed it's pathetic. Anyone can buy a bug and place it in a house and listen from a short distance. Someone is feeding you a bunch of bull. You stated 'If Mike Porter had been tried for the crime he committed, instead of whittling down his charges in hopes of getting Raye Dawn, the evidence would have come to light at trial.' Whittling down? 30 years is whittling down. I'm sure that Raye Dawn's won't be whittled down. You are evidently related to that family and they have fed you a line sister!...Gayla is a big let down...She is like the "mother from Hell"...Gayla contributed to the hatred against Kathie and just added fuel to the fire to Raye Dawn. Party, in Raye Dawn's defense, she would have never hated Kathie so much if it hadn't been for her mother. Her mother didn't like her so Raye Dawn didn't like her. Monkey see monkey do.*

The previous post was reminiscent of many posts that have been captured from various bash boards. Why would random people on a blog worry about "who hates Kathie"? A question to ponder...

Tab - July 18th, 2007 – Guilty!!! [article posted]
[Frances] - July 18th, 2007 – Mother convicted in child-abuse case
>*Raye Dawn was found guilty of enabling the abuse of her 2-year-old daughter and given a 27-year prison sentence, a jury decided today. After the verdict was announced, Raye Dawn lowered her head into her hands and sobbed, 'I don't understand. Help me.'*
Tiny - July 18th, 2007 - Wow, all the US observers in the state
>*couldn't convince this jury that she was innocent.*
Tiny - July 18th, 2007 – I guess the old saying is true 'What comes
>*around goes around. It went around TODAY. Thank God.*
[Whit] - July 18th, 2007 – [Frances] and Tiny, Where have you been
>*the last week, why speak up now? To rub it in? Admirable.*
Tab - July 18th, 2007 - The 27 years isn't definite,only a
>*recommendation by the jury.Ultimately,it is up for the judge to decide the length of her sentence.He could go less,he could go MORE.*
[Frances] - July 18th, 2007 - actually, i've been posting under the
>*name karen. why?? because i felt i had the right to. it was in my best interest to do so, as i had been attending the trial and i don't know who reads what on these sites. and i'm sure i'm not the only one who has done so. and in all honesty, i thought i had put karen when i posted. forgive me. regardless, i've been here posting the whole time and telling what i knew to be fact.*

The blog shut down within days of the completion of Raye's trial. The final post was from the blog owner explaining that it was time to let Kelsey rest in peace. Although I agreed with his statement, I felt that finding peace for Kelsey involved peace for her entire family, and in particular, Kelsey's mom.

Seeking the Truth about Kelsey

July, 2007

Raye Dawn wasn't charged with any crime until four months after Kelsey's death. These charges didn't come from an investigation or newly-discovered evidence. They were the result of months of plotting, planning, and pushing the district attorney to charge her with "something." Kathie Briggs and her followers clearly schemed and plotted to ensure that Raye Dawn would be imprisoned. They threatened and harassed anyone who dared stand up in Raye Dawn's defense, such as I. Remarkably, some still support Kathie Briggs today in her quest for "Justice for Kelsey." Her quest does not include Mike Porter facing a jury on murder and sexual assault charges, or having his name added to a sex offender registry, but instead a murder charge for Raye Dawn...the very charge Kathie Briggs wanted filed on Raye Dawn the night of Kelsey's death without knowing what happened, and without a review of the evidence. People blindly support her mission and add to the hate that is already overwhelming, causing a casual observer to fall into her well-planned pit.

Many akin the actions of Kathie Briggs and her followers to those of the angry mobs during the time of the Salem witch trials. The witch hunts reportedly started not because there were actual witches running around in Salem and doing evil deeds, but because the Pilgrims had moved to a new country with a climate unlike their own with a different type of soil, and a whole new host of environmental factors. When things went wrong, their faith was so strong that they immediately blamed Satan and thought his work was being done through "witches." These people didn't factor in the environmental or regional differences they encountered while growing crops and building communities. When something went wrong and crops died, they jumped to conclusions and blamed, judged, and murdered innocent people. Through this tragic part of our history, we've learned

458

that blame is at times associated with a specific, targeted person, not outside factors. When tempers get heated, the result is often the guilty walking free while the innocent is crucified. Someone has to pay and rational thinking is tossed aside in the name of "justice."

In the case of Kelsey, an innocent child was reportedly raped and murdered. The fact that this happened is appalling and disgusting and something that is heartbreaking for all. Consequently, the first thought that came to the minds of those following or closely involved in the case was to "burn the witch." Due to the hate that was already established for Raye Dawn from the paternal family, and since all of the fingers pointed toward Raye Dawn (aside from those who actually investigated the crime and were to prosecute the guilty party), she became the witch in this scenario.

In a typical case, one article can ignite a heated rage toward the perpetrator of a crime against a child. Multiply that rage by over 400 articles in print and in excess of 1,300 televised reports and imagine the amount of hate and anger and pure rage that has been centered on Raye Dawn...a mother who wasn't home at the time of her child's alleged rape and murder. As a logical person, wouldn't you question why the public was deceived in order to bring that type of hate for Raye Dawn while the torch-bearers worked to create sympathy for Mike Porter? I questioned this as well. I was an outsider who saw through the smokescreen and I was determined to bring the truth to light and fight the injustice that surrounded Kelsey's case. Therefore, in the last days of Raye Dawn's trial I started blogging about the facts as I knew them. Within days of the trial ending my blog was flooded with members of Kathie Briggs's Web site. I had previously met them on a random blog, but at the time, I didn't realize it was them. Like I stated, I knew the case, but I had no idea what I was stepping into with what we now term "Kathie Briggs's Purpose."

At the end of the first week of Raye Dawn's trial I created a blog titled "Seeking the Truth about Kelsey" and invented the character "Truth Seeker." The character I created was a mixture of various people that I knew. I drew from their lives as a basis for details I would share about me. I didn't want my identity known. I feared that people who knew me would recognize me if I were myself. I had a strong desire to help Raye Dawn, but I wasn't ready to commit myself to being the main person who spoke out on her behalf. The truth had started coming to light with an article in the U.S. Observer with the facts that had not been shared and the Judge's book. People were opening their eyes to the public deception. I viewed myself as nothing more than a messenger sharing the facts. I never dreamed it would grow into anything other than my original intentions.

After watching the negative media reports, I started searching online to see what was being said about the case. That's when I discovered the blog, videos, and other Web sites. It seemed that most of the Web sites that hosted posts from the paternal family also came with requests for donations. One Web site in particular was a military site on which the heading of the post was something similar to "A soldier in need" and a brief overview of the paternal family's version of Kelsey's story along with a request for donations. This Web site in particular upset me. It was one thing to deceive the general public and beg them for money, but to mislead our nation's soldiers who risk their lives for our safety was pushing it too far in my opinion.

One page on the Web site listed all of the board members and their contact information. I immediately drafted an email and addressed it to each and every board member with facts about Kelsey's case along with a summary of my disgust over the fact they put members of the military in the position to donate their hard-earned money to Kathie Briggs and her family. At the time of the email, I didn't know about the allegedly missing $6,000 they had collected from BACA (Bikers Against Child Abuse) or reported admissions to key members of their organization that they would "find a way to earn a paycheck from" Kelsey's story. However, I had been told that since Kelsey's death, multiple vehicles had been purchased. Witnesses who knew the paternal family told me that Kathie and Lance didn't work, but instead drew disability. People in their home towns questioned where the funds had come from to purchase vehicles when reportedly all they collected were disability checks. This has reportedly been a pattern since Kathie Briggs's husband never adopted her children so they could collect their father's social security. (Their father was said to be depressed after Kathie Briggs refused to allow him visitation for Christmas. He committed suicide.) Also, Kathie Briggs admitted on her Web site that her husband had not worked much since Kelsey's death. So where did they get the funds? Social security had ended since all of Kathie Briggs's children were over the age of eighteen. A witness stated that a private $10,000 donation was made to Kathie Briggs. Another witness has stated that Kathie Briggs was sent expensive gifts from multiple supporters. Also, rumors circulated that Kathie Briggs had gotten a facelift. There is a distinct difference in Kathie's face from pictures taken immediately after Kelsey's death to pictures taken just two years ago. Are the rumors true? I don't know. But if she collected donations and used them for a facelift and new vehicles, I felt it was beyond tacky. Today, my feelings are the same regarding the issue...nobody should profit from a child's death. To me, it's blood money.

Immediately after sending the emails, voicing my opinion, I received several responses from the military Web site's board members who assured me that the request for donations would be removed. Within days it disappeared from their Web site. To me, this was a small victory for Kelsey. Feeling as if baby steps were being made to rectify a great wrong, I forged ahead with the blog that would soon change the tide of hate against Kelsey's mom.

My first post was titled, "Meet Kelsey." I never thought anyone would read the blog. I merely sent my thoughts into cyberspace about the things I knew as fact and my opinion. There were no pictures of Kelsey or anyone in her family. I wasn't sure what I could legally use, so I kept it simple in the beginning. This was the introduction:

*Meet Kelsey - She was a beautiful two and a half year old child who
died of blunt force trauma to the abdomen. That much I know
is true. All the other things I've read, I'm not so sure about. I
do want to give my sympathies to her family. The loss of a
child or grandchild is so hard to bear. My sympathies to you.
My prayers are with Raye Dawn (Kelsey's mom) this week as
she faces a jury for either abusing Kelsey or enabling abuse.
I realize the hope of a fair trial has been tainted by the media
and the paternal family out for revenge. I do hope the jury
opens their ears and judges you according to the facts and
not preconceptions. I began this blog after being outraged at
the viciousness I've read on the Internet toward the Judge in
the case...and the mom, Raye Dawn. I would like to hear
some constructive, truthful comments about what happened
and suggestions or ways to prevent it from happening in the
future. There doesn't seem to be a neutral site anywhere that
I've found that isn't asking for money or ragging on someone
who hasn't been found guilty and someone who was doing his
job. If you've come here with those intentions, you've come to
the wrong place. I am looking forward to the book that was
written by the Judge. I think it's about time he told his side of
this story. If you want to know more about Kelsey, go to [link
given to the state newspaper's articles]. I look forward to
your comments. I hope some of you out there aren't media
zombies who believe everything you hear and read.*

My first response was from someone using the name
"LovedOnesRemembered." On July 12, 2007 this was posted:

*I wonder about the whole truth, too. It makes me very suspicious
when I see only one side of something out of the news
stations. Are they hiding something? Why don't they show
more than one side to the whole situation? It's very odd to
me. If it was so clear that Raye Dawn should be charged
after Kelsey died, why did it take so long to have that DA
decide to press charges? And why does the news keep making
Kelsey's dad out to be such a hero when he has been so
violent to women in his life? This history was printed by the
newspapers but I never heard one word about that on the TV
or radio. All they seem to want to do is blame Kelsey's mom*

and she hasn't even been convicted. You sure don't hear much about her step dad, even though he is in jail after pleading guilty to enabling abuse and is in jail for 30 years. He was the one the DA originally charged with murdering Kelsey. Now it is looking like a witch hunt to try to look tough. It just looks sad to me. I really wonder what is being hidden from the public. What else do they know that they aren't telling us? I hope they do eventually release those records, as even some of the reporters have mentioned in online stories that records have not been released to the public that should have already been released. It's all very sad and there's no way for any one of us to understand how hard it is for everyone involved. It's for sure that someone killed Kelsey. The real question to me is how could her mom have prevented it when she wasn't even there? It's very fishy to me and I know it's not right to try to convict someone in the press when they should be able to focus on their own trial. That's what it looks like from this side and it raises too many red flags when every media outlet says the same thing. What happened to innocent until PROVEN guilty in a court of law? I just hope Kelsey's mom gets a fair trial. I don't know how that is going to happen but I do hope it does.

Now I was conversing with someone who seemed level-headed and compassionate. What a change from everything I had seen. The posts below are included in their original format with me posting as Truth Seeker. Due to page constraints, only a few key posts are presented.

7/12/2007 8:20 AM Truth Seeker wrote: Thank you Lovedonesremembered! I was hoping that someone else out there had a real opinion in this case besides "string them all up!" It's just ridiculous how this whole thing has been allowed to get so out of control. Don't even get me started on how reporters like Cherokee Ballard and Britten Follett are in attack mode! They don't even listen to anything being said. They seem to be out for blood from Craig Key and Raye Dawn every time they do a report. What happened to the days when reporters were unbiased? It's nice to see that CBS and

ABC have remained professional in their reports on this case
    so far.

My blog had picked up more readers and participants so I posted
about various topics. One topic in particular was titled, "No, I don't
think Lance killed Kelsey." Because I was taking up for Raye and
bringing attention to Lance's violent past, I was told that I thought he
killed Kelsey. I posted:

Allow me to explain why I'm creating a picture of who [Lance] truly
    is:
    1. He killed Raye Dawn's first baby (I believe every fetus is a
    human being. [I know I'm going to get a lot of pro-lifers
    leaving comments now.] But even the pro-lifers must agree
    that a woman who is in a domestic violence situation does
    not have a choice in whether the baby lives or dies. She didn't
    choose that outcome.) So in my opinion, Lance killed one of
    Raye Dawn's babies.
    2. Raye Dawn was assumedly so focused on keeping her
    daughter away from an abusive man that she did not see
    what Mike Porter was really about.
    3. I'm sick and tired of seeing videos, articles and stuff on
    Lance as a war hero and someone who loved his child. I do
    not doubt he loved Kelsey. Even men who beat women have
    shown the ability to love their children. But, we know from
    valid sources that he was not in Iraq when Kelsey died.
    Anyone who would lie about something like that isn't a good,
    upstanding person in my book and I tend to doubt anything
    else they say.
    So now that we have all that out of the way, we can focus on
    why it's been proven that Mike Porter killed Kelsey.

KJ responded, taking up for Mike Porter:

I've been following your blog entries and agree with most of the
    things you say, but you lost me at proving Mike Porter
    murdered. Who murdered her has not been proven yet, so I'm
    a little lost on that one.
7/22/2007 8:39 PM Truth Seeker wrote: Thanks for your comment.
    I'm just looking at the facts. Fact 1: Mike Porter pleaded to a

30 year sentence instead of facing a jury. That tells me that he did something. Fact 2: Mike Porter was the one home when Kelsey died. Fact 3: Mike Porter sent Raye Dawn away from the home and then Kelsey was killed while Raye Dawn was gone. Fact 4: Mike Porter all but confessed to the preacher who was at the hospital with the family. That was brought forward in Raye Dawn's trial. Fact 5: The DA...told Mike Porter in Raye Dawn's trial that he knew Mike Porter sexually abused Kelsey and killed her. What do all of these facts say to you?

7/24/2007 2:39 PM iknowmore wrote: Truth seeker: First I have a question: How do you know that Lance is responsible for the miscarrige of Raye Dawn's 1st child? Do you have any evidence to back up that claim? Secondly, your correct Lance was not in Iraq 'when Kelsey died.'... he wasn't in Iraq when Kelsey died but he WAS IN IRAQ while she was being abused.

At the time of the blog, I didn't know all of the facts surrounding the case and to be honest, I had a different opinion of Mike Porter and his role. In my opinion, he had murdered Kelsey, but I didn't know he had abused Kelsey before the day of her alleged sexual assault and murder. Also, the paternal family claims that Lance was in Iraq while Kelsey was being abused. There is nothing to back up that claim. Lance was in Iraq in May of 2005 and he was in Georgia either in August or September of 2005. On May 3rd, the date that Lance allegedly landed in Iraq, Kelsey was removed from Kathie Briggs's home after she was added to the list of possible perpetrators of Kelsey's abuse. Kelsey was then put into the care of Gayla, her maternal grandmother, where she showed signs of improvement and there were no abuse allegations while in her care. In fact, no allegations of abuse were made until August after a drunk driver totaled the truck in which Kelsey was a passenger in the back seat. So when looking at the known facts, there is nothing to verify that Lance was in Iraq while Kelsey was "being abused." This point is still argued to this day. Lance's sister joined the discussion with the following post:

7/25/2007 7:09 PM Shirica wrote: ...As far as Lance's whereabouts on the day of Kelsey's death. Yes...Lance was in Ft Benning GA...I know it has been stated that Lance was in Iraq at the time of her death, but I do believe it was just meant as a paraphrase...

7/25/2007 8:45 PM Shirica wrote: The District Attorney's office issued a subpoena to the hospital that Raye Dawn was treated at for her miscarriage and NO WHERE in her records does it show that she lost her baby from being punched in the stomach...

It's my understanding that a person's medical records are confidential. Why would Lance's sister, Shirica, have access to what was or was not in Raye Dawn's medical records? Were the medical records presented as evidence in court, and if so, how would she have access?

7/27/2007 12:15 AM Tab wrote: Just wondering why Lance never attended any of the hearings for Kelsey when he was in Oklahoma the morning of one of the most important ones? Why did he decide to skip out, leave town and then return that night?

7/27/2007 6:34 AM Truth Seeker wrote: That's a question I think everyone would like to know. If you care for your child so much that you sue everyone and their dog after the child is gone and show up for the mother's trial, then why skip out when your daughter needs you, when she's still here and needs both parents? Is he unemployed now and can make time to show up now that money is involved? There is a (what was the amount?) 15 million dollar question.

Topics of conversation changed on the blog. It seemed that some came to the blog to discuss their beliefs and known facts, others only wanted to argue and find a hole in my statements that they could rip apart. Soon, my blogging turned into what I termed "rants." The nonstop arguing was getting to me. I'm not an argumentative person, but if I quit, I would be letting down Raye Dawn and her family. I was torn between doing what I thought was right and putting myself into a situation with people that were not the type I would invite into my life.

Unfortunately, I started "ranting" and taking my frustrations out on my posts. Looking back, I can see a lot of things that I did wrong and I wish I would have handled certain situations differently, but we live our lives in a forward motion that we don't understand until we can look behind us. Our lives are full of lessons and the most important one I've learned since 2007 is to not let what someone else does affect what I do or say. Now I know better, but at the time I was drowning and there wasn't anyone to toss me a life raft. Nobody knew who I was so I had no help in controlling the posts and I had a business to run and people who counted on me. Since I was accustomed to working on projects and not sharing the details with anyone due to confidentiality agreements, nobody in my life thought the change in me was anything but work related. They had been through tough projects with me and had seen how I would go silent if a certain project had affected me, but they never pressed for details. Therefore, I was on my own in dealing with the pressure and it started to show in my posts. My world was crumbling around me and I took my frustrations out on the people whose only purpose on my blog was to argue with me and tear down Raye Dawn.

Through the years and computer upgrades, some posts have been lost. One that I've yet to find was a post that claimed I couldn't discuss the case without Lance's permission. After that post I consulted with an attorney whom my parents had recently used in an unrelated issue. We had exchanged emails a few times regarding their situation and I thought he'd share his opinion with me regarding my right to free speech. In our short conversation, he told me that as long as I was discussing true events and not purposely lying or libeling anyone, I could in fact discuss the case. He also informed me that I could display a picture of Kelsey as long as I wasn't using it for profit. The blog soon changed its look and I added a picture of Kelsey with Raye Dawn. Those who came to my blog to start trouble were not happy that I didn't follow their orders. It wasn't long until threats of a lawsuit began circulating. To this day, I've been threatened so many times with a lawsuit that the words no longer have an affect on me. Despite the threats, the conversation continued as people came together to voice their opinions on the case, and others worked to silence our opinions. Although Raye Dawn had been found guilty of "should have known" and was convicted by a jury with a 27-year sentence, those who worked to put Raye Dawn into prison just couldn't let it go. It seemed like their hate grew stronger, especially as the facts they had spent years silencing were breaking through to the surface. Since Raye Dawn was in prison, the target for their hate soon became me…the one who dared to defy their orders to stop discussing the case and the one who ignored their threats. The battle that started over the custody of Kelsey soon turned into a battle of truth vs. lies. Each side thought their side was that of truth. When Kathie Briggs's supporters started abandoning ship, it soon became clear who fought for the truth and who just wanted to fight.

A Bright Idea

August, 2007

The first conversation I had with Gayla, Raye's mom, after the trial involved coming up with a "bright idea." Gayla was the only person in the family to whom I had spoken besides Raye. For months after my initial involvement, Raye's family members had heard of "Truth Seeker," but they didn't know if she was someone within the family or an outsider. My identity was a mystery to all. Not even my family knew. Since I didn't discuss business with my friends or family, they thought I was spending all of my time working. However, keeping up with the blog overwhelmed me and my business started to suffer.

Managing my business and overseeing all of the projects that were ongoing was an eighty-hour per week job. I had an assistant. She managed the contract labor and assigned projects, but I wanted to personally inspect every page of transcription that was presented to my clients because my name was on the work; it had to be perfect. Since I fell behind on my end, I found myself in the situation where I paid my contract labor thousands of dollars that they had earned, but I never collected from my clients. Every credit card was charged to the limit; my savings quickly became depleted; I was in a ship that was broadsided by a roaring tide of hate and I was swiftly being pulled into the darkness. Instead of putting myself, my family, and my business first, I never abandoned ship. I stayed on board with all hands on deck and lost everything I had worked so hard to gain in the process. Taking up for a person in need became stronger than my survival instincts, and looking back, common sense. To me, a person's life was worth more than all of the money in the world and I knew that one day I would be blessed in return, so I sacrificed in order to give. I didn't have any grandiose illusions that I could get Raye out of jail, but to assist her family in gaining support so they would no longer be smothered in the stifling hate was worth the risk.

Gayla told me, "We just need a bright idea."

Although I didn't know much about building Web sites, I could build one well enough to put up some facts about the case and start an online petition. Therefore, I offered to build a Web site and put up a form to collect petition signatures. Gayla was grateful and open to any suggestions, so *Free Kelsey's Mom* was created. The name was something that immediately came to me due to the fact that each correspondence I had seen from Raye was always signed, "Kelsey's mom."

The text on the first edition of the Web site was limited. As a professional, I was reluctant to write anything that could be misunderstood or argued. I knew some facts in the case, but I wasn't confident that documentation could validate all of them. At the time I hadn't seen much in the way of evidence. If my identity were ever revealed, it was my reputation on the line and I didn't want to be put into the position that my character could be attacked because I got something wrong. In turn, the case information on the Web site was restrained and there were only a few pages with the petition and pictures.

The Web site had been uploaded for just a couple of days with no Meta tags or keywords so it was not searchable on the Internet. It also wasn't submitted to any search engines since I was still in the process of building it. The only way someone could have found it at that time was by clicking on a direct link or typing in the exact address. After testing the form for the petition, I forwarded the link to the site to Gayla, who then shared it with family members and friends. Signatures trickled in with loving words of hope and faith, which instilled a reassurance that I was doing something right and good. During a shopping trip with Mom and my daughter the tone of the signatures turned dark as hate flooded my Blackberry's memory. While reading the words I felt stunned at not only the amount of hate directed at Raye and her family, but also over the fact that the people sending me the nasty messages felt justified in doing so. Raye's family was grieving the loss of Kelsey as well as her younger brother, the son of Raye and Mike Porter. The baby boy had been taken by child

471

protective services following yet another campaign from Kathie's group. Compound the loss of the two children with Raye's 27-year conviction—more than four times the amount of time the prosecutor thought she should serve (he offered her a five year plea), and just imagine the amount of pain the family felt. They were hurting. Why did these people feel justified in adding to their heartache?

I had no idea how to handle the situation so I created a post for my blog that included some of the nasty messages along with information that proved they had come from a link on Kelsey's Purpose. Following is an excerpt from that post:

After being posted on Kelsey's Purpose, the administrator was slammed with mean, spiteful, and hateful messages with names like Charles Manson, Bullshit, etc. and messages like,

'This entire case was a horrible tragedy, caused by Raye Dawn and her then husband Mike Porter. May she burn in hell, starting the day before she's due to be released from prison. In my eyes, 27 years isn't nearly enough... perhaps we should petition the court to increase it?'

'This site needs to be shut down, she got what she deserved. There is no way she wasn't abusing or knew about the abuse...I hope someone kills her in prison, but slow and suffer like Kelsey did!'

'they should be serving life in prison!!!!!...i wish when they are in their jail sells someone abuses them just like they abused Kelsey!!'

'I have pictures of Kelsey too. Of course they are of her with two broken legs and bruises on her sweet little face. You also may want to mention to people that Raye Dawn was ALSO charged and sentenced for ENABLING!!!'

'If poor little Raye Dawn is so innocent, she wouldn't be sitting in a cell waiting for the transfer to her new home.'

'My only hope for Raye Dawn is that everyday of her life is spent thinking over and over again about how she allowed that

little girl to suffer and die, whether by her own hand or her own will to let the abuse continue on through Mike Porter.'

'Maybe she can pen-pal with Susan Smith and Darlie Routier. You can delete this immediately, which I'm sure you will. It's obviously hard for you people to face the truth. Let me just say that I will save this message and start my own 'petition' for appeal denial and I guarentee my list is longer then yours!!!'

'i think she is giong to hell 4 what she did!!!'

'OK Hell no I do not support this at all, I can't even believe you have the gaul to have a petition!!!!! Besides the fact , that you have a picture of the murderer!!!!! Sick is all I can say! Oh and this is my Freedom of Speech!!!'

'I dont think the mom deserves anything but but to have her ass beat to helll sorry low life bitch why did you abuse that sweet baby?'

'HAHAHAHA!!!! SHE GOT WHAT SHE DESERVED!!!! HOPE SHE ROTTS IN PRISON!!!!!!!!!!!!!!!'"

A chart of traffic facts was posted that showed all direct links came from Kelsey's Purpose. Following are screen shots from the original report.

This first screen shot shows the date that traffic started on the Web site. I set up the traffic reporting as soon as I purchased the domain. Its original intent was to use for marketing purposes to determine what keywords were driving in traffic. That intent soon changed after the hate-filled messages started arriving.

	A	B	C	D	E	F
1	Report created by Traffic Facts for http://www.freekelseysmom.com on 07-26-07					
2						
3	Summary					
4						
5	Date	Visitors	Unique Visitors	Page Views		
6	Jul 19, 2007	0	0	0		
7	Jul 20, 2007	1	1	2		
8	Jul 21, 2007	3	3	5		
9	Jul 22, 2007	37	18	268		
10	Jul 23, 2007	97	66	423		
11	Jul 24, 2007	20	19	111		
12	Jul 25, 2007	308	230	1,214		
13	Total	466	337	2,023		
14						
15	Copyright © 2003 - 2007. All rights reserved.					
16						
17						

The second screen shot shows where the traffic came from—what links or search engines were used to discover the Web site. As you'll notice, the majority of traffic came directly from Kelsey's Purpose with some also coming from links within e-mails and from search engines.

	A	B	C	D
1	Report created by Traffic Facts for http://www.freekelseysmom.com on 07-26-07			
2				
3	Referring Domains			
4	2007-07-19 00:00:00		2007-07-25 23:59:59	
5				
6	Hostname	Referrals	Percentage	
7	www.kelseyspurpose.org	11	22.45	
8	search.yahoo.com	10	20.41	
9	bulletins.myspace.com	6	12.24	
10	thetruthaboutkelsey.com	4	8.16	
11	blog.myspace.com	3	6.12	
12	kelseyspurpose.org	2	4.08	
13	us.f611.mail.yahoo.com	2	4.08	
14	bored.com	1	2.04	
15	mailcenter3.comcast.net	1	2.04	
16	search.live.com	1	2.04	
17	us.f357.mail.yahoo.com	1	2.04	
18	us.f635.mail.yahoo.com	1	2.04	
19	us.f802.mail.yahoo.com	1	2.04	
20	us.f824.mail.yahoo.com	1	2.04	
21	us.f829.mail.yahoo.com	1	2.04	
22	us.f831.mail.yahoo.com	1	2.04	
23	us.f836.mail.yahoo.com	1	2.04	
24	webmail.aol.com	1	2.04	
25	Total	49	100	

The following screen shot shows that the only "key words" that were typed into a search engine was the actual Web site address.

Therefore, this Web site was not discovered through a search. The Web address was known.

	A	B	C	D	E
1	Report created by Traffic Facts for http://www.freekelseysmom.com on 07-26-07				
2					
3	Keywords				
4	2007-07-19 00:00:00		2007-07-25 23:59:59		
5					
6	Search Engine	Count	Percentage		
7	search.yahoo.com				
8	freekelseysmom.com	8	80.00		
9	www.freekelseysmom.com	2	20.00		
10	Total	10	100		
11					

The next screen shot proves that there were no keyphrases used to discover the Web site.

	A	B	C
1	Report created by Traffic Facts for http://www.freekelseysmom.com on 07-26-07		
2			
3	Keyphrases		
4	2007-07-19 00:00:00	2007-07-25 23:59:59	
5			
6	Search Engine	Count	Percentage
7			
8	Copyright © 2003 - 2007. All rights reserved.		

The final screen shot shows the amount of traffic that the Web site picked up within the first few days, and before it was finished being built or submitted to search engines.

	A	B	C	D	E	F
1	Report created by Traffic Facts for http://www.freekelseysmom.com on 07-26-07					
2						
3	Hits					
4						
5	Date	Hits	Percentage			
6	Jul 19, 2007	0	0.00			
7	Jul 20, 2007	2	0.01			
8	Jul 21, 2007	8	0.05			
9	Jul 22, 2007	1,064	6.51			
10	Jul 23, 2007	2,872	17.57			
11	Jul 24, 2007	847	5.18			
12	Jul 25, 2007	11,551	70.67			
13	Total	16,344	100			
14						
15	Copyright © 2003 - 2007. All rights reserved.					

The first response was from Lance's sister, Shirica.

*I have just read the above comments that were posted on
freeKelseysmom.com... When Kelsey's Purpose was started it
was with the intent to make changes to help other children
not suffer. A lot of the members feel very passionately about
this casue and sometimes get carried away. I have spent a lot
of time trying to keep our members focused on good and not
get caught up in the rest, but they are all individuals...we
have hundreds of guests that visit the site daily. Any one of
them could have happened upon the other site just by
browsing through ours...*

*7/25/2007 7:08 PM Truth Seeker wrote: Good points Shirica.
Hopefully those misguided individuals will recheck their
approach in making a positive change. My prayers go out to
your family for your loss.*

*7/25/2007 7:21 PM Truth Seeker wrote: I do have something else to
add. If you're someone, like me, who has not heard the name
Kelsey and you just happen upon the many sites, blogs,
articles, and videos about this story, your first assumption is
that Raye Dawn killed Kelsey and she was found with a
broken collarbone, broken legs, bruises, abrasions, etc. You
automatically are ready to string her up. I'm not making
excuses for those who sent those hateful messages, but it is
understandable to a point that they would be very angry with
Raye Dawn. The media and the way Kelsey's story has been
told up to this point have done this.*

*7/26/2007 5:20 AM kj wrote: ... It is sick that that anyone would say
these things to any grieving family, and the maternal family
is grieving the loss of 2 people. If people had said those kinds
of things to the Briggs, people would be outraged...*

*7/26/2007 6:21 AM Truth Seeker wrote: I agree! As far as I know,
it's still not searchable. I tried, and couldn't find it. But, I'm
happy to report that I received an email this morning and the
site is almost finished and the last hate mail they received
was at 5:15pm last night. As of an hour ago, the hate mail
had suddenly stopped flooding in. The administrator said
they knew it would be attacked so they put tracking features
in place. Good for them!*

476

Within minutes of posting the information on my blog that included tracking information for the petition signatures, the flood of hateful messages came to a sudden, screeching halt.

Shirica's formerly apologetic and empathetic tone suddenly changed with the next post. Reading it now, it's as if someone else were posting using her name. This would come as no surprise to me, knowing what I do now. Shirica wrote:

...Are you suggesting that Kelsey's Purpose members have ESP and have personal insight into the goings on of the Smith family. If that were the case then I guess we would all know who exactly committed what crimes, now wouldn't we?

7/27/2007 6:26 AM [Eloise] wrote: ...Those comments were very understandable. Convicted felons arent going to be COMMENDED by society for their crimes.

7/27/2007 8:00 AM KJ wrote: You don't have to commend them and no one asked you to, but you don't have to spread your hatred to a family in mourning either...If for some reason you just can't control your hatred and anger and you just HAVE to say something to someone, then send it to Raye Dawn, she's the one you're angry at. Stop torturing the families.

7/27/2007 6:39 AM [Eloise] wrote: One more thing, What is so wrong about posting the mug shots of the accused? If they weren't convicted felons, there wouldn't be a mug shot! The site is about Kelsey's abuse and murder. In my opinion, one would expect to see the mug shots of the perpetrators. I don't understand the way you view things in Oklahoma. It seems backwards or twisted.

7/27/2007 6:52 AM Truth Seeker wrote: I think people in Oklahoma, for the most part, are good people and we don't feed on someone else's pain. At least, that's what I used to think. I thought that site was dedicated to the memory of a little girl and to preventing child abuse and spreading love and peace for children. What part of saying those nasty things that I saw is positive or constructive? That, to me, would just drive away the very people you're trying to attract. Do you want an organization full of good people trying to make a difference

or an organization of back biting angry people who are
grinding their axes in your forums? That's what's wrong.
7/27/2007 8:21 AM Calling U out wrote: It's funny to me how you
keep saying that you are praying for the Kelsey's Purpose
members who sent nasty messages to Raye Dawn's grieving
family. Maybe you should have a special place in those
prayers for yourself...
7/27/2007 10:34 AM Calling U Out wrote: The juror or maybe 2
jurors who wanted to give her a year still thought she was
GUILTY...

The text on Raye Dawn's Web site has changed and expanded through the years. In the beginning, it was only a paragraph or two of the known facts. I was careful not to misstate anything and, as I recall, it took months before I would use the word "innocent" in anything I wrote or created on Raye Dawn's behalf. She was Kelsey's mother and she did have some culpability, but in my opinion, it was no more than that of dozens of other people in Kelsey's life. To me, if one were to go to trial on charges of "should have known," then they all needed to go. Every single person who had contact with Kelsey during the months in question during which abuse was alleged and just before her death needed to face the same charges and be treated equally. In my opinion, "should have known" is a state of mind. How can someone justify one person "should have known" when so many others were involved in Kelsey's life? This was something I argued repeatedly with those who only wanted to yell "string her up" without laying any blame on the paternal family, who in my opinion had abandoned Kelsey but chose to shout "foul" now that it's no longer about helping or saving Kelsey.

In August, 2007 the Web site had just been completed when its existence was announced on the news. An evening broadcast on our local CBS station relayed the following:

[Anchor] "Raye Dawn's friends and family are raising money for her legal fees." [Co-anchor] "They sat up a Web site and sent fundraising packets in the mail…"

[Reporter] "A woman called me after receiving these papers in the mail from Raye Dawn's family and friends asking for money. That woman's not the only one bothered by this."

A clip of Raye Dawn being placed into the sheriff's vehicle after her trial flashed across the screen with Raye Dawn crying, "I don't understand. I love my baby!"

[Reporter]: "One month after this moment when a jury found Raye Dawn guilty of enabling child abuse."

[Kathie Briggs] "I think desperate people do desperate things."

[Reporter]: "Raye Dawn's family and friends fight to pay for her appeal."

[Kathie Briggs]: "Had they fought this hard for a small child as they are for this adult who has been convicted of this crime, then we might not be here today."

[Reporter]: "Kathie Briggs, Kelsey's paternal grandmother, couldn't believe all of this. There is a Web site called, 'Free Kelsey's Mom' and letters going out to the community, both asking for donations to raise $25,000 to process Raye Dawn's appeal."

[Kathie Briggs]: "I would imagine that their legal fees are pretty expensive but I just don't understand why they would want the public to pay."

[Reporter]: "The letter signed by Raye Dawn's family and friends says she was dragged relentlessly through the legal system and media; that she will be exonerated because she is innocent, and that your donation will help right this terrific wrong in an attempt to provide a fair trial for Raye Dawn."

[Kathie Briggs]: "I understand that they want to support their family member, but they really need to acknowledge what Kelsey went through."

[Reporter]: "Our legal analyst…said this strategy is not entirely new."

[Legal Analyst]: "It's not unusual to see people find a way to raise money for a defense fund, but this organized of a manner, I've not seen it."

The Web site home page was shown.

[Reporter]: "According to the Web site, they have $4,000 so far. The battle won't end here."

[Kathie Briggs]: "And we know Kelsey fought and fought just to stay alive and now that she's not here, it's up to us to fight to make sure justice takes place."

[Reporter]: "I just talked to Sherri Heath who signed this very letter. She told me Raye Dawn did not get a fair trial. She said since the family has no more money for legal fees, they're reaching out to the community for support. The family does not want publicity and does not want to talk on camera."

[Anchor]: "Raye Dawn's lawyer…says he is not involved in the fund raising effort. He expects to file the appeal by the October 11th deadline."

I remember watching the report with a mixture of feelings including excitement that Raye Dawn's family's efforts in support of her defense were being shared, and angst over the fact that Raye Dawn's side of the story could never be told without Kathie Briggs

480

butting in with her opinion. It seemed to me that Oklahoma had forgotten the fact that Kelsey had two families who were suffering and grieving her loss. I questioned why the media didn't want to hear from the other grandma, the one who had shared in raising Kelsey.

With a feeling of hope that the public had watched, listened, and opened their hearts and minds to the other side of the story, I continued to work on behalf of Raye Dawn and Kelsey to ensure that her mom would no longer be crucified. I never imagined that the hate that had been building and brewing for years would soon turn on me. In 2007, I believed in the Constitution and my right as a citizen of the United States of America to have an opinion. I believed I should be able to voice my opinion without fear of retaliation or threats against me. However, since my opinion did not include hate or a public flogging for Raye Dawn, the rights I thought I had were soon turned against me with an underhanded and illegal plan from the opposition to silence me forever.

The Forum

August, 2007

Once our group moved to a forum, emotions were running high. People were outraged by the content of Kathie Briggs's Web site and bashboards. On many occasions they had tried to voice their opinions and state the facts, but found themselves censored and silenced. Things had been left unsaid and they were grateful for an open forum that was not controlled by Kathie Briggs's gang of cyber bullies. Therefore, for the first few weeks, nobody was censored. Our conversations were a continuous flow with hundreds of posts within days. Although at times things got out of hand when someone wanted to vent or the "others" came looking to start a fight, we were, at the core, a spiritual, open-minded group of individuals. We all had a different idea of what happened to Kelsey, but for the most part, respect was shown for a difference in opinion. Over one hundred active members participated, with only about one-fourth of those there for the wrong reasons. I was alone at the helm and I had no clue what I was doing. I made it clear in the beginning that I was new to forums and some participants understood and were, in turn, kind and helpful. Threats didn't come from any of us who were there to discuss the case or vent. The only threats were from the other side. However, Kathie Briggs and Lance were called to the carpet on their lies. On several occasions, they were boldly called "liars"—a term that seemed too "in-your-face" for me at the time, but it was a claim that I had also found to be true.

After moving to the forum, I reluctantly became acquainted with the cast of characters that had been posting on my blog. Some became confidants who, today, I consider my closest friends. Looking back, it's comical how hard I fought it in the beginning. I was lured into chat rooms, something I tried to avoid at all costs. I really didn't have time to socialize because my world was falling apart around me. I didn't want to like anyone, let alone trust them or let them into my world. I was the character that they all knew as Truth Seeker—the woman with several children who worked hard at being aloof, tough, and all of those things that in real life, I was not. I shared life experiences that were not my own in developing the character. I didn't want to remove the curtain or allow those who supported Raye Dawn and had come to know and like me to realize that I was a person who was in the midst of one of the most difficult times in her life. I was ashamed that I was failing miserably. I thought if they saw the real me—flesh, blood, and tears wrapped in a body that often betrayed me, they would no longer support Raye Dawn. I couldn't have been more wrong. I soon learned that some were also hurting and their lives consisted of different challenges from mine. They were searching for someone to throw them a life preserver and they found me--desperate, drowning, disappointing me. They didn't care that I wasn't the seven-foot-tall and tough-as-nails character I wanted everyone to see. The first time we met face-to-face, they expressed their relief that I was struggling, just like them.

Their image of me probably came from the avatars I had selected for intimidation. Unlike Kathie Briggs and her group who continually use pictures of Kelsey to be the face of their negativity, I chose a female warrior and then Keanu Reeves from the movie, *The Matrix* with his dark sunglasses and penetrating look. Kathie Briggs's supporters were hounding me with threats of lawsuits and constant harassment. I couldn't be the Girl Scout leader, Meals on Wheels driver, St. Vincent de Paul volunteer, homeschooling mom, former Mary Kay sales director that was the real me. I had to be someone who would be perceived as the type who wouldn't give in to the constant threats, someone who had been through hell and survived to tell about it. My intent wasn't for them to fear me; my character wasn't threatening. I just wanted them to know they had a true match in me. I wanted them to see me as someone who could not be threatened, someone who would not back down, regardless of how nasty their threats became, and they were constant and they were terrifying. The

483

flood of hate mail had shaken me to my core, and I could only imagine what life had been like for Raye Dawn's family for the two years before I became involved. It was overwhelming for me and I was an outsider. My heart broke even more for Raye Dawn's family as the gravity of the situation started to set in and I realized what I was getting myself into by dueling with Kathie Briggs's supporters.

In essence, I had stolen a move from Kathie Briggs's playbook and I created a fictional character to play David to her Goliath. As David, I stood tall on my single area of the Web against Goliath, Kathie Briggs and her supporters, ranking into the thousands, with hundreds of Web sites and videos spreading their message of hate for Raye Dawn. I stood with my slingshot and pelted small snippets of truth at their massive army of haters who shamelessly used Kelsey as their shield. I was in a no-win situation. They had a dead child and a "war hero" they treated as mascots. I had a mom who loved her child but was blind to what was happening in her own home. Due to what some see as her blind trust in her husband, her child was allegedly raped and murdered. There was no winning that battle. All I had on my side was the truth and my integrity, and on that issue, I would not bend.

In the following post, Kathie Briggs shares her opinion about our forum as well as Raye and her family. The highlighting was done by her in her original post.

kjbriggs
 Kelsey's Grandma
 Posts: 1,139
 Group: Super Moderators
 Joined: Nov 2005
 Status: **Offline**
 Reputation:
Post: #11
RE: That "Other" site
*I received a message from **Sherri Heath** recently asking me why this*
 site only tells one side of Kelsey's story. Have you noticed

*two sides on the Smith site? In my opinion there is only one side and it is Kelsey's side. All we can do here is comment on the facts as we know them and yes, they are all facts. **Raye Dawn** is just plain **backwards** if she as a mother could not see her child was in trouble. She blames any and everything for Kelsey's death. First it was our fault, then it was unexplainable accidents while in her care that she did explain, then a car accident, and the latest is a ride at an amusement park. They lash out at everyone, but the man that discovered Kelsey's lifeless body and the only other adult in the home. Why? Is it because they know something? Do they feel **Raye killed Kelsey** and they cannot point the finger at Porter? Geez...it makes so much more sense to blame the Briggs family. **Raye Dawn** will be **sentenced** next Monday. I hope she gets the full **27 years**. I might have a bit of sympathy for her if she took ANY **responsibility** for her actions. I might have a bit of sympathy if her family had not gone on such a bashing trip. **Raye's** family saw Kelsey before her death and did **NOTHING**. Now they want everyone to blame us. They should all be living with such **guilt**. I have **guilt** for not doing more and I wasn't present the last few weeks. **Sherri Heath** claims she saw Kelsey on a regular basis. Then why on earth did you let this baby die? You have all seen the pictures, they saw her in person and **did NOTHING**. As far as I am concerned they were **accomplices**. They should all be facing failure to report if they really saw her that often. **Gayla Smith** should be ashamed of letting her granddaughter **die**. She had first hand knowledge something was going on and she **did NOTHING**. "Watchin" someone commit a **crime** against a child and failing to report it is also a crime. I have heard on the "other" site they say it was only a game. What kind of game is it when you tape they eyes of a child? How many more children are in danger in that family if this is the games they play? Then you report a tear on Kelsey's eye as shampoo irritation? That was intentional **cover up**. Raye may not be the smartest kid on the block, but she was smart enough to **cover up** the truth time and time again. I have stated before if even HALF of what they were saying about me were true I would hide my head in shame. I certainly would not be living in this bubble. I would not put myself in*

485

*the public's eye to be questioned and judged. I have made many mistakes in my life. My family has made mistakes. None of those mistakes are connected with Kelsey's abuse or death. Can the Smith family say the same? **GUILTY**...that was the decision of twelve people. They heard the evidence and they came to the conclusion that **Raye Dawn Smith** should sit in **prison** for **27 years**. **Raye Dawn's** daughter is **dead** and she did **NOTHING** to stop it. Playing **DUMB** is not an excuse. It didn't work for Raye Dawn and it won't work for her family. In my opinion **Raye Dawn** may have gotten away with **murder**. That is the only explanation I know for her actions since Kelsey's death. These people are **grasping** at anything they can to make it appear this is our fault. Raye Dawn said if you tell someone something often enough they will repeat it. She stated this in court referring to Kelsey. Yet, it can apply to her family as well. Did she tell them this stuff so often they really do believe it? Or are they saying it so often they think the public will believe it? I have to hope the public has more common sense than they do. Once again, I am going against the purpose of this forum. Eventually at some point I will delete this thread. Our family has been slandered and bashed for two years. There comes a time you have to speak your mind. I hope you all understand our needed reasons to express our opinions. This post was last modified: Yesterday 01:36 PM by **kjbriggs***

Kathie further stated:

Michael Porter has not been convicted of murder. We will never know if Kelsey died at the hands of Raye Dawn or Mike.

And:

Mike Porter was originally charged with her murder and plead to enabling child abuse. We cannot call him a murderer or a sexual predator because he was not convicted of that crime.

Did she not just call Raye a murderer? Raye was never charged with murder, but Mike Porter was. Why call Raye a murderer and not Porter? In the following two posts, Kathie Briggs complained about Raye's family seeking donations to help the cost of her defense:

Post: #2
RE: That "Other" site
Thank you. We have chosen not to let the negative remarks get to us.
If you believe in what you are doing you can't be stopped by
another group. Kelsey only has ONE story and it stays
consistent on this site. My position is anyone wanting to make
a difference has come to the right place. Anyone that believes
ignoring the obvious and allowing abuse to occur before
your eyes should look else where. If you choose to donate
your money to Kelsey's mother it is your right to do so. I
personally would be embarassed to ask the public for their
money before I exhausted all my own resourses. That
includes jewelry and other items not needed to survive. I am
sure this is a sad position to be in and I cannot put myself in
their shoes. Raye Dawn has the right to file an appeal and if
asking others to pay for her mistake is the answer then to
each his own. I stand behind what we tried to do for Kelsey. I
feel comfortable going to my judgement day with my actions.
Those doing the devil's work are only fueled when we reply to
their false allegations. I made the decision to move forward
and put this is God's hands. I have met the kindest most
generous people through Kelseyspurpose. That could not
have happend if we had done all things wrong. So again,
thank you. This post was last modified: 08-30-2007 03:56
PM by **kjbriggs**

Post: #4
RE: That "Other" site
Raye's mother and grandmother are widows. They are widows with
"men" friends that has been reported by Gayla to have
"money". So why ask the public to help? They could sell one
of their many homes and live together. Their family could sell
the empty home of the great grandmother. Instead let's ask
the public to donate. Does Gayla work? Why not? She could
get two jobs. Mildred still works at age 75. Seriously, I
almost feel sorry for them. Raye Dawn has put them in
financial woes, ruined many lives, and put herself in prison. I
know this is not the future they had planned. Mildred has
allowed Raye Dawn's actions to keep her from knowing her
other great grandchildren all because they are my

*grandchildren. My granddaughter still asks about her each
time we pass her house. We dare not say anything ugly about
her as it is not the children's fault.*

*Personally I dont' care if the public donates the entire
$25,000 plus some. We expected an appeal, it is part of the
process. Just another hurdle for our family to jump in seeking
justice for a child that had no appeal. I have heard many a
person in this town state, if Ray Smith or Elvis Fowler were
still alive this would not have happened. These were great
men and I believe as most they would have cared about
Kelsey. This post was last modified: 09-03-2007 12:56 PM by*
kjbriggs.

kjbriggsKelsey's Grandma Posts: 1,138Group: Super ModeratorsJoined: Nov
2005Status: Offline Reputation: Post: #1Rumor or Not A Smith family member has
reported to us that Gayla Smith has sold her land. She reportedly received
$100,000. This should take care of the financial problems they have. It should also
put an end to the donation site that has so many concerned.

09-11-2007 05:06 AM

She referred to Free Kelsey's Mom as a "donation site." Why were
they so "concerned"? They call me a liar because I created a character
and I hid my identity. Imagine the hell I would have been put through
from the beginning if I had been myself all along. I can't say if I would
have backed down from them or not because I didn't do or say
anything that I'm ashamed of or that I wouldn't have done had I used
my name from the beginning. Does hiding my identity from a group
of people who did nothing but maim and destroy anyone in their path
make me a bad person? Even then, I realized that my identity would
eventually be discovered, so my integrity was on the line. So, I made
sure that every piece of the case I presented was the truth, but like
every other human being, at times, I was proven wrong. I admitted to
being wrong and rectified what I found to be untrue.

Some who came to the forum to destroy me, along with my
mission, quickly opened their hearts long enough to listen to what I

had to say and to them, it made sense. Many had questioned various parts of Kathie Briggs's story and they had seen her lack of integrity as her story changed with each lie in which she was caught. The difference in us was clear. She had been there and lived it. I never met Kelsey. I was piecing together the facts as I discovered them. Kathie Briggs had been a part of the madness that engulfed Kelsey's life. When pieces of Kathie Briggs's story didn't fit into the puzzle, they were changed until a piece was found that would fit. In the end, it was my integrity that won the support of those who had previously believed Kathie Briggs, or possibly it was the fact that I wouldn't back down and give in to the threats and hate that were thrown at me on a daily basis. Maybe they just wanted to support Kelsey's story and found a group of people who were open-minded and wanted to know the truth just as badly as they did, and their support had nothing to do with me. I'm not sure why the forum grew as quickly as it did, but I was thankful that it was no longer "David vs. Goliath," or myself against thousands. It soon became "us vs. them." Our numbers weren't as great because we refused to use Kelsey as a mascot or to feed into the constant negativity on which they thrived, but we soon took control of the forum and banned anyone who was negative, became threatening, or seemed unstable. We became a real force to be reckoned with; we were "Truth Seekers," who only wanted to dissolve the hate that had been started by Kathie Briggs and her supporters. Each day was a myriad of trials followed by never-ending drama. One never knew what to expect. At times, emotions and words were heated. It was like an uprising of the downtrodden. For two years, Kathie Briggs and her gang of goons had ruled the Internet, but there was a new sheriff in town and we collective few were no longer going to sit by and watch people be destroyed by the hate. It was time for it all to stop.

In an effort to see what the consensus was on our forum, I presented the following poll:

Post Info   TOPIC: Let's have a show of hands

May We Have Your Opinions Please? [13 vote(s)]

How many of you think Raye Dawn killed Kelsey?   0.0%

How many of you think Raye Dawn allowed Mike
Porter to abuse Kelsey?   7.7%

How many of you think Mike Porter killed
Kelsey?   92.3%

How many of you think Mike Porter allowed Raye
Dawn to abuse Kelsey?   0.0%

The general opinion from our forum members was worlds away from the poll taken on Kathie Briggs's Web site, and though we didn't agree on every aspect of the case, we were able to carry on peaceful conversations, even with some who came to the forum as Kathie Briggs supporters.

It soon became clear that not everyone involved in Kathie Briggs's group was involved in the hate. Some were just trying to make a difference and they thought they found like-minded people. They were wrong. I've often joked that the only way out of Kathie Briggs's support group is "in a box." This analogy came from one of my all-time favorite movies, *Malibu's Most Wanted*. The character, Brad, or B-rad as I like to call him, found himself a member of a street gang in which the only way out of the gang was "in a box." From the start of the forum to this day, each person who, at one time supported Kathie Briggs and then realized s/he was misled is attacked and inundated with hate mail when the "others" discover s/he is communicating with me. One of my arguments against Kathie Briggs and her supporters' behavior with these types of antics is the fact that they claim to fight child abuse, yet they've abused numerous adults who are parents, causing job loss, depression, and worse. How can a group that promotes itself as being concerned with the community act in an obviously abusive manner?

Kathie Briggs posted the following statement on her Web site when our forum was just getting started. This was one of the last public examples we would see of Kathie Briggs's unleashed hate for someone whom she thought "needed to pay."

We have not forgotten about Craig Key. He is still on our radar. He stated he would give up anything to have saved Kelsey? He is the one that sent her to her death. His words are meaningless, too little and too late. He has a bit of the Raye Dawn syndrome. Blame the ones that tried to save Kelsey. I am so glad I don't have to live with guilt. The thing is they don't either because they don't know how to take responsibility. He makes me absolutely sick. You send someone to die and profit from it. No matter how he spins it he is a joke. By the way, instead of buying the book you should just check it out at the library. I still have not read it. Does he still have a picture of himself in a robe? Someone needs to tell him he no longer holds that position. The title of his website shows he isn't living in reality. Hellooo Craig Key, you are not a Judge. However: you will meet the ultimate Judge and then you can tell your story only this time it won't be bought.

I remember reading her comments that were clearly harassment and lacked any type of remorse on her part, even though she made several mistakes that could have possibly saved Kelsey, had she not been so self-absorbed with concern over what people thought of her instead of the safety of her grandchild. It was then I realized she was an empty shell of a woman. I tried to feel pity for her and eliminate her participation in her granddaughter's death and Raye Dawn's wrongful conviction from our forum, and then she would make another sickening comment about someone else, never taking any responsibility herself. It was maddening to watch unfold. I'll never forget our discussion about the child pornography that was found on Mike Porter's computer and how she admitted to knowing about it, but still blamed Raye Dawn for Kelsey's alleged sexual assault and murder. She stated that Mike Porter's computer contained "disgusting filth" so she knew what was on it, yet her strongest supporters argue that it wasn't child porn because some of the Web sites in question contain the word "teen." During our heated debate of the sexual assault that Kelsey had reportedly endured, Kathie Briggs posted the following statement on her forum:

The second autopsy did show signs of sexual abuse, but no DNA was found. That doesn't say that Raye Dawn wasn't using an object and hurting Kelsey herself.

| kjbriggs
Kelsey's Grandma
🔲🔲🔲🔲🔲

Posts: 1,138
Group: Super Moderators
Joined: Nov 2005
Status:
🔲 | RE: Lance's Interview on Fox   Post: #93

Once again, Larissa this question has been answered. Mothers do use objects and have been convicted on sexual abuse. I would suggest you do some research on the subject and that will answer further questions.

Kelsey is not a character on a TV show. She is my granddaughter. She was a precious little girl that wanted to be loved like all children do. Please respect her memory and stop asking questions that continue to show you lack of compassion. If you will notice this thread is titled, Lance's Interview on Fox. Your question has nothing to do with that interview.

This post was last modified: 09-08-2007 01:29 PM
by kjbriggs. |

09-08-2007 01:28 PM

Every new piece of evidence we discovered was twisted into something that Raye Dawn could have possibly committed. The amount of hate and blame that Kathie Briggs and her followers spewed at Raye Dawn was sickening and nothing short of abuse.

Another example of an abuser, Lance (and his "war hero" status), was also a popular topic of discussion. On August 1, 2007, I posted the police report in which he cussed out a female officer. I followed the police report with this comment: "Some war hero!!!!!"

A Kathie Briggs supporter responded with the following comment:

I have a question, this accident you put up happend August 2, 2002 right? If so what does that have to do with Kelsey? I mean Kelsey wasn't even born yet when this happend. What I'm saying is what ever happend before Kelsey was born IT DOESN'T MATTER. Oh I can go to ODOC and bring up some stuff about Raye Dawn even before Kelsey was born if you are going to do this.

8/1/2007 8:24 AM Truth Seeker wrote: How can the fact that a man who is supposed to be serving in the military and be some kind of "war hero" cuss out a female police officer and call her names in front of his mom and two children not matter? We're not dragging up pasts here. I'm simply pointing out the true character of someone who has been treated as some kind of prince of the media instead of what he really is.

8/2/2007 11:24 AM unspokentruth wrote: There are several things that bothered me about this page...obviously he has a temper issue and no respect for the law or authority. I wonder if he also has issues with women in general. But what really got me was that if I am reading this correct, his whole family, so to speak, shows up at a fender bender to what?, support him? control him? I don't get it...I've heard of family support, but goodness!

8/2/2007 11:34 AM Truth Seeker wrote: Exactly! It doesn't really say who was with him in the van that I saw. But if they were there for support, why would they not be sure if they could control him, and why would he use that language in front of his mom, sister, and two small children? I've read a lot of his other police reports, but this one bothered me the most because of his disregard for authority and his disregard for his family. Not to mention the fact that he had been drinking. That explains the beligerant behavior to the officer.

In another report, Lance threatened a police officer and his family while being transported to jail. At the time of the forum, I had seen the reports and I viewed Lance as a violent man who had gotten away with being abusive to women. Therefore, I was disturbed that women were being duped into believing he was something he was not. It really became an issue of public safety to me since I advocate against domestic violence. For bringing awareness to his true character through documentation, I am called a "bully." It seems like anyone with a different opinion is a bully in Kathie Briggs's book, yet she can't recognize those traits in herself. Why?

An interesting post was by "Unspokentruth." She questioned some of the stories told by the Briggs as follows:

1 , 2, 3 Stories About the Same Thing. Which is True?
You know, I was reading Kathie's Testimony and remembered that
I had heard several versions of "the story" and thought I'd
do some research and see what I could find and why I
thought it was different. As it turns out, there are clearly 3
versions to this story and ALL by the Briggs family. I find
this odd, one would think it would be VERY CLEAR in the
memory of a grandparent and aunt as to how they learned
their grandchild died.....What do you guys think?
Kathie Briggs Testimony;
Smothermon: How did you find out she died?
Kathie Briggs: A friend from the beauty shop called and told me
Kelsey was at the hospital and may have had a seizure. So I
called the CASA worker and she told me that she believed
Kelsey had had a seizure. Then she called back and told me
Kelsey didnt make it.
Shirica's Version of how they found out Kelsey died; (post on KP)
ShiricaSuper Moderator Posts: 174Group: Super
ModeratorsJoined: Nov 2005Status: Away Reputation:
Post: #2RE: I'm CONFUSED First of all, Lance was in Ft. Benning,
Georgia on the day that Kelsey died.That fact has never
been disputed. Lance had been in Iraq and was sent to
Georgia to do his out process that they make soldiers
complete before returning home from war. He was set to
come home very soon and had been in Georgia for a couple
of weeks. We were very grateful that he was in Georgia on

the day Kelsey died because it allowed us to get him home by that night. If he had been in Iraq it would have taken a lot longer. On October 11th my mom, Kathie, received a call from a friend that Kelsey had been taken to the hospital by ambulance. Kathie contacted the CASA worker and asked her to find out what was going on. The worker assured mom that she would call her back after she knew. DHS and CASA was at the hospital and so was Raye's family. I happened to have a friend that worked in the area and she was willing to go and see what was going on. I received a phone call while at work that Kelsey was dead from my friend. NOT a family member, not DHS, Not CASA, no one. I then called my mom and had to tell her over the phone while she was home alone that Kelsey was dead. I called both of my sisters and told them to get to mom as fast as they could. It took me twenty minutes to get to her home from work. When I pulled in her driveway Lance was calling mom from a payphone in Georgia and was then told of the death of his daughter.

Kathie's Version of how she found out about Kelseys death: (NOTE: this speach was given approx 8 weeks after Kelsey died) (posted on KP was the copy of the speach, here is the portion of how she learned of Kelsey's death) Speach given by Kathie Briggs at the Justice For Children Rally at the State Capital in Oklahoma City,Okla.On October 11th, I received a call from a friend that Kelsey had been taken to the hospital. I contacted the CASA worker and asked her to check on the situation. I called her again and she told me Kelsey had a seizure and she would call me back. She never did.We heard from a friend at the hospital that Kelsey had died. My son called thirty minutes later from Ft. Benning, Georgia, and I had to give him the news that would change his life forever. Our family was never contacted by DHS. They did not make any effort to call the Red Cross to notify my son that his only child was gone. We made the calls necessary and got Lance home that night. A few days later we got the news; Kelsey's death was listed as a homicide.

Her post was signed, *"This is my OPINION and this is also America. American's have a right to 'Freedom of Speech'. If you have a problem with what I have to say, don't read it."*

Kathie Briggs and her supporters have referred to our forum as a "bashboard" and they have called us "trolls," "a hate group," and other colorful names. However, nobody on the forum made any threats or personally attacked anyone such as they had done on Kathie Briggs's Web site and bashboards. Unlike what I've seen from the mean-spirited group on the other side, Raye Dawn's cause seems to attract people who are kind-hearted and compassionate individuals. There were very few on the forum that I would consider mean. On Wednesdays, some of us prayed and fasted for Raye Dawn's swift release. We also participated in a motivational thread in an effort to keep focused and positive, which was targeted by a certain key member of Kathie Briggs's group…Debbie. She continuously started arguments in that specific thread. We discussed issues such as abortion and community service. Because we weren't the people that Kathie Briggs and her followers made us out to be, I believe people who came to destroy us instead grew to understand us and joined our mission to raise awareness to Raye Dawn's wrongful conviction. It was evident we weren't there to spread hate. The only interactions some members had with Kathie Briggs's group was termed "truth bombing," in which they would post on her Web site facts about the case and questions that everyone wanted to ask Kathie Briggs. Her members continuously harassed our people and inundated us with hate, so, in some member's minds turn-about was fair play. This was something in which I never participated because I didn't want to join Kathie Briggs's Web site or be accused of being mean. However, on several occasions, someone posted as "Truth Seeker" or something similar on her Web site and it was always a nasty post that was displayed as a badge proving my bad behavior. This would be the beginning of the ongoing impersonation of me in an effort to destroy my character.

496

At times, people got carried away, myself included. When one particularly annoying person who only wanted to cause problems posted personal information about herself on another public forum, some people did say inappropriate things about her. I believe my comment was: "Nobody would touch her with a ten-foot pole." It wasn't my proudest moment, but after months of being bombarded with hate mail and threats, I found myself a part of the negativity. Looking back, I don't know how I made it as long as I did without succumbing to the hate. It was a tough road to travel and, at times, I lost my temper, but I personally never ripped anyone apart or made threats, other than occasionally throwing their lawsuit threat back at them. Once, I even dared Kathie Briggs to file a lawsuit against me. I was tired of the threats and it was time for her to put up or shut up. I was never served.

Not a day went by when there wasn't new drama. For months, I was threatened day-after-day and called names, or someone found something new and horrible that had been done to Raye Dawn or one of her family members. I was living in a nightmare that I couldn't escape. By October of 2007, I had lost everything. I was unfocused. I couldn't write anything worthwhile and I had taken steroids for months, due to my bronchitis and then pneumonia. My life fell apart and all I had left, other than my wonderful family, were the friendships I'd made on the forum and members of Raye Dawn's family whom I felt were depending on me.

It wasn't long before my family learned what I had done. I was a failure, but I had a new purpose and I wanted to finish what I had started. I remember my husband begging me to let it go and let someone else help Raye Dawn. I was failing at everything else in my life, so I told him, "Just a few more months and then I'll quit." I'm not sure what I thought would happen. It's now been five years and I've lost even more as Kathie Briggs and her group have plotted to carry out their threats to destroy me. As time has passed, they've evolved. They still hide behind anonymous names to spread their hate, but now they've crossed the line by breaking laws and invading my privacy…something they claim to which I have no right anymore.

Man in the Hole

September, 2007

Shortly following Raye Dawn's trial and arrest, I made the two-hour trip to visit her in jail. Members of her family held jobs that didn't allow them to take time off during the week, so I thought a friendly face might cheer up Raye Dawn on days her family was unable to visit. Also, doing something productive, such as working on her book, would keep her mind busy.

I'll never forget that first visit. The county jail was in a small building that didn't have an intimidating appearance from the outside. I parked in the mostly empty parking lot and approached the doors with only my driver's license and keys, as well as a pen and pad to take notes. The foyer reminded me of a doctor's office. It was sterile, cold, and uninviting. The most remarkable difference was the bulletproof glass that surrounded the reception area and the bank-like slot that was only large enough to slide my identification through.

Every head in the room reacted as I was forced to yell the name of the person I was there to see through the small speaker box. "Raye Dawn!" I shouted and then quickly turned to see all eyes in the room on me. I wasn't the typical visitor. I was there to see a prisoner who was widely known in our state. I had a pen and a pad for notes. I had no children with me, and my appearance was maintained and clean. I'm not sure what the other people in the room thought of me. I felt as if I stood out from the crowd, but while I waited for the sheriff to bring Raye Dawn to the visiting room, I was entertained.

One woman in particular placed herself on the coffee table in front of me. I tried not to wince at her dirty, bare feet, cut-off shorts, and matted hair. "Is your man in the hole?" she asked me in a serious tone.

"What?" I replied, trying not to be rude.

499

"My man's in the hole." she proudly proclaimed.

"What's the hole?" I asked, curious about the new lingo I was learning. *Perhaps I could use it in a client's book*, I thought.

"He keeps gettin' in fights. He'll never get out." she informed me. "It's where they put the prisoners that don't follow the rules."

After a few moments of silence, she continued, "I've never been in the hole."

"Oh!" was all I could think to say.

She then explained why her feet were so dirty. Apparently, she had to be dropped off in the street by her friend who had given her a ride. She went on to explain that her friend had recently been released from jail, and for a certain number of days, the friend couldn't be on jail property. She furthered her story with the fact that she, however, had been out of jail for a long enough period of time that she was allowed to come onto the jail property and visit her boyfriend.

I'm not sure if she thought of me as rude, but I didn't know what to say or how to respond. This was a world unlike my own, and I was fascinated, but at the same time, repulsed. I smiled in response to her commentary and fielded her questions about the identity of the person I was there to visit. I called Raye Dawn "a friend" and left it at that.

Relief washed over me as my name was called and I was led into a tiny room with barely enough space for a chair, a small table built into the wall, and a phone. The door was locked behind me. On the other side of the glass partition, Raye Dawn looked tiny and helpless as she pointed to the orange receiver and raised her cuffed hands to pick up her end. My heart immediately went out to her and I grasped the germ-filled receiver and held it to my ear and mouth without thinking of the people who had touched it before me. My only concern was for the person sitting in front of me with tears streaming down her cheeks and pain visible in her eyes.

Before arriving at the jail, I had prepared myself not to cry. I didn't want to upset her more than she already was, and so I told myself over and over on the trip there that no matter what happened, I would not cry. Though tears streamed down her cheeks from the moment I sat down until the time I left, I remained calm and tried to cheer her up with stories of the forum and the characters that had become a part of her online support group. She enjoyed learning about the people who didn't know her and had never met her who were spending their time sharing the truth about what had happened to her daughter. She seemed to be grateful for the efforts of everyone involved. The conversation went well and I held it together until she told me about what the hate and the constant harassment had done to her. She stated that "if it wasn't for" her son, "things would be different." I knew what she was referring to and all of my Girl Scout leader training didn't prepare me for that moment. I was shocked and saddened that Kathie Briggs, Lance, and their group had driven her to that point, but I was disgusted when I thought of the pleasure that those same bullies would get if she had gone through with it.

I lost my internal battle and my eyes filled with tears as I asked for clarification. *Did she say what I thought she'd said?* She did. She told me, "I have nothing left. My baby is gone. She was my life. I lived for her. She was my best friend. How could he hurt her?! I don't understand how he could hurt Kelsey! She was perfect." She repeated, "She was perfect."

I hung my head in agreement with her disbelief. How do you understand what a monster like that is thinking? I didn't know how to explain it or what to say to alleviate her pain. I've always been more like a bull in a China shop when it comes to "touchy-feely" situations and I stick my foot in my mouth more times than not. I blurt out what's on my mind without thinking about the repercussions because I've always been taught that honesty is the best policy. For these reasons, I avoid funerals and anything to do with grieving, whenever possible. I don't want to be the one who causes more pain by saying something inappropriate. On that day, I was the only person on the other side of the glass and Raye Dawn was crying out for help and I felt terrible that she was stuck with me. *Why me, God?* I asked, trying to figure out why God would place someone like me in a situation like that. I was out of my element and I didn't know what to do.

Today, I can't recall everything I said and I'm not sure if I helped her or if I opened the wound even deeper. I wish I could remember. I just know that I cried with her and tried my best to be a shoulder for her (figuratively speaking, of course), if nothing else. The visit didn't last long. When it came time to leave, I was reluctant, but relieved. My only concern was to not cause her more grief. Her burden was already too much for her tiny body to handle.

I returned home and to the forum filled with both compassionate people and troublemakers and I didn't say a word about my visit. It was emotionally draining for me to realize that she was on the brink of suicide due to the hate she had endured, the same hate with which I had been dealing day and night, with no end in sight. I wrestled with what she had told me and wondered if I should pass on the information to her family or keep it to myself. In the end, I decided her family needed to know. If she was crying out for help and something happened to her after she confided in me, I would have been devastated. I would have held myself accountable. It was the hardest news I've ever had to deliver.

Making light of the situation with the "man in the hole" comment made it easier for me to make return trips to see Raye Dawn. I didn't want to abandon her, especially after my first visit. So, before my next visit, my daughter and I went shopping for what we jokingly termed, "Man in the hole" shirts. I wanted to make sure that I was dressed well enough that nobody would even consider that I was someone with a man in the hole. It worked. On each of my remaining visits I was ignored by all of the other visitors. I breathed a sigh of relief.

On my second visit, Raye Dawn had been spending a lot of time praying and writing, and although she still cried throughout the visit, she seemed to be in better spirits. She told me that she was worried about issues she was having with blood in her stool. I immediately thought she probably had an ulcer since her level of stress had been off the charts for quite some time, but since her father had died from colon cancer, she was concerned that she could have cancer as well. Raye Dawn's family worked with the sheriff's office and a scope was ordered. Raye Dawn told me that the nurse knew Kathie Briggs's story and that she was extremely rough when inserting her IV. She said that the nurse jabbed it into her arm so hard that it hit the bone. I winced as she described the cruel and unusual treatment she had received from the nurse, as well as from the person from the Pardon and Parole Board who interviewed her for her pre-sentencing report. It seemed certain people had judged Raye Dawn from what they had heard. Their minds appeared to be closed to the possibly that Raye Dawn was also a victim. It was terribly disturbing for me to watch the tyrannical turn of events unfold.

Kathie Briggs and her supporters, however, seemed to surpass everyone when it came to disturbing words and actions. They viewed Raye Dawn's possible illness as entertaining. They accused Raye Dawn of being pregnant and laughed at her. They relished in the fact that she was in pain. Granted, it was discovered that the pain was something minor that could be treated, but her diagnosis lends no excuse for laughing at a young girl whose life was ripped away from her.

I recall wondering at the time how Kathie Briggs and her followers knew about Raye Dawn's medical condition. Several times, Raye Dawn's family members and myself discussed the possibility of someone they trusted leaking information to Kathie Briggs. When we later discovered the email tampering, hacking, and other illegal means by which they gained inside information, things made sense. They were always one step ahead. They always knew the game plan before it was played. As I repeatedly reminded forum members in messages, "This is not a game! Someone's life is at stake." Looking back, I was so naïve. I had no idea that to some, it's only a game.

YouTube and Erin Brockovich

September, 2007

Before working with Raye Dawn and her family, I didn't have a clue about YouTube or how to make a video. Once, a friend had taken a cute video clip of her nephew that she wanted to upload to YouTube and she thought I should know how to do it. I laughed and stated I had never heard of the Web site. That was less than a year before I met Raye Dawn. Within just a few short months, I found myself in a position where I had to learn how to make a video and upload it to YouTube. Just weeks after Raye Dawn's trial, it was brought to my attention that Kathie Briggs was gaining a large amount of supporters from videos. Something needed to be done to counter the negative videos being made that didn't reflect the true story. So, I opened an account and created a video using Word and PowerPoint to create slides and then I incorporated the slides into the video software that came with my computer. It wasn't professional, but it was a video and it reflected the facts in the case. At the time, none of the other stuff mattered.

It wasn't long before I started receiving hate-filled messages on YouTube. One in particular accused me of trying to be the next Erin Brockovich. It was meant as an insult, but I took it as a compliment. Like Erin, I was fighting for the underdog and sacrificing everything I had in order to do so. I feel honored that I would be compared with such a courageous woman, though I still have a hard time seeing myself as someone so selfless. Unlike Erin, I wasn't confident or strong and the hate messages were tearing at my soul. With each new message, I could feel the hate and the passion in the person who wrote it and it overwhelmed me. I didn't know what to do or where to turn. Since I had exposed Kathie Briggs's gang for being a part of the bombardment, the messages slowed down, but I continued to receive ten to twenty a day for months. With each new Web site I joined or service I obtained, it seemed like a new venue for the haters to bombard Raye Dawn's family and myself. The hate got to be so bad that I eventually removed Raye Dawn's family members from the forwarding service so they wouldn't have to see anymore. The intensity of the messages was like bullets. I would recover from one, and then another, and then another, and it never stopped. Hate messages were coming at me from every direction, and Raye Dawn wasn't their only target.

I wouldn't sign this petition if my life depended on it. You are as much to blame as the bastard who killed that beautiful child. And you still have pics of that monster on this website. You are in denial you sick bunch of bastards! Rot in hell Raye Dawn....

You've got to be kidding me...any DECENT mother would have PROTECTED her child. There is no way in hell that this woman did not know that her daughter was being ABUSED and for that she should ROT IN HELL!!!!!! This was not one incident of abuse (which by the way is one too many) but this is many, many instances of abuse!!!! God help you for trying to protect a MURDERER!!!!

The following message came from someone in my county. I remember being frightened that someone within just a few miles of my own home could say something like this:

Her mother needs to burn in hell for not protecting Kelsey, not SAVED! Someone needs to break both of her mothers legs and then punch her in the stomach until she dies so she can know the pain and suffering her little girl went through that her mother didn't stop!!!

Murderer. That's all that is needed to be said. Even if Raye Dawn didn't land the fatal blow, she was absolutely an accessory. May she rot in jail then burn in Hell.

Are you fucking kidding!! No matter how it looks to you blind people, Kelsey was ONLY with the Smith for the last 6 weeks of her life. Pull your head out!

*I think she should get ready to burn in hell for the things she done to
    this baby. I think she is the one who killed Kelsey herself and
    Mike Porter took the fall for her.*
*YOU GUYS ARE RETARDED DO YOU NOT KNOW THAT THIS
    LITTLE GIRL DIED CAUSE OF THIS DUMB BROAD GO
    TAKE YOUR SORRY ASSES AND YOU DIE AND SEE HOW
    IT FEELS!!!! assholes!*

One petition signature had "fuck you" in every field except the
email address where it said, "fuckyou@starfucker.com." "Star" is a
favorite addition to many of the hateful messages on the Internet and
resembles Kathie Briggs's sidekick, Starla's name. She stated:

*god knows what she did, she killed her baby and tried to use a
    statistic to her advantage, and blame it on the step father, she
    killed Kelsey, if she couldn't have her, no one else would,
    how you make this site and sleep at night, enjoy your judas
    piece of silver, that poor baby*

The hate continued. They poured into my inbox day-after-day.
This message was one of the most disturbing of all. In order to get the
full effect, it's presented in its original form. I am sure you can guess
who I believe wrote this message.

Username: Burn in Hell
UserEmail: gofuckyourselves@yahoo.com
UserTel: 555-getraped
UserState: Put a Bullet in your Brain Raye Dawn, you fucking bitch
UserCounty: You never deserved Kelsey. She deserved a much
better mother.
Date: 15 Aug 2007
Time: 20:59:40
Comments:
Go fuck yourselves. If that fucking psychobitch had done
ANYTHING AT ALL to protect her daughter, Kelsey would be
alive today. I hope she fries. Or gets raped in prison. Perhaps then
she would finally understand everything Kelsey was put thru because

she refused to stand up to her psycho hubby Mike Porter. And to top it off, instead of being adults and admitting what those 2 monsters did, you trash her dad's family. Her dad defended this country, what the fuck did Raye Dawn do besides abuse children and get knocked up? Oh drugs, that's right. She was the druggie, not Kelsey's dad. I hope she fries.

In an effort to alleviate my stress from the ongoing hate, I found a way to cope in what I like to term, "video therapy." My "therapy sessions" resulted in the creation of close to eighty videos. At times when I felt frustrated, angry, or I had the often-overwhelming feeling of helplessness, I made a video. By the time I was finished writing, editing, and uploading my video, the frustration would subside. I had done something constructive with the excess energy that still makes my heart pump today when I read the messages. There were times when I was so frustrated that one video didn't do the trick and I had to make two, but the video therapy helped me through the pressure that was continually mounting.

In response to my first videos filled with facts about the case, a "new member" posted this message on Kathie Briggs's forum titled "ignoringtheTRUTH (videos)."

I was looking through all of the videos that are posted on YouTube. The ones being posted by the site that is supposed to be seeking the TRUTH,are actually full of LIES. I'm know they read here,so I just want to ask. WHY do you all CONTINUE to ignore the REAL FACTS,and put up unproven BS?? Do you bother to research,and when you do,are you skipping over what is FACT,and believing only what you want to believe?

A laundry list of arguments was included in the post followed by this statement:

To the Briggs family, I hope you do not see this post in a bad light.I only want answers from the people that are supposedly spreading the TRUTH and the REAL FACTS as they call it. All I see there is slander.

Kathie Briggs seconded the post by adding:

Those who think they can 'solve' this crime with unfounded and ridiculous theories apparently do not have compassion for Kelsey as a person.

Compassion was what kept me going when things became really rough. Soon after I started the forum, I realized that Kelsey's maternal family had not been allowed a memorial for Kelsey due to the hate messages. There were multiple memorials that had been purchased for Kelsey's paternal family and each memorial, of course, displayed their version of Kelsey's story along with negative comments about Raye Dawn. Members of Kelsey's maternal family informed me that they lit candles on the memorials, but their candles had been deleted. I thought it was a travesty, so I purchased two memorials and built them with pictures of Kelsey and Raye Dawn. I was astonished at the instant attacks and the number of hate-filled messages that were left on memorials for a dead child. It made me literally nauseous. I couldn't believe it. On September 16, 2007 this message was left:

your a fucking cunt you should die in jail

The tone of the hate was always the same, and it affected me deeply. It made me really question if there was any compassion from any of Kathie Briggs's and Lance's family or supporters. How could they be a part of the hate that was constantly surrounding Kelsey's family? Didn't they love Kelsey enough to want peace on her behalf?

By October of 2007, I was at my breaking point. My husband had just lost his best friend in a work-related accident. He was a man with a wife and small children. It was a very emotional time for us as my husband faced his own mortality and I was being pulled in different directions. Kathie Briggs and her supporters had been having fun at Raye Dawn's expense for weeks after seeing her pre-sentencing

509

report. Starla posted the following statement on her forum in response to the report:

> *I read the report a couple of days ago, and I would think the recommendation would stand. Uumm...the Judge knows everyone is watching this case...from ALL over. I believe **he probably remembers what happened to the judicial career of the last Judge** that did not pay attention to things related in this case. I believe he will sentence her to the 27yrs and not release her. **To do anything but** that, since it is also the recommendation from the investigators **would be suicidal to his judicial career**. I doubt he is going down that road.*[48]

After reading their vile comments, I was finished. I couldn't take any more of the hate. When one of our moderators received a message from one of Kathie Briggs's supporters about our members who were "truth bombing," I decided to share some of the hate mail with her that I had received. First, I informed her of the ongoing problems I had experienced with Kathie Briggs's supporters. She responded with the following message:

> *From: [Kathie Briggs supporter] Date: Sat, October 13, 2007 11:41 am To: Truth Seeker - I'm sorry they are calling her names. Unfortunately I have no control over this. People can be very cruel especially on the intranet. Since there identity cannot be discovered they seem hold themselves accountable for their actions. Hopefully they will settle down and discontinue their childish games.*

I replied:

> *From: Truth Seeker To: [Kathie Briggs supporter] Sent: Saturday, October 13, 2007 3:59:12 PM - Yes it is VERY childish and I've personally NEVER been on one of your chat rooms or on your forum, period! The only reason I've allowed a tiny bit of bashing to go on with our forum is because when I started my blog (which is what our forum originally was) I didn't want to say at the time because I was so bombarded but I had also*

---

[48] Emphasis by post author

set up the Free Kelsey's mom site. In the first two days, before it even went to a search engine I received 55 hate mails directly from Kathie Briggs's Web site. I have the proof that they all came from your people. I was disgusted and heartsick for several days until I made it public how nasty your people were and now they've slown down. I hadn't been a part of this at all until the end of the trial and I didn't know what was going on between the two sides. I just thought Raye Dawn got a very raw deal and I wanted to stand up for her. But after all the CRAP that was put on me by Kathie Briggs's people I did get a little bitter and very disturbed about what Raye Dawn had probably dealt with over the last two years. The more I've heard and read, the more sick I've become so when people came on the forum to voice their disgust I let it go on, but I'm putting a stop to all of it. I'm cleaning up the forum and not allowing any bashing, only discussions, opinions, and facts, yet your people will not stay off our forum. I know we've had a couple of people come to your forum but we've asked them not to and they weren't putting out the disgusting filth and name calling we've had to erase from your side. They wanted answers from Kathie Briggs. Last night one of your people who was hiding on our forum under the name restinpeaceKelsey talked to one of our moderators and told her to go to youtube so she could see how many people hate Raye Dawn. Why would we want to do that? She was trying to convince our moderator that everyone hates Raye Dawn so we should as well. I'm sorry, but I'm a Christian and I think that is WRONG! Today I've been called an evil bitch and a piece of shit. I'm called names like that EVERY SINGLE DAY by your supporters. How does that make you feel? I've received hate mail daily since the end of Raye Dawn's trial with awful, horrible things like 'Raye Dawn should be beaten and burned alive and then burn in hell.' This is what's making me fight harder for a woman that I don't even know because even if you people think she killed Kelsey why would Lance go on tv and say he hopes she's beaten every day in prison and that he hates her? That, along with all the nasty things I read every day give me an idea of what you're telling your people. Why else would there be so much hate? Kathie Briggs knows Raye Dawn

511

loved Kelsey. Kathie Briggs knows Raye Dawn fought for Kelsey. And Kathie Briggs knows that Mike Porter is a pedophile (he had child porn on his computer for God's sake!) and he murdered her grandchild, yet she's taking out all of her hate on Raye Dawn, why????? In closing, I will do what I can to keep our people off your forum and out of your chat room if you'll ask your people to stop sending hate mail (I can send you some if you'd like) and get off our forum and out of our chatroom. We don't want them there because they're only trying to spread their hate and we are coping with all the hate and it's the hate that is turning us all bitter toward Kathie Briggs and Lance…I'll pray that you do the right thing as I'm striving to do it on my side. ~ Truth Seeker

I followed up my passionate plea with some hate mail I had just received:

From: Truth Seeker To: [Kathie Briggs supporter] Sent: Saturday, October 13, 2007 7:20:03 PM Subject: RE: Message This is what I get every day. Do you think you'd become bitter and sick after reading stuff like this day after day? This is what Kathie and Lance and all their supporters are doing. Are you a Christian? Is this what you support? Did you know Raye Dawn has been stalked, harassed, and hated for two years? Mike Porter murdered and sexually assaulted Kelsey and I wouldn't even wish this on him. This is sick and it's coming from the hate Kelsey's Purpose is spreading. Why can't you people see that????????

I attached the latest hate mail I had just received as follows:

Username: BITCH U SHUD ROT IN HELL Comments: U CANT TELL ME THAT U DONT NO UR CHILD IS BEIN ABUSED WEN JUS ABOUT EVERY PIC U C SHE HAS BRUISES AND 2 BROKEN LEGS U CHOSE A MAN AND HIS DICK OVER UR BABY U SHUD B BEATIN EVEYDAY OF UR LIFE!!!!!!!

Her reply was, "I will forward to Kathie Briggs," and a second reply stated, "Again I have no knowledge of all of this and again I am not a member of this group. I will forward this email to Kathie Briggs hopefully she can handle this situation with you. Thank you" Immediately after I received her final email, her chat box was closed and she removed herself from Kathie Briggs's forum.

Kathie Briggs replied to me personally in the only direct contact I've had with her to date. In two separate e-mails, she stated,

Once again, I cannot control what the general public feels. I am only responsible for my own words and actions. Please do not send me emails that do not concern me. If someone sends threatening mail to you I would suggest you contact someone with authority to help you track it.

And,

So called hate mail cannot be considered coming from a Kelsey's Purpose member. Even if the link they last came from is Kelsey's Purpose, that does not make them a member. At the same time some of our members are also members of the Smith family. Regardless who is sending this garbage I can assure you we do not condone it. We are not responsible for individual actions other than our own.

She added, "Listen lady, I don't know what you're trying to pull." Her e-mails ended with a link to a video with the message, "Soldiers child…please watch."

High School Moment

September, 2007

From the instant our forum members realized that we were standing tall with arms locked against the giant, a handful of Raye Dawn supporters began to keep a close watch on everything Kathie Briggs and her group did in furthering their mission that seemed to be off-focus. Their sights seemed to be set squarely on Raye Dawn and her family, as well as any other cases that were brought to Kathie Briggs's attention. With every case there were new threats against lawmakers, public officials, and state workers. Kathie Briggs repeatedly boasted that she had a loud voice in our state. People were afraid of her. Anyone who dared to cross her found themselves in jeopardy of losing their job. She had an army at her disposal that was ready and willing to file complaints, write letters, and contact the media—all without looking into the other side of the argument— whatever it took to get their opinions heard. Her followers seemed to think that by doing Kathie Briggs's bidding, they were helping rid our state of child abuse. However, since 2005 when their group began their purported "mission," the number of deaths due to abuse, neglect, and murder among children under the age of eighteen had risen at a steady pace. Given the alarming statistics and the lack of change on behalf of children, it makes one wonder where their focus was aimed. If the group's true intention was to bring awareness to child abuse issues and put an end to children suffering, as they claimed, why weren't they successful in their efforts since, admittedly, their voices could be heard above all?

The truth of the matter is that Kathie Briggs and her group could be seen as nothing but bullies, not champions against abuse. The totality of abuse, which included the abuse Kathie Briggs's group carried out with various threats, was not a topic they wanted discussed. Any mention of the abuse that Raye Dawn suffered at the hands of

Lance or the abandonment of Kathie Briggs's children, which undoubtedly left scars from emotional abuse, were quickly squashed and silenced, and deemed "unimportant" and immaterial to the case. They were, and still are, bullies; they were, and still are, abusive. Evidence of their bullying could then and still be found everywhere, but mostly on the Internet. Their days and nights have been spent making threats and spreading hate for Raye Dawn and anyone Kathie Briggs didn't like. If they weren't actually spreading hate or making Raye Dawn out to be a monster, then why do I continue to be bullied by these same people and receive hate messages for supporting Raye Dawn even today?

I'll be the first to admit that our efforts to end the hate, threats, and bullying were not well-organized or without flaws. Some who joined us seemed to enjoy the fight. Most of us did not. As mentioned previously, the constant hate messages I received were getting to me. At times I was ornery. It was somewhat of a relief to throw some of their "crap" back in their faces through "video therapy" or by posting evidence that had been withheld from the public. But, as a good friend described it, "It was like taking spaghetti to a sword fight." I was being told I needed to die. In response, I threw their words back at them or posted facts. They were in the mud, and although I felt dirty for even participating in the fights with them, I maintained my integrity by sticking to what I knew was the truth. It was a no-win battle for me and at a time in my life when the hate had overwhelmed me and I searched for anything to escape it. Throwing their awful actions, words, and lies back at them was healing not only for me, but for members of Raye Dawn's family. They had been Kathie Briggs's whipping posts for years and their hands were bound in gag orders and threats of arrest; they had no way to fight back. Finally having a voice and finally watching the bullies squirm was beyond anything they could have hoped for at that dark time in their lives. The tide was changing!

Those supporting Kathie Briggs's mission needed to know exactly what type of people they were supporting. I do admit that at times it felt good to watch them backtrack and try to cover their lie-filled stories. So, when members of our forum found posts from Kathie Briggs and her supporters that were interesting or showed deceit, they were copied to our forum and we all gave our opinions on the content. Many of us had things to say, but we didn't want to join Kathie Briggs's forum. We knew that her spies read our forum. They always had multiple people who would join and pretend to be new. Therefore, the "game" consisted of posting comments to the "other side" on our respective forums. It was a silly, childish game, but it was what I had been reduced to…arguing via forum posts with a bunch of bullies.

One post in particular that caught our attention was from Kathie Briggs, in which she made an effort to explain accusations of stalking Raye Dawn that had been brought against her. The most intriguing part of the post was the fact that her explanation did nothing more than give the appearance that yes, she was in fact guilty of stalking both Raye Dawn and Mike Porter. She claimed:

At one point Mike was driving a Suburban and Raye Dawn owned an Explorer. As I pulled out of my daughters driveway one day I got behind Raye Dawn. She pulled up to the stop sign in Meeker and would not go. After I sat there a few seconds I noticed she had the tag from her Explorer on the Suburban. I knew her tag number as I had seen it sitting on Main Street so many times at her work. I knew Mike's tag started with a Q and this one was definitely hers. So I proceeded to have a high school moment and picked up the phone and called Meeker Police and reported it. Raye Dawn was letting several cars go and kept me behind her so I finally went around. Raye Dawn pulled into her grandmothers drive and later I found out she went in and called DHS to tell them I was stalking her. The…police officer…went to her grandmothers home to check out the report. He saw me drive by and told the DHS worker they needed to file a report on me. Then he proceeded to let Raye Dawn drive off in a vehicle that had a tag which expired six months prior and did not have insurance...I went on to the elementary school to watch the kids program. My main reason for making the call was to see if Meeker police would do anything that concerned Raye Dawn breaking the law and once again they did not. Later that day my daughter told her father-in-law about the incident. He was the Mayor of Meeker at the time and took some interest in our police department as he had several more complaints from other citizens. When he called the department and started asking the dispatcher questions this officer could hear her end and assumed it was me on the line. The Mayor could hear this officer in the background yelling for the dispatcher to 'tell Kathie Briggs to leave Raye Dawn alone.' She had to inform him it was not me on the phone. The following morning Mike's Suburban was again parked on Main Street... This time it has the expired tag back on it. I figured they had purchased a tag since Mike had called a friend of mine asking for an insurance quote that day. He told her he had not had insurance in nine months. I felt bad that I had made this call and put them in a financial bind. In reality I wasn't the one that put them in the financial bind, but I did make it worse with my call. If they had to take a tag from another vehicle they evidently were in a heck of a financial situation. Another day goes by and I get a call from a business in Meeker telling me flashing lights were sitting behind Mike's Suburban. Once again they put the tag from the Explorer back on the Suburban and parked it on Main Street. The Mayor noticed it and personally went to the police department and told them they should take action. I couldn't believe they would have so little regard for the law... Mike was allowed to walk down the block and purchase a tag and the vehicle was not towed in. When we went to Raye Dawn's trial I was questioned about this and her attorney made a big deal about my part in it. In reality she was the one that had broken the law and once again it was being blamed on me. I was not proud of the call I had made, but I made it and that was that...

A warrant was drawn up for Kathie Briggs's arrest for stalking Raye, but the district attorney denied it.

APPLICATION FOR WARRANT OF ARREST

Comes now the undersigned Affiant on this __17__ day of __MAY, 2005__, and hereby makes application to the Court for a WARRANT OF ARREST to issue against the following individual(s):

KATHIE J. BRIGGS

In support of this application, the undersigned Affiant, being first duly sworn, does now upon said oath, depose and say that the crime(s) of:

Stalking – Harassment

- - - - -

- - - - -

- - - - -

did occur in Lincoln County Oklahoma at __2:15PM__, on the __16__ day of __MAY, 2005__.

The Affiant believes that the above named individual(s) did commit the specified crime(s) by reason of personal knowledge, investigation and the reports of witnesses who have related their findings and observations of the facts and circumstances regarding the offense(s) hereinabove named.

THOSE FACTS ARE:

On 05-16-2005 at approximately 1415 hours, I Assistant Chief Matt Byers was traveling southbound on Hwy. 18 approximately ½ a mile south of Hwy. 18B. I overheard the Lincoln County Dispatcher notify Meeker Police Chief Don Conner to be on the look out for a black Chevy SUV displaying Oklahoma tag number LDB-937. The dispatcher stated he received a call that the vehicle was traveling southbound on Hwy 18 at Hwy. 18B. The dispatcher stated the caller advised the vehicle was traveling at an excessive rate of speed, passing in no-passing zones, and driving all over the road. I notified LCSO that I was ½ a mile south of Hwy. 18B and would look for the vehicle. I continued traveling southbound, believing that the vehicle was ahead of my location due to the amount of time that would have lapsed from the original call, I accelerated my patrol car to approximately 85mph until I reached Payson Road. I never observed any vehicles on the road matching the vehicle description. I then slowed my patrol car down and resumed traveling south at approximately 55mph due to traffic. As I approached Dawson and Red Hill Road in Meeker. I was notified by Don Conner that the vehicle was turning into a private drive on Dawson. I turned my patrol car around and went to the residence. I observed the vehicle displaying Oklahoma tag number LDB-937 sitting in the driveway, unoccupied. I made contact with the operator of the vehicle, known personally by me as Raye Dawn Porter. I asked Porter if there would be some reason she was driving recklessly on Hwy. 18. Porter stated that she had not been and appeared upset. Porter was also speaking to a person on the telephone at this time. I explained to her that I had received a call that she was driving recklessly. Porter asked who called and I stated that Conner informed me that he believed Kathey Briggs had made the call. Porter then pointed past me and stated "there she goes again". I asked who and Porter stated "Briggs. I saw her following me when I got to the 4-way". Porter then stated to the person on the phone that Briggs had been following since she left Chandler and was now driving past the residence again. Porter stated that she had observed Briggs drive-by 3 times since she arrived home. I then asked Porter who she was speaking with and she stated "Yolanda Hunter with DHS". Hunter then requested to speak with me. Hunter asked why I was there and I explained that I received a call of Porter driving recklessly, but was not able to substantiate the call and did not believe that Porter was driving recklessly because of my location on the highway when the call came in. Hunter then stated that Porter called her because she observed Kathey Briggs following her on the highway. Hunter then asked if this type of behavior has occurred in the past on Briggs' behalf. I stated that I was not personally aware of any incidents involving Briggs following Porter. Porter then stated to me while I was speaking with Hunter that there had been numerous other occasions, but only 1 was reported in January 2005 to the Lincoln County Sheriffs Department. Porter stated that she has observed Briggs and several members of Briggs' family following her around when she drives, parking at the end of driveways, and driving back and forth in front of hers and her family's residences. Hunter then stated that Porter has complained of Briggs and Briggs' family continually harassing her and that a report needed to be done on the events of today. Hunter stated that Briggs' had a supervised visitation appointment with Porter's daughter from 10:00am – 12:00pm today and that Porter had a supervised visitation appointment with her daughter from 12:00pm – 2:00pm today and that Briggs should not have been anywhere in the area of Porter while she was visiting her daughter. Porter also stated at this time that she had observed Briggs leaving the DHS center and waited to get out of her vehicle. Porter stated that Briggs drove around the parking lot 2 – 3 times before finally leaving. I then had Porter come to my patrol car so that I could begin a report and have her complete a voluntary statement concerning the events of today.

Kathey Briggs is known to Raye D. Smith through a marriage to Briggs' son, Lance. The marriage ended in divorce, but resulted in the birth of a daughter, Kelsey. A custody battle has been on-going since January 2005 between Briggs and Porter. Porter stated the harassment has been on-going since January 2005, when Porter's daughter suffered a broken collar bone. Briggs requested the Meeker Police Department to investigate the broken bone and an investigation revealed that no abuse or criminal act had occurred and the investigation was closed. Briggs has continued to fight for custody of Porter's daughter.

Kathie Briggs is known to Raye D. Smith through a marriage to Briggs' son, Lance. The marriage ended in divorce, but resulted in the birth of a daughter, Kelsey. A custody battle has been on-going since January 2005 between Briggs and Porter. Porter stated the harassment has been on-going since January 2005, when Porter's daughter suffered a broken collar bone. Briggs requested the Meeker Police Department to investigate the broken bone and an investigation revealed that no abuse or criminal act had occurred and the investigation was closed. Briggs has continued to fight for custody of Porter's daughter.

Porter stated to me while in the patrol car that Briggs and members of her family have been observed by Porter and her family doing the following:

Following members around in vehicles
Driving past residences continually
Calling in erroneous reports to law enforcement
Calling family members residences and hanging up

Porter stated that she is tired of looking over her shoulder and always seeing Briggs following her around and calling in false reports about her to law enforcement. Porter is worried that Briggs or her family members may become more aggressive in the nature of the harassment.

Another post that we found insightful was from Shirica, Lance's sister. She had exchanged e-mails with and met with Mike Porter in person. She also helped him in his defense. In this particular post, she shared her opinion regarding the OSBI interview of Mike Porter. This was the interview that was taken at the same time as Raye Dawn's. It's also the interview that ended with the investigators warning Raye Dawn that Mike Porter was a "sorry son-of-a-bitch." Neither Raye Dawn's family nor I have seen this interview. Shirica stated,

During Mike Porter's interview, he kept grabbing his heart and acting like he was having chest pains and he acted like he was going to vomit a time or two and was very dramatic. I have never seen such a drama queen. His body language was screaming guilt. He was beyond nervous and then toward the end he says he wants an attorney and he wants to see his wife. Watching the tape is so different from reading it. I truly feel that this man is responsible for the death of Kelsey.

Her post was followed by one from a die-hard Kathie Briggs supporter. To this day, she posts hateful comments about Raye Dawn. She responded, "Shirica, I have no doubt he did it."

Jeanna, Lance's older sister and co-conspirator with Mike Porter, couldn't allow the negative attention to sway from Raye Dawn to Mike Porter. She reasoned that her husband (Raye Dawn's first cousin) and Lance (Kelsey's father) had both walked away from witnessing Mike Porter's testimony with an overall feeling that the man was innocent. She reasoned,

Most of our family members were not allowed in the courtroom during much of the trial because we were subpoenaed as potential witnesses. My husband and Lance were able to witness Mike Porter's testimony. I understand that it was very compelling and he appeared to be genuine and believable...

Lance's girlfriend at the time and self-proclaimed "best friend" who has repeatedly continued the hate toward Raye Dawn and myself, followed up the posts with her interpretation of the events by sharing what seems like a rare moment of honesty. (A side note to consider while reading her comment was the fact that Mike Porter was transported to the district attorney's county jail nine days before the trial began so that the district attorney could prepare him for his testimony.) She stated as follows:

> There has been a lot of discussion about Mike Porter and also his testimony in court. As I previously mentioned, I had the opportunity to be in the court room while Mike Porter testified against Raye Dawn. As I said before, I wanted to believe what he said but started realizing that some things just didn't add up. I have read the OSBI transcript from Mike Porter's interview. After reading it and thinking about his testimony, it's clear to me that he had rehearsed his testimony for Raye Dawn's trial. I think he knew exactly what he was going to say and how to say it. I also think he had prepared himself for the attack from Raye Dawn's attorney. I was always surprised by how calm and collected he remained even though her attorney was screaming at him and accusing him of murdering and sexual assaulting Kelsey. I see major differences in the Mike Porter giving this OSBI interview and the man who sat in that court room. The man is obviously consumed by guilt and fear. His behavior both at the hospital, afterwards and during this interview make that obvious. I think he was scared to death that he was about to finally be caught. I personally think he was lying about the day he says he walked into the bedroom and found Raye Dawn punching Kelsey in the stomach. How convenient that she just happened to be punching her in the stomach and Kelsey died from abdominal injuries just a few months later. How convenient that she told him all she had to do was blame everything on him. I call BS on Mike Porter! For the first time in 2 years, I feel more certain than ever that I know what happened to Kelsey. I think the role that Raye Dawn played in her death will always remain a mystery but I think for most of us, we know who killed Kelsey. I find some small bit of peace in having some questions answered by these

interviews. I am so thankful that the Briggs family has been kind enough to share them with all of us.

Reading her comments from five years ago, it's difficult to imagine she's the same person that is so filled with hate for Raye Dawn today. She is one of the biggest bullies toward both Raye Dawn and I and she assists the other bullies in keeping the conversation away from Mike Porter. Mike Porter has never been the center of the conversation. Even when we brought him up on the forum, Kathie Briggs's gang members would join in the conversation and guide it back toward Raye Dawn.

In an effort to compete with the success of our forum, Kathie Briggs's supporters started a new bashboard. The picture they used was the one that Kathie Briggs has always displayed as her avatar, which is a Glamour Shot photo that Raye Dawn had made of Kelsey before her second birthday. On the bashboard, the same people who had declared that Mike Porter was, without a doubt, guilty of murdering Kelsey were taking up for him and ensuring all of the conversation focused on Raye Dawn. One of the creators even stated, "For the record, it is possible Kathie Briggs is reading this…" It was clear to me that she did more than read. Many posts by someone "anonymous" repeatedly took up for Kathie Briggs and swayed the conversation back to Raye Dawn.

One post that caught the attention of "anonymous" was so revealing that the blog disappeared. It was from Kelsey's step-grandmother, I call her "Susan"—a woman I've since found to be caring and upfront and who was Kathie Briggs's tie to the Governor…a tie that has since been severed. I suppose she was too honest for Kathie Briggs and her deceptive supporters. She stated,

I will be one of the first to stand up and say, I should have done more. People have asked, why I didn't go to court in September and my response is this, I honestly can't say why I didn't go to court in September and show Judge Key the pictures of Kelsey's condition…

523

One of the misrepresentations that Kathie Briggs had perpetuated was that the paternal family hadn't been allowed in the courtroom in September of 2005, a month before Kelsey's death. She also stated that they weren't informed about the hearing. The single post proved that the story had been part of the ruse that Kathie Briggs still wants everyone to believe—that she had fought to save Kelsey. Within mere seconds of the step-grandmother's post, a message from "anonymous" was posted, which stated simply, "OWNERS--PLEASE READ YOUR EMAILS!!" and then the entire bashboard disappeared. It was gone in a flash! Unbelievably, this wasn't the one and only time that something was said and then everything shut down. It was a pattern of events that seemed to repeat on a regular basis. If Kathie Briggs and her group were being honest, why would they have anything to hide?

As we watched Kathie Briggs's and her followers' actions, the trail of deceit grew beyond any of our expectations. There was no denying their mission. They had left plenty of evidence that could not be argued. Our entertainment came with their nonstop attempts at backtracking when caught in a lie that usually ended in more misrepresentations coming to light. Even though their tactics of misrepresenting facts have rarely ended in success, they still use the same underhanded strategies to this day. They're like rattle snakes, always searching for a new place to hide and when someone gets close to discovering them for what they are they get louder and louder, and then strike. With each strike, they show their true character. Many recognize them for what they truly are, but nobody wants to get in the pit with them. This is something I struggle with daily.

"Kathie, I forgive you."

September, 2007

It was two months after Raye Dawn's conviction for enabling child abuse when she appeared before the trial judge for her formal sentencing. Since she was taken into custody after the verdict, she had spent her days in prayer and contemplation over what she wanted to convey to the judge. Instead of throwing herself on the mercy of the court and begging for a lighter sentence, she stood and turned to the side of the courtroom, whose occupants were mostly dressed in pink, the color of Kathie Briggs's Web site.

Raye Dawn looked directly into Kathie Briggs's eyes and stated, "Kathie, I forgive you."

Laughter was heard throughout the courthouse as Kathie Briggs, her family members, and their supporters found Raye Dawn's act of forgiveness amusing. Interviews taken after the sentencing revealed Kathie Briggs's anger over the fact that she was forgiven. She also expressed her delight that Raye Dawn would be going to prison for twenty-seven years. The most shocking interview was from the juror who had immediately joined Kathie Briggs's Web site after the trial. She wore a pink shirt to the sentencing and spoke on behalf of the paternal family to members of the media.

As soon as Raye Dawn's trial was over, [Celia] joined the Briggs' "bandwagon" and jumped on the Kelsey's Purpose Web site. [Celia] wrote the following on this site concerning "The Trial for Raye Dawn Smith":

As one of the jurors in this heart felt trial, I have let my thoughts be known to many people. I have told Kathie that I believed Raye Dawn Murdered Baby Kelsey, and also I was one of few who wanted to give Raye Dawn a LIFE SENTENCE!!!!!! I

*BELIEVE SHE SHOULD HAVE GOTTEN A DEATH
SENTENCE. I TRULY HOPE THAT SHE GETS SOME
BEATENS JUST LIKE THE ONES SHE GAVE. I WILL
NEVER FEEL THE PAIN THAT THE BRIGGS FAMILY HAS
FELT, BUT I HOPE IN THE NEXT 27 YEARS IT GETS
BETTER. GOD BLESS THE BRIGGS FAMILY...SEE YOU
ALL AUG 23 AT 1:30 PM .... FLY Kelsey FLY*

The day of Raye Dawn's sentencing was a particularly emotional day for me. I had been to the county jail and I knew she was fairly safe there. However, I worried about how she would be treated in prison. I remember thinking that she would be transported back to the county jail and then on to our state prison for female inmates. Of course, some of our forum members had the inside scoop through Kathie Briggs, and they posted that she would be going to a prison in Southern Oklahoma first and she would be arriving at the prison that night. I was terrified for her, as well as her family. Thankfully, the process was swift. She was only kept in that specific prison for a day or two and then she was transferred to the all-female prison. On the day that I heard where she was transferred, I called the prison to inquire about how she was doing. An elderly gentleman answered the phone and told me that she was fine. He said that a roommate had been assigned to her who was very well-respected. He also stated that she seemed to be adjusting as well as could be expected.

I hung up the phone and wiped away the tears that had fallen for Raye Dawn. I could not imagine her pain; she was now dealing with circumstances that nobody should have to endure, especially a grieving mother.

I put my worry into action and I renewed my plan to help Raye Dawn by drafting a letter to the trial judge that I intended to attach to the collected petition signatures.

November 28, 2007
*Dear [Trial Judge], I am writing to you today to appeal to you on
behalf of Raye Dawn Smith. I realize the verdict has been*

cast, and she is now in state custody. However, I think a grave injustice has been made. I am not related to Raye Dawn's family. I do not live in Lincoln County. And I am not a long-time friend of Raye Dawn's. I am an individual who saw the mayhem that the Briggs family has caused in what I used to be proud to call my home state of Oklahoma. As a citizen of Oklahoma I feel it's time to stand up and do the right thing for the sake of an innocent mother who was denied counseling and has not been allowed to grieve the death of her child. I have seen all the evidence the jurors saw. I have read some of the testimony from the trial, and I have spent countless hours pouring over police reports. I know you're not interested in my opinion, but I believe this is a case of accidental death. I believe Mike Porter was trying to save Kelsey and injured her with his sloppy version of CPR and he teamed up with the Briggs to turn on Raye Dawn. The Briggs family members are out for revenge, fame, and money, and that's it. How long will we sit by and watch the injustice carry out? Mike Porter already sealed his fate with his plea, but Raye Dawn has continued to proclaim her innocence; an innocence that hundreds of people around the world believe in as well. I know you are a man of reason, so I am enclosing hundreds of signatures on a petition for a new trial for Raye Dawn. I beg you to read these petition signatures with an open mind and let your heart guide you in your decision. Raye Dawn deserves to have a fair trial. A fair trial will never be heard for her in the State of Oklahoma. You know that. The Briggs do not play by the rules. They violated the gag order that was in place before Raye Dawn's trial. They are still spreading their lies. When will they be silenced? When will the State of Oklahoma and Lincoln County take back control of justice? Respectfully yours, Truth Seeker

This letter was never delivered and neither were the petition signatures. I began to work closely with Raye Dawn's family members in doing what was best for Raye Dawn's defense. It was determined at the time that any direct contact with the judge while Raye Dawn's attorney worked toward an evidentiary hearing or a new trial could be seen as possible tainting. Since we strived to play by the rules, the petition signatures instead became words of support for Raye Dawn. I shared each positive message with her family members, which were in turn passed on to Raye Dawn.

At the time that I drafted the letter, it's clear that my perception of Mike Porter's culpability was a bit skewed. Shortly after Raye Dawn's sentencing, I was given documentation that was used in Raye Dawn's appeal so that I could upload it onto the Web site. One of the documents was a statement from Mike Porter's daughter's school counselor. In the statement, she described how Porter's eight-year-old daughter had told her that Porter had been mean to Kelsey when nobody was looking. According to the counselor, Porter's daughter had seen her father "spank Kelsey until her bottom was real red" and "bang Kelsey's head against a brick wall until Kelsey threw up." The idea that a man could do those things to a child was beyond disturbing to me. After reading the statement, I knew that Mike Porter was a monster. For months, I had been going back and forth due to the lack of evidence I had seen against him to prove without a doubt, that he had purposely murdered Kelsey. Also, I had been inundated with arguments from Kathie Briggs's gang. Evidence that later came to light of the child pornography and other disgusting videos, pictures, and instant message conversations that were found on Porter's computers further solidified my belief that he is undoubtedly a monster. My beliefs were evident in the text that was soon added to Raye Dawn's Web site. The word "innocent" was now a part of my vocabulary in connection with Raye Dawn. I now had evidence to back up my beliefs and my eyes were opened to exactly what had happened in Kelsey's home. Mike Porter was clearly not forthcoming to Raye Dawn about who he was. He manipulated her and she didn't realize it until it was too late. I grew even more passionate about ensuring Kelsey's true story was told.

In response to my efforts to help Raye Dawn, a "new member" posted the following on Kathie Briggs's Web site.

I agree, Mike Porter maned up and has taken his prison term like a
man, [Raye Dawn's prisoner number] well as cried, moaned
and well just look at this The Conspiracy Against Raye Dawn
[A video link was posted]

Starla responded in her usual manner:

I read on another site where Raye Dawn is actually housed now on
death row for her protection. Does anyone know if this is
true? They say she hardly comes out of her cell or socializes
with anyone anymore? This allegedly comes from someone
who's been to the prison to visit someone and was told that by
the inmate they were visiting. I'd like to know if that's true?
Anyone else heard this?

Kathie Briggs replied.

I have heard from more than one source that Raye Dawn is in
protective custody and is housed on death row. The women's
prison is a very short distance from Meeker and many people
either know a prisoner or someone that works there. Stories
about Raye Dawn circulate frequently in our small town. She
too has the option of being housed out of state for her
protection.

Being housed out of state would not protect Raye Dawn. Kathie
Briggs's and Lance's gang members have posted her address on
numerous occasions and she's received hate mail and dead flowers
since she's been in prison.

To this day, I hear stories that Kathie Briggs knows Raye Dawn's
every move, even though she's in prison. Of course, the reports of her
being housed on death row were false. Raye Dawn quickly moved up
in the prison system and is in the least-secure area. She has also
finished a program in which she learned how to counsel and mentor.
She now spends her days mentoring other prisoners. How could
somebody on death row earn trust from the guards and become a
mentor? As usual, certain people will say anything that paints Raye
Dawn in a bad light.

From looking at the mountain of evidence and reading all of the false stories, I know that Kathie and her followers have made up lies to misrepresent Raye and her family members as well as the chain of events. But when the stories suddenly became about me and then other Raye supporters—when the stories become personal and you know that you did not do what these people claim you have done—the gravity of the situation hits you. Anyone can make up anything and people believe them.

Obsession

October, 2007

It soon became clear that nothing was sacred or personal when it came to Raye Dawn. A letter that she had written to a childhood friend soon ended up in Kathie Briggs's possession. Either someone in the postal service tampered with the mail, or the letter was stolen at the prison or from Raye Dawn's friend's mailbox. Despite the circumstances, Kathie Briggs memorized the letter and distributed copies. The letter came to light when I was emailed a copy by Debbie, which I passed on to the intended recipient.

Kathie Briggs posted about the events.

One evening I was gone for less that two hours and as I pulled in my drive I noticed a plain white envelope leaning on my door. I was on the phone with Starla at the time and we were both shocked at what was inside. It took me a few minutes to understand who it was to and I still do not know why it was left for me. The letter was to [Raye Dawn's friend] and sent by Raye Dawn. It was four notebook pages handwritten front and back. I read the letter thinking there must be some information they wanted me to know, but I don't think that is the case. We were certainly baffled by this incident and do not know why it was left at my home. Raye Dawn expressed her disappointment in not getting a new trial and how unfair [the trial judge] was. She stated she felt the DA and I would allow Mike Porter to come home to his children on his one year review. She spoke of her upcoming ten year reunion and asked if any of her classmates would place one of her...stickers on their vehicles. She of course complained about me, but stated I never like her because she stood up to me. What surprised me is the fact she complained about our first Christmas together and our family traditions, but this was the first I knew of her concern. She spoke of a couple of other times when she stood up to me, but once again, she

531

never expressed those concerns to me either. She talked about how she felt Mike Porter was conspiring with us because he knew she and her family would be seeking the death penalty. All in all I could not figure out what the reason was for me to read this letter. A copy has been turned over to the DA for the simple reason that leaving this on my door step is a form of harrassment. The letter was written on Kelsey's birthday and she mentions that was a sad day for her. It is rumored that I have made copies of this letter and sent them out all over Meeker. That is not true. I have not made any copies at this time, but I won't say that couldn't happen. This letter was signed, your friend Raye Dawn...mommy to Kelsey and [Raye Dawn's son]. If anyone has any knowledge of why this letter was left for me I would be curious to know the answer. If there was a hidden message in the letter that I was supposed to get please let me know as I missed the point of it.

In the message, she stated that she had not made copies, but that a copy was turned over to the DA. Kathie Briggs's post was followed by one from Jeanna. She knew her mom would be called out on another lie. There obviously were copies made since one was scanned by someone other than their family members and e-mailed directly to me. Jeanna stated, "Actually mom, two copies of the letter were made--one for the DA and one extra, which was given to a family member of mine." This instance would be only the first sign of mail tampering we would see from Kathie Briggs's group. Privacy and laws regarding privacy seem to be something that has surpassed their comprehension skills. When confronted with this invasion of Raye Dawn's privacy, Kathie Briggs thought she should defend herself by stating the she was "no longer obsessed with Raye Dawn." She coupled this claim with seldom spoken words of disgust for Mike Porter. She stated,

I am no longer obsessed with Raye Dawn, she is in prison. Her fate is out of my hands regardless of any future ruling. I cannot say if we will fight against her when she comes up for parole. I am sure it will depend on how long the slander and accusations towards me and my family continue. As for Mike Porter and my desire for his early release. I will NEVER be

532

in favor of him getting out of prison. When he comes up for
parole in 25 years our family will be there to fight against it.
He is an evil monster that should never be free and allowed
around children. I do not regret the communication I had
with him because it helped Kelsey's case. If I had it to do all
over again, I would. It made me sick when he plastered his
place of business with Kelsey's stickers. I knew he was doing
it for a big show and we used his desire to please us to gain
information about many things.

Notice the threat toward us regarding the alleged "slander" against her family. If we would stop discussing the actual facts in the case, she would consider not fighting Raye Dawn's parole. Also, Kathie Briggs was the one who suggested to Mike Porter that he put the signs at his business. On January 24, 2006 she told him, "You could have a large one [sign] and attach it to the outside of your business." At the time of her post, the e-mails had not been publicized so nobody realized that the signs at Mike Porter's business were actually her suggestion. The public deception seemed to be never-ending.

Mail tampering wasn't the only law that Kathie Briggs and her supporters ignored. Impersonation of Raye Dawn's family members and supporters has been an ongoing problem. Whit described her experience with this issue in the following post:

The Shawnee News-Star comments below the article about Raye
Dawn's PSI report were disabled about a week ago because I
was posting at the same time as 3-4 other Kelsey's Purpose
members who started posting comments under my name, but
with opinions that were not my own. The site administrator
tried to sort it out, but ultimately closed the thread. Before it
was ended, I posted that Kelsey's Purpose members resorted
to childish games when they don't have valid arguments.
They're looking desperate and foolish to me, turning around
and accusing us of the very game they started. I've never seen
anyone post under the name Zoe'sMeemaw on
thetruth. Guess I know who was posting under my name,
now, eh, ZM and Kathie Briggs? Part of their game was
accusing me of sleeping with Craig Key because I think his

533

*insight is valuable to finding out why Kelsey died. I am a
happily married mother of two living in KC, MO. Unless,
we're astral projecting our spirits across hundreds of miles, I
don't see how this tryst is taking place.*

Accusations of affairs are another ongoing issue with Kathie
Briggs's group of supporters. An affair that is nothing but rumors is
possible. However, to continuously accuse multiple people of sleeping
with a person just because one shows respect for him is a mindset that
I will never understand. It clearly illustrates how these people process
information and to me, it's garbage.

In September, 2007, on Kelsey's Purpose there was a big
fundraising effort for the billboards. They raised an unknown amount
of money to pay for the billboards that would disappear one month
later. Where did the funds go?

Hopesanddreams, member
*9-01-2007 - New Kelsey-Billboard - In Elk City, Western Oklahoma,
we (really there is only me way out out in Kelsey's Purpose
out here)-lol! I have been talking to a lot of wonderful
members online about getting a Billboard as people come
into Oklahoma from Texas!! Now! Together have started a
Fundraiser-along with Heart of the Prairie Candles!! (In
Clinton Oklahoma) All The money raised will GO to the
Billboard!! We picked out 8 scents to sell as the fundraisers-
You in your different states may order them and sell them
there, this shop sent to ALL over!! They will be $14.00, All
checks will be made out to "Heart of the Prairie". Now the
WONDERFUL part!! All the candle will be in a pink color!!!
(some were first made in a brown and dirrerent colors and
the shop wishes to make them in the pink!!) Then the Heart
sticker will be on the lables!! YEA!! They are a Large jar,
with a lid. As I said ALL checks will be made out to Heart of
the Prairie, so NO question will be raised where the money
will be going!! THANK YOU!!! The MORE we sell the More
Billboard we can have!! (Yes this was OK by the Family)*

Kjbriggs, Kelsey's Grandma

9-01-07 – FYI - Before the other family runs to the Attorney General let me say....this billboard will contract under Prevent Child Abuse Oklahoma.

Hopesanddreams, Member
9-01-07 - One check will be made out to PCAO, from the Candle shop! Then the Billboard Co. will be paid! I hope EVERYONE will help!!-Hugs

Yhiannah, Senior Member
Post: #138 - RE: Kelsey Saturday—Your Help is Needed! - Charlie still has some of our stickers at the shop. If anyone has businesses or individuals who were interested in donating, several options are available: <u>FOR TAX DEDUCTIBLE RECEIPTS, DONATIONS MAY BE SENT TO:</u> Prevent Child Abuse Oklahoma – [address removed for privacy] *Please write kelseyspurpose in the memo space so it will go in her account.

<u>TO DONATE WITHOUT NEEDING A TAX DEDUCTIBLE RECIEPT, DONATIONS MAY BE SENT TO:</u> Kathie Briggs [address removed for privacy]

<u>TO DIRECTLY HELP WITH THE COST OF STICKERS, PLEASE CONTACT:</u> Charlie's Sign Shop [address removed for privacy]

*Payments can be mailed or made by debit credit card over the phone. If you are calling to donate specifically for Kelsey Saturday, please specify this when you call. Charlie has a separate list set up just for this event.

<u>TO PAY BY PAYPAL:</u> Ashley... has graciously offered us the option of sending money through paypal to her account and she will see that it gets to Kathie. Log in to PayPal (accounts are free). Ashley's email for PayPal is [email address removed for privacy]. Donations are appreciated and the money will go to stickers.

The Smith family wanted answers about the fundraising, considering the organization that was the umbrella for the Briggs stated they knew nothing about billboards. Sherri sent the following letter to the IRS.

July 23, 2007

IRS-EO Classification [address removed for privacy]
To Whom It May Concern: On June 8, 2006, I sent a consumer
  complaint form to the Office Of The Attorney General,
  Consumer Protection Unit Investigative Analyst in Oklahoma
  City, Oklahoma. It was concerning a "non-profit"
  organization called Kelsey's Purpose. The business contact
  and founder of the organization is Kathie Briggs. I was
  passed information today that this organization has never
  filed a 501(c)(3) with the IRS. They are not a tax-exempt
  charity. They have had problems with their donations coming
  to them directly, so they claim to be under another
  organization; Prevent Child Abuse Oklahoma but had their
  tax-exempt status revoked in February 2005. Kelsey's
  Purpose has had various fundraisers, donations and sales of
  t-shirts. In fact, at one large fundraiser, a check for almost
  $6,000 was handed to the son of Kathie Briggs. There has
  been 'Kelsey's Day' at Bell's Amusement Park in Tulsa and
  at the Wynnewood Animal Sanctuary where part of that day's
  proceeds went to Kelsey's Purpose. There has also been
  numerous jars left in fast food, quick stops, and video stores
  for donations. Kelsey's Purpose was founded because it is
  Kathie Brigg's belief that a two and a half year old little girl
  was an abused child. The courts have yet to prove that she
  was abused, but only murdered by her stepfather. Thus
  Kelsey's purpose was to die so that other children may not be
  abused like she was. I am Kelsey's cousin. I DO NOT want
  people profiting off of Kelsey's death. It is unethical and
  should not create Kelsey's memory with us as an abused
  child. I spoke with Micah…at Prevent Child Abuse Oklahoma
  the summer of 2006 and she assured me that Kelsey's
  Purpose was being handled properly. She did inform me that
  the organization does not condone the monies for supporting
  billboards and that she knew nothing of the $6,000

536

fundraising event. She did say she will be calling Kathie Briggs to inquire about the fundraiser and the billboards and explain to her so that she will understand that their organization does not support billboards and signs. I then spoke to The Consumer Protection Department of Oklahoma and they told me that Kelsey's Purpose was to cease and desist all donations. I have reasons to believe that the donations are still being asked for and innocent people are still giving. Please help us stop the abuse of the personal gains that Kelsey's memory is being used for now. Sincerely, Sherri S. Heath

Another issue arose after Raye was officially sentenced in September, 2007. The billboard discussion came up again in October, 2007 when the billboards, stickers, and signs started to disappear. Kathie Briggs's excuse for taking it down was due to the contract expiring. At the same time, she reportedly removed the huge signs from her fence and Lance Briggs removed the signs from his yard. Had justice for Kelsey been served in their eyes?

kjbriggs	**RE: Kelsey on I-40**	**Post: #68**
Kelsey's Grandma ☆☆☆☆☆☆	*The contract was up on the I-40 billboard. We chose not to renew it since we have some other projects in the works. We all knew it could not stay up forever.*	
Posts: 1,221 Group: Administrators Joined: Nov 2005 Status: Offline eputation: ▮▮▮▮▮▮▮▮▮		

Intimate Emails

December, 2007

In November of 2007 I succumbed to the requests of a local reporter who wanted to do a story about my business in the statewide newspaper. We originally discussed the story earlier that year, before my employment with the Judge or my involvement with Raye Dawn, also before I was forced to take a round of steroids so that I could breathe. I was puffy and battling yet another round of bronchitis and I didn't want Kathie Briggs and her gang to discover my identity. When the article was to be written, I presented multiple arguments in an attempt to cancel the interview. The reporter's attitude and kindness squashed my arguments. She needed the story and I wanted to help her. However, because I had been sick for so long, I wasn't thinking clearly during the interview. I brought out a stack of books that I had edited and I didn't notice that in the stack was the Judge's book. The article mentioned the fact that I edited the book. Once I saw my name in connection with the book in print, I knew it wouldn't be long before they discovered my identity, and, by December, I had pushed Kathie Briggs to the point that she didn't care what it took. She wanted to know who I was.

This determination came after I received the e-mails between her family and Mike Porter and I published them on Raye Dawn's Web site. I also included excerpts from the emails in a video. The emails had been in my possession for months before they were posted. Raye Dawn and her family had never read them, but after just skimming over them, I came to the conclusion that her family needed to be informed of their content. I met with Gayla, Raye Dawn's mom, and delivered the originals back to her. I didn't need them anymore because I had scanned them into my computer. Gayla, in turn, took the emails to Raye Dawn's new attorney and then she mailed a copy to

Raye Dawn. After months of consideration and a consultation with Raye Dawn, as well as her attorney, the consensus was that they needed to be published. I'll never forget Raye Dawn's reaction to those emails. She asked me, "How could Kathie do that to Kelsey?" I had no answer for her either. To me, it was the ultimate betrayal. She befriended the man who had been charged with the murder of her grandchild. Raye Dawn's family couldn't comprehend what Kathie Briggs was thinking and we all thought that her followers needed to know as well. The decision was made. We would publish them. But we questioned how it should be done.

In the following e-mail with Raye Dawn's family members and close friends, I discussed what we should do with the e-mails. The forum moderators and close supporters had seen them, but we had not released them to the public. In 2010, the following e-mail was posted on Starla's blog as her proof that I'm Truth Seeker. I suppose she forgot that it was an e-mail they had obtained through e-mail tampering. Although we've reported their illegal activities to the FBI and the police, no charges have been filed to date.

On December 20, 2007 I wrote:

I'm assuming you all know each other. This is the three from the forum who know who I am and Raye Dawn's family, so we're all safe. :) Okay, I've been thinking, praying, thinking, praying, and considering about the emails and what to do with them. This is my new thought: I agree that selling them is a great idea along with the rest of the prelim, but now I'm wondering if we shouldn't just put it all out there. I'm thinking that the more readily available they are, the more support we're going to get from releasing them and it will in turn give us more supporters who will donate to the fund. I think once people see and understand how Kathie Briggs and Mike Porter teamed up against Raye Dawn and we clearly point that out to them, they'll realize that Raye Dawn has been railroaded into prison. The biggest argument I'm getting now is that a jury convicted her so she must be guilty. I think we need to (along with our current approach) fill in

*those who are new to the game and let them know what they
missed and what it's been like for Raye Dawn and her family
for the last two years. New people watch the Briggs' videos
and hear their side and they assume that Raye Dawn's side
has been out there and nobody believes her. Even those who
have read Judge Key's book don't get the magnitude of what
has happened. I think we need to paint that picture and
supporters will flood us. What do you all think??*

The decision was unanimous. We would post the e-mails. I
announced it via e-mail to our forum members. The ornery tone of the
e-mail illustrates the attitude I had at the time. I was throwing their
crap back at them.

*We've recently released the emails between Kathie Briggs, Shirica,
and Mike Porter. It was an early Christmas present to the
Briggs family. What can I say? I'm a giver! The emails are
being posted five at a time at [Web site address given] and
there is a discussion of them on the forum at [forum address
given]. [A moderator] has worked hard at going through
them and making notes after each one to point out the lies
and clear cut case of a conspiracy to get a plea for Mike
Porter to leave Raye Dawn to pay for Mike Porter's crime.
These are a MUST READ! Happy Holidays! Truth Seeker*

The posting came with the following explanation:

*Since shortly after the death of two-year-old Kelsey, Kathie Briggs
has had a singular purpose – a vendetta against Raye Dawn
and her entire family. Kathie Briggs's vendetta was also
extended to others including Kelsey's doctor, DHS, the Judge
who heard the custody battle over Kelsey, CHBS, CASA, and
everyone else that had contact with Kelsey during the last few
months of her life. This vendetta has been proven time and
time again, but it has never been more clear than in the
emails that were exchanged between Kathie Briggs and her
daughters and Mike Porter, the man the district attorney said
sexually assaulted and perpetrated the murder of little
Kelsey. Kathie Briggs admitted to exchanging maybe a dozen
emails with Mike Porter, but in total approximately 90 were*

exchanged between Mike Porter and the Briggs. (Some
emails had missing pages and the conversation jumps. Cell
and home phone numbers were exchanged several times as
well.) At Raye Dawn's trial, Kathie Briggs was questioned
about the emails. She testified that she didn't ask Mike Porter
what happened to Kelsey. This is true, however her daughter
also exchanged emails with Mike Porter and she offered to
share information about the investigation and phone numbers
were exchanged numerous times, some emails referred to
conversations that were not in any of the emails. Kathie
Briggs's daughter told Mike Porter, "I welcome private
phone calls and I am very much into discretion."

One hour after the announcement that the e-mails were going
public, Kathie Briggs's forum shut down. A message was briefly
displayed that stated that the forum had been hacked. After just a few
minutes, the "hacked" message was replaced with the following:

This bulletin board is currently closed. The Administrator has
specified the reason as to why below. The forums are down
temporarily for maintenance. Merry Christmas and a Happy
New Year to everyone!!!

Moments before the forum disappeared, Jeanna posted a family
announcement that included excuses for the e-mails with Mike Porter.
She stated that she and her family members had used him and that they
had been a means to lure Mike Porter into providing information to
the family.

After reports that all of the e-mail addresses that were associated
with Kathie Briggs's Web site were also down, a good friend and
former Kathie Briggs supporter who had purchased one of the
memorial sites for Kathie Briggs sent to her the following as a "test"
e-mail:

Just wondering what is happening with the Kelsey's Purpose site. It
has been down for 'maintence' for quite awhile. Yall having
some kind of problem over there. Also, just curious as to
what your response on the emails that have been posted

between you and Mike Porter??? Hows that working for you now???

The email was answered by an overly polite email from Jeanna who stated that life was great.

From December 20th or 21st to January 8th, Kathie Briggs's forum remained closed. According to witnesses who had been closely watching Kathie Briggs's group from the beginning, this is something that had not happened since the day the forum opened. It had never closed for any reason, not even for Raye Dawn's trial, except to new posts. It remained open for people to read. On January 8, 2008, the forum reopened with this message from Shirica:

The intent of the emails were to lure him out by trying to gain his confidence and trust and then using that to gain some kind of understanding into the mind of this murderer.

In her statement, she reiterated her previous statement that Mike Porter was indeed the one who murdered Kelsey. Yet today Shirica and her family promote a story that leads the public to believe that they don't know who committed the murder, and, as usual, they work to shift the focus to Raye Dawn.

On the same day that Shirica made her announcement, Kathie Briggs made one of her own.

Raye Dawn's actions since at the trial and since has made me lean towards her. She is the one I originally thought killed Kelsey and now I am back to that thought.

After the trial, Raye Dawn was taken directly into custody. Her one and only action was to turn to Kathie Briggs and say, "Kathie, I forgive you." Kathie Briggs had not seen nor heard from Raye Dawn since making that statement. Raye Dawn knew who put her in jail. She knew why she was sentenced to twenty-seven years for "should have known." It wasn't for a crime. It was because of the hate that Kathie Briggs clearly has for Raye Dawn. On the day of Raye Dawn's sentencing, Raye Dawn forgave Kathie Briggs, who turned to the media and stated, "Take her away. Keep her. Let her think about what she's done." Kathie Briggs's statement of how Raye Dawn's actions lead her to now believe that Raye Dawn murdered her child is incomprehensible!

Not one to be overshadowed by her mom and her sister, Jeanna added her own misleading statement about the emails.

The emails that were available to be used as evidence in The State of Oklahoma vs. Michael Lee Porter and The State of Oklahoma vs. Raye Dawn Smith will be posted to this site as soon as time is available to get them posted. Michael Porter pled guilty after the emails were turned over to the District Attorney to be used against him. Raye Dawn and her attorneys felt they were not important and chose not to use them for her defense.

aunt bean
Administrator
Posts: 105
Group: Administrators
Joined: Nov 2005
Status: Offline
Reputation:
Post: #1Emails
The emails that were available to be used as evidence in The State of Oklahoma vs. Michael Lee Porter and The State of Oklahoma vs. Raye Dawn Smith will be posted to this site as soon as time is available to get them posted. Michael Porter pled guilty after the emails were turned over to the District Attorney to be used against him. Raye Dawn Smith and her attorneys felt they were not important and chose not to use them for her defense.

In actuality, the trial judge had refused the submission of the e-mails as evidence in Raye Dawn's trial. The judge continuously used the excuse that they were "attached to the wrong witness" although the witness Raye Dawn's attorney tried to attach them to had been one of the participants, Kathie Briggs. The e-mails have never been posted in their entirety on Kathie Briggs's Web site or in anything created by

Kelsey's paternal family. Only excerpts are used to portray their *claimed* intent.

Soon after the e-mails were published, Kathie Briggs's supporters started dropping like flies. A long-time supporter of Kathie Briggs who admittedly stalked Raye Dawn at the request of Kathie Briggs sent this message to me:

> *From: [Kathie Briggs supporter] Date: Mon, Jan 07, 2008 1:14 am To: Truth Seeker - Many people feel very betrayed by the emails between Mike Porter, Shirica, Jeanna and Kathie. They are extremely disturbing and I have some questions. 1. Why were these emails only released after Raye Dawn's trial? 2. Why did the DA announced that he was giving Mike Porter a plea because he didn't want to put the family through a painful jury trial. 3. Why did the same DA go after Raye Dawn and offered "no deal" per Lance while this family waited for the trial with baited breath. I have never posted on your web site but a Kelsey's Purpose member told me I am banned. Good day from An obsessed freak.*

In the emails between Shirica, Jeanna, and Mike Porter, they referred to their supporters as "obsessed freaks," which soon became the tag under all of our names on the forum. Other than being called a derogatory name by the people she had worked so hard to support, I believe it was posts like the following from Kathie Briggs that made this person believe that she had been mislead. On December 17, 2005 Kathie Briggs stated:

> *Two months ago yesterday we got the call that would change our lives forever. Our lives are now filled with questions, anger, and a mission for change. As I look back over the last two months I am amazed at all of the positives that have come out of this tragedy. We have heard from old friends and we now have new friends that have reached out to a family they have never met. Our family that has always been close has been our biggest source of strength next to the prayers that come from people near and far. To count our blessings would be an endless task. Yes, some days are long and hard, but we get*

*through them together. So many have shared their kind words
on this site and we appreciate all of them. We have even
allowed some to voice opinions we do not necessarily agree
with, but at this time I am asking that some of that stop. This
site was designed to honor Kelsey and the loved ones she left
behind. It was not put here to defend or attack the ones who
abused her. I agree there are many questions that need
answers. There are many facts that don't add up. The wheels
of justice are way too slow, but we have no choice but to
wait. I have to believe the truth will come out and justice will
be served. In the mean time, Kelsey was not the only victim of
this crime. I continue to not only think of how this has
changed our family, but the lives of Mike Porter's children. I
also want to mention Mike Porter has two sisters ages 27 and
22 that are alone during this time. Their parents are no
longer living and they do not have the support system we
have. It breaks my heart to think what these two girls are
going through. I would ask each one of you to remember
them in your prayers...*

At the same time that Kathie Briggs's supporters were struggling
to understand the facts that had been brought to light about a side of
Kathie Briggs that had been hidden from public view, my life was
continuing to spiral out of control. For me, no more business also
meant there was no money for extras, such as Christmas. Two
wonderful ladies from the forum who had trapped me in chat rooms
and broken down my barriers had gotten to know me. They knew I
was struggling and they wanted to help. Days before Christmas, while
Kathie Briggs and her closest supporters were plotting to destroy me,
my new friends who called themselves "Christmas elves" mailed my
family a box full of wrapped gifts. I told them:

*The UPS man just came and I have too many tears streaming down
my face and my glasses are all messed up so I can't type very
well right now. Pardon any mistakes! I don't know what to
say! There are no words to express my gratitude that you all
thought of us in this way. I'm speechless! I only dug a couple
of things out and put it back in until my daughter comes home
from sitting with my mom. We've never in our lives had*

*someone do something so kind for us! I can't even begin to
express how thankful I am for you! And yes, you are my
favorites!! LOL! Thank you so much!!! Thank you, thank you,
thank you and God bless you!!! I will repay your kindness
one day because you know I don't like to accept things with
nothing in return. But this came (now I'm bawling again) at a
time when I really needed cheering up! Thank you!!! I also
got a card from Raye Dawn today and she just spoke of how
much she appreciates what I've done. It's things like this that
make everything worth it. I wouldn't change a thing and I'd
make all these sacrifices all over again just to have people
like you brought into my life. Thank you and I thank God for
you and I'll keep praying for the baby to get well! Love, Jody*

Oklahoma State Bureau of

Investigation

January, 2008

In the case against Raye Dawn, Kelsey's paternal family members have mentioned hindsight on multiple occasions. They've stated that with hindsight they realize they "should have done more to save Kelsey." With hindsight, everything becomes clearer. All of our victories and mistakes are easily seen with hindsight. Odd behavioral patterns in people once trusted are suddenly visible when that person's true character is exposed. In fact, this was an issue brought up at Raye Dawn's trial. I'm sure that everyone who knew Kelsey would like to go back and change things, but it seems the only ones involved in the tragedy that are allowed to use hindsight are Kathie Briggs and her family. In their eyes, everyone is to blame except for them, even though, according to witnesses, their mistakes would also make them accountable for not protecting Kelsey.

After reopening her forum, instead of posting the e-mails as Shirica promised they would do, Kathie Briggs, with the help of Lance's girlfriend, transcribed Raye Dawn's confidential Oklahoma State Bureau of Investigation interviews. These were classified interviews that never should have been in her possession, but as you will recall, they had been given to her by Mike Porter's attorney. She then committed a misdemeanor crime and posted the "transcripts" on her Web site and called them "official" in a desperate attempt to deflect the attention from the damaging e-mails and back onto the one Kathie Briggs obviously hated most, Raye Dawn. Along with the few long-time supporters who hadn't abandoned ship, as well as the new supporters who didn't understand the significance of Kathie Briggs's betrayal of Kelsey in her correspondence with Mike Porter, posts were soon added to Kathie Briggs's forum that included several negative opinions about what Kathie Briggs claimed Raye Dawn had stated in her interviews. In these posts, Kathie Briggs's supporters pointed out all of the "red flags" that Raye Dawn had missed as she described Mike Porter's actions that had struck her as odd while she revisited everything that she could remember happening since Mike Porter entered Kelsey's life. These discoveries came to light while contemplating Mike Porter's actions after the first interview, when she had been told that her daughter was murdered and had not died from a seizure.

What struck me as odd was the fact that none of the people commenting took into consideration that the interviews on which they were basing their opinion of Raye Dawn were mere interpretations made by Kathie Briggs and Lance's girlfriend. There was nothing "official" about what they had transcribed and posted. Since I was familiar with the history of deception from Kathie Briggs and her group, I only glanced through their version of the interviews and decided to wait until something official was released before I made any judgments.

One thing that was never pointed out to those who trusted the validity of the interviews was the fact that Raye Dawn used hindsight in her second interview with the OSBI. In an effort to figure out exactly what happened to Kelsey, she reported the things that now seemed suspicious in Mike Porter's actions. With the loss of her beautiful, beloved daughter, and the realization that she never really knew her husband, memories took on new meanings. Once, they were of a man who was a good father and who would do anything to help her raise her child. Now, in the darkest depths of her imagination, she didn't want to see the memories in a new light or envision what the stranger in her bed had done to her child. She revisited her memories honestly and openly and reported what she knew to the officials in an effort to solve the murder of her child.

Upon reflection, she very naively discussed every detail of their lives with no holds barred and her honest and open admissions were eventually used against her. In a normal case where everyone follows the law and works together for the greater good, as the district attorney described it, her "full cooperation" would have helped to put the perpetrator behind bars and ensure he was listed on a sex offender registry. However, in this case, when the desired outcome is something other than justice for a dead child and the one "fully cooperating" is the ex-mother-in-law's main target, Raye Dawn didn't stand a chance. In hindsight, the release of the interviews was also a deflection of their latest scheme in which they would soon reveal my identity, breaking multiple laws in the process.

My Middle Name Isn't Sue

February, 2008

Despite tactics from Kathie Briggs's gang to break up our forum, we continued to attract new members and gained support with an ever-evolving set of rules and strong leadership provided by key people who had earned my trust. These members were soon assigned the task of moderator. At times, a few of them even took over the role of "Truth Seeker" while I took much-needed breaks from dealing with the ongoing stream of hate. This change was noticed by a Kathie Briggs supporter, who stated to one of our moderators, "One day Truth Seeker is nice and the next day she's not." She had no idea that it wasn't just me with whom she corresponded and I wanted to keep it that way. We never publicly announced the fact that a few of us answered Truth Seeker e-mails or that moderators would post on the forum as me, sometimes by accident. We called it the "Truth Seeker Plan" and it gave me time to rest. It also allowed others to take on more of the responsibilities, which I was eager to share. It was nice having people on board I could trust. My role in helping Raye Dawn was easier once some of the decision-making was taken off of my shoulders. Within just a few months I had gone from the lone wolf to having several people pitching in whenever needed. Everything we did on behalf of Raye Dawn turned into a group decision and life was slowly becoming easier for me. We had been acting as a team for quite some time, but after only a few months, our teamwork had stepped up to a level where I could disappear for a day or two and few people noticed I was gone. It was a nice change.

By January of 2008, mentally, I was finished. I needed to get back to my old life. Since Raye Dawn had gained strong supporters who seemed to care as much about her and her family as I did, I wanted to turn the reigns over to someone new and bow out quietly. I'm not proud of the fact that I wanted to quit Raye Dawn, but I couldn't take the hate anymore; it was really getting to me. My plan was to increasingly turn over more of the day-to-day responsibilities until I could finally go away and not be missed. At least, that was the plan. Kathie Briggs, Lance, and their supporters had another plan. They wanted to expose me and make good on their countless threats of lawsuits. Since the forum's inception, our leaders would get wind of lawsuit threats and make changes within the forum to ensure we were playing by the rules at all times so that none of us could be held liable. I never worried. We weren't breaking any laws so the constant changes were annoying to me. Lance had filed multiple lawsuits and even had his attorney draft a letter to the Judge's publisher claiming he was entitled to the proceeds of the Judge's book, which was unfounded. We all knew that wherever there was money to be had; Lance and Kathie Briggs would find a way to get their hands on it. For some, the constant threats became too much. Even though the threats against us were never backed up by anything tangible and Kathie Briggs and Lance had no basis for a lawsuit, we lost good supporters because they didn't want to take the chance. This was, presumably, another part of their evil plan to destroy us.

For months, Kelsey's Purpose members worked hard to convince us that we had no right to express our opinions on the high-profile case without Lance's permission. Each and every day we had to argue our rights. We also faced issues with Kathie Briggs's spies pretending to be supportive of Raye Dawn. In reality, they only wanted to harass us. These trouble makers were usually easy to spot and were banned from the forum, but they always returned. Every idea we had of how to rid ourselves of the pesky invaders failed. We went from an open forum where anyone could read or post to a closed forum—for members only—and then to a forum where all memberships had to be approved because sneaky haters joined the forum in the middle of the night and posted several vulgar messages. Keeping up with the hate was constant work. It finally got to the point where we required every member to join with an e-mail address through their Internet Service Provider. We hoped that no longer allowing members to use a free and easy-to-open e-mail account to gain access under a false identity would cut down on the intrusions and help us to weed out the bad eggs. When we initiated this plan, we heard a lot of excuses, and one in particular was from someone named "Starlady." Sound familiar? I was told that it was another one of "them," but as usual, I bought the sob story and let her join, only to later regret my decision.

From: Truth Seeker To: Forum members Sent: Monday, February 11, 2008 12:16:04 PM - Subject: isp provided email accounts - I wanted to first thank all of you for taking the time to join our forum and read the facts on this case and search for the truth. For those of you who have opened your hearts and minds to the obvious truth of Raye Dawn's innocence, I want to especially thank you. It's not an easy transition to go from believing the lies you've heard for over two years to facing the facts and the realization that only one person and his sick, twisted mind perpetrated the crime that took Kelsey's life. Since the end of July, 2007 I've struggled in a never-ending battle to get people to open up and look at the facts and not just what they've been told. For those of you who don't know, before July, 2007 the only story in the public anywhere was that of the Briggs. The first U.S. Observer article was published in June, 2007, the Judge's book was released at the end of July, 2007, and I began a blog which led to this forum at the end of July, 2007. There were 63 Briggs videos when I made the first Raye Dawn video in August, 2007. It was a hard, uphill battle and it's so nice to now have so many others who are fighting alongside me and to have such a dedicated and caring Raye Dawn army. I'll never be able to express my gratitude for all of you enough, but just know that you are appreciated and you will receive many blessings when you meet our Lord and Savior. God bless all of you. For the others who are still here and want to silence our message, what can I say except I just don't get it. If the Briggs were right and this wasn't just about their hate for Raye Dawn, then what harm are we doing? Why try and silence us? Why not concentrate on your 'purpose' which is supposed to be child abuse and don't give us a reason to even discuss your forum? If you think you're right, our time is wasted, right? So why continue to bother with us at all? Your continued presence on our forum just tells us and the entire world that we're on to something and that you don't want the truth heard. We can't keep you out, obviously, so keep proving us right. You're doing a great job of that. In the meantime, we're still tightening the forum by only allowing isp provided email addresses to be used for memberships. We extended the deadline to change to an isp email for some members, but now that deadline is up. For those of you with an aol, gmail, yahoo, hotmail, or any other free email account your membership will be deleted at 12:01pm CST tomorrow, February, 12, 2008. If you have an isp email address and haven't made the switch yet, click on your name on the forum, click edit profile, and change your email address there. If your account gets deleted, all you have to do is rejoin with an isp provided email address such as through your phone company, cable company, business, school, your own website, or any other provider that isn't a free one that anyone can get. You'll be asked to verify your email address after you sign up and you can rejoin with your current name. Again, we appreciate all of our members, but this is a necessary step to keep out those who are only here to disrupt our forum and report back to the Briggs. Thank you for your cooperation! Cheers, Truth Seeker

By manually approving the memberships, I was thrown into a position where I had to judge people and question their intentions. It was tough on me. In 2007, I entered a world that was unfamiliar and I didn't like it. It took too much of my time and energy and I very quickly grew tired of it all.

Because of our constant battles with the other side, our forum remained small with less than two hundred members. We deleted each inactive account and booted members from the forum at times for no reason other than the fact that they were "suspicious." It got to the point where, to me, it seemed ridiculous. I had a feeling that paranoia ruled over common sense. Every new member was seen as a possible enemy. The childish games the intruders were playing wore on us all and we argued and pointed fingers at each other on several occasions while trying to find out who was sharing information with the other side. I felt terrible for those who were put under a magnifying lens. It was a place I knew I would never be because I was obviously not sharing anything with the "others," but some of the trusted seemed suspicious at times and were questioned. I hated it. All I wanted to do was to help Raye Dawn and her family, but in the process, I found myself a soldier in an unwinnable war. It was nothing short of ridiculous.

There were two especially troublesome individuals whom we had to ban multiple times. Their leading questions were always the same. I wanted to give everyone the benefit of the doubt and treat them as they presented themselves to us—someone new to the case. However, our ever-watchful group of moderators could usually spot the intruders right away. To me, having someone on the forum that was there to spy wasn't that big of a deal because nothing was posted that I wouldn't say in person. However, because of Lance's history with lawsuits, others worried about their financial safety, even though all they did was voice an opinion. They also viewed the constant intrusions as a disruption in our typically-peaceful conversations. Another concern was that they posed a security threat for Raye Dawn and her family since, often, the discussion concerned helping Raye Dawn in her defense.

One of the particularly-annoying intruders was someone who seemed to be in the fight for the right reasons. We'll call her "Clay." Her mission was to bring awareness to child abuse and she was good at what she did. Clay's videos were popular on YouTube and she seemed to have a real heart for children. During Raye Dawn's trial, Kathie Briggs's forum was supposed to be closed, but evidence shows that Clay was recruited by a member of Kelsey's Purpose and she actually joined while Raye Dawn was on trial. I can't recall when I first had knowledge of the existence of this person, but at one point, we were in contact with each other and I presented to her the reasons why I supported Raye Dawn, as well as the inaccuracies in a video that she had made for Kathie Briggs. She based the video on Kathie Briggs's "story" of Kelsey, which has been proven to be misleading and partly untrue.

In the beginning, my communication with Clay was friendly with "God bless you" and "good luck." She joined our forum under a false identity after not feeling appreciated by Kathie Briggs and not understanding the e-mails between Kathie Briggs and Mike Porter. Kathie Briggs rectified the situation with this person by sending her a "thank you" card. Kathie Briggs then posted a statement about the card on her forum in her typically condescending manner.

The last time I counted there were 120 videos…It simply amazes me how many people take it upon theirselves to make a video about someone's deceased child without first contacting the family. I then thought how nice it was that they were taking the time from their day to make a tribute to Kelsey. Recently it was brought to my attention that some people felt we haven't given them the recognition they deserve. I want to apologize for anyone who feels that way. Out of all the videos that have been made I've seen approximately five. Of those five I sent a thank you via email. Then when [Clay, with her name spelled incorrectly] hit the 18,000,000 mark I sent her a thank you card with Kelsey's picture printed inside along with some keepsakes. It wasn't that I appreciated her more than the others, I simply do not have everyone's contact information. I had hoped these videos were being made for the compassion you felt for Kelsey and child abuse and not because you wanted personal praise.

Immediately after receiving the card, Clay forgave Kathie Briggs, but she remained on our forum. Her questions turned into never-ending arguments. She wanted to argue every minute detail of Kelsey's final months. No matter how hard we tried, we could never get her to look at the heart of the matter. She wasn't very young; she was twenty-seven or twenty-eight, but the fact that she had no children and she was immature made it difficult for her to understand anything from Raye Dawn's point of view. She frustrated every one of us, but especially me. I could see through to her heart and I felt a strong sense of compassion for her. It was clear she was being used, but she just didn't get it. Not one of my fellow moderators agreed with me. Even today, after everything she's done to me, I still feel only compassion and sadness for her. My friends don't understand and neither do I. She doesn't deserve my compassion, and although she is, at times, nothing but rude and horrible to me, I still pity her.

After realizing Clay was a lost cause, the moderators decided to give her the boot. In turn, she took her disappointment out on me. The communication between us was no longer friendly, and to this day, I consider her one of the main instigators of the continual bullying and hate against me. In a sworn deposition taken in the summer of 2009, Kathie Briggs denied knowing this person, yet she still supports Kathie Briggs and Lance. She refuses to believe that Lance abused Raye Dawn on several occasions and that he should not be portrayed as a "hero" or a loving father because of witnesses who told me that "he didn't want to be bothered with Kelsey." It's a travesty to me that Clay is still being used for a sick cause.

Another thorn in my side that was kicked off the forum on countless occasions was Starla. We jokingly stated on several occasions that her middle name was Sue to which she always argued, "My middle name isn't Sue!" We didn't know which part of her denial to find the most entertaining: the fact that she repeatedly threatened lawsuits against all of us on behalf of Lance and Kathie Briggs, hence the nickname, or the fact that she wasn't sharp enough to make the connection and would ramble on about how we knew nothing about her because we didn't even know her middle name. It was hilarious! At one point, she pretended to be "Taylor." On December 28, 2007, we emailed back-and-forth because she was having issues accessing the forum. She wrote:

I have been reading through some of your site. I am new to this story, having been sent a video of this story from myspace. I have not formed an opinion on any of it, and hope that does not pose a problem being on your site. From what I have read on your site, there is another site that has a problem if you don't form your opinion based on theirs [Kathie Briggs's Web site]. I have not as yet, seen this happening on your site. I like to form and have my own opinion and not have to play follow the leader. Thank you for your response. Respectfully, Taylor

I responded in my usually trusting manner.

Welcome Taylor, Glad to have you aboard. All we ask is that you do not bash Raye Dawn or her family and we all will get along fine. We have various opinions on our site. Please be sure to check out our other websites and read more of the facts on the case especially the emails between Kathie Briggs and Mike Porter. Thanks, Truth Seeker

On January 11, 2008 I sent the following message to the forum members.

This case is so confusing that we all get mixed up on who's who. So I built a page of participants. Hope it helps!

I ended the message with Scripture that I began to use often. John 3:19-21

This is the verdict: Light has come into the world, but men loved darkness instead of light because their deeds were evil. Everyone who does evil hates the light, and will not come into the light for fear that his deeds will be exposed. But whoever lives by the truth comes into the light, so that it may be seen plainly that what he has done has been done through God.

By January 19, 2008 "Taylor" had been exposed and banned from the forum. Kathie Briggs and Starla pretending to be Taylor sounded so much alike in the biting and cynical comments that I thought she was Kathie Briggs, and she could have been. I wouldn't doubt that they were sharing the same email address and membership.

Taylor asked, "Do you mind me asking why I am banned from your forum?"

I replied, "Apparently you didn't read the comment I left you on your other blog. I suggest you go check it out."

I was referring to a political blog that Kathie Briggs's gang members had been using to spread their hate against Raye Dawn. The hate ignited on that blog with an article that was posted about Cherokee Ballard that included reports of her over-consumption of alcoholic beverages. I've seen accusations against me for writing that article, but at the time it was posted, I wasn't in the fight. I had no idea of the reporter's ties with Kathie and Lance until the press conference when the reporter inappropriately commented on the Judge's description of Kathie Briggs's attire. At that time, I was just piecing the relationships together.

Starla responded.

My dear lady, If I had another blog I would...Thank you for letting me learn a bit of your side's side. I'm not sure for the banning and would have preferred to get the rest of that side, but I will be able to attain what I remain to need from others. Knowing my friends side, I wished to learn your side for myself before contacting the other family. Either way, will make an interesting story. Too bad banning me proved to me that maybe my friend is right in what she has tried to tell me about the Free Kelsey's Mom site. I tried to remain objective and seek answers for myself. Thank you for the help you gave until this point. Taylor

Soon after the first response, she added,

...I have no idea what you are speaking of. Do not worry, no further communication between us is required or wanted. Good Luck to you. Taylor

At the end of the e-mail, she added the following statement in an attempt to cover her tracks for what was to soon come. She stated,

I will be leaving soon and will let my friend assume this email
address as I have no further need for it. She may choose to
keep in communication with some of those that email this
account and she may not. Of no difference to me. Just wanted
to be 'up front' and let you know.

I was tired of her games. I had her pegged as Kathie Briggs. I told
her,

Haha! There is nothing up front about what you've done. I know who
you are. I just didn't put it out there. I baited you in our
private messages and said things to you that I haven't said to
anyone else to see if you'd run with it and you ran with it
straight to the political blog. I called you another name on
there, but I know who you really are. You made yourself a
public figure and we're discussing facts and our opinions so
there is no lawsuit to be had with us. Why don't you get to
what you're supposed to be doing and save some children? I
feel for you because I know you loved Kelsey, but I feel worse
for the other family because of what you've done to them. You
know in your heart that Raye Dawn didn't hurt Kelsey.
Doesn't it bother you that you've put her through all that you
have and that she could be in prison until you're almost dead
and gone? Don't you have a heart or a conscious
whatsoever? What will you regret on your death bed?
Haven't you learned yet that life is too short to play with
other people's lives? Have you destroyed enough people?

It seems that Kathie Briggs found a soul mate in Starla. Neither
one of them has compassion for anyone but themselves. They both
have an attitude like they can do no wrong. It's as if nobody could ever
find fault in either one of them when, in fact, the double-standard
seems to apply only to them. On numerous occasions, Starla has called
me an "outsider" and stated that I "positioned myself into the case"
and that I'm "butting in where I don't belong." For years, Raye
Dawn's family has tried to discover the connection between Starla and
the paternal family. She has always seemed to be out for blood with
her relentless attacks on Raye Dawn, Raye Dawn's mom, and myself

that have carried on for years, with nothing to ignite the attacks from any of us.

When sorting through saved posts and communications in piecing together the chain of events, I discovered a post from Kathie Briggs's Web site from August 7, 2007. Shirica was attempting to garner a renewed support from her members by posing the question, "Why are you here?" Starla answered.

When I first came here, it was because I saw a newsclip about a little girl named Kelsey who died as a result of child abuse…I googled her name and found this site… You know, when those against this Purpose are hollering their loudest…that is when you know you are really doing something right. I am proud to be one of those 'evil Kelsey's Purpose members…'

The question is answered. She saw it on the news and in turn, became immersed in the drama. The distinction between her and me is that I didn't seek out the case. It found me. I didn't watch the news and insert myself into the drama. I felt compelled to help someone who was being crucified after I was pulled into the case. My question is this: Who is actually writing the posts that call me an "outsider" when, clearly, the person who is supposedly making the accusation is more of an "outsider" than me? To my knowledge, she hasn't even attended a single event to "raise awareness against child abuse." So what is her true purpose and who is the one posing as her?

On March 21, 2008 the same email address that "Taylor" had used in connection with her membership on the forum, comfort_bears, sent this message to my Truth Seeker account:

So, Jody how the hell are ya? LOL We've known for some time who you are, now the world does. So, is your rally open to the public? I'm thinking about making the trip just for it. Don't worry, I won't hide, I'll introduce myself to you. And you thought the Grand Jury Investigation was far fetched! Details to follow… Starla Proud member of Kelsey's Purpose

A day later I replied.

Starla, So, you finally came out of the closet. Nice to meet you. But you have my name wrong. I see you're on a fishing expedition. LOL!

She responded with a threat and blackmail.

Jody, Seriously, do you really think you can start a website...trashing a DA, and seriously think that a subpeona can't be obtained without your knowledge? Do you really think that was a smart move? How many of the 12 websites that you owned at the time the subpeona was issued are nothing but www.trashsomebodysites.com ? How do you think the public will feel about you when the information really does go public about your identity with all the evil, filthy lies and twisted facts that you have posted all over the internet about Kelsey's paternal family?? How will that affect your business? From what I have been able to find out, you have nothing to compensate them if they do sue you. But...a couple of investigative stories published in the news will have such a lasting impact. Everytime someone "searches" your name when looking for a writer, editor, or voice over...well guess what? It will pull up a link to the newstories too. Personally, I think that would do you greater monetary harm than sueing you. Legit people won't want to hire an editor or writer with so much negativity and controversy publicly displayed by that person who has continually trashed and disrespected the memory of a murdered, innocent child by posting the evil lies all over the web like you have done about Kelsey's paternal family. Did you forget that the Briggs really do have connections? Do you doubt that the reporter that you all trashed as being a drunk maybe wouldn't jump at the opportunity to do a story on the revealing of truthseekers identity with all the facts that have been twisted and altered by that person? and with the connection to Craig Key? And just so you know, I hear the OCCY isn't very happy with the altered reports that have been displayed on your sites. I also hear there are 'important' people that aren't happy that you posted

SEALED DHS documents on [your Web site], or did the Smiths or Key forget to mention to you those records were sealed when they gave them to you? You know something to put some thought into...you have stated on [Raye Dawn's Web site] that you aren't perfect...how much would someone find out on you to be splasing all over the internet if they decided to take the time to dig into YOUR past? You started this battle, you can end it. You started the websites, you can end them and all of this can go away.

The End of My Peace

March, 2008

My journey in helping Raye Dawn has been fraught with twists and turns and valleys and mountain tops. I've experienced highs and lows, the likes of which had not entered into my previously-quiet existence of a work-a-holic writer and business owner who was fulfilled by being a mom and a wife. Not in a million years could I have imagined the stark difference in my life in just a few months. In February of 2007, I had been clueless about anything having to do with Raye Dawn or Kelsey. On the single occasion I'd heard their names, I immediately dismissed them from my mind because I didn't have time to get involved in anything that didn't serve to help with our pending adoption or to better the lives of my family and the children in Mexico we were trying to adopt. Just one year later, the compassion I felt for a grieving family in need had put me in the line of fire of a gang of bullies on a mission and there was no escape.

At one point in the preceding months, I was told by a journalist that the new story was now me. I didn't understand why. I'm the one who had started the blog and then the forum. I shared evidence of the true story of Kelsey and Raye Dawn. But almost immediately, it had turned into something bigger than just me. Many others hopped on board the ship once the waters seemed to be clear and the sharks were at bay, and we took turns at the helm. We all worked together for the same cause. Therefore, why would anyone be interested in me? I was nobody in the big picture of things. As Kathie Briggs and Starla pointed out, I was an "outsider."

The first sign of interest came in December of 2007 from a man who had followed Kelsey's story. He had written an article about our fight for Raye Dawn and his opinion of our shortcomings. He responded to an e-mail that had been sent to every forum member that discussed another case, of which Kathie Briggs's gang had listened to only one side of the story and then lit their torches and went after a judge and the father of the children in question. In the message, I used a two-letter acronym that had been the description of Kelsey's Purpose long before I entered the picture. I guess it was a term that was new to him. He asked me,

Forgive me, but who is KP? And why aren't you using your real name?

I responded.

KP is Kelsey's Purpose. But we like to think of the site as Kathie's Purpose.

I provided a link to Kelsey's Purpose and continued.

You'll see that they claim to fight child abuse, but they're really just out for anyone who disagrees with them and out for revenge on Raye Dawn, which is why I don't use my real name. If I did, we wouldn't have gotten as far as we have in our fight for Raye Dawn because it's harder to fight an unknown adversary.

He replied.

While I understand your desire for anonymity, when dealing with guys like me, it's nice to know with whom I am corresponding. I have leaned in your direction over the last few weeks, but find that some of your tactics could be refined to garner greater support for Raye Dawn. I appreciate you keeping me in the loop, but I really need to know your name before I go any further. Your identity is safe with me - and if you know me, you know that my word is good.

After the first contact from him, I had researched his involvement in the case and turned it over to the forum moderators. Their unanimous decision was against trusting him. They reasoned with me that he could find out the same things from me, whether he knew my name or not. I trusted their instincts and decided he didn't need to know my identity. My final response to him went unanswered, probably because I busted the bubble of any curiosity or mystery that possibly surrounded me. I admitted that I didn't have a clue about what I was doing. I told him,

> *I appreciate your advice, and definitely welcome it. I have no clue what to do from here because I've never done anything like this before and I just want to help right a wrong, but I can't tell you who I am. I don't know you, and unfortunately I can't trust my identity with a stranger right now. I'm nobody important, really. Just trust that I can't tell you who I am. If you want to know who you're talking to, I could put you in touch with one of the moderators on the forum who can use her real name. Either way, thanks for your support!*

Even with possible help from the media, I had carefully guarded my identity. Only a few people on the forum knew who I was and I trusted every one of them. It wasn't that I was really afraid of Kathie Briggs or her gang. I wasn't. Although I had seen the havoc they could wreak in people's lives, I really thought that they were nothing more than a strong-blowing wind that filled the sails and tipped the boat sideways long enough to cause fear in its occupants, but I hoped that the force behind the wind would give way with an opposing gust and everything would go back to normal. However, that didn't happen. They blew and blew and stormed across Oklahoma for two years, and even though we managed to temporarily knock them down, they came back even stronger.

Starla sent an email to one of our moderators from an email address that contained her real name. The subject said JODY ORTIZ and the message was blank. I forwarded the following message to Raye Dawn's family members, including her older sister, and in the subject line I put, "Deny, deny, deny." The post was Kathie Briggs's post on Kelsey's Purpose from March 21, 2008. At the time, her forum had 20,000 registered members.

During the past several months our family has been the victims of multiple websites and videos filled with slander. With the assistance of our attorney, through subpoenas, we now know most of the people behind them. Most would assume they are all at the hands of the maternal family. It is true they have some connection to most of them, but they have not created or do not own a bulk of the vicious material on the Internet. First and foremost the majority of the sites and videos are owned by a lady by the name of Jody Ortiz aka truthseeker. She is the editor of the book written by... the former Judge. She claims to have written up to 70 books and is a ghost writer. She works under the company name of Supplemental Office Services. http://www.supplementalofficeservices.com. Some have suggested she is the mouth piece for Craig Key. She makes her home outside of Oklahoma City. Mrs. Ortiz has posted that she won't stop until our family pays for what happened to Kelsey. This seems to be a strong statement coming from someone that never met Kelsey or our family. It has been our policy to take the high road during the past two years. We continued to work on behalf of children that could still be helped. All the while we were being stalked, harassed, slandered, and physically threatened. We will continue to make choices that are in the best interest of our family. That includes putting a stop to the madness of this lady and her small group of friends. We appreciate the continued support of so many that have come to Kelsey's Purpose with good intentions. Logging into this site is a choice each of you make. We hope it is to help other children and to support families in abusive situations.

After reading this statement on Kathie Briggs's Web site, my initial reaction was a chuckle. It was like a relief that I no longer had to hide my identity. It felt good. But after re-reading the statement, I realized that she had accused me of things I did not do. This would be the first of numerous false allegations that Kathie and Starla would make against me. I suppose she makes allegations to garner as much hate and distrust as she possibly can for me, hence she stated that I was acting on behalf of the Judge. This accusation is nothing short of ridiculous. I believe the Judge did a superb job of speaking for himself when he wrote a book about the case. She also accused me of saying that I wanted to make her family "pay" for what happened to Kelsey. I never made that statement. The only thing I've said that could resemble that statement would be that her family would "pay" for Raye Dawn's defense. They should. They're the ones who ensured that she was railroaded into prison. Also, she stated that her family had been stalked, harassed, threatened, and so on. This was a claim she had made within weeks of my involvement in the case. In her post about me, she insinuated that I had something to do with the allegations, but on August 19, 2007 Kathie Briggs posted the following on her forum:

> *...You may get personal messages or hear we are hiding facts...As you continue to learn more about Kelsey's case you will have questions. You will hear things that are so ourtrageous and irrelevant that you will question our sanity. As I have stated before we have been harassed, stalked, physically assaulted, threatened, and slandered for almost two years.*

A pattern of allegations was emerging, but at the time, I did not recall her previous statement. Thankfully, once the accusations against me were thrown my way, I started collecting posts and e-mails as evidence to build my defense against her lies.

In the same post from August of 2007, Kathie Briggs mentioned the hindsight that she and her gang don't believe that Raye Dawn has a right to use. She further stated as follows:

> *It is a difficult situation, but one we can handle. People who weigh the evidence and use their common sense will be able to detect fact from fiction. Mistakes were made in this case by both families. I admit we should have done more. In hindsight we can think of other avenues we should have explored, but it is called 'hind' sight for a reason...Mike Porter was originally charged with her murder and plead to enabling child abuse. We cannot call him a murderer or a sexual predator because he was not convicted of that crime. Many question which one actually did commit this murder. Many*

*people in our family and in our community believe Raye
Dawn herself beat and left Kelsey for dead. We will never
know the answer to that question. Her actions after Kelsey's
death validate the reasons some question her part. As you
hear facts, theories, and some lies you will have to come to
your own conclusion...Raye Dawn's family has chosen to
attack us to make themselves feel less guilty. They will never
admit they watched Kelsey die before their very eyes. They
are the ones that have to live with their decisions and their
failures to an innocent child. They should have pulled their
resources and fought for this child the way they are fighting
for this adult. Had they done that they would not have to beg
the general public for money now. It must be difficult to be in
their shoes and I ask you to pray for them and hopefully they
will be able to ask God to forgive them.*

When I read statements such as this from Kathie Briggs, I can
picture the venom dripping from her words. It was clear that she
wanted everyone to hate Raye Dawn and her entire family, and she
wanted pity for Mike Porter. I'm called an "evil monster" and "spawn
of Satan" because I pointed out the discrepancies and the lies. Do my
actions truly make me equal to anything her gang has done in
perpetuating hate against Raye Dawn and others?

Kathie Briggs's post about me was soon followed by a post from
Starla. In it, she stated,

*I am glad the information is finally out there. Hopefully, though a
little late, Jody will back down and stop the nonsense and
lies. Now that everyone knows who is behind twisting the
facts to fit their own agenda, maybe the embarrassment will
be enough to stop her. Hopefully when this is all said and
done, people will see her for what she is. This has went on
way too long. Now we also know why she was so adamant
about and protective of, the clueless FORMER Judge. Again
Kathie, I am sorry for all the nasty, hateful downright mean
lies that have been spread about you and your family. Your
strength amazes me still. You have put up with this bull way
longer than I would have.*

Someone posting as "Tommi" added, "thanks for posting this, Kathie. I hope you guys receive the protection from you deserve from the nasty venom that she is spewing."

A "new member," "Hillary" posted something that was right up Kathie Briggs and Starla's alley. She stated,

This week I watched a news report about a college website that slandered students. According to this expert you can sue for slander if you know who the poster is. Only if the poster is anonymous is it close to impossible to hold them accountable. After watching several of these videos I would highly recommend you file suit against this truthseeker. She says she is only giving her opinion and you cannot sue for an opinion. Some of the things in these videos are not opinions, but written as facts. Such as, Kathie is a prime suspect in Kelsey's abuse and has not been cleared to this day. That is not true and it is not an opinion.

It was and is true. Kathie Briggs was listed on the deprived child petition as a possible perpetrator of Kelsey's abuse when her legs were broken. She has stated that she was cleared of that allegation. As of the time of the video and the writing of this book, to my knowledge she has not been cleared. The OCCY even stated in their final report that she could have perpetrated some of the alleged abuse.

Several people chimed in to voice their opinions about what a terrible person I was for making up stories about Kathie Briggs. She needed them to believe they were stories so she wouldn't lose all of her support. Another "new member," "Scarlett," took a special interest in digging up whatever she could find about me. For someone who wasn't a very active member in Kathie Briggs's forum, she seemed to know a lot about me and everything I had done on my own forum. She posted,

I don't post much on here, but this has me fascinated. I have been so curious for so long as to who Truthseeker is. Now everything is falling into place. According to her website, Jody Ortiz is a

> *ghostwriter. That would explain some of the terrible*
> *inconsistencies and flat wrong, made-up information in Craig*
> *Key's book. She has even asked people to rewrite their*
> *reviews of the book and make them favorable instead of*
> *telling the truth about how poorly it was written and how*
> *repetitious it was in order to fill pages. After reading part of*
> *the book (I finally had to put it down, it was torturous to*
> *read) I would never hire her as a ghostwriter or an editor.*
> *What a waste of money.*

Her post went on to suggest a lawsuit against me and she made other statements about her disagreement with me in general.

"Scoobydoo" stated,

> *...Sick and twisted. Shame on all of the anonymous people who tell*
> *lies about others. What a coward you are Mrs. Ortiz.*

"Scarlet" then posted my picture and information from my business Web site about a book festival that I would soon be attending. When it came time for the festival, I alerted the coordinator of the fact that Kathie Briggs's gang members had posted the information about the festival along with my picture. An armed, plain-clothed police officer hovered near my table throughout the day in the event that one of the haters would come looking for me. They didn't.

scarlett
New Member

Posts: 5
Group: Organizer
Joined: Jan 2008
Status: **Offline**
Reputation: Π

RE: New Information   Post: #9

I found this announcement on Jody Ortiz's website along with her photo. For some reason she looks familiar to me.

Calendar of Events
On March 29th you can meet Jody in person at the Border Queen Book Festival in Comanche, Oklahoma.

Come and join in the fun at the Border Queen Book Festival on March 29th at the Asbury Complex in Comanche, OK. Meet the authors, get an autographed book, meet Miss Comanche 2008 and hear words of wisdom from Periwinkle VonSkittlebaum, a real live fairy godmother!

Writer set-ups start at 8 a.m. The Book Festival runs from 8 a.m. until 4 p.m.

The Book Festival is free to the public. In the adjoining dining hall hot food can be purchased.

Those traveling a distance can get a room at the Chisholm Suite Hotel on U.S. Hwy. 81 in Duncan (8 miles north of Comanche.) A discounted block of rooms is available for Book Festival attendees.

Attached File(s)
Thumbnail(s)

Scarlett

Kathie Briggs's gang posted for three days on thirty-three pages filled with nothing but attacks on my character and my professional abilities, and they didn't hold anything back. They copied my resume from a freelance Web site and posted it on the forum along with messages from a Yahoo writer's group that I was forced to quit shortly afterward due to them stalking it. They read where I had commented on the writer's group that I had pneumonia at the time I worked on the Judge's book and they made a joke out of it.

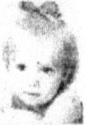

Starla
Moderator

Posts: 688
Group: Moderators
Joined: Feb 2006
Status: **Offline**
Reputation: ▢▢▢▢▢▢

RE: New Information   Post: #19

She writes "Christian" articles? With the way she tells and
promotes lies? Does this woman **NOT** have a conscience?

*"I edited a book last summer when I had pneumonia for a local,
former Judge and it's not my best work and I've been hammered
on that one. So I'm working on adding to and editing it again."*

Blaming having pneumonia for sorry work in editing? LOL (that's
my story and I'm stickin' to it) Please, Please, Please tell me they
aren't reworking that pathetic thing they call a "book"? Of course
that is just my opinion on what I've heard of the contents of her
"book". I personally haven't read it, the reviews were all so sorry, I

3/23/2008 4:55 F

They also posted laws about what they claim was my harassment
of them. It was a joke. These people had made a mockery of
themselves and had anonymously harassed Raye Dawn and several
other people for years, but they went on a full assault mission against
me for taking up for Raye Dawn and others with facts and
documentation to back up what I had to say. Did my actions in helping
Raye Dawn and her family warrant so much hate against me that it's
still ongoing years after Kathie Briggs set her hounds to my scent?

After three days, someone using the name "StarryEvenings"
attempted to snap them back to reality. This person stated,

*When is all this fighting going to stop?!?!? Is this going to bring
Kelsey back? Unfortunately no. I feel bad for Kelsey. No
matter who did what or who didn't do what, she loved all of
her family...I don't think Kelsey would want the ones she
loves so much to be fighting. I'm not nessasarily referring to
possible law suit. Just in general. It seems that you have to
pick a 'side' with this whole horrible mess...I saw that you
are trying to get approval for donations. Once that is
approved, what will the donations go to? If its for preventing
child abuse, I would love to help! But if its to fund law suits
like against TruthSeeker, you can count me out...*

Her post was answered by Jeanna who stated,

576

*...Absolutely none of the money is for personal use, personal gain, or
lawsuits of any kind. Any lawsuits that have been initiated
are personal issues and are personally funded. It is very
unfortunate that lawsuits and grand jury investigations have
become necessary. Our family has civil rights that have been
willfully infringed upon again and again. Defamation of
character, slander and libel are against the law. These laws
have grossly been broken for three years. We had hoped that
the situation would improve, but unfortunately it has
worsened. I understand that some people feel that Kelsey's
mother was wrongly imprisoned and are fighting for her
release. I have no objection to that; they have every right to
lawfully help her. However, laws have been broken in the
process. We have overlooked it time and time again, but with
the increasing severity with which they try to harm our
family, we have come to the point where we feel that legal
action must be taken to end it. We did not convict Raye
Dawn of any crime; 12 jurors that she and her chosen
council approved in a location that she and her council
approved convicted her. As far as we are concerned, justice
has been served and we are trying to move on with our lives.*

The first call that I made after reading Kathie Briggs's post about
me was to find out if, indeed, a subpoena had been issued. Although
Raye Dawn's family technically owned her Web sites, I purchased
them in my name and maintained all of the expenses for them. I made
three or four calls and asked different representatives and their
answers were all the same. There was no subpoena. Posts that were
made later by Starla clarified that Kathie Briggs's statement "with the
help of our attorneys" was actually referring to her district attorney.
Kathie Briggs had been known to call him "her attorney" but,
according to Starla, the district attorney in her county had issued the
subpoena for my identification because her family and I purchased his
domain name along with Raye Dawn's Web sites. The DA's Web site
was a single page with no active links, but with a picture or two of the
DA and requests for information about him. We had been
contemplating pulling together a grand jury into his actions in regards
to Raye Dawn's case and we wanted to know if there were any other

cases in which he had acted questionably. Only three or four people contacted us, and we eventually took the Web site down because nobody had the time to maintain it. Why would a district attorney subpoena information for the owner of a Web site that had no information about him and then turn over the identifying information to a known group of bullies? It made no sense. Also, Starla stated that I owned twelve Web sites at the time when, in actuality, I owned nineteen Web sites and every Web site name except for four or five that were for Raye Dawn and her family were clearly for business purposes. Things just weren't making sense.

At the same time that Kathie Briggs and Lance's gang members were harassing me on their forum, they used aliases to further trash me on the political blog. On March 23, 2008, "Justice_finally" posted as follows:

Just so all you people know...'Truthseeker' from Free Kelsey's Mom is Jody Ortiz. She is a 'ghost writer' and is the editor of the pathetic book supposedly 'written' by the former Judge...A subpeona revealed her identity. You can check this out on [link to Kelsey's Purpose was provided]. Very interesting information on the thread titled 'New Information'."
This person continued, "Just wanted to add, this is what happens (subpeona's) when people go around telling blantant lies."

Someone by the name of "Enough already Free Kelsey's Mom" added,

Jody Ortiz and ...the former Judge in Kelsey's case are trying to sell books. It isn't about getting Raye Dawn out of prison it is about saving his sorry reputation. I can see this all going to court this year to set the record straight. I have read the comments Jody Ortiz aka truthseeker has posted about the Briggs family. She needs to be held accountable. The Free Kelsey's Mom site is slanderous beyond words...

Keeping with the pattern of not very creative aliases, "Darla" posted using the typical "in the gutter" mindset of their gang,

So Jody Ortiz, the editor of that book, is the one behind all of this? How ineteresting. What is she in this for? Sounds like more than an editor and writer relationship to me. I wonder if their spouses are aware of this? She makes so many accusations towards the paternal family to be on the outside. I hope they copy every single word she typed and take her to the cleaners. I did some checking and she lives at [my home address was posted]. Her company is actually located at her home. I would love to see how many books she has actually written. Have any of you read that book Craig Key wrote? It reads likes someone had to cram a last minute essay for class the next day. It is repititious, and so poorly written that I felt sorry and embarrassed for Key. Now I really feel sorry for him because he wasted money on an editor that ripped him off. Then again, maybe she did not make him pay her. How could she? She should have paid him. Maybe this is why she is atamately trying to save his butt and attacks the Briggs family over and over again.

Just so all you people know..."Truthseeker" from FKM is Jody Ortiz. She is a "ghost writer" and is the editor of the pathetic book supposedly 'written' by the former Judge---craig key. A subpeona revealed her identity. You can check this out on www.kelseyspurpose.org
Very interesting information on the thread titled "New Information".
Justice_finally | 03.23.08 - 2:22 am | #

Just wanted to add, this is what happens (subpeona's) when people go around telling blantant lies.
Justice_finally | 03.23.08 - 2:24 am | #

Jody Ortiz and Craig Key, the former judge in Kelsey's case are trying to sell books. It isn't about getting Raye out of prison it is about saving his sorry reputation. I can see this all going to court this year to set the record straight. I have read the comments Jody Ortiz aka truthseeker has posted about the Briggs family.

So Jody Ortiz, the editor of that book, is the one behind all of this? How ineteresting. What is she in this for? Sounds like more than an editor and writer relationship to me. I wonder if their spouses are aware of this? She makes so many accusations towards the paternal family to be on the outside. I hope they copy every single word she typed and take her to the cleaners.

I did some checking and she lives at ███████████ Her company is actually located at her home. I would love to see how many books she has actually written.

Have any of you read that book Key wrote? It reads likes someone had to cram a last minute essay for class the next day. It is repititious, and so poorly written that I felt sorry and embarrassed for Key. Now I really feel sorry for him because he wasted money on an editor that ripped him off. Then again, maybe she did not make him pay her. How could she? She should have paid him. Maybe this is why she is atamately trying to save his butt and attacks the Briggs family over and over again.
Darla | 03.23.08 - 1:29 pm | #

I sincerely hope the people reading this do not believe one word the Observers says. They are a paid publication. It says so on the very paper it is printed on.
Terry | 03.23.08 - 5:53 pm | #

The attack continued with comments such as "go get her" and "somebody should pay her a visit." They again posted my business Web site address and made several disparaging comments about my professional abilities, just as Starla had threatened to do. It was as if they were wolves that had been starved for days and then let loose on a wounded animal. They were relentless and vicious in their attack. Someone had dared to stand up to Kathie and Lance, and exposed their lies. I was going down, and to hell with anyone who stood in the way.

The amusement and relief I initially felt soon turned to fear. After I was sent information that they were posting my home address and giving orders such as "go get her," I shut down. I was afraid. Their attack started on the week before Easter, as I recall. I had planned to work in my garden that weekend, but the garden could be seen from the road. I remember walking into the garden and jumping every time a car passed. *Was it them? Did they see me? Would pictures of me in my garden be posted on the Internet next?*

Over the weekend, I had several blocked numbers on my phone with hang ups on my voice mail. My cell phone number had been listed on my business Web site. A few months earlier, I had received an e-mail from a Raye Dawn supporter. Her phone number had been made available to Kathie Briggs and she had hang-up calls on her cell phone that had been blocked, but her service provided a reverse call trace. She told me, "The phone number I told you about earlier, well it belongs to Kathie Briggs's husband, remember she has all my contact info...lmao oh well......gees imagine that one, oh and here is my documentation...haha." She provided her account history that showed the following:

Call Information-- Type Incoming Call - Nature of Call Local - Number Called 1918xxxxxxx - Calling Number 1405279xxxx - Call Date 12/23/2007 - Call Time 01:06:47 AM - Timezone US/Central - Call Duration 0min 9sec - Call Location USA/Oklahoma

Her reverse number look-up gave the name of Kathie Briggs's husband as the owner of the phone number. The calls that were made to my phone were also in the middle of the night.

After the calls started, we discovered the bullet holes in our truck. I was visiting my parents when my dad noticed that it looked like someone had leaned into our truck. A day or two later, I was showing my husband what we had found and we saw two distinct holes where someone had shot what the police termed "bird shot" into the side of my truck that would have been facing the road. A few days after that, we discovered that the other side of the truck had been keyed. The order to "go get her" had obviously been taken seriously by someone and my fear grew even more intense. They had been to my home and had made a statement on the political blog to "watch out for her or she'll run over you in her little red car." Two of my neighbors drove red cars, but I did not have a "little red car." I knew Lance's history of drug use and I was frightened that with his history, he also had connections with shady characters and, with the way his mom and their supporters were attacking me on the Internet, what was next? How far would they go to silence me?

I invested in something I never thought I would need. I took out a life insurance policy on myself in case something happened to me to ensure that my daughter would be alright. It was a tough time for me, but I didn't want them to see me sweat. I remained on the forum and to my surprise, nobody cared who I was. Not a single Raye Dawn supporter questioned me or my identity. If anything, I believe the revelation of who I was made them trust me even more. They knew that I was someone respected and a professional and I had work ethic and integrity. I wasn't going to make up lies just to garner support for Raye Dawn. It would be a waste of time because once the lies were revealed, I would look foolish and nobody would believe another word I had to say. I wasn't going to risk that. The truth about the situation was enough to illustrate that Raye Dawn had been railroaded. All I needed was the truth.

I posted a message directly to Kathie Briggs on a blog on March 24, 2008. I had gone past the point of being amused and I was pissed, but I had not yet found the bullet holes so the fear hadn't fully hit me. I sent the statement in an email to Raye Dawn's family, including her older sister. At the time, I didn't realize that someone in Kathie Briggs's and Lance's gang had hacked Raye Dawn's sister's email account. I stated,

I told her off! They took the entire thread off Kelsey's Purpose about 20 minutes after I posted this, but there is still my address and stuff on the political blog. What a bunch of losers!!!

I included my message to Kathie Briggs as follows:

TOPIC: Kathie Briggs is LYING!
Kathie Briggs has convinced her band of cohorts that she actually has a subpoena and that she has identified me. That's a lie!!! Her minions are posting a home address on the Internet for this person that Kathie Briggs is dragging through the mud and it's time that those people are stopped! Kathie Briggs has lied, again, and is telling people that a subpoena has identified me. This is NOT true. There has been NO subpoena. This is but another lie that Kathie Briggs has stated, and she is, yet again, dragging innocent people through the mud. I will be producing another video that has facts about this case and brings attention to the many lies told by Kathie Briggs. File a lawsuit against me tomorrow Kathie Briggs. I dare you. The truth is an absolute defense to any claim of libel/slander. Can you say the same Kathie Briggs? Have you told the truth? Why don't you post a copy of your subpoena Kathie? I'd love to see it! Kathie, you and I know everything I've posted is the truth. Let me get this right Kathie, you've lost every suit that you and/or your family have filed against everyone and his brother. You've lost every single suit and now you're going after anyone and everyone you can to hide the REAL facts. But the truth will be my defense, and Kathie, you know that you don't have the truth on your side. It's time to take responsibility and realize that the blame lies on your shoulders as much as anyone else you want to blame. Your son didn't show up for a single hearing.

You did nothing when Kelsey couldn't walk while at your home. You keep blaming everybody for everything. Blame, blame, blame, that's all you do. You take ZERO responsibility for ANYTHING that's gone wrong in your life. It's time to admit that you FAILED as a parent and as a grandparent. Take responsibility Kathie and leave everyone else alone!

In the post I included the comment from Kathie Briggs's Web site from Starry Evening that was deleted from their forum immediately after it was posted, and I posed the questions, "What are they hiding? Can nobody ask you questions? Why did you ban one of your members and under reason put – 'bitch'?" I continued, "Those who are members of your forum have nothing to do with me or my forum - NOTHING! I've never posted on your forum and those who choose to post there are doing it because they want answers, just like the rest of us. What are you hiding from Kathie Briggs?"

Within minutes of posting this message to Kathie Briggs daring her to sue me, the thread about me on her forum disappeared. They had gone underground to talk about me. A friend who entered their chat room saw some of them had posted a link to my business Web site in the chat. When the friend questioned what it was, they responded, "It's my friend's business." I knew they would continue their mission against me. On April 3, 2008 I received a welcome e-mail from Reunions.com. Apparently, someone had opened an account in my name, and it wouldn't be the last.

Raye Dawn's sister told me, "They MUST BE WORRIED ABOUT U GIRL!!!!!!!!! They are trying like hell!!!"

My response was, "Yes they are!!! They know they have a worthy opponent in me. LOL!!!"

I wanted a legal opinion, so I e-mailed the attorney from whom I had sought advice previously. I sent him the message I had received from Starla along with the following message:

Sorry to bother you again. This came from the owner of Kelsey's Purpose. She's hiding behind a screen name. I'm told I should just ride it out, but she's already signing me up for things on the Internet and she's psycho. Any suggestions? BTW, I have about 20 sites, all but four or five are business related. She's still bluffing.

He answered.

Honestly, I, personally, wouldn't dignify her letter to you with a response. I'd keep doing whatever needed to be done behind the scene to keep the actions in as much check as possible; but keep a low and professional profile.

I responded.

Thank you. I'm not responding. I just don't want to quit helping Raye Dawn.

He advised,

Don't have to quit. Truth is an absolute defense to slander or libel. Couple that with First Amendment rights, and you're in a good position. However, First Amendment rights do not protect another party from a tort action of slander or libel IF you can proffer sufficient proof of the party.

I told him,

I'm collecting and printing. I keep googling my name to see what they're putting out there. If they do anything, I'll be sure to have evidence. Thanks again!

Rally for Hope

February through May, 2008

Before Kathie Briggs and her group shared my information, I had searched for and found a replacement for myself. One of the moderators that I loved and trusted took over the leading role in the fight for Raye Dawn and I stepped into the shadows. However, every time I tried to walk away and refocus on what I needed to do for myself and my family, "they" dragged me back into the fight. Their actions directly contradict what they claim they desire. If they wanted me to quit supporting Raye Dawn, all they had to do was leave me alone in 2008. I would have walked away. I planned to walk away. It's not something I'm proud to admit, but it's the truth. Once I realized the lengths to which Kathie Briggs and her gang were willing to go in their mission against Raye Dawn and everyone on Kathie's alleged "hit list," I wanted nothing more to do with them. I wanted no part in their game. From the moment I was bombarded with hate mail, it took everything I had to stay and fight. My sympathy for Raye Dawn and her family kept me going, but once Raye Dawn had other supporters who were willing to "go to bat" for her, I felt my purpose had been served. I had done my part.

Just weeks before they put a plan into motion that they thought would destroy me, they discussed "playing nice" in an email that a Kathie Briggs supporter forwarded to my replacement. From the moment they learned someone was replacing me, they bashed her and blamed her for her daughter's rape, which she had discussed on the forum. This group of vile people looked for any opportunity possible to tear us down and it didn't matter who got hurt in the process. An organization of people who promoted themselves as "preventing child abuse" mocked and taunted a mother of a teenager who had been raped. That was the "norm" for this group. They are nothing more than bullies. However, somehow, the people who had been bullying, badmouthing, and threatening others since 2005 had decided they were now the victims—a role they still play to this day.

From: Shirica Sent: Thursday, February 14, 2008 2:28 PM
Subject: RE: CORE GOSSIP/UNDERCOER/INSIDE INFO EMAIL
GROUP - I am going to ask that everyone please not make any reference at all to the other site on Kelsey's Purpose. Do not refer to it as Free Kelsey's Mom or the "other site" or anything of that nature. I think that maybe the new leader may play nice if we agree to play nice. I do not trust her one little bit but I do agree with her that the hostility has got to stop. I do realize that 99.8% of it is coming from them, but we do have to take a teeny weeny tiny part of the blame, and I do mean teeny...I think Kelsey's Purpose needs to really get caught up in the new stuff right now and let Raye Dawn and her ban of freaks be for the time being.

Just two hours before Shirica addressed the email to the core group (who received emails that were "NOT AS LOVELY" because they were "OH SO NOT PUBLIC"), Shirica messaged my replacement. She told her,

...about the emails...I in NO WAY am friends with Mike Porter and I do not think he is an innocent man. I truly feel he is the one who murdered Kelsey... Mike makes my skin crawl. He is a sorry, sorry human being...

I've never understood how Kathie Briggs or Shirica can justify the tone of their communications with Mike Porter or the fact that they didn't record anything to use against him such as the numerous phone calls or in-person meetings. Their mission was clear and they weren't happy when their actions were made public, which, in turn, placed a huge target on my back, even though I was removing myself from the picture. Starla had no intentions of letting me escape the punishment she thought necessary because I had exposed Kathie Briggs's true mission. She wanted me to pay and her first attempt was to try to convince my replacement that I had knowledge that a grand jury was being convened and that I only wanted to dump my "mess" on someone else. She told her:

From: Starla Sent: Sunday, February 17, 2008 11:38 AM - I am going to be upfront with you. I'm not as forgiving as some of the Briggs. I don't trust as unconditionally either, therefore, I don't trust you. And with good reason...You have come to our site in the past on the pretense of a "truce". Then went right to your site and posted how the post on Kelsey's Purpose was meant to be "condesending". Why are you so willing to do it now? What makes this time any different than the last time? Is it because you got wind of the possible Grand Jury Investigation of you, Truth Seeker and your website? Or is that why TS turned the site completely over to you? Because she got wind of it, and didn't clue you in, and just dumped this mess on you? Well, please inform her for me, that the damage has already been done. Everything that was needed for the Grand Jury Investigation has already been copied from your site. Doesn't matter if it's since been deleted or not, evidence has already been collected to be used in the GJ investigation, and believe me, there is plenty of evidence to support it. If you were truely sincere, you would have shut that site down after you posted on Kelsey's Purpose...The longer you keep the crap up, the more damage that is done...Keep digging yourselves deeper, and we will keep copying and collecting evidence for the Grand Jury. They absolutely "love a paper trail". Makes our job so much easier...We aren't worrying about Raye Dawn, because she is where she belongs, and where we want her...Kelsey's Purpose is a strong organization...and we will continue to grow and become even stronger. You cannot bring us down...Your site breeds hate and has caused stalking and threats to be made, which is against the law...You can also tell TruthSeeker for me, that dumping the site on you not only wasn't a very nice thing to do, since you have supported her and her twisted lies all this time, but now everyone will know exactly who she is. The Grand Jury will know and so will everyone else. Her "secret" will be out. LOL Most of us on Kelsey's Purpose use our real names, as I've stated before, we have nothing to hide and are not ashamed of what we say.

This was a surprising claim after years of "anonymous" posts on their bashboards, which were nothing like our site where we discussed facts. All they did was breed hate.

After receiving the forwarded message, I responded.

LMAO! They're trying to get a grand jury investigation going? What about one against them? I think we need to get one in the works, don't you?

She agreed.

I have the paperwork ready!!! Like how I offered...my info.....she is a stupid bitch - you dont' get a grand jury to investigate a civil matter!! We CERTAINLY have not done a THING that is illegal!!

Starla continued the conversation with the moderator telling her,

I've been to your site alot and see what goes on. If it weren't for your posts on KP and bitchin' about Kathie and Lance, then there wouldn't be much to your site. I will say the one time that I was posting on Free Kelsey's Mom, although truth twister was a bitch as usual, you were decent to me and answered the questions I asked.

The moderator responded,

Kelsey's Purpose is nothing more than a gossip trash can... I am sick to death of it. It behooves NOONE.

I agree with her statement. After the initial round of attacks from Kathie Briggs's gang, life seemed to come to a standstill for me. Starla had threatened to destroy my good name, and in turn, my business. Also, Kathie Briggs's forum members were sharing my business Web site information. I knew whatever they were plotting could not be good. I felt threatened, vulnerable, and as if I had no choice but to stop taking on new clients. I quit advertising my business and services online and I drove away the few potential clients who contacted me with questions about who they were and where they found out about my business. To this day, I rarely answer e-mails from my computer, which makes it difficult to send contracts, and so on. All communications are handled through my cell phone. I don't contact anyone from my computer until I know the person isn't just a "spy." It's a ridiculous way to run a business, but because of their threats and nonstop harassment, it's what I've been reduced to, which means my business is practically non-existent because of them.

My attitude by April 14, 2008 was not good. I told one moderator,

I think it's those people who are negative and just want to drain us. I'm so tired of them and tired of arguing with them. I just can't stomach all their lies anymore.

Although we were all beaten down and weary, the members of Raye Dawn's support group moved forward. My replacement started planning a rally against wrongful convictions and she lined up guest speakers and got the plans underway. In the meantime, Raye Dawn wrote a letter to the state lawmakers that we delivered to them in May of 2008, along with information that had not yet been made public about the case. I emailed Raye Dawn's family and we discussed the time and place we would meet to pass out the literature. To our surprise, when we arrived, a camera crew from Kathie Briggs's reporter-friend, Britten Follett's news station was waiting for us.

As we approached the stairs to the State Capitol building, we thought perhaps there was something else going on at the Capitol building that day and we didn't think much about their presence. However, they stopped us on our way into the building and then followed us around for at least an hour asking for a copy of Raye Dawn's letter, which we refused to give to them. Within two hours, and before any of us even made it home, the letter was posted on Kelsey's Purpose and she and her hounds were ripping it apart. It was also on the news that evening with Britten Follett displaying her disgust with the letter, and included quotes from Kathie Briggs and the district attorney. It was unbelievable! Every lawmaker received the following letter with their packet:

Dear Lawmakers: Kelsey Smith-Briggs was sexually assaulted and murdered at the age of two years and nine months. According to the Ryan Luke Law, her records should have been released after her death, but they've been suppressed and kept hidden. Why? Attached are just a few of the supervised visitation notes taken by DHS in May and June of 2005, just before Kelsey's death. As you can see, Kelsey showed no fear of her mother, but the same can't be said for her paternal grandparents. Could this be why her records have been suppressed? As lawmakers, you have the power to ensure your laws are followed and obeyed. Release Kelsey's records and allow the public that has judged her mother, Raye Dawn, so harshly to see what really happened to precious Kelsey. Thank you for your consideration. Friends and family of Kelsey Smith-Briggs and Raye Dawn Smith

Following are excerpts from Raye Dawn's letter:[49]

My name is Raye Dawn Smith and my daughter was Kelsey Smith-Briggs, the beautiful two year old little girl that was killed by her step-father... I have been wrongfully convicted of enabling child abuse, because the District Attorney...has made the statement that I "should have known." Not that I knew anything, but I "should have known." So many things went wrong in my case and they continue to go wrong to this day. I am trying to reach out to anyone who will listen to me...So many lies, stories, and half truths have been told, but very little has been told about what kind of a child Kelsey was and no one has ever heard of the wonderful relationship Kelsey and myself had. Just because Richard Smothermon, Pattye High (special prosecutor), Kathie Briggs (Kelsey's paternal grandmother), Mike Porter (step-father), and/or the media say something doesn't make it true. This is who Kelsey and I were..."

Raye Dawn's letter went on to describe Kelsey and all of the wonderful things that had made her mom one of the proudest moms I've ever met. She stated,

---

[49] The letter can be found at www.FreeKelseysMom.com

*Did I mention well mannered and very independent? She would tell
     you 'God bless you' if you sneezed. If she was trying to get
     past someone and it was a tight squeeze she would say, 'Cuse
     (Excuse) me' and if anyone tried to help her do something
     she would say, 'No, I do it.' Everything Kelsey did was an
     event to me....*

Her letter ended with this plea:

*So many wrongs need to be made right and it is long over do. I've
     always felt this way and I always will. I am asking you to
     please check more into the facts of this case and help my
     family and me. My family as well as myself, would be more
     than happy to speak with you. Please, I am asking you and
     your colleagues to please find it in your hearts to fix the part
     of the tragedy that can still be fixed. I pray this letter finds
     you well, and I appreciate you taking the time to hear me out.
     The truth is out there, someone just has to take the time to
     listen to it, read about it, and then act upon it. Please do the
     RIGHT THING.*

Raye Dawn stated in her letter that she had remained silent for two
years because of gag orders, and the fact that she was following the
law. She now wanted to have her voice heard, but not only was nobody
listening, but every word she said would be judged and ripped to
shreds by a gang of bullies.

A week or two after delivering the packet to lawmakers, Gayla
(Raye Dawn's mom) and I returned to the Capitol building alone and
we passed out flyers for the upcoming rally. It had been obvious to us
on our first trip there that Kathie Briggs had made friends in the offices
of some of the lawmakers. Among the warm welcomes, we also
received dirty looks and cold stares. After passing out all of the flyers
in record time (since we just went door-to-door and placed the flyers
on desks without saying much of anything to anyone), we were
stopped by three security guards on the bottom floor who were there
to arrest us. Apparently, "complaints" had been lodged by lawmaker's
assistants. We were led into the security room and, after a few minutes
and their realization that we posed no threat we were released with a

warning. Inquiries have been made since that day and we're told that people pass things out at the Capitol building all the time and nobody ever complains. We were targeted for a reason.

On the day of the rally, I made the last minute decision that I would attend. I didn't know if it would be wise since Starla had threatened to be there and had made multiple public threats about bringing the press and getting "in my face." Other than a few drive-by's from Lance with the local police following closely behind him, the rally was a success. We had Raye Dawn supporters visit from several different states and I got to know those who had found a place in their hearts for Raye Dawn and her family. They are, to this day, like angels to me with hearts that are pure and full of compassion. I don't know where I would be without them.

The rally ended with a candlelight vigil in a field near the prison. I had called the prison warden and asked for permission to bring a small group onto the premises to pray. She denied my request. Gayla scoped out a neighbor who said we could use his property to say our prayers. We weren't there for five minutes before a swarm of prison guards arrived in their vehicles and threatened to arrest us. It seemed everything we did was ending in possible arrests, although our intentions were pure.

Everything we had gone through seemed worthwhile when Raye Dawn's eighty-two-year-old great-uncle took my hand in his and told me, "I pray to God every day that he will let me hang on until Raye Dawn comes home." His words bring tears to my eyes even now and my heart went out to him as I vowed to hang in there and do what I could to help see that his prayers were answered.

Being Bad

April, 2008

In April of 2008, the ongoing, senseless argument with Kathie Briggs and her supporters moved to a public forum, which was not moderated, where they could post as much hate and lies as they desired and nobody could do anything about it. It was a playground without any supervision and the bullies wanted me to come out and play.

Clay posed the question, "Where's Truth Seeker?" and when I didn't respond, she followed with another post that accused me of starting the forum to further my career. Prior to the last few months, I never said a word about Raye Dawn publicly, so how would a forum that had nothing to do with me on a professional level further my career? The charges from Clay and Starla became so ridiculous that I finally posted under my real name. I was still denying that I was Truth Seeker because I was afraid of these bullies. The bullet holes in my truck and my home address being posted on the Internet with the order to "go get her" were more than I could take. I was also told horror stories about U.S. Observer reporters who had been attacked. With the history of violence, stalking, and harassment that their victims were sharing with me, I just wanted it to end.

On May 6, 2008 I told them off.

I see you people are throwing my name around and saying I'm using Judge Key's book to further my career. I'm only going to say this once as I don't have time for all this childish back and forth crap and you bitches have already done your part in destroying my career. I will take Kathie Briggs and Starla to court. They're LYING and have attempted to blackmail me and I'm sick of it!
1. I did not make $7,000 off editing Judge Key's book. That's stupid!
2. I had pneumonia when editing his book so say what you

want about it.
3. I did not author his book and I have NO part in any
proceeds from it! I do not get paid from his book sales. Grow
up and go back to school!
4. Although I thought Raye Dawn was guilty when I edited
Judge Key's book and I felt sympathy for the Briggs, I no
longer have any sympathy for them because of the way they
have trashed me. For the record, I would be honored to have
done something as selfless as Truth Seeker but no matter how
many times you try to call me her, it won't make me her.
That's all I have to say. I refuse to become a part of any
childish back and forth that Kathie Briggs's supporters seem
to live for. Leave me out of this because I have nothing more
to say to you people! You need to get a job and get a life!

The post was a bad idea because I'm the one who sounded like a bitch and they used it as open-season to continue to harass me by using my name now that I had used it. I wanted nothing more than to get them out of my life.

Things only got worse when Starla (using an alias) posted hurtful and false statements about Gayla and her family. She stated that Gayla had murdered her own husband, Raye Dawn's dad, who had died of cancer when Kelsey was one year old. She claimed that Gayla's husband wasn't actually Raye Dawn's dad and that Gayla had an affair. She also claimed that Gayla helped Raye Dawn pose Kelsey's body so that Mike Porter would be framed for Kelsey's alleged sexual assault and murder. The charges against Gayla and Raye Dawn and their family members were endless, but Starla used an alias and denied her true identity. At one point, someone tried to call her out and she threatened to sue them for even guessing it was her. Gayla wanted to know why someone would be so hurtful and lie about her family, so the members of our forum decided to research Starla and see if we could tie her to her alias and confront her. When that plan didn't work, Gayla called a family member of Starla's and asked if Starla was related to Kathie Briggs in any way and why she would have a vendetta against Gayla and her family. The family member took

Gayla's phone number and gave it to Starla's ex-husband, who then called Gayla. He must have told his adult daughter, who apparently lived with Starla, that he had spoken to Gayla because his daughter phoned Gayla and threatened her. Gayla was so frightened that she had to change her number. Presumably, this is the same daughter who would later attend a court hearing with Starla where she focused a video camera on Gayla and laughed at Gayla and Raye's family. Sherri and her husband had to pull in front of Starla's daughter and block her so that Gayla could get into her car without harassment. It was beyond belief. Gayla had been ridiculed and assaulted for months, but Starla is always the victim, so she turned the story of her ex-husband calling Gayla around and wrote several lengthy messages to Gayla on Kelsey's Purpose and on the open, un-moderated forum.

On June 5, 2008, she posted to Gayla:

you owe my daughter an apology. Seriously. She's taking a summer class and gets out of school a little while ago and goes to her older sister's house, and guess what? Her daddy calls and she says he is drunk again. Gayla why did you call him again today?? Do I need to call you? or DO I NEED TO FILE A RESTRAINING ORDER AGAINST YOU TO GET YOU TO LEAVE MY CHILDREN ALONE AND OUT OF THIS??? Gayla, my daughter already TOLD her dad that she called you last night. Why did you think YOU needed to call him and INVOLVE MY DAUGHTER again?? This is NOT a threat Gayla, I AM TELLING YOU .... LEAVE MY CHILDREN ALONE! It's me you really want, call ME. Seriously!! be a grown damn woman and call me, stop involving my minor daughter in your vindictivness and revenge against me. Your actions in this are despicable. He is just as despicable for allowing this and involving his daughter too. Gayla, Have you lost your mind totally? My email address is on this site, email me, we can hash it out on email if you wish, but you really need to leave my children out of this. [My ex] was on this site today. Coming here knowing I am here, is a direct violation of the PFA. Continually calling my daughter being drunk is also violating

595

a court order. And yes, I had him banned, of which he admitted to my daughter he was on here and got banned and he's mad about that too. You do not know what you have done or started Gayla. I will not let my family become a victim of yours in any way shape or form. STOP IT. People like you make me sick. I seriously feel sorry for your daughter and after your continuing efforts to cause trouble in my family, with MY children, I am saddened to tears that you were Kelsey's grandmother!! THAT IS AN OPINION OF WHICH I AM ENTITLED!! God, what is wrong with you??? Did you come to the realization that your daughter isn't getting out of prison and now you need something else to focus on? You picked the wrong one to mess with their children. I WILL be talking to the media, there WILL be letters written to the editor of all your local papers. You are already losing support for Raye Dawn because of this, so not only are you harming my daughter, but your own. Do you care about Raye Dawn? I think(my opinion again) you love the drama, are you that attention starved that you have to sink to this? One more time, read these words carefully....LEAVE MY CHILDREN ALONE AND OUT OF THIS!Maybe it isn't all Raye Dawn's fault she is where she is............(another opinion dear)

Newcomers to the drama are now being told that Gayla and I had Starla investigated and then we drove to Kansas and met with her ex-husband and gave him the address of Starla's home. The story had to change to include me and to make it seem more sinister—more dramatic—when, in actuality, it was a grieving grandmother and mother trying to end the vicious attacks against herself and everyone she loved. However, there was no end because her attacker wanted to be the victim, which is a role that Kathie Briggs and her gang members love to play.

At the end of March of 2008, less than a week after the vicious attack on me, Kathie Briggs decided to close her forum and, of course, she blamed me. She was applying for non-profit status, and I was leading a group of letter-writers who wanted to inform the IRS of exactly the type of "charity" that Kathie Briggs was running. I wrote the following letter to the IRS:

May 28, 2008

Dear IRS Agents: I'm writing to you regarding Kelsey's Purpose, an organization based in Meeker, Oklahoma that is filing for a 501c3. I ask that you attach this packet to their application and consider its contents when making your determination of their worthiness of becoming a charity. That organization claims to be fighting child abuse, but they have used the organization to threaten, harass, and stalk. I edited a book for a former Oklahoma Judge and they worked to get the judge out of office and they have now targeted me for their harassment. They've plastered my name, picture, business website address, and home address all over the Internet and have trashed my work. The sad part is that I'm not the first person they've attacked. Enclosed you will find several pages from a four page thread on their website where they trashed me and my business, and pages from a website at www.thetruthaboutkelsey.com that has worked at exposing the truth of what happened in the case that is the topic of the book I edited. The pages that I have enclosed from that site are all posts from Kelsey's Purpose in which they trash and threaten and ask their members to contact public officials. It's my belief that their organization should be shut down. They are stalking and harassing me on the Internet and have destroyed my business and I am the breadwinner for my family. Thank you for your consideration. Sincerely, Jody Ortiz

Kathie Briggs posted the following "goodbye" message and then finally closed the Kelsey's Purpose forum sometime around June of 2008.

As you all know the past three years have taken a toll on us that no individual should ever experience...Our private little world in Meeker became a fish bowl for all to see and judge...I went from being the grandma that sews and takes pictures to the one on the news. I was in a world that most people only read about...As each reporter called wanting me to speak, as

*much as I wanted to, I never said 'no'...I learned our so
called 'fame' brought out very peculiar people, some that
only wanted to touch me. I know that sounds bizarre, but I am
not kidding...I have been bashed beyond my wildest
dreams...In the past few weeks our spirit for everyday life has
dwindled...We were strongly encouraged by many of you to
obtain our own nonprofit status. A process that took weeks
and much work on a select few...All the while other problems
surround us. Two weeks ago during spring break I was at
Jeanna's with seven of my grandchildren. We were outside
playing t-ball and then went around back to pick up limbs.
Well, everyone, but two who considered it work. Making a
game out of picking up limbs was not something she was
going to fall for. I soon noticed a white Explorer sitting
straight across the highway from Jeanna's driveway. After
being stalked several times before I had had enough. I
literally walked across the highway and took down his tag
number. While I was walking back, the children said they
could see a lens pointed towards the house. He then pulled
forward just enough to see the backyard. Then backed up to
the original position. I made the children go into the house.
This went on for approximately fifteen minutes while I have
seven children reporting his every move as they peered out
the window. He finally left about two minutes before
Jeanna's husband could get to us. This is only one example of
the stalking we have experienced, but this one was the most
serious for the children...Misinformed freaks are coming out
of the wood work to trash the Briggs in their efforts to free
Kelsey's mom. That on top of the threats and stalking make
you wonder when they will no longer be threats and will
become another tragedy. I can only imagine them doing a
happy dance and taking credit for our decision, but in reality
they had little input. Now they can focus more on their
ultimate goal of freeing Kelsey's mom. In reality that is out of
all our hands and our family will accept the decisions made
by our judicial system...After a personal desire to step back
we had to make a decision. We sat for hours talking about
once again doing the right thing. This time the right thing
had to put our family first. It wasn't easy and I was a hard
sale. The final sales pitch so to speak was when Jeanna said*

Kelsey deserves to rest in peace. It was a major light bulb moment. We looked at each other and said, 'Kelsey is done.'...As long as her name is attached to this site the others will never let her rest. But we will. She deserves it and we are giving it to her...we will no longer have a message board effective sometime in April. We will dissolve the 501c3...Regardless of what you hear, the Attorney General's office has not nor have they ever shut us down. Our nonprofit status was not in jeopardy. This was a personal decision and no one forced our hand...By taking Kelsey's name away we open the door to other families to feel their loved one is just as important. We can add other faces to child abuse such as Olivia, Letha, Logan, and many many more. One of Kelsey's favorite sayings was 'I done'. I think it is time to let her rest in peace.

Kathie Briggs's message board eventually closed, but she was far from "done." The attacks continued on the open forum and, basically, anywhere that members of Kathie's and Lance's gang could voice their opinions.

Steven Morrow /......... - does comes around. That is why there is a special place in hell for her, where they shove pineapples top first up her analey. She will burn and you shall also.

Like

Shortly after Kelsey's Purpose closed, our forum did, as well. After the bullet holes were discovered in my truck, nowhere seemed like a safe place to me. Going to church even became an issue. I feared for my safety everywhere I went and I quit sleeping at night. I awoke to every noise and spent sleepless nights lying awake and listening. In an effort to alleviate some of the fear I faced, I went to confession and spoke with my priest who told me, "You can't save the world." I decided I needed to make a change.

Soon, a new forum opened with a new name and a new owner. I was only a member, and I was completely happy with no responsibilities. The back-and-forth continued, but not at the level it had been previously. At the time, I ignored most of what went on, so maybe things were just quiet in my world. Either way, I was getting back to normal.

Burglary

October, 2008

In mid-October of 2008, on the same day as the "Kelsey Fun Run" for Kathie, Lance, and their supporters, I drove my husband to meet his ride to Mexico. His grandfather was dying and my husband wanted to spend time with him before it was too late. On a typical Saturday afternoon, my daughter would have been home alone, but on that day, she decided to ride with me so that we could shop for groceries after we dropped off my husband. It would just be the two of us eating meals for a week and we thought we'd have some fun and cook things we normally didn't get to eat. We left our home at noon and returned at 4:00 pm to a busted lock on the front door. The back door was unlocked. We searched, but we could find nothing out of place or missing. It was one of my worst nightmares coming true.

On the day of the burglary, we had left the gate open. It was worn out from keeping it shut since the issues we'd faced earlier that year with our truck, and it was literally falling off the hinges. Once we arrived home to a busted lock, and my daughter and I were alone, my first call was to my dad. He fixed the lock and the gate and installed a deadbolt in the back door. We spent a sleepless night worrying if the intruder(s) would return. The next morning, I filed a police report. The officer looked at my truck and went through the house and told me what I needed to purchase to keep us safe until my husband returned home. I had to purchase locks for all of the windows and a kick-bar to go under the front door knob. I remember thinking that it's a shame that the victim of a crime is always the one who has to pay for the damages and for future protection.

At that time, I had been going to the gym three to four days per week. I worked with a personal trainer with the goal of being able to protect myself if any of Kathie's and Lance's gang members came after me. I was starting to feel healthy. The exercise and the sauna were good for my asthma and arthritis. My clothes started falling off of me for the first time since I had taken steroids in 2007; I was feeling good about myself. After the burglary, I no longer felt that it was safe to leave my home. I worried about what might be waiting for me when I arrived back home, so I quit going anywhere by myself. I made a transition from going out with my husband and not worrying about my daughter's safety to being fearful of leaving her alone. Our lives were forever changed and, because of everything that had been going on with Kathie Briggs and her gang, I didn't know if the burglary was related to my issues with them or if it was just a random act. I didn't have the alarm system active and I had no video surveillance, so, although I suspected it was them, I had no proof.

The most frightening thing about the ordeal is the fact that we couldn't find anything missing. Within arm's reach of the front door was a large plasma television and a Playstation 3. The intruder(s) didn't take them. Since we could find nothing missing, we had to wonder what the intent of the burglar was. Did (s)he plant a bug in my office or my computer? Was (s)he scoping out the place for a future attack on my young daughter? Was (s)he frightened away before (s)he could grab anything? I'm still perplexed to this day and, since my e-mails and my telephone conversations are often quoted in posts on the Internet, I have my suspicions about the intent of the break-in. Without proof, all I can do is speculate.

Due to my fear, I distanced myself even more from Kathie Briggs and her gang. I tried to find "normal" again in my life, but I found that the more I tried to get back to work, the more difficult it became. I was blocked and couldn't write anything that made sense, but I did my best and kept moving forward, only with more caution and without leaving my home.

Freedom March

March, 2009

In March of 2009, Wendy, a new and wonderfully compassionate Raye Dawn supporter had written on my Facebook wall, "There has to be something that we can do to help Raye Dawn." The plea was familiar; it was the same thing I had said in the beginning, but I was beaten down and I had run out of ideas. At the time, I was becoming aware that Raye Dawn wasn't the only innocent person in prison. This was a tough conclusion for me because I believed that everyone incarcerated belonged there. I also supported the death penalty. The idea of ridding the earth of people who posed nothing good for society was acceptable to me. However, since my eyes were beginning to open to wrongful convictions, my views were quickly changing and I started an online group that discussed Raye Dawn's case, as well as others. I believe it was part of a plan at the time among Raye Dawn supporters. If we discussed other cases and allowed people outside of Raye Dawn's case to join our group, maybe Kathie Briggs and her gang would get tired of us and leave us alone. When this plan was devised, I was open to the possibility of other wrongful convictions, but I didn't know of any cases that I personally felt justified the term "wrongfully-convicted."

Once the online support group gained members, a few cases that were brought to my attention touched my heart; I started making videos for the family members and I purchased and maintained Web sites, just as I had done for Raye Dawn. Since all of these things were happening and Wendy wanted to come up with something big, I thought that everyone marching on their respective State Capitols on the same day at the same time would undoubtedly get attention. The new owner of Raye Dawn's support forum came up with the name "Freedom March." In less than three months, we threw it together and it was a success! We had families of those who have been wrongfully

603

convicted find our cause, and people raised their voices against wrongful convictions in sixteen states. It was amazing!

In Oklahoma, we had several special guests. A man joined us who had been wrongfully convicted of murder and had spent eleven years in an Oklahoma prison. His case was the subject of a John Grisham novel. He had spoken at our first rally and was a dedicated supporter of Raye Dawn and her family. Also, family members of three other local wrongful-conviction cases joined us, as well as Laura, my "adopted" British daughter and a young lady who is a strong Raye Dawn supporter. She came from London all the way to Oklahoma to participate in and speak at our march. It was exciting! Not only was our march successful, but after spending a week with this young lady, we took her into our hearts and I unofficially adopted her. Through all of the trials and tribulations I've faced, the bonds that I've made with giving and compassionate people like Laura and Wendy have made it worth while. Other bonds were made as well. The Freedom March served as a network for family members of the wrongfully-convicted. As one of our founders put it,

> It doesn't matter if the evidence supports the conviction. Arguing evidence in a public forum gets us nowhere. The fact that the family is suffering and is fighting for their loved one is what matters. Showing support for family and loved ones of the incarcerated is sometimes all that's needed.

On the day of our first march, despite efforts to get media attention, only one news channel was interested and ran a story on our activities. Due to the fact that we carried signs for all of the wrongfully-convicted cases in which family members had joined forces with us nationwide, the media focused on the signs that did not involve Raye Dawn. Even though Raye Dawn's family members spoke, they didn't interview them and only covered our guest speakers who were involved in other high-profile cases. It was good coverage for the other cases, but a real disappointment for Raye Dawn's family. It seemed that the media had their story and, because our efforts threatened to change the story, they didn't want to take the risk in changing it.

A New Beginning

April, 2009

After two years of stress due to my involvement with the book that detailed the facts in Kelsey's case and then my support for Raye and the onslaught of hate that followed, it was time for a vacation. In the spring of 2009, my family decided to take a short trip to the beach. The coast of Texas is just a nine- to twelve-hour drive from Oklahoma City (depending on traffic) and it is a trip I had made often.

However, this trip would not be like the rest. While driving in the early hours of the morning on a wet and stormy highway, we were lifted off the pavement, spun around for what seemed like forever, and we thought we were going to die. As I closed my eyes and waited for the end to come, instead of feeling at peace, I felt like it was my fault and this was my time to pay. I regretted that my family had to be taken with me. But God had other plans. We survived with only severe dizziness from being spun around and there wasn't even a scratch on the truck. It was a wake-up call for me. While I stared out at the deep, blue water, I was happy to be alive. I searched my heart to discover why I felt guilty so that I could fix it.

My feelings of guilt could have come from my recent back-and-forth with Clay. Just before going on vacation, Clay had attacked me on YouTube. In her video tags, she used keywords such as "fuzzy kittens," "cute puppies," and "Jonas Brothers" to get hits on her video, which I found appalling because children should never be targeted to watch any of her videos. She had gained the attention of millions of viewers for her video of the Briggs story that promoted hate against Raye because she used the age group that controls what goes viral on the Internet…young teens and children. Her videos are all about dead or abused children. Why target children with such a dark and disturbing message? To make sure that the people she was targeting weren't sucked into the hate, I copied her tags, except for those I thought inappropriate and that targeted minors. I wanted her viewers to see the actual facts in the case, but I did not want to use children for my message. I assume she noticed our tags were almost identical because she erased all of her video tags and, instead, stated as follows:

Jody Ortiz aka Truth Seeker and Former Judge Craig Key suck they
are exploiting Kelsey's murder for money placing the blame
on her paternal family the very ones who tried to protect her.

Category: Nonprofits & Activism

Tags: Jody Ortiz aka Truth Seeker and Former Judge Craig Key suck they are exploiting Kelsey's murder for money placing blame on her paternal family the very ones who tried to save Kelsey

URL http://www.youtube.com/watch?v=uWow42T

She followed that bold statement against me and the Judge with another message on her profile with Kathie Briggs's statement from her forum in which she said that I had been stalking and harassing her and her family. I complained to YouTube and not only was the statements removed, but her account was also suspended. It was only down for two weeks, but, of course, that launched a firestorm against me. Clay then went after me on the public forum with a vengeance, stating that I had "no right to privacy" and so on. Starla followed her statements by calling me a "piece of shit."

are left...but only for now. Should... ....
the accounts suspended. Enjoy your crap TS tel what a piece of shit you are.

Praying for L...

Kathie Briggs
(Kelsey Briggs' Paternal Grandmother)

During the past several months our family
has been the victims of multiple websites and
videos filled with slander.

With the assistance of our attorney, through
subpoenas, we now know most of the
people behind them. Most would assume
they are all at the hands of the maternal
family. It is true they have some connection
to most of them, but they have not created
or do not own a bulk of the vicious material
on the Internet.

First and foremost the majority of the sites
and videos are owned by a lady by the name
of Jody Ortiz aka
truthseeker,(freekelseysmom)
She is the editor of the book written by,
Craig Key, the former judge.

03-21-2008

In retaliation, I uploaded a not-so-attractive picture of Clay on Raye Dawn's Web site which she had attached to her MySpace account and I also displayed pictures of her YouTube home page in which she had provocative pictures of herself surrounded by videos of dead children. I pointed out that the combination of the pictures and the dead children was inappropriate. I also added some of her vile comments that contained threats and hate against Raye Dawn that she was allowing on her video in an effort to get her video hits to a higher level. Since Starla had tampered with Raye's sisters e-mail account and had access to all of my private e-mails with Raye's family members, she informed Clay that her pictures were labeled "slut 1" or "slut 2" in my computer. I had sent copies of the screen shots of her home page to Raye's family members to keep for their files. I worked for days to try to discover how she knew what the pictures were titled on my computer after she complained about it on the Internet. I had changed the names of the files when I uploaded them to the Web site, so how did she know? I agree it was an inappropriate term, but at the time I was at my breaking point with all of the hate and it disgusted me to see pictures of cleavage and puckered lips surrounding dead children. Were the names I had for her pictures on my private computer that I sent through private e-mails to Raye's family members any of her business? To me, it is an invasion of privacy...something she claimed I had no right to.

Advocate4Kelsey
Fort Worth, TX

15 hrs ago   #8371 | ⚖ Judge it! | Report Abuse | Reply »

Judged: 🏆 ₃ 😈 ₂ ✖ ₂

HOW DARE YOU JODY ORTIZ!
YOU HAVE STOPPED KELSEY'S STORY, AND THE STORY OF OTHER CHILDREN!
CHILDREN WHO NEED HELP, LIKE LARA BOTA, WHO NEEDS A NEW HEART!
YOU HAVE VIOLATED MY PRIVACY SO MANY TIMES BY PLACING MY PICTURES AND THE PICTURES OF
OTHERS IN YOUR VIDEOS!
YET YOU COMPLAIN WHEN SOMEONE MENTIONS YOUR NAME?
YOU ARE PATHETIC, AND DON'T FOR ONE SECOND THINK THAT THIS WILL NOT BE REVERSED.
JUST SO OTHERS KNOW JODY COMPLAINED TO YOUTUBE AND THEY SUSPENDED MY YOUTUBE
ACCOUNT, THUS STOPPING KELSEY'S STORY, AND THE STORIES OF OTHER ABUSED/MURDERED
CHILDREN.
JUST REMEMBER JODY, WHAT GOES AROUND COMES AROUND!

Kelsey
Fort Worth, TX

Judged: 🌟 ₁ 💡 ₁ ✔ ₁

This is something Jody wrote to Repulsed on FB...

Jody Ortiz - I'm off to bed. Goodnight my friend!July 13 at 9:19pm · Comment · Like /
Unlike · View Feedback (1)Hide Feedback (1)

Jody has shown no mrecy towards anyone or their privacy, so I don't feel it wrong for
me to post this.

FYI there is no such thing as a private email.

I understand what you are saying, I really do, but I did not reveal anything to 'out'
Repulsed/Ginger. She told you her own name on
here. I posted a post of Jody's to Ginger.

Honest question, please give an honest answer....

Do you believe Jody has a right to HER own privacy by hiding behind various
screen names while she constantly invades the rights of others?

> ❝ hhhmmm wrote:
> <quoted text>
> She lied - and still bringing up "names".
>
> Hello little Troll.
>
> Jody's name doesn't count.

hhhmmm
Oklahoma City, OK

6 hrs ago   #12527 | ⚖ Judge it! | Report Abuse | Reply »

> ❝ Shonya wrote:
> <quoted text>
> Hello little Troll.
> Jody's name doesn't count.
>
> Then why do you constantly bring her name up SK? She's not here.

She had knowledge of the books I was working on from the e-mail tampering activities she had been participating in with Starla. The quoted text was from her. The text below was from someone who was taking up for me at the time.

When her Youtube account was reinstated, she used a statement I had made on someone's wall in an Oklahoma political group (she's from Texas) as her background on her Youtube page. Since she didn't use my name, she got away with it without being banned again. I started to refer to her as my "Red River Stalker" since the bedlam between Oklahoma and Texas is always referenced with the Red River that divides us. She further complained that I called her a stalker. Why was she on an Oklahoma political group and how would she find a post I had made to another member if she was not stalking me?

My BG Pic is a post from Kelsey's mother's, #1 Supporter, "Truth Seeker."

For almost 2 years now "Truth Seeker" has claimed that Raye is "Innocent", was "Railroaded" into prison by a hate campaign from Kelsey's paternal family, and was "Wrongfully Convicted."

But in a post she posted on the Oklahoma Public Education Network Website she stated this....

At 11:07 am on December 19, 2008, Truth Seeker said...
What do you mean by my "objectives"? They're still the same. I don't believe Raye Dawn should be in prison for 27 years. I could understand one to five. But 27 shows something clearly went wrong.

Who would want an "innocent" person to spend time in prison?
It's clear by this post that "Truth Seeker" believes Raye Dawn Smith should have served time in prison.

The picture of people pointing fingers was my avatar within the group and in the statement I had shared my true feelings. With all of the hate and the campaign by Kathie and her group, Raye did not have a chance at a fair trial. My words were, as usual, twisted into something they were not.

The back-and-forth from that time was beyond ridiculous and not like me at all. Once again, they had pulled me down to their level and I was acting just as childish as they were. Once our vacation ended and we returned home, my first task was to remove every trace of Clay from Raye Dawn's Web site. I vowed to stay out of the fight from that point forward. I developed the attitude that they could do whatever they wanted to me, but I would no longer give into their childish antics that they used to get me to come out and play. As mentioned previously, they have to keep things going. Although I had decided to walk away and I told Gayla and other family members, "I quit," the hate grew louder. "They" would never let me be free from the hate.

Putting a "Price Tag on" Kelsey

May, 2009

In the spring of 2009, Raye Dawn received a letter from Lance's attorney regarding the $15 million lawsuit Lance had filed against the state in connection with Kelsey's death. The letter asked that she not appear in court to make any claim to the $625,000 settlement that Lance had agreed to accept in lieu of the $15 million.

Raye Dawn called me about the letter and she was in great distress. "How can they put a price tag on my baby?!" she screamed into the phone. I had no answer. The only conclusion I could draw was that the evidence didn't support the lawsuit and the state offered a settlement so Lance took it. I had heard from someone who knew the paternal family that their attorneys had been working for years on a contingency basis. Since every lawsuit Lance had filed was thrown out of court, I'm sure his attorneys pressed for the settlement because they were entitled to forty percent.

Raye Dawn read the letter to me and what I gleaned from the language was that the attorneys were acknowledging her as Kelsey's mother, which meant she was eligible for half of the settlement, and Kathie Briggs's alleged plan to put Raye Dawn in prison so that her entitlement would be erased was in jeopardy. I encouraged Raye Dawn to send the letter to her attorney and seek his advice. My initial response was that she should go for it, and she had already decided to do just that.

She told me, "I don't want this money to go up his arm or up his nose."

After a few moments, she regained her composure and told me that if she were to get the money, she would donate it to St. Jude Children's Research Hospital in her father's memory, and in Kelsey's memory to

613

the local infant crisis center that had been on the news frequently discussing how they were in need of funding. She wanted to help save babies and children who were sick, in honor of Kelsey and her father. These were her plans from the moment she discovered she could be entitled to half of the settlement. Since I had been working with her on her book, I had my tape recorder ready and I taped our conversation. Therefore, proof exists that she had no other plans. Rumors, of course, began circulating that she wanted the money for herself. The media took these rumors and ran with them in a vicious attack against Raye Dawn's intentions for the money. The rumors were false. Raye Dawn wanted to honor her daughter, not collect "blood money," and her family supported her plans.

Shortly after Raye Dawn received the letter, Gayla saw a newscast in which volunteers were being requested to help the infant crisis center with car seat checks. The day the organization needed help just happened to be Gayla's day off from one of her many jobs so she spent a few hours volunteering. She felt it was a sign from God that Raye Dawn would be awarded half of the settlement and those who were struggling to save children would benefit. I was hopeful, as well.

The media frenzy surrounding the settlement included a petition that was created by a woman in Canada who has brutally attacked me online. Her comments are vicious and biting, and I've never even had a conversation with her. Her petition was covered by Britten Follett on a newscast and added to her news channel's Web site, which is our local Fox station. Someone took the liberty of signing my name to the petition and, when Kathie Briggs was asked about the petition in her deposition she stated, "It was inappropriate" and that she asked to have it removed. She also denied knowing the woman who created it. She said, "She's just some woman online." This random woman took part in creating a hate group on Facebook against Raye Dawn, which we were able to have removed. She then created another group that was to target both Raye Dawn and myself. She quickly gained over 400 members that were misled with lies; one was featured in her group's introduction. Note that the warden to whom she refers is, actually, a female. She stated:

The Warden at Mabel Basset Correction Center in Oklahoma, has
been contacted and he assure's us that it is not Raye Dawn on
Facebook or Twitter or Myspace.... He was not happy to find
out that someone was impersonating his inmate, and
promised to have the matter investigated further, as it is a
CRIME TO IMPERSONATE SOMEONE YOU ARE NOT
AND IT IS PUNISHABLE BY LAW...(THEY ARE NOW
ONTO YOU JODY MICHELLE ROBERTS ORTIZ, AND IT'S
ONLY MATTER OF TIME BEFORE WE ALL WATCH YOU
GO DOWN FOR YOUR CRIMES. I WONDER IF ALL YOUR
FIGHTING FOR RAYE DAWN'S FREEDOM WAS WORTH
YOU LOOSING YOURS, WHO KNOW'S MAYBE THE TWO
OF YOU CAN SHARE A PRISON CELL TOGETHER...YOU
BOTH DESERVE EACH OTHER!) I would just like to
remind everyone, that we can not leave death threats to Raye
Dawn in our wall posts or our discussion board Topic's,
post's or reply's... You are allowed to say that you think Raye
Dawn should have recieved the death penalty and the same
with Mike Porter, but you are not allowed to legally threaten
to do it...We all need to rally and protest and stand united
and be the voice for an abused child... We need Stricter
Sentences for Monster's like this... And they should not be
allowed to use facebook's social networking site, to try to
gain supporter's so she can get granted an appeal... This is
Morally wrong... Facebook know's it, Raye Dawn knows it,
and so do her supporters...They lie to everyone and then say
the Briggs are liars... I have read through weeks of DHS
reports, Police interigation Reports, OCYI Reports, I have
even viewed Kelsey's Autopsy Report and it made me literally
sick to my stomach...I have gone to the Free Kelsey's Mom
site, and viewed what they have posted on it, and I found out
that they have only posted half of the reports, and there are
some to that have been altered from the originals...Raye
Dawn is strongly supported by the editor of Craig Key's book
... Which he is the Judge that returned Kelsey back to Raye
Dawn and Mike Porter in June of 2005... He wrote this book
with hopes that he would get re-elected as a Judge, and to

615

line his own pockets off the earnings of the book... He did not get reelected....And the book failed miserably... It was a total flop, that some would only say was worthy of toilet paper! We had a group about getting Raye Dawn off facebook, and facebook decided to let her stay and shut our group down...Read what she is guilty of below, and you give us your opinion....

Like the other hate group, this group was soon closed, but has since been replaced with yet another group that targets Raye Dawn and me. It's a never-ending battle and the media only add to it. News reporters Cherokee Ballard and Britten Follett also host a group on Facebook that is made up of nothing but vile, mean-spirited comments. The following screen shot is from that group. One of the reporters had posed the same question about Mike Porter. Kathie Briggs could not allow the focus to be on him. She had to bring it back to Raye Dawn.

Kathie Batt Briggs If you could ask Raye Dawn a question, what would it be?

17 hours ago · Report

Will you allow me the honor of beating you with the same end result that you gave Kelsey??? I know it sounds harsh, but what she did to Kelsey doesn't even compare...
5 hours ago · Report

Why you didn't protect your child??? You don't suffer throw labor to give birth to your baby??? Whyyyyyyyyyyyyyyyyyyy you don't love her , the same way she loves her mommy. Do you not feel a hole in your soul???? How you can't sleep every nigh??? How you can live without her??..... So many questionsssss!!!
about an hour ago · Report

They allow bashing because drama is attractive to some people and it sells books, t-shirts, belts, and hats that are said to be a "fashionable way to spread the word about who killed Kelsey." Of course in their version Raye Dawn did it and Mike Porter was a victim.

Raye Dawn doesn't stand a chance against people with such poor taste in judging what's appropriate. The hate that is being generated from this group is immense and Raye Dawn isn't their only target. My name is commonly mentioned within every one of their groups as an example of "evil." Their form of logic makes no sense because they know nothing about me.

On Youtube, Clay created a video that attacked Raye and she opened up the comment section so that people could express their hate and threats. Following is just one of the comments. Clay responded to the comment, thanking this person for her opinion.

> My god, now this vile sick freak of a birth canal thinks she is entitled to half of this money...OMG, I hope that the judge who hears this case, see's past this bitches lies ! Even Lance say's that its not about the money, but this bitch only wants it,so she can pay her legal fee's to keep appealing her case...She is a vile piece of shit who deserves to die, and long and painful death, just like she allowed her baby to suffer...OMG, I am flipping out right now....

During the media frenzy regarding the settlement, Kathie Briggs lobbied for an emergency law to be inacted so that Raye Dawn wouldn't be entitled to claim any of the settlement. She contacted lawmakers and her plea to them was featured on the nightly news. My computer skills had improved by this point. I went from someone who could barely put together a Web site and who knew nothing about images to someone who could create PDF documents out of Web pages, screen shot statements to keep for evidence, and record videos from television and the Internet. This is one occasion where my newly acquired skills came in handy. I recorded the interview and paused the screen where it briefly displayed Kathie Briggs's letter written on July 8, 2009 to her State Representative. This letter had been forwarded to Britten Follet. I transcribed the letter and sent it to Raye Dawn's family members and her attorney. It stated as follows:

"I am looking for someone willing to write a new law or (adjust?) one already on the books. As you may know we will be going to court yet again in Kelsey's case. Raye Dawn Smith has filed a claim to receive half the wrongful death suit received

by the state. This is not something a family should have to face after all we have been through. She is in prison in connection with her child's death and now she wants to gain financially. It makes no sense to me. This could open the door for other inmates to claim or file wrongful death suits. It could also be a motive for a parent to sit back and allow a child to be killed. That may sound like a far stretch, but it is possible. Currently the law as I understand it states you cannot gain financially if you are convicted of murder or manslaughter. It should state you can not gain financially if you are convicted of a crime in connection with the death. Please let me know if you are interested. I will be doing a story tonight on Fox on this subject. (then it looks like a smiley face) Thanks, Kathie Briggs

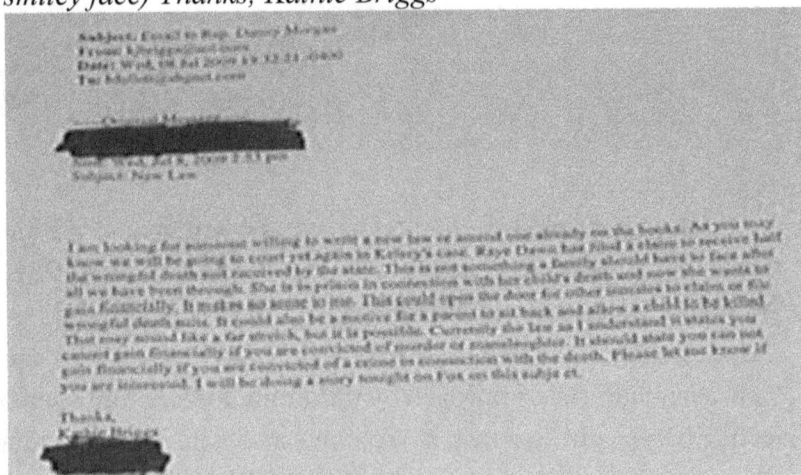

Cherokee Ballard and Britten Follett have admittedly written a book for Kathie Briggs and Lance that is filled with their excuses for certain actions and statements and it portrays Mike Porter as a loving father who was heartbroken over the loss of Kelsey and Raye Dawn as a cold-hearted slut with a bad temper and a drug addiction. On the Internet, Starla has been pushing for murder charges against Raye Dawn. Could this letter give us insight into their campaign? I think so.

At around the same time that Kathie Briggs pressed for a new law, Lance was on the news playing his usual role and crying for the camera. When asked what he was planning to do with the money, he stated that he was donating to Kathie Briggs's organization, which had been closed for over a year. However, as soon as the broadcast was over, the doors swung back open with a fury and Kathie Briggs began posting on her Web site and basically talking to herself in an effort to gain support. Kelsey would rest in peace no more. Since their new goal was to keep Kathie Briggs's Web site "clean" and not use it as a "bash board" and there was an un-moderated area where Kathie's and Lance's supporters could say whatever they wanted without reprimand or responsibility, only a handful of supporters joined Kathie Briggs's conversation. Kathie Briggs posted,

The message board is now open due to the large number of new members. You MUST be a member to read the Kelsey forum and the archives. As in the past we will monitor alll posts for inappropriate material. Anyone using content that is not suitable for Kelsey's site will be banned.

Kathie Briggs started posting on her forum that had been closed for over a year in an effort to appear to have an active organization. In the following screen shot, you can see where the author of every topic was "kjbriggs" and on most of the posts there were zero replies but multiple views. All of the posts were made within a two day period.

Kelsey's Purpose / Search / **Results**

	Post	Author	Forum	Replies	Views	Posted
	Thread: Kelsey Forum Post: Kelsey Forum *You must be a registered member to view Kelsey's forum as well as the Archives.*	kjbriggs	Kelsey Briggs Events	0	42	Yesterday, 07:55 AM
	Thread: Kelsey Forum Post: Kelsey Forum *You must be a registered member to view Kelsey's forum as well as the Archives.*	kjbriggs	Childhood Should Not Hurt	0	15	Yesterday, 07:54 AM
	Thread: Kelsey Forum Post: Kelsey Forum *You must be a registered member to view Kelsey's forum as well as the Achives.*	kjbriggs	Messages of Sympathy	0	44	Yesterday, 07:52 AM
	Thread: Kelsey Forum Post: Kelsey Forum *You must be a registered member to view Kelsey forum along with the Archives.*	kjbriggs	Announcements	0	24	Yesterday, 07:50 AM
	Thread: our pride and joy Post: RE: our pride and joy *This picture was taken on August 27, 2005 and it was our only visit with Kelsey after she was returned to Raye and the last time we saw her. According to Raye the bruises were from a car wreck eight d...*	kjbriggs	Messages of Sympathy	4	97	07-13-2009, 09:31 PM
	Thread: Jada Justice Post: Jada Justice *(CNN) -- The mother of a missing 2-year-old Indiana girl said police are working "around the clock" to find her daughter, who was apparently taken from a parked ca...*	kjbriggs	Childhood Should Not Hurt	0	11	07-13-2009, 09:02 PM
	Thread: Hayleigh Cummings Post: Hayleigh Cummings *This is a case that was on Nancy Grace for weeks. I found this summary on a site called After Hours Friends http://afterhoursfriends.com/ahfforum/viewtopic.php?f=6&t=329&p=3028 Haleigh C...*	kjbriggs	Childhood Should Not Hurt	0	11	07-13-2009, 08:46 PM
	Thread: Caylee Marie Anthony Post: Caylee Marie Anthony *ORLANDO, Florida (CNN) -- There was no trauma visible on the "completely skeletonized" remains of slain toddler Caylee Marie Anthony, but there were overlapping*	kjbriggs	Childhood Should Not Hurt	1	13	07-13-2009, 08:36 PM

Due to a lack of support, Kathie Briggs soon created a new organization, still using Kelsey's name, but under different management. However, Kathie Briggs and her daughters are all board members; the paid position that a witness told me she had been looking for all along.

In preparation for the settlement hearing that was scheduled for January of 2010, depositions were taken of key witnesses including Mike Porter, Kathie Briggs, and Lance. Raye Dawn was also deposed. Lance had been in an accident where he totaled his pickup just before Raye Dawn's deposition. According to a witness, he had been drinking and taking pills just before the accident, but no charges were filed against him. An officer on the scene also told witnesses that Lance appeared to be intoxicated at the time of the accident, but no investigation ever took place. The police chief is said to be a distant relative of Lance's family and Lance is treated as a hero and a grieving father, so everything he does that would normally be punished seems to be overlooked.

After Kelsey's death, Lance was charged with two counts of domestic violence in 2006 in connection with two different women.

These charges, along with the 2001 charge of domestic violence for assaulting Raye Dawn, were dismissed on September 23, 2008. Three charges more than five years apart regarding three different women were all dismissed on the same day by the same DA who charged and tried Raye Dawn, after telling witnesses that he only charged Raye Dawn because he "had to." Lance and his family members seem to be above the law, which is terrifying to a few residents in their county.

Despite arguments from Raye Dawn's attorneys that Lance not be allowed to attend Raye Dawn's deposition, he entered the prison on crutches and positioned himself across from Raye Dawn and mocked her. Raye Dawn's attorney posed the question, "Do you find something funny about the abuse and death of your daughter?" She told me that Lance did not act like the grieving father that he portrays on television. On that day, his mom must not have prepared him well, though she did wait for over four hours in a hot car outside the prison for him.

During that same time frame, Mike Porter was also deposed. Raye Dawn's attorney traveled to the Missouri prison where Mike Porter is housed "for his protection." The attorney didn't recognize Mike Porter when he was first brought into the room, and neither did I when I watched the video that was made that day. His formerly heavy frame, clean-shaven face, and round cheeks were now replaced by a thin face and a goatee. He looks like what we termed when I was in school "a hood." His current looks were a far cry from the clean-cut man I first saw on the news.

Mike Porter after his arrest in 2005 or 2006.

Mike Porter during a deposition with Raye Dawn's attorney on
September 9, 2009 after serving over two years in prison.

Through every question, he stared coldly into the camera and answered, "I respectfully decline to answer that question." No question asked of him caused him to shake his calm demeanor, not even when Raye Dawn's attorney asked if he had ever sexually abused his own daughter. However, he did attempt to cover smirks when asked about deceiving Raye Dawn. Conversely, while there was little reaction from Mike Porter, Lance's attorney, who also attended the deposition, had plenty to say. To the question of sexual abuse and his own daughter and many other questions asked of Mike Porter, Lance's attorney's voice took on a high-pitched tone and he screamed, "Are you kidding me with that question? You're badgering this witness!"

When the deposition first began, Mike Porter informed Raye Dawn's attorney that he would not answer any question. He claimed that his attorney had placed a call to Lance's attorney and informed him that no questions would be answered. At the time of his claim, there was no denial from Lance's attorney. However, once the judge was called because Mike Porter was not cooperating, and Raye Dawn's attorney informed the judge that Lance's attorney had been notified that Mike Porter was not going to cooperate but Raye Dawn's attorney's office was not informed, Lance's attorney denied that he ever received such a call. Mike Porter shook his head and denied he had made that statement as well. The entire deposition was a joke. Lance's attorney continually treated Mike Porter as his client and he left before the deposition ended with the parting words of, "I'm leaving with the understanding that you're going to continue to answer every question as you have been doing." He repeated this to Mike Porter several times and then shook Mike Porter's hand on the way out the door. Many wonder if Lance's attorney was only there to ensure that Mike Porter would keep his mouth shut. By his behavior, that would also be my guess.

In the weeks before the depositions, I actually joined Kathie Briggs's Web site and spent hours searching for evidence that would

623

assist Raye Dawn's attorney in deposing Kathie Briggs. The deposition was a slow process with every misstatement from Kathie Briggs argued with her own words to prove her statements were false. Immediately after her deposition, the un-moderated public forum sprung to life with posts about how people didn't realize how much I had helped Raye Dawn's attorney. *How did they know what I was e-mailing to her? Have they hacked into my email account, as well as Raye Dawn's sister's account?* Starla shared information that I helped the attorneys and she knew that it was shared with a female associate attorney and not Raye Dawn's main attorney, who is a man. *How did they know who I emailed?* The hate against me grew to a loud roar. I was being quiet and they were mad because they knew what I was doing behind the scenes. They were above the law and I was in their way. They began working day and night to ensure everyone hates me as much as they do.

Although I had quit Raye Dawn's family, the paperwork I started in January of that year so that I could occupy the "friend" position on Raye Dawn's short list of allowed visitors came through just after I quit. I was no longer saying anything publicly in support of Raye Dawn, but I had made a promise to her that I would help her tell her story. The appellate court judges had received her appeal in January and by May she was restless and wanted something to keep her mind busy. I thought it was the perfect time to get back to work on her book. The plan was for me to visit and ask questions, then come home and work on the chapters and mail them to her as we progressed, and to also email them to certain family members, including her sister whose email was being hacked.

The first time I went to see Raye Dawn in prison was a bad day for me. I didn't know what to expect and I imagined the fear and sadness that Raye Dawn and her family members had experience when seeing the prison for the first time. On the drive there, I called a dear friend of mine and she helped to keep me calm. My emotions took over, and the closer I got to the prison, the stronger the feelings became; I was almost in a state of hysteria by the time I reached the parking lot. My biggest fear was entering the prison in that panicked state and Raye Dawn seeing me and that my reaction would be upsetting to her. I just couldn't do it!

As I approached the prison, the exterior alone was quite intimidating. When I pulled into the parking lot and parked, a gentleman approached my window and asked if I had any change for a dollar bill. I hung up the phone with my friend and searched my truck for change, which took a few minutes. I don't know if it was divine intervention, but he was a young man and appeared to not have much in the way of spare money. Finding money for him to use to purchase whomever he was there to visit some snacks took my mind off my fear and my fast-beating pulse began to slow down. The throbbing in my ears also subsided.

I took my truck key off the key ring and grabbed my Ziploc bag full of quarters and my identification, and I concentrated on remembering my tag number as I followed the young gentleman up the steep, concrete steps that led to the main gate. The man pushed the buzzer on the gate and yelled "Visitor!" and the large steel gate squealed on its tracks and opened. My legs felt weak, but I moved forward, following his lead, and I stood with him between two gates that led into the building. I looked to both sides and saw a chain link fence with razor wire on top and rolls of razor wire in front of them that were taller than me.

After the gate behind us closed, the gate in front of us opened and we followed the path into the foyer where an armed guard waited at a desk with a sign-in sheet and a list of names and another armed guard stood by the metal detector and frisked visitors who had been approved to go inside the visitation area.

Although I was told I had been added to the list, my name wasn't there. I was turned away and relief washed over me as I made my way through the large gates and past the razor wire. I was going home and more relieved than disappointed. I told myself that the hard part was over because on my next visit, I would have already made it into the building and I knew what to expect. There would be no surprises.

The following week when I returned, my name had been added to the list and I was allowed to go inside and see Raye Dawn. She looked well. She had made some good friends and people were treating her nicely because she was a model prisoner. The guards were all very polite and helpful and I left the visit feeling even more relieved.

The hardest part of the visits was sitting across the table from Gayla, Raye Dawn's mother, and Mildred, Raye Dawn's grandmother. The pain was evident in their eyes and my heart broke for them. They shouldn't have to drive to a prison week-after-week to visit Raye Dawn. She should be home.

With each visit, I grew more at ease. Gayla and Mildred would try to keep the mood light and we talked about a variety of topics, not just Raye Dawn's book. After a few weeks, I had enough information from Raye Dawn to get a feel for who she was and what her book should include. It was a different environment than I was accustomed to working in, so it took more hours of work than usual. I would go in each week with questions, but since I could not take notes, I forgot a lot of what we discussed before I arrived back home. Also, most of the content of our previous discussions that took place while she was in the county jail were about Raye Dawn's and Lance's relationship before Kelsey was born, so we hadn't gotten very far. I recall one statement she made to me about the first time Lance had hit her. She told me that it was her fault. When I posed the question again after two years had lapsed and Raye Dawn had grown in her faith, she said she realized that it was not her fault; a man should never hit a woman. When she stated her new opinion, tears filled my eyes because I knew she was no longer a victim of Lance's abuse; she was now a survivor.

Raye's Book

626

After writing the first chapter, something inside told me to take a break. Comments were being made on the Internet such as "I'd love to read Raye Dawn's book" and I had a bad feeling but I didn't know what it was. Also, the hate on the Internet against me was getting worse and, with my resolution to not retaliate in the haters' childish manner, I was left with few options to use to combat them. Looking back, it's a true blessing that I stopped working with Raye Dawn when I did. The first chapter has been read by Kathie Briggs and her gang members due to their admitted crime of tampering with Raye Dawn's sister's email account. Kathie Briggs, Lance, and all of the other haters read the first chapter before Raye Dawn's attorney did. This could have jeopardized Raye Dawn's appeal, due to the fact that I was merely writing what I remembered Raye Dawn telling me, and my recollection is not always accurate. Although complaints have been made to the police and the FBI, those who are hacking into email accounts with the sole purpose of spying on Raye Dawn and her defense have yet to be charged.

Cyber bullies and Pleas for Help

August, 2009

In the fall of 2009, the online bullying was building and I felt helpless against the attacks. Accusations were being made against me that had no basis in truth. I was accused of hacking into Kathie Briggs's computer and giving her a virus through Facebook. They repeatedly brought up Gayla's conversation with Starla's ex-husband and said that I had stalked the woman and put her and her children in danger. Claims were also made that I was stalking and harassing people online and that I was stalking, video taping, and taking pictures of Kathie Briggs's grandchildren. The only thing that Raye Dawn's family and I knew was that someone was online telling heinous lies about Raye Dawn and her family members. We worked for months to try to find proof of that person's identity so that Raye Dawn's family could do what needed to be done to make it stop. We thought it was Kathie Briggs and Starla, but we weren't sure of whom it was and we needed proof. So, I created an alter identity on Facebook and sent friend requests to the gang members and I copied their lists of friends who lived near the location of the main bully. I emailed the lists to Raye Dawn's family members to see if any of them recognized someone who could fit the profile. At the time, I didn't realize that my emails to Raye Dawn's family members were being read by Kathie Briggs and her followers. Only a few of them accepted my request and I was dropped by everyone almost immediately. Things that seemed odd at the time now make sense.

As the list of allegations against me grew, so did their level of implausibility. On one occasion, the bullies stated that I would be arrested the following day for my alleged crimes. Although I knew I was innocent, since working with Raye Dawn's wrongful conviction and learning about others, I realized that I could be sent to jail as an innocent person and with no evidence against me. I knew that a wrongful conviction could occur due to the mere fact that people hated me, and there was nothing I could do about it. Add to the allegations their statements that "there is no such thing as private email" and "Jody doesn't deserve privacy," and you can only imagine the terror I felt. People have committed suicide over similar circumstances because, at some point, the terror becomes overwhelming. Do these bullies want to drive someone like Raye Dawn to kill herself? They almost got their wish. What did they hope to push me to do? Would the terrorizing and bullying have stopped had Raye Dawn committed suicide? Or would they have carried on with their agenda against Raye Dawn's family? At what point does law enforcement step in and put an end to the madness? When it's too late? I needed help and I reached out to several online abuse groups, but only one responded. For months, the volunteer worked with me to file complaints against several Web sites, as well as the Internet Service Providers of the two main bullies. Despite our efforts to get the bullying and harassment to stop, it continued.

On August 19, 2009, I sent the following e-mail to a contact person for the un-moderated forum with a list of post numbers that needed to be removed:

> I am not posting on your forum and posters on there are calling everyone me to justify smearing my name as they have threatened to do. They are stalking me, harassing me, and cyberbullying me. Please keep my name off your forums. Thank you!

When my pleas went ignored, on August 27, 2009, I followed up with another e-mail.

> I filed a complaint today with the FCC against your site since I couldn't find a phone number to contact you and no address. I have requested five times via e-mail and on your site with the individual links for you to not allow people to use your site to stalk and cyberbully me and you are ignoring my requests. I want my name removed from your site

630

immediately! I also want a physical address for law
enforcement officials to contact you.

This e-mail got a response that included an address to forward information to subpoena identities of the individuals posting threats. Since one of the bullies had posted that Raye Dawn should be "drawn and quartered," I forwarded the information to Raye Dawn's family and her attorney.

Starla soon started making threats about suing people who were trying to identify her and she discussed the fact that Gayla was going to request a subpoena for her information. She continued to deny her identity. As in the past, we assumed someone was sharing information, but after we tightened our communications and only shared information with the few we knew for sure weren't telling anyone anything, and they continued to discuss things we were discussing, I became suspicious. I soon pieced together our conversations that occurred just before they were mentioned on the un-moderated forum and most of the things that we thought were leaked could be traced back to emails sent to Raye Dawn's sister, Janet.

By August 28, 2009, I was so defeated that I had to speak with a therapist. I was getting tunnel vision when I would see my name online and I had a break down in the middle of Best Buy. I had also decided to go back to school and the online environment with my name on the screen where other people could see it and the questions being asked about me and what I did only added to my stress. Each time I looked at the computer screen and saw my name, my peripheral vision would start to go dark and my ears were filled with ringing. I had to get up and walk away, and the pounding in my chest wouldn't slow down. Many nights, I would lie in bed and feel pressure in my chest, and I would think that was it and that I was having a heart attack. Never in my life have I had such strong physical reactions to anything, and I was afraid that something serious would happen to me. I worried about my family. The therapist told me to start writing about everything that happened, so, with my husband's encouragement, I decided to write my own book, *The Naked Truth Bound in Scorn*. After I was notified by Facebook that my account had been hacked, I closed my account and worked at remaining under the radar. I sent an email to the online abuse group.

I had to start talking to a psychiatrist. The stalking was really getting to me and they're using my name to sign petitions, join writing sites, and argue with themselves. I was told as you told me to fall off the face of the earth so there is nothing to stalk online. It was hard to give up all my hard work but I created new accounts for new domains to work under and I'm going to work under a 'pen' name. I've reported [the forum] to the FCC for not removing my name when I've requested 6 times for them to remove it on over 70 posts and I've made contact with my district attorney. Anyway, thank you for all you've done. I really appreciate you very much and if you are set up for donations when I get back to where I can work I will make a donation to your very worthy cause. God bless you!

For months, I worked to restore my life, but to no avail. As I grew even more silent, they grew louder. They told new people that I was a moderator on the open forum and when posts disappeared, they blamed me. I was called the "spawn of Satan" and a "devil" and other choice words. While they were spreading hate against me, I did everything I could to get some help. I called the district attorney in my county and was told that I could get a restraining order against them and, when they violated it, something could be done. I knew that wasn't a plausible solution because there were just too many of them and they would create another alias in order to harass me. I called the police and filed reports, but after a certain point, the police no longer listened. I called several attorneys and was told that since I couldn't work because I had been crippled for years and, therefore, I had no money to pay them, and that the people harassing me obviously didn't work, they had nothing to gain, so I couldn't do anything. One attorney told me to use them for advertising. *Advertise what?* I asked. Even the

632

FBI told me it was "civil" and there was nothing they could do. I was on my own.

Stalking Blog

December, 2009

In December of 2009, the bullies recruited someone who stated that she was going to contact all of my clients and tell them that I'm the devil. She was convinced that the claims made by Starla about me were true. She actually believed the dramatic story that Starla had shared and that I had tracked down her ex-husband and put her adult children in danger. There were so many bullies who were repeating the lies that she believed them. To show her support for the bullies, she threatened to add to the destruction of my business.

Following are examples of some of the statements that were posted to me or about me at that time (I did not respond to any of the comments made, though it appears I had from the way their statements were phrased):

*I can be someones best friend or worst enemy…it all depends on how
     I am treated…I have access to amazing amount of
     information and ways to get it…you play in my life or that of
     my friends and I will play in yours…*
*Jody is the devil…My brother is looking into her online
     dealings…soon we will have answers and more evidence for
     my attorneys*
*If I ever find out who your stalker is, if you even have one…remind
     me to buy them dinner for making your life hell*
*You think your life is hell now..wait until you piss off the wrong
     person…A simple posting will be the least of your worries…*
*I'm done with you Jody Ortiz…You want to keep playing this
     game…Go ahead…You will have a miserable life…Your an
     evil woman and you know it…You're an empty woman. I'm
     sick of you and your boring…I may have wasted the last 2
     weeks of my life on you and I wish I could get them back…I
     will not waste anymore time on you…your a pity…..*

*I would feel sorry for you if you weren't so damn pathetic...Enjoy
        your sorry excuse of an existence...*

*Quit your sh*t Jody...Im not gonna hold your hand and make you
        feel all warm and fuzzy simply because your a coward piece
        of crap...You stalked and prey on peoples lives, like you did
        with Gayla...You two biotches deserve each other...I'm sick
        and tired of you crying like your the god damn victim..You
        brought this on yourself...Quit playing like you have no idea
        whats going on...You wanna play games...Now we are going
        to play games...Let's see how you like your own bullsh*t
        played back on you...Good luck finding where I or someone
        else post about you...Good luck with that...*

*Jody is a b!tch that takes pleasure in destroying lives...I take back
        my promise...I won't sink to her level...But when someone
        else does...I will celebrate and smile and laugh at Jody's
        misery...*

*This wench really thinks she is so smart...NOT... I would love to sit
        in a courtroom with Jody, to prove that all her lies are just
        that LIES...*

*I believe the facts in this case... Nothing More, Nothing Less.... You
        wanna believe your garbage and lies that is your problem...
        One you will live with for the rest of your sorry ass life... As
        for us being accused of breaking and entering into your
        home, shooting at your truck, and or keying your truck, well
        from where I live, that would be very hard to do... So maybe
        we aren't the only ones you have pissed off...I would check
        your enemy score card again...Oh and one more thing....The
        virus you gave the Organization that I am affilated with now
        has traced the virus back to where it came from... It is now in
        the our Legal Departments hands..... So you have not just
        messed with us as you call us, Kathie Groupies... You have
        now messed with an Organization, and one that has Lawyers
        who can have you tied up in civil litigation for the next 10
        years.... So lets see, criminal activity, stalking, defamating
        ones character, posting on a public blog that people are who
        they are not...... NEED I SAY ANYMORE... On that note, a
        very wise lady once told me to never argue with idiots as they
        will only beat you with experience, and I tend to live my life
        these days to those words.....So this is the last post that I will
        address to any of Raye Dawn's Supporters....You [another*

Raye Dawn supporter] seem to come on here like a highschool girl with a score to settle... And a fight to cause... So here is one for you, if you want to fight so much, Stick your head up your ass and fight for air.... Cause your a waste of it just like Raye Dawn......

Starla added,

I don't know what her problem with me is. She claims that I have blackmailed her which is a lie. My comment in the email, 'you started this, you can end it' I guess is what she is claiming was 'blackamail'. What I meant by that comment was she was the one who started the drama between her...group and Kelsey's Purpose members and she was the one who could stop the nonsense that was going on back then.

That was it! I could take no more. The fear that had taken hold of my life since early 2008 was replaced by anger. I became sick of hiding from the bullies. I was no coward. I started writing my first book and I started a blog. I was tired of being their victim. I was mad as hell and I was going to take control of my life. My daughter and I watched the movie *Julie & Julia* and I was inspired. It was based on a true story of a woman who cooked and blogged her way through Julia Child's cookbook. In 365 days, she made over 500 recipes. I thought to myself, *I wonder how many days of blogging it will take to make the bullies go away?*

On December 14, 2009 I posted a video I had just taken of a man in a truck who was parked outside my home watching me and I stated,

<u>Hello world!</u> *I started this blog to document my daily struggles with ending the hate on the Internet. Let's see how many days it takes me to finally be heard. Day one: I'm shocked at how people can read something and take it as fact and then jump on the hate parade. Why do people think that toying with lives and picking apart details about people they know nothing about is fun? What is missing in their lives that they spend hours every day harassing and stalking people? Why*

*won't the Web sites that allow the hate do anything about it?
Last week I arrived home to find a truck parked across the
street from my driveway. I questioned some men working next
door, and the truck did not belong to them. As I walked back
to my driveway, I could see the shadow of someone sitting in
the truck, watching me. Was he taking pictures? Was it a
scare tactic? Was he stalking me? Or was it someone casing
the area for a future burglary? Daily, thoughts such as these
go through my mind. Every engine noise, every stranger
becomes someone suspicious. Two years ago I would have
walked up to the truck and asked if the person needed help.
Two years ago my gate was always open to visitors. Today,
my gate is shut and locked with a variety of no trespassing
signs greeting each possible visitor. Today, my life has
changed.*

My new blog was quickly found by my bullies and they started
four of their own in answer to mine. Each day, I posted on my blog,
and they would find something to harass me about on their respective
blogs. The following post was from Starla.

---

1 hr ago   #24924 | ⚖ **Judge it!** | Report Abuse | **Reply** »

Ok, after much consideration and speaking to some others, I have a suggestion. I really
think that any of us that are/have been under attack on the new blog of Jody's, should
not post anything to her blog. The feeling is that this is only empowering her more in
her quest to portray the "victim" in this. My opinion. She is apparently trying to fuel the
fire and we don't want to be a part of that. Also my opinion. I have not posted and would
not post there because of the IP issue we all know about.
She has succeeded in drawing attention to herself and her blog and taken the topic of
conversation here on Topix away from Raye Dawn and has had it focused on herself.
Also remember that the more people go there, gives her more hits to her site.
I will say that I have been informed there will be a site shortly that will address the lies
and accusations on that blog. Maybe we should get back to the real topic here? Just a
suggestion. I'm sure not "ordering" anyone to do or not to do anything, nor telling them
they have to, only a suggestion. It's up to each of you what you do with it. I gave my
opinion is all, wanted to make sure and clarify that. LOL

Videos have been made about me; poems have been written; and
a screenplay was said to be created about a paranoid writer who, of
course, is murdered in the end. The torture is a game for them and one
that, to this day, they are still playing.

Kathie Briggs had Starla put a post to me on her blog. She stated that I had committed road rage against her husband and his two employees and that my truck had been identified. In the beginning, their comment was "Watch out or she'll run over you in her little red car" but now they had identified my truck. She also stated that she couldn't wait for my book so that she could sue me and that if anything happened to anyone in her family, they would have the police visit me first as a suspect. It was beyond ridiculous!

TUESDAY, JANUARY 12, 2010

From Kathie Briggs

Kathie Briggs asked me to post this notice to Jody Ortiz..

Enough is enough. You have spread lies long enough and now that you have written them using your actual name I will be filing a lawsuit. I have never harassed you and I have never posted, read, or logged into Topix. Since Raye's criminal trial I have made few posts and when I do it is with my name. You have twisted words, and flat lied about me and my family long enough. My suggestion to you: start working to prove everything you have said about me is true. If you only have to justify the lies on this site my case is strong. I might add you have also lied about the actions of our attorney's on this site as well.

You claim to be a victim. From what I see you seek the all the attention you can get. As for me: I am only responsible for my statements and my actions as are the other parties to this lawsuit. I have been preparing and saving for this for two years and will be well prepared for all the lies you have told. I honestly don't see the Smith family wanting to help you with your legal fees when they have a family member needing their help. You see, I don't blame them for working as hard as they can for Raye even though I am on the opposite side. You haven't helped Raye at all...and now you have your own legal battle to fight.

Do you remember the day you engaged in road rage against my husband and two of his employees on I-40? Had that not happened your identity would have remained secret for a much longer time. Since then we have been offered proof that you are "truthseeker" and that you used the name "Mary Thompson" to spy on KP members. So when this lawsuit is ready to file I will not be the only plaintiff listed. The list of people you have harassed and slandered is long. As with any good case we have been patient long enough to get all the facts and proof we need to build a rock solid case.

If you genuinely feel your life is in danger I feel for you. I too have a list for the authorities if anything should happen to me and your name is on the top of the list. All of this could have been prevented had you logged off your computer and left us alone.
Another suggestion: when you post the rest of your hearing testimony....remember we can get a copy of the transcript so it

From Kathie Briggs

needs to be accurate.

A final note: I can't wait for your book to come out. I will be first in line to get a copy in hopes I can use it in this lawsuit.

One more note:

You have made many incorrect statements on your notes about the depositions. I can prove your posts are lies. Your comments about the attorneys are uncalled for and also untrue. Keep posting and thanks.

Posted by Starla at 1:30 AM

4 comments:

satojos said...

I have waited for someone to do this for so long. Karma is such a hard thing to deal with when you reap the negative kind.

January 12, 2010 8:15 AM

Starla said...

I know satojos, we had hoped that it would not come to this, but as you see...it never stops. It's time to stand up and do what's right and stop the nonsense. We have asked for this to stop for over two years and it has fallen on deaf ears. Now that there can be no lying about "who" it is that is posting the lies, accusing us of doing things we have not, spreading and breeding the hate against not only us but against Kelsey's Purpose as a whole, it's time to get it stopped.
Gosh we have asked her for so long to stop stating her opinions as fact...good example being when she says that "800 Kelsey's Purpose members" returned Key's pathetic book to the distributor or publisher. I hope she can prove that 800 were returned and they were ALL KP members. Her harrassment and stalking of KP and its members is something else.

Insurance

I hear the much awaited "book" is soon to be sent to the publisher. I'm wondering if the author has the forethought to purchase the insurance policy that will protect them when/if they are sued over the content? Guess we will know soon enough. Seems like a small investment when writing something such as this. I know of a few attorneys that are anxiously awaiting the release of the book. This could get interesting. Time will tell.

Posted by Starla at 1:55 AM 1 comments

The accusations were shortly followed by multiple threats of lawsuits against me by several of the bullies. I received several cease and desist notices, as well. The bullies had pushed me too far and I was tired of sitting back and taking it, and they were worried.

The Bully is Revealed

January, 2010

Distance creates clarity and I tried to figure out why the haters were somewhat quiet and then started their attacks on me with brute force in the summer of 2009. With the recent discoveries of e-mail tampering, the fact that they knew I was helping Raye Dawn's attorney prepare for depositions just before it happened, and statements on a public forum where they stated that I went to extreme lengths to help Raye Dawn, it's crystal clear. The main bully had been denying her identity for years, but, suddenly, she knew she was caught. Starla admitted it was her all along, yet she called me a liar for denying my identity.

As evidence of her denial, Starla posted this reply on YouTube on February 2, 2009 with her real identity:

Yes, like usual your only defense of Raye Dawn is to lay blame with someone else or to turn the attention with your lies and slander/libel to someone else. This was sent to my attorney and she will be getting a subpeona to find out who actually posted this LIE so we know who exactly to sue. So....you. No clue who my friend Starla is, yet you make stupid implications like this, too dang funny. And she's probably forgot more than YOU EVER learned to start with. such a joke, the whole ignorant bunch of you. Yes, dear my opinion. Now run along and mark this as spam to peak others' curiosity.

As part of her plan to reveal my identity, she posted screen shots of the ill-gotten e-mails, along with private Facebook messages from the time period when my account was hacked, on her blog. She was busted! Her identity had been discovered and, to deflect attention from herself, she used tampered e-mail messages that I had sent to Raye Dawn's sister and private Facebook messages. *How stupid can one person be?* A police report was immediately filed now that we had proof that she was the one guilty of tampering, and the FBI was contacted. We're still waiting for charges to be formally filed.

Starla's alias was "NoUse."

KelseysVoice   10 hrs ago   #16046 | Judge it! | Report Abuse | Reply »

> **NoUse wrote:**
> KV, I have a question? You have the witness list of Raye Dawn's, do you have the Briggs' list? I heard from a VERY reliable source they are considering subpoenaing Jody and truthseeker! Have you heard anything about that?? Talk about "Breaking News!!!" lol

Let me go back and look at my lists. If they subpoena Jody, I will throw the largest block party in history. LOL, LOL, LOL!!

KelseysVoice
Parsippany, NJ   22 hrs ago   #20364 | Judge it! | Report Abuse | Reply »

> **NoUse wrote:**
> Thank you for posting this. I'm not surprised, this is how she operates. She's gotten away with it for so long, she just keeps going. Ever heard the saying, the "bigger they are, the harder they fall?", that quote doesn't just fit when you are talking about a physical fight, it also fits when you are talking about someone who's tried to make themselves big and important in something and they get out of hand, get caught, get charged and have to pay the price for their wrongdoings, as will she. Too many people are tired of her illegal, unethical and immoral tactics. We'll see what happens down the road a bit lol
> <quoted text>

The bigger they are, the harder they fall? Do I hear the loud noise of an FKM member hitting the ground with a really loud thud?

Starla posted my private e-mails with Raye's family members and private messages from my Facebook account at the time I was alerted by Facebook that it had been hacked.

In this message Starla posted, she discussed things that Raye's family had been discussing about their strategy for the depositions. Raye's family did not have a chance to defend Raye with the Briggs and their supporters breaking into private e-mails and watching every move.

40 min ago   #16067   Judge it!   Report Abuse   Reply »

66 NoUse wrote:
I knew you were responding to sue, somehow my post showed up, then was gone and back after sue's. It should have been right under yours. Sorry for the confusion.
Yes, Raye is listed on the witness list and they already did Raye's deposition. I can't wait to see Raye's testimony!! Her deposition was interesting, testimony time will be even better, I'm sure.
It would seem by RD's witness list that she is trying to get things on record that were not on record in the criminal trial, but I think they will be disappointed. I don't think this Judge is gonna play around, he already said he would not allow retrying the criminal case in his courtroom. This isn't a criminal hearing on the felony charges lol. She already had her trial, guess they just don't "get it". Will be interesting to see J.O. testimony too....will she tell the truth, the whole truth and nothing BUT the truth??? hhhmmm....inquiring minds wanna know....lol (and a lot of them at that! lol)
<quoted text>

I want them to bring out all of the lies and outright character assassination that J.O.(I can think of two other words that start with J.O.) engages in on a daily basis. They'd have people lined up for three miles to sue her for libel alone.

Dec 11, 2008   #314   Judge it!   Report Abuse   Reply »

                                              Judged:

Again? Oh yeah, like when I was right about TS/Jody, hhhmmm/RIP Angel. If you all don't want people to know who you really are then maybe you shouldn't feel so comfortable with the security you think is in place on those other websites. What? You think Hod is the only one who has someone that knows about computers? LMAO
And no, I'm not wrong, how much do you want me to reveal to prove it? hhhmmm???
Just generally speaking, sometimes it's better to cut your losses and quit while you're ahead.
It's not your business who I am. I don't go around spewing filth on other websites, patting my own back revealing who I am. Say what you want to try to divert the truth, but once again, your lies and cover ups, will not change the truth.

On January 9, 2008, I had received this email from Raye Dawn's sister:

I got booted and couldn't get back on. My computer has been doing this lately. Kathie Briggs probably has got a hold of it!!

It seems that, subconsciously, she already knew what was happening.

645

The Hearing

The hearing to decide the distribution of the lawsuit settlement took place in January of 2010 and, for the first time I came face-to-face with Kathie Briggs, who had nothing to say to me. In fact, we ignored each other. However, Lance's girlfriend gave me the evil eye throughout the entire hearing. Every time I glanced her way she was turned around in her seat and staring directly at me.

Throughout the hearing, I took intensive notes and made sure that the quotes were accurate and verbatim. Like Britten Follett's notes from Raye Dawn's trial, they weren't perfect. I didn't capture every word because I have forgotten shorthand and arthritis makes writing by hand something painful. When I began posting my notes to my blog, I was called a liar and, soon, members of the left side of the courtroom, none of whom took a single page of notes, suddenly posted their version of the hearing with notes that contradicted my own. Just like with Raye Dawn's Web site, they claim everything is altered or a lie, but my notes accurately portrayed what took place that day. How do you prove your integrity when vicious people work to destroy everything you do with claims of foul?

Raye Dawn testified at the hearing. Since it was a Federal Courtroom, she wasn't allowed to wear "street clothes" or to be unchained. For her protection due to ongoing threats from Kelsey's paternal family and their supporters, the two prison guards who had transported her to the hearing sat directly behind her throughout the day and a US Marshall sat within reach of her at all times, even when she was on the stand. The Marshall was seen admonishing Lance on more than one occasion because he was trying to intimidate Raye Dawn.

Raye Dawn took the stand in her grey prison scrubs and with both of her ankles shackled, and she relayed the events that happened on the day of Kelsey's death. Her emotions were raw and there wasn't a dry eye on the right side of the courtroom where I sat. However, smirks and giggles could be seen and heard from the paternal family's side, as well as from Britten Follett, who sat a couple of rows behind me. Raye Dawn poured her heart out and described her relationship with her daughter and the last time she saw her alive, and Kelsey's paternal family laughed. I didn't understand how they could be so cold and unfeeling. The judge watched Raye Dawn intently and I was hopeful that he had seen past all of the dramatics that had been played out earlier in the day when Lance's family member described him as a "broken man" who was suicidal and had no joy in his life. They also denied any claims of Lance doing drugs or being an alcoholic, even though these are aspects of his character that had been publicly admitted. Their description was a far cry from the man that Raye Dawn's attorney had described just months before who sat across from Raye Dawn and held up his fingers for "two" and "seven" as he laughed at the number of years Raye Dawn would be in prison while she was questioned about abuse allegations and her daughter's death.

As Raye Dawn's testimony progressed, I noted that she described events just as she had in Mike Porter's preliminary hearing that took place just months before Lance reportedly asked the district attorney to give him a plea for a lesser charge. My tears smeared the pages and my shoulders shook as I joined everyone around me in sorrow over the unthinkable loss of Kelsey. I stopped writing and listened to Raye Dawn's heartfelt testimony of the last day she spent with Kelsey.

After the hearing, Raye Dawn's attorney submitted the evidence that he did not present in court in an effort to spare the families from the added heartache. Although the judge stated that he would read through whatever was submitted after the hearing, it was apparent that he did not. He submitted his answer less than twenty-four hours after receiving the brief and the verdict was not good: Lance would get the entire settlement. Within days of the judge's decision, reports made their way to Raye Dawn's family from a family friend who worked at a local strip club. Lance had reportedly tipped a stripper $500 and ran up a tab of a near equal amount, spending just under $1,000 of the "blood money" from his daughter's death in just one night out on the town.

Now, Kathie Briggs has a new modular home; Lance has purchased ten acres of land and is building a home.

Someone close to the family recently told me,

I hope every time Kathie Briggs walks into her home she sees Kelsey's face.

I agree.

Conclusion

December, 2011

It's now the end of 2011 and not much has changed. I have been working at getting back to normal, while Raye's family still fights to prove her innocence.

It's been almost two years since I attended a public function with Sherri Heath in Shawnee. She wanted to go so that she could ask Cherokee Ballard and Britten Follett questions about their role in Raye's wrongful conviction. I wanted to be a witness for her. I started my recorder the moment I stepped out of the car and I didn't turn it off until we left. I was determined to have proof that we did nothing wrong, and we didn't. Still, stories appeared on the Internet within hours of us being there. It was said that I tried to get onto a radio program and that we were escorted from the building by four uniformed police officers. The imaginations of those who intend to do harm....

Sherri and her cousin passed out flyers for my book, *The Naked Truth Bound in Scorn.* When Britten Follett's mom was offered a flyer, she screeched, "I'm Britten Follett's mom!"

"So?" I thought as I watched her storm away. She had been standing with a young girl, glaring at me. I had no idea who they were. The only thing I had ever stated about Britten Follett was that she was a biased reporter, and I have concrete evidence to back up my belief. Did that statement constitute such a reaction to a flyer? Could it be that she was told stories about something I had supposedly done?

I had the same questions earlier that day as we waited for the music to quiet down so that Sherri could ask Britten Follett and Cherokee Ballard why they were telling untrue stories about Raye.

649

While watching performances on the stage and talking quietly amongst ourselves, Cherokee Ballard approached reporter, Nick Winkler, and whispered something into his ear while she pointed directly toward me. He then approached some bikers and other large gentlemen and they all lined up behind Britten and Cherokee as we approached. What were they expecting? Did they actually believe the stories that the Briggs and their supporters had circulated about us? Aren't reporters supposed to seek the truth and find out the real story before they jump to conclusions and believe hearsay?

From Amazon about my book "The Naked Truth Bound in Scorn." Debbie briefly introduced herself to me at a public event but I have never "been around" her and I have never had a conversation with her.

Don't Bother, completely ridiculous and all in the authors mind. December 19, 2010

By **Debbie Hammons** (MACOMB, OKLAHOMA, US) - See all my reviews
REAL NAME

The Naked Truth Bound in Scorn (Paperback)

This author has a mental problem that she thinks that people are after her. She creates things in her own mind, embellishes them and then, whoosh, they are real. She's a mental case that actually stalked the paternal grandmother and family of the Kelsey Briggs family. She needs a restraining order against her for the things that she has done. She ghost wrote another book that she made up things in that book also. It's too bad that she does have somewhat of a talent in writing, but it should be for cartoons. Don't take this book seriously. If you'd ever been around this author you would understand.

This post was left on my book page on Facebook. Like all of the others, I have never met this person nor have I had a conversation with her.

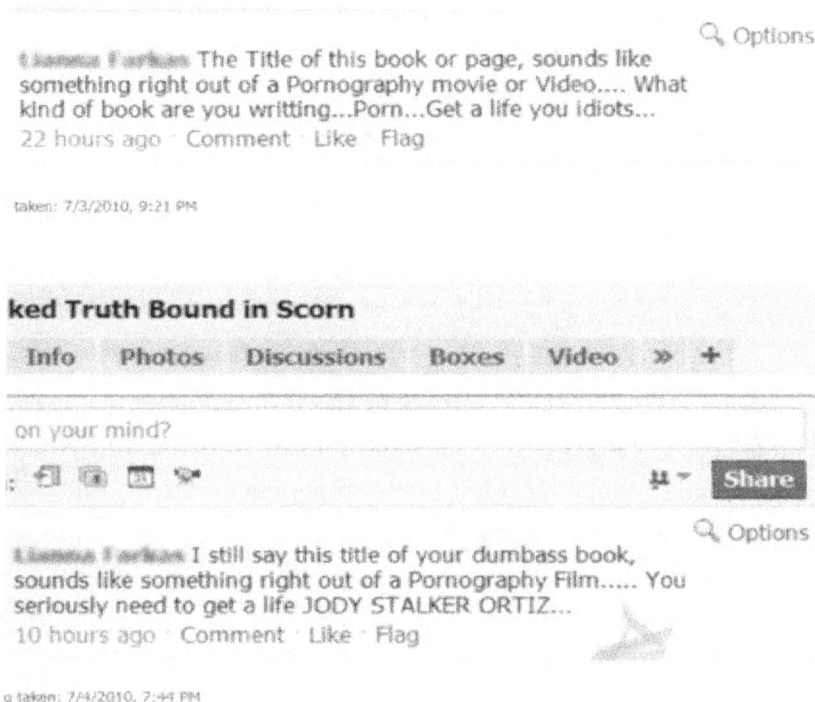

Q Options

~~~~~~ ~~~~~~ The Title of this book or page, sounds like something right out of a Pornography movie or Video.... What kind of book are you writting...Porn...Get a life you idiots...
22 hours ago · Comment · Like · Flag

taken: 7/3/2010, 9:21 PM

ked Truth Bound in Scorn

| Info | Photos | Discussions | Boxes | Video | » | + |

on your mind?

☰ ⊞ ⊡ ⚬   ♀ ▾ **Share**

Q Options

~~~~~~ ~~~~~~ I still say this title of your dumbass book, sounds like something right out of a Pornography Film...... You seriously need to get a life JODY STALKER ORTIZ...
10 hours ago · Comment · Like · Flag

g taken: 7/4/2010, 7:44 PM

On October 31, 2010 I received the following message from Debbie. She was responding to an e-mail from 2008 when we briefly communicated and I tried to reason with her about her hatred for Raye and her family. I had just announced that I was going to speak at an Innocence conference in Michigan.

I'm going thru deleting all this trash and ran across this.....How
Dare you Jody to question ANYBODY????? You're just white
trash. I'm happy with my life, in fact I'm so happy that I don't
think I could be much happier...can you say that? I can do,
go anywhere or buy anything that I want. The best thing for
me was to get out of Meeker and out from around "those"
people. I now know what lots of people thought about Gayla
(not Ray) because they have told me after finding out we're
no longer close. It's amazing. Some of Ray's own friends,

651

couldn't stand her. But that's another story.
I'll tell you how tight that family is.....my ex (Gayla's own
brother) spent 3 days in Branson with my husband and I,
Randy, Jeanna and kids AND Kathie and her
family!!! TOGETHER. We had a ball sightseeing, eating out
and listening to bands, etc. Plus he came into Shawnee for a
few days for my daughters surprise birthday party. Did he go
see his mom? No way.....I picked them up. He doesn't want
to put up or listen to their bull. Get a life, Jody.........yours
obviously from I've heard has been going downhill ever since
you got acquainted with them. They will cost you....more
than money. I can attest to that. They suck away on your
dignity and try to belittle you. Don't let them win.

Things became even weirder in the fall of 2010 when Dr. Phil invited me to be a guest on his show to discuss the bullying I had endured and overcome. One of the producers read my blog where threats and accusations from Kathie Briggs were posted for all to see. She asked me if I minded her reaching out to Kathie Briggs to also attend the show. I told her, "She makes up stories and lies. But I'm fine with it."

Within days, Starla posted on her blog that she was planning a trip to Los Angeles. This woman had threatened to destroy my business and then she threatened to follow me to Michigan when she found out I was going to an Innocence Conference to speak about Raye's case.

My heart jumped out of my chest, afraid of what these people who had stalked and harassed me and worked for years to destroy my life would do. I have since learned that they were conditioning me to be afraid to speak out. Everything I announced, they threatened to be there.

For several days I continued to work with the producers as they also spoke with Kathie Briggs. Weeks before the show was to be taped, a producer called me and asked me questions like "Are you missing any teeth?" "Do you have any visible tattoos?"

"Oh brother!" I exclaimed. *What had Kathie told them about me?*

I became even more apprehensive. As the producers tried to encourage me by stating, "Dr. Phil wants to help you," I saw images of Kathie on the couch across from me playing the grieving grandmother who was being harassed by me.

A day later I received an e-mail from the producer stating that the show had been cancelled. What happened? I will never know. What has been said about me to people? I don't really care anymore. Someone's opinion of me is just that. It's none of my business what people think of me. What matters is that I know myself and who I am. If someone wants to tell lies about me, as has been clearly illustrated in the pages of this book, it's their sin and not mine. This was a hard lesson for me to learn.

In the same year, I was asked to appear on radio shows. I spoke with a lady about my stalking ordeal. We did not discuss the case, just the stalking. Kathie Briggs contacted the host and told her that everything I said on the show had happened to her, not me. The host did not want to be involved so she deleted the show. Kathie then sent messages to the online abuse group that had helped me and to Survivors in Action, a group for which I volunteered. In these identical messages, she admitted to putting my home address on Kelsey's Purpose.

Below is the result of your feedback form. It was submitted by Kathie Jo Briggs [email removed for privacy] on October 18th, 2010 at 01:47PM (CDT).

realname: Kathie Jo Briggs
email: [email removed for privacy]
Over18: Yes
northamerica: Yes
harassername: Jody Ortiz
harasserage: unknown
harassercountry: United States

harasserstate: Oklahoma

relation: none

*whyHarrassed: After the murder of my 2 year old granddaughter she
helped write a book for the former judge that placed Kelsey
back in her abusive home where she was killed. She became
and advocate for him and then the mother of Kelsey and now
claims to be a victim herself.*

firstinteractiondate: 2007

firstinteractiontype: Website

firstharassdate: 2007

firstharasstype: Website

*beganhow: Not sure why she became so obsessed with this case, but
many have. Jody chose to side with the maternal family of
this case and has continued to harass my family even after
the mother was convicted.*

lastharassdate: 2010

harassment: Website

escalation: yes

physicalthreat: no

physicalattack: No

defamation: Yes

*defamationdetails: This lady has claimed I threatened to kill my
children, abused Kelsey. The list is very long.*

impersonation: No

evidence: Witnesses

*evidenceother: I would love to talk to you about Jody Ortiz. I
understand she is one of the directors with you organization.
My name is Kathie Briggs and I am the grandmother of
Kelsey Briggs. I have been a victim of Jody's for many years.
I hoped it would stop when I no longer posted on my own
web site Kelsey's Purpose three years ago with the exception
of helping another abused child on occasion. I do not post on
any other site nor do I read or login to these sites or read the
blogs. I get reports from others about the stuff reported about
me by Jody. The only place I post is facebook and I am
careful what I share there. In my opinion if someone is
scared of stalkers on the Internet they need to keep a low
profile as I have done. All the things Jody claims she has
suffered are the things she has done to me. She continues to
post down right lies about me on her blog. Jody started by*

ghost writing a book for the former judge in Kelsey's case. She became and advocate for him hiding behind the name of truthseeker. For months we had no idea who this person was. On the way home from work with two co-workers my husband came home telling me some woman tried to run him off the highway and was making gestures and yelling something. She got off on an exit for Anderson Road. We chalked it up to an isolated case. A few weeks later someone managed to find out who was behind the user name of truthseeker and it was Jody and they found a picture. When I showed the picture to my husband he was shocked to learn it was the same person that had tried to run him off the road. We then learned she lived on Anderson Road so that made sense when she took that exit. After all the things she stated about me behind her user name and the highway incident I called her out on Kelsey's Purpose and listed her address. The next day I felt it was wrong to list her address and I deleted it. She then became an advocate for Raye Dawn and someone wrongfully convicted. Her mission became an obsession. Soon she turned that obsesssion into becoming a victim herself. I don't doubt she has had many people address her posts on these web sites, but again, if you want it to stop you also must stop. I have asked people to stop and from my understanding when they do Jody comes back in a bigger vengance. We have proof of her admitting to posing as Mary Thompson and getting on my
facebook page so she could keep an eye on me. I pretty much accept everyone on my page because I do not know who is a legitimate child abuse advocate or one of her group. I have nothing to hide or be ashamed of so that is not a big concern of mine. Now that Jody is writing her book and speaking out publicly about being a victim and fabricating even more stories it concerns me that you organization is backing her. I am sure you are aware of the recent Dr. Phil request for us to talk about cyber stalking. At first I agreed to it in hopes it would make it stop. Then I realized there is nothing Dr. Phil could say to me that I am not already doing. I don't provoke her and Kelsey's story isn't about cyber stalking or Jody Ortiz and I felt it inappropriate to use Kelsey that way. I heard Jody's recent radio show where she claimed her emails had

been hacked into. The fact is another person named Janet gave her password to someone who then gave it to another person. That person read some of the emails and some to and from Jody were included. That is where the proof that she was impersonating others to spy on me. She also stated they needed to do more to discredit me. She even reported what I was wearing one night at the mall with my grandchildren. I have nine other grandchildren and it scares me that people are watching me while they are with me. Once when a car was parked across from my house I had some of the children with me. The kids were scared and I didn't want to get them out alone so I called inside the house to have my husband come get the children. We've had people taking pictures of my home and my daughters home twice. Jody has a picture of my home on one of her web sites and someone has screenshots. She altered state documents about Kelsey's case and posted them to make it look as if I was responsible for the abuse. A lady that worked for OCCY told me that they tried to do something legally about it, but the Attorney General stated they were not copy righted and he could do nothing. She claims the Attorney General stated I was the one that broke Kelsey's legs and that is not true. I have been told that she has cleaned up some of the provoking posts she has made when she decided to claim she is a victim. In the beginning she was an advocate for the judge, then for Raye Dawn and now she wants the attention for herself. I know this is long, but you should be aware that the person you are working with is not a victim other than of her own doing. I don't know how to make it stop and honestly I am the one that needs the support. Our family has endured so much with the death of Kelsey. We have done everything we know to do to make it our mission to work for abused children and founded the Kelsey Briggs Foundation to give out scholarships and build a Child Abuse Network facility in Shawnee, OK. As you can see this keeps me busy and I do not want nor do I need to be distracted with the constant attacks from Jody. I hope you will call me at
405-279-xxxx *to discuss this further.*

Thank you,

Kathie J. Briggs

reported: Yes
reportedto: Law Enforcement
reporteddetails: The District Attorney, FBI Internet Crime Unit, a
personal attorney.
harassercontact: Yes
harassercontactdetails: I recently did a radio broadcast about the
harassment, but do not remember if I used her name or not. Jody hid
behind a user name for many months while attacking our family.
> *When I learned her identity I called her out on Kelsey's*
> *Purpose. I posted her information that she had on another*
> *web site of hers. The following day I removed her address.*
> *This was about 4 years ago.*
hardwarefirewall: Yes
NAT: Unknown
softwarefirewall: Unknown
antivirus: Unknown
onlineprotection: I do not post on any of the sites that speak about
Kelsey's case. I stopped more than three years ago. As new
developments occur in the case I will post a link on my fb. Facebook
is the only thing I post on. Jody used a fake profile to spy on me.
Another person has an email where she admits to this.
offlineprotection: I don't know how to protect myself.
netexperience: 7
leveluser: Consumer
mycountry: United States
mystate: Oklahoma
gender: female
age: 41 or over
maritalstatus: married
race: caucasian
aboutus: From Jody's radio interview.

The e-mail that she referred to where I mentioned what she had
worn to the mall was a description from Raye's family member who
works at the mall and sees Kathie frequently. She is hard to miss when
wearing a t-shirt with Kelsey's picture on it. I sent an e-mail spoof to

a few people that I thought had their e-mails hacked by the bullies to see if it would be posted on the un-moderated forum. It was. It helped us to narrow down whose e-mail was hacked, which was Janet's.

Following is the e-mail:

From: Jody Ortiz
      Sent: Friday, December 18, 2009 3:26 PM
      To: [sent to five people including Janet]
Subject: The Real Truth aka Kathie

> *Kathie keeps posting on topix under the name the real truth. She was spotted yesterday with a Kelsey shirt on. Does she wear it to get attention so people will recognize her and give her some undeserved sympathy as the "grieving grandmother"? That's what some people think.*

> *HI KATHIE! Thanks for reading my email and posting on topix. We're always interested in your latest "story." Real truth my ass! This e-mail is confidential and is meant for the addressee only, not for Kathie and Starla. If you have received this electronic message by mistake or you are not the addressee, or if you've hacked into my email account, [Clay], please delete the message. Any forwarding, copying, or quoting from this message will be considered a violation of the addressor and addressee's right to privacy and will be prosecuted in a court of law. You can trust that is the truth.*

Recently, Raye's older sister, Janet, had a garage sale to raise money for Raye's defense. It was a typical garage sale with no surprises before Janet noticed a woman wearing a t-shirt with Kelsey's picture on the front. The woman also spoke to the other women in her party in a loud voice and mentioned the name "Kelsey" to ensure that everyone at the garage sale knew exactly who she was...Kathie Briggs.

Kathie purchased a candle holder that Gayla had originally bought for Janet. As Kathie handed Janet the money, she politely thanked Janet who was somewhat camouflaged in a hat and sunglasses.

Janet lowered her glasses and looked Kathie in the eyes and stated, "Thank YOU."

Janet laughed as Kathie drove away and she shared the story of how Kathie had unknowingly contributed to Raye's defense.

The moment I heard the story I was worried because Kathie now knew where Janet's mother lived. I knew it would be just a matter of time before she would experience what we all had experienced, such as the black rose in Janet's mailbox or the "have it your way" wrapper that was shoved in my truck grill or the outside door knobs that were busted at Gayla's home.

A few weeks passed and Janet's brother moved in with his mom. One night someone who claimed to be an off-duty cop knocked on the door. He informed Janet's brother that he knew who he was and that he was part of the Smith family, and that he had been watching him. It was just a matter of time before he would catch him doing something wrong and he would lock him up. He even knew that the brother had been away for several days.

Was this the same man that I captured on video sitting outside my home and watching me? Are these instances related? Or is it just a random act from vigilantes?

As everyone else works to move on with their lives, Kathie is still on a mission. These posts were recently forwarded to me from a Facebook group. This supporter of Raye is from France and she was disturbed that Kathie had called her a "moron." As you can see, Kathie is still hiding behind pictures of Kelsey as she assaults Kelsey's mom.

659

· Light a Candle For Kelsey's Profile ·

Kathie Batt Briggs- Your information is not accurate. Abuse was confirmed on Kelsey's mother.
Like · · *Tuesday at 6:20pm* · *7 people* like this.

Debbie ... Apparently wasn't really "years" of abuse either.
Tuesday at 6:34pm · Like · 5

In Loving Memory of Little Kelsey Shelton Smith-Briggs I'm sorry. A friend of mine wrote the descriptions... I'll ask her to change it.
Tuesday at 11:37pm · Like

[Raye supporter] raye loved her baby ,I know that a lot of lies are said but go here and read http://www.thetruthaboutkelsey.com/
Wednesday at 1:27am · Like · 1

Sharon ... After two broken legs she should have known something was wrong no matter what a child has died through abuse at the hands of scum and her mother shoud have protected her should know what is going on when you bring a new partner into your home more so if the last relationship was violent At the end of the day a child has died that should have and could have been saved there is no exuse for child abuse
Wednesday at 7:50am · Like · 7

[Raye Supporter] I'm a child abuse and it's very easy for a adult to said "she has fall " Raye was very worried for her ,she do a test to know if she has a anomaly.Read on the link to know the 2 version.
Wednesday at 10:42am · Like · 1

In Loving Memory of Little Kelsey Shelton Smith-Briggs - Everyone has read different articles, so everyone believes

different things. This event was made so people would remember Kelsey on her birthday, not so they could argue about her mother. ♥
Wednesday at 3:03pm · Like · <u>*7*</u>

Kathie Batt Briggs - Fact is she would be here to celebrate her birthday if not for her mother. Yes, there are many stories, but it takes little effort to research court documents for facts. As for Kelsey's paternal family we have learned to celebrate her short life and not focus on the abuse she suffered at the hands of her mother and stepdad. You can go to the above mentioned site and if you are a moron you will believe what is written. Don't read blogs for facts, get court documents.
Wednesday at 3:30pm · Like · <u>*9*</u>

As for everyone else, Oklahomans can now breathe a sigh of relief. Cherokee Ballard and Britten Follett are currently off the air. Cherokee Ballard works for Oklahoma Natural Gas, and Britten Follett has gone to work for her family's business. Aside from the journalist that Britten Follett is said to be dating, no other member of Oklahoma's media has relentlessly pursued a story against Raye Dawn.

Raye Dawn is patiently waiting for an answer to her Federal Appeal. Her state appeal was denied after Britten Follett and Cherokee Ballard hosted booths on at least three occasions at the State Capitol where the state appellate judge's offices are located. They shared the Briggs version of Kelsey's story to everyone in the Capitol building.

January of 2010 was my final visit with Raye at the prison. She can only have five visitors on her visitation list at a time, and the spaces are currently occupied by her family members. We've yet to get back to work on her book due to concerns with an ongoing issue of mail disappearing and e-mail hacking and tampering.

As for me, I am who I am and I don't believe that my defense of a woman whom I believe to be wrongfully convicted should cause a gang of bullies to target me for their hate. They see the case their way and I see it mine. We will never see eye-to-eye. Does that mean I am to be bullied, threatened, and destroyed? Do they have the right to destroy Raye Dawn's family for supporting her? What if their lives were to be dissected under a microscope on a public forum where everyone was allowed to voice an opinion about them? Every person makes mistakes. What makes them better than me or Gayla or Mildred or anyone in Raye Dawn's family?

In 2011 I closed my blog after learning that the best way to deal with the situation was to disengage. I started working with a spiritual advisor who has taught me the difference between acting out of love and acting from ego. When the bullies taunted me into responding, my ego got in the way. I wanted to defend myself. Once I disengaged and quit reading what the bullies had to say, I felt peace. Sometimes ignorance really is bliss.

When I announced the release of this book, and the fact that I would include some of the posts from the bashboards, I received another cease and desist notice. Misty, the woman who ran the bashboard with Mike Porter, claimed that she owns the posts from the bashboard and that by publishing them, I was harassing her. I have never met her much less harassed, stalked, bumped into, or anything else she claims she does not want me to do. She told me:

CEASE AND DESIST ORDER
This CEASE AND DESIST ORDER is to inform you that you and/or
    your associates harassing and intimidating actions against
    Misty... and the family and friends of Misty... have become
    unbearable. Such anti-social behavior is completely
    unacceptable and will not be tolerated in any way, shape or
    form. You are putting Misty...'s childrens' lives in danger by
    your continual harassment and public internet postings and it
    will no longer be tolerated. This letter is to demand that you
    and/or your associates continuing involvement in, planning

and encouragement of, information gathering, harassment and intimidation must CEASE AND DESIST immediately. Should you and/or your associates continue to pursue these activities in violation of this CEASE AND DESIST ORDER, we will not hesitate to pursue further legal action against you and/or your associates including, but not limited to, civil action and/or criminal complaints. You and/or your associates continued information gathering, harassment and intimidation of   Misty... and the friends of family of Misty... includes, but is not limited to, statements made by you on the multiple websites owned by you, including but not limited to www.TheTruthAboutKelsey.com and www.Jodyortiz.b logspot.com.   This also includes content from Misty... 's Bravenet blog,   ... , a site that was closed over three years ago,   being posted or published on any and all websites, (including Facebook) ran by you and your associates. This also includes any books, etc. being published, ghost written, edited, written or authored by you or your associates, now or in the future. You do not have permission to use any of its content. Misty... and her family and friends have legal rights to remain free from information gathering, harassment and intimidation by you, your associates and other persons and Misty... and her friends and family will take the responsibility upon ourselves to protect that right. Note that a copy of this letter and a record of its delivery will be stored. Also note, that it is admissible as evidence in a court of law and will be used as such if need be in the future. This CEASE AND DESIST ORDER demands that you immediately discontinue and do not at any point in the future under any circumstances do the following to Misty... and her friends and family: speak to ; contact (except in connection to answer this letter), pursue, harass, attack, strike, bump into, brush up against, push, tap, grab, hold, threaten, telephone (via cellular or landline), instant message, page, fax, email, follow, stalk, shadow, disturb our peace, keep us under surveillance, gather information on Misty... and her friends and family, and/or conduct any actions that may interfere with the privacy and peace of Misty... and her friends and family, or use or republish any of their websites or internet usernames, including but not

*limited to ..., MistyLT and Misty_LT. This letter also
demands that you remove any and all posts concerning
Misty..., her usernames or her website material from your
books, websites or anything else that you have control
of. Should you and/or your associates willfully choose to
continue your current course of action, I will not hesitate to
file a complaint with the proper authorities for your ongoing
violations of harassment and privacy laws. This letter does
not constitute exhaustive statement of my position nor is it a
waiver of any of Misty... 's rights or her family and
friends'rights and/or remedies in this and/or any other
related matter. I am emailing this letter to you as I have no
other contact information for you. My email does send a
"Read" report when the recipient accepts the e-mail and that
read receipt will be stored. We demand your immediate
compliance, and furthermore that you confirm in writing that
all violative activity will cease immediately. Very truly
yours, Misty*

On January 7, 2012 I was forwarded a comment from a blog owned by a victim survivor group. The blog owner had posted about a woman from Louisiana who has been recruited by the bullies to harass me. She told me that she wanted to come to Oklahoma and kill me so that she could go to prison and then kill Raye Dawn. The blog owner thought it was the stalker who posted the comment. After reading it, I informed her that it is indeed the same bullies that have harassed me for years. It stated:

Author : you're an idiot (IP: 141.0.10.133 , s41-07.opera-mini.net)
      E-mail : youaredumb@jodythatsyou.com
      URL   :
      Whois : http://whois.arin.net/rest/ip/141.0.10.133
      Comment:
      *"I rarely take the time to watch an entire video before
      sharing it and I NEVER look into who made the video."*

      Boy are you a stupid amatuer, any good journalist checks

*their sources. Got involved with someone you don't like out of
your own actions, YOU RARELY TAKE TIME TO WATCH
AN ENTIRE VIDEO?? how's that working out for
you? never even contacted the author for permission? hack
wanna be journalist, if you are going to play reporter maybe
you should review you Lou Grant DVD collection.*

Recently, I discussed perspective with a dear friend of mine. Her grandchild had questioned the validity of the Bible because of the difference in the way the stories were told by the Disciples. She described the differences in perspective by using a building as an example. She stated:

*If I'm directly in front of a building, I can see the front and some of
the right side and some of the left, but not the back. If you
were to stand a few feet to the right of me, you could see the
right side and possibly some of the back and some of the
front. With each different person's viewpoint, we're looking
at the same building, or the same events, but we will not
agree on what we see.*

This description was very fitting in the case of Raye Dawn and Kelsey because of the different relationships with the parties in question, as well as the differences in our life experiences that we bring to the table when reviewing the case; these will cause us to view the events according to our own perspectives, which will, undoubtedly, differ. Why should our differences in opinions cause such a firestorm of hate toward me or anyone else that stands in support of Raye Dawn? Until the current laws are changed, the bullies will continue to harass and stalk their prey.

Since voicing my opinion and exposing what some wanted hidden, my family had to move, and I can no longer vote because I don't want my new address to be known. I drive a mile out of my way if a vehicle is spotted in my rearview mirror on the way home. My bullies have no idea what it's like to live my life. To them, it's fun and games. This was evident at a recent hearing for Raye Dawn's appeal when Starla followed me around and looked for an opportunity to introduce herself to me. I ignored her, along with Kathie Briggs, Lance, and all of their supporters. I was there for Raye Dawn, not for them.

As more details of the case come to light and the amount of injustice that has occurred is exposed, I'm saddened beyond belief that nothing has been done to stop it. What is there to silence if Kathie and Lance Briggs are telling the truth? They obviously have something to hide.

Recently, Kelsey's paternal step-grandmother (Lance's ex-wife's mother) realized she had been lied to about what happened to Kelsey and she began to question the intent of Kathie and Lance Briggs and their "cause," and she "friended" me on Facebook. She soon received the following message from Lance, an echo of an ongoing warning for us all who dare speak the truth:

> *I can't believe how fake you have been and you would stoop to the level of the Smiths. I don't think you wana open that can of worms. You are truly a dissapointment and acting no better than Gayla. Honestly, nobody cares about your opinion and you need to keep them to yourself. You and your entire family have never TRULY cared about Kelsey. Go on with your life and* **keep your mouth Shut**. *"*[50]

It pains me that with all of the hate, the bullying, and the false allegations the only victim who matters is lost in the fray. She is used, abused, and her life and death are misrepresented by those who claim to love her and to have fought for her. But hate for the woman who carried her in her womb and cared for her while others sought their own agendas is stronger than any love they have for Kelsey. The precious memory of this innocent child is soiled by hate, lies, and greed. It's a disturbing reality that Kelsey is forgotten in all of this.

When you live in the world that I joined in 2007 when speaking up on behalf of Raye, you never know who is watching, following,

---

[50] Emphasis by book author

waiting to threaten you in some way. I took to heart every awful word that was said about me. I lived in a constant state of panic and fear. I had worked hard and I had built a business that I was proud of. I loved my life, despite anyone else's opinion of it. I went from being oblivious to the nastiness in the world to a person who lived in constant fear. I cannot say that I have walked in Raye's shoes or that I understand the amount of hate targeted at Raye and her family. I will never be able to fully comprehend their loss and it is my intention that this book will bring awareness to the real issues in the case and will help to free Kelsey's mom.

Through it all, I have learned that love is stronger than hate and I forgive those who have bullied and harassed me. They can take my life tomorrow, but hiding in fear will not change their plans. I no longer live in fear. Today I just live.

December 4, 2011
From: Sherri Heath
To: Jody Ortiz
Jody, While I was in church this morning, the pastor's sermon was
on 'acceptance.' Made me think about Raye Dawn.

Since it's the Christmas season, he was referring to Joseph
who had to go through the struggles of ridicule and social
standards of his community with Mary's condition. He wasn't
sure what to do, so God spoke to him through a dream and
assured him everything was going to be okay. Joseph
accepted Mary and her pregnancy knowing she was going to
be the mother of the Son of God. That had to be a struggle
socially speaking. I can imagine there were whispers about
him and Mary. His carpentry business probably dropped and
the social invitations didn't come anymore. Made me think of
how my family went through the media ridicule and the hate
blogs. I wonder how we did survive all that...the feelings of
worthlessness and looking over our shoulders in fear. It took
a long time to stand firm on the fact that we were not the
people they portrayed us to be. We are a good family with
Godly morals and virtues. Whatever they said about us, it
didn't matter. We knew who we were/are and nothing they
said could change it. Thank goodness for our Christian
background. A lot of prayers were said during that time. Not
only trying to get over a death of a little loved one, but facing
everyday the attacks of hate and harassment. Back to Joseph,
he stood on what he knew and took Mary to be his wife. He
protected her and accepted her. The ridicules of the town did
not interfere of who he was or what he needed to do.

I commend Raye Dawn at the time of her sentencing.....she
stood, turned to the courtroom and said, "Kathie, I forgive
you". She knew what Kathie did to get her to this point, but
accepted the responsibility of her deep rooted values and
morals to forgive her. Wow....Raye knew who she was/is, and
in no way was she going to let this situation change her. She
has moved forward with strength that only God could give
her. We all have....

Anyway, thanks for letting me share my thoughts with you on
this Sunday afternoon! Love ya! Sherri

Appendix A

Kelsey: The two-year-old girl who was sexually assaulted and murdered in 2005

Raye: Kelsey's Mommy

Gayla: Raye's mom and maternal grandmother to Kelsey

Lance: Kelsey's biological father

Mike Porter: Kelsey's step-father who was charged with Kelsey's murder and sexual assault and then met with and conversed with Kathie and her daughters in an effort to frame Raye. He was allowed to plead to 30 years for enabling child abuse, is protected in an out-of-state prison, and will never have to register as a sex offender

Kathie: Lance's mother and ex-mother-in-law to Raye

Mildred: Raye's maternal grandmother and Kelsey's great-grandmother. She was repeatedly attacked and harassed by Kathie and her supporters immediately following her great-grandchild's death

Judge Craig Key: The Judge who wrote a book about the facts in Kelsey's case almost two years after her death

Jeanna: Lance's older sister

Shirica: Lance's sister

Starla: Kathie's closest friend and the person who originally attempted to blackmail me and who threatened me. She has made good on her threats with an ongoing assault against me and my character

Britten Follett: Kathie's reporter/friend who posted notes online every day of Raye's trial

Cherokee Ballard: Kathie's reporter/friend who had Thanksgiving dinner with her

Appendix B

Exhibit 1 - Mike Porter's user account on Kelsey's Purpose:

Kelsey's Purpose / **Profile of seekingtruth**

seekingtruth
(New Member)
☆☆

Registration Date: 03-12-2006
Birthday: Not Specified
Local Time: 07-16-2009 at 09:09 PM

seekingtruth's Forum Info		Additional Info About seekingtruth
Joined:	03-12-2006	**Sex:**
Last Visit	02-01-2007 09:26 AM	**Location:**
		Bio:
Total Posts:	4 (0 posts per day | 0.02 percent of total posts) (Find All Threads — Find All Posts)	
Time Spent Online:	5 Days, 18 Hours, 42 Minutes	
Rating:	☆	

Mike Porter on Kelsey's Purpose

seekingtruth
New Member

Posts: 4
Group: Registered
Joined: Mar 2006
Status:
Reputation: ▓

RE: What is going on????   Post: ⁄⁄
When a visitation schedule is arranged child
support should be determined and ordered by a
court. With a court ordering someone to pay child
support, you can then refer the child support case to
Oklahoma's Child Support Enforcement Division(CSE). I
am fairly certain that payment of child support does not
depend on whether visitation happens with the minor
child. It is up to the custodian's lawyer in a custody case
to make sure the non-custodial parent provides accurate
wage information for child support computations and also
that any arrearages that may be owed are presented to
the court. The Judge normally will not order back support
without an order determining an amount for child
support. Make sure when visitation is ordered that child
support is included in that order.

This post was last modified: 11-02-2006 09:46 AM by seekingtruth.

11-02-2006 09:45 AM   EMAIL   PM   FIND   REPORT

Screen clipping taken: 1/17/2010, 9:21 AM

seekingtruth
New Member

Posts: 4
Group: Registered
Joined: Mar 2006
Status:
Reputation: ▓

RE: I'm new, please help me do this right....   Post: #22

The disorder you are referring to is called Munchasen by Proxy(MBP). That is when a caregiver contrives or causes illnesses to a child in their care to get the attention of family, doctors, and others. It is so sad to hear how it seems that the DA you are dealing with does not really seem to want to find out what really happened to Kayla or may be simply ignoring the facts, something I am sure happens far more than people would like to believe. So often it seems prosecutor's will choose the easy road, or even worse elect not to prosecute at all if there is no overwhelming public outcry for justice. I am deeply sorry for your loss, I will pray for you and your family.

10-25-2006 10:11 PM   EMAIL   PM   FIND   REPORT

kjbriggs
Kelsey's Grandma

Posts: 1,218
Group: Administrators
Joined: Nov 2005
Status:
Reputation: ▓▓▓▓▓▓▓▓▓▓

RE: I'm new, please help me do this right....   Post: #23

The attorneys in Kelsey's case also discussed Munchasen by Proxy. It is pretty sick when someone will hurt someone else to gain attention.

10-25-2006 10:37 PM   PM   FIND   REPORT

Mike Porter's charges are as follows:

IN THE DISTRICT COURT OF THE TWENTY-THIRD DISTRICT
SITTING IN LINCOLN COUNTY
STATE OF OKLAHOMA

AC

FOR THE PERSON OF:)
)
MICHAEL E. PORTER,   )   CASE NO. _CF 05-319_
P. O. BOX 185   )
MEEKER, OK   )
DOB: 04-04-80   )
SSN: 446 88 8938   )
            Defendant.   )

APPLICATION FOR WARRANT OF ARREST

Comes now the undersigned Affiant on this 20th day of October, 2005, and hereby makes application to the Court for a Warrant of Arrest to issue against each of the following individual(s):

MICHAEL E. PORTER

In support of this application, the undersigned Affiant, being first duly sworn, does now upon said oath, depose and say that the crime(s) of :

MURDER IN THE FIRST DEGREE (21 O.S. § 701.7)

did occur in Lincoln County, Oklahoma, approximately four (4) miles East of Meeker on Highway 62 and then North on top of the hill to the residence occupied by Raye Dawn Porter and Michael E. Porter on or about the 11th day of October, 2005.

The Affiant believes that the above named individual did commit the specified crimes by reason of personal knowledge, investigation and the reports of witnesses who have related their findings and observations of the facts and circumstances regarding the offense hereinabove named:

THOSE FACTS ARE:

I KEVIN GARRETT, of lawful age, and being first duly sworn upon an oath, deposes and says:

I am a Special Agent with the Oklahoma State Bureau of Investigation, State of Oklahoma, and have so for over eleven years. I have probable cause to believe that the following constitutes evidence of a crime:

On Tuesday, October 11, 2005, the Lincoln County Sheriff's Office requested OSBI investigative assistance involving a suspicious death that later was determined to be a homicide by the Office of the Chief Medical Examiner. The victim was KELSEY SHELTON SMITH-BRIGGS, WF, DOB: 12/28/02, Post Office Box 185, Meeker, Oklahoma.

On Tuesday, October 11, 2005, PATTY BONNER, aka JEAN, Family Care Provider for Services with Comprehensive Home Board Services (CHBS) reported the following information to OSBI Special Agent STEVE TANNER. On October 11, 2005, from noon until 1330 hours, BONNER arrived at the residence of RAYE DAWN and MICHAEL PORTER for a weekly visit with RAYE DAWN's daughter KELSEY. RAYE DAWN and KELSEY were the only people at the residence. BONNER observed KELSEY climbing on RAYE DAWN and KELSEY appeared and seemed normal. KELSEY was ornery just like a normal two-year old girl. BONNER had been visiting RAYE DAWN and KELSEY for a little over three months once and sometimes twice a

674

10/20/05 KG

IN THE DISTRICT COURT OF THE TWENTY-THIRD JUDICIAL DISTRICT OF
THE STATE OF OKLAHOMA SITTING IN AND FOR LINCOLN COUNTY

THE STATE OF OKLAHOMA,
    Plaintiff,

vs.

MICHAEL E. PORTER
ADDR: P. O. Box 185
    Meeker, OK 74855
SSN: --
DOB: 04/04/80
    Defendant(s),

Case No. CF-2005-219

FELONY WARRANT

STATE OF OKLAHOMA, COUNTY OF LINCOLN, TO ANY LAW ENFORCEMENT OFFICER:

YOU ARE HEREBY COMMANDED to forthwith arrest and take said **MICHAEL E. PORTER** into
custody for the offense(s) of:

COUNT 1:   MURDER IN THE FIRST DEGREE~ 21 O.S. § 701.7 a **FELONY**

and bring him before me or some other Magistrate having cognizance of the case, to be dealt
with according to law. You are further directed to execute this writ or warrant either in daytime or
nighttime.

Bond for the release of the above named defendant, to guarantee said defendant's appearance in
all the Court's proceedings herein, be and the same is hereby fixed in the sum of $___ NO bond
until the further Order of the Court.

Dated this __20th__ day of October, 2005.

_____
Judge of the District Court

Presenting Agency: OKLA. STATE BUREAU OF INVESTIGATION   Agency Case Number:

EXTRADITE / ENTER NCIC: **YES**   NO

Circle ONE: LOCAL ONLY   **ALL STATES**   SURROUNDING STATES

Identifiers: Gender: Male   Race: WHITE
              Height: 6' 1"   Eye Color: GREEN
              Weight: 250 lbs.   Hair Color: BLACK
              DL #: 082-06-4861
              Markings:

IN THE DISTRICT COURT OF THE TWENTY-THIRD JUDICIAL DISTRICT OF
THE STATE OF OKLAHOMA SITTING IN AND FOR LINCOLN COUNTY

FILED
2006 JUL 21 PM 3: 15

CINDY KIRBY CT. CLK.
LINCOLN CO., OKLA.

THE STATE OF OKLAHOMA,
          Plaintiff,

vs.

MICHAEL LEE PORTER

ADDR: P. O. Box 185
          Meeker, OK 74855
SSN: ~~~~~~~~
DOB: 04/04/80

          Defendant,

Case No. CF-2005-219

AMENDED INFORMATION

FOR:

    COUNT 1:   MURDER IN THE FIRST DEGREE~ 21 O.S. § 701.7 AND 10
    O.S. § 7115 a FELONY

    OR IN THE ALTERNATIVE TO COUNT 1:

    COUNT 1:   CHILD ABUSE ~ 10 O.S. § 7115(A) a FELONY

    COUNT 2:   SEXUAL ABUSE OF A CHILD ~ 10 O.S. § 7115(E) a FELONY

STATE OF OKLAHOMA, COUNTY OF POTTAWATOMIE:

    I, RICHARD L. SMOTHERMON, the undersigned District Attorney of said County, in the
name and by the authority, and on behalf of the State of Oklahoma, give information that in said
County of Lincoln and in the State of Oklahoma, MICHAEL LEE PORTER, did then and there
unlawfully, willfully, knowingly and wrongfully commit the crime(s) of:

COUNT 1: MURDER IN THE FIRST DEGREE ~ a FELONY, on or between the 1st day of
January, 2005 and the 11th day of October, 2005, A.D., the crime of MURDER IN THE FIRST
DEGREE was feloniously committed in Lincoln County, State of Oklahoma, by MICHAEL LEE
PORTER, who willfully or maliciously injured, tortured, maimed, or used unreasonable force
upon a child under the age of eighteen (18) years, specifically: Kelsey Smith Briggs, thirty-three
(33) months of age, to-wit: by MICHAEL LEE PORTER severely beating or using unreasonable
force upon Kelsey Smith Briggs, thereby inflicting blunt force trauma to her abdomen resulting in
bruising, lacerations and internal injury; and beating her on or about the head, face, chest, back,
buttocks, legs, inflicting mortal wounds which caused her death on the 11th day of October,
2005, contrary to the provisions of Section 701.7 of Title 21 and Section 7115 of Title 10 of the
Oklahoma Statutes, and against the peace and dignity of the State of Oklahoma.

DEFENDANT'S
EXHIBIT
42

676

– OR IN THE ALTERNATIVE –

COUNT 1   CHILD ABUSE ~ a FELONY, on or between the 1st day of January, 2005, and the 11th day of October, 2005, the crime of CHILD ABUSE was feloniously committed in Lincoln County, State of Oklahoma, by MICHAEL LEE PORTER, who willfully or maliciously injured, tortured, maimed or used unreasonable force upon a child under the age of eighteen (18) years, specifically: Kelsey Smith Briggs, thirty-three (33) months of age, to-wit: by MICHAEL LEE PORTER severely beating or using unreasonable force upon Kelsey Smith Briggs, thereby inflicting blunt force trauma to her abdomen resulting in bruising, lacerations and internal injury; and beating her on or about the head, face, chest, back, buttocks, legs, on the 11th day of October, 2005, contrary to the provisions of Section 7115 of Title 10 of the Oklahoma Statutes, and against the peace and dignity of the State of Oklahoma.

COUNT 2   CHILD SEXUAL ABUSE ~ a FELONY, on or between the 1st day of January, 2005, and the 11th day of October, 2005, the crime of SEXUAL ABUSE OF A CHILD was feloniously committed in Lincoln County, State of Oklahoma, by MICHAEL LEE PORTER, who knowingly and intentionally looked upon and touched the body and private parts of Kelsey Smith Briggs, who was at the time thirty-three (33) months of age or less, in a lewd and lascivious manner and in a manner calculated to arouse and excite sexual interests, to-wit: by MICHAEL LEE PORTER sexually assaulting Kelsey Smith Briggs in the anal and/or vaginal area with a part of his body or an unknown foreign object resulting in bruising and tearing to the anal and/or vaginal area of Kelsey Smith Briggs, contrary to the provisions of Section 7115 of Title 10 of the Oklahoma Statutes, and against the peace and dignity of the State of Oklahoma.

RICHARD L. SMOTHERMON
DISTRICT ATTORNEY

By: _____
Richard L. Smothermon
District Attorney

WITNESSES ENDORSED FOR THE STATE OF OKLAHOMA

Exhibit 2 –

        Q   Were you physically abusive to
Raye Dawn during the marriage?

        A   I hit her one time.

        Q   When did you hit her?

        A   I'm not sure on the exact date.

        Q   Okay. Where did you hit her?

        A   I slapped her in her face.

        Q   Why?

        A   Because she was embarrassing us.

        MR. WHITE: She's asking about during
the marriage.

        THE WITNESS: Yes, sir.

        MR. WHITE: All right.

        Q   (BY MS. TEBOW) Where was this at? Do
you recall?

        A   The Illinois River.

        Q   Okay. And you believe you guys were
married when you were at the Illinois River?

        A   No, I believe it was before our
marriage.

        MR. BURCH: Listen to her question and

```
 1   think about it.
 2          THE WITNESS:   Can we take a break?
 3          (A short break is taken.)
 4      Q   (BY MS. TEBOW)  Okay.  Mr. Briggs, we
 5   were talking about the Illinois River trip
 6   before we took a break.  Do you recall when that
 7   took place?
 8      A   Shortly before me and Raye Dawn got
 9   married.
10      Q   Was it during the summer of '03?  I'm
11   sorry.  That wouldn't be right.  Summer of 2000?
12      A   I believe so.
13      Q   And you said that you had slapped her
14   across the face; is that right?
15      A   Yes.
16      Q   Did it leave a hand print?
17      A   No.
18      Q   Was there ever a time that you bloodied
19   her nose?
20      A   Yes.
21      Q   When did that happen?
22      A   At the river.
23      Q   Was that the same incident, or did that
24   transpire later?
```

```
 1      Q   That caused her nose to bleed?
 2      A   Yes.
```

First Name	Last Name	MI	Soc. Sec. No.	Birth Date	Race
Raymond	Briggs	L		██████	White

Address	City	State	Zip	Phone No.	Sex
██████	Meeker	OK	74855	██████	Male

NARRATIVE
=========

On above time and date, I Officer Roland was dispatched to 527 South Dawson in reference to a domestic. Lincoln County Sheriffs Office advised me that the reporting party was Raye Don Briggs (██████ DOB. ██████). I arrived at approximately 1955 hours. I was the first officer to arrive. Shortly after, two Oklahoma Highway Patrolman (Jerry Treadwell and James Watson) arrived. Upon my arrival Raye Don approached me and told me what was going on. She stated that she and her husband (Ramond Lance Briggs DOB. ██████) got into an arguement over her not super sizing his value meal from McDonalds. She said that she was getting ready to go out with some friends and he got really mad and took her clothes, and keys away from her. She then stated that he pushed her up against the wall with his forearm at her throat. She said after he pushed her around and yelled at her, she then started walking northbound on Highway 18 to use the pay phone to call for help. While she was walking her grandmother picked her up and took her to use the phone, then took her back to the residence to wait on an officer to arrive. She stated that between the time she had left and the time she arrived back at the residence Ramond had gotten into his truck and was driving North bound on Highway 18. I, Officer Roland did observe visible injuries to Raye Don Briggs on her neck and collar bone area that were consistent with the type of assault she stated had occured. At this point Jerry Treadwell asked her if she wanted to press charges and she stated " yes ". The two officers drove around the Town of Meeker to see if they could locate him. Approximately five minutes later James Watson contacted me on the radio and said that he had found Mr. Briggs at the laundry mat in Meeker and needed me to come up there to talk to him. I left a voluntary statement for Raye D. Briggs to fill out and told her that myself or one of the other officers would be back to get more information from her. She said that she would stay at the residence until we came back. I then got into my patrol car and headed to the laundry mat to meet with the other officers. Upon arrival I noticed that the officers had already had Mr. Briggs in handcuffs and in the front seat of one of the patrol cars. Officer Treadwell advised me that he had already informed Mr. Briggs of his miranda rights and told him that he was under arrest for domestic assault and battery. Officer Treadwell then took Mr. Briggs out of his car and put him into my car. Officer Treadwell told me that he would go back to the residence and take a voluntary statement and get all the information from Mrs. Briggs, and when he was done he would meet me at the Lincoln County Sheriffs Office. I then told Lincoln County that I was enroute to their facility with Mr. Briggs. I arrived at Lincoln County Sheriffs Office at approximately 2043 hours. Shortly after my arrival Officer Treadwell arrived with Mrs. Briggs voluntary statement and other information.

   I then started going through the process of getting Mr. Briggs booked into the jail. I issued him citation # 004422. I charged him with domestic assault and battery. End of report.

Exhibit 3 – The following statement is from the State's answer to Raye's appeal about Kelsey's broken legs:

Furthermore, unlike other injuries, the leg fractures were less directly linked to the defendant and there was no link to Michael Porter. Taking this portion of

Exhibit 4- Repair order for Mike Porter's truck after August, 2005 accident:

Exhibit 5 - Kathie Briggs deposition, 2009, admits to giving up visits with Kelsey and denies having anything to do with the "justice for Kelsey" public cries (read depositions at www.RayeDawnSmith.com):

```
1   she was convicted that your family would now
2   receive the entire $15 million as opposed to
3   just half?
4       A    No.
5       Q    Would it surprise you to know that we
6   have witnesses that say that you did just that?
7       A    Yes, I would.
8       Q    Did you e-mail Debra Nguyen on
9   September 6, 2005, and tell her that none of
10  your family would be present at the
11  September 8th hearing or at any more supervised
12  visits with Kelsey?
13      A    Yes.
14      Q    So you did have supervised visits with
15  Kelsey, didn't you?
16      A    In May, not after June.
17      Q    Why would you be writing her in
18  September that you would not be at any more of
19  the supervised visits, then?
20      A    They allowed Ashley to have a couple of
21  supervised visits at the DHS office and said I
22  was welcome to come if I wanted to.
23      Q    And why didn't you come?
24      A    Because I didn't -- they were not
25  reporting accurately what happened in those
```

1   visits.

2   Q   What were they reporting?

3   A   They were stating -- they were not

4   telling the positive things. They would say

5   Kelsey would bite and hit, which she did, but

6   they wouldn't tell what she did on the other

7   visits.

8   Q   So instead of seeing your

9   granddaughter, you chose -- instead of dealing

10 with what DHS was saying and seeing your

11 granddaughter, you chose not to see her; is that

12 correct?

13   A   Not under supervised conditions.

14   Q   How is it you are affiliated with the

15 Concerned Citizens of the 23rd Judicial

16 District?

17   A   I don't know what you mean.

18   Q   Well, are you familiar with that

19 organization?

20   A   No.

21   Q   Are you familiar with the ad they

22 published in the newspaper encouraging

23 Smothermon to charge Raye Dawn?

24   A   I know who those people are, but it

25 wasn't me.

Exhibit 6 –

<pre>
24   Q   Can you explain to me why you would
25   have your military uniform on in a photograph at
</pre>

Young Reporting Services * (405) 236-8426

RAYMOND LANCE BRIGGS - 08/27/09
149

<pre>
1   Kelsey's grave site in December?
2   A   Because that was Veteran's Day.
3   Q   In December?
4   A   In December?
5   Q   Uh-huh.
6   A   No.
7   Q   And I can show you the photo.
8   A   I believe it was -- yes, I can say. It
9   was because a wreath was given for fallen
10   soldiers, and one was given to my daughter, and
11   I went out there in my soldier's uniform to give
12   it to her.
13   Q   Was this a ceremony, or did you just go
14   out there by yourself and do it?
15   A   There was no ceremony.
16   Q   All right. And then who took the
17   photograph?
18   A   I believe it was my mother.
</pre>

Exhibit 7 –

Shirica   Post: #106
Administrator
                               RE: Comments on OSBI interviews.

                               During Mike Porter's interview, he
                               kept grabbing his heart and acting like he
Posts: 175   was having chest pains and he acted like
Group: he was going to vomit a time or two and
Administrators   was very dramatic. I have never seen such
Joined: Nov   a drama queen. His body language was
2005   screaming guilt. He was beyond nervous
Status: Offline   and then toward the end he says he wants
Reputation: an attorney and he wants to see his wife.
                               Watching the tape is so different from
                               reading it. I truly feel that this man is
                               responsible for the death of Kelsey.
                               Shirica Kelsey's Aunt Rees

Exhibit 8 –

On 11-9-02 at approximately 2035 hours I Sgt. Leabo was stationary at Main and Fowler. I observed a vehicle west bound on Main at a high rate of speed. I activated my radar and it indicated that the vehicle was traveling at 38 MPH in a 30 MPH zone. I pulled my patrol car out behind the vehicle and activated my emergency lights. The vehicle stopped at approximately 1 ½ mile west of town on Hwy 62. I called the dispatcher and informed him of the stop and my location. I exited my patrol car and approached the driver and informed the driver why I had stopped him. I then asked him for his driver's license and insurance verification. The driver was identified as Raymond Briggs, DL# ███████ by his Oklahoma driver's license. I then returned to my patrol car and ask the dispatcher to check the status of Briggs's DL by number. The dispatcher informed me that Briggs's license was valid. Officer Combs Meeker #5 then notified me that we had a warrant on Briggs that had not been ▮ace on the warrant list. Officer Combs then informed me that he was at the Meeker Police ▮partment and that there was a warrant on Briggs. I then exited my vehicle and approached Briggs. I asked Briggs to step out of his vehicle and I informed him that Meeker had a warrant for his arrest and he was being placed under arrest for that warrant. I then placed him in double locked handcuffs and secured him in my patrol car. I then called the dispatcher and asked him to send the next wrecker to my location. I then completed an impoundment record on Briggs's vehicle and waited for the wrecker. Russell's Wrecker arrived and impounded the vehicle. I then transported Briggs to Meeker Police Department and pick up a copy of the warrant. I then transported Briggs's to Lincoln County Jail booked and jailed him for the Municipal Warrant # 02-341,342,343,344. Briggs's while in route to Lincoln County Jail made many verbal threats towards my family and me.
End of Report

Exhibit 9 –

Week later
September 6, 206
Shawnee
News
Star
Meeker
Paper

Justice demanded from District Attorney

To the editor,

This letter stems from news of the recent developments in the pending criminal cases involving the mother and stepfather of Kelsey Smith-Briggs.

After watching coverage of Michael Porter's preliminary hearing held on August 23, we were very disturbed by the news that Raye Dawn Smith, Kelseys' mother, is currently in plea negotiations with the District Attorney. This news is even more shocking given Mr. Smothermon's past public statements concerning the possibility of a plea negotiation between his office and Kelsey's mother. In that press conference, Smothermon spoke of society's demand that parents be held accountable when they do not uphold their moral responsibility to protect their children. He said that Raye Dawn Porter knew or should have known her daughter was being abused.

Smothermon also stated that he had no intention of offering Raye Dawn any kind of plea bargain, and that he had enough evidence to convict the stepfather without her testimony. His emphatic statements to the media make the recent development all the more surprising.

We would like to know why it seems that people who "ONLY" fail to protect or enable their children to be abused are not considered to be as culpable as the actual abuser? Why would Mr. Smothermon even consider any kind of plea negotiation for this woman after stating on TV he did not need her testimony? What would the reasoning behind it be? Why would he even consider using her testimony?

Her testimony is not credible. Of course she has to point the finger at Mike Porter. It seems Mr.Smothermon has made a deal with the devil.

Another recent child abuse case comes to mind, that of a very young child named Akaysha McGee. The mother and mother's boyfriend were both charged in the beating of this child, arrested and each subsequently jailed on a $250,000 bond. The mother in that case was able to give a time line for each individual bruise, and in exchange for her testimony she received a plea deal of two years from Mr. Smothermon.

Two years for a mother that stood by and watched as her child was savagely beaten. This leads us to wonder how light the punishment for the mother in Kelsey's case will be? We would be hard pressed to believe that she will ever admit any actual wrongdoing such as witnessing any abuse.

Why is Mr. Smothermon sending a message that it is not acceptable to beat children but it is acceptable to stand by and watch or not protect your child? More importantly, why are the citizens of the 23rd Judicial District allowing our District Attorney to send this message?

We would encourage all of you to take the time to let your feelings be known in regards to people being slapped on the wrist for allowing their children to be beaten and killed.

Mr. Smothermon, we demand justice.

Liana Rowe, Oklahoma City, Ok
Lori Watson, Tulsa, Ok
Lorri Justice, Little Rock, AR
Tina Moore, Broken Arrow, Ok
Jamie O'Dell, Tulsa, Ok
Julie Barto, Norman, Ok
Louella Ryan, Harrah, Ok
Daphne Spencer, Meeker, Ok
Beverly McKinney, Ninnekah, Ok
Frances Ferguson, Warr Acres, Ok
Barbara Troyer, Oklahoma City, Ok

(Note: This letter was e-mailed along with complete addresses and phone numbers of each name listed)

687

This letter stems from news of the recent developments in the pending criminal cases involving the mother and stepfather of Kelsey Smith-Briggs. After watching coverage of the stepfather's preliminary hearing held on August 23rd, we were very disturbed by the news that Kelsey's mother is currently in plea negotiations with the District Attorney. This news is even more shocking given Mr. Smothermon's past public statements concerning the possibility of a plea negotiation between his office and Kelsey's mother. In that press conference, Smothermon spoke of society's demand that parents be held accountable when they do not uphold their moral responsibility to protect their children. He said that Kelsey's mother knew or should have known her daughter was being abused. His emphatic statements to the media make the recent development all the more surprising.

We would like to know why it seems that people who "ONLY" fail to protect or enable their children to be abused are not considered to be as culpable as the actual abuser? Why would Mr. Smothermon even consider any kind of plea negotiation for this woman! What would the reasoning behind it be? Why would he even consider using her testimony?

Another recent child abuse case comes to mind, that of another very young child. The mother and mother's boyfriend were both charged in the beating of this child, arrested and each subsequently jailed on a $250,000 bond. The mother in that case was able to give a timeline for each individual bruise, and in exchange for her testimony she received a plea deal of two years from Mr. Smothermon. Two years for a mother that stood by and watched as her child was savagely beaten. This leads us to wonder how light the punishment for the mother in Kelsey's case will be? Why is Mr. Smothermon sending a message that it is not acceptable to beat children but it but it is acceptable to stand by and watch or not protect your child? More importantly, why are the citizens of the 23rd Judicial District allowing our District Attorney to send this message? We would encourage all of you to take the time to let your feelings be

...scan on the most surprising.

We would like to know why it seems that people who "ONLY" fail to protect or enable their children to be abused are not considered to be as culpable as the actual abuser? Why would Mr. Smothermon even consider any kind of plea negotiation for this woman? What would the reasoning behind it be? Why would he even consider using her testimony?

Another recent child abuse case comes to mind, that of another very young child. The mother and mother's boyfriend were both charged in the beating of this child, arrested and each subsequently jailed on a $250,000 bond. The mother in that case was able to give a timeline for each individual bruise, and in exchange for her testimony she received a plea deal of two years from Mr. Smothermon. Two years for a mother that stood by and watched as her child was savagely beaten. This leads us to wonder how light the punishment for the mother in Kelsey's case will be? Why is Mr. Smothermon sending a message that it is not acceptable to beat children but it is acceptable to stand by and watch or not protect your child? More importantly, why are the citizens of the 23rd Judicial District allowing our District Attorney to send this message? We would encourage all of you to take the time to let your feelings be known. MR. SMOTHERMON, WE DEMAND JUSTICE.

Please contact Mr. Smothermon at the following address, which is his office:
331 N. Broadway Ave
Shawnee, Ok 74801
(405) 275-6800

Paid for by Concerned citizens of the 23rd Judicial District, Daphne Spencer, Spokesperson

Exhibit 10 –

Below are two posts from the 30 pages about me that were posted on Kelsey's Purpose. (Notice the pictures of Kelsey used as avatars.)

Author	Message
kjbriggs Kelsey's Grandma ★★★★★ Posts: 1,219 Group: Administrators Joined: Nov 2005 Status: Reputation:	**New Information** Post: #1 During the past several months our family has been the victims of multiple websites and videos filled with slander. With the assistance of our attorney, through subpoenas, we now know most of the people behind them. Most would assume they are all at the hands of the maternal family. It is true they have some connection to most of them, but they have not created or do not own a bulk of the vicious material on the Internet. First and foremost the majority of the sites and videos are owned by a lady by the name of **Jody Ortiz** aka truthseeker. She is the editor of the book written by Craig Key, the former judge. She claims to have written up to 70 books and is a ghost writer. She works under the company name of Supplemental Office Services. http://supplementalofficeservices.com/ Some have suggested she is the mouth piece for Craig Key. She makes her home outside of Oklahoma City. Mrs. Ortiz has posted that she won't stop until our family pays for what happened to Kelsey. This seems to be a strong statement coming from someone that never met Kelsey or our family. It has been our policy to take the high road during the past two years. We continued to work on behalf of children that could still be helped. All the while we were being stalked, harassed, slandered, and physically threatened. We will continue to make choices that are in the best interest of our family. That includes putting a stop to the madness of this lady and her small group of friends. We appreciate the continued support of so many that have come to Kelseyspurpose with good intentions. Logging into this site is a choice each of you make. We hope it is to help other children and to support families in abusive situations.
03-21-2008 09:27 PM	💬 PM 🔍 FIND QUOTE
Starla Moderator ★★★★★	**RE: New Information** Post: #2 I am glad the information is finally out there. Hopefully, though a little late, **Jody** will back down and stop the nonsense and lies. Now that everyone knows who is behind **twisting the facts** to fit their **own** agenda, maybe the

Starla Moderator ★★★★★ Posts: 688 Group: Moderators Joined: Feb 2006 Status: Reputation:	**RE: New Information** Post: #2 I am glad the information is finally out there. Hopefully, though a little late, **Jody** will back down and stop the nonsense and lies. Now that everyone knows who is behind **twisting the facts** to fit their **own** agenda, maybe the embarrassment will be enough to stop her. Hopefully when this is all said and done, people will see for what she is. This has went on way too long. Now we also know why she was so adament about and protective of, the clueless **FORMER** Judge. Again Kathie, I am sorry for all the nasty, hateful downright mean lies that have been spread about you and your family. Your strength amazes me still. You have put up with this bull way longer than I would have. ~~If you are not part of the SOLUTION...you are part of the PROBLEM!!~~
03-21-2008 10:19 PM	✉ EMAIL 💬 PM 🔍 FIND QUOTE

Below are posts from blogs about me where Kathie's supporters state that the district attorney that charged Raye got a subpoena to identify me and then he reportedly turned my information over to Kathie Briggs, according to Kathie and her supporters.

> encouraged. Also, as I was told, Richard Smothermon issued a subpeona to identify who owned the http://www.richardsmothermon.com/ site when it was just in the beginning stages. The subpeona showed, according to what I was told, that SHE owned that site, along with the freekelseysmom site and others. If I remember correctly there were 13 sites altogether she owned at that time.

(Smothermon). He found out about it and had the website subpoenaed to find out who owned it. It was Jody.

The following posts are from a Facebook page that is administrated by Ms. Follett and Ms. Ballard. This is just a sample of the language that can be found on that page any day of the week. (Notice that Kelsey's picture is used as an avatar.)

and you....you are a pathetic, STUPID,selfish, obviously blind, sorry excuse for a mother! You make me sick...I wouldnt want to ask her anything....she would just play stupid and lie!! I just wonder what went though both of thier heads when they did it????? Did they actually think they were going to get away with it and live happily ever after without Kelsey?????? Did you ever think of the consequences????? Karma....its a bitch!!!! I also would like to know if either of them think it is going to be pretty when they get out??? So many know thier names....they are going to be HATED...it wont be pretty I can tell you that. Has anyone thought about ???? Imagine that poor kids life when he gets older and gets told the truth, both your parents are jail birds, they abused and murder your 1/2 sister when she was just a baby, your dad gave up all rights to you, you have another 1/2 brother and sister you will never meet. That poor kid is going to loose it when hes older. Best thing for him is to have no contact with the evil mother, be adopted, and NEVER be told. That is the only way that kid will ever have a NORMAL life!!!! I wonder if Raye/Porter even realized what they did to him!!!! That is 2 kids that they ruin thier lives. Lock them both up and throw away the friggin key!!!! I cant stand looking at either of them.....I want to vomit!!! Geez...Porter has a way with making people do that. All but dumb Raye... she cant see anything before her eys...or so she claims. Why dont you just bang your head against the walls and try to knock some sense into yourself. You classless POS!!!

about an hour ago · Report

is...

Paula Cuthbertson Holly, just shut up! No one here is interested in anything that you or any other of Jody's goons have to say.... We are only interested in the facts and not the bullshit that you trolls have to say.... Go stick your head up your ass and fight for air....
18 hours ago · 🖒 3 people · Flag

Christy Henshaw Holly –Making it about RD and not Kelsey is quite sad, and I hope that one day you and your family are not faced with a situation like this, and if so I hope you will protect your child, but seeing how you believe she is so innocent you probably wouldn't do anything yourself to save a child.

When it comes down to it, this is not about weather she killed Kelsey or not, it is she failed Kelsey as a mother, she FAILED TO PROTECT her child.

Please do not respond to this as you are being blocked, you all just don't even give up, and it is sad, use your energy to stop abuse, it will get you further!
9 hours ago · 🖒 2 people · Flag

Diane Lael It's so hard not to let idiots like Holly and Jody get under your skin, especially when they are posting the crap they dig right out of their hineys, but we know the truth. I say it just has to slide right off our backs. We can just look at those people and laugh-then say as many prayers as we can for their children if they have any.
8 hours ago · 🖒 1 person · Flag

Christy Henshaw Amen to that Diane! I agree with you, I used to try and argue points with them, and realized they are not even worth my time, that time needs to be put other places!
8 hours ago · Flag

d-Kelsey/1588708322271?v=wall&story fbid=110677292321797

Holly Dawn Brubaker What I don't get is the fact RD has hurt Lance and the briggs family enough. Why make them keep reliving that sad painful day?Make that murderer stay behind bars for the rest of her pathetic,meaningless life!! Lance,Kathie...I Stand behind you and your family ALL THE WAY!!
Yesterday at 6:47am · Flag

Courtney Briggs Yea I agree the bitch Raye Dawn SHOULD rot in prison where she belongs..what a piece of shit she is..looking at her face makes me want to punch it in even more
11 hours ago · Flag

d-Kelsey/1588708322271?ref=ts

✉ **Inbox > Message Detail**   **Print**   P

Subject: Lance Briggs sent you a message on Facebook...
From: Facebook <notification+ze66ldze@facebookmail.com> (Add as Preferred Sender) ⊙
Date: Thu, May 13, 2010 1:58 am
To: Raye Dawn Smith <truthseeker@thetruthaboutkelsey.com>

---

facebook

Lance sent you a message.

Lance   **Lance Briggs** May 13, 2010 at 7:58am
Briggs
          Subject: I Really Want To Be Your Friend

          Please except me so you can tell me all about your jail cell and all the
          new friends you have made. Is your big bed comfortable, is the food first
          class, how is the view from in there? I have so many more questions to
          ask, let's be friends and catch up stranger. Well I'm sure you won't
          except me so you better get use to being in there bitch cuz your gona be
          in there for a long long long time! :D

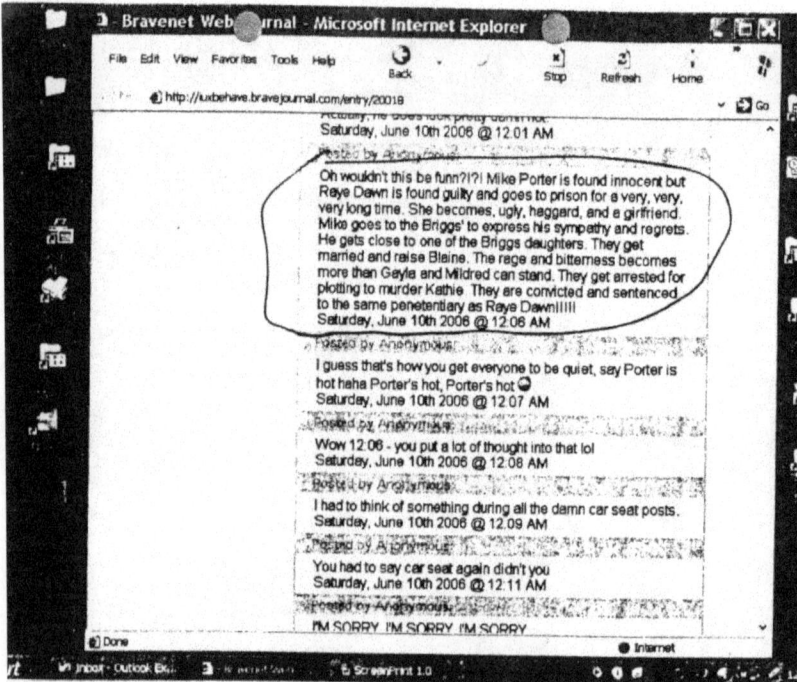

Bravenet Web Journal - Microsoft Internet Explorer

File Edit View Favorites Tools Help   Back   Stop Refresh Home

http://iuxbehave.bravejournal.com/entry/20018

Saturday, June 10th 2006 @ 12.01 AM

Oh wouldn't this be funn?!?! Mike Porter is found innocent but
Raye Dawn is found guilty and goes to prison for a very, very,
very long time. She becomes, ugly, haggard, and a girlfriend.
Mike goes to the Briggs' to express his sympathy and regrets.
He gets close to one of the Briggs daughters. They get
married and raise Blaine. The rage and bitterness becomes
more than Gayla and Mildred can stand. They get arrested for
plotting to murder Kathie. They are convicted and sentenced
to the same penetentiary as Raye Dawn!!!!!
Saturday, June 10th 2006 @ 12.06 AM

I guess that's how you get everyone to be quiet, say Porter is
hot haha Porter's hot 🙂
Saturday, June 10th 2006 @ 12.07 AM

Wow 12.06 - you put a lot of thought into that lol
Saturday, June 10th 2006 @ 12.08 AM

I had to think of something during all the damn car seat posts.
Saturday, June 10th 2006 @ 12.09 AM

You had to say car seat again didn't you
Saturday, June 10th 2006 @ 12.11 AM

I'M SORRY I'M SORRY I'M SORRY

694

Tuesday, June 27th 2006 @ 12:08 PM

We will have a booth at the Blackberry Festival this weekend with Kelsey stickers. Anyone in that area please come by and say "hello". The Blackberry Festival is in McLoud. One of our members will also have a BUG in the car show with Kelsey magnets on it.
Tuesday, June 27th 2006 @ 12:19 PM

Is it true that Raye Dawn is living in Tecumseh with her sister?
Tuesday, June 27th 2006 @ 12:37 PM

I saw the cutest lime green BUG on Saturday at Lake Stanley Draper for the Kelsey's Purpose rally. It had Kelsey stickers all over it. Is this the BUG? It was absolutely adorable.
Tuesday, June 27th 2006 @ 12:40 PM

Scary to think that DHS would let her be around Rachelle's baby with criminal charges pending. I heard that Rachelle had to get assistance for her baby too. Whatever happened to working?
Tuesday, June 27th 2006 @ 12:41 PM

Just curious? Do any of the Smith women (Gayla, Raye Dawn, Rachelle) currently work? How are they supporting themselves? And did I read correctly, Gayla Smith, actually embezzled from her own brother's company? Is this true??
Tuesday, June 27th 2006 @ 12:50 PM

Raye Dawn and Rachelle supposedly work. Gayla might show houses for her man if anything. They are supported by the men in their life as usual.

Where have I been? EBay?? What kind of things would anyone want to purchase from that family? Plus, I believe court costs, legal fees and attorney fees can be quite costly.
Tuesday, June 27th 2006 @ 1:33 PM

What are they selling Raedawgs scratch and sniff panites? Or Mildew Fowlers scratch and sniff dentures? I know Gala is making some money showing Prick Jame's homes. On her knee's.
Tuesday, June 27th 2006 @ 1:44 PM

WHAT!!!! The Smith's never paid for Kelsey's funeral??? You have got to be kidding me!!! My blood is just boiling! Now let me get this straight. They have money for cigarettes and alcohol. They have money to pay thugs to beat people up. They have money to run all over town harrassing people about displaying Kelsey stickers. They had money for bond for Raye Dawn. Yet, they could or would not pay for Kelsey's funeral services???
Tuesday, June 27th 2006 @ 1:44 PM

How evil and demonic do you have to be to hack a murdered childs web site? Just ask Judge Key! The red faced brat.
Tuesday, June 27th 2006 @ 1:48 PM

I heard they used the victims compensation fund to pay for her funeral. I guess they could do that since that was before the mother was criminally charged.
Tuesday, June 27th 2006 @ 1:59 PM

Why do you think Gayla should be charged?
I think that she may also be guilty, but I was just wondering what your view is.
Friday, June 9th 2006 @ 4:38 PM

Everyone in Meeker thinks that Gayla and Mildred both should be charged.
Friday, June 9th 2006 @ 4:39 PM

From what Gayla has told people and on the tv, she seems like the type that would lie for her own daughter just to protect her children from anyone else and in the meantime, she didn't protect Kelsey. If she truly was there and saw Kelsey often, she should have seen all the signs of abuse and by now changing her story and saying that she saw how Mike was jealous, etc., she is just as guilty as Raye Dawn.
Friday, June 9th 2006 @ 4:43 PM

I agree that Gayla seems like quite the B*tch in this situation.
Friday, June 9th 2006 @ 5:09 PM

I think it's a run for the money on who's the most responsible of that family, they are all non caring human feces.
Friday, June 9th 2006 @ 5:11 PM

does anyone know who's got the baby now? Does Gayla have it yet? Poor child, if she does. Surely Mike wouldn't allow that.
Friday, June 9th 2006 @ 5:13 PM

Mildred didn't "knowingly" harm Kelsey. That's the key word. She didn't know what she was doing. That's right...that's the ticket, she didn't even know that she didn't have a seizure at the funeral.
Saturday, February 4th 2006 @ 12:31 AM

Mildred is common knowledge around Meeker and especially around Lewis Mfg.
She used to be a fine upstanding woman.
Saturday, February 4th 2006 @ 12:32 AM

Mad - Mildred would be left out of it if she would just come out and tell the damn truth. If she would come out and say "I am just supporting my daughter and granddaughter. I do not know what went on in that house. I know Kelsey was abused and I do not know who did it. I know it was not Lance or Kathie. I will support my family and that is all. I will not lie for them, or withhold information for them. I will tell everything that I know, even if it makes my daughter or granddaugher look bad. Yes, Raye Dawn is an alcoholic and yes I tried my best to cover it up. Yes she has slept around and treated people like shit generally. No she was not a good mother most of the time. But I do not believe she killed Kelsey so I wil support her." IF MILDRED SAID THAT THEN I WOULD SAY "EVERYBODY LEAVE HER ALONE AND BASH RAYE DAWN AND GAYLA". BUT SHE WIL NOT DO THAT SO SHE DESERVES WHAT SHE GETS. SHE HAS DONE JUST AS MUCH TO COVER SHIT UP AS ANYONE.
Saturday, February 4th 2006 @ 12:33 AM

I think you are wrong. This site is for people who failed Kelsey. Mildred

You are right 2.25, Gayla is really messed up. She still keeps secrets from her mother so she can missuse her. They like to keep Mildred in the dark.
Tuesday, February 14th 2006 @ 2:31 PM

Posted by Anonymous:

Poor poor Mildred. They better hold a press confrence for her. She needs peoples sympathy for her getting left out in the dark.
Tuesday, February 14th 2006 @ 2:40 PM

Posted by Anonymous:

How could Gayla see poor Kelsey abused and not do or say something. Poor little Kelsey. Did you ever think maybe Gayla was rough with Kelsey too? It is possible. I think of that baby every day and cry alot. I know all of you do too! Thanks for trying to get justice for Kelsey. I wish I could do more.
Tuesday, February 14th 2006 @ 2:42 PM

Posted by Tired of Waiting for Justice:

So true. Mildred has ALWAYS been in the dark pertaining to what the Smiths are doing. She IS a good woman, but she has been misguided by all this and stands by someone, or some people that she should not stand by and she SHOULD know better. But you've got to remember, she IS 74 years old and I'm sure that her mind is starting to fail her. I just hope she doesn't think that her darling Gayla will take care of her when she needs it.
Tuesday, February 14th 2006 @ 2:44 PM

Posted by Anonymous:

anon - 2:42. If you are in Oklahoma you can do more. Do you check Kelsey's purpose for upcoming rallies and events?
Tuesday, February 14th 2006 @ 2:44 PM

Posted by Anonymous:

I am sure that Gayla will take care of her - the same way she took care of her "beloved"

Bibliography

Jon, Barry. '"Oklahoma Prosecutor Smothermon Pushes False Charges? The Murder and Exploitation of Kelsey Smith-Briggs" *US Observer*. July 18, 2010.
<http://www.usobserver.com/archive/june-07/Kelsey-smith-briggs.htm>.

Jon, Barry and Ron Lee. "Sentenced for Another's Crime: Jury Convicts Mother Despite Evidence*." US Observer. July 18, 2009.* < http://www.usobserver.com/archive/july-*07/raye-dawn-verdict.htm>.*

Key, Craig. *A Deadly Game of Tug of War: The Kelsey Smith-Briggs Story*. Garden City, NY: Morgan James Publishing, 2007. Pp. 60, 86.

Morava, Kim. "Kelsey's Father Gets Deferred Sentence for Domestic Violence." *Shawnee News-Star*. May 24, 2010. <http://news-star.com/stories/011307/new_46279.shtml>. (online article has since been removed)

Ortiz, Jody. *The Naked Truth Bound in Scorn*. Oklahoma City, OK: Jody Ortiz Publishing, 2010.

About the Author

Jody Ortiz is a wife and a mother who currently works as a freelance writer. She has written for various fields including: financial, insurance, mortgage, construction, religion, inspiration, how-to, memoir, education, and academic. Her resume includes ghost writing over 70 books (she's lost count); several have been published in the business genre, and she has ghost written a four-hundred page novel.

Jody's experience has opened doors to clients from all over the world including: Hong Kong, Switzerland, Australia, U.K., Wales, Turkey, Canada, Mexico, South America, Israel, South Africa, and so on.

In her spare time, she has volunteered as a Girl Scout leader, delivered meals for Meals on Wheels, and volunteered with St.

Vincent de Paul where she delivered food to those in need and developed a database to keep track of donations.

Jody's recent exposure to wrongful convictions has led to her position on the board of Raye of Hope, an Oklahoma based organization that gives a voice to those who claim to be wrongfully convicted.

Although Jody was paralyzed for over two years from the overwhelming amount of hate she receives on a daily basis from her attackers, through her strong faith and encouragement from her family as well as her loving supporters and friends, Jody learned to face her fear and her harassers head-on. She is now reclaiming her life through telling her story of survival to the world and is working to change laws in the process to assist other victims of stalking and cyber bullying.

Contact Jody at jo@jodyortiz.com to schedule speaking engagements and book signings. Read *Murdered at the age of 2: Mother convicted of "should have known"* also by Jody Ortiz for more information on the case.